The Culinarians

The CULINARIANS

LIVES AND CAREERS from THE FIRST AGE OF

American Fine Dining

David S. Shields

THE UNIVERSITY OF CHICAGO PRESS
CHICAGO AND LONDON

The University of Chicago Press, Chicago 60637
The University of Chicago Press, Ltd., London
© 2017 by The University of Chicago
Published 2017
Printed in the United States of America

26 25 24 23 22 21 20 19 18 17   1 2 3 4 5

ISBN-13: 978-0-226-40689-3 (cloth)
ISBN-13: 978-0-226-40692-3 (e-book)
DOI: 10.7208/chicago/9780226406923.001.0001

The University of Chicago Press gratefully acknowledges the generous support of
the University of South Carolina toward the publication of this book.

Library of Congress Cataloging-in-Publication Data

Names: Shields, David S., 1951– author.
Title: The culinarians: lives and careers from the first age of American
fine dining / David S. Shields.
Description: Chicago: The University of Chicago Press, 2017. | "A biographical
reference book about two hundred of the most influential cooks and restaurateurs
from 1790 to 1919"—Publisher. | Includes bibliographical references and indexes.
Identifiers: LCCN 2017028446 | ISBN 9780226406893 (cloth: alk. paper) |
ISBN 9780226406923 (e-book)
Subjects: LCSH: Cooks—United States—Biography. | Restaurateurs—
United States—Biography. | Cooking—United States—History. | Restaurants—
United States—History.
Classification: LCC TX649.A1 S54 2017 | DDC 641.5092—dc23
LC record available at https://lccn.loc.gov/2017028446

♾ This paper meets the requirements of ANSI/NISO Z39.48-1992
(Permanence of Paper).

For Sean Brock

Contents

The Third Era 1865 to 1885

THE FRENCH HEGEMONY AND THE NATIONALIST REACTION

The Gilded Age 1885 to 1919

FAME AND THE MASTER CHEF

INDEXES

A Note to the Reader

Some peculiar features of the following performance should be explained. Menu French in America abounded in orthographic perversions and in the manhandling of diacritical marks. I had proposed silently correcting the deviations from Parisian linguistic and spelling practice; but the University of Chicago faculty Board of Publications thought reproducing the original barbaric Franglish more informative. So that is what you find here in all its lurid deviancy.

In biographical compendia, the use of academic annotation regimens is distracting and overblown. So following each entry one finds a list of the most significant sources arranged in chronological order. I have attempted to supply in the body of the entry some indication (date, publication name, commentator name) that will link direct quotations to the source annotation. For every entry, a good number of other primary sources and commentary were consulted.

Finally, certain of these culinary artists possessed more than a usual element of vanity in their self-projection; consequently, the stories about their lives and works is troubled with more than a little fancifulness. Not as much as the early silent motion picture personalities I discussed in my earlier book, *Still: American Silent Motion Picture Photography* (Chicago: University of Chicago Press, 2013), but enough that I attempted to corroborate the often remarkable claims in memoirs. I have jettisoned stories that I've discovered to be lies, unless the lie itself reveals something signal in the subject's character.

Introduction

Here are the lives and works of those who made cooking an art in the United States. Here are the careers and creations of the chefs, caterers, and restaurateurs who made cuisine a profession from 1793, when Julien's Restorator, America's first restaurant, opened in Boston, until 1919 when the Volstead Act prohibiting the sale of alcohol destroyed the financial basis of fine dining in the United States.

After 1919, the great temples of cuisine in the metropolitan areas shuttered: Sherry's, Mouquin's, Rector's, Shanly's, Jack's, and Delmonico's in New York; the Old Poodle Dog in San Francisco; the Café Royale in Chicago; the Old Absinthe House and Francoise's in New Orleans. Only the great hotels championed the experience of fine dining through the 1920s and '30s, keeping it alive until the beginning of the second age of fine dining in the wake of the Second World War. Some of the final lives recounted here will treat persons central to keeping the ideal alive from the first to the second age—Oscar Tschirky, Louis Paquet, Louis Diat, Emil Altorfer.

Here I've presented 175 lives of chefs, caterers, and restaurateurs arranged in chronological order by year of birth (when known). The most influential professional cooks, the most visionary restaurateurs, and the most active organizers of public banquets from 1793 to 1919 will be found, as well as a number of lives illustrating the challenges, serendipities, rewards, and penalties of the culinary life. The cast of characters is ethnically diverse—12 are Italian; 20, German; 4, Chinese; 30, African American; 28 combined are Britons and Anglo-Americans; 2, Hispanic; 1, Jewish; 1, Native American; 2 are from eastern Europe; and there are, not surprisingly, 77 of French descent (counting persons born in Alsace and Switzerland as well). The works of 18 women are chronicled here. The cosmopolitan mixture of expert practitioners in the culinary profession was only rivaled by that of musicians during this period. My hope is to communicate the extraordinary labor, discipline, economic savvy, creativity, and collaborative skill necessary to make a difference in the world of food.

How is it that the artistry, sacrifice, and accomplishments of so many generations of professional culinarians have gone unrecognized? Where is the great history of the cooking profession in the United States? American poets, painters, architects, composers, musicians, industrial designers, printers, photographers, and dancers all have their celebrants, their historians, their informal or formal halls of fame that keep memory and tradition vibrant. But not cooking. Despite our living in an age when chefs have become cultural celebrities, we have not honored the masters of the culinary profession by keeping their memories. In a strange way, the memory of cooking has condensed around recipes, dishes that are performed in a general kitchen repertoire, while their creators have vanished into the ether. Can we imagine performing the *Jupiter Symphony* without referencing Mozart, or *Giant Steps* without considering John Coltrane? Yet in the kitchen we revive oysters Rockefeller without recognizing the soul of Jules Alciatore; vichyssoise, without acknowledging Louis Diat; and deviled lobster, without mention of Isaiah Le Count.

The Culinarians is a corrective to amnesia. It recollects the work of the masters who brought gastronomy to the cities of an expanding United States. To teach new pleasures, to supply spaces of conviviality and celebration, to reveal how basic biological functions, such as olfaction and ingestion, can be rendered conscious, indeed, trained to become conduits of knowledge—these have long been the great gifts bestowed by culinarians in the name of nourishment and hospitality. These gifts are worth recalling and revering.

What distinguished the culinary professionals who emerged in the 1790s from the vocational cooks who have existed since time immemorial? How do they differ from the military camp cooks, household servants, and innkeepers who peopled colonial America and remained numerous in the early republic? This: three gifts that the professionals had very particular ways of preparing.

Gift 1: For the culinarian, the pleasure of novelty lay in providing choice for the diner, a range of offerings that explored the seasonal variety of the market. In the old world of the inn, choice was restricted to beverages—the guest had to content himself with the dish prepared for everyone on the day's bill of fare. The restaurant was distinguished by variety, offering the diner a choice of possibilities that would be prepared à la carte. In hotels, variety in the early nineteenth century worked in another way—the table d'hôte, the set offering for all diners at a meal, announced a range of dishes arrayed on stations at the perimeter of the dining room. Diners chose among the offered items (the buffet, if you will) those they wished. A multiplicity of offerings satisfied a diner's wish for variety.

Gift 2: Just as Americans needed sacred spaces—churchyards and meeting-houses in which spiritual elation, gravity, and purity might bind a community—so they needed spaces of conviviality and celebration, zones in which sociability, specialness, and play might be shared. To make the food tasty and the drink agreeable was a base upon which to construct an atmosphere conducive to shared well-being. The décor, the stemware, linens, flatware, and silver, the politeness of the waiters, the cleanliness of the house, the acoustics of the space—all contributed to the experience of enjoyment. Before the French and American Revolutions, cooks attached to aristocratic households had learned the complexities needed to make an effective social occasion. In these households, however, the invitees were all known and invited by the host, the aristocratic owner of the house. After the revolutions, when the chefs found themselves unemployed, they set up spaces in which a social occasion might be had on every night by the public at large, that is, persons unknown to the host. The public host—the restaurateur, the hotelier, the maître d', the headwaiter, the steward—operated as the Boniface, the polite enabler of everyone's good times. So the experience of dining began to bifurcate, with cooks being unseen, and restaurateurs or stewards fronting the house. What these men and women lacked in lineage, they compensated for with stylishness and politeness.

Gift 3: Jean Anthelme Brillat-Savarin—the father of gastronomy and author of the landmark *Physiologie du goût* (1825)—spent the 1790s in exile from Revolutionary France in the United States and contributed a recipe to "Julien" (Jean Baptiste Gilbert Payplat) that contributed materially to the success of the first American restaurant. His exposition of gastronomy as the "knowledge and understanding of all that relates to man as he eats," with the end of conserving men "using the best food possible," expressed the unarticulated impetus of many of the early culinarians. They operated when agricultural innovation led to the explosion of new plant varieties; when livestock breeding improved a range of pig, cattle, and sheep breeds; when the roads and coastal shipping routes developed a dynamic internal trade in the United States; when chemical science fostered an understanding of emulsification, fermentation, and infection; and when cookstove technology permitted a more exquisite control of fire and thus cooking temperature. Brillat-Savarin promoted intellectual engagement in "all that relates to man as he eats" and a questing spirit in the aesthetics of taste. These cooks became the most active exploiters of the new fruits and vegetables coming to market. When they moved into the growing cities of the West, they became the driving force for the establishment of a diversified gardening system—indeed, Jules Arthur Harder contributed largely to the enrichment of California agriculture in the 1870s when he was the chef of the Palace Hotel in San Francisco.

The culinarians were intellectually curious, aesthetically experimental, and gastronomically evangelical. They strove to inspire devotees among their customers—persons whose tastes became so enriched by their experiences of the creations put before them that they become savants possessed of a special knowledge of "the best food possible." They became faithful communicants at the chef's table. This community of devotees lurks in the background of a number of these profiles and go by several names—the epicures, the bon vivants, the gourmets, the gastronomes, the good livers. I have quoted several of them to provide a contemporary public response to menus or dishes. In one case, that of Sam Ward, I have provided a biography, since he was a cook as well as a consumer of genius. His greatest creations found themselves in the repertoire of restaurant cooks. He was an exceptional figure in that he would be invited into the kitchen by chefs and allowed to work at the ranges.

One popular perception of fine dining arose from the enthusiasms of the gastronomes—that cuisine was a kind of gnosis, an occult, an upper-crust pursuit that offended prudence and indulged human carnality. There was, of course, no riposte to accusations that fine dining turned one to the senses, for it was true; but the culinarians (many of whom were French and Italian) believed that the parsimony and asceticism of sumptuary Puritans (many of whom were Anglo-American), offended God's endowments to human physiology of sensitivity in taste, smell, and touch. Was it "carnal idolatry" to make fullest use of the body God gave us? Or was it a kind of worship to sample and appreciate the full bounty of creation?

The gastronomes made consumption a path of knowing and superlative living. This offended the Protestant ethical conviction that work, the labor of production, and cooking were where meaning and moral worth lay. The figure of the chef confused the distinctions between *bad* consumerism and *good* productivity, because tasting was intimately involved in the work of cooking, and the end of production was to render emphatic the quality and sumptuousness of "the best food possible." The restaurant was successfully established in the United States in 1793 Boston (the old capital of Puritanism) when Julien ingeniously presented his establishment as therapeutic, restoring the health of invalids, and promoted food's good taste as a requisite for restoring good health, since illness often produced loss of appetite. "Restorators" were the name of the most ambitious eating houses in New England through the 1820s.

Coupled with Reformed Protestant anxiety about the sensuality of consumption was the political anxiety about the seemingly aristocratic character of fine dining. Classical republican ideologues insisted upon simplicity, egalitarianism, and lack of the symbolic distinction in public conduct. That the restaurateurs' pursuits of excellence entailed making their spaces different, more stylish, more special than plain public spaces seemed suspicious. While certain of the restaurants—Delmonico's, Sherry's, Rector's, Marchand's, the New Poodle Dog—consciously cultivated a blue-book exclusivity and fashionability, particularly during the final quarter of the nineteenth century, a number of houses recollected in the following pages were invitingly demotic in character. Alexander "Sandy" Welsh's Terrapin Lunch, for example, Coppa's Restaurant hosting the Bohemian Club, and Madam Bégué's in New Orleans were neither costly, nor snooty, nor plain in their fare. Price point did not determine the quality or professionalism of food. The skill of the cook and the care of the restaurateur did.

Furthermore, one truth about superb cooking was that its finest creations were intelligible to the vast majority of people once in the mouth. The common fellow might not understand the technique enabling a turkey to be boned and jellied, but that did not matter much when a forkful melted on the tongue. Indeed, an argument could be made that the novelty of a chef's creations would register more meaningfully on the tongue of a routine eater, one who cycled the same few dishes week after week. The new taste might expand that eater's desire and explode unthinking habit. Turning a feeder into a diner performs a social good. Certainly from the perspective of long-term cultural practice, the incitement to expand one's pantry has been beneficial. That experience of restaurant food gives rise to demand for a more diversified range of ingredients, countering the industrial tendency to concentrate on fewer crops grown more extensively.

Cooking has been a vocation for thousands of years, and the practices of meal preparation have been widely inculcated in populations in many cultures over vast stretches of historic time. The sort of culinary career explored here has existed for a relatively short time, only since the end of the eighteenth century. It came into being with the rise of the restaurant in France in the late 1760s and with the hotel in the 1790s in the modern West. The careers recovered here were all shaped by a sense of professionalism directed toward public service. All understood their activity to be something more than feeding those who need to be nourished. At a minimum, pleasure and alimentation—aesthetics and hygiene—were what these creators wished to give their boarders, guests, and customers.

The self-understanding of these culinarians can be seen in the way they presented themselves in advertisements for employment. Here is an October 15, 1856, advertisement in the *New York Herald*: "Wanted—A Situation, by a Capable Woman, who is a professed cook (understands French and English cooking, game, soups, and side dishes, des[s]erts, pastry, and confectionery of all kinds, and can get up dinners and suppers) as head cook in a hotel or first-class boarding house; has been accustomed to the same; best of city references given." The professed cook was schooled, either by a rigorous kitchen apprenticeship or by a cooking school, in pastry cooking, confectionery, and the preparation of roasts and entrées. He or she knew the styles and ethnic inflections of cuisine.

He or she sought a place in an institution (hotel, restaurant, hospital, school, store that served the public in preference to, say, a family). The professed cook championed an ideal of quality of performance—hence only sought places in which a commitment to being "first class" existed.

In the world of advertisements, the professed cook contrasted with the plain cook, someone who prepared meals learned usually at home by emulation and performed a limited repertoire. The plain cook could be a household servant working for lodging and small wages, or a kitchen worker in a second-class boardinghouse, tavern, or inn. Before 1863, they could be slaves with rudimentary training in cookhouse techniques. Slaves, too, were ranked in terms of accomplishment: plain cooks were expected to do laundry and were sold at regular auctions; "complete cooks" were trained in pastry cooking and sold privately. Furthermore, "French cooks"—the highest category of complete cooks—were especially valuable. Eighteen such "French cooks" were advertised in Charleston newspapers from the end of the American Revolution until 1840. In the following pages, we will meet Eliza Seymour Lee, a free black pastry cook who was the greatest teacher of cuisine to enslaved and free African Americans in the antebellum South.

Most cooks were plain cooks, black or white, northerner or southerner. Truth be known, since most housewives who prepared meals for their own households also learned "at home by emulation," they might be reckoned plain cooks too. Since "the greatest curse a man can have in his house is the self-styled 'plain cook,'" housewives and servant girls suffered cultural pressure to become something more. It was to improve these that the cookbook industry burgeoned in the 1800s. Cookbooks were in large part written by women who were professed cooks—whether matrons of cooking schools, like Eliza Leslie or Fannie Farmer, or onetime hotel or boardinghouse head cooks, such as Mary Randolph of Richmond, Virginia; Sarah Elliott of North Carolina; or Maria Parloa—simplifying preparations for home use. The purely literary cookbook author Marion Harland, for instance, was a rarer creature.

Contrasted to this abundance of print instruction was the paucity of print generated in America by and for professional chefs until the late 1880s. High-end cooking was learned by observation and practice during a four-year apprenticeship in an older master's kitchen. Signature dishes and chef's creations were proprietary matters, preserved with great secrecy. Most were not written down on purpose. Even those dishes considered the standard repertoire of fine dining—vol-au-vent or chicken à la financière or breast of canvasback duck—were made distinctive by a chef's take on seasoning. One did not give away the information upon which one's distinction in a marketplace depended. Hence one did not publish recipes. Rarely did one write them down. After the 1880s, when publication of recipes became commonplace, one often withheld the secret of the seasoning (see Jeanne Marie Bouisson Esparbe's recipes in "The Gilded Age" section).

The first cookbooks putatively presenting recipes by "name" chefs—Pierre Blot's *What to Eat and How to Cook It* (1863) and William Vollmer's *The United States Cook Book* (1858)—hardly reflect professional practice in the great kitchens of the 1860s and '70s. Both targeted housewives as their primary readership, simplified recipes accordingly, and presented vast stretches of elementary instruction about, say, making preserves or carving meats that would hardly have registered on a contemporary chef's imagination. Vollmer, a German who was chef at the Union Club, had interests in a farina company whose product appeared conspicuously in his printed recipes, so his book was an experiment in using print to diversify revenue streams. Blot is an odder case, a political exile and Parisian man of letters who had never been a chef, but who taught gastronomy to a largely female public in the Northeast as an academic. His attempt to set up a catering service in metropolitan New York was a dismal failure.

So what exactly is wrong with the books by Vollmer and Blot? Exactly the same thing wrong with most recipe books: they did not capture the full knowledge of an experienced chef about ingredients. In cookbooks, whether by Marion Harland or William Vollmer, a recipe will call for "one large onion, diced" or "three fine large tomatoes": What kind of onion? What variety of tomato? During the entire period covered in this book, only one chef revealed the secret wisdom of chefs regarding vegetables. Because the genius of American horticulture during the nineteenth century expressed itself in breeding an extraordinary variety of kinds of grains, fruits, berries, and vegetables, a sense of which ingredient was optimum for a particular dish was the most valuable sort of knowledge, a kitchen comprehension gained only through long experience and access to the richest produce markets. Jules Arthur Harder, chef at the Maison Dorée and Delmonico's in New York and the Palace Hotel in San Francisco, privately published the Rosetta stone to American vegetable cookery in 1885 as *Physiology of Taste; Harder's Book of Practical American Cookery*. It began the revelation of the professional mind to an American readership.

Three other volumes rendered a full exposition of that mind—the first was written by Vollmer's successor as chef of the Union Club. Felix J. Déliée published a year of menus with appended recipes in his 1884 masterwork, *The Franco-American Cookery Book*. This fascinating work, because of its organization by calendar, explored the seasonality of American ingredients while expounding on French techniques and formulas for cooking them. In 1890 Alessandro Filippini, a branch chef at Delmonico's in New York, simplified the presentation of the year and the exposition of the ingredients in *The Table: How to Buy Food, How to Cook It, and How to Serve It*. He provided the chef's seasonal repertoire, albeit simplified for home use. Since he had been an ingredient buyer for the network of Delmonico's restaurants in New York during the 1880s, his grasp of markets could not be excelled. Meats, fruits, produce, cheese, and grocery goods surface in the book with encyclopedic casualness. For all the knowledge offered in the volume, the cooking of dishes languished. Filippini despaired that a home cook, a household servant, or even a boardinghouse caterer could perform the sorts of preparations that were matters of course in the greatest restaurants on the continent.

So it remained for the greatest chef of the nineteenth century in America to provide the final reveal. Chef of chefs at Delmonico's, Charles Ranhofer, after he had departed from the institution, published in 1894 *The Epicurean*, a magnum opus intelligible only to master chefs but available to all, expounding in exquisite detail the way things were cooked in the great hotels and restaurants of America during the final twenty-five years of the nineteenth century. It is a stupefying book—one hurtful to read for its revelation of the variety of dishes, ingredients, flavors, and seasonings put into play in response to public desire. Perhaps more astounding than anything to a twenty-first-century reader is Ranhofer's imaginative accommodation to the tastes of his contemporaries—his willingness to experiment to bring the finest ingredients, most suitable techniques to engage with the peculiar tastes of persons who appeared at his restaurant. It is a surprisingly American book because it takes so serious the task of serving the tastes of a cosmopolitan American clientele.

Publication of *The Epicurean* in 1894 presented permission for many chefs to distinguish themselves by exposing their signature dishes to the public. Indeed, it became a mark of superlative cuisine to have a dish named after a hotel, restaurant, chef, or dedicatee printed and replicated by chefs and home cooks across America. Whether it was Louis Diat's vichyssoise or Madam Eugène's crawfish bisque or Gus Jaubert's burgoo, the revelation of the secrets of preparation became newsworthy. One task of this composite biography of the first age of fine dining in America is to secure and publish recipes from the period before the exposure of the repertoire of haute cuisine.

While Ranhofer's magnum opus is a rich deposit—containing a cosmopolitan array of dishes and a powerful exposition of the stocks, extracts, and sauces that built flavor in haute cuisine—it did not communicate the regional styles of cooking that had developed over the nineteenth century. French-style fine dining in the 1890s was only one in a variety of cuisines that had developed in the United States.

So we face a peculiar challenge when reconstructing the lives and works of the major practitioners. Not only do we not have dishes from their hands before us, we for the most part lack their instructions on how to replicate their creations prior to 1885. The cookbook—the most consulted form of evidence in culinary history—only gives us insight into the final thirty-five years of the period under review. So we look to what does survive in some profusion—reports of meals from contemporaries in manuscript and periodical print, menus from the 1840s on, and occasional autobiographical meditations by some of the cooks. That these miscellaneous evidences have not been gathered, taken up, and shaped into lives and histories until now arises from the immense labor in research such a synthesis has entailed, at least until the rise of the great print digitalization projects of the past two decades. Yet there have always been scholars willing to undertake vast projects of research. There are other reasons why it is only now that such a project seems somehow needful.

The philosopher Carolyn Korsmeyer, in her rumination *Making Sense of Taste: Food and Philosophy* (1999), has called attention to the way Western culture has valued the distance senses—sight and hearing—over touch, smell, and taste. When in the sixteenth century taste was taken up by thinkers and critics in discussions of aesthetic judgment, the gustatory experience had to be metaphorized. The sensations of pleasure and disgust in the mouth were too subjective and primal for rational reflection, yet their immediacy and their presentation of varieties of qualities was something that could be referenced since they were broadly intelligible. The connection of tasting with ingestion and the physical processes of being an animal struck philosophers as insufficiently sublime to be treated as idea or apperception. The Kantian distinction between bodily sensation of pleasure and the aesthetic pleasure in beauty made taste always a figure of speech rather than a direct frame of understanding.

Given traditional aesthetics' investment in the eternal verity of beauty, one can understand why a philosophy embracing universals and ideals would have difficulties with something as ductile as taste. Individual tastes can be quite peculiar, so much so that the ancient adage holds: *De gustibus non est disputandum* (There is no disputing taste). Yet since the ancients, there has been an alternative path of inquiry, one that finds capacities of understanding in the educability of taste, the ability to learn to savor the new, or to refine one's enjoyment of foods and to discriminate with great delicacies concerning its qualities. Archestratus of Gela—who accompanied Alexander the Great on his conquest of the world, along with Pyrrho the father of skepticism—articulated the potentials for this understanding in his masterful poem "Hedypatheia" (Life of Luxury). Archestratus's work might be seen as a counter-inquiry to Pyrrho's conclusion that no principles or ideas operate in the thinking of all cultures universally. Archestratus engaged in a world inquiry into the foods that every culture encountered in Alexander's conquest, surmising that experiencing the pleasures of others and testing the bounds of disgust worthily built the broadest sort of human *sensus communis* (common sense).

Archestratus's thought would be revived in the early nineteenth century by Jean Anthelme Brillat-Savarin in his landmark *Physiology of Taste*. The father of modern gastronomy understood the philosophical trepidations about the subjectivity of taste, when weighed weakly in the face of the historical demonstration of the planetary establishment of a community of shared tastes, and in the wake of the Columbian exchange. Brillat-Savarin also challenged contemporary thought to recognize that food was a matter of the utmost importance. The service of the stomach had organized the world system of trade and stood at the center of the modern economy. Of all the senses, taste and touch were those needful for survival. The blind and the deaf can live and thrive without sight and sound. But humans need to eat to live and touch to reproduce.

In the twenty-first century, as the crisis of the global industrialization of agriculture, the technological processing of edible matter, and the expansion of fast and convenience food have forced thoughtful people to wonder whither natural flavor, whither terroir, whither the slow experience of cooking and dining; and along with chefs and restaurateurs, they now lead the effort to preserve traditional ingredients and methods of growing and herding. They insistently assert the primacy of flavor. They continue to champion alimentation married to pleasure.

When I first undertook this project, I began collecting notices of the work of early culinarians promiscuously. My initial body of persons of interest numbered around 780. This initial collection included categories of professionals that I eventually excluded from this collection—bakers, headwaiters, riverboat stewards, common boardinghouse cooks (Elizabeth Englehardt is documenting their labors), food processors (pickle makers, sausage manufacturers). Of these excluded communities, the bakers were of most consequence, since they impinged upon the domain of pastry cooks and confiseurs at times. Yet the history of baking in the 1793-1919 period is so rich, so different in terms of financial and institutional organization, and peopled with so distinctive a set of significant figures, that I concluded it required its own book. I also excluded a group of culinarians who did not cater to the public—chefs such as Joseph Dagnoll, hired by millionaire W. K. Vanderbilt to oversee cooking in the Vanderbilt household; or Hercules, President George Washington's personal chef. In the wake of the Civil War, wealthy American families trekked to Europe to hire trained chefs for private dining, luring them to the United States with extravagant salaries. About two dozen such individuals have been recorded in newspaper reports of the time. Yet if they did not subsequently exercise their skills in a public venue, they do not appear here.

As the various biographical sketches began to coalesce, I realized that my final selections had to speak to certain themes in the development of national cuisine: the transmission of various European regional cuisines to and through North America, the engagement of European-trained chefs with American ingredients and American markets, the consolidation of the African American catering community and their immense influence on public banqueting in the nineteenth century, the development of a sense of a distinctive American and American regional cookery that was both refined and locally expressive, the development of culinary institutions that oversaw exchange, training, and job placement in the world of restaurants and hotels, and the rise and fall of iconic eating places in American cities. I composed 245 biographies, because the number was ample enough to cover the temporal and geographic ranges that the first age of fine dining in America entailed. It could communicate the variety of contributions to the development of "the best food possible." Furthermore, the number was sufficient to show that certain endemic problems—racism, sexism, French culinary chauvinism, the declining populations of indigenous game and fish (sturgeon and eastern salmon particularly)—gave rise to very complex responses politically in society at large and within the culinary profession. Yet the size of such a compendium required that I trim lives, even lives of "name chefs." I cut the biographies of a number of French fine-dining chefs in American hotels who did little more than perform the repertoire for an urban clientele, accomplished professionals such as Jean Berdou of the Hotel Astor, E. C. Perault of the Planters Hotel in St. Louis, John Chiappano of the Auditorium Hotel in Chicago, Louis Pfaff of the New Willard in Washington, DC, John Juillard of the Hotel Adolphus in Dallas, and John Bicochi of the Hotel Piedmont in Atlanta. Because Adrian Miller was preparing a comprehensive account of the African American chefs who worked at the White House, I eliminated several of my profiles of these cooks, knowing that they would be well treated. Also eliminated were a group of figures who were culinary specialists of sorts—a roast meat and game man such as William Clarke of New York, or seafood specialists such as Thomas Barr of Boston, or southern food promoters such as Simon Peter Gross. Among the 245 original biographies were those of a number of African American chefs, such as Abraham Cobb, of Savannah, Georgia, who presided over major restaurants yet contributed little new to the repertoire of regional cuisine. I eliminated these but have posted my biographical sketches on the blog of the Black Culinary History group so that they receive some recognition. Eventually I distilled the collection to the 175 lives that appear here.

In the following biographies, I provide the salient contribution of the subject to the development of fine dining in the country. If menus, recipes, descriptions of the signature features of a person's or restaurant's culinary approach exist, I've sought to incorporate them. Digital archive projects at the New York Public Library, the American Antiquarian Society, the University of Nevada, Las Vegas, the Los Angeles Public Library, the Culinary Institute of America, and Henry Voigt's extraordinary blog, *The American Menu*, have enabled us to understand much about the repertoire of fine dining.

For restaurateurs and hoteliers, I've attempted to show how the institutions they brought into being and managed materially contributed to the shaping of the experience of superlative food, whether in terms of kitchen technology, dining room design, or rearrangement of diners in space (those persons, for instance, responsible for supplanting refectory-style seating at long tables in gentlemen's dining rooms to the small-table café array in the 1850s). I also desired to say something about the shape of a person's life—their mobility, their fixity, their self-renovations, their growth in curiosity and mastery. There are many dates, places, and facts encountered here, derived from an extraordinary number of contemporary sources. Yet for certain persons it was difficult to secure even basic information, despite his or her immense influence. Baptiste Moreau, for example—reckoned by some to have been the greatest chef in antebellum New Orleans—left a surprisingly faint paper trail. A passing reference here, a census taker's note there, a fugitive advertisement, a memoirist's fond recollection, a rival's brief assessment. Gathering these things into a life is a curiously satisfying exercise. I've tried to present here more than factitious stick figures.

Invariably, I drafted a biographical sketch of a subject from primary sources before turning to secondary sources and recent histories to learn what other persons have found out. This way, I have been able to dismantle some hoary fantasies and correct details of lives and institutional histories. Yet I've found a number of studies edifying, informed, and valuable. We now live at the dawn of a great age of culinary history writing. I offer these lives as the dramatis personae of the culinary histories yet to come.

The First Era 1790 to 1835
The Restaurant, the Coffeehouse, and the Oyster Cellar

As an aid to reading these biographical sketches, I provide some general observations about the institutions and historical circumstances marking the development of fine dining. The earliest phase of this development—mirrored in the first twenty-five biographies—saw the development of several distinct institutions and styles of gastronomy. The restorator—or the restaurateur (the metonymic confusion of the institution with its creator)—made claims about the healthfulness of fine-flavored foods and wines, tended to be homosocial in its clientele, featured soups as well as chops, and boasted a Gallic genealogy of influence. An ordinary—or regular sitting for boarders—was held in midafternoon. Available dishes were ordered off a menu à la carte.

The coffeehouse, in contrast, advertised an English orientation to food, with meats and pastries (pot pies, particularly) featured on the menu, a commercial ambience (a broad subscription to continental and European newspapers adorned the public rooms), with coffee and ale as the chief beverages. The company was predominately male. Business mixed with pleasure within a large and well-appointed space. Service did not tend to regular seatings. Rather, breakfast, dinner, and sometimes supper were available at various hours.

The hotel was an institution at which one could lodge as well as board. It invariably offered breakfast, dinner, and supper. Men, women, and families were accommodated. Cuisine was a draw and offered in the form of a table d'hôte, a range of set offerings for the day from which a diner could select. Game and spirits were particular attractions in terms of offerings. The size of the dining hall enabled public entities to hold balls and banquets on the premises.

The oyster cellar was an urban phenomenon associated particularly with Philadelphia, Baltimore, and New York. Located below a public building, this homosocial space offered porter and bivalves, fish and turtle in season. Soups and chowders assumed an increasingly important role with each decade. African Americans were particularly significant in developing the cookery associated with these spaces. And food was consumed standing as well as seated. Speed of service became a hallmark of cellar fare.

The confectionery shop also emerged as an important urban center of pleasure. Women confectioners and pastry chefs operated in Charleston, Philadelphia, and New York in some number. These shops performed dual functions: retailing sweets and savory pies for home consumption, as well as offering sit-down service. These shops popularized ice cream and made the service of women a matter of emphasis.

British American culinarians dominated the 1790 to 1835 era of professional cookery. It would be the only period when they would do so.

The Second Era 1835 to 1865
The Great Hotel, the Saloon, and the Black Caterer

Antebellum America saw the transformation of the restorator into the restaurant, the hotel into a massive center of urban hospitality and luxury, the emergence of the saloon (or large room dedicated to a specific purpose, whether dancing, drinking, or dining), and the efflorescence of event and on-site banquet catering. The scale of provision expanded. The competition to offer in a city the best spread, the most resplendent service, the most exhilarating experience drove caterers and restaurateurs to greater effort and more creative management of hospitality. The recruitment of talented collaborators became a hallmark of managerial excellence. John and Peter Delmonico in New York launched a century of restaurant supremacy in America by astute recruitment in the 1830s, including their nephew Lorenzo, the restaurateur with as fine a judgment about character and skill as existed in the nineteenth century. The Delmonico family's penchant for orderliness and competence made them compartmentalize functions and staff: the steward, the waiter, the chef, the cooks, the butcher, the baker, the dishwasher—all had clearly defined roles, responsibilities, lines of communication, and protocols of behavior. The rationalization of the restaurant was mirrored in the organization of the high-end hotels that came into being in the late 1820s and '30s in the major cities of America.

Hotels began taking on a variety of forms in the nineteenth century, from modest lodging houses, to respectable midsize hostelries, to the spectacular public palaces. Each form of the hotel had its characteristic cuisine—the low end had boardinghouse fare; the middle range could have fine cuisine, particularly if run by a restaurateur who transmuted into a hotelier; and the famous hotels had to have superb cuisine if they wanted to attract a cosmopolitan patronage. Because of the scale of service, the hotel kitchen became the locus of technological innovation during the century.

Within the commodious spaces of the great hotels, certain rooms took on specific functions—a space where females could lunch without the distraction of male attention or a room devoted to male bibulousness. The latter were designated saloons. The emergence of the saloon—a room tricked out to promote a particular kind of hospitality or food and drink service—was one of the signal developments of the second phase of the history documented here. Common parlance has made the saloon synonymous with a drinking house; but it originally meant a room outfitted and decorated to promote a specific kind of human action. At racetracks, for instance, the saloon was where men and women might refresh themselves and converse away from the track and insulated from the business of betting.

When the oyster cellar emerged from belowground and spread from eastern cities to New Orleans, Mobile, Galveston, St. Louis, and Cincinnati, it became the oyster saloon. Two men from New Orleans profiled here—Walter Van Rensselaer and Anthony Astredo—drove this development. That oysters could grace the saloons of interior cities indicated that modes of transportation had greatly developed from the 1830s onward. The canal projects, the development of river-borne steamship traffic, the rise of the railroads, and the coastwise steam-packet trade enabled goods to traverse hundreds of miles rapidly. The rails enabled the great hotels to provision their tables with game from the western wilds, exerting a pressure of incessant harvest that would endanger many species over the course of the century.

In the competition for the epicurean high roller, hotels exerted themselves to secure rare ingredients, wines, and liquors to distinguish themselves from competitors. To publicize and memorialize offerings, chefs began to cultivate the art of the menu on both sides of the Atlantic. More than a simple card listing the bill of fare, the menu was the subject of calculation, decoration, and personalization—with watercolor drawings, impromptu epigrams, and novel dishes scribed in the chef's or steward's hand. From the 1840s onward, not a public banquet, anniversary feast, or holiday passed without a paper celebration of the foods and wines brought to the table.

And hotels did not exert a monopoly on the banquet trade. The second quarter of the nineteenth century was, after all, the great age of American association—a time that Alexis de Tocqueville characterized as rife with club formation, the institution of societies and corporations. Many such bodies had their own meeting halls and rooms. Why pay for space in a hotel when one had as impressive a hall oneself? It was for this world of on-premises dining that caterers plied their trade. The great caterers of this era, many of whom were African American, provisioned, transported, erected, cooked, and served 500-person feasts on site. They booked entertainment, supplied bartenders, and hauled in their own flatware, stemware, serving dishes, and china. Sometimes they hauled in portable stoves as well. James Augustin, Nat Fuller, and Joshua B. Smith were among the most resonant names during the antebellum period. Their menus compare favorably with those of the great hotels for spectacular fare, graphic beauty, and seasonality.

The political situation of the African American caterers stands in bold outline with the war that would disrupt American society in the 1860s. Some (Nat Fuller, for instance) were slaves operating on a "work for hire" basis with their masters. Some had been freed and departed the slave states so as not to risk having liberty deprived them again. Some were active abolitionists (Thomas Downing and Joshua B. Smith), some (James Wormley and William Walker) took pains not to be forward in the insistence on civil rights. In every case, the Civil War transformed the political rules by which these caterers and hoteliers operated in the United States.

The Third Era 1865 to 1885
The French Hegemony and the Nationalist Reaction

The European revolutions of 1848 set many young people on the move, seeking a better, less repressive social and cultural scene. A diaspora of musicians, urban artisans, and culinarians crossed the Atlantic seeking employment and space to exercise their conscience in North and South America. French chefs came in some numbers, having heard of the success of early generations of emigrants in Boston, New York, Philadelphia, Washington, DC, Charleston, and New Orleans. Persons trained in pastry cookery, in particular, won immediate honor and custom. By the Civil War, the population of French-trained chefs had reached such density in New York that the organization of a voluntary association would serve the interests of the professional community. The Société Culinaire Philanthropique was organized on April 22, 1865. It celebrated its 150th anniversary on the day I wrote this paragraph.

From the first, the Société took a liberal view of who might become a member (Alsatians, Belgians, Swiss, and French-trained Italians found their way on the rolls at various junctures) and held a strict view of its purposes: to enable the smooth insertion of professionally trained French cooks into American positions, to assist any member suffering financial or health reverses, to promote friendly sociability among professional rivals in the hotel and restaurant world, and (in the later 1870s) to promote a public mystique about the skills of French chefs by public food exhibitions. In imitation of the New York Société, communities of French and German chefs in other major cities organized similar associations.

Organization enabled the spread of French cuisine into the American interior. Curiously, associations parallel to the Société proved to be among the most congenial venues for placing newly arrived European cooks. Clubbing had burgeoned across America in the 1850s, and gentlemen's clubs took on the cultural importance that they had long had in London and Paris. For many men, these clubs were a home away from home, where one took meals, enjoyed conversation, and sought respite from business. A building boom began in the 1850s that would continue unabated throughout the remainder of the century, producing an urban landscape full of architecturally imposing club buildings. Unlike the Masonic halls of an earlier era, the new club headquarters all possessed in-house kitchens and dining spaces. In the period after the Civil War, there were cities (Baltimore, St. Louis, Pittsburgh, and Milwaukee) where the best cuisine outside of hotels was to be had in men's clubs, not restaurants. Unless the clubs were German or Italian ethnic sodalities, the chef would be French, the food French with added American specialties (particularly fruit pies), and the menu language Franglish.

While menu French had existed in the antebellum period, it became ubiquitous among restaurants with any pretension to quality in the post–Civil War decades. The association of French cuisine with quality was accomplished largely without professional chefs addressing the public in cookbooks, articles, or recipes. The literary celebration of their accomplishments fell to literary men—American gastronomes who had a facility with the pen, such as Nathaniel

Parker Willis and Sam Ward. The most potent literary counterforces to the gastronomic rhapsodies were the writings of the literary Bohemians—the ragtag assortment of young iconoclasts who haunted any place that was cheap, filling, and good; and so a Germanic rathskeller such as Pfaff's or an Italian pasta house with inexpensive palatable wine such as Coppa's in San Francisco would become the haunt of poets, painters, and periodical writers. Bohemians did not care if the red wine was Chianti or Burgundy, so long as it produced elation with minimal hangover.

The saturation of fine dining with French cuisine began to prompt a pushback within the culinary profession in 1874, shortly before the nation's centennial. The tour of Grand Duke Alexis of Russia and his observations (derived from an extensive course of hotel dining) that "there were no American dishes" and that American chefs "were all French," caused confectioner and chef James W. Parkinson of Philadelphia to publish a manifesto, *American Dishes at the Centennial.* He begins with a diagnosis of the state of affairs in 1874: "So deeply rooted is this sentiment in the public mind, that Paris is the great fountain-head of all art and all taste in these departments, that when an American confectioner or caterer makes any invention in his craft, he feels that to secure its sale and to establish its popularity, he must give it a French name." Where, then, is authentic American cooking? "Nearly all the good cooking in the United States is in private houses." Parkinson then proposed that at the centennial exhibition there be an American restaurant devoted to American things. He follows this recommendation with a catalog of the ingredients distinctive to America or cultivated with superior results in the United States than in Europe. Home cooking and local ingredients—a hundred years before Craig Claiborne reclaimed his southern heritage in print in the *New York Times*—Parkinson stated the grounds from which an American cookery might arise.

The French, however, were an imperial power, and they understood that the incorporation of the local ingredient into the metropolitan cookery was the means to keep powerful traditions, such as Parisian haute cuisine, vibrant. And so the canvasback duck, terrapin à la Maryland, the Saratoga chip (potato chip), the blackfish, the sweet potato, and maize found their way into Delmonico's kitchen and onto the French menu. Every new vegetable variety that American horticulturalists and seedsmen introduced to the seed catalogs and markets of the United States would be tried, assigned to particular sorts of preparations, and filed away in the secret preserves of professional memory.

During the period when French chefs established their hegemony over the institutions of American fine dining, they maintained secrecy over their recipes. The cookbook publishing industry had expanded substantially from the 1840s through the '70s. In the United States, it was, for the most part, a literature compiled by women for women—by women of letters and boardinghouse cooks for housewives and would-be boardinghouse cooks. Some of the cook-books codified the teaching of cooking schools, matron-led cooking acade-mies that taught the mysteries of baking and pastry cooking while inculcating principles of economy and promptitude. The most innovative of the matrons—Elizabeth Goodfellow, Esther A. Howland, Sarah Tyson Rorer, Juliet Corson, Maria Parloa, Mary Lincoln, Fannie Merritt Farmer—became celebrities.

The cookbook literature involved massive reprinting of recipes from earlier culinary compendia. Only recently have the digital tools become available to trace the genealogy of recipes through various books and decades. But even a cursory examination of major titles makes certain things apparent. American cookbook authors were most beholden to early French authorities in the realm of confection, pastry cooking, and soup making. Nineteenth-century English translations of the works of Louis-Eustache Ude and Marie-Antoine Carême, and the English-language books composed by Antoine Beauvilliers and Alexis Bénoit Soyer, supplied the basic information. English cookery books supplied much of the information on the cooking of meat, fish, pickling, preserving, and the making of cakes and puddings. What was most American in this literature? In the South, it was the African American and vernacular dishes that found their way into print; in the North, the vegetarianism and gymnosophist cookery of various pure food and ethical sects.

In 1885 the culinary profession reversed its attitude about keeping knowl-edge of cookery secret. The public exposure of the professional mind was one of the hallmarks of the final phase of the first age of American fine dining, the Gilded Age.

The Gilded Age 1885 to 1919
Fame and the Master Chef

At the end of the nineteenth century, no city could regard itself as culturally ad-equate unless it boasted a hotel with a name chef. No millionaire could reckon himself a baron of wealth and industry unless his or her household had a chef poached from a top-ranked restaurant or hotel in Paris, London, Baden-Baden, or Monaco.

As disparities of wealth burgeoned across the United States, the divide be-tween the home cooking of the common people and the dining of the privileged orders grew increasingly stark. Perhaps the differences were most apparent in terms of beverages. Restaurants celebrated with wine; hotels, spirits; and urban taverns, beer. But across America, a vast population regarded alcohol as a sign of moral failure. Temperance was a demotic movement with strong Protestant inflection. It looked upon the habits of the great urban temples of consumption as dissipation. The discipline of Delmonico's had always mitigated criticism. The emergence of a younger, racier, and more unbuttoned style of fine dining pioneered by Louis Sherry and Charles E. Rector heightened the anxieties of the hinterlands. After Broadway began celebrating the carnal pleasures of stage-door Johnnies wooing showgirls at lobster palaces in musicals such as *The Girl from Rector's*, a full-fledged culture war broke out that would not be resolved until the moral majority had pressured the Volstead Act into existence.

Prohibition brought a wrenching end to the first age of fine dining in America. The markup on champagne had kept many a restaurant afloat in the 1890s and 1900s. The tide of bubbles was staunched. Of all the strategies devised about what must be done to replace alcohol as the financial linchpin of dining, the most promising were (a) replacing alcohol with sugar as the drug that would make diners return repeatedly, making dessert a more emphatic component of the meal; (b) making entertainment—dancing, music, or even theatrical performance—a component of the evening's experience; or (c) specializing in an ethnic tradition that was not French and transforming the restaurant into a site of community identity. Each of these paths forward had limited success. Only the hotel dining rooms continued to make a go of fine dining. Their advantage lay in the necessity of serving the visitor to a city, rather than the local resident; they could regard the dining facility as a loss leader, while making a profit on lodging.

The ethnic turn of dining to some extent had taken place during the Gilded Age, a function of the wave of immigration taking place at the end of the nineteenth century. Germans had successfully established restaurants with a non-French focus in Cincinnati, Chicago, New York, and St. Louis in the wake of the Civil War. German culinary training—particularly in the spa resorts of Baden-Baden, Karlsbad, and Marienbad—had not differed greatly from Parisian training, particularly in terms of pastry cooking. An admixture of signature Germanic dishes—sauerkraut, sauerbraten, and wursts—to the cosmopolitan fish, roasts, and soups was the common strategy of Faust's in St. Louis, Lüchow's in New York, and Lew Boman's in Cincinnati. Italian restaurants tended to be one of two sorts: the spaghetti and sauce cookshop, inexpensive with modestly priced wine; and the regional houses that featured the favored dishes of a distinct region. While the former might occasionally rise from the status of neighborhood eatery if adopted by artists or writers, gaining some fame, the latter became beacons of Italian cuisine in America: Louis F. Mazzetti, Nunzio Finelli, Dominico Paretti, and Francesco Martinelli were the most luminous of a galaxy of stars to operate in American cities in the latter part of the nineteenth century. In San Francisco, New York, and Philadelphia, Chinese trading communities burgeoned in the wake of the Civil War. A place of entertainment and banqueting became requisite for these enclaves, and at least one regionally authentic restaurant emerged in each major city. Because these communities were fraught with faction struggles, the histories here invariably speak of restaurateurs allying with one or another group; misinformation, false names, and contradictions in police records abound. No histories were more difficult to retrieve. The biographies of Wong Ah Cheok, "Harry" Lee King, Lee Chit, and Der Doo are the most plausible and confirmable constructions of the messy bodies of evidence. Hispanic restaurants emerged in several locales in the United States during the Gilded Age—Los Angeles, Tampa, San Antonio, and New York had scenes. Yet few of these pioneering restaurants had aspirations greater than feeding the local immigrant population. Two restaurateurs, however, won a measure of fame with their efforts: Jose Gestal brought fine Basque cuisine to Boise, Idaho; and Jose Sanroman synthesized the best dimensions of a robust Southern California scene in his Los Angeles restaurant-tienda complex.

One measure of the success of these ethnic culinarians was their appearance in print. Professional solidarity among culinarians gave rise to a national print culture devoted to cuisine. James W. Parkinson's *The Confectioner* and his later periodical *The Caterer*; Gustave Nouvel's French-language newsletter devoted to Gallic cuisine, the twentieth-century *Table Talk*; and the emergence of food columns in newspapers, such as the *New Orleans Times-Picayune*'s "The Caterer" in the 1880s—all attested to the growing cultural interest in food preparation. Some literary chefs—Jessup Whitehead and Parkinson, particularly—grew wealthy off the proceeds of their columns, magazine articles, and cookbooks. Whitehead was probably the first person hired to be as chef de cuisine of a resort largely on the basis of his printed oeuvre rather than his record of hotel and restaurant work.

A final word about the kind of notice a chef received in the last years of the first age of fine dining in America—articles in the professional press had a different tenor than those in the general press. The latter has a very few categories of interest in chefs: exalted salaries for famous chefs, pronouncements by foreign chefs about American foods and eating habits, crimes committed by chefs, technological innovations pioneered by chef inventors, and chefs changing major venues. In the 1890s, newspapers developed an interest in recipes, and food columns began featuring several chefs' treatments of dishes in holiday menus or breakfast menus. In the early twentieth century, newspaper series would feature major chefs offering housewives guidance on how to make great food inexpensively or how to shape menus with variety.

Finally, we should think about how chefs and restaurateurs turned increasingly to branding a line of food, for example: James W. Parkinson's and Louis Sherry's launching lines of ice cream and confection; James H. W. Huckins's commencing the mass marketing of soups; or Henri Mouquin's brokering escargots to restaurateurs across America. Ironically, the most creative things that the chefs of the Gilded Age did—the creation of new, immensely popular dishes—invariably did not carry the name of the creators. Charles Ranhofer's baked Alaska, Jules Alciatore's oysters Rockefeller, Louis Diat's vichyssoise, Jules Arthur Harder's green goddess dressing—these became fixtures in a thousand kitchens, and knowledge of who their creators were evaporated.

The
FIRST ERA
1790 to 1835

THE RESTAURANT, THE COFFEEHOUSE,
AND THE OYSTER CELLAR

"Julien" (Jean Baptiste Gilbert Payplat) 1753–1805

Boston

The legendary originator of the restaurant in the United States, Julien arrived in Boston in the late summer of 1786 as steward to M. de Letombe, the Consul of France for the Eastern States. In July 1793 Julien left Letombe's service and on July 10 established a hotel named the Restorator opposite the Quaker Meeting House on Leverett Street in Boston. Conceiving his hotel in terms of the accommodations found in European spas, where guests imbibed healing waters and renovated themselves in the baths, he styled the Restorator as "a Resort, where the infirm in health, the convalescent, and those whose attention to studious business occasions a lassitude of nature; can obtain the most suitable nourishment." The other model for his restorator was the new Parisian style of eating house, in which chefs displaced from aristocrat households by the French Revolution supplied the desires and needs of the public à la carte. Julien declared that "Excellent Wines and Cordials, good Soups, and Broths, Pastry, in all its delicious variety, Alamode Beef, Bacon, Poultry, and, generally, all other refreshing viands, will be kept in due preparation: And a Bill of Fare will be constantly for exhibition; from which each visitor may command whatever may best suit his appetite."

The excellence of his dishes, the seriousness of his claims concerning healthfulness, his wines, and his refined manners immediately made his eating house a favorite resort of Boston's literati and young businessmen. He became a town celebrity, portrayed in prose on multiple occasions, admired for making something so worthwhile when he arrived in America "with little or nothing to support himself" except his talent and industry. A portrait describes him: "His person is very graceful and his hair toupeed. In conversation he is affable, accommodating and polite; his voice is pleasing, and sonorous; he still, however,

"Julien's Restorator." Wood engraving. From James Henry Stark, *Antique Views of the Towne of Boston* (Boston Electrotype Engraving Co., 1882), 75.

retains his provincial dialect, and the same sign over his door which indicated the place of his former residence. Julien may be called the Prince of Soups."

His soups were famous. Invariably, Julien commended them for their curative and nutritive power. Julien would "procure every luxury" a customer wished, but with a soup would provide the requisites of life. When flu came to Massachusetts in November 1793, Julien advertised "Soup of Barley, particularly salutary for those who are afflicted with the present prevalent Influenza." His brown soup, a beef consommé, became his signature. He made a clear turtle soup—"efficacious in remedying the numerous diseases incident to the Spring"—on the same model: "The Soup made of Turtle, like the Brown Soup of Mr. Julien's, will be free from ingredients, and with but a small quantity of spice. Good lean Beef, Veal and Fowls with the Turtle-flesh are the basis." Julien prepared two sorts of turtle soups: land turtle soup and green turtle soup. The former Julien commended for its "efficacy in purifying the blood," citing Samuel Auguste Tissot and Comte George-Louis LeClerc de Buffon.

In June 1794, John Magner advertised the three-story building occupied by Julien for sale. The Boston Restorator moved in midsummer to the Thomas Clements House on the corner of Milk Street and Dalton's Lane, a site agreeable because of its access to "fresh air." This is the building illustrated above. At this juncture, Julien came to the notice of Jean Anthelme Brillat-Savarin, who was touring America while in exile from the French Revolution. Brillat-Savarin taught Julien to cook a cheese omelet (*oeufs brouillés au frommage*). It proved popular and Julien sent Brillat-Savarin the carcasses of two roebucks in recompense when the latter settled in New York.

Julien's success inspired imitators. The Messrs. Dorival and Deguise opened their restorator at Oliver's Dock, near the Exchange. It offered its own "rich and well seasoned Brown, and other Soupes" to restore health to invalids. The partnership did not last six months. Isaac Deguise opened a "new" restorator that failed within two months of opening. John L. Dorival opened a boardinghouse in a building at the bottom of the Mall, offering "a great variety of pies." By summer of 1798, it too had failed. The Parisian cook M. Le Rebour opened the Shakespear Hotel and Restorator on Water Street in 1797, promising soups, pasty, and cookery of every description that is "in the American, English or Paris style." Note that there was no medical framing of the fare. He was obliged to move almost immediately to the vicinity of the Boston Theatre. He soon realized Bostonian conscience required luxury to be lashed to hygiene, so he began advertising his own "nourishing, restoring Soup" so that "the generous epicure, the strengthening convalescent, and the fainting valetudinarian, may constantly find gratification, confirmation and salvation." The Disciples of Epicurus, however, preferred their old champion, Julien, and Le Rebour was forced to remove to Salem in 1800.

Though Julien made it known that gambling was not permitted in his establishment, and that nutrition was the raison d'être of his restorator, the ability to prepare delicious fare attracted men of appetite. In 1803 the *Boston Commercial Gazette* published a mock epic, "Battle of the Bucks," describing a visitation by a band of boastful bachelors to the Restorator:

> Julien, now doz'd, when Ten the Old-South struck,
> Upon his ears a thundering tumult broke;
> In rush at once a well-known, noted band,
> The kitchen throng, and round our landlord stand;
> For brandy, wine and steaks, aloud they call,
> Obsequious Charles now shews them to the Hall;
> The table spread, the chairs arrang'd around,
> With steaks and wine the festive board is crown'd.
> Now not a noise is heard, as mute they sate,
> Save the knives sound against the clattering plate;
> Now flies the cork, the purple claret flows,
> And in the glass the sparkling liquor glows;
> Quick to the lips the bumper each applies—
> As the wine sinks, the mounting spirits rise.

The most interesting moment in the verse is the reverent silence when the bucks consumed their food.

Julien's eminence in the world of letters can be judged by the adoption of "The Restorator" as the title of a column of cultural commentary in the *New-England Palladium* in 1801. "In imitation of Mr. Julien, I mean to open a house of public entertainment, where every intellectual epicure may be gratified with his favourite dish."

In October 1797, Julien married Hannah Horne of Boston. The couple lived in the Restorator, with Hannah managing the house's books.

After the turn of the century, a challenger for culinary supremacy emerged in Boston in the person of Othello Pollard, an African American caterer. As a contemporary observed, these two giants treated each other with respect free of jealousy. The supremacy of Julien in soups was acknowledged, while Pollard's precedence in creams won common consent. "Each seemed conscious of his own greatness, and exalted above the feeling of envy."

In 1805 Julien died, and the Restorator came into the hands of Hannah, who ran it for a decade before selling it to Frederick Rouillard. When Rouillard took over, he paid homage to its creator, Julien: "This long established house is well known throughout the country. Its celebrity was first acquired by the original proprietor, whose obliging disposition and gentlemanly deportment, united with a thorough knowledge of the art, we may almost say science of cookery, brought to his house, a constant and overflowing bevy of bon vivants, as well as invalids." Since 1816, Julien has been perpetually remembered as the originator of one of the fundamental institutions of American gastronomy, the restaurant.

※ ※ ※

SOURCES: "Restorator," *American Apollo* 2, no. 42 (July 19, 1793): 4; "Restorator," *American Apollo* 3, no. 8 (November 15, 1793): 4; "Boston Restorator," *American Apollo* 3, no. 47 (August 21, 1794): 3; "Restorator. M. Julien," *Columbian Centinel* 21, no. 15 (April 30, 1794): 4; "Boston Restorator," *Columbian Centinel* 25, no. 15 (April 27, 1796): 3; "New Restorator," *Massachusetts Mercury* 8, no. 19 (September 2, 1796): 4; "New Restorator," *Massachusetts Mercury* 26, no. 9 (October 5, 1796): 3; "John L. Dorival," *Columbian Centinel* 26, no. 32 (December 24, 1796): 3; "Shakespear Hotel," *Massachusetts Mercury* 9, no. 21 (March 14, 1797): 4; "Fresh Turtle Soup," *Boston Price-Current* 155 (August 31, 1797): 4; "Removal," *Boston Price-Current* (October 19, 1797): 3; "Married," *Newburyport Impartial Herald* 5, no. 379 (October 24, 1797): 3; "Turtle Soup," *Columbian Centinel* 31, no. 17 (May 1, 1799): 4; "British Spy in Boston, No. 2, Restorator," *Salem Gazette* 15, no. 986 (January 30, 1801); "Battle of the Bucks," *Boston Commercial Gazette* 13, no. 36 (January 3, 1803): 2; *Boston Repertory* 2, no. 4 (January 11, 1805): 4; [Mortuary notice,] *Political Observatory* 2, no. 87 (July 13, 1805): 3; "Julien's Restorator," *Boston Commercial Gazette* 45, no. 39 (May 2, 1816): 1; Arthur Wellington Brayley, "The Shoe and Leather Trade in Massachusetts during the Past 274 Years," *The Bostonian* 1 (October–March 1894–95): 278; "John Baptiste Julien," *Boston Herald* 8, no. 4 (March 9, 1922).

Othello Pollard 1765?–182?
Boston; Cambridge; Halifax

"The politest man in Boston"—"a polished piece of ebony"—an unrivaled creator of creams and cheesecakes—a master of ceremonies at parties, meetings, and funerals—a wit—an entrepreneur—the foremost champion of elegant living in a city haunted by its ancestral Puritanism: Othello Pollard's culinary career was brief but brilliant, spanning approximately from 1796 to 1806. It was almost briefer. On a frigid January night in 1803, fire broke out in Daniel Bowen's Columbian Museum on Common Street in Boston. A wooden edifice, the building ignited instantaneously and spread to the William Doyle House on one side, used as a boardinghouse by the widow Pollard, and on the other side, her son Othello Pollard's refectory and store. Both burned to the ground, and the residents barely escaped with their lives. "This fire commenced by the falling of a light upon the bed in which the wax figure of Desdemona was placed. The flames immediately communicated to the curtains and spread so rapidly that those who were present (four persons) could not stop their progress." Another commentator explained that some country folk jostled the lit taper that a wax statue of Shakespeare's Othello held, making it fall upon the wax effigy of Shakespeare's tragic heroine. Town officials estimated the total loss at $50,000. Othello came close to ruining Othello.

The fire forced Pollard to leave off retail sales to embrace wholeheartedly his true calling as chef and restaurateur. He moved across the river to Cambridge, since he had catered Harvard College class events since 1800, and opened his Classic Hotel or Attic Bower at the north side of the Common, two doors north of Packard's Tavern.

> In chusing an appellation for his Hotel, he has endeavoured to attract the notice of Gentlemen of elegant leisure, or of delicate health; and he trusts he shall, in pursuance of his motto, be enabled to combine in his social retreat, all the invitations which the politest palate may require, with all wit-inspiring ingredients of

TO BE SOLD BY
OTHELLO POLLARD,
ONE DOOR NORTH OF THE COLUMBIAN MUSEUM,
BOSTON,
SOLID ARGUMENTS,
CONSISTING OF
Bread, Butter. Cheese. Ham, Tongue, &c. &c.
ready cook'd.
AGITATIONS,
Cider, Vinegar, Salt, Pickles, Sweet Oil, &c.
GRIEVANCES.
Peppersause, Mustard. Black Pepper, Cayenne.
PUNISHMENTS.
Wine, Gin, Brandy, Ice Punch, Cordials, Spirits.
Bitters. Porter.
SUPERFLUITIES.
Ice Creams, Custards, Strawberries and Creams,
Whip-Sullibubs, Pies, Jellies, Olives,
All kinds of Fruits, Snuff,
Tobacco and Segars.
N. B.—Any of the above articles to be exchanged
for
NECESSARIES,
Viz. French Crowns. Spanish Dollars. Pistareens,
Cents, Mills, or Bank Bills.
Credit given for
PAYMENTS,
30, 60, and 90 seconds, or as long as a man can
hold his breath.
RUDIMENTS GRATIS, VIZ.

Those indebted for	Arguments,
Must not be	Agitated,
Nor think it a	Grievance,
If they should meet	Punishment,
For calling for such	Superfluities
And not supposing it	Necessary
To make immediate	Payment.

I have trusted so long, it is to my sorrow;
It's now. pay to-day, and I'll trust tomorrow.

Othello Pollard's "Bill of Fare." *Gloucester Telegraph* (January 6, 1838): 3. From the *Boston Evening Transcript*. Original from October 1803.

intellectual festivity. A mere bon vivant is a sad dull dog, and a mere philosopher a sad wise one. Blend the two characters, and you follow the receipt to make a Gentleman.

One of Harvard's litterateurs supplied a prose portrait of this African American caterer and wit. "His countenance is dark and penetrating; his eye quick and animated; his nose retreating; his hair short behind, and in point of stature he is somewhat less than the emperor of the Gauls. His manner is extremely engaging, his language correct, and harmonious." He was styled a genius and "the erratic comet of cookery." His forte was pastry and confections. His winter cheesecakes were famous; and he became a familiar figure on Boston's streets in summer, wheeling a vehicle dispensing ices.

In early 1805, Pollard moved from Cambridge to his New Coffee-House on Congress Street. He lasted there for perhaps four months. The last public mention of Pollard dates from December 1805 when S. Bradford announced the sale of the Brick Building on Congress Street occupied by Othello Pollard. Whether his finances failed or his health, we do not know. In 1824, a Boston antiquarian, recalling Pollard, remarked that "in a short time Othello's occupation was gone, and both he, and his fair Desdemona, with it." Because Pollard's widow, Essame, died in Halifax, Nova Scotia, in early March 1828 at age sixty-three, it is likely that he removed to Canada, where a robust population of New England loyalist expatriates lived.

> Pollard lived and worked in Philadelphia prior to coming to Boston. He appeared on the membership rolls of Philadelphia's African Episcopal Church of St. Thomas in 1794, the first African American congregation in the United States. Sometime between 1794 and 1798, he moved to Boston. In a biographical sketch of Pollard contained in Peregrine's 1834 "Memoirs of a Sensitive Man about Town," details of his background emerge: He had been principal cook and head waiter in one of the first families of Boston—one that stood at the very head of the elite—the most noble of the Bay state nobility—the most aristocratic of the Essex aristocracy—the most consequential of the metropolitan patricians. [The family in question may have been that of merchant Samuel Pickering Gardner.] Othello was a polite, well-educated and shrewd negro, having laid up a sufficient proportion of his wages and perquisites to become a large stockholder in the Mechanics' bank. As a waiter he was unrivalled in civility: and, by the advice and assistance of several of his master's friends, backed by the warm recommendation of the gentleman himself, he was now the principal of a first-rate refectory, near the spot where the late Haymarket theatre once stood.

Sometime during this period of family service in the 1790s, romance entered Pollard's life, and on December 22, 1799, Reverend William Walter of Boston officiated in the marriage of Pollard and Eupha Brown.

Pollard operated as a kind of major domo for civic events, something on the order of Robert Bogle, the Philadelphian master of ceremonies at funerals, wedding receptions, and association picnics. Pollard was recalled by long-lived Bostonians for printing and distributing invitations to funerals and fetes. "I have heard it stated of Othello, that, having in hand two bundles of invitations, one for a fandango, of some sort, and the other for a funeral, and being in an evil condition, he made sad work in the delivery." Like Bogle, he was considered the politest man in the city, famous for his dandyism and fastidiousness. He was all about show, and his attraction to museums and exhibitions led to side ventures and to the restaurant business, including, in 1802, the displaying of the first leopard shown in North America, imported from Bengal, at his place next to the museum.

We know roughly seven years of his life and work in detail. In that time, he appears a legendary creature, a self-educated black savant who promises to instruct the undergraduates of Harvard about the finer things of life.

> A little learning is a dangerous thing;
> Then while you visit the Pierrian Spring,
> Oh! let Othello's 'Attic Bower' allure,
> Instruct your palates, and your taste mature.
> Here, streams, tho' not from Helicon, you'll find,
> To raise the genius, and inspire the mind;
> When Science has consum'd her classic hour,
> Othello courts the Muses to his bower;
> Each of the Nine his rich libation gives,
> Hence Harvard flourishes, and Pollard lives.

During the period of his culinary eminence, only Julien, the proprietor of the Restorator, stood as a rival. "The cake of Othello is much sweet than that of Mr. Julien, but his soup has not the better savour." Such discriminations graced the pages of the city gazettes in the columns that the town wits penned. Genius often requires another brilliant spirit with whom to contend in order to advance the bounds of creativity. So it was in early Boston.

※　※　※

SOURCES: [Commencement notice, Pollard caterer,] *New York Herald* 69 (August 28, 1802): 2; "A Young Leopard," *Massachusetts Mercury* 19, no. 44 (June 1, 1802): 1; William Douglas, *Annals of the First African Church* (Philadelphia: A. Baird, 1803), 109; "Fire!—Again—Fire!" *Baltimore Republican* (January 28, 1803): 2; "Fires," *Dartmouth Gazette* (January 29, 1803): 3; "British Spy in Boston, No. 1," "Attic Bower," *Boston Independent Chronicle* 35, no. 2340 (August 29, 1803): 3; "Private Bills," *Massachusetts Spy* 33, no. 1642 (September 26, 1804): 2; "Turtle Soup," *New-England Palladium* 26, no. 34 (October 25, 1805): 2; "Reminiscences," *New England Galaxy* 7 (April 23, 1824): 341; [Death notice, Mrs.

Essame Pollard,] *Boston Commercial Gazette* 22 (March 10, 1828): 1; Peregrine, "Original Auto-biography: Memoirs of a Sensitive Man about Town," *New-York Mirror* 11, no. 49 (June 7, 1834): 390; Lucius Manlius Sargent, "Number Eight," *Dealings with the Dead by a Sexton of the Old School* (Boston: Dutton & Wentworth, 1856), 29.

Stephen Simonet fl. 1791–1803
Paris; Philadelphia

A Parisian-trained pastry cook and chef, Stephen Simonet was the founder of restaurant culture in Philadelphia. He and his brother, confectioner and distiller J. C. Simonet, arrived in Philadelphia in 1791 during the political tumults in France. Settling in the vicinity of New Market near Fourth, he opened a shop selling "ham pies, fowl, and game of all kinds; pies at a quarter and half dollars, cakes at different prices, first courses and dainty dishes; he also makes little French pies when desired, hot pies, veal pies." The offerings indicated a classical culinary training—roasting, stewing, the creation of pastry for savory dishes as well as sweet, and the assembly of entrées. The "dishes and dessert" formula proved successful, and he quickly expanded to processing foods that could be kept on sea voyages. He was a master of conserving cooked meats in fat or jelly. He specified that he had entire "beef and geese legs in daube, particularly fit for exportation over the sea." He also made Italian macaroni on premises. For much of 1794 and 1795, he produced food from his residence at 245 South Second Street, New Market. His wife ran a millinery shop out of the same building.

In autumn of 1795, he began taking boarders. The success of his business prompted him to enter into partnership with the performer M. Jaymond. He secured the commodious building across Second Street, No. 254, where customers might lodge as well as board. He held a regular ordinary at 2:30 in the afternoon, publishing daily a bill of fare announcing the differing dishes available, indicating that the customers "may take their choice." Thus the first à la carte restaurant came to be in Philadelphia. "Beefsteaks & Restorative Broths may be had at any time of the day, and any of the dishes mentioned in the bill of fare will be served up when called for." He also indicated that on Sunday and Thursday there would be pastry specials. Cold pâtés were available daily. He also invited "large or small parties" to come to No. 254 for dinner or supper. The distinctiveness of the experience afforded by Simonet may perhaps best be seen in the alcohol served:

	Dollar	Cents
BORDEAUX WINE, common	0	8
Do. do. Old	1	00
White Wine of GRAVE	1	00
MADEIRA, first quality	1	00
PORT WINE	0	75
SHERRY	0	75
LISBON	0	75
MALAGA	0	75
MUSCADEN WINE	1	00
WINE of LUNELLE	1	00
Do. of CYPRUS	1	00
COGNIAC BRANDY	1	00
French Liqueurs of all kinds	1	25

The most surprising item listed was the American vintage—the muscadine wine made from sweet *rotundifolia* grapes. Pricing it above the similarly sweet Malaga suggests the item's rarity.

Simonet's partnership with Jaymond scarcely lasted the winter of 1797. A performer at heart, Jaymond left No. 254 entirely in Simonet's hands while joining Lailson's Circus and becoming a regular performer there in the final years of the eighteenth century. Simonet, meanwhile, further transformed his business into what we now recognize as a restaurant. Indeed, in November 1797, he adopted the designation that Julien had pioneered in Boston, advertising his place of business thusly: "Simonet. Pastry Cook and Restorator." There was a retail pastry shop at the front and "two very large parlours, where he can give repasts of twenty-five or thirty covers, also particular repasts, the bill of fare will be on the table." A separate shop at 104 North Third Street sold olive oil, mustard, vinegar, and liquor. At the pastry shop attached to the restorator, Simonet offered "cold pies, brioches, meringues, tourtes d'entremets" as well as pot pies and oyster pies.

Through 1797, Simonet expanded the capacity of his dining establishment. He indicated an ability to serve seventy to eighty persons and reiterated his intent to deliver meals to lodgings within Philadelphia. This was important during the season when yellow fever ravaged the city—as it did annually in 1797, 1798, and 1799. When the disease was about, the desire to congregate in public places languished. When mortality ran particularly high, Simonet advertised "Broth for Patients"—"according to the direction of the Physician." When the threat abated, Simonet was sure to recapture public curiosity by introducing new dishes to the menu. In 1799, for instance, he promised that "any quantity of ice cream may be obtained" at his business.

At the beginning of the nineteenth century, Simonet maintained his mixed model of operation—part pastry shop, part victualer, part restaurant, part wine merchant. Stephen's brother J. C. Simonet created gin and cordials in the city, concentrating his efforts on alcoholic beverages, with occasional side excursions into chocolate and sugar. Both men suddenly disappear from the record in the early 1800s. Stephen Simonet's building on South Second Street came into the hands of Isaac Carpenter, sometime before the summer of 1807. One hopes that Simonet did not succumb to one of Philadelphia's seasons of disease. Whatever his fate, to him belongs the honor of presiding over Philadelphia's first freestanding restaurant.

☀ ☀ ☀

SOURCES: "A Pastry Cook," *Federal Gazette* (November 25, 1793): 3; "Mr. Simonet," *Philadelphia Gazette* (December 11, 1794): 1; "Mr. Simonet," *Aurora General Advertiser* (December 15, 1794): 1; "Simonet, Pastry Cook," *Aurora General Advertiser* (October 19, 1795): 1; "Simonet & Jaymond," *Aurora General Advertiser* (January 3, 1797): 1; [Notice of partnership dissolution,] *Aurora General Advertiser* (May 2, 1797): 2; "Simonet. Pastry Cook and Restorator," *Aurora General Advertiser* (November 21, 1797): 1; "Simonet, Patissier & Traiteur," *Aurora General Advertiser* (November 15, 1798): 3; "Broth for Patients," *American Daily Advertiser* (September 5, 1799): 1; "Stephen Simonet Pastry-Cook & Confectioner," *Aurora General Advertiser* (November 15, 1799): 3.

Ann Poppleton 1770?–1840?

New York; Baltimore

Ann Poppleton introduced the luncheon as an institution of women's refreshment and sociability into the United States in 1816. A wit, a fashionable matron, and a London-trained pastry chef and confectioner, she became a culinary celebrity in New York's beau monde, catering the annual Bachelor's Ball in the city and collaborating with the famous African American cook and master of ceremonies Simon in many civic celebrations. The public generally conceded that she stood foremost among the creators of cake in the city—her dark, moist plum cake enjoying particular mystique. Yet her training had been thorough, and she won patronage upon first opening her shop in 1815 for her nutritive soups and roast game as well as her pastries. "Mrs. Poppleton" was the spouse of Thomas Holdsworth Poppleton (1765–1837), New York's surveyor and mapmaker.

Both Thomas and Ann Poppleton remained New York institutions for two decades.

The first advertisement appeared on October 19, 1815, in the *New-York Evening Post*:

> Mrs. Poppleton, Restaurateur, Pastry Cook and Confectioner, next door to Washington Hall, respectfully begs leave to inform the public, she has opened a store for general accommodation, where families may be supplied with all kinds of Soups, savory Patties, single and double dressed Entre[e]s, Chicken, Eel, and Game Pies, Puff Pastry in variety, sweet and savory, Jellies plain and ornamented, Omelettes, Creams, Blanc manges, almond, caramel and gum Paste Ornaments, Italian Sallads, potted and collared Meats, Fish Sauces, cold ornamented Hams, Tongues, Fowls and savory Cakes with every article in the Kitchen and Pastry business.

She indicated that those expecting a European standard of luxury would find satisfaction with her work. She highlighted her cleanliness and her suitability for christenings, weddings, and ladies' parties. She began serving hot English cheesecakes at 11:00 a.m. daily and maintained a "refreshment room" where customers might have "mock Turtle and other Soups, savory Patties, anchovy Toasts, and other relishes." The service ceased at 3:00 p.m.

Poppleton's second season as a restaurateur and confectioner began in late autumn 1816. The primacy of soup in her luncheon offerings was acknowledged by designating in her ads the dining room as the "Soup Room." Yet in addition to soup à la reine and almond soup (white gazpacho?), she recommended lobster pudding, lemon cocoa nut, marrow, and her Italian salads (antipasti?). Her statements made particular acknowledgment "to those ladies whose patronage" had supported her the previous season, and, as a particular reward for their support, she was making English macaroons and maids of honor (a jam-filled tartlet with a cap of almond paste created at Richmond Palace in the sixteenth century). Poppleton was clearly exploring the wishes of women when it came to her food. On May 17, 1817, she moved her refectory to 8 Wall Street and expanded her service, setting a dinner table for eight regular male boarders. She also indicated that married couples would be accommodated with a handsome private chamber, if so desired.

In spring 1819 Fitz-Greene Halleck, New York's poet of the bon ton, penned an ode to the caterer Simon in which Poppleton figures as provider of one of the accoutrements of fashionable life—candy kisses.

> Taught by thy art, we closely follow
> And ape the English lords and misses—

For music, we've the Black Apollo,
 And Mrs. Poppleton—for kisses;
We borrow all the rest, you know;
 Our glass from Christie, for the time,
Plate from our friends, to make a show,
 And cash, to pay small bills, from P[ine].

Configured in the shape that Hershey's imitated and built into a source of fortune, kisses in New York were famous for dispensing a printed motto on the wrapper. Irked at the banality of these sentiments, Poppleton announced a contest to the citizens of poetic temper. The notice would be reprinted in a dozen papers.

TO POETS

Whereas the printed mottos which now envelope the kisses and comfitures, that are handed about at parties, are so devoi[d] of taste, so unpoetic, and so inelegant, that Mrs. POPPLETON, desirous of combining delicacy and talent, and giving an impuse to poetic merit, hereby offers a PRIZE CAKE of 10 pounds, for the best *one hundred* original mottos which shall be handed to her in one month from the date hereof, to be decided by ladies and gentlemen of poetic taste. Apply at the Confectionary Store, Broadway, nearly opposite St. Paul's.

In August 1821, the papers announced that "a lady residing in New-York, writing under the signature of Aspasia[,] has been the lucky laureate" who won the contest and the cake.

In autumn of 1819, Poppleton migrated to 206 Broadway, relocating to the new locus of fashionable commerce opposite St. Paul's Church. Realizing that continued success lay in making her pastry a topic of city conversation, she fashioned a 300-pound plum cake for New Year's 1820. It went on display on December 29 in her Broadway window and was cut for carryout on the holiday. The two-story brick pastry shop and restaurant caught fire on Monday, March 5, 1821, but speedy action by the fire brigade limited the damage. In gratitude, Poppleton fed the firefighters from her stock, provoking a city critic, who disliked the notion of giving volunteers food as a tip because it led to an expectation of receiving something and thus stimulated looting, to observe: "Mrs. Poppleton's confectionary must have suffered prodigiously in the efforts made to save it, for all the boys that could obtain admission, carried off as much preserves as they could eat. A confectionary store on fire, may be considered as a dead loss—a druggist shop, on the contrary, is not in danger." Poppleton reopened for business on March 8. Wittily, she suggested that old clients come by to "perceive her pastry, pure, perfect, pleasant and palatable, rising, phoenix like, from the flames, delightful to the eye, and delicious to the taste."

In 1822, at the request of newspaper correspondents, Poppleton added rum jelly to her stock of standard vendibles. Here is a recipe that was published at that time:

RUM JELLY

Among the novelties of the Parisian circles, rum jelly has become a universal favorite. It is made in the following manner. To a quart bottle of common white wine take a pound of sugar, which is to be reduced to a sirup and clarified. Then take an ounce of isinglass, which put on the fire till it is thoroughly melted, pass it through a cloth, and mix it with the sirup half warm. When this mixture is nearly cold, pour it into the white wine, and stir it well, so as to mix it completely. Then add a spoonful or a spoonful and a half (according to the strength which you desire to give to the jelly) of Old Jamaica rum. Stir again this mixture, and pour it into the mould that it may take the shape in cooling which you design to give it, if intended as a plat for the table, or into glasses if designed to be handed round at an evening party.

In spring of 1823, Poppleton moved her business to 142 Broadway above Cedar Street. There she reigned over the fashionable world of women's food for a decade. Yet the woman-centered business did not neglect the desires of the male population. In 1824 city bachelors instituted a ball on St. Valentine's Day. A success, they sought to improve the second version to an event irresistible to any fashionable woman in New York, so they hired "the triumvirates of good cheer, Simon, Mrs. Poppleton, and Abby Jones" to run the entertainment in 1825. Success gave rise to a paradox: the ranks of the bachelors were decimated in the wake of the celebration.

The last chapter of Poppleton's career took place in Maryland. Baltimore had been Ann Poppleton's first home in America, when she and husband, Thomas, emigrated from Great Britain in 1810. During the early 1810s, Thomas surveyed Baltimore, producing the most famous early map of the city in 1822. From 1814 to 1815, he took concurrent employment in New York. Thomas and Ann relocated to Manhattan in late 1814, but in 1830 the couple returned to Baltimore, and Thomas appeared before the US magistrate to become a citizen. Ann opened a confectionery, but this shop burned in the great Baltimore fire of 1833. She relocated to a large brick store on South Calvert Street, but the property was sold out from under her a year later. At this juncture, she apparently retired. Thomas Poppleton died in 1837; Ann lived in widowed retirement for several years. Because she did not appear in the 1842 Baltimore Directory, we must presume she died in 1840 or early 1841. Their presence in the monument city was memorialized by the naming of Poppleton Street.

SOURCES: "Notice," *New-York Evening Post* (October 19, 1815): 3; "Notice. Mrs. Poppleton," *New-York Evening Post* (December 7, 1816): 3; "Notice—Mrs. Poppleton," *New-York Evening Post* (May 17, 1817): 2; "Mrs. Poppleton Has Removed," *New-York Daily Advertiser* (May 19, 1817): 3; Croaker & Co. "To Simon," *New-York Evening Post* (April 20, 1819): 2; [Notice,] *New-York Evening Post* (November 9, 1819): 3; "Another Mammoth Cake," *National Advocate* (December 29, 1819): 3; "Fire," *National Advocate* (March 7, 1821): 2; "Mrs. Poppleton," *New-York Evening Post* (May 9, 1821): 3; "To Poets," *National Advocate* (June 18, 1821): 3; "Mrs. Poppleton," *National Advocate* (August 17, 1821): 2; [Notice of removal,] *National Advocate* (May 21, 1823): 1; "Bachelor's Ball," *Boston Daily American Statesman* (February 15, 1826): 2; "Baltimore Fire," *Philadelphia Inquirer* (February 18, 1833): 2; "Positive Sale," *Baltimore Patriot* (May 24, 1834): 3; "Thomas Poppleton (1765–1837)," MSA SC 3520-2757, Archives of Maryland, Biographical Series, http://msa.maryland.gov/megafile/msa/speccol/sc3500/sc3520/002700/002757/html/02757bio.html.

James Prosser 1782–1861
Philadelphia

A legendary founder of Philadelphia restaurant culture, African American caterer and provisioner James Prosser was a native of South Jersey. He came to Philadelphia in 1810 and, in rivalry with Thomas and William LeCounts, became the city's source of wholesale terrapins and oysters. Originally stationed at 120 on the south side of Market Street below Eighth, Prosser's refectory became a cherished resort of Philadelphia's business community. At first the service was periodic, with "Superior Turtle Soup" served on Wednesdays and Saturdays at 11:00 a.m. Prosser competed against D. Rubicom of the Washington Hotel, who dispensed his turtle soup on Mondays, Wednesdays, and Fridays; John Doyle of the Leopard Tavern in Laetitia Court, who offered his on Mondays, Wednesdays, and Saturdays; and Charles Newman at 10 Library Street, on Tuesdays, Thursdays, and Saturdays. That Prosser eventually prevailed over every rival and became the city's foremost maker of both Caribbean green turtle soup and local terrapin stew can be attributed to his peculiar sensitivity to the ingredients. A lover of Prosser's terrapin transcribed an interview with the cook in which he rhapsodized over the turtle and detailed his

James Akin, "Philadelphia Taste Displayed, or, Bon-Ton Below Stairs" (1828). Colorized lithograph, Kennedy and Lucas. James Prosser's Oyster House. Photograph: HSP Medium Graphics Collection, Historical Society of Pennsylvania.

treatment of it. Recorded in the 1850s, it would be republished at the end of the century:

TERRAPIN STEW

You can't enjoy terrapin unless the day is nippin. Temperature and terrapin go hand in hand. Now, as to your terrapin. Bless you, there is all the difference in the world in them. The more northerly is the terrapin found the better. You eat a Florida terrapin—you needn't despise it, for terrapin is terrapin everywhere—but you get a Chesapeake one or a Delaware bay one, or, better still, a Long Island one, and there is just the difference between $10 a dozen and $36. Warm water kinder washes the delicate flavor out of them. Don't you let Mr. Bergh know it, but your terrapin must be boiled alive. Have a good big pot, with a hot fire under it, so that he shan't languish, and when it has got on a full head of steam pop him in. What I am goin to give is a recipe for a single one. If you are awfully rich and go in for a gross of terrapin, just use your multiplication table. Just as soon as he caves in watch him and try his flippers. When they part when you pry them with your fingernail, he is good. Open him nicely with a knife. Bilin of him dislocates the snuff-box. There ain't overmuch of it, more's the pity. The most is in the jints of the legs and side lockers, but if you want to commit murder just you small his gall, and then your terrapin is gone forever. Watch closely for eggs and handle them gingerly.

Now, having got him or her all into shape, put the meat aside. Take three fresh eggs—you must have them fresh. Bile 'em hard and mash 'em smooth. Add to that a tablespoonful of sifted flour, three tablespoonfuls of cream, salt and pepper (red pepper to a terrapin is just depravity) and two wineglasses of sherry wine. Wine as costs $2, no. 50 a bottle ain't a bit too good. There never was a botega in all Portugal that wouldn't think itself honored to have itself mixed up with a terrapin. Now you want quite a quarter of a pound of the very best fresh butter and put that in a porcelain cover pan and melt it first—mustn't be browned. When it's come to be oily, put in your terrapin, yolks of egg, wine and all. Let it simmer gently. Bilin up two or three times does the business. What you are after is to make it blend. There ain't nothing that must be too pointed in terrapin stew. It wants to be a quiet thing, a suave thing, just pervaded with a most beautiful and natural terrapin aroma. You must serve it to the people that eats it on a hot plate, but the real thing is to have it on a chafin dish, and though a man ought not to be selfish there is a kind of divine satisfaction in eatin it all yourself.

One had to descend into a cellar to enter Prosser's eatery, and there, over a table heaped with oysters, Prosser stood for decades, dressed in a snow-white apron, wielding a famous knife of tremendous weight and sharpness. In the kitchen behind the counter, vats of turtle soup, clam and turtle soup, and railroad oyster stew simmered, all celebrated dishes of nineteenth-century Philadelphia. The dining room tended to service an all-male clientele, but Prosser's stand would also supply households with soup and fixings, or sell ingredients retail to home cooks, so women were seen below grade much of the morning, purchasing live turtles and bushel baskets of bivalves.

Prosser cooked for mixed society at various public banquets that he catered in the later 1820s and '30s. In public memory, his most memorable meals were those staged for large societies, such as the March 1832 banquet founding the Musical Fund Society of Philadelphia or the 125th anniversary of the Schuylkill Fishing Company. He also regularly catered the Philadelphia City Council feast. In the 1840s, Prosser purchased space on the site of the current post office, erecting an open hall for the general public and stalls for genteel customers. His two locations drew extensive custom, and his Market Street restaurant—which operated for a half century, including a rebuild after an 1858 fire—was the finest in the city from the 1840s to the '50s.

Prosser, when not cooking, cultivated fast horses. Riding his racing buggy about the city and on the tracks, he boasted that he "never took any driver's dust." His audacity as a driver inspired great pride in Philadelphia's African American community, as did his honesty, industry, and finesse as a caterer. In March 1861, James Prosser died of apoplexy. His estate and business, valued at $40,000, eventually passed to his son-in-law John McKee (1821–1905), a Virginian whom Prosser employed as a waiter. McKee would manage the restaurant until 1866, when he went into real estate speculation and began amassing a huge fortune.

Prosser's passing inspired Joseph William Miller, a city wit and epicure, to honor his memory in verse. "Prosser's Journey to Heaven; or, The Triumph of Terrapin" recounts the hero's passage over the Styx, through the Underworld, and finally through Saint Peter's gates, offering the dishes for which he had been famous in lieu of passage money. At each station when his presents win him passage, the monitor shouts, "Jump!" The journey reveals Prosser's entire culinary repertoire.

> "Oh, good Chayron, Massa Chayron,"
>   Quoth old Jeems in voice subdued,
> "I'se forgot to bring my money,
>   Won't yer take a 'dozent stewed'?
>
> "Buckwheat cakes an' Jarsey sassage,
>   Nothin else has I to pay."
> "Jump!" cries Charon, "you've free passage
>   Every time you come this way."
>
> So he crossed that fearful water,
>   But he met on t'other side
> Direful Furies, unto whom he
>   Offered vainly "roast" and "fried,"
>
> "Chincoteagues," and "Coves of Maurice,"
>   Lying plump in wounded shell;
> But the Furies, dire, refused them,
>   And his grief we may not tell.
>
> "Here's 'soft crabs' jis fried in buttah,
>   'Reed birds' too, am nice an' plump."
> Scarcely he the words did utter
>   When the Furies, dire, cried, "Jump!"

Prosser wends his way out of the underworld and encounters Saint Peter at the gate.

> "All my gold I'se left behind me,
>   But I has some 'oysters br'iled,'

Canvis bag, sah, steak ob tortle."
    Peter shook his head and smiled:

"Won't do, Jeems, that's not the ticket!"—
    "Glass ob ale, an' dozen raw?
Lobster salad?" "Won't do here, sir."
    Sunk great Prosser's heart with awe. . . .

"From salt Del'war's reedy margints,
    From de shores ob Sheapeake,
Comes our Terrapin, good Petah,
    Spose o' dem I needn't speak?"

"What! STEWED TERRAPIN, Jeemes Prosser!"
    Open wide the gates are borne—
"Here come Terrapin and Prosser!
    Make him Welcome as the morn!"

※   ※   ※

SOURCES: "Superior Turtle Soup," *Poulson's American Daily Advertiser* 45, no. 12382 (July 24, 1816): 4; "Turtle Soup," *Poulson's American Daily Advertiser* 46, no. 12607 (April 22, 1817): 3; "Green Turtle Soup," *Poulson's American Daily Advertiser* 49, no. 13565 (May 19, 1820): 2; "Celebration of the Foundation of the Musical Fund Society of Philadelphia," *National Gazette* (March 8, 1832): 1; "Improvement—Prosser's," *Philadelphia Inquirer* (November 1, 1858): 1; "How a Philadelphia Negro Made a Fortune," *Providence Evening Press* 5, no. 8 (March 22, 1861): 3; "The Colored Upper Ten of Philadelphia," *Boston Traveler* (January 3, 1862): 1; [Obituary notice,] *Philadelphia Inquirer* (March 15, 1861): 5; "Old Caterer on Terrapin," *Irish American Weekly* (January 24, 1898): 4; Joseph William Miller, "Prosser's Journey to Heaven; or, The Triumph of Terrapin," in *Mars Hill and Other Poems* (Philadelphia: Published by his Friends, 1879), 146–50; William Milnor, *History of the Schuylkill Fishing Company of the State in Schuylkill* (Philadelphia: The State in Schuylkill, 1889): 197; William C. Bolivar, "P, James Prosser, Jimmy Prosser," *Philadelphia Inquirer* 169, no. 40 (August 9, 1913): 8.

William Sykes 1782–1833
New York; Paris; London

TURTLE DINNER

WILLIAM SYKES respectfully presents to the public the following bill of fare for the ORDINARY at the New-York Coffee House THIS DAY. Dinner on the table precisely at half past 3 o'clock [January 6, 1823].

FIRST COURSE
Green Turtle and Vermicelli Soups
Boiled and Barbacued Fish
Quarter of Lamb
Boiled Chickens and Turkeys
Roast Ducks and Geese, Hams and Tongues
Lark, Quail and Oyster Pies
Roast and Corned Beef

SECOND COURSE
Turtle Callipash, Callipee and Steaks
Snipe, Quails, Wild Pigeons, Brant, Teal
Canvas-back Ducks
Saddle of Mutton—with a rich DESERT

Fine dining in New York before William Sykes opened the New-York Coffee House in 1822 consisted of green turtle feasts at the Tontine Coffee House or the Philadelphia Hotel, perhaps a game dinner at the City Hotel on Broadway. Sykes's menus, published in the pages of the *Commercial Advertiser*, threw down the gauntlet to the cooks and caterers of Manhattan. Their ambition, their variety, their abundance of rare ingredients, stunned his commercial rivals and provoked comment in the press. Indeed, the era of fine dining in New York was shocked into existence by Sykes's incandescent four-year career. But ambition had its costs. The expense of game and wild fowl, expansion, and sponsoring banquets mounted; in late autumn 1825, it would seem they became insurmountable. Before the creditors came with their demands, Sykes fled to Paris. Or he was obliged to go to Paris for some other cause when news of someone forging bills of credit in his name surfaced in Manhattan. His business imploded and he was not there. In Paris, destitute, he became an object of charity and eventually consented to hire on as a gentleman's butler, while in Manhattan his properties were auctioned off. He returned to New York in 1833, attempting to recuperate his reputation. By April he was dead of an accidental gunshot wound. Sometimes the careers of culinary artists are short and brutal. In Sykes's case, the career was also memorable.

His name first appeared before the public on July 19, 1822, in an invitation to partake of a collation at Sykes's newly opened coffeehouse and hotel at 10 William Street. The New-York Coffee House matter-of-factly stated, "Dinner and supper parties accommodated in a superior manner, with every delicacy the market affords." The superiority of his offerings prompted a group of merchants within two months to finance a new isolated branch office during an outbreak of yellow fever, the Merchant's Exchange and New-York Coffee House, at the corner of Asylum and Hammond Streets. Sykes's makeshift refectory had a single kitchen serving a public dining room (75 by 25 feet) and a private hall (50 by 25 feet) for the use of the merchants. The schedule of sittings mirrored the traditional English schedule:

Breakfast	8 o'clock
Dinner	3 o'clock
Tea	6 o'clock
Supper	8 o'clock

In order to build custom at the Merchant's Exchange in then-underdeveloped Greenwich, he sent anything rare coming into New York, such as a Galapagos turtle in October 1822, to that location. Yellow fever abated by mid-autumn, and the temporary outpost was no longer needed. On November 8, 1822, Sykes informed the public he was shuttering the Greenwich branch and consolidating his efforts at his original location at 10 William Street.

A native of England, Sykes made the New-York Coffee House as close in style to a London coffeehouse as he could manage. The coffee room stood separate from the bar and dining rooms. It served soups and modest dinners as well as the bitter brew, and would serve single diners. The major metropolitan and London papers were available gratis in the barroom. In the dining rooms, Sykes periodically celebrated the holidays of his homeland. On New Year's Day 1823, he invited his neighbors to partake of a collation on January 6 to honor Twelfth Night. A visitor to this celebration remarked, "Such a display of wines and delicacies has never been surpassed in this city." Another of the attendees recorded the bill of fare and published it in the *New-York Evening Post* on January 8, 1823:

First Course—green turtle soup, white soup, boiled and stewed cod, barbecued bass, chickens, ducks, turkeys, hams, partridges, tongues, green turtle, calipee, quail pies, oyster pies, calf's foot custard, and roast beef.

Second Course—saddles and venison, wild turkeys, green turtle callipasch, gallipagos turtle steaks, do. white and brown fricassee, Canada hares, and canvas back ducks.

Desert—Plum puddings, orange puddings, mince pies, tarts, puffs, jellies, blumage [blancmange], syllabubs, ice creams, custards, trifles, fruit, &c.

Wines—Madeira, Port, Claret, Champaigne.

This menu galvanized New York's bon vivants and forced Sykes's rivals—William Niblo of the Bank Coffee House and Chester Jennings of the City Hotel—to reconsider the nature of their offerings. Sykes's habit of announcing the seasonal offerings in the advertisement pages of the Manhattan papers kept the pressure on his competitors. Every week had its specialty: a week after this banquet, for instance, a shipment of terrapin and oyster arrived from the James River in Virginia. For beverages, he served Juno Madeira, old Port, and Racey's Pale Ale.

On March 5, 1823, Sykes published the menu of a public dinner. At the three o'clock dinner, Sykes offered three courses:

Green Turtle Soup

Royal Soup

Boiled Trout

Trout and other Fish

Turkeys boiled and roasted

Hams and Tongues

Oyster, Chicken, Quail & French Pies

* * *

Green Turtle Calipee

Turtle Steaks

Bear Steaks

Bear's Feet, stewed

Wild Geese

Brant

Canvas Ducks

Saddle of Venison &c &c &c

* * *

Dessert

The menus from Sykes's first year of operation tell us a great deal about the first era of fine dining in New York. The orientation was generally English—

protein heavy, yet with glimpses of French kitchen practices in the quail pie and the tortoise fricassee. No vegetables are noted, even garden peas and celery, those typically cherished by Anglo-Americans. The American character of the feasts lay primarily in the ingredients—in the game and wild fowl. Yet it also appeared in Sykes's adoption of the West Indian division of turtle meat into steaks, calipee (the yellowish meat and matter contiguous to the lower shell) and calipash (the greenish meat and matter contiguous to the upper shell). The appearance of bear on the March menu attests to Sykes's special relation with men in the New York game market. Indeed, Sykes's purchase of bear on February 2, 1823, made the news columns of the *New-York Spectator*.

By spring of 1823, Sykes had become New York's fashionable caterer for public banquets, and the long room of his coffeehouse was the preferred venue for concerts and commercial demonstrations. Later on the Fourth of July that year, the nine hundred firemen of New York dined at Sykes's. He obliged them by decorating the façade of his coffeehouse "with an illuminated transparency of a Fire Engine, surmounted by a blazing star." Sykes also hosted the cotillion that honored the launch of the steamboat *Nautilus* in September 1823, and the anniversary dinner of the Erie Canal in October. This banquet featured a baron of beef four feet in length and weighing 122 pounds. He secured another Galapagos tortoise for the table. The year climaxed with his work catering the Mount Vernon Fair in late October. A price list for his fair food survives, with prices noted in shillings. The cost ranged from 6s. per dozen for fried or stewed oysters and 4s. for ducks down to 6d. for cold meat or fruit pies. Sykes also supplied alcohol, including Newark Cider.

Months of civic dinners, bachelor suppers, and catered balls passed until October 1825, when Sykes advertised a "Grand Canal Dinner," marking the "confluence of waters" with the completion of the Grand Erie Canal, and charging $3 a head. The banquet, held on November 4, was the last great occasion over which Sykes would preside in Manhattan, and by all reports it was magnificent. In the following weeks, something went wrong. What happened next is difficult to adduce. In the third week of November, a young man, John R. Powers, was arrested for passing counterfeit checks subscribed by Sykes. Sykes meanwhile was forced by circumstances (never sufficiently explained) to go to France. The conjunction of his departure and the appearance of counterfeit bills of credit spooked his creditors, of whom there were many.

Why he didn't return to allay fears is a mystery. He had failed once before in his life—as an English silk merchant—before coming to New York. The trauma must have been great, for he left off that business entirely, using his talent at cookery to serve as an assistant for William Niblo at the Bank Coffee House. His self-renovation had taken years, and the prospect of facing disaster again must have been horrifying.

On December 14, 1825, a notice appeared in the papers that business was going on per usual. On December 20, the Court of Chancery announced that Joel Post had failed in several attempts to have a summons served on Sykes and that the court had ordered defendant Sykes by public declaration to appear in court within four months. Sykes had absconded. On December 25, the eleven years remaining on the lease was offered for sale by T. Gibbons.

The following scene was said to have taken place on December 30, 1825. A well-dressed stranger entered the New-York Coffee House and requested to see Sykes:

> "Where is Mr. Sykes?"
> "Gone—failed—decamped—Non est inventus." . . .
> "Failed!" said the stranger—biting his lip, and looking grave.
> "Yes, sir."
> "For how much?"
> "Only the small matter of 150,000 dollars."
> "Is that all! A mere trifle. I wish I had known of his troubles. Forty thousand pounds—is nothing. I would have assisted him to any amount."

The visitor claimed to be Charles Montagu, son of the Duke of Montagu. But the visitor was probably an impostor. Sykes's career in New York was over. The amount of debt, $150,000, suggests that the first efflorescence of public haute cuisine in New York took place on a credit bubble.

> Sykes took nothing with him went he left New York. Indeed, New Yorkers did not know whither Sykes had traveled until late 1826, when rumors surfaced that he was in Paris. Then in a letter from Paris dated January 30, 1827, the first concrete report surfaced: Your old friend Wm. Sykes has been in this city, in distress and wholly destitute, and had not some of our countrymen taken pity on him would have starved or done worse. There was some talk of making up a little purse for him, among those here, to whom his favors and good dinners have been dispensed in William Street, and had it been done, I certainly should have given him twenty francs on your account, for old friendship sake and a like sum myself; but one of his friends obtained him a situation as a servant to an Englishman who was travelling, and he has left the city.

For five years, Sykes labored as an English butler when Edward Windust of the Shakespeare House in Park Row engineered his return to New York in January 1833 to assist Sarah Windust with the growing crush of diners. Sykes returned to New York in part to exonerate himself from the imputations that had hung over him.

On March 31, 1833, in front of Windust's Shakespeare House, Edward Laverty was showing Sykes a pair of pistols he had purchased when one of the guns fired, piercing Sykes between the stomach and groin. Sykes lingered for two days. "[A] few hours before his death, and while under the full sense of his approaching dissolution, he dictated, signed, and made oath, in the most solemn manner, of his innocence." He died on April 2.

※　　※　　※

SOURCES: "New-York Coffee House," *New-York Evening Post, no.* 6257 (July 19, 1822): 3; "Merchant's Exchange and New-York Coffee House," *New-York Evening Post, no.* 6289 (August 26, 1822): 2; "Galapagos Turtle," *New-York Evening Post,* no. 6338 (October 22, 1822): 3; "Williams Sykes," *New-York National Advocate* 10, no. 27 (November 8, 1822): 3; "Bill of Fare at a New-York Coffee House," *New-York Evening Post, no.* 6402 (January 8, 1823): 2; "New Year," *New-York National Advocate* 11, no. 2837 (January 6, 1823): 2; "Terrapin and Oysters from the James River," *New-York Evening Post,* no. 6406 (January 10, 1823): 3; "Harmony and June Wines, and Racey's Ale," *New-York Evening Post* 49 (February 21, 1823): 3; "William Sykes," *Albany Argues* (February 28, 1823): 3. [Public dinner menu,] *New-York National Advocate* 11, no. 28 (March 5, 1823): 2; "Wild Meats," *New-York Spectator,* February 4, 1823, 2; "Firemen's Dinner," *New-York National Advocate* 11, no. 2995 (July 10, 1823): 2; "Canal Celebration," *Albany Argus* (October 14, 1823): 3; "Mount Vernon Fair," *New-York Daily Advertiser, no.* 2026 (October 29, 1823): 2; "Grand Canal Dinner," *Commercial Advertiser* (October 24, 1825): 3; [Notice of the Court of Chancery,] *New-York Commercial Advertiser* (December 20, 1825): 4; "Forgery and Theft," *New-York Daily Advertiser* (November 22, 1825): 2; [Montagu story,] *New-York Commercial Advertiser* (December 31, 1825): 3; "Accident from the Careless Handling of Firearms," *New-York American* 13, no. 4433 (April 2, 1833): 2; "The Verdict of the Coroner's Jury," *New-York American* 13, no. 4344 (April 3, 1833): 2; "Unfortunate Accident," *Poughkeepsie Independence* 2, no. 61 (April 3, 1833): 3; [Obituary notice,] *New-York Spectator* 36, no. 46 (April 4, 1833): 2.

Frederick Rouillard 1783–1843
Boston; Nahant, MA; Newport, RI

If Jean Baptiste Gilbert Payplat ("Julien") was the legendary originator of New England restaurant culture in 1794 with his Restorator on Milk Street in Bos-

"Old Tremont House, Boston, Massachusetts" (1830). Lithograph, Print Department, Boston Public Library. Frederick Rouillard served as kitchen master here for hotelier Harvey D. Parker. Photograph: Boston Pictorial Archive.

ton, then Frederick Rouillard was his successor, the conduit through which French cuisine would be communicated from the Revolutionary era to the Civil War. Rouillard brought haute cuisine from the one-room restorator to the grand dining salon of the Parker House Hotel. Indeed, early in his Boston career, Rouillard purchased the "Restorat Julien," revitalizing its French fare; he closed his career as chef for Harvey D. Parker, making his Parker's Restaurant the byword of Boston dining and supplying Parker with the ideal of cuisine that the famous restaurateur would pursue when founding his namesake hotel in 1855.

Rouillard came to Boston in his twenties, establishing sometime in 1811 a confectioner's shop at 51 Marlboro Street. Besides sweets, he manufactured charcuterie, stimulating the city's taste for bologna. In 1815 Rouillard secured the lease of Julien's Restorator from Julien's widow (the caterer had died a decade before in 1805), and for six years enjoyed steady success with the public, so much so that he ventured in 1821 to open a summertime resort in Nahant, Massachusetts. Opening on May 25, 1821, the resort served guests until September 15. The summer seasons at Nahant became regular during the early 1820s. He assured visitors taking the steamboat *Eagle* to Nahant that "his tables will be bountifully supplied with all the delicacies that the City Market can supply, and all the varieties that the surround sea will afford. His Wines, Liquors, &c will be of the choicest kind."

In 1823 Rouillard found the Milk Street eating house too confining. He closed Julien's Restorator and moved down the street into the Stackpole House on the corner of Devonshire and Milk Streets. He began serving breakfast as well as dinner and supper—"the greatest delicacies of the season, cooked in the most approved taste." To back up the promise on his card, he purchased in late April 1823 a 21-pound salmon from the Kennebunk River, the first of the season, at the enormous price of $40 to serve at his restaurant. The price was so astounding that news of the transaction was reported in seven provincial papers. Whenever choice items were procured from the market, such as "Fresh Green Turtle" or "Canvic Back Ducks," Rouillard would publish a note in the *Columbia Centinel* to that effect.

Rouillard's evenings of winter game inspired a poetic appreciation in the mid-1820s:

> I knew by the glow that so rosily shone
> > Upon Frederick's cheeks, that he lived on good cheer;
> And I said, "If there's steaks to be had in the town,
> > The man who loves venison should look for them here."
>
> 'Twas two; and the dinners were smoking around,
> > The cits hastened home at the savory smell,
> And so still was the street that I heard not a sound
> > But the barkeeper ringing the *Coffee-House* bell.
>
> "And here in the cosy *Old Club*," I exclaimed,
> > "With a steak that was tender, and Frederick's best wine,
> While under my platter a spirit-blaze flamed,
> > How long could I sit, and how well could I dine!"
>
> "By the side of my venison a tumbler of beer
> > Or a bottle of sherry how pleasant to see,
> And to know that I dined on the best of the deer,
> > That never was *dearer* to any than me!"

Wishing to get into the catering business, Rouillard secured the services of an assistant, a French cook, so he could "furnish families, and others, with such

Dishes as the moose to order, at short notice." This took place in September 1823. Though unnamed in the public notices, the cook was Louis Charrier.

In August 1826, when the rebuilt Faneuil Market opened its doors, the editors of the gazettes wondered who would be the fortunate fellow to be the first purchaser of goods. The *Commercial Gazette* reported that "Mr. Rouillard, of the Milk-street restorator, was the first purchaser of beef, mutton, poultry, fish, &c." Rouillard's success stimulated his ambitions further. Taking Louis Charrier as a full partner, Rouillard left Stackpole House in autumn of 1827, turning it over to the caterer William Gallagher, for an even larger and more fashionably located house next to the Boston Latin School on School Street, opposite the new Court House. Pastry and confectionery joined the list of the usual attractions—soups, dinners, liquors. The stress of the move, however, strained the partnership. Not two months had passed before notice appeared that the partnership between Charrier and Rouillard had dissolved. In the wake of the breakup, business did not go well on School Street. After a year of struggle, Rouillard closed the business and left Boston.

On July 1, 1828, Rouillard opened the Bellevue Hotel in Newport, Rhode Island. Offering a "table d'Hote," Rouillard assured the public he would also accommodate private supper parties with special requests and serve soup and coffee at all hours. There would be a reading room stocked with the major American papers and a bar supplying the best wines and liquors. To show his culinary talent, he held a public banquet featuring a turtle. This feast inspired the following verse:

> The turtle that but t'other day
> Was swimming in the sea,
> Is caught, turn'd over on his back,
> And destin'd soon to be
> On Monsieur Rouillard's table seen,
> Drest in the finest style,
> And season'd so delightfully,
> You'll nose it half a mile.
>
> The New Hotel is on the hill,
> Where purest breezes blow,
> There the larder teems with fatness
> And the choicest liquors flow,
> And there upon the glorious Fourth,
> Shall joy and mirth abound,
> And business, care, and politics,
> In rosy wine be drown'd.

Over the summer, the rooms and dining hall overflowed with the fashionable, but by fall Rouillard realized he had become attached to a money pit. On October 4, the *Providence Patriot* ran a notice from C. Windsor proposing the disposal of the hotel and grounds, or the erection of a stock subscription scheme for its support. In January 1829, the furniture was sold at a great auction.

The Bellevue misadventure caused Rouillard's financial ruin. What he did from 1828 to 1833 cannot now be determined. He probably attached himself as a private chef to one of the wealthy Rhode Island families. But in 1833 Harvey D. Parker brought him back to Boston to serve as chef at his Tremont Restorator (later, the Tremont Coffeehouse). Parker's success with his eating house and its successor Parker's restaurant were enabled by a decade of work by Rouillard in the kitchens, labor acknowledged in print on several occasions in newspaper appreciations of Parker's eating house.

After providing Bostonians the finest cuisine they would experience during the first part of the nineteenth century, Frederick Rouillard died in late spring of 1843. Poets hymned him while he lived; no one wrote his elegy.

✳   ✳   ✳

SOURCES: "Boulogne Sausages," *Columbian Centinel, no.* 2899 (January 18, 1812): 4; "Nahant, Frederick Rouillard," *Boston Repertory* (May 14, 1821): 2; "Nahant," *Boston Commercial Gazette* 61, no. 39 (May 27, 1822): 3; "Frederick Rouillard," *Columbian Centinel, no.* 4068 (April 9, 1823): 3; "The First Salmon," *New-York Evening Post* (April 29, 1823); "Notice—Frederick Rouillard," *Boston Commercial Gazette* 63, no. 30 (September 18, 1823): 3; "Fresh Green Turtle," *Columbian Centinel*, no. 4286 (May 11, 1825): 3; "Communication," *Boston Commercial Gazette* 71, no. 21 (August 18, 1826): 2; "Notice: Mr. F. Rouillard," *Boston Commercial Gazette* 72, no. 46 (November 29, 1827); "Notice [partnership dissolution]," *Boston Commercial Gazette* 73, no. 8 (January 17, 1828): 4; "Bellevue Hotel," *Rhode Island Republican* 20, no. 13 (June 19, 1828): 3; "A Public Dinner," *Rhode Island Republican* 20, no. 14 (June 26, 1828): 2; "Bellevue Hotel, Newport," *Providence Patriot* 26, no. 80 (October 4, 1828): 3; "Tremont Restorator," *Boston Traveler* 9, no. 3 (July 9, 1833): 3; "Boston Coffee House," *Boston Traveler* (May 10, 1839): 2; "The Stackpole House," *Boston Traveler* (December 9, 1842): 1; "Deaths," *Boston Recorder* 28, no. 23 (June 8, 1843): 9; Samuel Adams Drake, *Old Boston Taverns and Tavern Clubs* (Boston: W. A. Butterfield, 1917), 66.

Joseph Boulanger 1787–1862
Washington, DC

Caterer and restaurateur Joseph Boulanger was the most successful of a generation of chefs who came to the United States attached to a diplomat's entourage, glimpsed opportunity, and stayed. The decision was always risky. The great majority of Americans had never been nurtured on French cookery and had grown content with their beef, bread, mutton, and peas. To succeed, one had to capture the fancy of the cosmopolitans who peopled the burgeoning cities of the United States. Some who tried and failed included Bertrand La Touche in Boston, Louis Charrier Jr. in Boston, George Benoit in New York and Boston, and Henry F. Doyhar in New York. Joseph Boulanger, however, met with immediate favor and enjoyed enduring success. He came to Washington, DC, in 1825, and for thirty-seven years pleased the palates of the more discriminating diners in that city.

After a career in Great Britain as household chef to Sir Charles Vaughan, Lord and Lady Kennedy, and the Marquis Tremaine of Ireland, and after extensive tours of the Continent to school himself in the refinements of French and Italian cuisine, Boulanger came to the nation's capital and was employed by President Andrew Jackson as White House steward and national banquet cook on state occasions. Much of the first part of his Washington career was spent catering state dinners and governmental parties. He prospered because the majority of cooks in Washington, while capable of feeding boarders, could not manage the logistics of mass seatings.

Boulanger arrived in America as steward to Sir Charles Richard Vaughan, Great Britain's envoy extraordinary and minister plenipotentiary to the United States. He accompanied Vaughan during the minister's extensive tours of the country and left his service in April 1831, when Vaughan returned to London to conference with the Crown on American affairs. In 1833 President Jackson secured Boulanger's services to be steward at the White House. Boulanger not only managed the running of the dining facilities but also the operation of the entire household. He served in this capacity for three and a half years, retiring shortly before Jackson left office.

In January 1837 Boulanger opened his American and French Restaurant on Pennsylvania Avenue, nearly across the street from Gadsby's National Hotel. He promised that his "larder will always be supplied with the delicacies of the season, and the cooking will be of the most superior description, as a French and an American cook are attached to the kitchen." He did not note that the French cook was either himself or his wife, Jane. The American cook was one of a rotating series of persons good with the fry pan and griddle. In the upper stories of his building, Boulanger lodged visitors, so the restaurant operated as a small hotel. But Boulanger's became renowned for its "excellent refectory," not its living spaces. His reputation as a caterer helped his business, drawing associations to his parlors and dining rooms. "Mr. B. keeps a good table and is famous for his style of preparing sumptuous dinners for parties meeting at his house." How good a table? A commentator expatiated after the restaurant had been open a month. It was not the American, but the French cuisine that excited:

> Members of Congress and strangers from all sections of the Union, while they are sojourning in the metropolis will doubtless pay their devoirs to his *Potages*, his *Bouillis*, his *Rots*, his *Volaille*, and his *Gibier*, with bones and without bones, but all *tres bon*, his *Salmis* and *Sautes* of poultry and game, flavored with the exquisite truffle and the delicate mushroom, his Oysters in all the varieties of cookery, his *Entremets*, his *Petite pates*, his *Pulissini*, his *Pommes-de-terres frits*, or *a le Maitre d'Hotel con multis alile*, with fine wines and spirits, and delicious coffee and Liqueurs, to keep all quiet and harmless.

This is not to say that Boulanger neglected the local bounty. Advertisements appeared regularly when the latest rockfish, oysters, terrapin, or venison became available.

In January 1848, Boulanger relocated his business into a double brick building with adjoining stable on G Street, between Seventeenth and Eighteenth Streets (a site now occupied by the World Bank). Fronting on G Street, the buildings contained eighteen rooms, including a large dining room on the west side and a saloon on the east. A suite of five private dining rooms made up the second floor. The top-floor rooms were rented to lodgers. Boulanger and his wife, Jane, lived in an apartment in the west building. He ran the business with a staff of seven—a waiter, a barkeeper, an oyster shucker, an assistant cook, a housekeeper, a helper, and an errand boy. The lot contiguous to the stables enjoyed fine tidewater soil; this enriched with horse manure permitted Jane Boulanger to plant a superb vegetable garden. Boulanger's May asparagus, artichokes, and breakfast radishes were famous in the city. When the lot and structures were put up for sale by owner James H. Collins in autumn of 1851, Boulanger purchased them, enabling Boulanger's American and French Restaurant to remain a fixture of the First Ward until the Civil War.

Amicus, writing in the *Washington Daily National Intelligencer*, commented on the beverages and fare at "Monsieur B's" during the restaurant's heyday: "The oysters and other eatables that grace his tables are of very superior quality, and are dished up most temptingly." Though abstemious himself, Amicus included a report that "his wines are old and superb, his brandies of most excellent 'bead and brand.' " One peculiarity of Boulanger's conduct of the restaurant was his invariable rule to close on major holidays "and public occasions calculated to collect a large assemblage of people." On these days he would hire his services out to cater balls and parties happening in the city.

Boulanger remained a steadfast host of Washington gastronomy into the first year of the Civil War. In early summer of 1862, Boulanger's health began to decline. An arsonist torched his back stables. This event provoked a health crisis, and he died in on August 21.

✳   ✳   ✳

SOURCES: "Notice," *Washington Daily National Intelligencer* 19, no. 5669 (April 7, 1831): 1; "The Subscriber Particularly Requests," *Washington Daily National Intelligencer* 24, no. 7349 (September 1, 1836): 3; "American and French Restaurant," *Washington Daily National Intelligencer* 25, no. 7461 (January 10, 1837): 3; "American and French Restaurant," *Washington Daily National Intelligencer* 25, no. 7490 (February 13, 1837): 2; "Metropolitan Hotels Again," *Washington Daily National Intelligencer* 31, no. 9608 (December 4, 1843): 1; "American and French Restaurant," *Washington Daily Union* (January 22, 1848): 4; "American and French Restaurant," *Washington Daily Union* (March 13, 1848): 4; "For Sale, or Lease," *Washington Daily Union* (October 8, 1851): 7; Amicus, "Social Retreat—Monsieur Boulanger-First Ward," *Washington Daily National Intelligencer* 39, no. 11880 (March 31, 1851): 1; "Acknowledgement," *Washington Evening Star* (May 12, 1855): 3; "Wanted," *Washington Evening Star* (February 28, 1857): 2; "Take Notice," *Washington Evening Star* (December 27, 1858): 4; "Death," *Washington Daily Intelligencer* 50, no. 15607 (August 22, 1862): 1; "Very Valuable Improved Property Near the War Department," *Washington Evening Star* (March 25, 1864): 3; John DeFarrari, *Historic Restaurants of Washington, D.C.* (Charleston: American Palate, the History Press, 2013), 19–20.

Eliza Leslie 1787–1858
Philadelphia

The greatest of the antebellum matrons of American cookery, Eliza Leslie was born in Philadelphia into a family of extraordinary talent. Her father, Robert, trained in Scotland as a watchmaker and possessed a mechanical genius that entranced Benjamin Franklin, Thomas Jefferson, and Benjamin Rittenhouse. Her mother, Lydia, kept house but enlivened her mind with mathematics. Lydia

Thomas Sully, *Eliza Leslie* (1844). Oil on canvas, 36 × 26 in. (Acc. No. 1861.1). Photograph: Courtesy of The Pennsylvania Academy of the Fine Arts, Philadelphia. Pennsylvania Academy purchase.

was a baker of exquisite precision, and after the death of Robert in 1803, Lydia ran the Philadelphia Boarding House to keep the Leslie family solvent. She managed to support the schooling of son Charles Robert Leslie and daughter Anna in the fine arts. Charles would become a successful English literary genre painter who visualized scenes from Cervantes to Sterne. Eliza's younger sister, Anna, supported herself copying paintings in New York. Eliza's youth was spent assisting her mother in managing the boardinghouse.

Homeschooled, Eliza Leslie excelled at reading and drawing, and enjoyed free run of an extensive library as a girl. Yet when it came to the practical arts of the kitchen, the Leslie family's penchant for formal instruction asserted itself. Eliza Leslie enrolled in Mrs. Goodfellow's cooking school in Philadelphia and received a systematic instruction in household arts, with special instruction in pastry cookery. Elizabeth Baker Goodfellow (1768–1851) had learned pastry cookery in the French mode from her husband, Alexander Pearson, and succeeded to his business upon his death in 1803. She remarried and held her classes in her shop on 64 Dock Street.

The novelty of Goodfellow's pastry academy lay in its concentration on the education of women. European culinary education tended to be conducted through kitchen apprenticeships, and men were the dominant recipients. In the early republic, employment as a cook tended to be tracked by gender. Men worked the kitchens of hotels, restaurants, coffee shops, and refectories. Women tended to be hired as domestic cooks, doing laundry and food for a propertied family or running boardinghouses out of their own homes. It was a rare person who, like Ann Poppleton in New York, set up a retail pastry shop or made and sold confections in markets to the public. There was no apprenticeship system in place to learn an advanced field of culinary art such as pastry cooking; it was not something mastered watching one's mother work in the kitchen. Since making pastry was a bankable skill, giving one advantage over other cooks seeking employment, Goodfellow armed female students with state-of-the-art knowledge. Leslie received a thorough grounding in the practice of pastry cooking and confection.

Leslie possessed one skill that Goodfellow lacked—fluency with the pen. Leslie collected the heart of Goodfellow's syllabus in *Seventy-Five Receipts for Pastry, Cakes, and Sweetmeats*, published in 1828. Leslie was forty when it appeared in print. Her final years in Goodfellow's school had not been spent preparing to tend a boardinghouse cookstove (though she had and could do it), but to gain a sense of the order of the culinary arts, so she could make a narrative epitome and put the art on paper. By the time Leslie had enrolled in the pastry school, she had long settled on her vocation: writing. What she needed was matter to convey in her writing. Having come from a family that valued knowledge, skill, moral purpose, and utility, she had little inclination for writing for the amusement of audiences. Women, in particular, needed information and direction. She was twenty-four when she decided that her task in life would be to provide that information and advice. In 1803 she had published an anthology entitled *The Young Ladies' Mentor*, most noteworthy for its inclusion of extracts about natural history.

The early anthology had not been a success. The mystery that she had been expounding to her readership had not been sufficiently compelling. But pastry cookery—that was a potent art, indeed—and those who mastered its mysteries could compel man and woman, child and adult, with the power of pleasure. *Seventy-Five Receipts* proved a great success. Its sales provided her the credibility in the marketplace to float long pending projects—for instance, *The American Girl's Book* (1831). If one did not know how earnestly she held her convictions about the need to convey life knowledge to girls and women, one might think the volume an odd production for a childless, indeed unmarried, middle-aged woman from a respectable family, with good connections in Philadelphia society.

There was something incisively judgmental in Eliza Leslie's makeup that bridled at aspects of the culture she inhabited. Though she loved the professional hospitality of hotels and admired the utility of politeness, on the one hand, the world of courtship, family rivalry, social reputation, and classism that prevailed in America's cities rankled, on the other. She won an avid female readership in 1832 by publishing fictional sketches of polite society. Her breakthrough piece was "Mrs. Washington Potts," which appeared first in *Godey's Lady's Book* and highlighted the volume *Pencil Sketches* (1833). She excelled at fictions in which a woman protagonist had to negotiate social minefields. She had a lively vision of social disaster.

Besides her manuals elucidating the household arts, Leslie earned much of her income from editing lavishly illustrated annuals, such as *The Gift* (1837), given by beaus to belles, or sensitive young gentlemen to sensible young women.

Leslie's dislike of artifice and her preference for clarity, simplicity, and practicability of manners translated into her approach to cooking. She had little tolerance for the French aristocratic penchant for cooking for display. Taste, nutrition, and economy framed her approach to the household arts. As she wrote in the Preface to her *Complete Cookery* (1851), "A sufficiency of wholesome and well-prepared food is absolutely necessary to the preservation of health and strength, both of body and mind." Securing "good ingredients" was a requisite to preparing wholesome food.

A brief review of a recipe drawn from her 1851 edition of *Directions for Cookery* will convey the signal features of Leslie's style: simple diction with little technical vocabulary, imperative mood, narrative flow, thoroughness in treating processes, and a rather generalized indication of the heat at which a dish is cooked and the duration. This is an American recipe, okra soup in the South Carolina style, rather than the Louisiana gumbo:

OCHRA SOUP

Take a large slice of ham (cold boiled ham is best) and two pounds of the lean of fresh beef; cut all the meat into small pieces. Add a quarter of a pound of butter slightly melted; twelve large tomatas pared and cut small; five dozen ochras cut into slices not thicker than a cent; and a little cayenne pepper to your taste. Put all these ingredients into a pot; cover them with boiling water, and let them stew slowly for an hour. Then add three quarts of hot water, and increase the heat so as to make the soup boil. Skim it well, and stir it frequently with a wooden or silver spoon.

Boil it till the tomatas are all to pieces, and the ochras entirely dissolved. Strain it, and then serve it up with toasted bread cut into dice, put in after it comes out of the pot.

This soup will be improved by a pint of shelled Lima beans, boiled by themselves, and put into the tureen just before you send it to table.

The basic recipe is quite simple—indeed it is a minimalist approach—with ham as the protein, cayenne as the spice, lima beans as the starch, okra, tomatoes, and water. As with other okra soup recipes pre-1870, no mention is made of making a roux.

This adherence to the basics in her recipe writing ensured their favorable reception by the broad public desiring commonsensical approaches to the preparation of daily meals. "Her various receipt books have probably attained a larger circulation than almost any other American books ever written." A trio of titles dominated her contributions in the domestic realm: 1837's *Directions for Cookery*, 1840's *The House Book*, and 1847's *Lady's Receipt-Book*. These were all published by H. Carey of Philadelphia, Leslie's brother-in-law, husband of the youngest Leslie sister, Martha ("Patty").

In these books, Leslie repeatedly declared that recipes had been tested, yet as an unmarried woman with no household per se, the question presents itself under what domestic conditions were these dishes prepared? (She lived in hotels during the final twenty-five years of her life. Did she have access to the chef's kitchen?) She did not create dishes. Rather, she codified a repertoire circulating in the world of respectable households and reputable boardinghouses, a world in which she had participated during the first decade of the nineteenth century.

Family correspondence indicated that Leslie possessed personality traits that made cohabitation with her difficult. She was eccentric, particularly in the later 1840s and 1850s when she lived at the United States Hotel, given to extreme judgments, biting sarcasm, alternating with bouts of warmhearted benevolence. She had numbers of obsessive-compulsive rituals that interested casual acquaintances but maddened persons having to be in her company for protracted periods. One biographer noted that "she was loved by her family, but they could not cope with her peculiarities in her last years." To her vast readership, she seemed the most sensible and even-keeled of human beings.

Leslie's culinary works include the following: *Seventy-Five Receipts, for Pastry, Cakes, and Sweetmeats by a Lady of Philadelphia* (Boston: Munroe & Francis, 1828); *Domestic French Cookery, Chiefly Translated from Sulpice Barué, by Miss Leslie* (Philadelphia: Cary & Hart, 1832); [with Mrs. N. K. Lee,] *The Cook's Own Book, and Housekeeper's Register* (Philadelphia: Carey, Lea, and Blanchard, 1833); *Directions for Cookery* (Philadelphia: E. L. Carey & A. Hart, 1837); *Miss Leslie's Lady's New Receipt-Book* (Philadelphia: Carey & Hart, 1847); *Indian Meal Book* (Philadelphia: Carey & Hart, 1847); and *More Receipts by Miss Leslie* (Philadelphia: A. Hart, 1852). Each of these titles was reprinted in multiple editions, altered, and expanded.

※ ※ ※

SOURCES: Alice B. Haven, "Personal Reminiscences of Miss Elizabeth Haven," *Godey's Lady's Book* 56 (1858): 344–50; "Death of Miss Leslie," *Philadelphia Press* 1, no. 131 (January 4, 1858): 2; Ophelia D. Smith, "Charles and Eliza Leslie," *Pennsylvania Magazine of History & Biography* (October 1950): 526–27; Becky

Libourel Diamond, *Mrs. Goodfellow: The Story of America's First Cooking School* (Yardley, PA: Westholme, 2012).

William Niblo 1789–1878
New York

On June 1, 1813, William Niblo opened the Bank Coffee House on the corner of Pine and William Streets, holding a welcoming feast of cold prepared dishes. This commodious building would host many of the memorable feasts of the 1810s held on Manhattan Island and inaugurate a memorable career in New York hospitality. While remembered in the later nineteenth century for erecting Niblo's Garden in 1849—a composite hotel, music hall, pleasure garden, and café—Niblo commenced his public career as a restaurateur.

A native of Dublin, Ireland, who came to New York in his young manhood, Niblo married in 1819 Martha King, the daughter of David King, keeper of a public house on Sloat Lane in New York. Intelligent, energetic, and possessed of the acutest business sense, Martha Niblo proved the best sort of partner in William's various enterprises. The expansion of the Bank Coffee House in 1817 began what would be thirty years of "improvements," intent on making consumption as rich a human experience as could be imagined.

Doubling the number of his dining rooms in 1817, Niblo converted the largest space into an ordinary where city bachelors could board at a regular dinner at 3:00 p.m. Breakfast was served between 8:00 and 10:00 a.m., and drop-in customers could order "Beefstakes, Mutton Chops, Veal Cutlets, Relishes . . . at ten minutes notice" all day long. While clubs had met and dined in the Coffee House since 1813, Niblo inaugurated a catering service in 1817. To counter the drop-off in business occasioned by summer, that same year Niblo opened the Marine Bath at Arden's Wharf next to the battery. It included two showers for ladies and stressed the purity of the water employed. "Refreshments of every description necessary for such an establishment will always be kept."

In 1821 Niblo decided to expand his summer enterprises, opening the Kensington House on the banks of the East River four miles from the city. Outfitted fashionably in a federal mansion known as Mount Vernon, the Kensington was equipped with baths. "Dinner and tea parties, clubs and societies, can be furnished with all the delicacies of the season." Niblo believed the hotel would be particularly attractive to "turtle clubs," the gentlemen's societies devoted to rural feasts on terrapin and sea turtle stews. Niblo set up his own carriage ser-

"Niblo's Garden (rear view)," New York (ca. 1820). Lithograph. Photograph: Museum of the City of New York.

vice from the Bank Coffee House to Kensington House for the convenience of citizens. The traffic proved sufficient to keep the Kensington House open year-round.

In summer of 1822, Niblo erected a new building for his Bank Coffee House on the corner of Asylum and Perry Streets. He was almost immediately engaged in a culinary war with William Sykes over the high-end dinner trade. The ammunition was green turtle soup. The armament escalated as the 1820s wore on with grouse, venison, and canvasback duck. The war continued until 1828, when Niblo decided to sell the furnishings of the Bank Coffee House. He retained the building for two years before tearing it down, and he moved the famous wine cellar to his new headquarters on Broadway.

In the later 1820s, Niblo had a vision of a new form of entertainment combining the old English public gardens (e.g., Vauxhall et al.) with the modern hotel and theater. In 1828 he contracted for 576 Broadway, styling his new space as Niblo's Garden. To advertise the place, he began contracting novel entertainments. As in all show business ventures, the results sometimes did not pan out. Madame Johnson, the aeronaut, contracted to ascend in her balloon from the garden in July 1828 for $300. The gas failed, the balloon remained earthbound, and Niblo lost the $55 advance paid to Johnson. The garden itself featured over two thousand "rare and valuable plants" in an open ground and in a greenhouse with well-graded walkways and gas lighting. Admission to the grounds was a shilling. In its early years, the saloon contiguous to the greenhouse featured an evening display of panorama paintings, huge canvases unrolled on spools treating such topics as "The Greek Struggle for Liberty" (10,000 square feet of canvas), "The Battle of Waterloo," and "The Battle of Algiers." While the greenhouse and saloon were open year-round, the exterior garden opened on June 1 and hosted evening band concerts by the Boston Military Band or similar ensembles. In 1834 Niblo erected a brick building on Broadway to display dioramas, the first being "The Departure of the Israelites Out of Egypt." In 1835 a fire destroyed part of Niblo's complex. In order to assist in rebuilding of the Niblo's Garden, his friends staged a benefit on September 30, 1835; this would mark the first time the musical entertainment in the garden was expanded to include singing and spoken comic monologues. It took until 1836 for the rebuilt saloon to be enclosed.

In the 1840s, Niblo's migration from the world of food to that of entertainment became irrevocable. Yet disaster intervened in 1845 when his building complex was destroyed by fire; the devastation was total—a loss of $50,000, according to assessors. In 1848 he rented the Astor Place Opera House to stage variety shows. On July 4, 1849, he opened the "new" Niblo's, a hotel, theater, ballroom, and restaurant complex on his old Broadway site. Despite the gesture at dining in his new building, a sign of his move away from culinary matters in his concerns was the sale in 1849 of the contents of his cellars at the Bank Coffee House. It would be one of the most memorable sales of old Madeira, port, and sherry of the antebellum period in New York. Another sign of his mutation into a showman was his $50,000 suit against the editors of the *New York Sunday Courier* for libel concerning "unwarrantable criticism upon performances in Niblo's Theatre." In 1852 Niblo sold his interest in Niblo's Garden theater to A. T. Stewart. He remained, however, a theatrical producer of some activity. In 1855, in the face of the financial depression, Niblo paid off his performers and shut his theater. He had approximately $400,000 in the bank, so he could afford to wait out bad times. By 1857 he was staging pianist Sigismond Thalberg, soprano Louisa Pyne, and others. For twenty years Niblo's Garden was the most popular house of entertainment in America.

Niblo was one of the distinct personalities of the nineteenth century. He erected an ornate tomb in New York's Green-Wood Cemetery, an aesthetic masterpiece, and during the last decades of his life he spent hot summer afternoons in its shady vault reading novels. He loved the "finer things of life," collecting books, paintings, relics, and fine wine. After the death of his wife in 1853, he became an avid traveler, crossing the Atlantic on several occasions.

When he died at age eighty-nine in August 1878, the obituaries characterized him as a "veteran theatrical manager." His contributions to New York gastronomy had been completely forgotten. One must turn to that wit of the first age of Gotham dandyism, Fitz-Greene Halleck, to understand how central "Billy Niblo's" was to the man of fashion. In "Ode to Fortune," a gentleman with some means observes:

> I'm quite contented as I am,
>> Have cash enough to keep my duns at bay,
> Can choose between beefsteaks and ham,
>> And drink Madeira every day.
>
> . . . .
>
> The horse that twice a week I ride
>> At Mother Dawson's eats his fill;
> My books at Goodrich's abide,
>> My country-seat is Weehawk hill;
> My morning lounge is Eastburn's shop,
>> At Poppleton's I take my lunch,
> Niblo prepares my mutton-chop,
>> And Jennings makes my whisky-punch.

Jennings, Niblo, Poppleton, Weehawk, Goodrich, and Dawson—all in all, a round of pleasures in America's most cosmopolitan city during the 1820s.

⁂ ⁂ ⁂

SOURCES: "Bank Coffee House," *New York Columbian* 4, no. 1092 (May 28, 1813): 3; "Bank Coffee-House," *New-York National Advocate* 5, no. 1357 (May 2, 1817): 1; "Marine Bath," *New-York National Advocate* 5, no. 1400 (June 21, 1817): 4; "Kensington House," *New-York National Advocate* 9, no. 2395 (May 21, 1821): 3; "Bank Coffee House," *New-York Evening Post*, no. 6294 (August 31, 1822): 3; "Green Turtle Soup," *New-York National Advocate* 12, no. 3227 (April 22, 1824): 3; "Grouse & Venison," *New-York Evening Post* (October 29, 1827): 3; "[Sale of] Bank Coffee House," *New-York Evening Post*, no. 8024 (April 10, 1828): 3; [Madame Johnson,] *New-York Commercial Advertiser* (September 23, 1829): 2; "Niblo's Garden," *New-York Evening Post*, no. 8695 (June 12, 1830): 3; "Splendid Novelty at Niblo's Saloon," *New-York Evening Post*, no. 8851 (December 24, 1830): 2; "Niblo's Garden," *New-York Commercial Advertiser* (May 31, 1831): 3; "The Original Diorama," *New York America* 14, no. 4962 (December 22, 1834): 3; "Niblo's Garden-Proprietor's Benefit," *New-York Evening Post*, no. 10301 (September 3, 1835): 3; "Benefit to William Niblo," *New-York Evening Post*, no. 10320 (September 25, 1835): 2; "Astor Place Opera House," *New-York Evening Post* 46 (May 27, 1848): 2; "Mr. William Niblo," *New London Democrat* (April 22, 1849): 2; "City

Intelligence," *New-York Evening Post* 47 (April 9, 1849): 2; "A Night in a Tomb," *Cleveland Plain Dealer* 34, no. 204 (August 28, 1878): 2; "Death of Mrs. William Niblo," *Irish American Weekly* (February 15, 1851): 3; "Sale of Old Wines," *New-York Evening Post* 47 (April 23, 1849): 2; "Revolution among the Theatres," *Boston Herald* (January 8, 1855): 2; Fitz-Greene Halleck and Joseph Rodman Drake, "Ode to Fortune," in *An American Anthology*, ed. Edmund Clarence Stedman (Boston: Houghton Mifflin, 1900), no. 71.

William Walker 1790–1853?

Washington, DC

In 1825 Joshua Tennison, the mercurial early hotelier of the nation's capital, first proposed the idea of a national restaurant, a refectory in which "the temporary occupant of Massachusetts need not hesitate to call for a pumpkin pie, the Virginian for his favorite bacon, or the Pennsylvanian for his caul slaugh." Yet Tennison's experiment—the LaFayette Refectory, or Table d'Hote—lasted a season at most before he ventured on to his next project, the Canal Hotel in Georgetown. A decade would pass before the idea of a "National Eating House" would be realized in Washington, DC. African American caterer William Walker, who "from his long and practical experience in this department," assured the public that he could satisfy its tastes. Outfitting a cellar on the corner of Sixth Street and Pennsylvania Avenue, a suite of subterranean rooms that snaked beneath Gadsby's and Brown's Hotels, Walker advertised in December 1835 the one dish that dissolved the regional peculiarities of the New Englander, Pennsylvanian, and Southerner: "Oysters which will be taken from the shell during every moment of every day, constantly on hand, to be sold by the gallon or smaller quantity."

Walker from the first intended his National Eating House to be something more than an oyster cellar. The bar, instead of selling the usual accompaniment of oysters and porter, offered a range of tipples, including the best mint juleps in the city. The kitchen served up the entire range of Atlantic and Chesapeake delicacies. In 1839 Walker made Washingtonians devotees of the Lynnhaven oysters that grew in a creek at the mouth of the bay in Virginia, establishing the variety as a national brand. Nor was it only to local residents that Walker suited his fare; periodically, he published a notice "To Members of Congress and Visitors" inviting them to board at his restaurant. In the 1840s, Walker expanded his repertoire—salmon, fresh lobsters, green corn, and green peas, "three extra fine young Deer," and oysters from the North River graced a single midwinter advertisement in 1845. More interesting than the ingredients was the notice that Walker would serve these up "a la mode Francaise" if wished. Walker had noted the popularity of J. Boulanger's restaurant in Washington, DC, and took pains to compete. In the later 1840s, as the railroads snaked westward, Walker's supply of game birds diversified. In winter of 1847, he announced he would serve a brace of grouse.

Summer menus at the National Eating House featured seafood—the invariable sea turtle, "sheepshead, hogfish, salt-water terrapins, soft, hard and devilled crabs." In summer of 1847, after a dozen years of business, Walker thoroughly renovated the building. The repairs and refitting lasted into the fall season and cost Walker more than he had bargained for. The doors opened on November 23, 1847. In 1848 Walker established a connection with Captain Dorry's barque that plied the route from St. Thomas in the Caribbean, securing for his eating house the most regular supply of green turtles south of New York. It supplanted oysters as the signature dish of the restaurant, appearing in every advertisement published over the next three years.

In early spring of 1850, Walker decided to retire and leave Washington. He sold the National Eating House to his protégé, the tavern keeper Bonaventura Shadd. In homage to his old master, Shadd listed the proprietors as "Walker & Shadd" for the duration of his ownership. The bill of fare remained the same—the finest seafood in summer, game and oysters in winter. But in 1853 the Corporation (government council) of Washington, DC, revoked Shadd's license on that grounds that persons of color could not run eating houses. Shadd was forced to sell the National Eating House to David Fuller. Fuller was the first of several white proprietors who could not make a go of the business, and by 1859 it was offered for sale and repurposing. Shadd in the meantime opened an ice warehouse (where he happened to serve lager beer) and catered public events. He died in 1858, a year before the National Eating House expired.

※ ※ ※

SOURCES: "The LaFayette Refectory, or Table d'Hote," *Georgetown Metropolitan* 5 (January 7, 1825): 1; "National Eating House," *Washington Daily National Intelligencer* 23, no. 7119 (December 5, 1835): 3; "Fresh Shad and Oysters," *Washington Daily National Intelligencer* 27, no. 8122 (February 24, 1839): 3; "Notice—to Members of Congress and Visitors," *Washington Daily National Intelligencer* 27, no. 8362 (December 3, 1839): 1; "National Eating House," *Washington Daily National Intelligencer* 33, no. 9944 (January 2, 1845): 2; "National Eating House—Sea Turtle," *Washington Daily National Intelligencer* 34, no. 10414 (July 9, 1846): 3; "National Eating House—Reopened," *Washington Daily Union* (November 23, 1847): 1.

Thomas Downing 1791–1866
New York

Antebellum New York's most famous oyster caterer, Thomas Downing, built a potent cultural presence in the city over his forty-year career. His dignified ethos, his active participation in the world of associations, his commercial success, his forwardness in projecting himself in various public arenas, his culinary skill, and his careful cultivation of print and visual media—all gave rise to a celebrity whose reputation spread beyond Manhattan to the nation in the decade before the Civil War. As a culinarian, he championed professionalism and quality. As a politician, he championed civil rights for African Americans. As a cultural leader, he championed education and social organization. He lived long enough to see the slave system abolished and his sons established in commerce and politics. Upon his death in 1866, newspapers memorialized him as a Gotham landmark, an African American leader, and a paragon of self-cultivation and self-discipline. "His death, though at the maturity of life, cannot but excite lively emotions. For industry, patient energy, and heroism, he had few superiors."

A native of Chincoteague on the eastern shore of Virginia, Thomas Downing was born to parents manumitted by a master, Captain John Downing, who had been inspired to free them by the Methodist evangelical teachings about Christian brotherhood. Downing grew to manhood in Accomack County, a premium tidewater grounds for seaside oysters. While a boy, he attended the same small school as Henry A. Wise, who would later become governor of Virginia. When Captain Downing died, his heirs attempted to revoke the ex-slaves' liberty, including that of young Thomas. This attempt at repossession was resisted by force. The resisters killed one of the white Downing heirs during an attempted seizure. "Thomas Downing left Virginia during these troubles and came North, enlisting in the Army and fought in the War of 1812." In 1813 he moved to Philadelphia, where he reached his majority, married, and worked as a housepainter. He lived in Philadelphia through 1819.

In 1820 Downing moved to New York, secured a space at 5 Broad Street, near Wall Street, connected with several coastwise traders at the waterfront, and, using connections with oystermen at his old home, began shipping oysters to Manhattan, serving them at his stand in the business district. Oysters, being a seasonal product, required that Downing undertake other business during summers. The earliest advertisements Downing published in New York papers alerted readers that, besides oysters, he was a "White-Washer, Water-Colourer and House-Cleaner."

Enduring preeminence in a market requires securing a majority of custom by

Alfred M. Hoffy, "The Great Fire of the City of New-York, 16 December 1855" (Merchants Exchange). Lithograph, Charles G. Swasey, publisher. Thomas Downing carries water bucket in the street in front of the building farthest right. Photograph: Library of Congress (LC-DIG-pga-01587).

price or by quality. Downing chose the latter path. In the late 1820s, he informed the city that he had "a first rate article, such as has been seldom exhibited in this city, Cold-spring, Mill Pond and Oysterbay Oysters. They are salt, fat and well flavored, and fresh from the ponds—The Coldspring Oysters are very large." Downing's celebration of the three West Long Island merroirs burnished the mystique of these varieties of oyster to the level of brands. This is the first occasion they appear in print in New York newspapers, though word of mouth had probably created their cachet before 1828. About this time, he began styling his oyster parlor as Downing's Refectory. It would remain in operation until 1857.

Downing became a full-fledged restaurateur in 1842 when he opened his Oyster Saloon at 245 Broadway. This three-story building accommodated clubs and private families on its top floor, the general public ("ladies and gentlemen") on its second, and sold oysters in the shell and jarred pickled oysters retail on the ground floor. Assuring the curious that he was "perfectly acquainted with the best method of preparing Pickled, Stewed, Fried or Boiled oysters. He will also provide, in the most modern style boned Turkies, Alamode Beef, Hams, Tongues, jellies, etc."

While a fixture among the businessmen of Wall Street throughout the 1820s and early 1830s, Downing became a hero of Manhattan during the great fire of 1835: "On the night of the 17th of December, 1835, part of New York was devastated by the great fire. The water froze in the hose, and the firemen were powerless.—Downing broke into a vinegar cellar near Garden street, opened several barrels of vinegar, and assisted by Mr. Hale of the *Journal of Commerce*, succeeded in using it to put out the fire. Several buildings filled with valuable property were thus saved." Downing's ingenuity in the crisis and his forward-ness in action made him the talk of the town.

Downing's insistence on being respected, his dignified demeanor, and his public renown made him a flash point in the cultural conflicts over racism. In 1841, when taking passage in an empty railroad car, the agent and driver order him to leave. "We don't allow niggers to ride inside." Downing refused and was beaten. Downing complained to the police, and his attackers were jailed. On a later occasion in 1855, in an occupied car, the conductors of the Sixth Avenue Railroad attempted to expel him and a woman companion from the car, the pas-sengers objected, and when force was threatened, a riot came close to erupting before the train continued its journey. Downing was known to persons in the cabin, and their sympathy for him occasioned a public resistance. Sometimes the valences of race, rights, and public responsibilities moved Downing's ac-tions in less starkly oppositional ways. In 1855 Downing, mistaken for a white citizen of the same name, received a warrant to appear before the court of ap-peals for failing to appear at a muster of the New York State Militia. Because Downing was exempt from militia duties by reason of his race and age, he chose to appear before the justices as an exercise in cultural theater and a demonstra-tion of his agency and responsibility. A New York bard celebrated the occasion:

> Have you heard how Thomas Downing
> Downing, publican, of Broad street,
> Downing, he whose famous oysters,
> Drawn from Chesapeake and South Side,
> Lie upon his shilling saucers,
> Fat and large as the ear of Pete—
> How this Downing hoaxed the collectors
> Of the fine for non-appearance
> On the tented field of carnage?
> Now, this Downing is a black man,
> Or a rather dark mulatto

Sixty years his head have frosted,
And the oysters so well know him,
That they leave their shells with pleasure,
And no knife he ever uses,
Well, one day a requisition
Told him he must go to prison,
'Cos he wouldn't leave his bivalves
Just to join the city train bands.
So this venerable man of color
Went to court at once, and showed 'em
That, at least at that time, they had
The wrong passenger awakened.

Downing was singularly cognizant of the power of the law and the symbolic importance of appearances in court. In 1860 he appeared in US court on supplementary proceedings to take an action that, for the first time, made the Supreme Court's *Dred Scott* decision consequential in an action. "He objected to being sworn, on the ground that, by the Dred Scott decision, he had no rights as a citizen, but was merely a chattel." The judge ruled that he should be considered a human being and a citizen.

Downing's concern for the condition of African Americans found many expressions. He used his Broadway restaurant as a way station of the Underground Railroad. He was a conspicuous subscriber to *Frederick Douglass's Paper*. He belonged to the New York Anti-Slavery Society, the African American branch of the Odd Fellows, the Freemasons, and spoke at abolitionist meetings with fire and conviction. Yet his authority in these arenas was underwritten by his success as a businessman. He amassed a fortune, owned Manhattan real estate, educated his sons George W. and Peter in Europe (both would become famous caterers and George a famous politician), and monopolized the high-end oyster trade until the Civil War. His pickled oysters, sold in stoneware jars bearing his name, became ubiquitous. Indeed, New Year's Day in Manhattan was not considered sufficiently celebrated unless Downing's pickled oysters appeared on the table. He catered several of the most famous banquets of the era, including the famous "Boz" banquet honoring Charles Dickens.

In 1857 the Broad Street property was closed for demolition and rebuilding. The business migrated to a space in the Custom House, the famous "hole in the wall," and fell to the management of Thomas's son Peter. Thomas Downing suffered a stroke sometime in the early 1860s; his speech suffered impairment, and he had difficulty with the logical organization of his thoughts. His death in April 1866 produced an outpouring of grief and nostalgia, for he was one of the most recognizable persons of "Old New York."

He died the patriarch of a dynasty of politically active and aesthetically refined caterers. The Downing name inspired respect and reverence in New York,
Newport, Rhode Island, and Washington, DC, well into the twentieth century.

☀ ☀ ☀

SOURCES: "White-Washer, Water-Colourer and House-Cleaner," *New-York
American* (April 24, 1826): 4; [Ad for oyster varieties,] *New-York Evening Post* (October 21, 1828): 4; "Downing's Oyster Saloon," *New-York Evening Post* (December 29, 1842): 4; "Police," *New-York Spectator* (January 2, 1841): 2; "Downing and
the Pine Collector," *The Liberator* (December 21, 1855): 3; "Almost a Riot on the
Sixth Avenue Railroad," *New-York Evening Post* (September 25, 1855): 1; "From
the City of New York," *Washington Daily National Intelligencer* (March 31, 1860):
3; "Interesting Biographical Sketch of the Late Thomas Downing," *Providence
Evening Post* (April 16, 1866): 2; John H. Hewitt, "Mr. Downing and His Oyster
House: The Life and Good Works of an African-American Entrepreneur," *American Visions* 9, no. 3 (June–July 1994).

Alexander "Sandy" Welsh 1793–1857
New York; Hoboken, NJ

The presiding genius of the Hoboken Turtle Club, the "immortal" restaurateur
who "appeased the generous appetites of . . . mediaeval knickerbockers in the
glorious 'terrapin' lunch," Alexander "Sandy" Welsh was one of the legendary
founders of the epicurean world of Manhattan. Ensconced in the cellar beneath
the Scudder's American Museum, Welsh's eating house—known either as Terrapin Lunch or Sandy Welsh's—made seafood and game the twin temptations
that beguiled the public below grade. A flash bachelor in his youth and a merry
fellow who loved drinking and joking, Welsh became increasingly a victim of
alcoholism until converted to the temperance cause. He then became the most
trenchant, funny, and dynamic temperance speaker in the country during the
1840s and '50s.

Welsh's eating house had entrances on both Nassau and Ann Streets, the latter across the street from the office of N. P. Willis's *The Mirror*. At lunch, Welsh's
became the resort of newspapermen and writers. Among them was Willis's
employee Edgar Allan Poe, who, according to legend, in 1844 composed "The
Raven" in the dim depths of the restaurant, testing sections with the assembled
newspaper reporters.

"Scudder's American Museum, originally the first New York Poor House stood in the Park facing Broadway" (ca. 1830). Lithograph. Its lowest level housed Sandy Welsh's Terrapin Lunch. Photograph: Museum of the City of New York.

Welsh began the practice among New York restaurateurs of having a Latin motto for his eating house. Welsh's was "Dum Vivimus Vivamus"—While we live, let us live. When he opened his famous restaurant is a matter of debate. But it could not have existed prior to John Scudder Jr.'s installation of the American Museum on the corner of Broadway and Ann Street in December 1830. By 1836 the restaurant had become a well-known station of the high life and Welsh a national character, purchasing for $1,000 a huge ox from Madison County, New York, and serving it up in his restaurant. On January 7, he ventured onto the New York stage as a variety act to deliver a comic "oration in low Dutch, in the character of the Flying Dutchman." Welsh's reputation as a "character" grew greater in July when Colgate, proprietor of a rival eating house, brought suit against him for violating the New York Game Protection laws, serving a woodcock out of season. Colgate's cross-examination established the fact that he could not explain the material differences between a woodcock, a wood hen, and a woodpecker, and may have imbibed too much champagne at Welsh's on the evening in question to be considered a reliable witness. The reportage of the trial was a widely reprinted newspaper comic set piece.

Something about Welsh inspired humor. A wit himself, and an artful mimic of a multitude of voices, he enlivened the company about him. When traveling to other cities, he was feted, and often "the wit of the company sparkled brighter than their champagne, and the bon mot took precedence of the bonne bouche." Yet his greatest triumphs often took the form of long comic narrations—several of these survive, transcribed by the newspapermen who heard them. "Billy Patterson—A Story of the Broad-Street Riot" is perhaps the longest of these, printed in two columns in the August 11, 1837, issue of the *Boston Traveler*.

Given his equal skill as a cook and raconteur, it is little surprising that Welsh was elevated to the presidency of the Hoboken Turtle Club, that ancient club of connoisseurs who, since the 1790s, met in the riverside grove in Hoboken in September to revel around pots of steaming turtle stew. Presiding over the stew pots, employing all the ancient "Knickerbocker implements of the Cuisine," Welsh regaled the brotherhood with tall tales and jests.

The dishes served at Sandy Welsh's restaurant were seasonal. His green turtle soup, his fish chowder (that inspired a comic disquisition on the ideal fish chowder in the *New York Gazette*, a recipe so splendid that Welsh would add 33⅓ *per centum* in his reputation and purse if he emulated it), and his terrapin soup were mainstays. Welsh understood that the quality of ingredients directly influenced the sumptuousness of one's cuisine. He was the first American culinarian to publicize the farms, orchards, husbandmen, and seafood harvesters that sourced his food—now standard practice in farm-to-table restaurants. In March 1839, for instance, he announced, "The following forms a small part of what he has on hand, and for quality, he challenges the world, viz.: Beef from G. Haws, P. Valentine & Son, Wheeler & Montgomery, A. Smith, C. Green, Fulton Market; Terrapin from Messrs. Rogers & Middleton, Fulton Market; Cellery, Lettuce, &C from Messrs. Mills & Co. of New Jersey; Hams of superior quality, cured by the celebrated Horton, of Reade Street; Pickerel, Shad, and Perch, from a newly discovered river in the vicinity of Goose Pond Mountain; Crabs from England, received by steamer Liverpool."

The invariable liquid accompaniment to Welsh's soups and seafood was champagne. While he offered "approved brands," such as Sillery Mosseux and Heidsieck, he arranged for bottlers to supply "the favorite rich and delicate 'Terrapin' brand Champagne." Clarets came out in winter when the venison and beef made their appearance on his board.

Certain of Welsh's assistants became significant figures in the world of Manhattan cuisine. Welsh's barkeep, J. Adams, became proprietor of Knickerbocker

Hall, next to the Park Theatre. His chief cook, Peter R. Steile, became his successor in the mid-1840s when Welsh turned temperance crusader.

Welsh's cuisine exerted influence in other ways. His conception of what constituted a sumptuous board provided a model for the Poughkeepsie Hotel in 1838 when it determined to become a first-class establishment. The hotel "secured a splendid turtle and a fresh salmon, of the description used on like occasions by the renowned Sandy Welsh, of New York. Turtle soups, turtle steaks, and fresh salmon, then formed the base of operations." Any rival establishment in New York that secured a particularly large turtle would trumpet in the papers "Sandy Welsh Out Done."

Welsh called his style of fish and game cooking "Knickerbocker Cookery." It vied in the late 1830s and '40s with French cuisine as defined by the Delmonico brothers. In the summer of 1838, the contest of styles came to a head when Delmonico's secured the contract to cater the New York City Corporation's annual Fourth of July feast. "Unfortunately, as it turned out, these remarkable delicacies, and rare and unmentionable dishes, did not suit the tastes of our Knickerbockers, who were taken all aback, and sighed for the good old days of the roast beef, the alamode, the pig, the round, the lobster, and the turtle soup of Sandy Welsh." Welsh catered every subsequent Fourth of July dinner for the corporation.

Welsh was an active politician, affiliated with the Whig Party, and a vocal enemy of the Locofoco faction. He knew how to perform political theater, such as sending a sumptuous dinner with wine to feed the inhabitants of New York's debtors' prison, as well as to make a humorous set speech. His activity won him more than the contract for corporation dinners. He was made inspector of canvasback ducks at the city market in 1839, enabling him to get first view of the wildfowl entering the city.

In December 1841, Sandy Welsh joined the Temperance Society, converted by the Washingtonians, a singularly talented and ingenious group of temperate young men. It was national news. In his conversion testimony, he declared that he "had worked hard to make drunkards," but he was going to work as energetically "to make sober men." Welsh's humor galvanized the temperance movement, taking it away from the earnest pleading and shaming that had characterized its discourse. Here is a taste of Welsh's temperance satire, entitled the "diary of a moderate drinker." The day begins with

An Eye-opener.
Gum-tickler.
Stomach-settler.
Treats Resolution.
(Breakfast.) Another to feel better.

Gin and Peppermint.

Brandy with Friend No. 1.

Eleven o'clock.

Friend No. 2.

Lunch Nip.

Champagne.

to 20.—At Theatre. And 21. to 30.—Each one for last, and so on till daylight.

For a decade, Welsh's temperance tales and satires of alcoholic stinky thinking graced American newspapers. He died in 1857, remembered as one of the true Knickerbockers.

※　　※　　※

SOURCES: "Thousand Dollar Ox," *Hampshire Gazette* (March 1, 1837): 3; "Terrapins, Terrapins, Terrapins," *Albany Evening Journal* (April 18, 1837): 3; [Welsh and the woodcock,] *Baltimore Gazette and Daily Advertiser* 88, no. 14477 (July 8, 1837): 2; "Fish Chowder," *Charleston Courier* (July 26, 1837): 6; "The Dinner to Sandy Welsh," *Newark Daily Advertiser* (August 4, 1837): 2; "Hoboken Turtle Club," *Boston Traveler* (September 26, 1837): 3; "Knickerbocker Hall," *Boston Traveler* (October 6, 1837): 2; "Poughkeepsie Hotel Entertainment," *New-York Evening Post*, no. 11072 (June 14, 1838): 2; "Turtle Soup," *Baltimore Sun* 3, no. 43 (July 6, 1838): 2; "French Cookery," *Charleston Courier* (July 28, 1838): 3; "An Excellent Appointment," *Baltimore Sun* 4, no. 69 (February 6, 1839): 2; "News from Maine-Sandy Welsh," *Hudson River Chronicle* (March 26, 1839): 3; "More Cruelty to Animals," *New York Herald, no.* 10867 (June 1, 1866): 4; [Obituary notice,] *Salem Register* (June 11, 1857): 2; Appleton Morgan, "Edgar Allan Poe in New York City," *Valentine's Manual of Old New York, n.s.,* 5 (1921): 83–85; Edward Ruggles, *A Picture of New York in 1846* (New York: Homans & Ellise, 1846), 82; Joseph Norton Ireland, *Records of the New York Stage*, 2 vols. (New York: T. H. Morrell, 1867), 207.

John Weller 1795?–1870
New York

City Hotel on Broadway in New York was the first purpose-built hotel in the United States. Opened in 1794, it pioneered many of the practices of commercial hospitality, including the tripartite division of executive power in the offices of hotelier, steward, and chef de cuisine. Operating in the wake of the French Revolution, its first chef was an unnamed refugee of the breakup of the aristocratic households. City Hotel initiated the tendency of hiring trained European cooks to preside over hotel kitchens in Manhattan. John Weller was the first such chef we know much about. He was the City Hotel's chef de cuisine in the 1820s and early '30s. He supplied dishes for some of the great public banquets of the period, from Lafayette's tour feast of 1824 to the literary banquets honoring Washington Irving and James Fenimore Cooper. He chose to leave the hotel during its closure after the substantial fire of 1833.

We know about Weller because he opened his own business in June 1834 at 204 (later 264) Broadway, strategically positioned two doors up from Peale's Museum. "In addition to the ordinary Confectionery business, he will dress Dinners at home or abroad. Soups and made dishes, in all their varieties, made and sent out to order, with every article necessary to furnish an elegant table." This combined restaurant, catering business, and sweet shop was modeled on one maintained by Gunter in London. Weller's contemporaries, the Delmonico brothers, followed this business model as well when founding their famous restaurant in Manhattan.

Weller made known that he had served "a regular apprenticeship to the above business in Europe." That is, he had undergone the traditional four-year stint learning kitchen work from dishwashing to saucing, and had performed the additional year's labor as a pastry chef. His experience was international—London and Paris at a minimum—with exposure to "a hundred artists of different nations" during the course of his training in Europe and his working life at the City Hotel. Of the foods he prepared, he noted "Truffles, Sauces, &c." to advertise his adherence to French cuisine.

In 1838 Weller opened a dining room on the ground floor of the New Brighton Pavilion summer resort "a half hour from Wall Street." He partnered with confectioner James Thomson, who created the pastry, ice creams, and baked goods, while Weller handled the entrées. Their "names alone are a guarantee that every delicacy will be served with all the latest improvements in English and French Cookery. To which may be added every refinement of the pastry Cook or Confectioner, accompanied by the greatest variety of choice wines of every country and clime." The upper floors were rented as summer apartments.

After the finish of the summer season, Weller and Thompson returned to their Manhattan headquarters at 235 Broadway. Sometime in the summer of 1840, a branch of the confectionery store/restaurant opened at 579 Broadway, across from Niblo's Garden theater. They catered to the city's ice cream craze, offering several flavors as well as fruit ices, Roman punch, charlotte russe, and blancmange. They also sold ceramic pots of preserves—black currant, raspberry, blackberry, and quince jelly. When New York high society became smitten with food displays ("Pyramids and Ornaments of Nougat, Grapes, Oranges, Ratafias, Macaroons, Cocoa Cakes, Kisses &c.") in the winter of 1844, Thompson and Weller expanded their catering department to service parties in "any part of the city."

In 1845 Weller had his lease of the 579 Broadway property bought out from under him, so he moved up Broadway to 713, at the corner of Washington Place. The business in dinner and evening parties expanded so greatly that in 1847 the partnership opened a branch at 20 Clinton Street in Brooklyn. During this decade of expansion, Weller would travel to Paris in the autumn to secure the finest bonbons and "fancy articles" for the Christmas season. But the next year Thompson's health began to fail. The Brooklyn shop was closed, and Weller advertised for a young confectioner to assist him. In 1850 Thompson retired, and Weller trained his son W. Henry Weller in the business. Weller and Son continued the business for five years, expanding to include imported fruits, until John Weller retired in early 1855. Henry Weller, headquartered in the 713 Broadway shop, kept the business going until 1868, when he moved to 19 Amity Street and made over the confectionery into a restaurant. In the end, the business resembled the one launched by his father in 1834.

SOURCES: "J. Weller," *New York American* 15, no. 4802 (June 17, 1834): 1; "New Brighton Pavilion," *New-York Commercial Advertiser* (April 12, 1838): 3; "New Brighton," *New-York Commercial Advertiser* (June 13, 1838): 3; "Ice Cream, etc." *New-York Evening Post, no.* 12048 (October 14, 1841): 3; "J. Weller's New Ice Cream Saloon," *New-York Evening Post, no.* 11742 (August 12, 1840): 2; "Confectionery for Parties," *New-York Evening Post* 42 (March 8, 1844): 4; "Bon-Bons," *New-York Evening Post* 45 (December 28, 1847): 3; "A Situation Wanted," *New-York Evening Post* 46 (April 3, 1848): 3; W. Henry Weller, "Just for the Holidays," *New-York Evening Post* 54 (December 29, 1855): 3; "W. Henry Weller," *New-York Evening Post* 67 (December 22, 1868): 4.

Joseph Letourno fl. 1812–1840
Philadelphia; Washington, DC

Arriving in Philadelphia in 1812, French Canadian caterer and restaurateur Joseph Letourno belonged to that species of public man—like William Niblo in New York—intent on enriching every dimension of a guest's experience under his care and hospitality. Entertainment, service, cuisine, companionship—all fell under his imaginative auspices. He began his career as a proprietor of Philadelphia pleasure gardens and ended it as the master of the Congressional Refectory in the United States Capitol building.

Letourno's first American enterprise was the organization of the Philadelphia Garden at 328 Race Street, a modest array of lawns and shrubs punctuated by booths dispensing cordials or ice cream. It opened in April 1813 but proved insufficiently rural to attract much custom. Searching for a broader expanse of picturesque greenery, he crossed the river to Camden and created Vauxhall Garden, audaciously drawing comparison with England's most famous pleasure garden. He arranged for the steamboat *Atlantic* to ferry customers between Philadelphia and Camden, and added to the rural charms a more extensive bill of fare to satisfy hungry excursionists: "Coffee, Chocolate, Tea, and all sorts of Relishes, including Oysters cooked to order; also cakes and Ice creams of every kind—Dinners for parties will be served up at any hour, at a short notice."

At Vauxhall Garden, Letourno provided entertainment. In a pavilion theater, phrenologists lectured on heads, elocutionists recited favorite passages of literature, child dancers performed hornpipes. Like the proprietors of the English pleasure gardens, Letourno discovered that managing open-air amusement grounds taxed one's sanity. Bad weather, the prevalence of mosquitoes, damage to plantings, and prostitutes ("Females unattended by Gentlemen, cannot be admitted") troubled the proprietor. But the aggravations came to a climax in September 1819, when aeronaut Michel had difficulty with the gas apparatus to his balloon. The restive crowd outside the fence started throwing stones, damaging the balloon. A riot broke out and the pavilion theater burnt to the ground, witnessed by the 30,000 in attendance. Letourno endured at Vauxhall Garden long enough to see a successful balloon ascent in the autumn of 1820, before leaving the garden and Philadelphia for good to settle in the nation's capital.

Letourno became a hotelier, opening up a commodious house near the offices of the *National Journal* on Tenth Street. He secured the notice of the residents of Washington City by catering balls and parties. His favorite venue for staging the events was Carusi's Assembly Rooms. In 1826 he moved out of his Tenth Street hotel (which quickly became the Washington Coffee House under different ownership), leasing the Fountain Inn on Pennsylvania Avenue, opposite the National Hotel. He had scarcely owned it a year before he grew tired of it and offered it for rent in August 1827: "Wishing for greater relation from business than the necessary attention to the duties of the Fountain Inn afford me, I offer the establishment for rent, for the unexpired term of my lease." He held on to the lease, however, rebranded the house as Letourno's Refectory and Tavern, jettisoned the lodgers, and cultivated boarders and street traffic for food and refreshment. It served as a coach depot as well. In the early 1830s, his wife opened a public house next door called Mrs. Letourno's.

Letourno's Refectory and Tavern became a favorite gathering place for retired military officers and the mayor of Washington, DC (General Van Ness), during the 1830s, the home of "wine, and wit, and repartee, and song, and story." For balls and other large events (such as Washington's Birthday celebrations), Letourno continued to use Carusi's Assembly Rooms through the 1830s. The balls were dominated by dancing until 11:00 p.m., when the supper room doors were opened for a cold collation and confections.

In September 1832, Letourno turned over his lease to George W. B. Blackwell, who renamed the building the Congress Hall Hotel and Refectory. Letourno migrated to his wife's public house next door, and in the following year Madame Letourno traveled to France, turning over her building to M. Justa.

From 1832 to 1838, the caterer operated Letourno's Refectory in the US Capitol building. During race season, he also set up in the tavern at the Washington Race Course. Because Letourno was known for the quality of his wine and spirits, his Capitol building office became a cause of agitation for the temperance movement. "When you approach the great Hotel of the people, the Capitol and enter its doors, the first thing that meets your eye on each side of the marble steps leading to the Rotunda, will be 'Letourno's Refectory.' This is another specimen of the 'veritas in vino.' You would think it an eating place. It is so nominally, but really is a groggery under the patronage of congress." More circumspect descriptions of Letourno's Refectory reveal that it was something more than a political grog shop.

The first object which presents itself after entering the Refectory, is a little circular bar in one corner, with upright slats, like Yankee toddy-rooms, where Monsieur Letourno presides with his busy sugar stick, with all the paraphernalia of his office. He is gracious as you please, and polite as Chesterfield, and compounds a dozen glasses of "sling" and "jule" and "wine bitters" at the same moment. This room is perhaps fifteen feet long and ten wide, and opposite to Monsieur, a long bench is laid, where two or three glossy skins are busily engaged in opening oysters. As a sort of connecting link between the liquids and solids, numerous edibles hang, in the form of raw steaks, dead fowls and sausages, ready to be impaled upon the spit or stretched upon the gridiron. In front of these appendages, is the culinary department, with the soiled plates and broken victuals, and a fire-place, before which two or three blacks are roasting meat or stewing oysters, their skins glistening with heat and perspiration. From the dimensions of the room, it will be seen, but a small territory is left for the accommodation of guests and distinguished strangers—yet amidst this congregated mass of blacks and cooking apparatus and oysters tubs and raw meats and steam from the fire and fumes from the hot slings and brandy bottle, twenty or thirty individuals often are congregated there, verging from the dignified Senators and Representatives down to the smallest errand boy of the Capitol.

In January 1847, the political heat caused by the temperance movement prompted a congressional ban on the sale of alcohol at the refectory. By this time, however, Joseph Letourno had retired and turned the business over to John West. Exactly when Letourno retired or when he died has not survived in the District of Columbia or Capitol records. His son George continued in his father's footsteps, maintaining a hotel in Washington through the 1850s and '60s.

❉ ❉ ❉

SOURCES: *Index to Records of Aliens' Declarations of Intention and/or Oaths of Allegiance, 1789–1880, in United States Circuit Court, United States District Court, Supreme Court of Pennsylvania, Quarter Sessions Court, Court of Common Pleas, Philadelphia*, compiled by WPA, Project No. 20837 ([Harrisburg,] Pennsylvania Historical Commission, [1940]), 25 vols. in 11, vol. 6, Letter L, 185; "The Philadelphia Garden," *Democratic Press* (April 22, 1813): 3; "Camden, June 11, 1819, Vauxhall Garden," *Democratic Press* (June 16, 1819): 1; "Grand Gala," *Franklin Gazette* (June 1, 1819): 2; "Great Mob," *Baltimore Patriot* (September 10, 1819): 2; "May Ball," *Washington Daily National Intelligencer* (April 13, 1826): 3; "For Rent," *United States Telegraph* (August 16, 1827): 3; "Commemoration of the Eighth of January," *United States Telegraph* (January 15, 1831): 2; "The Complimentary Ball to M. Roux de Rochelle," *United States Telegraph* (March 17, 1831): 3; "Notice of His Taking the Tavern at Washington Race Course," *Washington Daily National Intelligencer* (May 9, 1835): 2; "Congressional Groggery," *Knoxville Register* (August 9, 1837): 5; "Two Refectories," *Alexandria Gazette* (August 23, 1837): 2.

Edward Windust 1795–1877 and
Sarah E. Windust 1804–1891
New York

When Edward Windust opened his Phenix Coffee House at 149 Water Street in Manhattan in spring of 1823, he little realized he was commencing a career as a restaurateur that would mark him as one of founders of New York cuisine.

ATHENÆUM HOTEL, BROADWAY, NEW YORK.
E. WINDUST.

A. Fleetwood, "Athenaeum Hotel, Broadway, New York. E. Windust" (ca. 1836–37). Lithograph. Photograph: Eno Collection, New York City Views, from the New York Public Library.

A native of Southampton, England, he had emigrated in 1816. Newly married when he opened the Phenix, his nineteen-year-old wife, Sarah, a trained cook, had come from London in 1821 seeking employment in something other than an aristocrat's town house. Her genius at the griddle made the name Windust resonant in the annals of Knickerbocker epicureanism. The Phenix advertised that "Beef steaks, lamb and mutton chops, veal cutlets, chickens, oysters, relishes, and soups of various kinds" were always available. At 11:00 a.m., morning soups (green turtle soup was advertised by name in season) became available.

In 1825 the Windusts moved to 11 Park Row and renamed their establishment the Shakespeare House, in honor of the Park Theatre two doors away. The 1820s were the heyday of the subterranean eating house—the oyster cellars, rathskellers, and below-grade restaurants such as Alexander "Sandy" Welsh's Terrapin Lunch beneath the American Museum. Just as the politicians had adopted Sandy Welsh's as their den, New York's actors and literati adopted 11 Park Row as their resort. Convenience, of course, played a part in this. After a performance, it was the closest place of public refreshment in the neighborhood. But part of it had to do with the courtly congeniality of Edward Windust. In January

1826, he sent an invitation to his patrons to partake in New Year's punch and a cold collation on January 6, England's "Old Christmas Day."

As soon as the Windusts had become established in 11 Park, they began catering events, particularly during the summer hiatus in the city dining trade. In spring of 1829, they supplied the club dinner in the Pavilion at the Long Island Race Course. Inevitably, contact with theatrical personalities began turning Edward Windust into "Ned," a lively fellow. In 1831 he claims to have found a bill when dismantling an old trunk describing the exhibition of the "Bididden [Biddenden] maids, who were born in 1100, joined together at the hips and shoulders and lived 34 years." This was precisely the sort of humbug in which the American Museum reveled. Windust showed the trunk and bill on the stage there all through the Christmas season of 1831. The bill prompted a collecting mania that transformed the cellar into a museum of the theater, with engraved portraits, a cast of Shakespeare's monument, and other relics of the stage, including, after the Park Theatre fire of 1848, the cornerstone of the Park Theatre.

In 1833 as Edward's trade increased and the couple's ambitions swelled, they contracted William Sykes, who had been New York's greatest caterer in the early 1820s but had since suffered exile and disgrace, to come from England and assist in the kitchen. He worked at Shakespeare House for almost three months when an accidental gunshot wound cut short his life in early April of that year.

Sometime in 1835, the Windusts decided to emerge from the cellar and enter the hotel trade. In New York, Philadelphia, New Orleans, and Boston, a hotel boom had commenced with huge architectural structures designed to accommodate and impress the public. The Windusts did not possess the funds or bank credit to undertake new construction, but they did purchase two four-story edifices on the corner of Broadway and Lombard Street, connected them, and outfitted them "with great taste and elegance" as the Athenaeum Hotel. While convenience played in favor of the hotel's success, the erection of other more commodious, modish, and better-staffed hotels in the city had the Windusts fighting for trade. In March 1841, rumors that the Athenaeum was going under prompted Edward to publish that these impressions were "entirely unfounded." The truth was that the couple remained solvent only through aggressively seeking catering jobs for events in the metropolitan area. They struggled for another year, shuttered the Athenaeum, and returned in spring of 1842 to the Shakespeare House at 11 Park Row.

Edward was welcomed back with hallelujahs by his friends. Actor John Brougham later recalled the Shakespeare House so beloved by his brethren: "You descended a flight of stairs and found yourself in an ample saloon, on one side of which was a long bar, while the wall on the other side was decorated with all sorts of old dramatic and sporting pictures. I remember particularly a fac-simile of Shakespeare's tombstone. . . . Further down was a very long table, round which the actors of the Park Theatre and other congenial lovers of the drama were wont to congregate, and opposite this were a series of small boxes for private suppers."

And what of the suppers? If Sandy Welsh's stood as New York's prototype for the seafood house, Windust's stood as the first of the great steak houses. Brougham attested:

> It was commonly said that you could nowhere get as good a steak as at Windust's. He cut them thicker than anybody else, and they were tender, succulent and delicious. . . . Beside the splendid steaks and the genial conversation I should also mention as one of the principal attractions the exquisite cleanliness of the place. The drapery and all that sort of thing was always faultless. Much of this was owing to Windust's wife, a buxom and comely English woman, who personally attended to the cooking and attendance, and who contributed a great deal to the popularity of the place. She was about forty at the time I remember her.

In the later 1840s, the Windusts took possession of the upper stories of 11 Park Row, converted the street level to a store, and outfitted the second story "as an extensive dining-room, with large, wide windows, which in the summer time were thrown wide open. In the centre of this room stood a long dining-table, while at the end and sides of the room were other tables, accommodating four persons each." The cellar became a saloon. In the later 1840s, writers and magazine editorial boards began using the private rooms for dinner meetings—including Lewis Gaylord Clark and the writers for the *Knickerbocker Magazine*, and sportsman William T. Porter, editor of the *Spirit of the Times*. Edgar Allan Poe frequented the cellar. Indeed, every significant author, actor, and sportsman (particularly the cricketers) in New York dined or drank at Windust's.

After the great Park Theatre fire of 1848, magazines began publishing short glimpses of the company and hosts of Shakespeare House. The theater's cornerstone, excavated from the rubble of the building, was embedded into the wall near the clerk's counter and served as a stimulus for editorial ruminations on the history of New York's stage. Since the editorial staff of many publications dined there, the congenial atmosphere of the cellar bar or the dining rooms became something they venerated in print. Ned became something of a literary character, and his Latin motto, "Nunquam Non Paratus"—Always at the Ready—became a shorthand for the Shakespeare House itself, invoked in a dozen comic sketches of drunk Knickerbockers who, after Ned's oyster feasts and lubrication, burst onto Ann Street gunning for bullfinches or tales of visiting rubes trying to parse the motto's meaning. Even Sarah Windust made an appearance in these sketches, called out of the kitchen to tell Fred, an 1850s foodie, that she didn't have time on New Year's morning to instruct him on turkey boning for his New Year's open house feast. Only occasionally did food appear in these sketches, a dish of coleslaw in "A Scene at Windust's" or a pork roast with or without mustard in the recollections of actor John Gilbert. Only the beefsteak was a perpetual theme.

The Windusts retired in 1865 and turned Shakespeare House over to Mr. Barry, a loyal employee who began as a boy in the cook room and who was the young man who saved Horace Greeley from a murderous street mob in 1863 by hiding him beneath a linen-clad table in the dining room where customers were in the process of eating. Barry closed Windust's in 1870 and enjoyed his own fame as steward of the Everett House in the 1870s.

Edward and Sarah retired to a cottage on Long Island. He died in 1877, she in 1891. Both were woven deeply into the story of dining in New York in the days of the Knickerbockers.

※ ※ ※

SOURCES: "Phenix Coffee House," *New-York National Advocate* 11, no. 2946 (May 13, 1823): 2; "A Card," *New-York Evening Post*, no. 7325 (January 4, 1826): 2; "Look Out for the Races," *New-York American* 10, no. 2880 (May 8, 1829): 3; "American Museum," *New-York Evening Post*, no. 9140 (December 12, 1831): 3. [Notice on Athenaeum Hotel,] *New-York Evening Post*, no. 10646 (October 13, 1836): 2; "The Athenaeum Hotel, 374 Broadway," *New-York Commercial Advertiser* (March 12, 1841): 4; "Shakespeare 11 Park Row," *New-York Commercial Advertiser* (June 3, 1842): 3; "Windust's," *New York Herald* 42, no. 78 (March 19, 1877): 6; "Old Times at Windust's," *Record of the Year, A Reference Scrap Book*, vol. 2 (1877), 103-6; "Extract from a Letter from Paris," *New-York Commercial Advertiser* (March 21, 1827): 2; "Theatres in New York," *Spirit of the Times* 25, no. 48 (January 12, 1856): 567; Deintical, "Nunquam Non Paratus," *Spirit of the Age* 19, no. 41 (December 1, 1849): 482; "Bull-Finches: A Sporting Sketch," *The Knickerbocker* 20, no. 4 (October 1842): 354-58; "The Tale of a Boned Turkey," *Spirit of the Times* 23, no. 50 (January 28, 1854): 593; "A Scene at Windust's," *Spirit of the Times* 20, no. 5 (March 23, 1850): 49.

Eliza Seymour Lee 1800–1874?

Charleston, SC

The freeborn black pastry chef and restaurateur Eliza Seymour Lee inherited the shop and skill of her mother, Sally Seymour, the founding matriarch of the greatest of South Carolina's African American cooking dynasties. Eliza's mother

"Eliza Lee, Pastry Cook." Advertisement, *Charleston Mercury* (March 2, 1851): 3.

had been the cook and mistress of planter Thomas Martin and mother of his mulatto son, William Seymour. During the period of Sally Seymour's enslavement, Thomas Martin had her trained by Adam Prior, one of Charleston's two professional pastry chefs in the early 1790s. Martin manumitted her in 1795. She immediately set up an independent business as a pastry cook. Her recipe for plum pudding became a fixture among Charleston's home bakers. From Catherine Lee Banks Edwards's recipe manuscript:

SALLY SEYMOUR'S DIRECTIONS FOR MAKING PLUM PUDDING

Slice a four penny loaf of stale bread—put it in a bowl. Boil a bottle of porter and pour it over it. When completely saturated with porter, chop it with a spoon and let it stand until cold. Beat up twelve eggs, and stir them in with a saucer of flour—a teaspoon of powdered ginger, a grated nutmeg, and a little salt. Have a pound of suet shred fine, to which add a pound of stored raisins, a pound of currants, some citron, and three spoonfuls of brown sugar. Dip your towel in boiling water, flour it, pour in the pudding and tie it up tightly, plunge it into boiling water, and let it boil five hours.

Eliza Seymour was born in 1800 and was homeschooled to read and write. Sally Seymour's reputation as a cook had grown so prodigious that elite townspeople had young house slaves article to her to learn the arts of meat cookery and pastry making. Seymour had anywhere from six to nine slaves in her kitchen at any time from 1805 to her death in 1824. If any of these would later come to sale, the transaction would be private and notice given that the person being sold was "a first rate meat and pastry cook" or "a complete pastry cook." There was no higher commendation. Eliza learned oven craft in the company of a crowd of youthful, enslaved assistant cooks (Peter, Betsey, Liddy, and Laura) under her mother's tutelage. By the time of her majority, Eliza had absorbed her mother's entire art.

In 1823 Eliza married the free black tailor John Lee, whose shop was a block from Sally Seymour's shop at 35 Tradd Street. He was ambitious, fashionable, and eight years older than Eliza. They were married in St. Phillips Church, one of the very few African American marriages recorded on the church's register.

Upon Sally Seymour's death in 1824, the shop at 35 Tradd Street and its servants came into the possession of John and Eliza Seymour Lee. Eliza took over its management, opened a dining room for club meetings and boarders, and began expanding the offerings. The Society of the Cincinnati met regularly at her establishment on Tradd into the mid-1830s. During the 1830s, John secured the contract with the Charleston City Council to provision the assemblies of the Citizen Guard. Given his wife's talent as a caterer and his own administrative ability, John Lee determined to change vocations, becoming both a public caterer and boardinghouse proprietor.

From 1840 through 1851, the Lees collaborated in running a hotel opposite Washington Park on the south side of Broad Street. It bore different names at different times: the Mansion House (1840–45), Lee's Hotel (1845–48), and the Jones Hotel (1848–50). In the last enterprise, Eliza's brother, William, undertook the preparation of cuisine. In August 1848, Eliza secured the old Seymour residence on Tradd, outfitting it as an eating house, pastry shop, and domicile to raise the Lee children. To remind old customers of the familiar pleasures, she promised "Hot Buns and Tea Cakes every Evening." During the summers of 1850 and 1851, John Lee shuttered the Jones Hotel and conducted Moultrie House, a seaside resort on Sullivan's Island. The death of Eliza's husband, John, in 1851 forced Eliza on an independent course. William Seymour, too, went his separate way, becoming the caterer at the Madison Springs resort in Georgia.

From 1848 to 1856, Eliza maintained her Tradd Street restaurant. Yet her most pronounced influence on Charleston cookery may have been her society banquets, spectacular feasts for the Hibernian Society (1850–53), the Jockey Club of South Carolina (1848, 1860), the St. Andrew's Society (1848) , and the Washington Light Infantry (1846). After 1848 she used the Tradd Street building as a catering office. It was a large multistoried building broken into separate apartments—not ideal above the ground floor for accommodating guests, yet it was entirely suitable for lodgers. In 1856 Eliza secured a small building at 18 Beaufain Street and moved her restaurant there. She converted Tradd Street to a lodging house to supply a second revenue stream. A notion of her daily offerings may be had from an 1856 advertisement (see p. 000), in which it can be seen that Eliza's sense of vocation conforms exactly to that of most pastry cooks. Cakes, pies, and jellies stood foremost among the creations at her command. Hosting society dinners was her primary evening business, not boarding diners. Drop-in customers would be served at all hours, but lunch was commended particularly to the public. Of savory dishes, oysters—the signature dish of coastal eating houses from Portland, Maine, to Galveston, Texas—was the only savory item receiving particular mention. If turtle had been in season, it too would have been mentioned.

Pastry cookery was a cosmopolitan art, its tenets codified in majestic tomes, such as M. A. Carême's *The Royal Parisian Pastrycook and Confectioner*, whose English edition was advertised in the *Charleston Courier* in May 1837. The premium placed on complete pastry cooks in slave sales strongly suggests that persons apprenticed and trained by literate cooks, such as Sally Seymour and Eliza Lee, made up the majority of the skilled listings during the final decades of slave culture in South Carolina. Nineteen advertisements from 1784 to 1840 indicated a skilled "French Cook" being put up for private sale in the city. The other free black pastry cooks who owned slaves—Camilla Johnson, Eliza Dwight, Martha Gilchrist, Hannah Hetty, Elizabeth Holton, Mary Holton, and Cato McCloud—performed similarly. Perhaps the greatest testimony to Eliza Lee's work as instructor in the mysteries of cookery was the success of her protégé Nat Fuller, who advanced to the first rank of his profession while the slave of William C. Gatewood. Fuller would extend the lineage of African American culinary art, training his own protégé Tom R. Tully. Tully, in turn, would train a generation of black chefs, including Alfred Castion and William Barron, the two greatest caterers in the city during the 1880s and 1890s.

Lee did not wish to reside in Charleston during the Civil War. She left for New York, where her daughter Sarah Barquet lived. She then relocated for the bulk of the war to Cleveland, Ohio. Lee family legend holds that Eliza sold a recipe for dill pickles to John Henry Heinz. But Heinz did not get into the pickle business until 1860—in Pittsburgh, not Cleveland. Lee did not wish to reside in Charleston during the Civil War. She left for New York, where her daughter Sarah Barquet lived. She then relocated for the bulk of the war to Cleveland, Ohio. Lee family legend holds that Eliza sold a recipe for dill pickles to John Henry Heinz. But Heinz did not get into the pickle business until 1860—in Pittsburgh, not Cleveland. One difficulty with judging whether Lee's recipe was appropriated is the absence of any written collection of Lee's creations. Indeed, only one of Lee's recipes has survived in the manuscript collections of Charleston's matrons:

BLACK CAKE

Three pounds of currants, two pounds of raisins, one and a half pounds of citron, one and a half pounds of butter, one pound of sugar, and one pound of flour; mace, cloves, nutmet, all-spice, cinnamon, brandy and rose water, and twelve eggs. To make a browning for the cake use a half pound of moist sugar, two ounces of butter, add a little water and simmer till brown. A little of this mixture will give a rich color to the cake.

Shortly after the war, Eliza returned to Charleston intent upon occupying her properties. Much to her shock, the Tradd Street house had been sold by her trustee, triggering a bout of litigation. Eliza received only a token payment for the loss. Her son's increasing mental illness absorbed her time. The coming of Reconstruction found her petitioning Charleston's Committee on Retrenchment and Relief to have him sent to an asylum. In the secretarial introduction to the petition, it was noted that "she was in old age and poverty, and that her son had lost his reason." The committee ruled that he was not crazy, but "if he should become worse the City Hospital is amply sufficient." Neither was she as impoverished as her lawyers represented her as being. A lifetime as a businesswoman had taught her to have caches of resources in unsuspected places. In 1868 she left Charleston for good to live with her daughter Sarah Barquet in New York. Circumstantial evidence indicates that she died there at the age of seventy-four.

✳︎   ✳︎   ✳︎

SOURCES: Larry Koger, *Black Slaveowners: Free Black Slave Masters in South Carolina, 1790–1860* (Columbia: University of South Carolina Press), 39; "Society of the Cincinnati," *Charleston Courier* (January 1, 1833); "Proceedings of Council," *Charleston Council* (July 26, 1838); "Lee's Hotel," *Charleston Courier* (February 17, 1845): 3; "Under Decree in Chancery," *Charleston Courier* (March 2, 1847): 3; "Jones Hotel," *Charleston Courier* (February 18, 1848): 2 (see also March 10, 1848; February 2, 1850; and March 2, 1851); "The Madison Spring, Georgia," *Charleston Courier* (June 30, 1852): 1; "Petition of Eliza S. Lee," *Charleston Daily News* (December 29, 1866): 5; [Committee ruling,] *Charleston Daily News* (January 16, 1867): 3; *1870 United States Federal Census, New York, Ward 18, District 4*, 13; Jane W. Fickling, *Recipes from Old Charleston, an Edition of the Letters and Receipts of Catherine Lee Banks Edwards (1793–1863)* (Birmingham, AL: Banner Press, 1989): 88; David S. Shields, *Southern Provisions: The Creation and Revival of a Cuisine* (Chicago: University of Chicago Press, 2015), 129–42.

Isaiah Le Count 1803–1853
Philadelphia

The audacious and talented African American restaurateur Isaiah Le Count vied with Robert Manners in 1830s Philadelphia for preeminence as the greatest cook in the city. During the years 1835 to 1837, Le Count's United States Refectory at the corner of Fifth and Chestnut engaged in a style war with Manners's Merchants Coffee House. If Merchants installed a marble floor, Le Count would pave over his wood floor with marble tiles. The accidental death of Manners in a sleighing accident in winter 1837 left Le Count standing alone as the champion of fine dining in the city, beyond the seafood offerings of James Prosser. Le Count would labor to maintain this exalted status at the United States Refectory from 1835 to the 1840s, and at the revived Franklin Refectory at 262 Market Street throughout the 1840s.

Born in Delaware, Le Count trained as a seaman, spent his twenties in transatlantic stints, and learned cooking in France and Spain. He left off the ocean in the early 1830s and sought employment in one of the city's oyster cellars as a cook. He characterized his experience in circumspect third person: "He had dipt into the modes and perfections of countries other than his own"—and had acquired experience in Philadelphia. In spring of 1835, he opened up his United States Refectory and announced that his aim was gentility in dining. He was assisted in his enterprise by an expert African American staff—Henry, the headwaiter, and John, the oyster specialist, who shucked, roasted, fried, or stewed the bivalves as customers wished.

The portrait we have of Isaiah Le Count from this time is one of the richest that survives of any cook of 1830s America:

> Le Count is a fine, square built fellow, with a noble front and bearing with dancing eyes, black hair and black whiskers, which fringe like a dark forest his chin and neck, and would, if he chose, make his upper lip most magnificently charming. He is all attention, and has a world of heart, and knows by experience how to cook "duck or plover"—or snipe, or teal, or oysters, or beaf steak, or mutton chops, or canvass back ducks, or venison—in a word, any thing that a human stomach can digest.

If Le Count had a signature dish, it was deviled lobster—chopped lobster in a salty cream sauce laced with cayenne. "A New Yorker" in May 1835 observed that "it merited a name more congenial to our notion of pleasure-giving contrivances. The fact is, it was about the most delicious thing I ever tasted." Soft-shelled crabs, sourced from the Severn River in Maryland, also graced Le Count's springtime table.

Like every other ambitious caterer, Le Count invited persons staging public events to contract his services: "Balls, Routes, and Galas, served with spiced oysters, prepared in the first style. Game of all kinds in season. Dinners and Suppers provided." He also kept books of subscription for regular boarders who dined on a monthly plan. To these subscribers he promised "perfect cooking—absolute cleanliness—variety—punctuality, and cheapness."

Le Count conducted business on these grounds for five years, until he realized that the moneyed classes were migrating in Philadelphia. He sold the United States Refectory to Godfrey Lainhoof and P. W. Milligan. In September 1840, he hailed his clientele: "Epicures, Attention! Franklin Refectory, 363 Market Street, Revived." This business, however, did not attract the custom he envisioned. Perhaps the presence of James Prosser's refectory in the next block diverted would-be diners.

He remained in business at least five years, training his son James Le Count in the art of cuisine. James would keep the family name associated with first-class dining until the late nineteenth century.

※ ※ ※

SOURCES: "Le-Count's," *Philadelphia Inquirer* 12 (May 2, 1835): 2; "Lobsters and Le Count," *Philadelphia Inquirer* 12, no. 122 (May 19, 1835): 2; "Le Count," *Philadelphia Inquirer* 12, no. 137 (June 5, 1835): 2; "Communication—Le Count's," *Philadelphia Inquirer* 12, no. 149 (June 19, 1835): 2; "United States Refectory," *Philadelphia Inquirer* (September 16, 1835): 4; "Rivalry," *Philadelphia Public Ledger* 2, no. 195 (November 9, 1836): 2; John Gardener, Opener General at Le Count's United States Refectory, *A Short Treatise on the Habits and Character of the Oyster* (Philadelphia, 1837); "Epicures, Attention!," *Philadelphia Public Ledger* 9, no. 150 (September 19, 1840): 3.

John Wright 1804–1860?
Boston

In the era before the rise of the Parker House in Boston, eating houses with ambitions to artistry in cooking were exceedingly rare. John Wright's Tontine House at 7 Wilson Lane near State Street was the choice of New England's epicures. The small hotel boasted apartments fitted up in "neat and excellent style." His willingness to serve late suppers as well as an early breakfast made it a favorite refectory for commercial men forced to dine at non-standard hours.

Little is known of Wright's background aside from the fact that he was born in Maryland, migrated to Massachusetts in the 1830s, and immediately proved successful as a caterer. Wright's managerial skills made him a significant figure in the public banquet trade. His Barnstable Centennial feast of 1839 lingered long in New England memory as a festival of "good things." He also catered the annual Lexington Fourth of July ceremonies, one of New England's most unbuttoned public celebrations in the 1830s. He was a singularly cagey politician when dealing with the sumptuary Puritans who peopled Massachusetts. In an 1843 political dinner in Charlestown, Wright delighted the assembly by not supplying alcohol. "Cold water and warm coffee were liberally provided, and no other stimulus than that was needed to awaken the eloquence of the speakers or the pleasure of those who heard." At the Tontine House, of course, wine, beer, cider, and spirits flowed at the volume a customer dictated.

In 1845 Wright, noticing the migration of genteel society in the city, sold the Tontine House to A. R. Campbell, a restaurateur and pastry chef of nine years' experience who owned a contiguous building at 5 Wilson Lane. Campbell connected the two structures, creating the largest public dining establishment in Boston. Wright, meanwhile, purchased two recently erected private mansions facing the Boston Commons on the corner of Boylston and Tremont. He consolidated them into a new temple of hospitality, Winthrop House. It opened in November 1845, and Wright quickly realized that the facility could not accommodate the crush of diners. Over the next eight months, he built an addition on the rear of the buildings housing his refectory and kitchens. The dining area could seat 125. He hired George W. Pearson to superintend the space as steward. In early January 1847, however, arsonists intent on setting Boston ablaze set four fires in the city, including one in Wright's stables at the Winthrop House. They were quickly extinguished.

In August 1847, the strain of being a hotelier finally prompted Wright to sell his fashionable property. His successor, William Spooner, purchased Winthrop House with the intention of converting it from a hotel that housed visitors to Boston to upscale apartments for permanent residents. Wright, meanwhile, returned to food, opening the Bank Coffee House in the Merchants' Bank Building on Exchange Street. "Oysters served in great variety. Coffee, Tea, Chocolate, always hot. Cold Cuts and every luxury of the season, to satisfy the appetite and quench the thirst." Cold cuts—sliced ham, turkey, and roast beef—were staples in caterers' cold collations, typical party food in the antebellum era. He noted that the Bank Coffee House would be closed on Sunday, meaning he had the luxury of a day off.

Wright's move to the Bank Building enabled the reactivation of his career as a public event caterer. Boston's grandest ball, the May 1st Spring Ball at the Howard Athenaeum, was supplied by Wright in 1848. He enjoyed a full calen-

dar of events in his first year back in the business: the reunion of the Massachusetts Volunteers, the triennial exhibition and meeting of the Massachusetts
Horticultural Society, the October Levee, and the November Whig Ball. By this
juncture, Wright's principal rival in the Boston trade was the talented African
American caterer J. B. Smith. Their rivalry, particularly concerning the cost of
public dinners paid by taxpayer money, would periodically ignite in the papers.
Smith charged more than Wright in the late 1840s.

Sometime during the twelve months in which Wright reinstalled himself
into the world of public dining, he rebranded his stand as the Bank Coffee
House. In 1849 the inauguration ball of President Zachary Taylor and Millard
Fillmore at Faneuil Hall proved the most brilliant occasion of the winter season. The attendance would only be matched by the 1,000 people who attended
the Fourth of July Festival at Leicester that Wright catered. The *Worcester Spy*
opined "that every thing was arranged in the most perfect order, and in a style
unequalled by any public table we have ever before seen." While news reports
typically enthused about Wright's banquet fare, they rarely offered a bill of fare.
An exception was the account of the "Great Supper" given on New Year's Eve
1850, at Boston's Clarendon House by Wright for R. S. and J. H. Baily: "The bill
of fare comprised roast turkies, the largest one weighing twenty-two pounds,
roasted geese, chickens, roast beef, green turtle soup, celery, cranbury sauce,
plum pudding, queen's pudding, blanc mange, jellies, fruits, nuts, and champaigne. Every dish was prepared in the perfection of cookery, and the game appeared to be the fattest and most delicious that the market could afford." Celery
at the end of December could only be had by the most ingenious exertions of
Boston's hothouse gardeners.

By 1850 Wright's income from the banquet trade—particularly after contracting to erect the Mammoth Pavilion on the Boston Common for the Massachusetts Horticultural Society—enabled him to step away from the management
of the Bank Coffee House. He sold it to A. Decoster, whose motto "Food for
the Million" suggested he was taking the cuisine in a more demotic direction.
Wright's huge tent became a hallmark of his festival catering thereafter, making
its appearance at Burlington's Railroad Festival, the 75th Anniversary of Bun-
ker Hill, and other occasions. The Railroad Festival for local political reasons
proved a fiasco, with Wright losing $5,000.

Wright's business continued apace for six years, with summer exhibitions and
fetes under his pavilion tent and winter balls in the city halls. In 1858 suspicions
were raised that he was prone to binge drinking. At a Mass Meeting for John C.
Frémont in Manchester in September 1856, it was alleged in Boston district court
that he made "too free use of intoxicating beverages," making him incompe-
tent to superintend the barbecue. The facts of the case were intensely debated,
with strong suspicions that the host committee in Manchester was attempting

to stiff the suppliers (the plaintiffs) for the event. The court found for the plaintiffs, and Wright was by implication exonerated. If indeed Wright was drinking, there is the exculpating circumstance that his wife, Elizabeth, was declining toward death and would indeed expire within a fortnight of the Manchester event. Regardless, his business was hurt by the "Chowder Case." There was a falloff in events over 1858, and in October 1858 the newspapers recorded what would be his final public event, a meal prepared upon the completion of the chimney at the Charleston Navy Yard in October 1858. Wright prepared the meal on a wooden platform erected at the summit of the chimney for the forty workmen and ten guests. The newspaper story was archly titled "Getting High." From 1858 onward, Joshua B. Smith supplanted Wright as the chief caterer of Boston.

✳   ✳   ✳

SOURCES: "Eating Refectory in Boston," *Dedham Norfolk Democrat* 4, no. 17 (May 27, 1842): 2; "A. R. Campbell," *The Stranger's Guide in the City of Boston* (Boston: Andrews & Company, 1848), 39; "Winthrop House," *Boston Courier* (November 3, 1845): 2; "Things in Boston," *New Bedford Register* 5, no. 7 (February 15, 1843): 2; "Winthrop House," *Boston Evening Transcript* 17, no. 4925 (August 14, 1846): 2; "The Winthrop House," *Boston Evening Transcript* 18, no. 5068 (February 3, 1847): 2; "Fires in Boston," *Springfield Republican* (January 5, 1847): 2; "Bank Coffee House," *Boston Evening Transcript* 8, no. 5268 (September 27, 1847): 3; "Ball at the Howard Athenaeum," *Boston Herald* (May 1, 1848): 2; "The Public Dinner," *Boston Herald* (July 8, 1848): 4; "The Levee," *Boston Evening Transcript* 19, no. 5584 (October 5, 1848): 2; "Grand Taylor Festival," *Boston Herald*, February 17, 1849, 4; "Celebration, at Leicester," *Worcester Spy* 78, no. 28 (July 11, 1849): 2; "Great Supper," *Boston Herald* (January 3, 1850): 2; "Food for the Million," *Boston Herald* (April 19, 1850): 4; "The Railroad Jubilee at Burlington," *Boston Evening Transcript* (June 27, 1850): 2; "The Chowder Case," *Boston Herald* (March 1, 1858): 4; "Getting High," *Lowell Daily Citizen* 8, no. 752 (October 8, 1858), 2.

Harvey D. Parker 1805–1884
Boston

Restaurateur and hotelier Harvey D. Parker opened Boston's Parker House in 1855, establishing a standard of accommodation and refreshment that became legendary over the last half of the nineteenth century.

John D. Perry, *Harvey D. Parker* (1874). Bust in white marble. Photograph: Courtesy of the Museum of Fine Arts, Boston.

His was a rags-to-riches story of the sort that delighted Americans in the age of Horatio Alger. Son of a Maine farmer, he came to Boston with $10 in his pocket, the clothes on his back, and a change of underclothes tied in a handkerchief. As a teenager, he worked in a mill, in his twenties as a coachman in Boston's suburbs. Handsome, friendly, and witty, he haunted places of public conversation. He became a regular habitué of Boston's restaurants. He worked briefly as a waiter in 1832 at Hunt's Eating House. One restaurant, the Tremont Restorator, attracted him particularly. When he accumulated $400, he purchased its lease from John H. Hunt and began his career in hospitality in 1833.

Parker announced that "his establishment shall be inferior to no one in the city," and he promised "to superintend in person to every branch" of the business. He was true to his word. He performed whatever task was most needful to keep the place afloat—manning the cash register, waiting on tables, acting as steward, even preparing the meals when the cook was absent. The Tremont Restorator opened at 7:00 a.m. for breakfast, began serving soup at 10:00 a.m., provided hot dinners from 1:00 to 3:00 in the afternoon, and served suppers until midnight. Since oysters formed an important part of every restaurant bill of fare in Boston, Parker took care to secure and then advertise the New York varieties (York and Prince's Bay) from Long Island that Sandy Welsh had made famous in Manhattan's Terrapin Lunch. "Mr. Parker's modes of cooking too, are worthy of a passing remark; we have never elsewhere seen oysters taken from the shell and broiled in his epicurean way; and certainly for frying, roasting, stewing &c. the Tremont Restorator 'can't be beat.'" His industry brought profit, and he determined to secure a larger space. He found it on Court Square, where he opened Parker's, famous in the late antebellum period for its food.

In 1834 Parker attempted his first expansion, entering into partnership with George Corey and opening the Tremont Coffee House opposite the courthouse in Court Square. It did not serve breakfast. The partnership lasted two years, and 1837 found the Tremont Restorator name restored, a new partner in E. Whitney, and an aggressive print campaign to build interest in the restaurant. "The first venison brought to the city this season was on the blazers of the Tremont Restorator, Wednesday. Parker & Whitney have come to be celebrated for monopolizing the rarities of the market." What was fresh and new had a premium in the world of dining—in March the metropolitan craving for fresh vegetables began to rise. Parker announced in 1840 that the "'Tremont Restorator' has supplied the first cucumbers, first radishes, and first young pigeons of the season." Having fresh ingredients was only half the battle; one had to have someone to prepare them in a manner that displayed their quality. Parker found Frederick Rouillard, a French chef who had attempted and failed to run the Stackpole House in Boston in the 1820s. "Parker, with Rouillard at his elbow, does not yield even to Sandy Welsh in the preparation of Turtle Soup."

With Rouillard in the kitchen and business expanding, Parker decided to renovate his business while rebranding it. Parker's Eating House, at the corner of Court Street and Court Square, offered the public breakfasts, dinners, and suppers. It had an expansive main-floor dining room and kitchen, and a pair of second-story club rooms for private dining. These were outfitted "in a very superior style."

Enduring institutions seldom prosper because of the efforts of a solitary individual. Parker recruited talent. Chef Rouillard was the first important collaborator. He had supported Parker through the 1830s. His time at the Parker Eating House would be short; he died in 1843 at age sixty. Next was Charley Gray, "a man of the strictest integrity" and tact, who manned the bar at Parker's throughout most of the 1840s. He was the attentive confidant of many a Boston bachelor. Of even greater consequence was John F. Mills, first employed as a waiter at Parker's Eating House. Efficient, personable, and imaginative, Mills took on increasing responsibility for managing the house until Parker made him a full partner in 1848. At this juncture, the establishment was renamed Parker's Restaurant. Mills would be his collaborator in the launch of the Parker House in 1854. It was probably Mills's suggestion that Parker raise the wages of waiters to $18 a month in 1853, while the move was being contemplated, in order to retain as many as possible over the non-working transition period.

On March 2, 1854, Parker paid $55,000 for a 7,200-square-foot plot of land on School Street occupied by Joshua Seward's livery stable. Parker presented his plan before Boston's municipal authorities. He would clear the lot, then "erect on the site a splendid granite-front building, six stories high. The new building will be occupied by Messrs. Parker & Mills as a hotel, the first floor to be used for dining rooms for both ladies and gentlemen. The second floor will be divided into elegant suites of club rooms, and the upper floors appropriated to lodging rooms." Political forces within the city sought to thwart Parker's project. In the summer of 1854, temperance zealots initiated a prosecution of Parker for violating the recently enacted city liquor law at Parker's Restaurant. The grand jury brought forward two indictments in late summer. The attempted prosecution ignited a political firestorm. In May 1855, an "immense gathering" of merchants and opponents of the "Maine Liquor Law" took place in Faneuil Hall. One orator declaimed:

> If Harvey D. Parker is sent to the House of Corrections every man among his customers ought to go with him; if they do not they are not the men I take them to be. If the law must have a victim, let it have victims in plenty. A man who sells to his customer honestly, his responsibility ceases, and then if the customer is called upon as a witness he should be dumb as marble! But they will send us to jail if we do not answer. Let them. Let them glut the jails and station houses. . . . Soon one half of the Commonwealth will be kept by and boarded at the expense of the other half.

While Parker's conviction was being appealed, the Parker House Hotel opened on October 7, 1855. Parker's conviction was eventually quashed.

The most striking feature of the interior of the hotel was the spacious and elegantly furnished principal dining hall. Its ceiling extended 16 feet in height, and the hall extended 67 feet in length and 41 feet in width. Within this space were twenty-four tables for the accommodation of two, four, or six persons each. In this famous dining room, many of the fabled banquets of the latter half of the nineteenth century took place. The first of Parker's distinguished series of chefs was James W. Huckins, noteworthy in the annals of gastronomy for perfecting the canning and mass marketing of soups.

It was during Huckins's reign in the Parker House kitchen in the 1850s and early '60s that the buttery Parker House roll came into being. His baker was probably the inventor. The first published recipe for this classic roll appeared in the November 6, 1868, issue of the *Cape Ann Advertiser* in Gloucester, Massachusetts, and makes it sound as though the reputation of these rolls was already well established. Indeed, I suspect that N. P. Willis, the famous dandy and man of letters, may have been referring to them in his 1859 appreciation of breakfast at the Parker House: "Every French roll still captivatingly a-crisp with its tender memory of the oven, every butter-pat irreproachably virginal, every ruby drop from the coffee-pot worthy the lip and nostril of Mahomet."

GOOD ROLLS

The famous Parker House Rolls are made in the following described manner: Make a hole in two quarts of flour, and pour in one pint of curd milk that has been boiled, with half a cup of butter melted in it. Add a quarter of a cup of sugar, and a half a cup of good yeast. Let it stand without mixing, two or three hours. Salt to taste. Then knead it, and set it to rise a few hours; then mould it, and rise again in the pans before baking. The rolls require about fifteen minutes to bake in a quick oven.

The Parker House kitchen and bakery took their final form after the 1861 renovation that added the ladies' wing to the hotel. The complex was described in February of that year:

The kitchen is situated on the same floor as the dining hall and directly in the rear. On one hand is a series of ranges and furnaces, forty-four feet long, with compartments for various kinds of cooking. But the most prominent feature of this apartment is the roasting furnace. This mounts six spits, and is capable of roasting a flock of wild fowl at once.... The kitchen is well lighted and ventilated by means of a "bonnet" above the furnaces, late which ascent the smoke, steam and gasses. The larder is on the same floor with the kitchen; also the bakery.

It was during the post–Civil War period that Harvey D. Parker specified that guests could secure meals at times of their own choosing. He reasoned that possessing so well stocked and equipped a kitchen staffed by so professional a cadre of cooks meant that a resident's wishes should be accommodated. Leading the staff was chef August Anezin.

Parker's life as a hotelier was relatively free of frustrations. The periodic attempts to prosecute him for the sale of liquor invariably resulted in hung juries. A recalcitrant woman who owned the corner of Tremont and School Street would not sell her lot to him so he could make the Parker House symmetrical on the block. She would eventually die. Chefs would come and go. Yet Parker enjoyed the respect of Boston's commercial community, the goodwill of his employees, and the gratitude of his partners. In 1880 he handed over practical management of the hotel to a partnership. In 1882 he endured an honorary supper. Though his final years were somewhat troubled by heart disease, he managed to travel widely and enjoy the world with great gusto. He died from coronary failure at the end of May 1884, surrounded by his family.

SOURCES: "Tremont Restorator," *Boston Traveler* 9, no. 6 (July 19, 1833): 3; "Tremont Restorator," *Boston Traveler* 9, no. 3 (July 9, 1833): 3; "Tremont Coffee House," *Boston Traveler* 10, no. 48 (December 12, 1834): 1; "Turtle Soup!," *Boston Traveler* (August 23, 1837): 3; "The First Venison," *Boston Traveler* (September 29, 1837): 3; "New York Oysters," *Boston Traveler* (November 15, 1839): 2; "First Cucumbers," *Boston Traveler* (March 20, 1840): 2; [Parker and Rouillard,] *Boston Traveler* (June 5, 1840): 3; "The Stackpole House" [death notice F. Rouillard,] *Boston Recorder* 28, no. 23 (June 8, 1843): 91; "Death of Noted Landlord," *Baltimore Sun* 95, no. 14 (June 2, 1884), Supplement 2. [Notice on waiters' wages,] *Boston Herald* (April 21, 1853): 4; "Parker's Eating House," *Boston Traveler* (May 2, 1845): 3; "Parker's Restaurant," *Springfield Republican* (November 22, 1850): 4; "Charley Gray," *Boston Herald* (January 11, 1851): 4; "Improvement," *Boston Daily Atlas* 22, no. 208 (March 3, 1854): 2; "Great Faneuil Hall Meeting," *Boston Herald* (May 22, 1855): 2; "The Parker House," *Boston Evening Transcript* 26, no. 7752 (October 5, 1855): 1; "Good Rolls," *Cape Ann Advertiser* (November 6, 1868): 4; "Addition to the Parker House," *Boston Daily Advertiser* 97, no. 14518 (February 18, 1861): 4; N. P. Willis, "Parker's," *Boston Evening Transcript* (October 14, 1859): 4.

Lucretia Bourquin 1807–1882?

Philadelphia; Bethlehem, PA

Philadelphia boasted few caterers with French training in the antebellum era; Lucretia Bourquin—who in the 1830s serviced Rubicam's, Saint's, and the Philadelphia Eating House—was the greatest. Her motto, taken from Alexander Pope's translation of Horace, referenced her training in kitchen science and her creativity: "The feast of reason and the flow of soul."

At Daniel Rubicam's Washington Hotel kitchen, Bourquin made her first impression while still a teenager. There on Sixth Street, she came under the tutelage of Mrs. Rubicam, an amateur naturalist expert in game birds and fowl who imparted a detailed knowledge of ingredients. Bourquin mastered the hotel's signature dish, and a city favorite, green turtle consommé. When Colonel Daniel Saint took over Rubicam's in autumn of 1831, he kept Bourquin on as head cook. When the first green turtles shipped from the gulf in midsummer, Saint set Bourquin to the kettle, and the Philadelphia papers would feature announcements that "Turtle Soup of a superior order will be served up." In spring of 1835, Saint decided to move into a more modern and spacious building, founding American House. Bourquin thought the moment propitious to venture out on her own.

With the opening of the Philadelphia Eating House at 10 South Seventh Street in March 1835, she claimed a public reputation. Answering the challenge that R. G. Herring's American Coffee House had issued to Philadelphia's caterers, Bourquin manifested an ambition equal to Herring's: "Every description of Game may be obtained, cooked in the best possible manner, and at but a few minutes notice." She also announced the heart of her repertoire of dishes: "French Soups, B. Mange Creams, Beef A la mode, Hams, Jellied Hams, Iced Hams with Vegetables. Boiled Beef. Sweet Breads. Turkeys, boned, partridges. Canvas Back Ducks. Terrapins. Oysters. Snipe. Fish, of various kinds. Pies, Tarts, and every thing, in short, that the most fastidious taste may require at such an establishment."

In 1836 Bourquin renamed her house the Franklin Institute Restaurant. The bill of fare remained the same, with the added benefit of a soup she made available every day, beginning at 11:00 a.m. In the summer, this tended to be turtle. One lack that she felt in her offerings was dessert. In 1837 she advertised for two confectioners. Discontented at the amount of traffic she received on Seventh Street, Bourquin moved to 283 Chestnut Street in 1838. She fitted up the lower story in such a manner that "Gentlemen with Ladies can be accommodated." She wished to break the masculine aura of public dining and offered those inducements to female patronage thought most attractive: "Fruit, Jellies, Ice Cream." Bourquin had recognized that Philadelphia was undergoing an ice cream boom, with James B. Parkinson's setting the standard. She contributed her own talents to the world of cold confections from 1838 onward. Unfortunately, many shared her thought, and she found herself in a crowded market. After a year of struggle, she shuttered her shop and signed on as chef of S. M. Ogden's Star Hotel in Harmony Court. In advertising the opening of this establishment, Ogden observed of Bourquin that her "skill is too well known to need commendation." She remained with the Star Hotel until Ogden put it up for sale in July 1840.

Throughout the 1830s, Bourquin undertook the catering of public banquets and festivals. Her managerial abilities are best seen in her successful conduct of the Democratic Whig Festival on July 4, 1837. This *fête champêtre* featured a sit-down dinner for 2,000 in a grove in Leaming's woods near the city. According to reporters on the scene, it "was served in the best and most satisfactory manner."

Lucretia's husband, Louis, died on April 22, 1845. The widowed Bourquin worked for a period superintending the Moravian Kitchens in Bethlehem, Pennsylvania. She ended her life as chef by marrying Philadelphia physician Jeremiah Preisol.

⁂　⁂　⁂

SOURCES: D. Rubicam, "Green Turtle Soup," *Poulson's American Daily Advertiser* 49, no. 13567 (May 22, 1820): 2; "Reed Bird, Rice Bird, or Ortolan," *Philadelphia Inquirer* (October 28, 1829): 2; "The Norfolk Herald States," *Philadelphia Inquirer* (October 17, 1831): 3; "Turtle Soup," *Philadelphia Inquirer* 11, no. 15 (July 18, 1834): 3; "A Refectory," *Philadelphia Inquirer* 12, no. 17 (January 19, 1835): 2; "Philadelphia Eating House," *Philadelphia Inquirer* 12, no. 68 (March 16, 1835): 1; "Wanted," *Philadelphia Public Ledger* 2, no. 210 (March 23, 1837): 3; "Green Turtle Soup," *Philadelphia Inquirer* 18, no. 153 (June 28, 1838): 3; "Fruit, Jellies, Ice Cream," *Philadelphia Inquirer* 18, no. 153 (June 28, 1838): 3; "Ice Creams and Confectionery," *Philadelphia Inquirer* 19, no. 6 (July 9, 1838): 2; "Anniversary of American Independence," *Philadelphia Inquirer* 17, no. 7 (July 10, 1837): 2; "Star Hotel," *Philadelphia Public Ledger* 8, no. 15 (October 14, 1839): 3; "Died," *Philadelphia Inquirer* 32, no. 99 (April 25, 1845): 2; *U.S. Federal Census of 1870 for Philadelphia*, Ward 14.

Robert Manners 1809–1837
Philadelphia

Before his death in a sleighing accident in January 1837, Robert Manners was the most visionary and active caterer in Philadelphia. In 1832 at age twenty-three, he took control of the City Oyster House, a cellar opposite the City Hotel on North Third Street, and repaired, repainted, and expanded the space. On August 1, he reopened it as the Fish Refectory (44 North Third), promising to serve every variety of fish available in the Philadelphia market.

Manners, born in England, had come with his father to Pennsylvania as a young boy. He learned the art of dressing seafood and wildfowl while working for William Neil, who maintained an oyster cellar on the corner of Dock Street and Goforth Alley in the late 1820s and early '30s. While Manners owed to Neil his knowledge of cooking technique, his ambition, taste, and sense of décor were native endowments. The Fish Refectory instantly became "one of the handsomest and best arranged" eating houses in Philadelphia.

Because Manners sought in autumn 1833 to expand the offerings of his eating house to include game in the winter months, he renamed his restaurant Cornucopia. He also announced his intention to prepare dishes with finesse. Instead of the usual terrapin soup, Manners would present terrapins "served up in French style," that is, stewed in a gravy laced with Madeira—what would be called Terrapin à la Maryland in the 1850s. "Mountain Venison" made its first appearance in December 1833. His daily fare: "Chops, Steaks, Cutlets and Fish; Tea, Coffee, Chocolate, Buckwheat Cakes." His favorite oysters hailed from Milford Haven and Egg Island. And his ale of choice was Troy, which only became available around the first of the year.

Manners's ambitions grew every year, and by 1836 he had determined he wished to control the most important public eating house in the city. He found a successor in Robert Harmer, selling the Cornucopia to him. The old Merchants Coffee House—the most popular site for public auctions, business meetings, and news gathering in the city—was undersized and old-fashioned. He erected "a new establishment"—a Merchants Coffee House on Dock Street across from the post office. His success is attested by the fact that Manners never felt compelled to advertise for custom, while his chief rivals—William Edwards of the Bank Coffee House and E. J. Stout's Adelphia Coffee House—did. In terms of cookery, Manners had only one rival, Isaiah Le Count of the United States Refectory. Their rivalry found humorous expression in a sketch published in the *Philadelphia Public Ledger* in November 1836. A customer is torn between the splendors of both houses:

> Le Count laughed, rolled up his sleeves, and went into the cooking apartment. I saw there was a storm brewing. Coming out presently, he said, "There, taste that wine, and then tell me if Manners has any thing like it." It was cordial. I told him so. He snapped his fingers and laughed outright. Presently Henry came in with a bird, and then with some of John's best oysters. "O," said I, "Manners can never beat this." The forks (silver) were in fine order, so were the plates, knives, &c.
>
> A few days after I had occasion to step into the Merchants Coffee House. There was Manners, all politeness, all attention. "Will you taste this Wine, sir? I have just opened this house, and mean to keep it the best." The wine was at least equal to Le Count's. In came a duck, fat, well-cooked, delicious; and with it the needed accompaniments. This, thinks I, beats Le Count. All was fine. A few days after I stepped in to see Le Count and to get dinner. "So," said he, "You have been to see Manners?" I told him I had. "Well, how do you like him?"—"Very well," said I. He gave a shake of his head, rolled up his sleeves, looked a little agitated, and seemed to say d—m him. Presently he returned, and on being questioned I told him my fare. The moment I said, "Duck," he added, "Teal I suppose?"—"Yes." That moment I saw a canvasback fly out of Le Count's eye; and in a twinkling there was the bird, as if just shot on the Susquehanna, wine, chafing dish, &c. "There,"

said he, "Let Manners beat that." I said nothing, for I saw there was gunpowder between them.

On a snowy day in late January 1837, a sleigh in which Robert Manners rode went out of control. Manners was thrown twenty feet from the cabin and struck his head against a chunk of hard ice. Despite surgery, Manners did not survive twenty-four hours and died on January 29. His death left Isaiah Le Count to reign uncontested as the king of the bon vivants.

✳ ✳ ✳

SOURCES: "The Death of Mr. Robert Manners," *Philadelphia Inquirer* 16, no. 25 (January 30, 1837): 2; "The Subscriber," *Philadelphia Inquirer* (July 11, 1832): 2; "Card—Robert Manners," *Philadelphia Inquirer* (August 1, 1832): 3; "The Well Known Oyster House," *Philadelphia Inquirer* (August 3, 1832): 2; "Terrapins, Cornucopiae," *Philadelphia Inquirer* (September 24, 1833): 4; "Venison, Game, and Oysters," *Philadelphia Inquirer* (December 22, 1833): 3; "Milford Haven Oysters," *Philadelphia Inquirer* (December 28, 1833): 3; "The Merchants Coffee House in Dock Street," *Philadelphia Inquirer* 16, no. 23 (January 27, 1837): 2; "Rivalry," *Philadelphia Public Ledger* 2, no. 195 (November 9, 1836): 2.

Lorenzo Delmonico 1810?–1881
New York

The most famous restaurateur of nineteenth-century America and manager of Delmonico's—the restaurant that from the 1840s through the 1880s supplied the standards of service and cuisine for American fine dining—Lorenzo Delmonico came to the United States from Berne, Switzerland, in 1831 at the behest of his uncles John and Peter Del'Monico. In late 1827 they had organized a confectionery and catering office at 21–25 William Street in Manhattan. Their success enabled them in 1832 to open a second location on 76 Broad Street, offering both room and board.

In 1832, Lorenzo became a clerk maintaining the financial records of the restaurants. When the William Street building burned in 1836, Lorenzo was tasked with overseeing the erection of a new restaurant on the corner of South William and Beaver Streets. Completed in 1837, the structure would serve as the headquarters of the Delmonico empire through most of the nineteenth century. In his memoir, Pierre Morand supplied a view of the place:

"J.B.," "Hard times in New York—the soup-house, no. 110 Centre Street, one of the number instituted by Commodore James Gordon Bennett, and Superintended by L. Delmonico." Lithograph. From *Frank Leslie's Illustrated Newspaper* 37 (1873): 429.

From necessity and for convenience it was a genteel combination of restaurant, coffee-room, bar-room and bakery. On the right, as you enter, a narrow counter, about twelve feet in length, extended along the wall, loaded with a variety of international pastry in single cakes, square, round or in triangular sections.... When a client had regaled himself with delicacies in this line he advanced to the opposite counter, or bar, where plain and mixed drinks were dispensed, at from sixpence to a shilling per glass.

In the later 1830s, Lorenzo assumed different roles during the course of the day. In the morning he was cashier in the bar and coffee room. At noon he became barkeep, assembling juleps, cobblers, and sangarees. In the evening he was steward of the dining room. Absorbed in learning the entire operation of every dimension of the hotel and restaurant business, he had no life outside of the Delmonico buildings. His name did not appear in print in the 1830s.

Lorenzo became a full partner in the family firm upon the death of his uncle John in 1842. As partner, he felt his role had changed, that he needed to become a public figure. He launched into the world of civic associations, particularly those concerned with supporting firefighters. He chaired the Fireman's Ball of 1845 and campaigned for a pay raise for Fire Chief Anderson. Restaurateurs possessed anxiety about fire, the element that enabled them to perform their work, yet could destroy everything in the workplace if uncontrolled.

In 1845 the Delmonico Hotel at 76 Broad Street burnt to the ground. Peter and Lorenzo Delmonico rebuilt the hotel on Bowling Green. Three years later, Lorenzo purchased his uncle Peter's share in the business to become sole proprietor of every enterprise bearing the Delmonico name. Needing trustworthy assistance in the management of the empire, he turned to family, bringing brothers Constant and Siro from Switzerland. Siro would prove to be a valuable adjunct to the business.

The Delmonico's Hotel on Chambers Street at Bowling Green hosted the majority of the banquets and balls staged by New York high society in the 1840s and early '50s. Here Boss Tweed and the Tammany politicians would gather and feed (and here Tweed had Delmonico cater his daughter's wedding feast on impromptu notice). Old plutocrats, such as John Jacob Astor, feasted at tables next to young swells, such as Diamond Jim Brady, or worldly savants, such as the eccentric Henry J. Raymond. Lorenzo tickled the proprieties of this rarified company by assigning a woman to the cashier's drawer. Lorenzo opened a restaurant on the corner of Broadway and Chestnut Street in 1854, and it too became the center of public revelry but never on the scale of the Chambers Street venue. None of the early establishments bore any external identification. You either knew where Delmonico's was or you didn't. No sign needed.

In winter of 1860, Lorenzo became involved in a partnership for processing coal into oil. Its financial collapse led to a brief period in which, after failing to satisfy creditors of the company, the Delmonico dining empire was put on assignment as compensation for the liabilities. This financial reverse was short-lived, and Lorenzo's creditable reputation, social connections, and industry brought him out of peril within months. His personality and character served him well in this crisis and he made no enemies. His instinctive sense of honor, his orderliness, his carefulness and tact, his lack of condescension, his ready smile, his laconic yet friendly conversation, his sincere concern for the pleasure and well-being of his guests, his charity to New York firefighters and French and Swiss causes, and his exquisite good taste made him a unique figure—a man who worked miracles of collaboration in the name of gastronomic art and social delight without resorting to threat. He loved mastery in cooking, and his praise rang with such authenticity that many world-famous chefs felt authentically appreciated only when commended by Lorenzo. Even the vainest kitchen artists found his simple words of praise more compelling than their own self-celebration.

The Civil War dampened the spirit of the city elite. During the real estate recession occurring late in the war, Lorenzo secured Moses H. Grinnell's mansion located on the corner of Fourteenth Street and Fifth Avenue. Over the course of two years, he outfitted it into the most splendid place for eating in the Western Hemisphere. After the armistice, and with the election of Grant, the "large livers" felt like a splurge, and Delmonico had prepared a splendid new culinary palace in which to do so. It was in this location where a succession of European chefs—Jules Arthur Harder, Charles Ranhofer, Louis Ragot, Alessandro Filippini, Eugene Laperruque, Prosper Grevillot, Charles Lallouette, Louis Mazzetti, Adrien Tenu, Jean Roth—made Delmonico an enduring byword of American cuisine. It was also the first restaurant in the United States to feature elaborate floral displays and Parisian-style exhibition food. Yet this floral and comestible spectacle drew much of its effect from the classical austerity of the décor of the interiors—for there were no paintings on the walls, no lavishly ornamental sconces, and no lavish window treatments.

Lorenzo Delmonico grasped several truths about running a metropolitan restaurant business: citizens prospering from boom economies need spaces in which to live out their aspirations for the good life—so style mattered more than convenience in settings. Fine dining could only be accomplished by the best ingredients prepared by the best culinary talent and served in the most congenial setting. He would consult the networks of European epicures for tidings of new kitchen prodigies and hire them for his restaurants. A strict attention to cleanliness and economy, a firm authority and decisiveness in matters of personnel management, and a management staff made up of the most trustworthy and efficient of one's blood relations insured the long-term health of a culinary institution.

The year of the American centennial marked a revolution in the Delmonico empire. The branches of Delmonico's in the Broadway mansion and the Chambers Street branches were shuttered and new locations at Fifth Avenue and Twenty-Sixth Street and 112 Broadway were opened, equipped with state-of-the-art kitchen technology, and sited more conveniently to the new foci of the moneyed population in Manhattan. The new locations were outfitted with club rooms to reflect the explosion in associations and corporations.

In the 1870s, Siro and nephew Charles Delmonico served as his lieutenants. To Siro fell the task of provisioning all four restaurants; every morning found him up at 5:00 a.m. in the produce and fish markets. Siro managed the uptown locales; Charles, the downtown. Lorenzo, meantime, invited a grandnephew, Charles Crist, to intern. The young Charles Crist began showing the aptitude for logistics and public address that Lorenzo understood to be requisite for the future of the restaurant empire. He became Lorenzo's shadow—an assistant, amanuensis, confidant, and devil's advocate. The explosion of wealth created by stock speculation and finance had spawned a generation of big spenders with big egos. The challenge facing Lorenzo and Siro was how to accommodate their desire for lavish gestures while maintaining the decorum of a genteel world. Charles Crist, who had the flexibility of youth, was better able to negotiate the minefields of status and ego than the more rule-bound Lorenzo and Siro.

In 1880 Lorenzo had a stroke and began handing over daily management of the restaurants to Siro. His habit of smoking in excess of twenty custom-made Cuban cigars a day may have contributed to his physical failing. (Smoking would be the bane of all the Delmonico men.) After several months of incapacity, Lorenzo Delmonico died in early September 1881. Siro died a few months later. The empire came into the hands of nephew Charles Delmonico, but immense wealth activated dangerous impulses in Charles. He parlayed with stock speculators, began losing money, and the money he did not lose, he gave away to a legion of needy folk and hangers-on. Finally, in 1884, his mind broken, Charles wandered into the countryside in midwinter, fell into a ditch in the Orange Mountains, and drowned. His frozen body was recovered after an extensive search.

Fortunately there was one family member who could assume the burdens of management. Charles Crist changed his name to Charles C. Delmonico, assumed control of the dining empire, and guided it elegantly into the twentieth century. He would maintain the honor of the house until his sudden death in 1901. During Charles C. Delmonico's tenure, he maintained Lorenzo's rule of a house that a reputable customer never be presented a bill and that no one in arrears would ever be sued for remuneration. He honored his seniors by preserving their prohibition of music performed during dinner services. His contributions to the latter stages of the Delmonico empire appear later in the "Gilded Age" section below.

❋ ❋ ❋

SOURCES: "The Treasurer of the Fire Department Fund," *New-York Spectator* 48 (December 27, 1845): 3; "The Prince of Caterers," *Cleveland Plain Dealer* (September 1, 1881): 7; "Delmonico's Then and Now," *New York Herald* (April 26, 1896): 5; "Prince of Good Fellows," *Denver Post* (September 30, 1901): 4; "The Failure of Delmonico," *New York Herald*, no. 8551 (February 4, 1860): 8; Walter German Robinson, "Famous New York Restaurants," *Town and Country*, no. 3019 (March 26, 1904): 22; Pierre Morand, "Reminiscences of Foreign Residents and Old Times in New York City," *Frank Leslie's Popular Monthly* 4 (October 1890): 436–40; "Delmonico's," *The Illustrated American* (May 16, 1891): 625–31.

Victor LeFort 1810–1892
New York; Columbia, SC; Mobile, AL; Evansville, IN; Indianapolis

Genius in gastronomy was no insurance against evil. The literature of the nineteenth century was obsessed with the figure of the evil genius—the binding of great mental or physical powers with great moral depravity. Louis Victor LeFort was the monster who excelled in the kitchen.

In 1890, while LeFort lived in retirement in Chicago, he told the story of his career to a reporter. The syndicated autobiography ran in newspapers coast to coast under the title "Has Cooked for Kings" and told a tale full of honor and incident: a nine-year-old boy in Paris, he trained in the Restaurant de Chevail, among the best in France, and was immediately enrolled in the households of the Duc de Choiseu, the Duc de Reichstadt (Napoleon's son), and the Count St.-Hilaire. By a curious happenstance, while working as a chef, he encountered and signed on to the staff of wealthy planter Meredith Calhoun of Alabama, who carted him around the world and finally to America. He arrived in New York on September 17, 1838, and immediately signed up as a confectioner at Delmonico's in New York. "During the war he was located at Richmond, Va. Then he went to Mexico and superintended the cuisine of Maximilian until the ill fated emperor met defeat and death." The detail at this juncture goes out of focus, alluding to "various hotel enterprises." It was a strange trajectory—royal household to private chef to a southern slaveholder, to Delmonico's chef, to chef in the Confederate capital during the Civil War, to steward for the doomed Emperor Maximilian I of Mexico. A swerve from the culinary path of light in Manhattan to the loser's bracket.

There were problems with this story—first, the Austrian court chef Giuseppe Ranieri served as Emperor Maximilian's steward and cook. Why, then, the lie about the evacuation of the Confederacy for Mexico? Why this Confederado fantasy? Second, where in Richmond was he working? What was the pathology behind this concocted life? Perhaps the records would tell.

Findings: He was not in the Confederate capital during the war—his southern sojourns in the late 1850s and early '60s had him installed as a confectioner in the capital of South Carolina, Columbia.

Did LeFort go to Mexico? No. In 1862—two years before Maximilian I was installed as emperor—he had gone to Mobile, Alabama, and established the French Restaurant at 35 and 37 St. Michael Street. Yet in early 1862, he had told acquaintances, the De Scheppers in New York, that he was heading to Mexico. He had abducted their seven-year-old daughter, Augustine De Schepper, and informed them he was taking her to Mexico City with him. The tale is told in a French-language story in the January 30, 1862, issue of the *Courrier des Etats-*

"Victor La Fort" [Victor LeFort]. Wood engraving from "Has Cooked for Kings," *Trenton Evening Times* (September 2, 1890): 2.

VICTOR LA FORT.

Unis entitled "Enfant Perdu." LeFort (then calling himself Louis Victor LeFort) had befriended the De Scheppers on shipboard during their emigration to New York. He, a naturalized US citizen, was returning from a trip to Paris. At the time, the De Scheppers' child was ten months old. Over the subsequent years (from 1855 to 1862), LeFort had gone southward, kept in touch on periodic visits to New York, and always admired the young girl, Augustine. Sometime after the outbreak of the Civil War, LeFort moved to Plainfield, New Jersey, mourning the death of his young wife whom he had met and married in the South. His affection for young Augustine grew quite expansive. The parents interpreted it as a paternal regard. He asked whether he might take the seven-year-old on a trip to Plainfield but hesitated to act on the suggestion for some months. Finally, the De Scheppers dispatched Augustine to Plainfield with him. He did not return her and four days after the trip sent a letter telling the De Scheppers he was taking the girl with him to Mexico—that she was well equipped. The alarmed parents rushed to Plainfield and contacted the police, who informed them that LeFort had departed, presumably south into the Confederacy, then perhaps to Mexico. The French newspaper published a description of the seven-year-old and expressed the desire that other newspapers publish the story in order to locate LeFort and Augustine. There is no child listed in his household in Mobile, Alabama.

A pedophile, a probable child murderer, and an inveterate liar, LeFort could not abide being in any one place for too long a period. He made his way northward after the war, of course, avoiding New York and the eastern cities. His name mutated from Louis V. LeFort to Victor LeFort. When he gave his life story to reporters in 1890, he spelled it "Victor La Fort" (see illustration above).

He settled in Evansville, Indiana, in 1868, accompanied by Sophie LeFort, a woman described as being in her twenties. (Augustine would have been thirteen.) He opened the Paris Restaurant on the corner of Second and Locust Streets in 1868. His stay in the river metropolis was relatively short because tidings of the explosive growth and commercial strength of Indianapolis lured him thither in 1871. He was immediately hired by Simon McCarty for a new restaurant on the corner of Washington and Illinois Streets. Despite the restaurant's splendid appointments and novel placement of the kitchen above the dining room, LeFort wished to own his own establishment. On March 24, 1873, he opened the Restaurant Victor LeFort (his preferred spelling after the Civil War) at 26 North Illinois. It won immediate favorable notice: "The delightful meals gotten up by Victor LeFort, 23 North Illinois street, up stairs, are the pride of the epicures who most appreciate real French Cookery."

Unfortunately, the number of epicures who would eat regular at LeFort's table were not sufficiently great to pay his bills. In 1874 he closed his restaurant and hired on as chef at Louis Lang's restaurant on South Meridian Street. Creative differences caused him to part ways with Lang and hire on with Lang's rival, George Mowl, whose restaurant at 22 South Illinois became the most prestigious in the city for a short time.

In 1877 the Brunswick Hotel opened its doors on Circle Street in Indianapolis. "First Class in every respect," it sought to make its cuisine equal to the best in the city, so it hired the cook in the city's finest restaurant—Victor LeFort. That he was a superb chef was the one immutable truth of his life. All the rest was obscure and perverse.

✳ ✳ ✳

SOURCES: "Enfant Perdu," *Courrier des Etats-Unis* 25, no. 2 (January 30, 1862): 1; "French Restaurant," *Mobile Register* (March 16, 1862): 1; *Evansville City Directory, 1870–71* (Evansville, IN, 1870), 92; "Opening Day," *Indianapolis Journal* (February 7, 1871): 5; "Items of Interest," *Indianapolis People* (July 20, 1873): 6; *Swartz & Tedrowe's Indianapolis City Directory* (Indianapolis, 1873), 403; "Glittering Generalities," *Indianapolis People* (May 3, 1874): 1; *Swartz & Tedrowe's Indianapolis City Directory* (Indianapolis, 1876), 293; *Polk's Indianapolis City Directory* (Indianapolis, 1882), 363; "Has Cooked for Kings," *Trenton Evening Times* (September 2, 1890): 2.

Lucien Boudro 1811–1867
Mandeville, LA; West End, New Orleans

Boudro! The greatest of the seafood chefs at the lake resorts outside of New Orleans, Lucien Boudro became a single-name celebrity in the 1850s and '60s

Adolph D. Rinck, *Lucien Boudreaux* [Lucien Boudro] (1855).

for his court-bouillon, his grilled fish, and his Caribbean green turtle stew. Born in Quimper, Bas-Bretagne, in France, he came to Louisiana at age thirteen as a sailor boy and secured employment as a dishwasher in an eating house on Chartres Street. When the proprietor died, he assumed control and eventually bought the place. In the summer season, he began working in the kitchen of the Davis Hotel in Mandeville. Closing his in-city cook house, he devoted his talents to burnishing the culinary reputation of the new resort of Milneburg, serving as cook at the Washington Hotel. In 1843 he began his storied career as a resort restaurateur, taking over the Shell Road Hotel in the West End. Located near the terminus of the Pontchartrain railway, the hotel became the favorite destination of day trekkers from late April through the end of September. Fire destroyed the building in late 1848. He opened his new establishment, the Arcade, in April 1849.

Designed for summer use, the Arcade eschewed windows and was more a great wooden pavilion with broad airy piazzas. The landscape surrounding the building was extensively planted and earned it a second name, "Boudro Gardens." In the central part, Boudro's large charcoal-fired cookstove dominated. There he grilled pompano that made gastronomes travel from as far away as New York. The temperature control afforded by his stove permitted him to cook his court-bouillons at low heat for long durations enabling them to gelatinize. The fish would seem suspended in the dark briny amber sea. Periodically, Boudro would return to France to secure a sense of the latest innovations in cuisine. He spent the entire winter of 1857 in Paris. Whenever he took these excursions, he took care to return by April 1 to open the Arcade, or the "Little Trianon," as he would call it after a visit to his native land.

The seasonal splendors of Boudro's restaurant were interrupted in June 1865 when the great Lakeport fire consumed it. The rebuild occupied half the summer and the new building—still open and wooden—expanded the seating to suit its fame.

Boudro trained two assistants into mastery, Henry Borno and Philip Billman. The former would from 1863 preside over Boudro's winter season station, Boudro's Confectionary and Lunch Saloon, in New Orleans. Located on the corner of Canal Street and Carondelet, it served as both a catering office for event dining and a lunch saloon for ladies and gentlemen shopping in the city. Lunch was construed broadly, as Boudro advertised that he would "keep his Ladie's Lunch Saloon open until the close of the Theatres." Boudro sold the Confectionary to F. Kuntz in December 1866, and Borno became the caterer of the newly christened French Confectionary.

Billman would become the chef's successor when yellow fever felled Boudro in October 1867. Billman proved an energetic preserver of Boudro's legacy, repairing the Arcade after the hurricane of October 1868 and preserving the dozen signature dishes for which the restaurant was famed. Boudro's à la Billman continued until late in the nineteenth century.

At his death, Boudro inspired rhapsodies of grief among the gastronomes of the Crescent City and elsewhere. "There were epicures in Europe—Thackeray and George Peabody, both of whom dined at the Lake End—who pronounced him unsurpassed by any transatlantic cook." A memorialist in the *New Orleans Times-Picayune* declared, "No other man has ever arrived at such perfection in the art of cooking fish. Pompano were not pompano without Boudro cooked them. Court-bouillons were tasteless unless seasoned by Boudro." One foreign attester to the greatness of Boudro's cooking was William Russell, the British man of letters who sampled Boudro's cuisine on the eve of the Civil War. "The dinner was worthy of the reputation of the French cook; the terrapin soup was excellent; though not comparable, as Americans assert, to the best turtle. The bouillabaisse was unexceptionable; the soft crab worthy of every commendation; but the best dish was unquestionable the pompinoe, an odd fish, something like an unusually ugly John Dory, but possessing admirable qualities in that makes a fish good."

Boudro's fame for pompano would pose problems for him, because the fish was not commonly landed at New Orleans and everyone demanded it, whether in season or not. If Boudro suspected that the diner had little experience with the fish, he would substitute a sheepshead or a snapper. Occasionally, he would be caught out in his substitutions, and a bemused story would appear in the newspapers.

Of the famous resort chefs of antebellum Louisiana—Baptiste Moreau, Miguel Bresolara, and Lucien Boudro—Boudro's repertoire would have the greatest ongoing influence on New Orleans cuisine. Its marriage of regional seafood with French technique would mark the path forward. The enduring force of Boudro's cooking can be adduced by a menu prepared nearly a decade after his death by his disciple Philip Billman (I exclude the wines):

MENU

HORS D'OEUVRE
Salade D'Anchoix

POTAGES
Bisque D'Ecrevisses
Printaniere

POISSON
Pompanos Grilles, Maitre d'Hotel
Filets de Sole farcis, Parisienne

RELEVES
Filet de Boiuf pique, Sauce Perigueux
Petites Bouches a la Reine
Croquettes de Pommes a l'imperiale

ENTREES
Pigeons, a la Royale
Atterean de Ris-de-Veus, a la Villeroy
Cotelette d'Agneau, a la Pompadour

ENTREMETS
Fonds d'Artichaux, a l'Italienne
Asperges de Lubeck
Petits Pois, a l'Anglaise

ROTIS
Lelie d'Agneau, Sauce a la Menthe
Crabes Moux   Salade

DESSERT

Omelette Souflee   Beignets Souflee
Fruits   Cantaloup   Mendiants
Roederet Frappe
Café et Liqueurs

✳   ✳   ✳

SOURCES: "The New Canal," *New Orleans Times-Picayune* (April 27, 1844): 2; "L. Boudro, The Arcade," *New Orleans Times-Picayune* (April 13, 1849): 3; "L. Boudro," *New Orleans Times-Picayune* (October 1, 1863): 2; "Boudreau's Restaurant," *New Orleans Times-Picayune* (April 28, 1854): 4; "Lake Pontchartrain," "Boudro's Confectionary and Lunch Saloon," *New Orleans Times* 5, no. 739 (October 8, 1865); "Boudro's Restaurant," *New Orleans Times-Picayune* (September 27, 1868): 1; "Boudro Is dead!" *New Orleans Times-Picayune* (October 18, 1867): 1; [Obituary notice,] *Cleveland Plain Dealer* (November 18, 1867): 1; William Russell, *My Diary North and South* (London, 1861), entry for May 24, 1861; "Mobile Correspondence," *New Orleans Times-Picayune* (July 2, 1855): 1; "Great Fire at Lakeport," *New Orleans Times* 4, no. 613 (June 3, 1865): 3; [Advertisement,] *New Orleans Times-Picayune* (October 9, 1864): 2; "The Flood," *New Orleans Times-Picayune* (October 4, 1868): 1; "When Great Cook Was a Great Artist Honored by All His Patrons," *New Orleans Times-Picayune* (February 25, 1923): 5.

The

SECOND ERA

1835 to 1865

THE GREAT HOTEL, THE SALOON, AND
THE BLACK CATERER

Louis Galabran 1811–1847
Washington, DC

In Washington, DC, African American caterers played a major role in managing hotels, clubs, and restaurants over the nineteenth century, despite periodic legal restrictions on their participation in the business. Yet as the nation's capital, Washington served as the temporary home for a community of European diplomats and a stream of transatlantic visitors—persons who did not share most Americans' predilections for ducks, hominy, oysters, and terrapin. In the 1840s, French chef and hotelier Louis Galabran monopolized the accommodation and boarding of this non-American community. His European House, operating on the French plan, became a home of cosmopolitan taste. "All the foreign diplomatists who have not private residences, live at this house. . . . The cookery is precisely that which you can get in the first rate hotels in Paris."

A native of France, trained in cuisine and confectionery, Galabran came to Washington in the mid-1830s, setting up a restaurant with an appended pastry shop and confectionery store. On December 19, 1837, he opened an expanded business on the corner of Thirteenth Street and Pennsylvania Avenue. In an advertisement, he testified: "As a Cook, he is proud to say that he will give satisfaction to those who will favor him with their custom. Dinner, supper, or any parties where his services will be requested, shall be attended punctually. L.G. engages himself to supply those who will call on him with every thing that can be provided in the season, such as chickens and game of every description. Pastry of every kind will be found at his store every day." He was assisted by his new bride, Louise Gabriel Galabran.

The ambition of most French-trained restaurateurs was to become a hotelier. In March 1840, Galabran began letting furnished rooms to persons in a property he leased on F Street between Eleventh and Twelfth. This was the modest beginning of a residential hotel. His plans were threatened when in November of that year this elegant three-story brick building was auctioned as part of a trustee's sale. The purchaser, fortunately, was willing to have it remain an income property and renewed Galabran's lease.

Galabran's abilities as a chef de cuisine were so generally recognized that he need not advertise. His chief rival, John Prevaux—whose Franco-American restaurant on Sixth Street angled for a congressional clientele—also aspired to serve the European diplomatic corps. On Pennsylvania Avenue and Nineteenth, one A. Favier had the additional attraction of pastry, but by 1842 he was increasingly absorbed in real estate, less with cuisine. Galabran moved to Pennsylvania Avenue and Thirteenth in 1843, and his European House quickly installed itself as a landmark of conviviality in the federal metropolis. The papers of the 1840s feature some of the festive occasions he hosted, such as the visit of the Lancaster Fencibles to Washington City: "A detachment waited upon Col. Samuel Stambough, at Galabran's European House, by whom they were treated to a choice collation, with the most excellent liquors, to clear their throats of the dust of the avenue."

In certain respects, a chef confined to a kitchen may thrive more than a hotelier, for the manager of a rooming establishment must interact with people. Some of those people are not well. In 1847 the world suffered an influenza epidemic. Someone carried it into the European House, and Galabran contracted the illness and died.

Restaurateur Frederick Lakemeyer took over the business in spring 1848. Almost immediately he began emphasizing the attractions of his bar over his table. It remained open for a decade, with Thomas Meushaw taking it over in November 1859.

※　※　※

SOURCES: "Hotels for Travelers," *New York Herald* 11, no. 76 (March 18, 1845): 2; "L. Galabran," *Daily National Intelligencer* 25, no. 7763 (December 30, 1837): 1; "Furnished Rooms to Let," *Daily National Intelligencer* 28, no. 8438 (March 2, 1840): 4; "Trustee's Sale of Valuable Improved Property," *Daily National Intelligencer* 28, no. 8665 (November 21, 1840): 1; "John Prevaux, Restaurateur," *Daily National Intelligencer* 28, no. 8390 (January 6, 1840): 1; "Furnished Houses, Rooms," *Daily National Intelligencer* 28, no. 8693 (December 24, 1840): 1; "Washington, July 9, 1845," *New York Weekly Herald* 10, no. 28 (July 12, 1845): 220.

Edward Marchand 1811–1871
San Francisco

Chef and restaurateur Edward Marchand was the greatest French cuisinier in San Francisco in the decades after the gold rush. A native of France, he emigrated to the United States, arriving in New York in 1844. He trekked across the continent as a forty-niner. Marchand's first establishment was the French Restaurant at 837 Dupont Street, which he co-directed with his wife, Félicité, who managed the dining room. Madam Marchand was a stylish, imperious woman with a volatile temper. In 1856, when a customer, John A. Fleming, balked at paying for a whole roasted chicken when he claimed he only ordered half, Félicité "and her servants struck and scratched him." He paid for the whole chicken, fled, and swore out a warrant for her arrest. While Madam Marchand's personality stood front and center in this tale, we should not neglect the other character—the chicken. It was a whole roasted bird prepared by the "pioneer of the revolving spit in San Francisco," for Edward Marchand had introduced rotisserie cooking to the California public. Alas, Marchand's ambition and pricing proved too exalted for the citizenry, so he sold out to Leon Dingeon and Alexandre Finance, two waiters employed by F. Martinez at the Barnum House before he went east to found La Maison Dorée in New York in 1857. Dingeon and Finance toned down the offerings, styling their eatery as the French Cook Shop.

One quirk of Félicité Marchand as she managed the front of house at the French Restaurant was to keep her French poodle with her at all times. This poodle became the emblem of the restaurant and the public referred to it as the Poodle Dog Restaurant.

The Marchands migrated several doors down to the southwest corner of Dupont and Washington, where grocer Nicholas Richet and partner Augustus Esnault opened in autumn of 1858 an eating house called the Union Rotisserie. A "round the clock" restaurant, "under the superintendence of Mr. Marchand," it offered breakfasts, dinners, and suppers à la carte from a daily bill of fare. A fire in winter of 1859 drove Richet out of business. The repairs and renovation were financed by Jules Vermorel, who reopened the restaurant as the Louisiana Rotisserie in the second week of March 1859. Marchand remained "Director of the Cooking Department," and an assurance was published that care would be taken "to serve Fresh Oysters every morning." He presided over the Louisiana Rotisserie for two years, during which time he stockpiled sufficient money to risk becoming a proprietor once more.

In 1861 Edward and Félicité Marchand left the Louisiana Rotisserie and established a restaurant-café on Merchant Street near the new Fruit Market: Marchand Rotisserie, Coffee Saloon. Edward assured the public that "his establishment offers all the comforts that can be desired." Meanwhile, Augustus Esnault and the staff of the Louisiana Rotisserie joined Alexandre Finance at the French Cook Shop at 837 Dupont. When they moved to 825, they took to calling their new establishment the Poodle Dog Restaurant in homage to Félicité's pet and the spirit of Marchand's restaurant in the 1850s. The Poodle Dog would endure through several changes of venue and owners as a landmark of French cuisine in San Francisco well into the twentieth century. (The myth cited in a fiftieth-anniversary brochure of the restaurant that Eugene Peguillan was the founder of the Poodle Dog, and that the poodle belonged to his wife, Françoise, falters on the fact that Peguillan was listed as a butcher in the city directories throughout the last half of the nineteenth century.)

The success of the small-scale Marchand Rotisserie convinced Edward in 1862 to open the Union Hotel at 607 Kearney Street, the boulevard of fashionable promenading in the city. The name of the house advertised his political sympathies during the Civil War. He expanded his hours, promising that dinners and suppers "can be had at all hours of the day and night." He also promised to deliver food to any part of the city. Having learned that oysters were the sine qua non of American restaurant trade, he advertised them conspicuously among his offerings. In 1865 he added a suite of private rooms above the dining rooms. Throughout the city, "private rooms" became a restaurant code phrase for places of private assignations.

After five years as a chef-hotelier, Marchand decided to dispense with the labor of accommodating overnight guests. A suggestion of some of the headaches of a hotelier's life can be had from news reports of a court proceeding in 1862. Mr. H. C. M. Ely, a "free luncher and bummer," was forcibly ejected from the hotel by Marchand and two servants when Ely struck Marchand with his cane, demanding entrance "to see his friend." Ely sued. He was awarded a small amount for Marchand's rough handling of him. Marchand sold the Union Hotel and opened the Theatre Rotisserie at 325 Dupont in 1867. The public, however, took to calling it Marchand's Restaurant.

Marchand's Restaurant was one of the finest in the city. He wished it to remain a family legacy, so began training Edward Jr. in the art of cuisine. In 1871 at the age of sixty, Edward Marchand died of a heart attack. Félicité Marchand kept the restaurant operating until 1876, when she secured Pierre Priet (1837–1909) to become co-owner and partner of Marchand's Restaurant. Priet, who had come to San Francisco from France and found employment as a waiter in Lick House during the 1860s, possessed exactly the sort of demeanor and knowledge of cuisine needed to front a first-class restaurant. Priet would keep the reputation of the restaurant lustrous into the twentieth century and would head the French Restaurant Owners Association during the San Francisco government extortion scandal of 1905.

✳ ✳ ✳

SOURCES: New York Ship Passenger Lists, 1820–1957, ship: *Iowa*, date of arrival: June 10, 1844; "Difficulty in a Restaurant," *San Francisco Bulletin* 3, no. 43 (November 26, 1856): 3; "French Cook Shop," *San Francisco Bulletin* 4, no. 123 (August 29, 1857), 4; "Union Rotisserie," *San Francisco Bulletin* 7, no. 60 (December 17, 1858): 1; "Louisiana Rotisserie," *San Francisco Bulletin* 7, no. 132 (March 15, 1859): 2; "Marchand Rotisserie," *San Francisco Bulletin* 12, no. 93 (July 25, 1861): 4; "A Character Assailed, Defended, and Authoritatively Vindicated," *San Francisco Bulletin*)June 11, 1862): 2; "E. Marchand & Co.," *San Francisco Bulletin* 20, no. 139 (September 18, 1865): 3; Erica J. Peter, *San Francisco: A Food Biography* (San Francisco: Rowman and Littlefield, 2013), 114–15.

ℳiguel ℬrisolara 1812–1889
West End, New Orleans

Son of a Genoese pasta maker, Miguel Brisolara became one of the famous resort chefs of New Orleans in the mid-nineteenth century. Originally a disciple of Lucien Boudro, working under him at the Arcade at Lake End, Miguel went independent, married, and secured the backing of Daniels and Bidwell to create Phoenix House—a picture gallery, bowling alley, and oyster saloon at 96 St. Charles in the French Quarter. In 1853 he built a pavilioned dining hall on Lake Pontchartrain, also called Phoenix House. There he served "fresh fish and turtle soup and soft shell crabs, and game of all kinds, with the earliest vegetables, berries, and fruits." When yellow fever felled both Lucien Boudro and Baptiste Moreau in 1867, Brisolara alone survived of the trinity of caterers who created the seafood-inflected version of French cuisine that typified New Orleans summer fare.

Born in Italy, Miguel Brisolara spent his boyhood in Barcelona, Spain, and learned that city's approach to seafood cookery before coming to Louisiana as a young man. He initially fished the Gulf of Mexico, one of the supply fleet for New Orleans. He was apparently one of Boudro's suppliers of pompano when the chef invited him to serve as assistant at the newly constructed Arcade in 1849. After his marriage, Miguel and his wife worked together in the kitchen of the Arcade and every subsequent venue of Boudro's. Some debate attends the question whether Brisolara or Boudro cooked the bouillabaisse that William Thackeray extolled during his 1853 tour. Since the event took place at the Arcade, the odds are that Boudro did the honors.

When Brisolara erected his own wooden temple to fish in 1853–54, he presented the same repertoire of dishes offered at the Arcade, including court-bouillons, grilled blue fish, green turtle soup, and game. Like the other wooden structures at Lake End, the Phoenix House went up in flames in the 1865 fire, necessitating a rebuilding. Brisolara took the opportunity to expand and redesign the eating hall. In 1868 he began publishing bulletins in the newspapers about what was fresh in his ice chests. A May 21 notice was typical: "A few fine, fresh Spanish mackerel, the first of the season, have been received by that prince of restaurateurs, Miguel, at the Lake End of the Pontchartrain Railroad, and will be served up in the highest style known to the art. Miguel has also in his ice chest some splendid specimens of Blackfish, together with an assortment of fresh fish of all kind."

After the Civil War, Brisolara trained Leon Dubuc Sr. to be his grill manager. Sarah Brisolara, Miguel's daughter, married John Tresconi (1837–1902), an Italian-born caterer whose business acumen, ambition, and energy enabled him to build a culinary empire. He took over management of Phoenix House in 1874, enabling Brisolara to concentrate entirely on cooking until his death in 1889. Tresconi's empire included the Washington Hotel in Milneburg and the proprietorship of the French Market in New Orleans.

⁕   ⁕   ⁕

SOURCES: "Phoenix House," *New Orleans Times-Picayune* (March 30, 1853): 4; "Great Fire at Lakeport," *New Orleans Times* 4, no. 613 (June 3, 1865): 3; "A Few Fine Fresh Spanish Mackerel," *New Orleans Times-Picayune* (May 21, 1868): 1; William Makepeace Thackeray, "A Mississippi Bubble," in *Roundabout Papers* in *The Works of William Makepeace Thackeray*, 24 vols. (London: Smith, Elder; Philadelphia: J. B. Lippincott, 1879), XXII, 147; "Miguel's Restaurant," *New Orleans Times-Picayune* (May 23, 1866); "Phoenix House," *New Orleans Times-Picayune* (April 30, 1879); "At the End of the Lake, a Restaurant on the Water," *New Orleans Times-Picayune* (May 2, 1875); "Death of Miguel," *New Orleans Times-Picayune* (October 6, 1889); "Why You Should Go to the Old Lake End," *New Orleans Times* 12, no. 6547 (May 9, 1875): 2.

Nat Fuller 1812–1866
Charleston, SC

At age fifty-four, Nat Fuller, "the renowned presiding genius" of Charleston cuisine in the nineteenth century, declined to flee the war-battered city as the

Present-day building on the corner of Church Street and St. Michael's Alley, Charleston, South Carolina, that Nat Fuller outfitted as a restaurant, the Bachelor's Retreat, on October 8, 1860.

Union army gathered to invade in February 1865. He witnessed the panicked exodus of families to Columbia, South Carolina, and their straggling return when they realized that General Sherman had taken and pillaged the inland city and had no intention of torching Charleston.

Four days after the surrender of Charleston on February 18, Fuller, a lifelong slave until liberated by circumstance of war, hosted Union generals Webster and Gillmore at a Washington's Birthday celebration at his residence on Washington Street. A mixed-race company attended, and a report of celebration appeared in the news section of the *New York Tribune*. "The dinner was held at the house of a colored man, noted (like the New-York Downings and the Boston Smith) for being the chief of the class of caterers in Charleston." Fuller's long connection with shippers and New York marketers, Philadelphia brokers, and railroad clerks during his time running Charleston's game market in the 1850s gave him the lines of communication needed to secure food at a time when daily rice rations were dispensed to the city's 15,000 remaining inhabitants. Fuller's old acquaintances had become the supply staff for the Union army.

Three weeks later, Fuller took possession of the building at 78 Church Street, housing his famous restaurant, the Bachelor's Retreat, which had been taken from his control in March 1864. Fuller's aggressive projection into the new social circumstances was noted by certain old white Carolinians. Mrs. Frances J. Porcher reported: "Nat Fuller, a Negro caterer, provided munificently for a miscegenat dinner, at which blacks and whites sat on in equality and gave toasts and sang songs for Lincoln and Freedom." This grand dame of Charleston planter society knew exactly the significance of such a mixed assembly. It heralded a new vision of civil society and promised new grounds of civility: for an African American stood as host at a table around which blacks and whites sat subject to his hospitality and generosity. This generosity meant something in a city lacking meat, a city fed on daily rations of beans and rice. Feasts matter most in the midst of famine.

The child of a Charleston planter and an enslaved African American mother, Nat Fuller was born in West Ashley in Charleston in 1812. We do not know which of three landowners—Christopher Fuller, Benjamin Fuller, or Thomas Fuller—located west of the Ashley River was his father. For the first years of his life, Nat Fuller grew up on a plantation in St. Andrews, across the Ashley River from the peninsular city. He may have been one of the eighteen slaves auctioned from the estate of Mrs. Jannet Fuller in Charleston in March 1821. He would have been eight or nine years old at the time. He came into the possession of Colonel Daniel Stevens, who sold him in turn to Robert Dorrill when Fuller was fourteen. For some reason, Dorrill was dissatisfied with Nat—perhaps he was seeking a laborer and found himself dealing with a thinker and reader. Dorrill initiated legal proceedings to return Nat to Stevens, but the two negotiated an arrangement wherein the boy would be sold at public auction and the cash value turned over to Dorrill. The auction occurred in early August 1827. Fuller was fifteen. The purchaser was a twenty-year-old lottery agent from Virginia, William C. Gatewood.

At this juncture, Fuller's experiences as a slave diverged from the common narratives of ordeal and perseverance. One can hardly speak of good fortune when speaking about the happenstances of a person's life that were determined by someone else's wishes and not one's own will, yet there were distinct benefits to becoming a house servant to William C. Gatewood. Fuller had been purchased by an urbane young southern capitalist, not a planter, not a tradesman. Gatewood had Fuller trained to be a butler and cook. As a means of advancing this master's commercial and social ambitions, Fuller was encouraged to pursue mastery in cooking and was provided a venue to demonstrate his art at his master's widely frequented table. In the 1850s, Gatewood permitted Fuller to offer his services to the public for a percentage of his proceeds. In 1860, realizing that Fuller could increase his business by securing a building to serve as a high-end eating house, Gatewood arranged a trusteeship arrangement so that Fuller could occupy 103 Church Street. Because property could not own property, Fuller paid installments and interest on bonds and a mortgage and became a de facto owner. Gatewood died in 1861. Fuller litigated with Gatewood's widow after the Civil War to secure the property fee simple.

Gatewood's conception of the master-slave relationship was hardly conventional, even in the urban South. After serving in Gatewood's town house for a decade, Fuller negotiated the right to dwell and work in the city; he had the quasi-liberty of a "self-hire." He married a woman of his own choosing, pastry chef Diana Strobel (1823-1883), and worked in the market as an event caterer and a restaurateur. Strong circumstantial evidence indicates that Fuller accompanied Gatewood on business trips to New York and benefited from Gatewood's influence among the city associations.

Nat Fuller exclusively engaged in the marketing and preparation of sumptuous fare from the time he set up business in 1854 until his death from typhus in the autumn of 1866. As the chief marketer of game in Charleston (1854-57), as a caterer for society banquets (1855-62), and as restaurateur of the city's premier restaurant, the Bachelor's Retreat (1861-66), Fuller worked with the finest and most costly ingredients. Even during the weeks of deprivation after the Union army occupied Charleston in February 1865, Fuller secured meats and vegetables from the Union supply steamers, fashioned public dinners, and operated a full-service temple of fine dining amid streets of rubble.

The surviving bills of fare dramatize his thorough training as a banquet chef. The spectacular menu for the Memphis and Charleston Railroad Pageant in March 1857—a bill of fare for a feast of 600 diners—showed that he staged *pièces montées*: food sculptures and edible exhibition pieces such as ships made of nougat, a "Pyramid of Rice and Bales of Cotton," baskets of glacé fruit, pyramids of almond and meringue, and train cars crossing the bridge from Memphis to Charleston. Virtuoso display food had become important in transatlantic fine dining after Marie-Antoine Carême made them an emblem of culinary professionalism. The body of the railroad menu revealed Fuller's mastery at the entire range of banquet food. There were the cold dishes expected of caterers— the chicken and lobster salads, the cold cuts, the boned turkey in gelatin, the foie gras. Yet hot dishes abounded: successive services of fish, roast meats, fowls, game, and vegetables. His fish, fowl, meat, and game were attuned to the seasons—green turtle soup in summer, venison in fall and winter, canvasback in late autumn, lamb in the spring. Yet his vegetables indicated that he had access to the most expert glasshouse gardeners who could force asparagus at Christmastime and artichokes in late winter.

Enough survives in the way of bills of fare to reconstruct the core of Nat Fuller's repertoire—something that cannot be done with any other African American caterer of the nineteenth century.

Soups: Calf Head Soup, Cooter with Eggs Soup, Green Turtle Soup, Mock Turtle
  Soup, Oyster Soup, Oyster & Celery Soup, Terrapin Soup
Cold Dishes: Chicken Salad, Duffield Ham, Westphalia Ham, New York Corned
  Beef, Smoked Tongue, Boned Turkey in Jelly, Pate de foie gras, Lobster Salad
Savory Pies: Chicken Pie, Macaroni Pie, Oyster Pie, Oyster Patties, Shrimp Pie
Fish: Boiled Bass, Boiled Fresh Cod, Boiled Fresh Salmon, Fried Halibut, Fried
  Whiting, Fresh [Grilled] Mackerel, Sheepshead
Sauces for Fish: Anchovy Sauce, Mushroom Catsup, Walnut Catsup, Worcester-
  shire Sauce
Entrées: A la mode Beef, Capons with Mushroom Sauce, Capons with Oyster
  Sauce, Fricasseed Chickens with Truffles, Haggis, Lamb with Caper Sauce,
  Mutton with Caper Sauce, Oysters Vol au Vent, Pigs Feet stewed with Toma-
  toes, Sweetbreads with Truffles, Turkey with Oyster Sauce, Turtle Fins and
  Steaks with Madeira Sauce, Fricandeau of Veal
Roasts: Beef [New York], Capons, stewed with Truffles, Chickens with Tomato
  Sauce, Ducks with Olive Sauce, Goose [New York], Lamb, Pork, Whole Pig,
  Quail, Turkey [boned], Turkey [New York] with Mushrooms, Veal
Game: Canvasback Ducks, Black Ducks, Red Headed Ducks, Grouse, Partridges,
  Pheasants, Snipes, Venison with Currant Jelly, Wild Turkey, Woodcocks
Vegetables: Asparagus [Philadelphia], Beets, Carrots, Cauliflowers, Green Corn,
  Green Peas, Potatoes [Irish], Rice, Spinach, Sweet Potatoes, Turnips, Salad
Pastry: Apple Pudding, Cocoanut Pudding, Cranberry Pudding, Plum Pudding,
  Orange Pudding, Macaroons, Tarts
Desserts: Almond Rings, Biscuit glace a la Framboise, Blanc-mange, Charlotte
  Russe, Cocoanut Drops, Gateau glace a Rhum, Glace Fruit, Foam Cake, Pound
  Cake, Jellies, Meringue, Nougat, Almond Ice Cream, Lemon Ice Cream, Pine-
  apple Ice Cream, Rose Ice Cream, Vanilla Ice Cream
Fruit & Nuts: Almonds, Apples, Brandy Apricots, Bananas, Figs, Brandy Green
  Gages, Nuts, Oranges, Brandy Peaches, Raisins

Though Nat Fuller had been fully trained as a banquet chef and had married a complete pastry cook, his first public role after coming to an agreement
with Gatewood about public work in 1852 was not as a caterer. Rather, he advertised himself of a vendor of game imported from New York. There were reasons for this: to operate as a first-class caterer, one needed a substantial array of
equipment—china, silverware, punch bowls, chafing dishes, and serving plat-
ters. Absent a loan, he had to earn sufficient capital to purchase these items.
Only in January 1857 did he announce that he "has imported from Europe a
supply of china-ware (sufficient for the largest balls) and table ornaments, such
as candelabras (plated and gilded), fancy skewers, punch bowls, &c. &c., which
can be taken to any part of the country on demand." A second reason to enter

the game market may have been more compelling. Thomas E. Baker, the city's foremost marketer of game, had come into financial trouble. Fuller filled a vacuum in the city's food supply system.

Fuller first advertised "Fine Turkeys, Pheasants, Grouse and Capons" from New York on January 18, 1854, having secured a stall in the Fruit Market and cold storage at a house near the intersection of New and Tradd Streets. By April he had gained control of a stall in the small portion of the meat market devoted to game. Meanwhile, he had shifted his cold storage and off-hours sales to 78 Tradd Street—Eliza Seymour Lee's pastry shop, residence, and catering office. He would maintain this arrangement until autumn of 1855, when Lee moved her restaurant to Beaufain Street. Fuller then leased 68 King Street with the intention of opening a catering business as well as selling New York game.

In late 1853, Fuller lacked some of the requisites to become a caterer. He lacked the capitalization and the equipment, the storage, and the staff. Yet he possessed certain very strong recommendations for success. He had already served food and received the approval of many of Charleston's elite. He had prepared food for large parties. He knew the ingredients for markets and had connections with suppliers. And he had a network of free African American food preparers and waiters. His full-scale entry into catering simply required waiting until he had amassed enough money from the game market to purchase china and other equipment, and to secure a space to use for storage and an office. He began his career as public caterer in 1855 before he had secured the equipment, no doubt borrowing Eliza Lee's china and flatware to serve the Anniversary Dinner of the Medical Society of South Carolina on December 6, 1855. The dinner took place at the auctioneer's hall maintained by T. C. Hubbell at 33 Broad Street.

The 1855–56 social season in Charleston proved to be critical in setting up Fuller in business. The city's chief event caterer, Adolph John Rutjes—a French pastry chef who married Théonie Mignot, owner of the city's premier confectionery and women's luncheonette—fell financial victim to his uncontrollable impulse to speculate in real estate. Consequently, in 1856 a number of very major societies—the South Carolina Jockey Club and the St. Cecilia Society—found themselves searching for a caterer. William C. Gatewood, steward of the Jockey Club, knew where to look. Consequently, Fuller, who had been working private parties for much of the year, found himself thrust into the most conspicuous culinary arena in the city, catering the two most important social events of the season. In 1857 the *Charleston Courier* observed, "Any one who had the pleasure of assisting at the St. Cecilia and Jockey Balls of last year, not to mention many private parties, can testify to the talent which our own people can display with encouragement."

During the three and a half years he operated out of 68 King Street, Fuller was assisted by his wife and his assistant, Tom R. Tully. Certain of Fuller's efforts impressed his clients sufficiently to warrant published thanks. The chronology of the satisfied included:

The Charleston Fire Company of Axmen	*Courier* (January 10, 1857)
Vigilant Fire Engine Company	*Courier* (February 4, 1857)
Society of the Cincinnati	*Courier* (February 23, 1857)
Jubilee of Southern Union	*Courier* (May 30, 1857)
Society of the Cincinnati	*Courier* (July 2, 1857)
Aetna Fire Engine Company	*Mercury* (December 15, 1857)
Charleston Chamber of Commerce	*Mercury* (February 9, 1858)
Washington Artillery	*Mercury* (February 23, 1858)
Chamber of Commerce	*Mercury* (June 2, 1858)
St. Andrews Society	*Courier* (December 1, 1858)
Aetna Fire Engine Company	*Mercury* (December 15, 1858)
Phoenix Fire Company	*Mercury* (January 19, 1859)
Charleston Light Dragoons	*Mercury* (April 2, 1859)
Medical Society of South Carolina	*Courier* (December 10, 1860)

Of these highlight performances, two were so superlative in terms of the food supplied that a bill of fare was published in the newspapers. The more of elaborate of these was the Jubilee of Southern Union dinner, a feast celebrating the completion of a rail linkage between Memphis and Charleston. Six hundred invited guests proceeded from the Charleston Market Hall to the dining room decorated at Military Hall:

> "All hands and the cook" were busy from an early hour in preparation at the Military Hall, which had been generously tendered for the reception dinner, which was contracted and built up by that well known caterer, *Nat Fuller*. The approach to the Hall was a characteristic and highly appropriate symbol of the day and its occasion. From the gate on Wentworth street to the vestibule, there was erected a roof of evergreens imparting an aspect of coolness and shady retreat most prepossessing and inviting. This roof was supported on either hand by walls composed of barrels of rice, supported on bales of cotton. On entering, the main Hall showed decorations and appointments no less significant and appropriate, of which we can only make passing mention, as our space and other pressing topics warn us.

In the Military Hall, a long head table (six parallel clerestory tables) running the length of the hall flanked a live cabbage palmetto tree hauled into the space as a centerpiece.

One dimension of Fuller's catering business that becomes apparent when one reads through the notices carefully is that certain of the groups he served wished that he had his own dining rooms to accommodate meetings. The smallest of the listed groups, the Society of the Cincinnati, with less than twenty members, indeed took to meeting in Fuller's rooms at 68 King, making his private parlor a club space. But this state of affairs could not endure.

Fuller opened the Bachelor's Retreat restaurant on October 8, 1860. Gatewood had arranged the purchase in June. A summer was occupied in outfitting the building so that it could retail game and prepared food, as well as accommodate clubs and boards. He published a notice in the October 5 issue of the *Charleston Courier* and the October 10 issue of the *Charleston Mercury* announcing his ability to serve the public. Among the first to avail themselves of Fuller's hospitable spaces was the Charleston Chamber of Commerce, which adopted the space as its regular meeting place, and the Medical Society of South Carolina, which held its anniversary meeting at the Bachelor's Retreat on December 10, 1860. In short order, his old clients signed on as well: the Society of the Cincinnati and the Fellowship Society. As an encouragement to further business of this sort, Fuller announced in February 1861 that "the use of a convenient Room . . . is respectfully tendered to Military Companies, Committees or Clubs without Charge."

Beginning on April 12, 1861, the supply of loose bachelors began to dwindle in Charleston. In subsequent months, they would diminish greatly as the Civil War drew men to battlefields beyond the Lowcountry. Indeed, the Retreat's connection with the world of young men made it a favorable site for recruitment. Colonel Orr, for instance, recruited much of the manpower of his Regiment of Rifles there. "Col. Orr addressed the volunteer company at the Bachelor's Retreat on Saturday last. Fifty-six men responded to the call." With the disappearance of the bachelors, Fuller had to adjust his mission and began seeking family trade and drop-in diners. He expanded his hours of meal service from 6:00 a.m. to 5:00 p.m., the evening hours being reserved to serve those societies that remained operative in the city from 1862 to 1864.

> An excellent breakfast can always be obtained between the hours of six and eleven, A.M., at the Bachelor's Retreat. . . . A good lunch and oysters constantly on hand, and furnished any hour through the day. Travelers or others desiring it will be supplied with an early dinner from 10 A.M., and a regular meal from three to five o'clock. Everything will be served up in the best style directly from the heating furnaces, and worthy of the reputation of the Retreat.

We know what Fuller served guests at his restaurant because he would publish bills of fare for "extra dinner," a meal over and above that served for his regular boarders during the 3:00 to 5:00 p.m. dinner period. These were enticements for new customers: "All Gentlemen, whether over or under forty-five, are liable to find a GOOD DINNER and LUNCH at the BACHELOR'S RETREAT.... The Bill of Fare Tuesday, 2d inst., includes Oyster and Calf Head Soups, Turkey, Wild Duck, Roast Beef, A la Mode Beef, Roast Lamb, Chicken Pie, Oyster Pie, Vegetables and Desert Courses." There would be season adjustments to these extra dinners, with lamb and peas appearing in the spring, turtle steaks and fins in the summer. When dessert was specified, plum pudding or mince pie was most commonly cited. While these bills might seem rather restrained when contrasted with those surviving from the banquets of the 1850s, one must realize that from Lincoln's Proclamation of Blockade on April 19, 1861, until the end of the war, access to quality meats and vegetables was an extraordinary challenge. Indeed one mark of Fuller's ability as a restaurateur was the maintenance of his "style" of cooking throughout a general period of dearth. This required the sympathy of Confederate authorities who believed the fine things of their old way of life had to endure during the war as reminders of what they were fighting for. It also required having a network of procurers and suppliers of long-standing bound by deep covenants of trust.

Fuller was unwillingly dispossessed of 78 Church Street in 1864. Since cooking was his livelihood, he needed another venue—a house with water, space, a sizable kitchen, and an ice house. He found a marginally useful building at 25 Washington Street, well out of the business district. He announced turtle soup for sale on June 28, 1864, for $2.50 a quart. Rumors circulated over the summer that Fuller had left the business entirely. In September Fuller addressed the credulous public: "The Subscriber respectfully informs the public that his establishment, at No. 25 Washington St. still continues open (rumors in the country to the contrary notwithstanding) and that his bill of fare for dinner today, at three o'clock, will be as follows: Green Turtle Soup. Shrimp Pie. Wild Turkey." Though this menu was curtailed, it bore resonant names.

As Union general William T. Sherman carved through Georgia from Atlanta to Savannah over the final months of 1864, panic began to seize Charlestonians. Citizens began evacuating the city, attempting to dispose of property on the best terms that they could obtain. In January 1865, Fuller took advantage of the situation. "That ancient and well-known caterer, Nat Fuller, has just occupied a larger and more commodious house, next door to his late establishment on Washington street, where he continues to serve up wild turkey, venison, and all the delicacies of the table in his usual excellent style." Even in this larger space, Fuller could not apply the cherished name of his old establishment to it. He called it Nat Fuller's Restaurant and Eating House. He was biding his time.

On February 18 the mayor of Charleston surrendered the city to Union brigadier general Alexander Schimmelfennig. On February 21 the African American troops of the Massachusetts Fifty-Fifth Regiment marched into Charleston to occupy the city. The occupation enforced the Emancipation Proclamation. Fuller had become a free citizen of the United States. On Washington's Birthday, February 22, Union general Webster (Sherman's chief of staff) celebrated with a party at Fuller's Eating House. One of Fuller's commercial connections, a Mr. Getty, was in charge of the invitations. The dinner was "probably the best that has been in this lean and empty-bellied city since the blockage began." The company was informed that the dinner service employed was the same that had been used when General Beauregard held a ball celebrating the capture of Fort Sumter in 1861.

On March 15, 1865, the *Edgefield Advertiser* noted in its "Charleston News" section that "Nat Fuller advertises that he has resumed business at his old stand." Within three weeks of the Union takeover, Fuller again possessed the Bachelor's Retreat. It was then he staged his famous feast.

※   ※   ※

SOURCES: "Under Decree in Equity," *City Gazette* (March 8, 1821): 3; "Estate Sale," *Charleston Courier* (December 2, 1834): 2; "Wild Game, etc.," *Charleston Courier* (April 11, 1854); "Christmas! Christmas!," *Charleston Courier* (December 24, 1856); "Communication: What We Are to Eat," *Charleston Courier* (January 19, 1857); "The Elmore Mutual Insurance Company," *Charleston Mercury* (July 20, 1860); "Estate Sale," *Charleston Mercury* (March 21, 1864); "Nat Fuller," *Charleston Courier* (December 23, 1863); "Turtle Soup and Wild Turkey," *Charleston Mercury* (September 21, 1864); "Our Fireman at Charleston," *Daily Constitutionalist* (May 1, 1866); Benjamin Quarles, *The Negro in the Civil War* (Russell and Russell, 1868), 329; "To Companies and Committies [*sic*]," *Charleston Mercury* (February 27, 1861); "Notice," *Charleston Courier* (October 10, 1860); Simons and Simons case records, box 19, Fuller V. M. Gatewood legal papers, South Carolina Historical Society Manuscript. 0431.02 (F).

Charles Gautier 1812–1884
Washington, DC

In certain respects, Charles Gautier was the spiritual successor to Louis Galabran, the French confectioner and restaurateur who made the European House the temple of French cuisine in the nation's capital in the mid-1840s. Gautier arrived from France in 1838 and moved almost immediately to Washington, DC. A trained pomologist and kitchen gardener, he sought employment as a gar-

dener and florist. But he could not support himself doing ornamental gardening, so became a fruiterer and confectioner. Like Galabran before him, Gautier
captured the taste of the city with sweetness. He, too, was a confectioner, adept at concocting bonbons, pastries, and candied fruits. But his greatest public recommendation was his virtuosity in flavoring ice cream. Throughout the
1840s, a shop called La Ville de Paris on the corner of Pennsylvania Avenue and
Eleventh Street featured kisses imported from Paris, preserved fruits of his own
manufacture, and ice cream processed from "the best Cream of the State of
Virginia," all served at small tables in the shop.

His career nearly derailed before it had fully started when he was arrested for
manslaughter in 1842. On September 29 of that year, Gautier hit George William
Lacy, a black boy, stealing chestnuts from a bin outside his store. Lacy fell and
his head hit the pavement; he died from the effects of the concussion the next
day. Because Gautier had chased Lacy before hitting him, the authorities held
him on $1,000 bond. The jury eventually concluded that though Gautier was
culpable for Lacy's death and liable to financial penalty, witness testimonies indicated that "there was no intention on the part of the said Gautier to kill or injure the said George William Lacy, but to inflict upon him a moderate chastise-
ment." Gautier was released and returned to his fruit and confection business.

In summer and autumn of 1853, Gautier had John C. Harkness design and
erect a restaurant—Gautier's Saloon—intended to define the institution for
Washingtonians. Located between Twelfth and Thirteenth Streets on Pennsylvania, near the European House, it was a commercial complex. Upon entering,
"you find yourself in a handsome Confectionery, and Comestible Store, the
counters of white marble, the floor of chequerwork, the walls and ceiling highly
embellished, and lighted, at night, by gas emitted from a chandelier of much
taste and great costliness." One had to pass through the store to enter the saloon, a 75-by-21-foot space, with marble-topped tables, intended for ladies and
gentlemen to lunch. The second floor housed the gentleman's dining room, a
more austere place; on the third floor, there were three supper rooms or private
spaces. In the basement was an ice cream parlor and the kitchen. Gautier expended $60,000 on its building and fitting out.

In November 1855, he revamped the gentleman's dining room at 252 Pennsylvania Avenue, making it more fashionable. Periodic improvements to refresh
the saloon would become Gautier's habit in the coming years. In 1859 he traded
out the chandeliers, replaced the chairs, and upgraded the ventilation system
so the building wouldn't swelter in summer. In 1865 he did another extensive
refitting. One dimension of the rebuild was the conversion of some of the retail
space to liquor sales. "Old Wines, Brandies, Old Bourbon and Old Rye Whiskies" lined the shelves, "forming the largest and most complete stock of Liquors
to be found in this capital."

Fashionability was important. It became the resort "for nearly all the ladies in Washington on a morning's walk or returning from a concert, opera, &c." Gautier periodically advertised that he employed four "superior French cooks, perfect artists," dedicated to serving fashionable dinners. Louis Vavans was one of these cooks who would become a significant caterer. Citizens could secure the services of one of Gautier's cooks for private dinners at one's home for $2.00 an evening. Gautier's own catering career climaxed in two inaugural balls and dinners of the 1850s: the 1853 inaugural ball of President Franklin Pierce in Washington, DC; and the March 1857 inaugural ball for President James Buchanan. Gautier's bill of fare for the latter survives.

Pate Truffe
Saddles of Venison and Mutton
Boar's Head, stuffed and decorated
Boned and roasted Turkeys
Spiced Rounds of Beef
Filets de Boeuf en Belle Vue
Boned and roasted Pheasants
Tongues and Hams, decorated
Aspic de Volaille
Lobster, Chicken and Russian Salad
Terrapins and Oysters
Cream and Water Ices, in fancy moulds
Marons Glaces
Charlotte Russe
Meringues, Plombieres, Bavaroises
Jellies and Puddings
Fancy Cakes, Preserved Fruits, Confectionery
Roman Punch, Apple Toddy
Wines, Liquors and Cordials

A tally of the quantities of materials also survives: 400 gallons of oysters, 500 quarts of chicken salad, 1,200 quarts of ice cream, 500 quarts of jellies, 60 saddles of mutton, 4 saddles of venison, 8 rounds of beef, 75 hams, and 125 tongues. Gautier and his partners lost $3,000 on the job. Payment was always a problem. During the Civil War, the $600 bill for a dinner that Gautier prepared for the Lincolns when hosting Prince Napoleon provoked consternation among officials on how to pay it, until Mrs. Lincoln sold the manure from the Union horses camped on the White House lawn to the Department of the Interior for fertilizing Washington's parks.

The Civil War taught Gautier one thing clearly—if one sought profit serving the public taste, the greatest was to be had by slaking the popular thirst for alcohol. In 1866 he transformed his business, ramping back the restaurant service and embracing the bottling of champagne, the manufacture of "Native Wine Bitters," and the brokering of C. Gautier Cabinet Brand Rye Whiskey. Of these various businesses, the creation of herbal nostrums most pleased him, calling upon his early horticultural training. As early as 1855, he was hawking Gautier's Compound Herb Drops for sore throats.

Gautier wholeheartedly entered the retail liquor trade after the war and succeeded well in the business. One pause in good business occurred in 1881, when his name became confused by some with the assassin of President Garfield, Charles Guiteau. Charles Gautier died in 1884 a wealthy man. His son kept the liquor business going for a term before moving to Manhattan.

※ ※ ※

SOURCES: "A Gardener and Florist," *Daily National Intelligencer* 28, no. 8686 (December 16, 1840): 3; "City News," *Daily National Intelligencer* 30, no. 9244 (October 3, 1842): 3; "Dead," *Baltimore Sun* 11, no. 116 (October 4, 1842): 1; [Gautier bond,] *Middletown Constitution* 5, no. 251 (October 19, 1842): 3; "Important from Paris," *Washington Daily Union* (December 22, 1846); "Gautier's," *Alexandria Gazette* (November 5, 1853): 2; "Gautier's Saloon," *Washington Evening Star* (November 12, 1855): 2; "Gautier's Saloon," *Washington Evening Star* (December 10, 1856): 3; "Gautier's French Restaurant," *Washington Evening Star* (January 2, 1857): 1; "Bill of Fare," *Frank Leslie's Illustrated Newspaper* (March 21, 1857): 7; "Ice Cream," *Washington Evening Star* (April 14, 1857): 3; "The Reopening of Gautier's Restaurant," *Daily National Intelligencer* 47, no. 14718 (October 5, 1859): 3; "Gautier's Restaurant Renovation-Reopening," *Washington Evening Star* (October 28, 1865): 1; "The Prince Napoleon Dinner at the White House," *Columbus Crisis* 7, no. 42 (November 13, 1867): 334; "Charles Gautier Champagne," *Daily National Intelligencer* (February 23, 1867): 3; "Native Wine Bitters," *Washington Evening Star* (July 12, 1867): 2; "Charles Gautier's Native Wine Bitters," *Washington Critic-Record* 1, no. 245 (June 11, 1869): 2.

Victor Martin 1812–1865
New Orleans; Bagdad, Mexico

Victor Martin was the most important restaurateur in mid-nineteenth-century New Orleans. The French-born chef and restaurateur brought his family from

France to Louisiana in 1838 intent on establishing a house of fine dining. By common accord until 1870, Victor's Restaurant ranked first in the tastes of New Orleans's epicures among the independent restaurants of the city, greater than Moreau's, than Antoine's, than John's, than anyplace, except perhaps the great hotels on a fine day. Indeed, its devotees declared that "during its heyday it far excelled Delmonico's famous establishment in New York." The original restaurant managed by brothers Victor and Jules Martin (1819–1873) was at 15 Madison Street in the French Quarter. It served only two meals—late breakfast and dinner.

While Baptiste Moreau in the St. Louis Hotel in the 1840s or Fritz Huppenbauer in the 1840s and John Michels at the St. Charles Hotel in the 1850s could supply as splendid a cuisine—seasonal, varied, and precisely prepared—no other chef or caterer rivaled Victor Martin for the versatility of his preparations from soups to confections.

The role of Victor's Restaurant before the war was attested in many recollections of the 1870s. Memoirists observed, "Then New Orleans was a hard place to get out of. There were the dinners at Victor's and Moreau's and Pino's, with the little game after the table was cleared; there were sirens from Maine, Massachusetts and New Jersey, who charmed young Lonstaple's tender heart and his willing purse; there was the box at the opera, the races at the Metairie. . . . They were gay days, the last rapid days of the old regime, and New Orleans waxed fat."

Sometime before the war, Victor left to develop a hotel in Mexico, leaving Jules in control.

> A model French dinner, equal to the best served in Paris, could always be obtained at Victor's. Fashionable Parisians who partook of Victor's dinners esteemed them as fully equal to those of Very's, the Provencaus Freres, and other famous Parisian restaurants. The superiority of French cooking, supplemented by many Creole improvements, was thus demonstrated to even appreciative American stomachs, so that a taste for the gastronomic art became largely developed among our people, and Victor's receipts and style became the highest standard and tests of excellence in the preparation of viands, in the quality of the wines, and in the style of serving a feast.

The restaurant moved to the Place d'Armes on St. Peter's Street in 1844, then relocated to 27 Toulouse Street in September 1849. This larger space included private dining saloons as well as the public areas. In the late 1850s, Victor and his brother Jules and nephew Georges expanded to Baton Rouge in 1860, taking over the Gem Restaurant of Madame Eugène, the finest restaurant in Louisiana outside New Orleans. This space included a ladies' saloon and the best collection of wines in the Louisiana interior.

In 1865 the changes in the commercial organization of the city prompted Georges Martin to convince his uncle Jules to move Victor's to 185 Canal Street on the boundary between the old French city and the American commercial district. This new location, so "spacious, capacious and most commodiously fitted up," presented Victor's classically French cuisine in a new venue. In 1866 the Martins sought to grab some of the summer resort trade by opening Victor's Cosmopolitan Restaurant in Carrollton. One of the issues that provoked the reorganization of the Martin family enterprises was the Mexican venture that Victor had begun during the Civil War. Worried that the Civil War might mean economic disaster, Victor traveled southward and built a hotel in Bagdad, Mexico. He died in 1865 while putting this venture in order, requiring Jules to come southward and consolidate the business. From 1865 onward, Georges Martin became the major force at Victor's until his death in 1873. Then the restaurant came into the hands of employee Victor Bero. Bero would head the restaurant during its period of decline in the final quarter of the nineteenth century when Moreau's, under Madame Eugène, eclipsed its cuisine, and Antoine's, with Jules Alciatore as chef in the 1890s, took the crown when Madame Eugène retired in the late 1880s.

The restaurant was the center of elite culture in the wake of the war and consequently became the arena of struggles between the occupying powers and the old Confederate establishment. In 1868 a conspicuous murder—the stabbing of Confederate officer Major Richard Manning—occurred after the Martins rebuked Manning for drunkenness. A quarrel between Manning and his companion Colonel Luckett of Mississippi led to Manning's death by puncture from a gimlet knife.

※　※　※

SOURCES: "Victor's Restaurant," *New Orleans Times-Picayune* (September 5, 1849): 3; "Victor's Restaurant," *New Orleans Times-Picayune* (September 5, 1849): 2; "Victor's Restaurant, Boulevard Street," *Baton Rouge Daily Advocate* (October 16, 1860): 2; "Victor's New Restaurant," *New Orleans Times-Picayune* (April 30, 1865): 10; "Victor's Cosmopolitan Restaurant," *New Orleans Times-Picayune* (May 26, 1866): 2; "Homicide at Victor's," *New Orleans Times-Picayune* (June 26, 1868): 1; "New Orleans, as It Was and Is," *San Luis Obispo Tribune* (May 21, 1871): 1.

Antoine Alciatore 1813-1874
Marseilles; New York; New Orleans

Antoine Alciatore, the legendary patriarch of the Alciatore cooking dynasty in New Orleans and founder of Antoine's Restaurant, received his training in cuisine in the South of France, completing his apprenticeship at the Hotel de Noailles in Marseilles. There, according to family lore, he impressed Tallyrand at age sixteen with a rare roast beef dish of his own creation that he named "Filet de Boeuf Robespierre," referencing that revolutionary's raw face when he was led to his execution. Tallyrand's chef, Marchand, became Alciatore's instructor, engineering his appointment as cook of Château d'If, the fortress famous for being the prison occupied by the Count of Monte Cristo in Dumas's novel. Somehow the prospect of supervising cuisine at so grave a bastion of state justice did not thrill Alciatore, so he boarded a ship for America. After a short sojourn in New York, he headed to New Orleans in 1839.

Antoine's grandson Roy Alciatore said that the young man became convinced that he would succeed as a chef when he ate a meal at the St. Louis Hotel prepared by the famous Baptiste Moreau, then the city's great cook. If so, this happened in 1840 or after Antoine had established his first eatery. Moreau sold his namesake restaurant on Chartres Street to F. Moulin in 1839—he only became affiliated with the hotel in late 1839. Since Alciatore had already founded his own restaurant-hotel in 1840, the episode probably served as a confirmation of the rightness of his path. It is worth noting, too, that Moreau was two years younger than Alciatore.

The small restaurant that Alciatore oversaw at 50 St. Louis Street became famous for a half dozen dishes—French classics such as bisque d'écrevisse à la Cardinal and oysters Bordelaiese—and his own creations: tomatoes frappés à la Julius Caesar and dinde à la Tallyrand. Of these latter dishes, he exploited the 1840s craze for tomatoes in one and the wide availability of turkey caused by the domestication of America's indigenous big bird. New Orleans culinary lore attributed to Antoine the introduction of pommes soufflés to America, but Jules Arthur Harder of Delmonico's was the protégé of the dish's French inventor, Jean-Louis-François Collinet, and surely preceded Alciatore. The first era of Antoine's Restaurant closed with the Civil War. Antoine Alciatore accepted a commission as an officer in the Lafayette Guard and marched off to war, shutting his restaurant. He returned after the defeat, determined to rebuild the disrupted, occupied city. He opened a new Antoine's Restaurant at 713 St. Louis Street, the address that would eventually become world famous, particularly under the direction of Antoine's son, Jules, in the 1890s.

Sickening of tuberculosis, Antoine Alciatore returned to France, where he

Antoine Alciatore (ca. 1860). Oil. Photograph: Courtesy of Antoine's Restaurant, New Orleans, Louisiana.

died in 1874, he was understood to have been a capable practitioner of la cuisine française. Though reputable, his restaurant did not have the cachet among epicures possessed by Victor's (founded by Victor Martin), Moreau's (founded by Baptiste Moreau), Boudro's (founded by Lucien Boudro), or Miguel's (founded by Miguel Brisolara). It would be under the superintendence of Jules Alciatore that the incorporation of Italian risottos and pastas, and the addition of Louisiana-African dishes, made Antoine's a flagship of a *new* New Orleans style of restaurant Creole cookery. Antoine's widow, Julie Freys Alciatore, ran the restaurant for fifteen years with Louis Bezaudun as chef before Jules bought control. Jules operated as chef and also as steward during the period when his mother was directress.

✳   ✳   ✳

SOURCES: "Master's Famed Dishes Are Linked with City's Name," *New Orleans Times-Picayune* (September 16, 1934): 18; "Funeral of Mlle. Alciatore Held," *New Orleans States* (September 15, 1917): 3; "Antoine's Ten Secrets—They'll Taste Just Like Antoine's," *Cleveland Plain Dealer* (April 25, 1848): 112.

John Galpin 1813–1868
New Orleans

Butcher, grocer, and caterer, John Galpin became the most versatile figure in New Orleans's nineteenth-century food culture. A native of Bethlehem, Connecticut, he brought an expertise with meat to Louisiana nurtured in the most advanced locus of herding and livestock breeding in the United States.

Entering into a partnership with his brother Samuel as a grocer in July 1840, John Galpin learned about the production networks that brought vegetables, fruits, seed, flour, and cured meats into New Orleans. His first shop, located at 7 Dimond's Row (on the corner of Tchoupitoulas and Delord Streets), became the city's primary outlet for fine northern dairy goods—Goshen butter, cheese, and cream. His interest in dairy cattle turned his attention to livestock and meat in 1843. He thought the quality of produce available in New Orleans inferior to what he had seen in the North. Boldly, he determined to become the butcher of premium beef, lamb, and pork in New Orleans. He rented stall No. 1 and No. 3 in St. Mary's Market, and when success met his efforts, surrendered No. 1 for stalls Nos. 3 and 5; later he would occupy stalls Nos. 1 and 3 in the Old French Market. Galpin sold prime cuts of meat from cattle and sheep sourced in Indiana and Kentucky. Writers waxed poetic on viewing the cuts laid out in his stall— "rounds of beef that would have thrown Friar Tuck into a delightful enthusiasm, and saddles of mutton that might have been rode by Heliogabalus." Galpin was "the only premium sausage-maker . . . in the South." His meat processing followed an annual cycle, with beef steaks and corned beef being available with the October 1 opening of the season and charcuterie in December. The cold-weather months marked the peak of butcher work, with hams being salted in January. Fish supplanted meat in the spring, and Galpin's attentions turned to produce.

Much of his processed meat and some of his produce were stored in a refrigerated warehouse at 17 Commerce Street, one of the wonders of the city when first opened in 1848. In an instant, his cold store transformed the food dynamics of the city. He could store perishable items shipped from New York, and so, via steamship, he supplied "fresh Lobsters—Codfish—Blackfish—Eels, and Pheasants" as well as butter and cream. The city's restaurants turned to him as a primary supplier. By 1850 Galpin became chief supplier of meat, dairy products, and fish to the Mississippi River steamboats. During that year, he perfected his skill in charcuterie as well. "He cures only the best kinds of meats, and he has always on hand Spiced and Corned Rounds."

In 1854 Galpin partnered with hotelier H. P. Ensign in leasing the Verandah Hotel. They closed the building, refitted it, and designed the renovated house

John Galpin's meat advertisement. *New Orleans Times-Picayune* 15, no. 263 (November 30, 1851): 5.

to be a premium hostelry. Galpin sought to elevate the cuisine of the hotel by supplying the best ingredients through his supply networks. His brother Samuel took over most of the work managing the market stalls. In December, Galpin rearranged his contract, becoming sole proprietor of the Verandah. "As a landlord, [he] has already made himself well known by the excellence of his table and his cellar." With O. J. Noyes as host, and Ensign as manager, Galpin provisioned the kitchen and oversaw food operations at the hotel for five years. During the latter years of his proprietorship, Galpin diversified his businesses by setting up a Whale Oil Refinery at 60 Poydras Street.

Upon severing his connection with the Verandah Hotel in summer 1859, Galpin launched a full-service restaurant at Exchange Place below Canal. It would be one of the nodes of an ever-expanding retail produce, meat, wine, and grocery network. In December 1860, he established Galpin's Restaurant at 32 Royal Street, with Paul Viel as maître d' and E. Coutreau in the kitchen. The restaurant's show window was "an index of what is to be found in the way of fish, meats, and game in this market, and the transfer of these luxuries from the window to the kitchen and from thence to the table makes a complete and entirely satisfactory transaction." Given the superior meat being supplied to the establishment, there is little wonder that "Galpin's beef steaks have a genuine tenderloin reputation."

After the war, Galpin experienced a psychological crisis. In 1866 he closed the restaurant, which was taken over by his friend and successor, Philippe Forget, then moved to New York. His large family, some of whom remained in New Orleans, picked up the pieces of his empire, even opening a produce stand at

Terpsichore and Prytania Streets in 1868. He died in May 1868, in New York. McClure and Jonte took over his butcher stalls in the French Market. As the city's master of curing meat, Galpin's place was filled to some extent by Peter Forshee.

⁂   ⁂   ⁂

SOURCES: [Partnership notice,] *New Orleans Times-Picayune* (July 23, 1840): 3; "Notice-Goshen Butter," *New Orleans Times-Picayune* (June 4, 1841): 2; "To Epicures," *New Orleans Times-Picayune* (October 15, 1848): 2; "New York Luxuries," *New Orleans Times-Picayune* 13, no. 250 (December 15, 1848): 2; "Prize Stock—Galpin's Extra Beef," *New Orleans Times-Picayune* (December 27, 1849): 5; "Superior Meats," *New Orleans Times-Picayune* 16, no. 281 (December 20, 1850): 6; [Advertisement,] *New Orleans Times-Picayune* 15, no. 263 (November 30, 1851): 5; "John Galpin, of Stalls No. 3 and 5," *New Orleans Times-Picayune* (December 25, 1852): 2; "John Galpin Is in Better Spirits," *New Orleans Daily Delta* 8, no. 71 (December 31, 1852): 4; "Hotel Change," *New Orleans Times-Picayune* (May 17, 1854): 2; "The Verandah Hotel," *New Orleans Times-Picayune* (December 29, 1854): 1; [Galpin's new restaurant,] *New Orleans Times-Picayune* (September 30, 1859): 2; "Galpin's New Restaurant," *New Orleans Times-Picayune* (October 9, 1862): 3; "John Galpin's Shop Window," *New Orleans Times-Picayune* (February 28, 1864): 8; [Peter Forshee,] *New Orleans Times-Picayune* (October 17, 1865): 1; "Forget's Restaurant," *New Orleans Times* (January 10, 1867): 2; "Death of John Galpin," *New Orleans Times-Picayune* (May 16, 1868): 4.

Cary B. Moon 1813–1895
Saratoga, NY

The Saratoga caterer who popularized the potato chip (Saratoga chip) in the 1850s and made it a culinary fixture in the resort and then in the nation, Cary B. Moon presided over the Lake House from 1854 to 1884. On the eve of the Civil War, this wooden Greek Revival tavern on the road by Lake Saratoga became famous for game and wine dinners.

As early as 1856, Moon's "fried potatoes" appeared in print as one of the culinary attractions of Saratoga. Their first mention in connection with him is in "A Trip to the North," a *New York Herald* story from July 30, 1856: "There has been no event worth notice except a Sunday dinner party at the Lake House, where numerous trout, woodcock and fried potatoes were got up splendidly, and eaten up voraciously." By the next year, newspapers spoke of the venue and dish as established attractions: "the Lake House—where 'all the world' go to drive, or to dine on the famous 'fried potatoes.'" By August 1857, the famous African American caterer George Downing (later steward of the United States Congressional Dining Room) had adopted the dish, serving it at Newport fetes, rebranded as his own creation: "potatoes fried a la Downing, that is to say, sliced so thin and cooked so crispily without being browned in the least as to become, as an epicure tells me, the very poetry of fried potatoes."

Moon's Lake House enjoyed a situation that inspired rhapsody in visitors: "A hotel almost shut out from the light of day by surrounding trees crowns the top of the abrupt hill that descends to Saratoga Lake. The very fairies and nymphs, who gave delight to the gods in their ambrosial valleys, would envy such a spot." Moon's potatoes inspired a similar delight:

> Fried potatoes are an institution specially created so at the Lake, and so long as they last the moon, our particular friend, Moon, the proprietor of the Lake House, we hope will continue to shine. Imagine, dear reader, if you can, the largest and best of potatoes sliced so fine and thin that it would be no detriment to the rays of the sun passing to the earth—imagine them cooked and served up before you, hot and crisp, and so delicious that a monk would die in a delirium of epicurean joy at the first mouthful, and then you can form some faint conception of how palateable and delicious they are. Strange as it may seem, no visitor ever mentions the Lake without mentioning potatoes.

The potatoes served as the chief adornment of a table d'hôte that defined Saratoga resort cuisine: "We must not forget those miraculous dinners which run the gamut of delicacies, from fried potatoes up to green figs, the intermediates being trout fresh from the pond, bass boiled to a nicety, woodcock, snipe, quail, partridge, in fact game in such endless variety that Audubon himself would take a week, to describe them ornithologically. Then there are fresh figs, pineapples, tamarinds, pomegranates, lemons, peaches, apricots—in brief, all the gifts of Pomona." In spring of 1865, the reputation of Moon's table brought the king of American restaurateurs, Lorenzo Delmonico, to the Lake House: "After a natural dinner of green turtle, lake bass, trout and other fish, game in the shape of woodcock, partridge, quail, frogs, all washed down with delectable Carte d'or and Las d'or, &c., and fried potatoes celebrated for their exquisiteness—(Moon is said to have made a fortune on his fried potatoes alone)—Delmonico . . . declared that Moon had outdone him." Almost immediately Saratoga fried potatoes became a fixture on Delmonico's menu. At Moon's, crisps were served piping hot in a foot-long white paper cornucopia. They could also be procured cold.

"Our Fashionable Resorts—The Lake House, Saratoga Lake, N.Y., C. B. Moon, Proprietor.—From a sketch by our own Artist." Wood engraving from *Frank Leslie's Illustrated Newspaper* (July 26, 1862): 11.

Other Saratoga dining rooms imitated Moon's, offering their versions of fried potatoes—the United States Hotel as early as 1858, and Myer's at the Lake in the later 1860s—but none could achieve the proper lightness and crispness. When they had become a general offering of the resort circa 1870, they ceased to be called Moon's fried potatoes and were called "chip-fried potatoes." In the late 1860s, a journalistic game of "securing the secret" commenced. The *New York Herald* revealed one dimension in June 1869: "The first process before frying is to take all the starch out of the slice of potato by soaking it in a succession of many waters until it becomes so transparent that one can read the editorials of the Bohemian New York papers through it." In 1870 the *Albany Evening Journal* spoke further on the subject: "The potatoes should be cut to a wafer-like thinness, and immersed in cold water from four to six hours; then dried quickly by placing them between cloths, and dropped separately into hot lard; stir constantly with the skimmer; when done the lard will stop simmering, and the potatoes should be placed in a cullender that the grease may drip away; afterward salt to the taste." The heat of the lard was an important consideration. Later revelations—the widely republished "The Secret of Saratoga Fried Potatoes" in July 1874—followed the *Albany Evening Journal* account in most particulars.

The wide republication of the recipe in 1874 led to the first attempts at large-scale production. The Centennial celebration of 1876 in Philadelphia saw Saratoga chips featured as an indigenous American food. By 1878 newspapers reported: "The manufacture of Saratoga fried potatoes, or chips, as they are now called, has become quite a business. Heretofore this luxury was rarely found outside of a few hotels and first-class restaurants, but loads of potatoes are now sold every week for the production of this article, and Saratoga fried potatoes are to be found at all first-class groceries, and are on the tables at most of the summer hotels at the mountains and seaside."

In 1879 Cary B. Moon became deathly ill. His long convalescence determined him to turn over management of the Lake House to others. He hired Hiram S. Thomas to be his manager. Upon Moon's retirement in 1884, the Lake House was taken over entirely by Thomas, an African American caterer who had come to public notice in Washington, DC, during the Grant administration. He would use his connection with the Lake House at the end of his life to claim the invention of the Saratoga chip.

Moon died of heart failure in 1895 at the age of eighty-two, the same year that the Lake House burnt to the ground. Obituaries lauded him as the creator of "Moon's fried potatoes" and a signal figure in the resort's history. He did not create the potato chip—but his assiduous promotion insured that it would become a signature American food.

* * *

SOURCES: "A Trip to the North," *New York Herald*, no. 7274 (July 30, 1856): 8; "Curious Story Afloat—Robert Schuyles Reported to Be Alive, and in Saratoga," *Boston Herald* (August 11, 1857): 4; "Newport," *New York Evening Post* 55 (August 12, 1857): 2; "Trout Dinners and Fried Potatoes," *Frank Leslie's Illustrated Newspaper* (September 3, 1859): 9; "Moon's Lake House, Lake Saratoga, N.Y.," *Frank Leslie's Illustrated Newspaper* (July 26, 1862): 11; "Saratoga Lake—a Fortune from Fried Potatoes," *New York Herald*, no. 10491 (May 20, 1865): 2; "Our Watering Places, *New York Herald* 34, no. 165 (June 14, 1869): 8; "A New Kind of Confectionery," *Cleveland Plain Dealer* (September 28, 1870): 5; "From Saratoga," *Albany Evening Journal* (July 29, 1870): 2; "The Secret of Saratoga Fried

Potatoes," *Philadelphia Inquirer* (July 8, 1874): 4; "New Article in the Groceries," *Philadelphia Inquirer* (July 10, 1878): 6; "The Parting Glass," *Troy Times* 34, no. 8 (September 19, 1889): 5: "Famous Roadhouse Burned," *Boston Herald* (May 12, 1893): 3.

Joshua B. Smith 1813–1879
Boston

From 1842 to 1879, J. B. Smith reigned as the first-call caterer in Boston. Nearly every civic banquet, town anniversary, convention, political rally, and Harvard class day that featured a cold collation, buffet, or sit-down supper employed Smith. A genius at kitchen craft, this African American cook and steward won general recognition as the supreme practitioner of pastry cooking in New England during his heyday. Those who disbelieved in the capacity of Africans to master refined arts concocted a fiction that he was the offspring of an Englishman and a Native American woman. Smith always identified himself as African American, agitated for abolition, became a personal friend of Senator Charles Sumner and William Lloyd Garrison, and provisioned the African American Massachusetts Twelfth Regiment during the Civil War on his own account for half a year. When Senator Daniel Webster spoke on behalf of the Fugitive Slave Act, Smith refused his request to supply a dinner for a gathering of dignitaries.

Details of Smith's ancestry remain obscure. What is known for certain is that he was a mulatto who was orphaned in Pennsylvania at age fourteen. His abilities even at this age attracted the notice of a Quaker widow in Pennsylvania who fostered him (he repressed her name in every autobiographical memoir at the request of her daughter whom Smith assisted when she fell into poverty), educated him, and treated him with the respect and care that imbued in him a conviction of a special destiny. When Smith turned twenty-one, he hired on as a servant of Mr. John C. Craig and toured the South in his company, witnessing the culture of slavery firsthand. He departed Craig's service to head north to Massachusetts and was immediately hired as headwaiter of the Mount Washington House in South Boston. One of the patrons of that eatery, Francis Shaw, struck by Smith's abilities, hired him to run his household at a salary that made a waiter's wages seem paltry. During Smith's time as steward in the household, Shaw's son, Robert Gould Shaw, went from toddlerhood to boyhood in the presence of an omni-competent African American. Later, when Robert was martyred as the officer of the "Glory" regiment of African American soldiers in the

"Joshua B. Smith, Boston" (1871). Photograph from the online collection Portraits of American Abolitionists, 1850–1890. Photograph: Massachusetts Historical Society (#81.587).

Civil War, Smith became the moving force in the creation of the monument in 1866 to honor Shaw. The resulting Augustus Saint-Gaudens sculpture became the masterpiece of Civil War memorial art.

Superintending a household did not answer Smith's desire for an outlet for his creative impulses. He left Shaw's house to serve as assistant to A. Thacker, Boston's foremost black caterer in the late 1830s. There he learned both the logistics of banquet setup and the repertoire of baked goods and banquet dishes. In 1842 Smith set up business under his own name. Almost immediately his competence at management, his tact in negotiations, and his skill as a chef distinguished him from the brotherhood of Boston caterers.

An accounting of the important banquets Smith served over the four decades of his career would be a list too ample to convey much meaning, other than that he presided at nearly every great event occurring in the vicinity of Boston during the mid-nineteenth century. We turn, instead, to what he served—for menus survive for a handful of occasions. The earliest description of a spread dates from a ball in March 1849 celebrating the inauguration of President Zachary Taylor: "The supper was served at half past ten o'clock and continued to be served during the rest of the night. It was a most recherché and epicurean repast, by which J. B. Smith, the colored caterer, has made himself famous. His tables groaned with tempting luxuries, such as game, oyster pies served hot, ice creams, French bon bons, hot coffee, etc. The tables were tastefully ornamented with greenhouse flowers." Two months later, for the bicentennial of Malden, Smith prepared a sit-down banquet for 2,000 that included "roast, fowl, tongue, pig, pies, ice creams, pastries, etc. The tables were tastefully arranged with flowers." When tasked with serving a wedding banquet or a midday reception, Smith prepared a "cold collation"—a "recherché repast of fruit, cake, ices, pastry, lemonade and other articles of luxury." Given these rather general characterizations of the bills of fare, it is something of a surprise to learn that sixty-five different dishes were served at Boston's Fourth of July banquet for 1,600 at Faneuil Hall in 1850. What precisely did Smith offer in a banquet?

Commentators would sometimes particularize the viands (the meat dishes) thusly: "cold roast and boiled fowls, cold roast beef, ham, tongues, oyster pie, lobster salad." But the earliest surviving complete bill of fare dates from March 5, 1866, for the Grand State Ball. The following supplied a crowd of 1,600:

OYSTERS
Raw   Fried   Stewed   Scalloped   Pickled

ROAST AND GAME
Quail   Squab   Duck   Turkey
Prairie Hens   Chicken

COLD DISHES
Boned Turkey   Roast Chicken   Roast Turkey
Pates de Foie Gras
Chicken Salad   Lobster Salad
Ham   Tongue
Pickled Salmon   Sardines   Anchovies

CONFECTIONERY
Charlotte Russe   Meringues and Macaroons
Brandy and Preserved Fruit
Wine, Lafayette, Sponge and Plum Cake
Blanc Mange and Wine Jelly
Peaches   Pears   Grapes   Apples   Raisins
Almonds   Mottoes

ICE CREAMS
Lemon and Strawberry Water Ices
CHOCOLATE, TEA AND COFFEE
ORNAMENTAL PIECES

Smith's take on banquet food is cosmopolitan rather than regional. The absence of fish reflects the difficulty of processing and keeping fresh sufficient numbers to feed 1,600 at a site removed from one's home kitchen. The menu suggests that on-site carving stations and chafing dishes supplied the hot items, while a substantial amount of the food was precooked and carted to the hall. Smith maintained a staff of at least ten and contracted a corps of waiters. In the antebellum era, these were often fugitive slaves whom he had trained and established in the city personally.

Of the surviving menus from Smith repasts, that of the centennial of the Battle of Lexington—engraved and printed by the John A. Lowell Company—is the most elaborate. Given his near-daily involvement in festivals and rites memorializing places, events, or people, Smith developed a particular focus on matters of public memory. He was particularly drawn to public statuary and in 1851 petitioned the legislature to erect a memorial to Crispus Attucks, the black martyr of the Boston Massacre. Smith would become the moving force behind the Captain Robert Gould Shaw monument and, later, the Charles Sumner monument.

Though politically active all of his life, Smith did not seek public office until 1873, when he put himself forward as representative for Cambridge in the Massachusetts legislature. He was elected for two terms.

When Smith turned sixty in 1873, a newspaper reporter observed:

> He is still really a handsome man, even in comparison with his Caucasian associates. His face and figure are among the most familiar in Boston, where he has catered for two generations of distinguished people in public and in private. He has never had his equal here for excellence in this line, and, in view of the very large business that he has done, he should be a rich man, and I presume is very comfortably off in worldly matters. He has always been respected. I have seen him invited by a company of cultivated gentlemen to leave his kitchen, where he was cooking in person (as he is in the habit of doing on extraordinary occasions), to take a glass of wine and sit at the board with them.

His fame was such that a body of lore circulated through New England about him. Typical is the account of the reluctance of a bank clerk to cash a check payable to Smith. "Who are you?" asked the teller. Smith retorted, "The fact that you don't know me shows that you haven't been in good society for the past ten years."

When Charles Sumner died in 1874, he bequeathed Tintoretto's painting *The Miracle of the Slave* to Smith. Smith hung it in his great house at 37 Norfolk Street in Cambridge near a marble bust of the senator that he had commissioned. Sumner said of Smith, "Had Smith my own intellectual advantages [i.e., formal education] I know of no man who could have surpassed him, and I never feel the evil of slavery more keenly than when I see its power to limit the opportunities of a man like him." Since Smith had known slavery only from observation, a more apt statement would have substituted racism for slavery. Witnesses at Sumner's memorial service observed that Smith's tender eulogy "broken off by his inability to control his grief, was one of the most touching incidents of the occasion."

An 1875 fire destroyed a substantial portion of Smith's residence, including $10,000 worth of supplies connected with his catering business. At this juncture, to repair his fortunes, he submitted a bill of $17,000 to the legislature for compensation for his provisioning of the Webster Regiment of the Twelfth Massachusetts during 1861. The bill was debated hotly in the legislature, particularly because of Smith's tardiness in submitting it. Finally, in March 1879, the legislature handed the matter over to Governor Andrews for action. The debt remained unpaid when Smith died of gastrointestinal inflammation four months later in July 1879.

※　※　※

SOURCES: "Fashionable Intelligence," *Boston Herald* (March 7, 1849): 2; "The Bi-Centennial Celebration at Malden," *Boston Herald* (May 24, 1849): 2; "Universalist General Reform Association Festival, at Winthrop Hall," *Boston Herald* (May 31, 1850): 4; "Last Day of the Jubilee," *Boston Evening Transcript* 2, no. 1 (September, 20, 1851); "The Grand State Ball," *Boston Evening Transcript* (March 6, 1866): 1; [Mr. Joshua B. Smith,] *Massachusetts Spy* 103, no. 48 (November 28, 1873): 4; "Back Pay for Rations," *Boston Herald* (March 1, 1879): 1; "J. B. Smith Dead," *Boston Herald* (July 5, 1879); "Joshua B. Smith," *Boston Daily Advertiser* 133, no. 22109 (July 7, 1879): 2; "Joshua B. Smith," *Wayside Gleanings for Leisure Moments* (Cambridge, MA: University Press, privately printed, 1882), 90; "Mr. Sumner's Will," *Boston Daily Advertiser* (March 16, 1874): 2.

Sam Ward 1814–1884
New York; Washington, DC

Gastronome, arbiter of taste, supremely talented amateur chef, the paragon of elite American hospitality—"Uncle" Sam Ward, became volunteer steward of the Manhattan Club immediately after the Civil War. He made this Democratic Party political association in New York the most famous society devoted to fine

"Uncle Sam Ward." Woodcut engraving from *New York Daily Graphic* (December 20, 1876).

eating in the United States. He joined the club on January 22, 1866, two years
after the society's formation. He was aided by a circle of theatrical men whom
he recruited into the company—John Brougham, Joseph Jefferson, Oakley Hall,
and Dion Boucicault. Ward "used to devote a good part of his time to thinking
up a sauce, a salad dressing, or a tempting way to prepare everything that a man
who is fond of his stomach could wish for." The membership of the club served
as guinea pigs for his culinary fancies.

Sam Ward was heir to the Wall Street banking firm of Prime, Ward & King.
His life began with the usual stations on the path to privilege, but fate would
drive him on to a stranger path. He excelled in his studies at Columbia University (class of 1831), then married the granddaughter of John Jacob Astor. He
was taken into his family's firm when, suddenly, the firm failed and his wife
died. Ward then departed the United States on a spiritual, or maybe aesthetic,
journey. He disappeared from genteel life, only to resurface mysteriously some
years later in California, wealthy and politically connected. Friendship with and
financial support by James R. Keene had returned Ward to glory. He resettled
in New York, worked as a Democratic lobbyist, and built a mansion on Clinton

Place, where he became famous as the most splendid of hosts. His sister Julia Ward Howe was a frequent conversationalist at his parlor. In the 1850s, he perfected his culinary skill. His favorite haunt, the old Brevoort House, became the venue for offering several of his signature dishes including boiled ham. "First, the ham should rest upon a bed of new-mown hay. When it was thoroughly cooked, a pint of old port, some brandy, and some liquors should be poured upon it to give it the 'true Ward Flavor.'" By the Civil War, he was generally reckoned the greatest of New York's gourmets—or at least the most vocal and best connected gastronome.

Ward's well-designed dinners became the key to his success lobbying in Washington, DC. Some referred to him as "Rex vestibule," and rumor said his influence probably prevented the impeachment of President Andrew Johnson. No one refused an invitation to his dinners, and he would arrange the seating order to ensure deals would occur. If the negotiations flagged, Ward unlocked his legendary liquor cabinet to distribute the proper lubricant. His expertise in identifying liquors and detecting adulterations of beverages gave rise to a popular tale of an occasion in which he was at a loss to identify the tipple during a rural expedition when a farmer served him metheglin.

Ward made it a habit in his entertainments to have a focal dish. "This specialty was always something decidedly unique. It was either a wonderful haunch of venison, a remarkable roast of beef, an exquisitely carved piece of frozen cream, or some rare old wine." Henry Borel, chef at Delmonico's, was Ward's particular friend and invited him into the kitchen on the corner of Fifth Avenue and Fourteenth Street whenever he wished to prepare food with him. "He had a wonderful palate and could tell every ingredient that might enter into the composition of a ragout or sauce, and would spend almost any time in preparing a dressing so that it suited him. He did not use old recipes, but invented new ones, and to this day dishes named after him are to be found frequently on bills of fare all over the country." These include baked terrapin. Borel speculated that Ward's culinary training came in Italy. Yet macaroni was the only dish Ward was known to abominate.

He made breakfast at the Manhattan Club an elaborate rite. His favorite morning menu was recalled by Borel, including the wine pairings:

RUDESHEIMERBERG

Eggs à l'aurore   Stuffed Oysters

VEUVE CLICQUOT

Lamb chops, en surprise   Potato soufflees

ROMANEE CONTI

Fresh musrooms sautés au beurre

Broiled chicken on toast

COS D'ESTOURNEL
Macedoine salade   Omelette au rum
Fruit
Liquors and cognac   Coffee

The alcohol intake specified here makes the Bloody Mary mornings of the American 1980s seem like a Sunday school social.

When Oscar Wilde toured the United States in 1882, he dined at Ward's Clinton mansion in a room adorned with lilies. Ward composed a poem, "The Valley Lily," in Wilde's honor that was sung by Stephen Massett. Wilde rewarded Ward by staying the night.

In his later years, Ward was a portly Pickwickian gentleman with imperial sideburns, a mustache, and gray hair. His habit of wearing tall collars made him appear to have no neck. But his kindly expression, effusive personality, and impromptu wit won over strangers. His fellow clubman said that the only time he appeared stationary was when planning a repast. He would sit motionless in a chair with a pencil hovering over a blank sheet for a half an hour, contemplating the proper order of march for the viands before inscribing the first word. Ward died in Pegli, Italy, surrounded by friends. He was seventy years old.

Several of his recipes were internationally famous. The Prince of Wales swore by Ward's Terrapin Stew. He prepared it thusly:

> Immerse live terrapin in boiling water. Let it boil half an hour. Then take out, remove lower shell, carefully cutting out the meat. Take out gall bag without cutting or breaking, and throw it away. Remove liver and cut it into cubes. Remove meat from upper shell, disjoint and place in iron pot with the cubed liver and a pit of the liquor in which terrapin was boiled. Catch carefully and cook until tender. Serve in a sauce made of two ounces best butter, a pinch of flour, half a pint cream, cayenne pepper and salt. On the bottom of each plate place a piece of bacon cooked crisp, so that it will easily break all to pieces.

※   ※   ※

SOURCES: "The Famous Sam Ward," *Denver Mirror* (February 7, 1875): 1; "Logan and Sam Ward," *Patriot* (January 22, 1891): 3; "Recollections of Sam Ward," *Springfield Republican* (July 15, 1891): 7; "The Home for Democrats," *Omaha World Herald* (January 14, 1894): 2–10; "Tales of Some Old Timers Operating on Wall Street," *Omaha World Herald* 38, no. 45 (November 24, 1902): 4; [Sam Ward's recipe,] *Biloxi Daily Herald* (December 12, 1902): 5; Kathryn Allamong Jacob, *King of the Lobby: The Life and Times of Sam Ward, Man-about-Washington in the Gilded Age* (Baltimore: Johns Hopkins University Press, 2009).

Baptiste Moreau 1815–1868
New Orleans; Bayou St. John

One of the great French chefs shaping the nineteenth-century New Orleans style of restaurant cuisine, Jean-Baptiste Moreau (he preferred styling himself Baptiste Moreau in public communications) founded a restaurant—Moreau's—that would become an iconic outpost of Louisiana French cuisine and presided over the kitchen of the rebuilt St. Louis Hotel, a world-class hostelry, during its antebellum heyday. In the 1850s, Moreau would retire from the city, establishing a rural resort at Bayou St. John. In all three venues, he created cuisine of such quality that they constituted the standard against which any chef measured his or her accomplishment.

A native of France, Moreau emigrated to New Orleans upon reaching his majority. In 1837 he founded his first restaurant on Customhouse Street in 1837, an establishment that carried his name. In 1839 he moved the premises to Chartres Street and sold controlling interest to his assistant, F. Moulin. He immediately hired on as chef of the St. Louis Exchange Hotel. The restaurant bearing his name remained open, Moulin eventually ceding control to his chef, Charles Rhodes, who would take up Moreau's repertoire of dishes and make it the mainstream of city cookery. Rhodes moved the restaurant to Canal Street in 1850, and there it long prospered. Moreau's Restaurant enjoyed particular repute under the direction of Madame Eugène in the 1880s.

Almost immediately Moreau's skills were challenged at the St. Louis Exchange. He was called upon to cater the reception for General Andrew Jackson, visiting New Orleans in late January 1840 to lay the cornerstone for his monument at the Place d'Armes. Though Moreau's name did not appear in newspaper coverage of the event, reportage agreed that the dinner had been splendid and the civic ceremony and procession impressive. Scarcely three weeks later, an early morning fire consumed the marble four-story hotel, a $1.6 million loss. The edifice, however, had been insured, and the proprietors acted promptly to rebuild the ruin. It opened in 1841 under the direction of Edward Milford, with its named shortened to the St. Louis Hotel. Because of the slave sales in its ornate rotunda (recall the auction of Uncle Tom in Harriet Beecher Stowe's novel), it was also known as the St. Louis Exchange. To reestablish its bona fides against its culinary rival, the St. Charles, management again secured Baptiste Moreau to superintend the kitchen of the St. Louis Hotel. The new hotel offered two meals daily, a breakfast at which claret was served and a 3:00 dinner that lasted until 5:00. The management assured a "constant supply of fish and Biloxi oysters." For boarders who were not lodgers, the price was $8.00 weekly in 1842. Yet the greatest culinary challenges for Moreau were the public receptions and

"St. Louis Exchange, New Orleans" (ca. 1842). Lithograph. Manouvrier and Chauvin, printers.

dinners, particularly during the season of the great balls. When Mrs. Hawley assumed management of the hotel in 1843, Moreau agreed to stay on. He remained head of the kitchens through 1846.

On January 1, 1847, Moreau severed his relationship with the St. Louis Hotel, entering into partnership with L. Tournoi in establishing Restaurant du Cardinal at 43 Natchez. At first it declared that meals were prepared in the French style. Wishing more custom, the partners expanded their culinary range in summer of 1847: "Meals are reserved at all hours in both American and French styles." In late 1848, Moreau jettisoned his partner and entered 1849 as sole proprietor. While it boasted the best cuisine in the city, the Restaurant du Cardinal suffered from a less than fashionable location. Moreau scouted spaces and discovered that the old Commercial Exchange Building on St. Charles Street was vacant. He secured the space and in late 1849 advertised the closing of the Cardinal on Natchez. He occupied this St. Charles space until early 1853, when he decided he needed a fundamental change of pace. He shuttered the restaurant and moved from the city.

The final phase of Moreau's career would see him transforming the cuisine of the lake resorts. He would move to Bayou St. John and with assistant cook Jean Chiffer opened one of the great temples of resort cuisine. Besides seafood, the house was famous for its signature dish, gelatine truffée à la gelée, a dish he taught to Moulin and Rhodes. After the Civil War, he devoted great effort to improving the resort at Spanish Fort, but his efforts were curtailed by illness and eventually his death in spring of 1868 from the aftereffects of yellow fever.

During Moreau's final years, a midwestern visitor to his bayou resort requested a recipe for a soup. This transcript, published in 1899 by the *Boston Cooking School Magazine*, is a rare surviving instruction from one of the great antebellum chefs and caterers of New Orleans.

OKRA GUMBO SOUP

Put a spoonful of lard in the soup pot on the fire. Cut up a chicken, a few onions, and a little ham. Brown, add sliced okra, mix, add a few tomatoes, cut up, and a small quantity of flour. Put all over a quick fire for a minute or two. Add water or beef broth, according to number of persons to be served. Season with salt, pepper, thyme, and bay leaf. Veal will do instead of chicken. Serve with boiled Rice.

Offhand and conversational, no doubt dictated on the fly, it interests now because of its suggestion that roux was a standard component for gumbo among the great chefs of the first age of New Orleans fine dining. The lack of information about cooking times must have led to interesting results among persons attempting to follow the formula.

⁂ ⁂ ⁂

SOURCES: "General Jackson," *Richmond Enquirer* (January 25, 1840): 2; "Destructive Fire in New Orleans," *Baltimore Sun* 6, no. 83 (February 22, 1840): 2; "St. Louis Hotel," *New Orleans Times-Picayune* (December 7, 1841): 3; "St. Louis Hotel," *New Orleans Times-Picayune* (December 17, 1841): 2; "St. Louis Hotel," *New Orleans Times-Picayune* (July 7, 1842): 3; "Cardinal Restaurant," *New Orleans Times-Picayune* (February 26, 1847): 3; "Restaurant du Cardinal," *New Orleans Times-Picayune* (September 17, 1847): 3; "Restaurant du Cardinal," *New Orleans Times-Picayune* 12, no. 289 (December 28, 1848): 1; "Reception of Ex-President Polk," *New Orleans Times-Picayune* (March 22, 1849): 2; "For Rent," *New Orleans Times-Picayune* (May 22, 1853): 4; [Recipe for Gelatine Truffée à la Gelée,] *New Orleans Daily Picayune* (October 20, 1853): 3; *United States Federal Census, 1860*, New Orleans, 7th Ward, 137; "Moreau's Restaurant, Bayou St. John," *New Orleans Times-Picayune* (July 8, 1866): 4; "Okra Gumbo Soup," *Boston Cooking School Magazine* (1899): 73; "Canal Street Still the Battleground," *New Orleans Times-Picayune* (June 22, 1899): 8.

Balthazar Roth 1815–1888
Cincinnati, OH

In 1883 a correspondent of the *Chicago Journal* could not understand why Cincinnati, a city of great commercial wealth and cultural richness, could support only one restaurant of the first rank, the St. Nicholas, on Fourth and Race Streets. The Longworth family of Catawba wine fame had attempted to build a

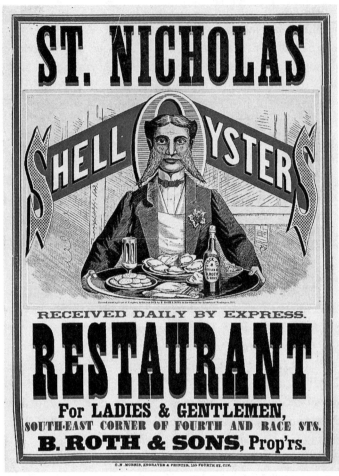

"St. Nicholas Restaurant. Shell Oysters, Received Daily by Express" (ca. 1878). Poster. C. S. Morris, Cincinnati, printer. Photograph: Library of Congress, Prints and Photographs Division (LC-DIG-pga-02243).

palace of cuisine, the Ortiz, on the corner of Fourth and Sycamore. It was run by a steward of long experience, ornamented in the latest style, manned by a crack wait staff, and offered excellent food at modest prices. "After a trial of a few months, the place had to be closed for lack of patronage." The reporter concluded that, for the most part, that the Cincinnatian was a "plain feeder." Only the St. Nicholas could tempt a citizen to pay $1.00 or more for a meal.

Since its opening in 1863, the St. Nicholas was regarded as "The Delmonico's of the West." Created by Balthazar Roth, it was intended to be the greatest restaurant in the Midwest.

Born on March 10, 1815, in Göcklingen, Rheinland-Pfalz, Germany, Balthazar Roth manifested an entrepreneurial spirit early in life, selling eau de cologne in the small towns of southern Germany from age sixteen to twenty-four, making a handsome living but growing increasing restive because the guild system restricted the scale of his manufactures and sales. He emigrated to America in 1839, intending to settle in New Orleans. When he arrived, however, yellow fever gripped the city. He immediately set off upriver, eventually settling in Cincinnati on May 26, 1840. He worked as a bartender, then as steward of George Selves's Bank Exchange Coffeehouse. An imposing six feet four inches tall and gifted with dignified features, Roth became a presence in Cincinnati's hospitality industry. With Selves he organized the St. Charles Restaurant, which would become Cincinnati's foremost restaurant of that period. Roth also catered banquets at Mozart Hall. Yet these activities did not suffice to quiet Roth's ambitious spirit. In 1860 he resigned, then bought the location on the corner of Race and Fourth Streets. There he constructed a palace of hospitality designed to dominate the social life of downtown Cincinnati—the St. Nicholas.

The St. Nicholas restaurant largely succeeded in presenting both the image of magnificence that would make it fashionable and the cuisine that would warrant an outlay of money that eclipsed other Cincinnati eateries. The original restaurant encompassed several sorts of space: a reading room, a confectionery, the ladies' saloon, the gentlemen's café, the bar, and the dining rooms. These last—lit by tall floor-to-ceiling windows, grounded by a mosaic floor, and dominated by a court painting of Pauline Bonaparte—were as grand a set of public spaces as the city boasted. The kitchen was originally headed by chef Louis Shultz. (Roth tended to repress the names of his chefs in order to focus public attention on himself as the conjuror of diners' experiences.) Shultz's kitchen was a well-ventilated forty-by-twenty-foot space lined with modern ranges and iceboxes.

Roth retired in 1878, handing the restaurant over to his son Edward N. Roth, who had been overseeing the hotel operations. In 1881 Edward managed to secure a six-year extension of his lease from the Carlisle family and expanded the portion of the edifice used for accommodation. The cuisine of the renovated restaurant was overseen by chef Chris Sponset. He would be succeeded by F. J. Nothhelfer in the 1890s.

The ladies were no doubt served the famous ice cream, the recipe for which came to a confectionery cook purportedly when visited by the ghost of Mrs. Louderback, who had made a fortune off her ice creams in the city early in the nineteenth century.

※   ※   ※

SOURCES: "The Great Social Exchange: St. Nicholas," *Cincinnati Daily Inquirer* 34, no. 50 (February 19, 1870): 8; "The Delmonico's of the West to Be Enlarged," *Cincinnati Commercial Tribune* 41, no. 356 (September 14, 1881): 4; "The New St. Nicholas," *Cincinnati Commercial Tribune* 42, no. 209 (April 23, 1882): 4;

"How Cincinnati Feeds: Only One First Class Restaurant in the Paris of America," *Cincinnati Commercial Tribune* 43, no. 331 (September 4, 1883): 5; "Death
of B. Roth," *Cincinnati Post* (January 23, 1888): 1; *Jahresbericht des Vorstandes des
Deutschen Pionier-Vereins von Cincinnati, Ohio 1887-1888* (Cincinnati: S. Rosen-
thal & Co, 1888), 37-38.

James Augustin 1817–1878

Philadelphia; Trenton, NJ; Cape May, NJ; Wilmington, DE

In the early decades of the American republic, intense debates occurred over the
level of ceremony that should attend civic events. Should public occasions be
conducted with a republican austerity, or should they be festivals that pleased
the senses, engaged the imagination, and elevated the mind? Philadelphia was
the center of these culture struggles. Martha Washington's national drawing
room—the Republican court—stood at one end of the spectrum. The meetings
of the Democratic-Republican clubs at the other. Should politeness or politics
frame public events? In a strange way, the world of public ceremony became
inflected by this dichotomy. Polite performers—persons whose elegance of gesture, verbal tact, distinction, and sense of occasion—enjoyed a premium in the
nation's capital during the 1790s. For this reason, the first African American caterers in Philadelphia—Robert Bogle, Peter Augustin—operated more as masters of revel or majordomos than culinarians. Bogle—the "politest man alive"—
spent more time superintending funerals and weddings than public banquets.
At banquets, he did not prepare food per se, but carved, orated, arranged the
décor, and secured the musicians. The second generation of African American
caterers—Isaiah Le Count, Henry Jones, and James Augustin—had more to do
with food preparation.

Son of Philadelphia renowned African American caterer Peter Augustin and
Mary Frances Augustin (1799–1890), James was born in the year before his parents established a small restaurant on Walnut Street in Philadelphia. James's
mother, a confectioner, schooled him in the culinary arts. When Peter died in
1841, his widow Mary continued the business, then at 1105 Walnut Street, taking
James Augustin as her partner as M. F. Augustin & Son. Under the direction of
Mary and James, the restaurant became the favorite haunt of theatrical personalities during the mid-nineteenth century. James Augustin supplemented his income by serving as the steward of the Philadelphia Club. By the 1840s, the position of steward had become less a master of ceremonies and more a provisioner,
headwaiter, and menu planner. In James Augustin's case, it meant chef as well.

During the summers when most Philadelphia restaurants shuttered, Augustin worked the summer seasons at Columbia House at the resort at Cape May, New Jersey. This was one of four first-class hotels on the island, with a spacious dining room seating 500 and the best wine cellar in the resort city. He also worked at the Brandywine Springs Hotel outside of Wilmington, Delaware.

M. F. Augustin & Son became the favorite meeting place of many of Philadelphia's clubs and societies. The Society of the Cincinnati held its anniversary meetings at 1105 Walnut every Fourth of July. The St. Andrew's Society and the St. David's Society considered the second-story dining room as their club home. The Philadelphia Club, before erecting its clubhouse, met there as well. Augustin's ability as a banquet cook made him a collaborator in some of the important celebrations of the 1860s and '70s. He assisted in catering the Philadelphia evening banquet for Russia's Grand Duke Alexis in 1871. He partnered with Peter Katzenbach of the Trenton House in staging the banquet for George M. Robeson, then Secretary of the United States Navy, an event that in 1877 was regarded as the greatest public feast ever conducted in New Jersey.

Upon Augustin's death in 1878, his brother Peter Jerome Augustin took over the management of 1105 Walnut Street. Like his brother, he kept the name M. F. Augustin & Son. Though Mary had retired from the active conduct of the business, she lived on the premises and her wishes remained important in its conduct. In the 1890s, Eugene Baptiste and James K. Augustin of the next generation took over conduct of the restaurant.

⁂ ⁂ ⁂

SOURCES: "The Dog on the Doorsteps," *Philadelphia Evening Telegraph* (February 1, 1867): 2; "St. David's Day," *Philadelphia Inquirer* (March 2, 1869): 3; "Cape May," *New York Herald* 34, no. 174 (June 23, 1869): 8; "St. Andrew's Society," *Philadelphia Public Ledger* 69, no. 60 (June 1, 1870): 1; "Robeson's Welcome Home," *Jersey Journal* (July 3, 1877): 1; "Died," *Philadelphia Inquirer* (April 17, 1878): 5; [Obituary notice,] *New York Herald*, no. 15212 (April 16, 1878): 6; "Notice. M. F. Augustin & Son," *Philadelphia North American* (May 1, 1878): 2.

Orra A. Taft 1817–1893
Boston

For many male diners in nineteenth-century America, the finest feasts had to feature game. Each region had a caterer or a restaurant that specialized in

"The Late O. A. Taft."
Wood engraving from
"Well Known Boniface
Dead," *Boston Herald*
(March 9, 1893): 9.

THE LATE O. A. TAFT.

dressing wild meats and wild fowl. In Massachusetts, O. A. Taft was the lustrous name for game from 1848 until his death in 1893.

A native of West Roxbury, Orra Taft went to Brighton School in South Boston and graduated from Chauncy Hall. Working after school, he learned his trade at home from his father, who kept the Brighton Hotel and the West Roxbury Tavern. He first made his name in Boston as a caterer in the 1840s, when he became steward of the Cornhill Coffee House. Orra gained a reputation for seasonal fish—smelts in November, shad in March, winter flounder, and black sea bass in summer. National fame began in 1848, when he took over the rustic dining sheds at Point Shirley, where summertime fish fries and clambakes had been held for a decade. Orra transformed the Cornhill facilities, expanding and upgrading them, then adding game to the menu. The renovated pavilion lasted a year before the 1851 gale blew it away. He procured the backing to erect a hotel on the site. In 1854, however, this structure was consumed by fire. Yet the fame of his dinners was so great by this time that the Boston city government gave him two buildings that were transported to Shirley point from Deer Island. These buildings were connected with a breezeway and named Cotton House, so called because the patchwork exterior was sheathed in cotton cloth. "It is said that no finer fish and game dinners were ever served on this continent than those served in the Cotton House."

During the regular hotel season, Taft relocated to his restaurant on Brattle Street in Boston. On May 15, 1856, Taft opened the Point Shirley House a short distance from the Cotton House and shuttered his town dining room. A hotel with forty rooms, equipped with "modern conveniences," and supplying boats and tackle for fishing parties, Taft's hotel became a weekend summer retreat. The East Boston Ferry provided the quickest way from city center to Point Shirley, but the five-mile drive was one of the more picturesque in the metropolitan area. After the Civil War, he renamed his establishment Taft's Hotel and extended its season into mid-October. He also assigned himself the rank of colonel.

Colonel Taft's banquets became frequent fodder for the news columns of New England's papers in the late 1860s. When the diplomats of the Chinese imperial embassy toured Boston in 1868, they dined at Taft's. "Not less than forty-two variety of birds, together with almost as many varieties of fish, were on his table on that occasion, and each cooked feathered and finny individual had its duplicate uncooked, ready for the inspection of the company." In another instance, clubs of men from New York and Boston laid a wager on how many varieties of fish and game could be had at restaurants in their respective cities, if a company dropped in on the restaurant without notice. The Boston Club won when Taft produced, besides soups and chowders, "Spanish Mackerel, Turbot, Chicken Halibut, Deep Sea Flounder, Mullet, Blue Fish, Rock Cod, Tautog, Rock Bass, Sole, Plaice, Scup, Perch, White Bait." Then, he produced "Erie Black Duck, Teal and Summer Duck, Prairie Chicken, Chicken, Partridge, Woodcock, Doughbird, Upland Plover, Golden Plover, Redbreast Plover, Beetlehead Plover, Godwit, Willet, Curlew, Brant Bird, Winter Yellowlegs, Summer Yellowlegs, Redbreast Snipe, Sand Snipe, Jack Snipe, Rail, Peeps, Reedbirds." Taft, a noted angler and wild fowl shooter, had a schooled amateur's knowledge of ichthyology and ornithology. He hunted with the great men of New England from Daniel Webster to Augustus Saint-Gaudens. Indeed, in the 1860s, he closed his downtown Boston office and devoted the autumn and winter to field sports and fishing. He also visited Europe to learn methods of preparing game and fish. As contemporaries observed, "He always superintended the preparation of the dishes served in his hotel." One of Taft's ambitions was to serve every sort of wild game and fish available in North America and Europe. Moose and arctic char appeared regularly on the menu. In 1882 he bet a company of friends that they could not name an edible North American bird that he could not produce instantly.

Taft trained his son George in the caterer's art. In December 1883, George opened a city center Taft's Hotel at 6 Norfolk Place. Employing cooks Henry Collins (who had been trained at Point Shirley) and Thomas Porter, George Taft's hotel specialized in game and good wine.

In 1890 the construction of the metropolitan sewer basin forced the closure of Taft's for the season. It would not reopen. Because Orra Taft's son predeceased him, the estate after his death in 1893 would provoke family disagreement among various grandchildren. The hotel changed hands and remained an attraction until 1930 under the name the Point Shirley Club.

SOURCES: "Fresh Shad," *Boston Evening Transcript* 13, no. 3562 (March 7, 1842): 2; "Smelts," *Boston Evening Transcript* 17, no. 4999 (November 10, 1846): 2; "Point Shirley House," *Boston Herald* (July 4, 1856): 3; "Taft's Hotel, Point Shirley," *Boston Traveler* (August 27, 1866): 4; "Notable Banquets," *Springfield Republican* (September 7, 1868): 2; "A Wonderful Game Dinner," *Cleveland Plain Dealer* (September 7, 1870): 1; "Taft's in Boston," *Boston Herald* (December 27, 1883): 2; "Death of Col. O. A. Taft, the Veteran Hotel Keeper of Point Shirley," *Springfield Republican* (March 9, 1893): 5; "Taft's Point Shirley, Closed," *Worcester Daily Spy* 45, no. 149 (June 23, 1890): 5; "Well Known Boniface Dead," *Boston Herald* (March 9, 1893): 9; "Col. O. A. Taft" [obituary notice], *Boston Journal* 60, no. 19563 (March 9, 1893): 2; Christopher W. Leahy, *The Birdwatcher's Companion: An Encyclopedic Handbook of North American Birdlife* (New York: Bonanza Books, 1986), 213.

Walter H. Van Rensselaer 1817?–1849

New York; New Orleans

New York born and trained, "Walter" emerged as a name in New Orleans cooking as caterer of the Bishop's Hotel (the City Hotel) in his teens circa 1836. Shortly after the opening of the St. Charles Hotel—perhaps as early as 1839—Walter Van Rensselaer was hired away from the Bishop to preside over the second-floor dining saloon, an immense hall accommodating 300 seats arrayed along three lengthy tables.

Van Rensselaer confronted a difficult task, adjusting the cuisine to the tastes of the army of Mississippi Valley cotton brokers and traders and foreign merchants who occupied the hotel from October through May, while securing sufficient local diners to tide the hostelry over during the summer season. The multitude of commercial men employed the chief second-floor dining room. A second saloon, styled the women's ordinary, serviced female customers so they did not have to suffer the presence of the masculine herd. Upcountry taste tended toward meats, breads, and seafood prepared without flourish. The residents of the city expected Parisian fare. There were but few places where tastes coincided: the Creole beefsteak, roasted wild fowl, and oysters.

On November 8, 1843, Van Rensselaer took leave of the St. Charles to create a more intimate setting for fine dining. He purchased from Daniel D'Arcy the Crescent Coffeehouse at 46 St. Charles Street. He renamed it the Crescent

"St. Charles Hotel, New Orleans, Louisiana" (ca. 1855). Albumin photograph.

Restaurant and renovated the meal plan, serving breakfast, lunch, and dinner. It was, perhaps, the first restaurant in New Orleans to make lunch a fixture on the daily cycle of meals. He counted upon the "friends" he made during his time at the hotel to lunch on "turtle soup, red fish chowder, and other 'fixin's.'" His experience in hotels had instructed him that the yearly tidal influx of Americans into the city required some adaptation in the local institutions to suit the non-Francophile tastes of men of trade. Since the season of commerce directly coincided with the season when oysters were available, and since the oyster had been a focus of American delectation at the St. Charles, Van Rensselaer pioneered the adaptation to New Orleans of a culinary institution famous in Philadelphia, Baltimore, and Washington, DC—the "oyster cellar." In those cities the man hungering for bivalves stepped below grade into enclaves located under stores, museums, and offices to feast on oysters and drink Philadelphia porter and Scottish ale.

Almost overnight in autumn of 1846, the oyster saloon became a fixture of masculine dining in New Orleans. Up and down St. Charles Street, these bivalve-and-beverage halls sprang up. Antonio Caytano's Oyster House followed the Baltimore model, being located beneath the Live Oak Coffee House. Lazzaro Dancevich's Palo Alto Oyster Saloon offered its wares above grade. A. Holbrook's New Oyster Saloon at 97 St. Charles boasted attentive waiters and oyster shuckers. Thomas Mile's American Oyster Saloon alerted customers to the national taste being served at his establishment. Van Rensselaer's Grand Oyster Saloon, located next to the Crescent Restaurant, promised quality and variety:

> In the Oyster Saloon will always be found the fattest and finest Oysters from Cat Island, Brand Pass, Barataria, Biloxi and Mobile, which will be served up at all hours, day and night, in every variety of style. In the Restaurant, Game of all kinds of Fish, fresh from the Lake, of every variety—Beefsteaks—Mutton Chops—Poultry—Turtle Soups, etc. etc. will be found at all hours, and they will be served up on short notice in a style to suit all palates.

Van Rensselaer took the serving of oysters a long way from the open-air oyster stand at the French market that had served the populace before flush times came to the city. Since he also introduced lunch to the Crescent City, it is a matter of interest what he advertised as a bill of fare for this meal. This comes from midwinter of 1848: "Green Turtle Soup, Oyster Gumbo, Baked and Boiled Redfish with oyster sauce, Roast Wild Turkey, Roast Venison Steaks with cranberry sauce, Fried Oysters, Roast Beef, Marshall's celebrated Spiced Beef, Pig's Feet, &c., &c."

Van Rensselaer functioned as proprietor of the Oyster Saloon, securing the services of first J. F. Teepell of the Florence Hotel in New York, then Harris Lyons as masters of cuisine. In late 1848, Walter began to sicken. He visited New York with his wife, Emeline L. Gladding, then returned to Louisiana and died in May 1849. He was mourned by the volunteer fire department to which he belonged, the Masonic Lodges, and the city epicures. Oyster bars thrived as a permanent fixture of cosmopolitan American dining in New Orleans into the twenty-first century.

※　※　※

SOURCES: "The Crescent City Coffee-House," *New Orleans Times-Picayune* (November 8, 1843): 2; "Notice," *New Orleans Times-Picayune* (November 10, 1843); "Walter Respectfully Informs," *New Orleans Times-Picayune* (September 4, 1846): 2; "Walter's 1 Grand Oyster Saloon and Restaurant," *New Orleans*

Times-Picayune (October 23, 1846): 4; "Lunch at the Crescent," *New Orleans Times-Picayune* (February 1, 1848): 3; "Crescent Restaurant and Oyster Saloon," *New Orleans Times-Picayune* (February 15, 1848): 3; "Walter," *New Orleans Times-Picayune* (November 8, 1848): 3; "Walter van Rensselaer," *New Orleans Times-Picayune* (May 26, 1849): 2.

David Canter 1817–1897
London; New York

Born in Leewarden, the Netherlands, on June 17, 1817, David Levij Canter was Manhattan's foremost Jewish confectioner and kosher caterer in the mid-nineteenth century. Trained in his native Friesland, he then moved with his sweetheart Sophia to London in the 1840s. They married there before emigrating for America. Carter settled in New York and opened a confectionery in 1854. The confectionery would remain a fixture in New York life for over three decades, the most reliable source for matzo in uptown Manhattan, and the preferred source for Passover confectionery. In the final twenty years of his career, he and his brother Alexander became caterers to many of the significant celebrations of Manhattan's Jewish community.

Canter opened his first office at 26 Ludlow Street near the intersection with Hester, styling himself a "fancy cake baker" and announcing the availability of the "best cakes in the city." His initial specialty list included the following items:

Superior English Rout Cakes	Ground Almonds
Superior English Almond Cakes	French Maccaroons
Superior Filberts & Walnuts	German Maccaroons
Superior Ratafie Cakes	Madeln Stangen
Shelled Almonds	Portugal Tea Cakes
Superior Almond Puddings (to order)	
Prelatos	Sponge Cakes
other basket Cakes	

During the Civil War, he expanded his offerings to include the following:

Chocolate Cakes	Lady Fingers
Hollande *Bitterkoekjes*	Cinnamon Cakes
Superior Burnt Almonds	

As the Portuguese items on this list suggest, Canter's cultural background was from the Ladino-speaking Portuguese Jews who migrated to the Netherlands. In New York, he affiliated with the Portuguese synagogue, yet performed wedding banquets and sold products servicing the larger Jewish community.

In winter of 1863, Canter moved his business to 146 Eighth Avenue, adding an "Ice Cream Saloon" to the confectionery. He made a point of advertising the availability of *pièces montées*—display food meant to impress guests in social settings: "Constantly on hand: plain and meringue pies, Charlotte de Russe, Meringues a la Crème, Jellies, Pyramids &c. &c. made to order." In 1870 he moved again, more "uptown" to 738 Eighth Avenue. While Canter made items with almond paste as Passover confections, he did not make unleavened bread—matzo—until 1871. "The Jewish community of New York City are hereby notified that the objections for so many years made as regards going down town for Matzos has been remedied, as Matzo will be sold for the coming season."

While much of the written record of the 1850s through the '80s presented David Canter as a confectioner, there are episodes in which he appears in the more cosmopolitan role as caterer, indeed as the one reliable caterer in the city who could prepare a public banquet within the stipulations of the dietary laws. In 1866 the Independents Social Club held a ball in mid-November. The organizers published the following commendation: "It is with great pleasure we here record the fact that the supper was strictly kosher, having been superintended by the caterer, Mr. Canter. We trust we shall never be again called upon to find fault in this department, for, if societies give entertainments which rely for support upon the Israelites, it is a great outrage upon their patrons to offer them forbidden viands, independent of Divine Commands." In 1879, during the meeting of the Sixth Council of Jews in America, Delmonico's turned over its staff to Canter's direction in order to serve a kosher banquet. The prepared *pièces montées* were all scenes from Jewish history. Throughout this period, David's older brother, Alexander L. Canter, his assistant in the confectionery, made a specialty of managing kosher banquets.

Throughout his career at the center of New York's world of Jewish public food, David Canter saw many rivals rise and fall. Indeed, his most talented competitors appeared jinxed. In winter 1859, the Jewish hotelier Ralph Benjamin installed "cook and ornamental confectioner" S. Myers in the restaurant at 94 Chatham Street, having pried him away from Baron N. M. de Rothschild's staff. Perhaps the bill of fare savored too much of London banquet food and not enough of Jewish cuisine:

Mock Turtle Soup, 75c. per quart, always on hand
Boned Turkey, from $4.00
Ragout Duck, $1.50 each

Boned Fowl, Mushroom, $2.00

Tongues, Glazed, $1.25

Entrees to order

Roast Poultry

Chicken Salads, from $1.00

Calves Feet Jelly, 75 c. per quart

Jellies prepared with Fruit and cannot be surpassed for Transparency, Flavor, and
Beauty

Orange Jelly, 75 c. per quart

Maraschino Jelly, 75 c. per quart

Punch, $1.00

Jelly in Oranges

Almond Pudding, from 25 c.

Wet Pudding 50 c.

Charlotte de Russe

Blanc Manges

Bolar D'Amour from $5.00

Bolar Pheado, from $3.00

Bolas 6 c. each always on hand

Pyramids, Devises, Chantilly Baskets, Wreaths, Flowers, Ice-Creams, Water Ices,
Ice Puddings, for wedding breakfasts, &c. Pastry. Almond Cheese Cakes,
Curd Cheese Cakes, Cream Tarts, Vanilla, Meat Pastry equal to Butter, Crystal
Fruits, Preserved Pine Apples

When spring arrived in New York, so did yellow fever. Benjamin shut down his hotel. Myers evacuated the city and opened a dining room in the Chestnut Grove House at Clifton, Staten Island. At the same time, Canter expressed a willingness to cater any sort of wedding or public event. When autumn came around, Myers had no fixed position in the city and catered one important event, the Ladies Fair at the Academy of Music. He opened a confectioner's shop at 121 Bleecker Street. But business expired by spring 1860. He disappeared, Benjamin moved to Philadelphia, and Myers's place in the Jewish culinary firmament was taken by Isaac Sommers and Mrs. J. M. Pach. Installed at Jones Wood Hotel on Third Avenue, Sommers proposed to stage "[Déjeuners,] Dinners and Suppers, For Weddings, Parties, and Banquets," but as a later commentator observed, there was more money to be made catering "large political assemblies than the merry Hebrew weddings and parties." Sommers eventually became a politician.

A more durable rival was the transplanted Berliner Mrs. J. M. Pach. Pach forever searched for an ideal situation, moving from Boston to Manhattan, from Manhattan to Philadelphia, from Philadelphia back to New York. Despite her frequent recourse to the advertising columns of newspapers, we know little about her culinary repertoire. Indeed, nothing, except the fact that "especial attention paid to Boned Turkey, Duck, French Fricassee." She endured throughout the Civil War by focusing upon the family trade rather than the balls and banquets of the major societies, such as the Purim Association. Servicing these public occasions could be dangerous to one's reputation, for they were notorious for harboring grumblers who found fault with the food. Many who set up as cooks for the Jewish community found themselves roasted: M. Goetz, I. Jacobs, S. Kochmann, Mrs. S. Appel, M. Keppler, L. Weil. Indeed, when someone did superlatively well—as Herman Danziger did at the Hebrew Free School Association Ball in 1870—the *Jewish Messenger* observed, "His food was abundant and well cooked, and the grumblers were for once silenced."

The most fundamental challenge to the enduring hold of David Canter on the culinary imagination of New York's Jewish community was not posed by the dozen bakers and confectioners who sidelined as caterers during the 1870s and '80s, but by the partnership of Jewish cooks who opened the first kosher restaurants in the city of any repute, Blaut and Minsesheimer. Opening branches at 45 Lispenard Street and 100 Duane Street in spring of 1870, and an uptown branch at 440 Broadway in winter of 1872 (upon which the Lispenard branch closed), their dining rooms offered both table d'hôte and à la carte dishes that were stylish and observant. The partnership was comprised of Lazarus Blaut (who had an interest in the Duane Street eating house) and father and son David and Leon Minsesheimer (who had an interest in both the Duane and the Broadway restaurants). They cultivated an extraordinary family trade by offering strawberry shortcake in season below cost. Their success encouraged them in October 1870 to enter into the banquet trade. The catering was done out of the Duane Street branch of the restaurant. The first great catering success was the luncheon of Grand Lodge 1 of B'nai B'rith in February 1871.

The importance of the Blaut and Minsesheimer restaurant for the Jewish community is best attested by a newspaper commentary run in 1870 shortly after the first branches opened:

> Where rabbinical lectures and newspaper scoldings have failed, in bringing our Jews to a proper sense of their position as regards the dietary enactments, it seems the young caterers of No. 100 Duane street, Blaut & Minsesheimer, have succeeded. By a proper attention to the requirements of a first-class restaurant, moderate prices, the best viands, and other edibles, good liquors, cleanly appointments and polite waiters, they have drawn into the fold many Israelite merchants, to whom kosher eating has been a dead letter for years past. If good dinners will save Jewish souls, by all means give good dinners. . . . Let us hear no more complaints about the "impossibility" of living in Jewish style.

From winter 1870 until winter 1873, Blaut and Minsesheimer maintained their temple of pure Jewish cooking. Then, like so many fine things in New York, it was swept into oblivion by the global financial panic of 1873. All three young men were ruined. Of the culinary professionals who served the community, only the oldest, cagiest, and most versatile survived: Mrs. Pach and David Canter. Indeed, Canter's business would prosper through the 1870s and most of the '80s. When he turned seventy, Canter shuttered his business. In 1892 he celebrated his golden anniversary with Sophie. He died revered in 1897.

✳ ✳ ✳

SOURCES: "The Late David Canter," *Jewish Messenger* (May 14, 1897): 2–3; "Ralph Benjamin," *Jewish Messenger* (March 4, 1859): 71; "Chestnut Grove House," *Jewish Messenger* (April 29, 1859): 126; "Confectionery for Passover," *Jewish Messenger* (April 15, 1859): 118; "S. Myers," *Jewish Messenger* (December 2, 1959): 162; "Notice to Jewish Families," *Jewish Messenger* (September 28, 1860): 102; "Notice to Families," *Jewish Messenger* (June 14, 1861): 182; "Isaac Sommers," *Jewish Messenger* (September 1, 1861); "Confectionery for Passover," *Jewish Messenger* (April 11, 1862): 114; "Removal," *Jewish Messenger* (February 21, 1863): 63; "The Independents Social Club," *Jewish Messenger* (November 16, 1866): 4; "Local Items," *Jewish Messenger* (March 11, 1870): 5; [Commentary on Blaut and Minsesheimer,] *Jewish Messenger* (April 8, 1870): 6; "The Most Elegant Kosher Restaurant in America," *Jewish Messenger* (June 10, 1870): 3; "Messrs. Blaut & Minsesheimer," *Jewish Messenger* (October 21, 1870): 3; [The B'nai B'rith,] *Jewish Messenger* (February 3, 1871): 2; "Long Wanted! And at Last Come!" *Jewish Messenger* (February 17, 1871): 3; "Confectioner—Alex. D. Canter," *Jewish Messenger* (May 5, 1871): 3; "Established 1854," *Jewish Messenger* (March 13, 1885): 6; "Persons and Places," *Jewish Messenger* (October 7, 1887): 4–5.

James Wood Parkinson 1818–1895
Philadelphia; New York

In May 1842, James W. Parkinson notified the public that he had expanded the confectionery shop at 180 Chestnut Street, Philadelphia, by opening a refectory in the rear. Parkinson's Restaurant would become one of the great houses of gastronomic resort in the United States. Here Parkinson and his staff won the famous $1,000 contest between the antebellum gastronomes of New York and Philadelphia, besting the chefs of Delmonico's in preparing the superlative

"Parkinson's Ice Cream Saloon and Confectionary Store, south side of Chestnut below 8th in 1839." David Johnson Kennedy Watercolors. Photograph: Historical Society of Pennsylvania.

feast. Here Parkinson perfected dishes that used American ingredients and embodied American approaches to preparing and consuming food—dishes that would be memorialized in his publication of a guide to American cuisine for the Philadelphia Centennial in 1876. Here Parkinson experimented with fruit, exploring the culinary uses of the strawberry, popularizing the juicing of oranges for breakfast, and extolling the health benefits of fresh fruit. And here, after forty years of restaurant life, he picked up a pen, wrote, and edited two of the greatest culinary periodicals of the nineteenth century: *The Confectioner's Journal* (1873–95) and *The Caterer* (1880–84), both magazines designed for culinary professionals.

Born in Philadelphia, the son of George Parkinson, an English confectioner who came to Philadelphia in 1808 to make his fortune, James W. Parkinson learned his art in the most famous pastry shop in North America. The building at 380 Chestnut was a landmark, a deluxe town house with a tessellated Italian marble floor, a ceiling painted by Monachesi, and outfitted with marble-top tables, banked mirrors, and suites of engravings. In 1838 James's father wished to sell the business and retire. James convinced him not to and urged expansion, and furthermore urged his father to be more ambitious in his business. James possessed several qualities over and above his father George's mastery with sugar and pastry. The young man was adept with a pen. He was curious, experimental, and acquisitive of information about areas of culinary art other than confectionery. He captured the vast knowledge his mother, Eleanor, had about confectionery, recording from her lips all the fundamentals of the craft of sugar baking. This James organized into *The Complete Confectioner* (1843), "Plain and practical directions for making confectionery and pastry, and for baking; with upward of five hundred receipts [recipes] for making all sorts of preserves, sugar-boiling, ornamental cakes, ices, syrups, jellies, muffins, rolls, tarts, pies, &c &c.; by Parkinson, greatly lauded in Philadelphia newspapers as *the* confectioner." It remained the chief reference about confectionery for American cooks in the 1840s.

James's ascendancy in the business is visible in the expansion of the premises into a restaurant in 1842. At Christmastime 1846, he moved the confectionery to a separate premises, at 38 South Eighth, temporarily named "Old Kriss Kingle's [sic] Head-Quarters," where French bonbons and sugar drops abounded. He created an instant tradition by throwing open the doors of the confectionery on Christmas Day and welcoming families with children in to sample wares. Meanwhile, 380 Chestnut became Parkinson's refectory.

In 1851 one of the most famous dinners of the century took place at Parkinson's restaurant. Fifteen gentlemen of New York challenged fifteen gentleman of Philadelphia to host a dinner at the finest restaurant in each city to determine culinary supremacy. "Money was of no consequence." The New Yorkers took the Philadelphians to Delmonico's. The harvest entertainment that Lorenzo Delmonico gave "was a great one, and, as we then supposed, unsurpassably fine." On April 19, the company met in Philadelphia at Parkinson's. "As this dinner was given in April, it took the caterer greatly at a disadvantage, as to both game and vegetables. It was 'between season.' He could only obtain what he did by special use of both telegraph and express. His lettuce, green peas, cauliflowers, etc., had to be ordered from Georgia. His reed-birds came from South Carolina. He sent anglers and hunters to the woods and waters of Virginia. The salmon of the occasion were swimming the night before in the Kennebec, in Maine." The feast had seventeen courses, each paired with a separate wine. The company sat down at 6:00 in the evening and rose from the table at 6:00 a.m. the next morning. The menu became a sacred relic of American gastronomy:

EMPIRE & KEYSTONE

BEFORE DINNER
Cognac of 1821, wine bitters, with Madeira (150 Years Old) and Sherry   La Carte

FIRST COURSE
Oysters—Morris River Cover on shell
Wines-Sauterne, vintage of 1846, specially selected from the stock of
Washington Morton, a Bordeaux

SECOND COURSE
Soups—Green turtle, Pottage a la reine
Wines—Snider's imperial cognac (in pint bottles)

THIRD COURSE
Fish—Fresh Salmon, lobster sauce; baked rock, a la Chambord
Wines—Extra cabinet, Steinberg, vintage of 1834, specially selected from the
cellars of the Duke of Nassau

FOURTH COURSE
Boiled—Turkey, celery and oysters sauce, Chicken and egg sauce, Beef tongues
Wines—Champagne—Sparkling, of Peuvrel a Avize
Specially on table, Medoc—Haut Brion, 1841
Burgundy, Cote roti, 1839

FIFTH COURSE
Cold dishes—Galatine de dinde a la gelee
Salade a la russe en bordure de gelee, Boeuf a la mode,
Salade de Volaille, a la mode anglaise
Jambon decore   Aspic des huitres   Mayonnaise of lobster,
Aspic de volaille aux truffes
Wines—Rare old cask, Amontillado—Pale sherry, Specially selected from
the private stock of Thomas Osborne, Esq., of the house of Duff, Gordon & Co.,
Port Andalusia, Spain

SIXTH COURSE
Entrée No. 1—Filet de boeuf aux champignons, Ris de veaux, sauce tomate,
Vol-au-vent, a la financiere, Cotelettes de deouton, Croquettes de volaille

SEVENTH COURSE
Entrée No. 2—Pigeons braise, sauce Madere, Arcade de Volaille, Fricassee de
poulets a la Chevalier; lamb chops, milanaise; turtle steak, callepash
Wines: Moet—Extra Sparkling Champagne; Vintage of 1846, Snider's special
importation

EIGHTH COURSE
Roast, spring chicken on toast, capons, bardet, spring lamb, mint sauce
Wines: Extra Sparkling Moselle, Scharzberg
Vintage of 1846, special importation from the cellars of Dienhard & Hordan, Coblenz

NINTH COURSE
Pieces montees, Swiss basket, pannier en nougat, cottage basket, vase monte with
fruit glace, Flora's offering, Moorish fountain, Indian temple
Vegetables: White potatoes, sweet potatoes, corn, hominy, tomatoes, celery, green
peas, spinach, cauliflower, asparagus, dressed lettuce

TENTH COURSE
Coup du miflieu, Sorbets au vin de Tokay

ELEVENTH COURSE
Game—Jack snipe, Teal duck, Woodcock, Plover, Rice birds
Celery hearts, Saratoga potatoes
Wines—Oeil de perdrix

TWELFTH COURSE
Diamond-back terrapin, roast potatoes
Wine—rare old Amontillado pale sherry
Specially selected and bottled in Europe, Imported October, 1850

THIRTEENTH COURSE
Pastry—Lemon pudding, peach pie, cocoanut pudding, Charlotte Russe, Gateaux a la
parisienne, Meringue de pomme, Gateaux a la napolitaine, Meringue a la crème,
Wafers a la francaise, Gelle au Madere, blanc-mange, Italian cream, Gateaux allemande
Wines: Sherry—Rare old mellow case wine, pale, of Duff, Gordon & Co.
Madeira—Soft, old; vintage of 1811
Port—Burmester, extra, Special importation

FOURTEENTH COURSE
Confectionary—Mint drops, Cream candy, Celery seed, Raspberry balls, Burned almonds,
Chinese almonds, Cream drops, Nougat de Provence, Port wine drops, Brandy drops

FIFTEENTH COURSE

Ice cream and water ices—Biscuit glace, Cream au burre, Caramel, Vanilla, Harlequin, Strawberry, Lemon, Orange water ice, Punch a la romaine, Champagne frappe a la glace

SIXTEENTH COURSE

Fruits and nuts, apples, oranges, figs, raisins, walnuts, almonds, pecan nuts, filberts
Wines—Rhenish, soft old, very rare extra cabinet
(Marcobrunn of 1834, specially obtained from the cellar of the Duke of Nassau)
Medoc (Montrose of 1840, very choice and delicate, bottled in 1844, and especially selected from the stock of Vale & Co., at Bordeaux)

SEVENTEENTH COURSE

Café noir, liqueurs, Maraschino, curacao

Wines and liquors selected for this occasion from the stock of
Jacob Snider, Jr., Philadelphia

Parkinson was assisted in preparing this banquet by several of Philadelphia's greatest caterers, including Joseph Head of the Mansion House. The New Yorkers at the end of the banquet conceded the supremacy of Philadelphia cooking à la Parkinson.

During the Civil War era, Parkinson's saloon was augmented with a garden that served during the summer months as an outdoor café. Contiguous to the Academy of Fine Arts and across from the new St. Lawrence Hotel, Parkinson's enjoyed a location second to none for cultural cachet. In the wake of the war, Parkinson decided to gain a foothold in Manhattan, signing a three-year lease at $45,000 on a site on Broadway and Amity Street. There his ices became a favorite refreshment of city women shopping and lunching. As a novelty and a relief from the lemon ices and vanilla ice cream favored by Philadelphians, Parkinson premiered pistachio ice cream at the Broadway saloon, the first commercially sold in the United States.

By the 1870s, Parkinson was becoming bored. He had accomplished all that one could accomplish professionally as a practicing cook. His ice cream brand was a mass market phenomenon. He had won recognition among the community of chefs for his mastery of cuisine. He was rich. He turned away from the range and toward the writing desk. He would supply in print that sort of useful conversation that culinary professionals needed to further their art. Furthermore, he had a cause—the validation of American food as a cuisine. To this end, he prepared a pamphlet celebrating American dishes for distribution at the Centennial in Philadelphia. He contended in print with the Grand Duke Alexis of Russia's critique of American cookery, and he edited *The Confectioner's Journal*, the most circumspect and informed chronicle of cookery composed during the nineteenth century in the United States. He became, in effect, the central man of letters in the culinary world.

No practice aggravated him more than the dumbing down of cuisine for household cooks. If a home cook had an aspiring spirit, she or he should be provided the information requisite to make a superlative dish. A signature recipe he formulated in the 1880s epitomizes what Parkinson stood for at the end of his career. It was a characteristic preparation of his native city—it posed a challenge to make—and it formed something artful, distinctive, and tasty. Note the care with which the instruction is laid out.

CHICKEN CROQUETTE

This formula for their preparation is for a pair of fowls weighing not less than six pounds the pair. Choose always those having the largest amount of breast meat. Boil the fowls in sufficient water to cover them, with two onions, two carrots, a small bunch of thyme and parsley, a few cloves and half a grated nutmeg. After the chickens are boiled tender and have become quite cold, divest them of all skin, fat, gristle, bones and tendons, and chop the meat as fine as possible. Put half a pound of the best table butter, and cook together, stirring constantly to prevent its burning; when these are fully incorporated add a gill of the stock in which the chickens were boiled and a tumbler of rich cream; boil for eight or ten minutes, stirring constantly; remove from the fire and season with salt, pepper, grated nutmeg and a little finely powdered sweet marjoram; then add the chopped chicken meat, stir and mix well together then add the yolks of four eggs, stir rapidly in; set all on the fire and evaporate the mixture for one moment; stir briskly, after which pour the mass out upon a flat dish and let it remain until perfectly cold. Then make it up into pear-shaped cones or into rolls, with the assistance of a little flour to prevent sticking to the fingers. When all ready dip each one separately into the yolks of eggs, beaten with a little cream, and roll them as fast as dipped into fresh bread crumbs made from day old bread. Let them stand for an hour or so to dry; then fry them to a delicate brown color in plenty of hot boiling lard and lay in a colander to drain. Serve in a napkin laid on a warm dish.

No one during the first age of American fine dining wrote better instructions for cooking dishes than James W. Parkinson.

❋   ❋   ❋

SOURCES: "Excellent Stand for Business," *New York Commercial Advertiser* (June 25, 1838): 1; "Parkinson's Restaurant," *Philadelphia Inquirer* 26, no. 112 (May 11, 1842): 3; [Advertisement,] "The Complete Confectioner," *New York*

Commercial Advertiser 46 (December 20, 1843): 2; "Old Kriss Kingle's Head-Quarters," *North American* 8, no. 2408 (December 24, 1846): 2; "St. Lawrence Hotel," *Washington Reporter* (June 14 1860): 4; Jennie June, "Parisian Fashions in New York," *Philadelphia Age* (June 15, 1866): 1; "Les Bon-Vivants," *Cincinnati Daily Gazette* (September 17, 1874): 3; "Much in Little," *Philadelphia Inquirer* 110 (May 14, 1884): 3; "Autograph Recipes from Eminent Authorities," *New York Herald* 19 (January 19, 1890): 23; [Mortuary notice,] *Philadelphia Inquirer*, May 15, 1895, 11; Mary Anne Hines, Gordon Marshall, and William Woys Weaver, *The Larder Invaded* (Philadelphia: Library Company of Philadelphia, Pennsylvania Historical Society, 1987), 26, 31, 61; Anne Cooper Funderburg, *Chocolate, Strawberry, and Vanilla: A History of American Ice Cream* (Bowling Green, OH: Bowling Green State University Press, 1995), 77.

Antonio Sivori 1818–1893
New York; Las Vegas; St. Louis

Born in Genoa, Italy, and trained as a cook in his native city, Antonio Sivori came to New York upon completing his kitchen apprenticeship at age fifteen. For six years, he worked in the kitchen of Delmonico's before going off on his own. During his fifty-year career as a caterer in the United States, no one had a more varied and active employment. As chef de cuisine, he prepared the banquet that opened the Union Square Hotel in Manhattan in 1860 and presided over the cuisine of the Barrett House during its brief heyday as a culinary destination.

When the Civil War broke out, Sivori joined the Fifty-Fifth New York Zouaves. This company initially represented itself as French but in reality was a multi-ethnic crew. Sivori, who spoke six languages fluently, passed himself off as French and called himself Soyer, after the famous French chef. On the battlefields of Virginia, he learned to handle the logistics of supply. This experience equipped him for the next phase of his professional life as a caterer and event cook, operating out of a hotel headquarters, yet managing events and cookery in remote locations.

Henry Voigt, the historian of American menus and student of Sivori's career, documents this phase of his career with particular richness. Using six menus from his time as chef at the St. James Hotel from 1869 through 1872, we can see the variety of Sivori's banquet work. In 1872 Sivori became proprietor of his own restaurant—the St. Marks—inside the Stevens House. His tenure there was curtailed by the financial crisis of 1873, forcing him to work a stint at Delmonico's as head of the on-site banquet work. He did this for several years, according to Voigt. This entailed a transformation into a steward, a more public office than

MENU

Oysters on Half Shell. — 3.00

SOUP.

Bisque aux Ecrevisse.   A la Cresy. 10

FISH.

Boiled Salmon. 6.60   Fried Smelts Tartar sauce. 3.00

RELEVEE.

Sweetbreads larded aux Petit Pois.   18.00

COLD AND ORNAMENTAL DISHES.

Boned Turkey aux Truffles.   30   Patèe de fois Gras,
Horn of Plenty,   Bass, sur Mer,
                 Ham, en Bellevue.

ENTREES.

Filet of Beef aux Champignons.   25.00
      Capons à la Godard aux Truffles,   15
      Lamb Chops à la Jardiniere,   8.00

Punch Napolitaine.   5

ENTREMETS.

Asparagus, String Beans, Stewed Tomatoes, Green Corn, 10
        Baked Mashed Potatoes,

ROAST.

Saddle of Mutton, 5   Turkey. 16

RELISHES.

Anchovies,   Olives,   Pickles,   Spring Radishes. 3

GAME.

Canvas Back Duck.   16

SALADE.

Mayonaise of Chicken. 5   Mayonaise of Lobster. 5

ORNAMENTAL PASTRY.

Harp of Ireland,   Temple of Liberty,   Pillar of Flora.
Column of Fame,   Sultanes of Fruit,   Washington.

ENTREMETS SUCRES.

Meringues Imperiales,   Charlottes Modernes,
Champagne Jelly,   Blanc Mange.
Assorted Cakes.   Tutti Frutti Ice Cream.

Fruits and Dessert.

COFFEE.

ST. JAMES HOTEL,   NEW YORK.

Antonio Sivori, "Menu, St. James Hotel, New York" (St. Patrick's Day, 1870). Henry Voigt Collection, "The Life and Times of Antonio Sivori, Part 1, New York, 1869–1881," *The American Menu*, http://www.theamericanmenu.com/2014/02/the-life-and-times-of-antonio-sivori.html (accessed February 14, 2014).

that of chef. He worked in this capacity for the Astor House, then the Metropolitan and Westminster Hotels. After the Civil War, when genteel society in Manhattan became smitten with balls, he catered three of the most lustrous for over a decade: the Charity Ball, the Old Guard Ball, and the Purim Ball.

The managers of the Atchison, Topeka and the Santa Fe Railway attended these social occasions. Impressed with the skill with which Sivori deployed hot and cold food in spaces not equipped for cooking beyond a bank of chafing dishes, they hired him as purveyor for their railroad. Sivori's work on the railroads took him to remote corners of the United States. His sense of adventure led him to work in 1882 as steward at the Montezuma Hotel in Las Vegas, where he managed the early festivals at Hot Springs for which that desert town became famous. The Las Vegas papers praised his skill at decorating and illuminating festive spaces particularly.

Sivori's menu, despite its Franglish, was equally impressive:

HOT
Bouillon Royal, en tasse, Deviled Crabs
Chicken Croquettes, a la Careme
New York Oysters, Fricasseed

COLD
Filet of Beef, a la Macedoine
Boned Turkey, a la Jele
Lamb's Tongue, a la Ravigotte
Spring Chicken, au Cresson
Lobster Salad
Westphalia Ham
Mayonnaise of Chicken
Sandwich Varies

DESSERT
Vanilla Ice Cream, Lemon Water Ices
Charlotte Russe, Wine Jelly
Assorted Cakes, Maccaroni
Ladies Fingers, Pretty Kisses
Fruits, Desserts, Coffee

Only the efficiency of the Atchison, Topeka and Santa Fe Railway could have enabled crab to be on this menu. After Sivori left Las Vegas in January 1883, he served in a similar capacity at Planter's House in St. Louis.

Membership in the Freemasons gave Sivori an instant connection with masculine society in every locale in inhabited. In the later 1880s, Sivori returned to New York, residing at 252 East Sixty-First Street. At his death in 1893, his colleagues in the Italian Benevolent Society honored him for having been the oldest Italian in terms of residence in New York. He was working as a steward until weeks before his death.

✳   ✳   ✳

SOURCES: "Antonio Sivori" [obituary notice], *New York Herald* 84 (March 25, 1893): 3; "Breakfast Briefs," *Las Vegas Daily Gazette* (September 19, 1882): 4; "Personal," *Las Vegas Daily Gazette* (January 5, 1883): 4; "Oriental Summer Night Festival," *Las Vegas Daily Gazette* (August 15, 1882): 3; "Magnificent," *Las Vegas Daily Gazette* (August 16, 1882): 4; "Fifty-Fifth Regiment in Camp," Civil War Newspaper Clippings, New York State Military Museum: http://dmna.ny.gov /historic/reghist/civil/infantry/55thInf/55thInfCWN.htm; Henry Voigt, "The Life and Times of Antonio Sivori," 4 parts, *The American Menu*, http://www .theamericanmenu.com/2014/02/the-life-and-times-of-antonio-sivori.html.

James P. M. Stetson 1818–1874
New York

If the Delmonico brothers redefined the restaurant as an institution of fine dining in 1830s and '40s New York, James P. M. Stetson, steward of the Astor House, did the same for the hotel as a place to gormandize. The younger brother of manager Colonel Charles Stetson, James was brought in as an assistant when the hotel came under Charles's management in 1837, a year after opening. In 1860 James would succeed Charles as manager. His greatness as a hotelier was revealed in the 1840s when he oversaw the hotel dining rooms and kitchens during the period when the Astor House redefined deluxe banqueting. He set the menu and organized the greatest hotel banquet of the antebellum period in the United States, the 1841 feast honoring the Prince de Joinville, son of King Louis Philippe, France's final monarch.

James Stetson was in his mid-twenties when he ruled over the culinary department of the Astor House. Answering to him were three chefs: "a Frenchman for the side dishes, an Englishman for the roast meats, and an Italian for the patisseries." Stetson provisioned the kitchens and in the 1850s organized the Astor House farm and dairy, an agricultural complex that supplied the hotel with "eggs, butter, milk (the real genuine article), fowls, hams, meats, vegetables and fruits."

"Astor House, New York" (1840). Engraving. Photograph: Museum of the City of New York.

Stetson's innovations regarding service were as consequential as his schemes for provisioning. He dressed the wait staff in uniforms, drilled waiters to a military precision in terms of movements, made low-modulated speech the standard "waiter's voice" in American luxury restaurants, and institutionalized the late-morning wait staff meeting as a rite of daily instruction.

In the 1840s, hotel guests had three options in terms of dining. Most sat at the stated dining period and partook of the table d'hôte. A bill of fare sat before every seat on the long tables, offering "a great variety of choice meats, prepared with much art and skill." One could order a private dinner—the same dishes as appeared on the bill of fare, except cooked to order—at twice the price of the table d'hôte. Or one could repair to the oyster cellar beneath the restaurant and consume at one's leisure. Typically, four hundred or so guests gathered for the general dinner or supper seating. For every six persons at the table, there was a server to manage dishes. Dishes were laid at a great table, the servers, after assaying the wishes of the diners, took the joints to carving stations flanking the hall, secured cuts, and brought plates to the diners. Breakfast was a more casual affair, being served from eight in the morning until eleven. It was an ample meal with much protein. Tea was served an hour after dinner service ceased. Supper service—a collation of cold dishes—began at 9:00 p.m.

In 1857 Stetson transformed the dining arrangements at Astor House. The central courtyard bar was glassed over and fifty café-style tables installed. He instituted a scale of prix fixe options for the men who boarded there. Women, whether in groups or accompanied by gentlemen, dined in a separate ladies' dining saloon. Stetson did not wish to embrace à la carte dining entirely, so devised this "middle way" of food preparation.

During the 1840s and '50s, the Astor House dining room accommodated many of the great civic banquets held in New York. Political luminaries—Henry Clay, Daniel Webster—made it their New York headquarters. Of all the banquets held, none exceeded the splendor of that accorded the heir to the French throne in 1841. Indeed, of all meals served in the United States prior to the outbreak of the Civil War, only James W. Parkinson's wager feast in Philadelphia surpassed it in finesse, and only because of the rarity of the wines Parkinson served.

CARTE DU DINER

POTAGES
Potages a la printaniere   Potage a la Turque

POISSONS
Bass pique a la Chambord   Cabillaud a la Parisienne

RELEVES
Filets de boeuf a la financiere garui d'atelletes
Tete de veau en tortue a la modern, garnie d'atelettes
Dindon a la perigore garni d'atelettes
Gradin de filet de volailles garni d'atelettes
Jambon au champagne

PIECES FROIDES
Bastions ornees
Pain de volaille a la reine historie sur un socle
Chau-froide a la belle vue sur un socie
Chaudmier d'anguille au beurre de monpiller sur un socle

ENTREES
Ris de veau a la St. Cloud aux petits pois
Cotelettes de mouton sates a la jardinière
Epigram de cotelettes d'agneau a la Toulouse
Petit noix de veau pique sause tomate
Cervelle de veau bigareer aux truffes sauce supreme
Turbans de filet de volailles a la babilonne
Cotellets de pigeons aux truffes en croustade
Petit poulet pique en bordure de legume aux champignons

Filet de faisans farie a la d'artois sauce perigueux
Chartreuse de gibier a la printaniere sauce demi glace
Salmi de becasse en croustade a la parisienne
Pate chad d'ortolans desossee a la montabello
Timbale de macaroni a la milanaise
Casserolle de pommes de terre garnie de cailles a la reine
Bordure de gibier a la richlieu sauce champagne
Aspic de filet de bass au truffes
Pain de volaille a la reine
Mayonnaise de sole a la gelee

HORS D'OEUVRES
Salade d'anchois   Sardines
Olives   Cornichons

ROAST
Filet of beef   Turkey   Lamb
Poulet   Ducks   Geese

GIBIER
Canvas Back Ducks   Brandt
Cailles   Perdreaux
Poulet de guinee pique   Oie Sauvage

ENTREMETS DE LEGUMES
Macedoine de legume   Celeri au just
Petits pois a la financiere   Choux fleur au gratin
Epinards   Navet au sucre
Croute au champignons

PIECES MONTEES
Trophe unis surmonte par la deesse de la liberte
Casque romain sur un socie
Croquet bouche a la reine
Lyre en pastilage
Vase en nougat garni de petites meringues

ENTREMETS DE SUCRE
Madedoine de fruit au champagne
Charlotte Russe a la vanilla
Gelee au rhum

Charlotte parisienne a la fleur d'orange

Blancmanger au marasquin

Bavaroise au kirch wasser

Pudding de cabinet

Crème a la Chantilly

PIECES FONDS

Biscuit de savoie decore   Gateaux de cedrat glace

Nougat   Gateaux milles heulles

ENTREMETS DE PATISSIRIE

Meringe a l'Italienne   Croquet aux amandes

Marspam aux amandes   Chous a la crème

Petits bouchees a la reine   Doigt dame decore

Champignons   Couronne d'amandes

Genoise a la gelee de caen   Rissoles aux confitures

Feuillet glace   Tartletts de peaches

DESSERT

Café et Liqueur

When Stetson took over management of the hotel in 1860, the tides of fashion were leaving the old granite dowager in its wake. A wholesale refitting of the hotel in 1868 attempted to stem the drift into anachronism, but the space itself was so fraught with associations of the days of enmity and political struggle before the war that it could not, despite the expenditure of $292,000, alter public perceptions that it was somehow a relic. When Stetson staged a reopening banquet for the Astor House, the dishes were named in English with one exception, the bill of fare contained only a third as many dishes as the 1841 banquet, and not a single dish was unique to the Astor House's menu. The cuisine of the Astor House would not be revived until the arrival of chef Ferdinand Fere, who assumed control of the kitchen in the 1870s.

Stetson died of paralysis in the hotel on April 18, 1874.

❋   ❋   ❋

SOURCES: "A Voyage of Discovery in the Astor House," *Alexandria Gazette* (May 7, 1841): 2; "Magnificent Farewell Dinner at the Astor House to the Prince de Joinville, by the Corporation," *New York Weekly Herald* 6, no. 11 (December 4, 1841): 81; "A Frenchman's Idea of the Astor House," *New Orleans Times-Picayune* (September 14, 1843): 1; "Astor House Restaurant," *Albany Evening Journal*

(May 2, 1857): 2; "Hotels and the Hotel System in New York," *New York Herald*, no. 7575 (May 28, 1857): 4; "The Astor House Farm and Dairy," *Frank Leslie's Illustrated Newspaper* (July 10, 1858): 10; "The Astor House," *New York Commercial Advertiser* (June 12, 1868): 2; [Obituary notice,] *Lowell Daily Citizen* 24, no. 5593 (April 23, 1874), 2.

Charles Ignatius Pfaff 1819–1890
New York

The host of New York's Bohemia in the 1850s and '60s, Charles Pfaff turned a Manhattan rathskeller whose vaults extended under Broadway's sidewalks into a legendary space of shared gustatory pleasures, audacious wit, and lager beer. "He was a genial and kindly German, and a fairly good cook and caterer." His memorable qualities were his hospitable sympathy, his generosity, and his love of camaraderie. The profession of authorship was not greatly remunerative during the 1850s. Many an out-of-work or underemployed writer was allowed to order and receive meals for which he could not pay. Indeed Pfaff's open-handedness became so legendary that an occasion in 1869 when he took deadbeat Edward Lingham to court for not paying a 35-cent lunch tab made the pages of the *New York Herald*.

Critic Edmund Clarence Stedman honored Pfaff's unparalleled generosity to New York's literary artists. He noted that the hard work, the pace, the irregular hours, and intermittent income drove many Bohemians to bad habits and early deaths. The meals and homey sociability of Pfaff's operated as the one constant of comfort in their lives, something that could be counted upon, even when one was broke. And Pfaff himself—"big, broad, large featured, shaggy browed . . . with a heavy voice and kindliest gray eyes"—was the loving and indulgent father of what seemed at the time a cellar of lost boys. He did not judge the vocal atheists, the injured cynics, the manic humorists, or the "man lovers": Walt Whitman, Fitz-Greene Halleck, and their set. Pfaff gave the greatest consolations of all unsparingly: food and drink. Bohemian poet George Arnold hymned Pfaff's famous lager:

> Why
> Should I
> Weep, wail, or sigh?
> What if luck has passed me by?
> What if my hopes are dear,—

Frank Bellew, "The Bohemians at Pfaff's Cellar." Lithograph from *New York Illustrated News* (February 6, 1864): 3.

My pleasures fled?
　Have I not still
　My fill
　Of right good cheer,—
　Cigars and beer?

It was the beer that had first drawn the attention of the circle of writers. Pfaff's coffee, too, exerted a strong attraction to Henry Clapp, who was addicted to caffeine. In 1859 Clapp was so delighted at the beer Pfaff served him that he praised it lavishly among his circle and importuned them to come. When Pfaff agreed to erect a plain wood table seating thirty at the far end of the restaurant, Bohemia gathered. According to William Winter, a Bohemian who eventually became the great critic and historian of the American theater of the 1880s and '90s, the restaurant when first seen had a Spartan simplicity: "The place was roughly furnished, containing a few chairs and tables, a counter, a row of shelves, a clock and some barrels. The long table was erected on the east end of the restaurant. Then, nightly, a crew of newspapermen, poets, dramatists, critics, humorists, and painters descended the stairs and sought out the long table in the far vault. The portion under the sidewalk was dimly illuminated before nightfall by sunlight filtering through glass bricks imbedded in the pavement. The walls were field stone and plank. Sawdust covered the floor." The company took to calling itself "the Bohemians," borrowed from the title of Henri Murger's 1851 novel about the artistic underclass in Paris, *La Vie de Bohème* (*The Bohemians of the Latin Quarter*). The company was predominately male, but one woman, the "Queen of Bohemia," actress and novelist Ada Clare, regularly sat at the head of the table, the muse of the company. The "King of Bohemia," Henry Clapp (editor of the witty and short-lived *Saturday Press*), sat on a throne-seat under a crack in the sidewalk deep in the vault so that his pipe smoke could escape upward in that ill-ventilated space.

Pfaff's food by all accounts somewhat exceeded the norm for New York saloons. He intended it to be more hearty than fine (liver and bacon, German pancakes, grilled mutton chop, beefsteaks, oysters in season), and because of its low prices offered the greatest value in the city. His wines were good, his lager beer plentiful.

Pfaff was born in Baden, Germany, learning his trade there before coming to America in 1855. He immediately opened a beer cellar and coffeehouse near the corner of Broadway and Amity Street. Shortly before the Civil War, he relocated to 653 Broadway, the subterranean locale where Clapp first sipped Pfaff's beverages. The Bohemians met through the war, but mortality thinned their ranks, and marriage forced some onto more regular paths, so that by the armistice, old Bohemia had for the most part vanished. The postwar period saw an influx of playwrights and performers intermingled with the staff of the comic periodical *Vanity Fair*. Theatrical producer Augustin Daly became the reigning eminence. The cellar kept in business until about 1874, when Pfaff retired to the country. To the extent that a Bohemia remained in Manhattan, it had relocated the Taverne Alsacienne in the Grand Vatel on Greene Street, with its twin parrots spouting leftist slogans and its cheap French fare.

By 1876 boredom with greenery set Pfaff back on the road to Manhattan, where he opened Pfaff's New Restaurant on Twenty-Fourth Street. It enjoyed modest success, for Bohemia had moved to other venues and the neighborhood was not as thirsty and hungry as the corner of Bleecker and Broadway. In 1887 he left off work, having put away only a modest retirement fund. Pfaff died of acute gastritis on April 23, 1890.

※ ※ ※

SOURCES: A. L. Rawson, "A Bygone Bohemia," *Frank Leslie's Popular Monthly* 41, no. 1 (January 1896): 32; "A Restaurant 'Beat,' " *New York Herald* 34, no. 78 (March 19, 1869): 5; Edmund Clarence Stedman, "Bohemian Days at Pfaff's," *New York Herald* 116 (April 26, 1890): 8; George Arnold, "Beer," in *The Poems of George Arnold*, ed. William Winter (Boston: Houghton, Mifflin and Company, 1889), 139; "The Bohemians and Their Host," *New York Herald* 34, no.

79 (March 20, 1869): 6; Rufus Rockwell Wilson, *New York: Old & New*, 2 vols. (Philadelphia: J. B. Lippincott, 1902), 2:141; William Winter, *Old Friends* (New York: Mofat, Yard, and Company, 1914), 63–67; "Pfaff, Charles Ignatius," *Appleton's Annual Cyclopedia and Register of Important Events* (New York: Appleton's, 1890), 660; Arthur Bartlett Maurice, "The New York of the Novelists," *The Bookman* 42, no. 3 (November 1915): 301; Dink Freer, "The Bookman's Mail," *The Bookman* 64, no. 1 (September 1926): 117; "The Vault at Pfaff's," http://digital.lib.lehigh.edu/pfaffs/p39/.

Henry Jakes 99 1820–1881
Baltimore

The great cities of the eastern seaboard each boasted at least one multigenerational dynasty of African American caterers. In Baltimore, three generations of the Jakes family served the public taste for the entire nineteenth century. From the 1850s until his death in 1881, Henry Jakes of the second generation was the city's foremost event cook.

> Jakes was not only in active demand for entertainments on public and private occasions in Baltimore, but he was frequently called to Washington to serve Senators, Congressmen, Ministers and others. . . . He also went as far as New York, at the summons of the Racket Club and others, to minister especially in that part of the entertainment where the terrapin and other Maryland luxuries figures as the pride of the feast and of the epicurean host.

Jakes began his career attached to his father's business, operating out of Jakes's Barber Shop, 2 Bank Lane, near Barnum's Hotel in Baltimore. The Barber Shop, being a social outpost of news in the city, provided a convenient public face for the catering business, the back rooms being used as storage for flatware, cutlery, and stemware. In the mid-1850s, Jakes established an independent caterer's office at 121 St. Paul's Street. He retained the Barber Shop and schooled his daughters to become hairdressers and wig makers. He announced himself "Superintendent of Balls, Dinner and Evening Parties." Besides the usual equipment for staging a banquet, Jakes provided waiters and cooks. In the Civil War period, we know that the chief assistant cook was Benjamin Franklin Simms, and his headwaiters, Jerry Mahammett and William Jackson. Jakes's business grew steady until an accident on a city railway car put him out of commission for the latter part of 1859. On March 31, 1860, he notified the public that he was "enabled to resume his duties again as a public caterer."

From the late 1850s on, Jakes conducted a concurrent business brokering terrapin, oysters, and game, shipping the Chesapeake's delicacies to restaurants in Chicago and cities and towns in California.

Henry's engagement in religious, civic, and political life befitted a man of property. His wife, Mary Jakes, belonged to the Holy Family Society, his daughters attended the St. Frances School for Colored Girls, and his son and heir, Henry Jakes III, attended the St. Frances Male School. Henry himself entered fully into the Roman Catholic faith on his deathbed. His civic engagements can be registered by the events to which he donated his services. Significant among these was Baltimore's Southern Relief Fair of 1866. His promotion of civil rights can be determined by his subscription as Baltimore's principal attester on the masthead of *Frederick Douglass's Newspaper*.

Baltimore dining centered upon a half-dozen dishes: stewed terrapin, canvasback duck, ham, crab, oysters, and fritters. These were the dishes for which Jakes grew famous. His assistant, Benjamin Franklin Simms, provided the ice creams, confections, and pastries. At times Henry employed his brother Frederick as a partner. A third brother suffered mental problems, becoming a notorious street character in Baltimore. Frank Blackwell Mayer's painting of *Crazy Jakes* dated from 1853, long after Henry Jakes had established himself as the city's foremost caterer.

When he died of heart disease in 1881, Jakes left an estate worth roughly $12,000; yet at various times in his life, he held property assessed as much as $18,910. He was among the wealthiest African Americans in Baltimore during the 1800s.

※　※　※

SOURCES: "Henry Jakes, Barber," *Baltimore Sun* 15, no. 62 (July 27, 1844): 2; "The Southern Relief Fair," *Baltimore Sun* 55, no. 124 (April 12, 1866): 1; "Henry Jakes, Caterer," *Baltimore Sun* 46, no. 116 (March 31, 1860): 2; "Ein befannter Farbiger gestorben," *Der Deutsche Correspondent*, June 24, 1881, 1; [Jakes estate,] *Baltimore Sun* 89, no. 56 (July 21, 1880): 4; "Death of Henry Jakes, the Caterer," *Baltimore Sun* 89, no. 33 (June 23, 1881): 4; Diane Batts Murrow, *Persons of Color and Religious at the Same Time* (Chapel Hill: University of North Carolina Press, 2002), 239.

Frozine Madrid 1820–1874
Mobile, AL

Mobile's greatest Creole cook and restaurateur in the wake of the Civil War, Frozine Madrid opened her namesake restaurant near the corner of Royal and Government Streets in December 1867. Declaring it a "No. 1 Eating House," Madrid lived on the premises and so promised "meals at all hours." Her specialties were fresh fish (particularly pompano in season), crabs, oysters, and game during the winter months. The restaurant occupied both 47 and 49 Government Street in the Lewis Buildings and supplied lodging as well as board.

A *creole de couleur*, Madam Madrid first cooked at her husband Manuel's boardinghouse on 11 North Jackson in Mobile, until she engineered the move into the Lewis Buildings during the Christmas season of 1867. Upon opening, the restaurant became known among epicures throughout the Gulf Coast. The *New Orleans Times-Picayune* took note: "The lovers of good eating, at moderate prices, are respectfully informed that Frozine, the well known cateress, opened her new Restaurant on the northwest corner of Government and Commerce streets, up stairs, on the 21st instant." Manuel ran the front of house and poured the wines.

A freeborn native of Alabama, Frozine, a mulatto, was raised in a Francophone household. As a girl, her family moved to Pointe Coupee in Louisiana, and there she learned to cook in the best Creole household style. As a grown woman, she was kidnapped, along with seven other female *creoles de couleur*, and forcibly transported to Mobile by a pair of white scallywags, Mabley and Long, who intended to sell them as slaves. The would-be slavers were captured and the eight women freed. Frozine chose to stay in Mobile. Shortly thereafter, she met and married Manuel Madrid and gave birth to a daughter, Pauline.

While her virtuosity at the cookstove found its most exquisite expression in the game stews, oyster dishes, and court-bouillons that lay at the heart of the Creole tradition, she gained a particular local fame for her coffee and caramel custards, the envy of Alabama housewives. She would not divulge her recipes, so the editors of the *Mobile Register* cribbed some boilerplate versions from recent cookbooks, printing them in their January 24, 1860, issue.

Manuel Madrid died in late 1869. Madam Frozine kept the restaurant operating an additional three years before illness forced her to close Mobile's signature French-Creole eating house in late 1873. She did not live through the subsequent winter. She was fifty-three years old when she died.

※　※　※

SOURCES: "Extensive Kidnapping," *New Orleans Times-Picayune* (March 1, 1853): 6; "Frozine Madrid's Restaurant," *Mobile Register* 1, no. 103 (May 28, 1868): 2; "Board and Lodging," *Mobile Register* 2, no. 119 (June 17, 1869): 2; "Frozine's Restaurant, Mobile," *New Orleans Times-Picayune* (December 8, 1867): 8; *United States Federal Census, Mobile, Alabama, 1870.*

François-Winceslas Pelletier 1820–188?
Philadelphia

The nationally famous chef of James Sanderson's Franklin House in the 1840s, Canadian-born François-Winceslas Pelletier alone rivaled James W. Parkinson and Joseph Head as masters of French haute cuisine in antebellum Philadelphia. Just as Parkinson in later life built a fortune by selling a brand of ice cream, Pelletier built a fortune in selling wholesale and retail wine.

Few chefs became celebrities in antebellum America. Pelletier was one. Canadian records suggest he was born in Quebec in 1820; at his naturalization declaration in 1857, he listed France as his place of nativity. He first appeared in Philadelphia in 1842, when James Sanderson inaugurated his hotel on Chestnut Street, the Franklin House, with a banquet for Philadelphia's publishing industry. Pelletier's distinctive way with cuisine won the approbation of visitors from New Orleans who indicated that Franklin House "is in the style of our southern *restaurateurs.*" He remained in the kitchens of the Franklin House after Sanderson sold the hotel to D. K. Minor in 1846. Minor added a ladies' ordinary to the dining saloon and retained Pelletier's friend and former employer, James Sanderson, as maître d'hôtel. When a New York editor published a criticism of the cuisine at the Franklin House early in 1847, complaining of his inability to get a piece of beefsteak, Minor's colleagues in the Philadelphia press riposted, "By referring to the bill of fare of the day, when the editor dined there, there were no beef steaks on the table! There were venison steaks, however, then in the delicacy of their early season, and our New York friend had eaten one without a chaffing dish and the accompaniments of currant jelly and the castor cruets!"

Pelletier had a knack of piggybacking his own creativity on popular enthusiasms. The Benjamin Harrison and John Tyler ticket inspired a good deal of passion among American expansionists. When Pelletier created a meaty "Tippecanoe Broth" in 1841, as homage to Harrison, it received wide play in American papers. The recipe indicates just how elaborate a dish could be in an eastern restaurant at the beginning of the fourth decade of the nineteenth century. The opening sentence also suggests the scale of public event dining:

John Rubens Smith, *Southwest View of Sanderson's Franklin House, Chestnut Street, Philadelphia* (ca. 1844). Watercolor. John Rubens Smith Collection. Photograph: Library of Congress, Prints and Photographs Division (LC-USZC4-3672).

TIPPECANOE BROTH

To make this Soup for from 50 to 150 persons, you proceed in the following manner: Cover the bottom of your sauce-pan or pot (to contain about five gallons) with 4 thin slices of larding pork, 4 large onions sliced, 4 large carrots, also sliced, and two large slice of Ham, say one pound; then add 2 knuckles of Veal, 2 fine chickens (trussed as for boiling), and 1 pint of water. Set your pot on a hot fire, and throw in a bunch of parsley and thyme half of each, and a handful of salt, 4 whole cloves, and 6 grains of allspice. Let it remain on the fire until it gives forth an aromatic smell, which will happen in about 20 minutes; then fill the pot to within two inches of the top with water, and boil it 4 hours, taking care that it does not boil over. In the meanwhile to make the Force meat Balls, or "Quenelles de Veau," as the French term them—you take one pound of Clear Veal, (that is perfectly free from fat, skin, or any stingy substance) and having trimmed it, scrape it to a thick pule, with a dull knife. Take also a half pound of larding Pork, and scrape it in like and half a nutmeg, grated. Beat them well with a pestal until they acquire the pieces into the shape of musket balls, which you mush poach in this manner: Put about 4 quarts of the broth from your soup pot into a frying pan, and whilst it is boiling throw in your balls which you have previously rolled in flour; when they are sufficiently done they will rise to the top. Take them out then, and throw them into cold water, in which they will sink, and return the broth to the sauce pan. These balls must be added to our soup above five minutes before serving. You must also make the Potato Balls or "Quenelles de pommes de terre," whilst your Broth is boiling. To do this, you roast a dozen large mealy potatoes, and when they are done, skim them and take from them all impurities—add to them the yolks of 3 eggs, quarter of a nutmeg grated, and 8 tablespoonfuls of cream; mash them well and pass them through a fine sieve, then sprinkle with flour and rolling out, cut into small pieces and moulded into balls. Ten minutes before serving throw them into your soup. After your broth has boiled four hours, put into another sauce pan, a pound of fresh butter and 12 tablespoonfuls of corn meal, mix them well together over the fire, stirring them continually for five minutes to prevent scorching; when you have thoroughly amalgamated them, add a bottle of Champaigne Cider (or Champaigne Wine if it is handier), and pass your broth through a sieve into this sauce pan which should be large enough to hold all the broth, and let the whole boil over a slow fire, for an hour and a half stirring it frequently to prevent any lumps being formed. At the proper time add your Potatoe Balls, then your Veal Balls, and finally, just as you are about to serve, add another bottle of Champaigne Wine or Cider, and you will then have a soup fit to serve "Old Tip," himself.

In 1848 Pelletier severed his connection to Franklin House and opened his own hotel and restaurant, Pelletier House, at 421 Walnut Street below Fifth. This became a favorite resort of newly arrived Europeans. The ground floor housed a bar and two oyster boxes. In 1851 Alfred Taylor, whom Pelletier hired as second bartender, robbed him, and the papers celebrated the young man's capture, although the $40 worth of pinched goods disappeared permanently. On November 21, 1857, Pelletier advertised the restaurant for sale, including the building, furnishings, and the contents of his wine cellar. The sale went sour when L. E. Goldsmith—New York cigar dealer but, unbeknownst to Pelletier, a forger and confidence man—involved the caterer in a confidence scheme. Elisha McCarty eventually secured the property, leasing it as a variety store to R. E. Agnew in 1858. McCarty's death in 1860 caused the house—still known as Pelletier House—to be sold by the administrator of the estate on March 28, 1860.

In 1857, some months before advertising his restaurant for sale, Pelletier went before the US Court in Philadelphia and announced his intention to naturalize. He listed his place of origin as France at this juncture. For much of the period from 1858 to 1859, he appears not to have been in residence in Philadelphia, but resurfaced in January 1861, residing in the St. Louis Hotel. He and his wife, Jane Lavinia, took up residence at 138 South Fourth Street. During the Civil War, he became a director of the Philadelphia Park Association.

Pelletier's postwar business was entirely concerned with the retail sale of wines and liquors. He Americanized his name to William.

❋   ❋   ❋

SOURCES: "Tippecanoe Broth," *Alexandria Gazette* (March 9, 1841): 2; "Opening of the Franklin House" *New York Commercial Advertiser* 45 (June 21, 1842): 2; "Franklin House, Philadelphia," *New Orleans Times-Picayune* (August 28, 1842): 2; "Sanderson's Franklin House," *Philadelphia North American* 8, no. 2256 (June 27, 1846): 3; "Sanderson's Franklin House," *Philadelphia Ledger* (October 25, 1846); "Not a Man of Taste," *Philadelphia North America* 8, no. 2441 (February 2, 1847): 2; "A Daring Theft," *Philadelphia Ledger* 32, no. 54 (November 27, 1851): 2; "Restaurant for Sale," *Philadelphia Public Ledger* 44, no. 37 (November 2, 1857): 4; "Local Affairs," *Philadelphia Ledger* 44, no. 51 (November 18, 1857): 1; "Philadelphia Park Association," *Philadelphia Age* (February 3, 1864): 2.

Louis Schultz 1820–1894
Paris; New York; Cincinnati, OH; Saratoga, NY

Few nineteenth-century chefs boasted the credentials of Louis Schultz, an Alsatian who presided over the kitchens of the greatest restaurants in Paris and New York, and in the most famous spas of Europe and North America. His training took place in Paris, where he eventually rose to become chef of the Maison Dorée in its heyday. He moved to Phaelzer Hof in Mannheim, Germany. From 1845 through 1849, he spent the summers preparing spa food at Baden-Baden. In 1849 Lorenzo Delmonico contracted for his services at his famous restaurant in Manhattan.

Schultz's stay at Manhattan's temple of fine dining lasted a single season. Seeking the congenial world of German cuisine, Schultz moved to Cincinnati to serve as the inaugural chef of the Burnet House. Opened in 1850, the Burnet House was the premier hotel in the city for a generation. Its annual income in the early 1850s was $227,000. A Cleveland visitor in September 1850 was granted a glimpse of Schultz's realm:

> Every thing is on a mammoth scale. In the grocery department we found goods enough for a respectable retail store—a clerk in attendance to fill orders for the laundry, the cook room and other departments of the house. A large bakery in full

A. Frobiger, "Burnet House, Cincinnati, Ohio" (1850). Lithograph. Onken's Lithography, Cincinnati. Photograph: Library of Congress, Prints and Photographs Division (LC-USZC4-7368).

blast, confectionary establishment, meat room, wine and liquor cellar with barrels and bottles enough to stock every store in Cleveland. . . . They heat all of their water, principal rooms, and cook most of their victuals by steam.

The ladies' salon and the main dining had a seating capacity of 1,200.

In 1863, when restaurateur Balthazar Roth determined to create a restaurant that rivaled Delmonico's in Cincinnati, he resolved to poach the one chef in the city who had actually worked at Delmonico's—Louis Schultz. When the St. Nicholas opened in 1863, Schultz directed its kitchen. He worked for Roth for four years before the proprietor's insistence upon repressing public notice of Schultz's accomplishments became irksome. In August 1867, Schultz opened a restaurant under his own name on 151 West Fourth Street. That restaurant remained open for over a decade. Sometime in the late 1870s, he returned East and joined a number of chef's social clubs, including the Hoboken Turtle Club. His final culinary station was the chef of the Planter's Hotel in Saratoga, New York. There, in the employ of the mercurial hotelier Girardi, he distinguished himself from the constellation of star cooks in the spa by cooking anything an epicure might wish to order.

In 1890 police in Elizabeth, New Jersey, took Schultz into custody after a night wandering the streets and lodged him in the Morris Plains Insane Asylum. He died on February 3, 1894. Obituaries noted he was responsible for popularizing lager beer in the United States during his time in Cincinnati. He was not the first to produce it but was instrumental in establishing its cachet.

✳ ✳ ✳

SOURCES: "Editorial Correspondence," *Cleveland Plain Dealer* (December 20, 185?): 2; "An Opening," *Cincinnati Daily Gazette* (August 29, 1867): 2; "The Hoboken Turtle Club," *Truth* (September 30, 1881): 1; "Palate Tickers: A Few of the Men Who Cater to the Epicure," *St. Louis Republic* (April 21, 1889): 4–26; 1853 Menu, Ladies' Ordinary, Burnet House, in Henry Voigt, *The American Menu*, http://www.theamericanmenu.com/2011/07/enduring-traditions.html.

Pierre Trapet 1820?–1880?
San Francisco; Portland, OR; Salt Lake City, UT; Helena, MT; Pioche, NV; Prescott, AZ

Gold lured many people to California in 1849 and the early 1850s—prospectors first, and then those who would service the needs and desires of the ones who "struck it rich." Parisian Pierre Trapet was one of those chefs convinced that wealthy prospectors needed haute cuisine. A trained French cook, Trapet operated on the faith that possessing a fat bank account instantly transformed one's taste for the better. He first set up as a hotelier in San Francisco in 1853, running a hotel with a name that played upon the locality's mineral obsession, L'Hotel de la Cote d'Or, on Pacific Street. He served brunches and dinners with varied seasonal offerings and much seafood; the charge: 75 cents a dinner.

On December 1, 1857, Trapet opened Richelieu's Hotel and Restaurant on the corner of Clay and Commercial Streets in San Francisco. He declared that his house would be conducted in a "new style, with all the comfort and *bon gout* wanted by the society of California." The idea that San Francisco needed fine dining, however, occurred to others throughout the 1850s, and the city exploded with restaurants and small hotels. Competition beat down many a restaurateur in San Francisco. If one was under-capitalized, located on an unfashionable street, disconnected from the best market suppliers, or lacking any distinction in fare, price, or stylishness, one's career in the city could be as brief as a season. Trapet was a first-class French chef. But the city in the 1850s boasted other talented practitioners in that line. A branch of Delmonico's had opened in 1850. Chef Vives—first of the Lafayette Restaurant, later at the Sir John Franklin Restaurant and Coffeehouse on Long Wharf—built a following during the 1850s with his cuisine. Gavreau and Boutinon of Hewlett's Exchange Restaurant on the corner of Battery and Jackson Streets had popularized the ladies' luncheon. Chevalier and Soudry maintained the Café de Paris on Spofford Street and performed catering duties for neighborhood households. Trapet staked his fortune on the quality of his fare and a novel arrangement of meals. He would eliminate supper, push back the dinner hour to five, and serve breakfast, a midday lunch, and dinner. Trapet provided the prototype for an arrangement of meals that would enjoy increasing popularity in urban centers during the 1860s and '70s. Like other restaurateurs in the city, he catered private parties as well.

By July 1, 1858, Trapet's debt running the hotel forced him to seek the protection of the insolvency law. He listed his liabilities as $4,317. It took six months to secure backing for his next venture, the Sansome Coffee Saloon and Restaurant at 112 Sansome Street. It offered "Breakfast, Lunch and Dinner as per bill of fare." The success of this venture emboldened Trapet to resurrect the Richelieu, this time in restaurant form on the corner of California and Battery Streets. During its initial months of operation in the winter of 1861, the Richelieu secured enough traffic to prompt Trapet to a wholesale renovation of the building's second floor into a suite of private salons that he opened on July 18. The fare on the second floor cost $1 and was more deluxe than that in the public dining room on the first floor, which was offered at 75 cents per diner with wine. Trapet managed to conduct this restaurant until autumn of 1862, when the disruption of business caused by the Civil War led to a downturn, forcing him to shutter his doors. He then reasoned that there must be a city on the West Coast more insulated from the vicissitudes of commerce caused by the war. In late 1862, he determined that Portland, Oregon, needed French cuisine.

Because restaurants were and are particularly sensitive to downturns in the general business climate, Trapet thought to diversify his business, opening a grocery-eatery at 97 First Street in Portland. By late 1863, the number of groceries and restaurants had doubled in the city, and B. Gutekunst's Delmonico's had monopolized the high-end trade. Trapet was forced to look elsewhere for opportunity. He headed to Salt Lake City, the Mormon metropolis, to supply the hunger of the Latter-Day Saints for French fare. At 8 North Second Street, Trapet's Parisian restaurant supplied a novel form of cuisine, divested of wine and coffee. His experiment ended in late 1867.

In 1868, seeking the next western center of mineral wealth, Trapet ventured to Helena, Montana, buying out E. M. Hoytt's National Restaurant on Main

Street. As ever, Trapet advertised that he operated a "first-class restaurant" and invited the residents to "come and judge for yourselves." For a year, the National remained a novelty before declining business set Trapet looking elsewhere. His explorations of western mining country sent him southward, to Pioche, Nevada (then Arizona territory), where he set up a saloon and eatery. This enterprise was destroyed by the Pioche fire of May 8, 1872. Trapet suffered uninsured losses of $2,000. After the destruction of Pioche, he trekked farther southward.

Trapet's final establishment was the National Restaurant and Chop House in Prescott, Arizona, which became the territorial capital in 1877. Ten years in western territories had adapted his cuisine to western tastes. The National featured pies and advertised the quality of his beefsteaks and pork. His advertisements in Arizona newspapers ceased in 1879.

Trapet had two sons, whom he trained during his San Francisco years to be chefs. John P. Trapet and François Trapet remained in the city and worked as chefs, having received a thorough culinary education under their father. They both enjoyed significant careers. When and under what circumstance Pierre Trapet died cannot be determined. But his career as an itinerant evangelist of fine dining throughout the West, bringing Parisian technique and San Franciscan style to mining towns, was part of the civilizing process in the boomtown West.

※ ※ ※

SOURCES: "Richelieu's Hotel and Restaurant," *San Francisco Bulletin* 5, no. 46 (December 1, 1857): 4; "Richelieu's Restaurant," *San Francisco Daily Globe* 3, no. 153 (December 4, 1857): 2; "Insolvency," *San Francisco Bulletin* 6, no. 72 (July 1, 1858): 3; "Sansome Coffee Saloon & Restaurant," *San Francisco Bulletin* 9, no. 89 (January 23, 1860): 2; "Richelieu Restaurant," *San Francisco Bulletin* 12, no. 87 (July 18, 1861): 4; "French Store," *Portland Oregonian* (March 28, 1863): 1; *Portland, Oregon City Directories*, 1863, 1864 (65; 10–12); *Salt Lake City Directory* (1867), 116; "National Restaurant," *Helena Weekly Herald* 2, no. 25 (May 14, 1868): 6; "Losses by the Pioche Fire," *Weekly Journal Miner* 9, no. 21 (May 25, 1872), 1; "The National," *Salt River Herald* (January 23, 1879): 1.

James Wormley 1820–1884
Washington, DC

Two African American caterers laid out the two paths to success in Washington, DC, after the Civil War. George Downing, the steward of the US Congress,

Henry Ulke, *James Wormley* (ca. 1865). Oil. Photograph: Collections of the Historical Society of Washington, DC.

used political influence, his skill as a communicator, and his outspoken political pronouncements to secure investment and custom. James Wormley—notoriously reticent about politics (aside from the simple attestation that he was a Republican)—made his expertise as a cook, his good taste as a caterer, and his suavity as a hotelier the means of earning fame and fortune. Both died wealthy, respected, and, indeed, revered.

Wormley's paternity has the aura of southern legend:

> His father was owned by a rich gentleman who resided at Charlotte, Va., named Cleo. According to one of the current stories, the daughter of that gentleman, said to be a very handsome and accomplished girl, became infatuated with her father's slave, ran away with him, concealed him in this city [Washington, DC] for a year and a day, when he received his freedom, and she married him. The senior Wormley was himself light in color, while the wife was of the purest Caucasian types.

They came to Washington, DC, in 1814. James Wormley was the fourth of the six children the couple had, born in 1820.

A native of Washington, DC, James Wormley was born free. From his youth, he reaped the benefits of two natural endowments: his good looks and his intelligence. Livery stable keeper Allison Nailor liked the young James so much, he lent him a carriage and a pair of horses, giving him time to earn the cost of purchase so he could set up as an independent hack driver. By dispatching and picking up guests at Washington's hotels, he glimpsed a world where African

American waiters, stewards, and caterers earned greater remuneration in more gracious settings. He determined to become a provider of hospitality.

He signed on as steward of a US naval vessel captained by Allen McLane. There he learned the art of catering. When, after substantial experience at sea, he decided to leave the service, he signed on as steward of the Metropolitan Club in Washington. This provided him the steady income needed to underwrite his project of opening a restaurant-hotel in August 1858. His restaurant, located on 314 I Street, was informally known as "the Clubhouse," since it was the resort of the Washington Club and became during the Civil War a favorite resort of the Union Army general staff. "Fresh Ortolan and Reed Birds are received every afternoon and served up in the best style by James Wormley." In 1860 Wormley began manufacturing ice cream at his dining room.

When Reverdy Johnson was appointed minister to the United Kingdom to negotiate the Johnson-Clarendon treaty in 1868, he contracted with Wormley to serve as his steward. While in England, Wormley introduced British epicures to the pleasures of terrapin à la Maryland. One benefit of the sojourn was the opportunity to visit Paris and experience French cuisine firsthand. The experience inspired him to elevate his cooking. Upon his return to the nation's capital in the autumn of 1868, he secured a row of houses—Nos. 310, 314, 318, and 320 on I Street—and opened "Wormley's Celebrated Dining Rooms: Having returned from Paris, is now prepared to furnish Dinner Parties, Suppers, &c, in the finest style. He purchased when in Paris a superb Dinner Set, which cannot be equaled in this country."

The several houses making up the row were outfitted as residences or temporary suites for visiting diplomats. The arrangement was not efficient. Wormley was determined to construct a purpose-built hotel. In 1869 he set in motion the financial arrangements, including a partnership with Congressman Samuel Hooper of Massachusetts, that enabled the erection in 1871 of the Wormley Hotel. Situated at 1500 H Street on the corner of Fifteenth and H Streets, the Wormley Hotel was the finest in the city at the time of its building and remained a favorite place of accommodation for visiting diplomats and overseas delegations. Opened in June, it offered lunches for transient guests and a late-night supper for theatergoers. One conspicuous feature of the décor was a large oil painting of Senator Charles Sumner that adorned the overmantel of the ground-floor dining parlor. Wormley would give the portrait to the Commonwealth of Massachusetts in spring of 1884. Another Washington relic dominated the office: the crimson velvet chair used by the Speaker of the House of Representatives from 1823 to 1868. Wormley purchased it for $96 at an 1873 auction.

Wormley declined to put himself forward as an activist for civil rights or associate with any of the many clubs, committees, or movements that sprang up among African Americans during the Reconstruction. He dismissed efforts at enlistment in the cause as being "bad for business," and his strict attention to commercial and professional concerns was the hallmark of his character. His single-mindedness was interpreted by many as aloofness. Wormley provoked suspicion among some members of his race, and the number of his white friends and associates prompted accusations of him "turning his back on Negroes." Yet Wormley was the only black man present at the deathbeds of the two greatest white champions of civil rights of the era—Abraham Lincoln and Charles Sumner.

One reason that Wormley stood at the deathbeds of Lincoln and Sumner (and President James Garfield's, for that matter) was that his famous "beef tea" was the sole nutrition ingested by the politicians as they approached their demise. This was not the standard bouillon of French cuisine. Rather, Wormley broiled a porterhouse steak, "and while the meat was yet steaming," put it into a heated iron receptacle. "A crank was then turned which brought hundreds of pounds of pressure on the steaming steak causing every particle of its juice to stream forth. A little seasoning and the tea was ready." This would be the last food tasted by Lincoln, Sumner, and Garfield.

A chronic sufferer of kidney stones, Wormley died in Boston, where he had undergone surgery for the freeing of a urinary obstruction.

❄ ❄ ❄

SOURCES: "James Wormley," *Boston Journal* 51, no. 16938 (October 21, 1884): 4; "Famous Caterer Dead," *Philadelphia Inquirer* 111 (October 20, 1884): 1; "Death of James Wormley," *Macon Telegraph*, no. 10854 (October 21, 1884): 1; "A Romance," *Cleveland Gazette* (August 24, 1889): 2; "Wormley's Beef Tea," *Canton Repository* (October 13, 1885): 6; "The Illness of James Wormley," *Washington Evening Star* (October 18, 1884): 1; "Charles Sumner: The Portrait Given to the State," *Boston Journal* 60, no. 16785 (April 25, 1884): 1; "Auction Sale at the Capitol," *Washington Evening Star* (April 29, 1873): 1; "Wormley's Celebrated Dining Rooms," *Washington Evening Star* (January 11, 1869): 2; "Colored Men of Washington," *Weekly Louisianan* (May 18, 1871): 1; "Visitors to Washington Will Find at Wormley's," *Washington Critic-Record* 3, no. 864 (June 3, 1871), 2; "A Talk about Terrapin," *Washington Evening Star* (April 26, 1884): 2.

Pierre Blot 1821–1874
New York

In the 1860s, the refugee and French man of letters Pierre Blot put himself forward as the public oracle of culinary matters in the United States. A proponent of cooking by rule, and a self-appointed crusader against the evils of dyspepsia, Blot imported knowledge of French cuisine into an American scene dominated by moral and nutritional debate about consumption. He projected himself into the institutions of American culinary authority—the cooking school, the athenaeum, the cookbook, and the magazine in the 1860s. He was the first *man* to run a cooking school in the United States. He was the first European-trained cook to lecture on the athenaeum circuit. He was the first European chef who sought to engage an American food readership composed largely of literate housewives. And he was the second European culinary celebrity resident in the United States to publish a cookbook.

Blot saw America as an opportunity for culinary reform in the name of "the science of cookery."

> No country in the world presents a greater abundance and variety of good than America, and in no country are the means of obtaining good materials so equally distributed. If the reform which has commenced in the great cities spreads to the country towns and villages, America will not only conquer its great enemy—dyspepsia—but it will also grow rich out of the savings which scientific cookery affords. Too much meat is eaten in America. The Anglo-Saxon race loves muscle, and therefore eats most the food that produces muscles. . . . When I see men who never or very seldom use their muscles live entirely on steaks and roast beef, which is exactly the opposite of what nature demands, I cannot help pitying them and wishing that they would listen to nature.

In truth, the science Blot championed had little relation to contemporary scientific work—the nutritional chemistry of his contemporary Justus von Liebig, or the fermentation chemistry of Louis Pasteur. Rather, Blot was a home economist with an aesthetics of cookery not too different than the physical culture devotees of New England, Sylvester Graham and T. W. Hutchinson.

Blot's preachments concerning meat—he wished it cooked well done and consumed less frequently—reversed the recommendations of Alexis Soyer, the oracle of French cuisine in England, who championed the rare roast beef of Britain and rare meats generally.

Blot arrived in the United States in 1857. The circumstances surrounding his immigration are unclear. He "began his career as a teacher of French in one of our up-town schools. But as an 'amateur gastronomer' as he loves to call himself, so soon as he had thoroughly acquired the English language, he stopped teaching French and began to teach us how to live as well as learn." His success as a lecturer depended on several things: a respectable display of learning in his presentations, with allusions to ancient Greek and Roman practices when characterizing modern modes; an insistence on the possibility that one could enjoy food, even French cuisine, without expending great amounts of money; a repeated celebration of science as an ideal of food preparation, a recourse to schematic surveys of subject matter, and a harping on nutrition; a rejection of vegetarianism and Dr. Sylvester Graham's sumptuary philosophy as extremist; and eloquent abuse of the popular demons that haunted the imaginations of American eaters—dyspepsia, food adulteration, meat spoilage, and uncleanliness. Most importantly, he conveyed to his largely female audience a sense that they were worthy to receive gastronomic information. His success as a lecturer led to success as a periodical writer, first in *Galaxy* magazine immediately after the Civil War, then *Harper's Bazaar*.

Blot's periodical essays have much more to do with domestic consumption and food preparation than the profession of cooking. He surveys produce and meat markets to suggest how a housewife might best select items for home use (a recapitulation of material found in Thomas De Voe's 1866 *The Market Assistant*). He lays out a multi-installment plan for learning to be a home cook. He offers menus for supper parties and a "Gastronomic Almanac" of seasonal menus. Finally, he presents ideas on how to use "broken victuals" (i.e., leftovers). As a culinary man of letters, Blot had his moments of insight. In a trenchant piece published in the May 1868 issue of *Galaxy*, "Native Wines and Native Game," Blot argued that the various wines made in the United States from native grapes should be judged by different aesthetic criteria than those of Europe. He also excoriated the unsanitary practices of hunters dressing game for shipment to eastern markets. Both matters needed addressing. His meditation on the debilities of American cookery also had its points. While it depended too much on the legacies of Puritan plainness in eating (what did Southerners make of this recourse to Puritan origins of American eating?), it hit the mark when Blot observed, "Nature produces here hundreds of different kinds of food, and yet, in many parts of the country, people live on but about half a dozen kinds." The besetting sin of American consumption was routine feeding: the serial ingestion of the same few dishes using the same few ingredients. One task of the restaurant experience throughout American history has been to inject novelty and variety into diners' relation to food.

In 1868 Blot's authority in the world of print had been established sufficiently to float a book. *The Handbook of Practical Cookery for Ladies and Professional Cooks* aspired to an authority that bridged the very different needs of two distinct constituencies. While certain of the principles espoused—the minimization of waste in food preparation, for instance—spoke to both audiences, the recipes themselves were couched in such a way as to favor the household cook. Among professionals, only the modest boardinghouse cook would have found his recipes useful.

Within the professional community, some grumbled that Blot's authority on matters culinary had little power, since he did not cook for the public. In late 1869, Blot determined to answer these criticisms by setting up the experimental Brooklyn Central Kitchen. From a small house on Hamilton Street, Blot organized a cooking office "supplying and delivering warm cooked food to families in any part of the city, in a better manner and at cheaper rates than they could prepare similar (by no means precisely the same) dishes in their own homes." The economic idea driving the plan was twofold: buy cheaper in bulk, cook more efficiently in quantity. He floated the idea in the New York metropolitan newspapers, was deluged with enrollees, and began putting the plan into operation in January 1870. Blot's kitchen ran from 7:00 a.m. to 10:00 p.m. filling orders. He invited reporters into the kitchens so that descriptions of Blot as practical chef could be published and quash the criticisms of the restaurant chefs. What the visits revealed, however, was that Blot acted more in the capacity of a steward. Manning the two ranges and boiler at the headquarters was Jean. "Jean, by-the-by, is the chief cook, and has been the faithful attendant of the Professor for more than five years. He accompanied him through all his courses of lectures from this city to Chicago, and is one of the best of the very best cooks in this country."

Blot's experiment eventually failed. The difficulty of transportation in inclement weather, the vicissitudes of demand, and the price volatility of the marketplace were manageable; the financial depression of 1873 was not. In the obituary notice that appeared in the pages of *Harper's Bazaar*, the editor noted that "four months before his death his reason gave way under the pressure of overwork—a sad ending for a useful career." Blot appeared on the American scene at a time when there was a public hunger for a culinary oracle who could speak to the changes taking place in the equipment of the kitchen (the coming of the cookstove), the understanding of nutrition (the advancement of Justus von Liebig's nutritional chemistry), the chemical management of baking (the rise of the quick breads), the growing awareness of infection and poisoning, and the education of women. Blot put himself forward as that oracle. After his death, one memorialist observed, "Pierre Blot, the Frenchman who visited this country as the apostle of a purer and better cookery, is dead. He was a clever and well-educated man in certain respects, but the various enterprises which he undertook here were nearly all failures. Whether this was due to the apostle himself, to his doctrine, or to his hearers, we need not decide. There is no doubt, however, that he undertook a gigantic task."

※　※　※

SOURCES: Pierre Blot, "The Art of Dining, I," *Galaxy* (May 15, 1866): 120–22; Pierre Blot, "The Art of Dining, II," *Galaxy* (June 1, 1866): 225–27; Pierre Blot, "The Art of Dining, III," *Galaxy* (June 15, 1866): 320–22; Pierre Blot, "The Art of Dining, IV," *Galaxy* (July 1, 1866): 460–62; Pierre Blot, "American Cookery," *Galaxy* 4, no. 6 (October 1867): 748–50; Pierre Blot, "Ancient and Modern Cookery," *Galaxy* 4, no. 7 (November 1867): 865; Pierre Blot, "Native Wines and Native Game," *Galaxy* (May 1868): 631–32; "The Brooklyn Central Kitchen," *New York Evening Post* 69 (January 8, 1870): 4; "All about Blot," *New York Evening Post* 69 (February 25, 1870): 1; "Personal," *Harper's Bazaar* 7, no. 38 (September 19, 1874): 603; "Pierre Blot, Cook," *New York Daily Graphic* (August 27, 1874): 6.

John Dabney 1821–1900
Richmond, VA; Old Sweet Springs, WV

John Dabney presided over Virginia's great political barbeques for the last half of the nineteenth century, taught the young Prince of Wales to crave mint juleps in 1859, catered to Virginia's mountain spas, and fed two generations of Richmond epicures with terrapin and turkey. Yet he became legendary throughout the South as "the honorable Negro," the man who fulfilled his prewar agreement with his owner to pay for his and his wife's manumission after the defeat of the Confederacy obviated any need to do so. His keeping his pledge became a cherished tale of the remnants of the old plantocracy, and the story's many elaborate mutations as the century drew to its close were an indicator of the potency and effervescence of white Virginia's fantasy life.

Born as a slave in Hanover County, Virginia, on the DeJarnette plantation, John was the son of London Dabney, a carriage driver on a neighboring plantation, and Elizabeth, Cora Williamson DeJarnette's house servant. Young Dabney did not receive schooling and worked for William Williamson, a planter, horse-breeder, and hotelier. As a teenager, Dabney rode Williamson's racers as a jockey and worked as a waiter in Hanover Junction and Gordonsville. His mannerly demeanor, competence, and expanding waistline determined that the saloon rather than the stables would be Dabney's working place. Williamson brought him to Richmond to tend bar at the Ballard House, his hotel. While tending bar, Dabney sought instruction from Jim Cook, the hotel's chef, and mastered cooking for the public.

John Reekie, "Ballard House, Richmond, Virginia" (1865). Stereograph. Photograph: Library of Congress, Civil War Glass Negative Collection (LC-DIG-cwpb-00477).

Dabney's first fame attached to his abilities as a mixologist, more specifically, as a mixer of mint juleps. While Kentucky now claims the cocktail as its own-most beverage, it is well to remember it learned the drink in its perfection from John Dabney. Colonel Burt Clark, who won fame playing the quintessential Kentucky colonel in the stage hit *Old Kentucky*, avowed that the only fine one may be had in Richmond from the hands of John Dabney. "It's not only delicious and exhilarating, but a work of chemical art, unique as it is beautiful. . . . Each year, at special times, Dabney, of Virginia, constructs one of his marvels, and I never miss the opportunity of being present."

In the wake of the Civil War, Dabney performed the deed that would make him a byword of honor in Virginia. He applied to Cora DeJarnette to purchase freedom for him and his wife, and she agreed, stipulating the amount. Dabney had worked enough to obtain his wife's liberty and was $200 short of securing his own when the war ended. Instead of availing himself of the general liberation, he kept his contract. "Despite the hard times, John discharged the obligation in full. Such conduct evinces a regard for honor which would ennoble any man, and John will stand (and deservedly) higher the ever in the estimation of every Richmond gentleman." This newspaper oracle proved true. From 1866 until his death, John Dabney received the first call for any association dinner, ball, or wedding in the region bounded by Richmond, Alexandria, and Norfolk.

The story of Dabney's fulfillment of his contract quickly began accreting details. An 1868 elaboration revealed that the total amount of the contract was $2,000, that half was paid in depreciating Confederate currency, and that his postwar final payments amounted to $600 in greenbacks. By the 1890s, the amount owed at the cessation of the war had swelled to $1,000, and the depreciation of currency had prompted his owner to request a cessation of payments until the currency situation stabilized. In the final versions of the legend, Cora DeJarnette returned payment by mail, prompting Dabney to return to Hanover and make the payment in person. Her straitened circumstances forced her to accept. Thomas Nelson Page supplied his own polish of Dabney's legend as the exemplary "Old Time Negro" in the pages of *Scribner's Magazine*, versifying the tale as "Little Jack."

After securing freedom and establishing his reputation for honor, Dabney obtained a bank loan permitting his purchase of a space at 1414 East Broad Street in Richmond. Dabney and wife, Elizabeth, set up a restaurant and catering office. As years passed, the restaurant became decidedly ancillary to the operation. He advertised himself as a caterer: "Suppers, Dinners, Weddings, or Single Dishes, for public or private entertainments furnished in full or part, with tableware, silver, and all pertaining to complete and first-class service."

Dabney's catered meals featured a numbered of staple dishes. An 1873 meeting of Richmond Railroad stockholders had the following note appended that reveals his usual stock in trade: "After the adjournment the stockholders proceeded to an adjoining room, and were regaled with a sumptuous repast provided by the celebrated caterer, John Dabney, in his best style. The viands embraced splendid mutton, roast turkey, terrapin stew, fried oysters, etc. Dabney is unquestionably one of the best and most artistic purveyors in this country." Memoirs of the period further note that Dabney boned his turkey before roasting, so that it could be sliced without hindrance at the carving station.

In June of every year, John and Elizabeth trekked to Old Sweet Springs, West Virginia, where he spent the summer months mixing juleps and preparing chafing dish versions of his banquet fare. (In the antebellum period, he went to Montgomery Springs.) Making the julep at the spas became a ritual endeavor: employ a "sterling silver goblet fourteen inches high" domed with shaved ice, sprays of mint, and "decorated with fruits and flowers, in magnificent style." The beverage was sipped through solid silver straws. In winter, when chilly juleps didn't suit, Dabney served apple toddies.

Sue Mason Maury Halsey described the ingredients for the julep that she was presented one morning at Old Sweet Springs: "Crushed ice, as much as you can pack in and sugar, mint bruised, and put in with the ice, then your good whiskey, and the top surmounted by more mint, a strawberry, a cherry, a slice of pineapple, or as John expressed it. 'Any other little fixings you like.' On mine was a pink rose." Dabney died at his home in Richmond on June 7, 1900, at the age of seventy-nine. Obituaries noted that he "concocted more mint juleps than any man in the country."

SOURCES: "City Items," *Richmond Whig* 36, no. 41 (May 24, 1859): 3; "Honorable," *Alexandria Gazette* (September 26, 1866): 1; [John Dabney,] *Galveston Flake's Bulletin* 4, no. 23 (July 17 1868): 2; "Meetings of Railroad Companies," *Richmond Whig* (December 19, 1873): 4; "John Dabney, Caterer," *Richmond Dispatch* (December 4, 1892): 10; "How Dabney Bought Freedom," *Charleston News and Courier* (October 28, 1893): 9; [Mint julep,] *Lincoln Courier* (September 19, 1896): 3; "Theatrical Gossip," *Evening Star* (January 16, 1897): 11; "Famous Julep Mixer Dead," *Baltimore Sun* 27, no. 20 (June 8, 1900): 7; "Mr. Thomas Nelson Page's Conclusion," *Richmond Planet* (December 31, 1904): 4; "John Dabney's Mint Julep," in *Famous Old Receipts Used a Hundred Years and More in the Kitchens of the North and South*, ed. Jacqueline Harrison Smith (Philadelphia: John C. Winston, 1908), 179–80.

August Louis Sieghortner 1821–1890
Düsseldorf; New York

A New York restaurateur for over forty years, August L. Sieghortner learned the whys and wherefores of cuisine from the front of the house. Born in Furth, Bavaria, he commenced his career as a waiter at the Breiten Bacherhof in Düsseldorf. During the political disturbances of 1847, he emigrated to America, taking a position as waiter at Delmonico's (Beaver Street). Four years of service thoroughly acquainted him with the highest standards of cuisine, service, and décor. He opened his first restaurant, Sieghortner House, at 58 Pearl Street in Manhattan, a venture so successful that he would twice have to move to more commodious quarters on Pearl Street (Nos. 71 and 72) and, eventually, like Delmonico's, opened another branch to satisfy demand (No. 32 Pearl Street).

The money ($200,000) that Sieghortner made from his restaurants tempted him with the prospects of immense wealth as a capitalist. He entered a partnership with Edward Weissenborn to establish the American Lead Pencil Company at Hudson City. Over the course of eight years, both partnership and venture soured. He sued his partner, but the New Jersey Court of Errors and Appeals in December 1869 ruled against Sieghortner, finding him liable for the venture's obligations. He lost his fortune, his restaurants, and his interest in manufacturing. The case became a fixture in handbooks of partnership law.

The year 1870 found him creating a new restaurant. He knew the business so well that his new Sieghortner House at 9 Lafayette Place eclipsed the success of his pre–Civil War situations. The postwar period was given to much innovation in style and manners. Sieghortner opted for a kind of Knickerbocker classicism in his arrangements, eschewing fashionable cosmopolitanism. This retro New York aura became further pronounced when he moved the restaurant into the old William B. Astor Mansion at 32 Lafayette Place during the centennial year. The Authors Club adopted it as their home. The king of the lobby, Sam Ward, regularly brought his political friends to partake of the beefsteaks, the marble steps, the heavy mahogany doors, and the Moorish revival décor. Presidents Chester A. Arthur and Grover Cleveland numbered among those friends.

The cuisine? English actor Henry Irving, who came to love the place during his tours of the United States, supplies a glimpse: "Shrewsberry oysters, gumbo soup, cutlets, canvas-back ducks, a soufflé, Stilton cheese, an ice, a liqueur, a dish of fruit and a bottle of hock." On another occasion, Irving discovered terrapin and the Saratoga potato chip. Sieghortner also included classic German dishes among his offerings and was regarded as the finest house for Bavarian fare in New York prior to the opening of Lüchow's.

In his final decade, the short, open-faced, and portly restaurateur became "Pappa Sieghortner." He personally served longtime customers, carving their ducks and pouring their port. In 1889, when physical debility prevented his travel to Lafayette Place, he opened a restaurant at his residence at 535 Fifth Avenue. After his death from pneumonia in 1890, Papa's son A. L. Sieghortner took over the business, maintaining the restaurant into the twentieth century.

✳   ✳   ✳

SOURCES: "August L. Sieghortner," *New York Tribune* (December 15, 1890): 7; "Mortuary Notice," *New York Herald*, no. 349 (December 15, 1890): 1; "Court of Errors and Appeals," *New York Herald* 34, no. 342 (December 8, 1869): 11; Joseph Hatton, *Henry Irving's Impressions of America* (Boston: James R. Osgood, 1884), 78–80, 169–74; " 'Pappa' Sieghortner Is Dead," *New York Times* (December 15, 1890); "The Lounger," *The Critic* (December 20, 1890): 324–25; George Cary Eggleston, *Recollections of a Varied Life* (New York: Henry Holt, 1910), 274.

Gustave Feraud 1822–1899?
Boston; New York

The chef of Manhattan's Fifth Avenue Hotel for thirty-five years, Gustave Feraud witnessed the maturation of fine dining in New York over the last half of the nineteenth century. He came to the United States in 1847 after a thorough training in French cuisine, to preside as chef at the newly opened Revere House hotel in Bowdoin Square in Boston. After provoking the sumptuary Puritans of Boston for a dozen years, Gustave Feraud moved to New York in 1859 to be installed as head of the kitchen in the newly built Fifth Avenue Hotel, then the most luxurious in the city. There he made the hand-decorated menu one of the defining emblems of haute cuisine and delighted two generations of Manhattan epicures.

His initial triumphs in America were dinners that he served at the Revere House in Boston, including the famous repast prepared when the remains of John Quincy Adams were brought back to Boston in 1848 and memorialized in a civic feast. Daniel Webster and Martin Van Buren attended that historic feast. The ancient Harrison Gray Otis spoke. The papers were so agitated by the fact that intoxicating beverages were served that no particular notice appeared of the menu, though "at the festive board were displayed highly seasoned French dishes and quantities of that objectionable article of food known as pate de foie gras." At least three dishes from the table have been identified from other informants: oyster patties, vol-au-vents, and chicken with truffles. In his old age, Feraud recalled it as the finest meal he had ever created. Fortunately, the bills of fare of a number of his Revere House dinners survive: an 1852 banquet for the Honorable Thomas Baring, an 1854 banquet for the directors of the Boston Theater, and one for the Boston and Sandwich Glass Company held in February 1853. Daniel Webster savored his dinners and made the dining room his particular haunt. Jenny Lind praised his cuisine on her 1850 tour.

If a portion of the Boston public fretted over the pleasurable indulgences that Feraud enabled at the Revere House, Manhattanites suffered few moral qualms. Paran Stevens, the presiding genius of the Revere House, was the moving spirit in the creation of the Fifth Avenue Hotel. He, no doubt, engineered the transfer of Feraud from Boston to New York. Feraud would superintend cuisine at the Fifth Avenue Hotel from 1859 to 1894.

A force in New York's culinary circles, Feraud assisted in the organization of the Société Culinaire Philanthropique during the late 1860s and served as its president from 1870 through 1872. He excelled at the creation of the *pièces montées*—the spectacle food exhibits—that the Société's balls made famous. A rendering of gigantic chessmen made of edible substances in 1877 was particularly well remembered. He was also an active participant in l'Union universelle de l'Art culinaire, a body greatly concerned with kitchen sanitation and hygiene. They were also the group that endorsed the exhibition of gas cooking ranges staged by Ferdinand Fere at Tammany Hall in 1887.

Feraud had a particular love of vegetables, and among his extensive repertoire of regular preparations, several dishes became justly celebrated.

STUFFED EGG PLANT À LA PROVENÇALE

Take two egg plants, cut them in halves, loosen the insides from the shells without removing them, boil five minutes, and put the pieces in cold water to cool, then remove the insides, press out the water, and chop fine with a little chicken, adding one onion fried in sweet oil, a little bread soaked in milk, three eggs, a little chopped parsley and garlic, and season to taste. Put the stuffing back into the shells, and brush a little beaten egg on top. Sprinkle on some grated parmesan cheese and bread crumbs; add a little sweet oil, and bake one hour.

Over the course of his cooking career, Feraud grew to appreciate certain dimensions of American taste and several ingredients. His appreciation of the American breakfast in particular can be seen in a winter menu he published in 1892:

Hominy

Broiled Shad

Tenderloin Steak

Fried Potatoes

Fried Oysters

Rum Omelet

Coffee

This might be had, sans rum omelet, at a southern hotel brunch in the twenty-first century. The rum omelet—a plain omelet sprinkled with sugar, lashed with rum, and flambéed—was the one gesture at Gallic flare in the meal. He expressed no great love, however, of other staples of the American breakfast—sausages and pastries.

In 1894 Feraud retired. The next year, he and his wife, Hannah, moved to a house on 126th Street where he lived out the remainder of his life.

❋   ❋   ❋

SOURCES: "Drunken Riot," *Emancipator and Republican* 12, no. 48 (March 22, 1848): 2; "Congressional Degeneracy," *Boston Evening Transcript* 19, no. 5411 (March 15, 1848): 2; "The Fifth Avenue Hotel," *Alexandria Gazette* (August 25, 1859): 2; "Annual Ball of the Société Culinaire Philanthropique," *Frank Leslie's Illustrated Newspaper* (February 26, 1870): 7; "Le Bal des Cuisiniers," *Courrier des Etats-Unis* 33 (February 8, 1872): 2; "The Refinement of Dining," *New York Daily Graphic* (April 15, 1876): 9; "Balls Last Evening," *New York Herald* (February 7, 1877): 10; "Stuffed Egg Plant à la Provençale," in *Société Culinaire Philanthropique de New York to Their Patrons and Friends* (New York: Société Culinaire

Philanthropique, 1882), 37; "Winter Breakfasts," *New York Herald*, no. 304 (October 30, 1892): 31; "Ferdinand A. Feraud," *New York Herald-Tribune* (September 6, 1895): 7.

James H. W. Huckins 1823–1884
Boston

Down-easter James H. W. Huckins, the first chef de cuisine of the famous Parker House on School Street in Boston, served from its opening in 1855 until 1865. After his stint at the Parker House, he became the first major manufacturer of canned soups in the United States.

Harvey Parker hired Huckins to manage the two dining rooms in the hotel, the Ladies' Restaurant (with midday hours and a private entrance on School Street) and the general dining room, serving à la carte at all hours of the day. During his tenure, numbers of the Parker House traditions took shape: the weekly meetings of Longfellow and Boston's literary luminaries of the Saturday Night Club, the Harvard Commencement banquets, the political conclaves, particularly among the abolitionist and republican parties, and the annual feasts of the Massachusetts State representatives.

That Huckins had mastered the techniques of banquet cuisine is apparent from a menu he formed for General Benjamin Butler in 1863.

SOUP

Green turtle; a la Julienne

FISH

Boiled cusk, cream sauce; baked pickerel, claret sauce

BOILED

Leg of Mutton, with capers; turkey, oyster sauce; capons and pork,
celery sauce; beef tongue

ROAST

Sirloin of beef; mongrel goose; turkey, giblet sauce; saddle of mutton, jelly sauce

ENTREES

Sweet Breads, larded, with peas; fillet of beef, with mushrooms;
lamb cutlets, a la Marachel; curry of chicken, with rice; venison cutlets,

Joseph L. Bates, "Huckins's Restaurant, Horticultural Building, Boston and Vicinity" (1865). Stereograph. Photograph: Boston Public Library, Photographs Collection.

jelly sauce; vol au vent of oysters; stewed terrapin; macaroni, fritters, croquettes, kidneys

COLD DISHES

Galatine of turkey, au foie gras; truffled duck, in jelly; capon au truffe; pate de foie d'oie au gelee; mayonnaise of chicken; salmon marine

GAME

Canvas back ducks, black ducks, widgeon, grouse, partridge, larded quail

PASTRY

Souffle a la vanilla, apple Charlottes, Charlotte russe, wine jellies, fruit pies, cream meringue

Ornaments—Dessert

Almeira grapes, pears, oranges, apples, almonds, walnuts, raisins, shellbarks, figs, olives, ginger, coffee, ice cream; Roman punch

The Parker House's avoidance of a French menu does not deflect a reader from noting the French ordering of dishes and the parade of sauces, the hallmark of Parisian cuisine.

In June 1865, after ten years of serving as Harvey Parker's chef de cuisine, Huckins left the Parker House to establish the James H. W. Huckins's Restaurant at the Horticultural Building, No. 43 Bromfield Street in Boston. He announced his independent status thusly:

It was in this office that Huckins experimented with formulating a savory soup that could be canned. Later in 1865, Huckins applied for a patent for tomato soup, the recipe using a beef stock, butter, mashed tomatoes, flour, brown sugar, pepper, and four root vegetables. It was quickly approved, and Huckins began canning in earnest in 1867. His first important customer was Z. M. P. King's King Palace restaurant on the corner of Fifteenth and Vermont Avenues in Washington, DC.

Huckins's soup presented another face of his cookery. The advertisements lauded the elegance and nutrition of his soups and salad dressings. Other chefs had tried their hands at mass sales of prepared foods. James W. Parkinson of Philadelphia had established his family's ice creams as a regional brand. William Vollmer sold Hecker's Farina. But it was the peculiarly New England sumptuary commercialism that Sylvester Graham had set into motion around Graham flour—the insistent linking of nutrition and quality—that provided Huckins with his model. By 1868 he affixed the Parker House name to his products for the gourmands and the insistence on nutrition for the diet cultists. His canned terrapin soup gestured to the tastes of the bon ton. Located in Boston, Huckins spent the remainder of his culinary career as a successful manufacturer of canned goods. His motto—"Huckins! Huckins!"—meant soup well before "Mmm Mmm Good" became planted in the American consciousness. Campbell followed four years after Huckins in canning soups.

The roster of flavors at the time of Huckins's death in 1884 were tomato, ox tail, pea, beef, vermicelli, mock turtle, okra or gumbo, green turtle, julienne, chicken, terrapin, macaroni, consommé, soup and bouilli, and mulligatawny. The brand survived into the twentieth century.

SOURCES: "Parker House, Boston," *Boston Daily Atlas* (October 8, 1855): 3; "John Galpin, What Do You Think of This," *New Orleans Delta* 18, no. 82 (February 7, 1863): 1; [Announcement,] *Boston Evening Transcript* (June 30, 1865): 3; "Huckins Parker House Soups, and Salad Dressing," *Boston Traveler* (May 11, 1869): 3; [Obituary notice,] *Boston Journal* (January 7, 1884): 1; "James H. W. Huckins's Restaurant," *Boston Herald* (June 28, 1865): 2.

William Vollmer 1823–1871
Philadelphia

When he died on September 4, 1871, of sudden illness at his residence in Philadelphia, William Vollmer finished a life of odd successes. A German-trained culinarian, he was embraced as a brother by the French chefs who dominated fine dining in the eastern United States. Indeed, the members of l'Union Française in New York were invited to assist in his funeral. As the first resident professional chef to publish a cookbook in the United States, he instructed American housewives on English and German cuisine, rather than American, despite calling his volume *The United States Cook Book*. It went through several editions. While housewives and plain cooks were the intended audience for his cookbook, some of the recipes would require the staff and equipment of a restaurant or club kitchen to execute. Vollmer won renown as a steward and cook at the Union Club in Philadelphia, but he made his fortune as a wholesale liquor seller in the city during the Civil War.

A native of Bavaria, Vollmer came to the United States in 1848, after being trained in hotel cookery in Württemberg, Germany. He may have left because of his political convictions. He married Swiss-born Anna Barbara Lindenmayer the next year on July 28 at St. Michael's and Zion Church. He spoke little English in his first years as a resident in Pennsylvania. In 1855 he became steward and chef of the Union Club, a social organization with pro-Northern political biases that would be a precursor organization to the more famous political action organization, the Union League. The Union League mobilized in the midst of the Civil War.

Vollmer found the culture of Pennsylvania curious. The Pennsylvania Dutch were somewhat displaced from current Germanic culture, while the Anglo-American population had grown insulated from the German elements in the city and state. He first served the German population of the city, composing and publishing in 1856 a German-language cookbook instructing housewives how

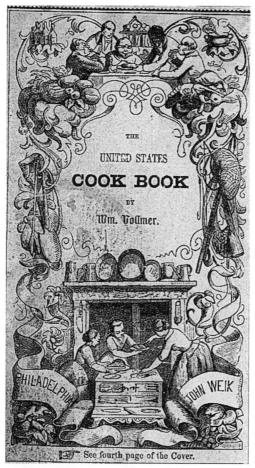

THE

UNITED STATES

COOK BOOK

BY

Wm. Vollmer.

PHILADELPHIA

JOHN WEIK

See fourth page of the Cover.

William Vollmer, *The United States Cook Book* (Philadelphia: John Weik, 1856), title page.

to prepare modern German fare using American ingredients, such as Hecker's Farina. (The Hecker Mills at 204 Cherry Street in New York was a pioneering processor of cracked wheat, cream of wheat, and buckwheat groats.)

In 1860 an English-language version of this volume issued from publisher John Weik in Philadelphia. This is the version now cited in culinary histories. Vollmer's cookbook had several novel features for a production printed in America: an extraordinarily rich collection of cold fruit soups, a chocolate soup, an entire section of recipes based on milk and flour (arising from Justus von Liebig's theories of invalid cooking and health), including a number of methods for making noodles from scratch and the largest early collection of dumpling recipes found in print before the Civil War. Quick-bread chemistry; the use of cheap sugar to preserve fruits by making preserves, jams, and jellies; and a presumption about fine temperature control enabled by cookstoves evince Vollmer's familiarity with the transatlantic state of the art in cookery.

During the Civil War, Vollmer apparently enlisted, then discovered that he lacked the stomach for violence. In August 1863, the Provost Marshal's Office in Lancaster, Pennsylvania, listed him among approximately eighty deserters from B Company of the Nineteenth Pennsylvania Cavalry. He was not in Lancaster; rather, he had set himself up in Philadelphia as a merchant of wine and liquor. Like Henri Mouquin in New York and François Lagroue in Baltimore, he reoriented his business to the brokering of high-end beverages. His wine and liquor business enjoyed a prime location at 141 South Front Street. He enjoyed great success until felled by a sudden fever in 1871 at his home at 1126 Wallace Street in Philadelphia. His brother Henry Vollmer took over the business.

✳ ✳ ✳

SOURCES: District of New York, City of New York, *Passenger List 1820–1957* (June 18, 1856), 199; William Vollmer, *The United States Cook Book* (Philadelphia: John Weik, 1856); *United States Federal Census, 1860*, Philadelphia, 8th Ward, 209; "Notice," *Lancaster Inquirer* (August 27, 1863): 3. *McElroy's Business Directory, Philadelphia, 1863*, 905; *McElroy's Philadelphia City Directory, 1866*, 899; MS Records, St. Michael's and Zion Church, Philadelphia, 2914; [Obituary notice,] *Philadelphia Public Ledger* (October 30, 1871): 2.

Augustin François Anezin 1824–1881
Marseilles; Boston; Philadelphia

Boston, despite its Puritan heritage, enjoyed a lineage of French chefs that spanned the nineteenth century. At every juncture, there was one generally regarded as preeminent, the master of refined cookery. Augustin Anezin was that master in the 1860s and '70s.

Born in Marseilles, France, hotelier Paran Stevens brought Anezin to Boston in 1849 to work with chef Gustave Feraud of the Revere House, one of the three temples of the city's cuisine in the mid-nineteenth century. He took over as chef when Feraud left in 1859 to run Stevens's Fifth Avenue Hotel in New York. Anezin remained in charge of Revere House until May 12, 1862, when he partnered with John Horan in operating a restaurant occupying the rooms at 3 and 4 Court Square that once accommodated Harvey Parker's Tremont Coffeehouse. The partnership lasted a little over a year. On July 1, 1863, Anezin departed for Philadelphia to become chef of the Continental Hotel. Horan assumed complete control of the restaurant.

John P. Soule, "Parker House, Boston, Massachusetts" (ca. 1880). Stereograph ("Boston and Vicinity #553"). Photograph: Boston Public Library, Photographs Collection.

Anezin headed the kitchens of the Continental from summer of 1863 through the end of the Civil War. As the grandest hotel in the city, it hosted an extraordinary series of civic banquets over which the chef presided: President Lincoln's visit in June 1864; the December 1864 banquet by the Union League for Captain Winslow, hero of the USS *Kearsarge*; and the "heroes" banquet of June 11, 1865, at which General Meade presided.

In late 1865, Harvey D. Parker hired Anezin away to head the kitchen of the Parker House in Boston. Then a culinary institution in the city, the Parker House had undergone a period of turmoil in the kitchen after the departure of James Huckins and then John Michels. Anezin imposed a reign of competence and injected variety into the Parker House menu. Over the course of his fourteen-year rule over the kitchens, Anezin expanded the offerings on the bill of fare until in 1879 when 300 items appeared. Some of Anezin's creations enjoyed wide popularity, particularly Chicken Salad, à la Parker House and Parker House Sausages (a breakfast staple).

In 1871 a reporter from the *Boston Traveler* ventured into the Parker House kitchens to view Anezin's realm. Here is his account:

Nine male cooks are employed, under the direction of Mr. Anezin, with six girls for assistants, whose duty it is to prepare the food, but none but men have a hand in the cooking. In the kitchen are four ranges: one of extra large size for roasting; one for broiling; one devoted exclusively to frying; and a range of copper kettles for soups, three in number, and with a capacity of one hundred gallons each.

The kitchen is a pattern of neatness—a model of cleanliness. . . . Passing from the kitchen we enter the Larder, over which an epicure cannot fail of going into ecstasies, for here are huge joints, sirloins, and barons of beef; legs, shoulders, and saddles of mutton; veal as delicate and as white as snow; fresh pork of the finest quality, and fed with an especial reference to the wants of the establishment; there is beef in steaks, mutton in chops, veal in cutlets; here are ten royal-looking deer, fresh from Aroostook county in Maine; there are great refrigerators, freighted with turkeys, chickens, geese and domestic ducks; here are the best sugar-cured hams attainable; and there are two freezing chests, which will keep their contents in perfect condition throughout the entire season, with a capacity of a thousand pounds each, filled to the brim with game birds—with partridge and quail, with widgeon and teal, with prairie-check and plover, with woodcock and English pheasants, with black, mongrel, mallard, red-head, and canvas-back ducks; while close by there are bears from Maine and Canada, and antelope from the Rocky Mountains.

As long as Harvey D. Parker asserted control of the Parker House, Anezin remained superintending the hotel's culinary department. When Parker retired from business in 1880, Anezin cast aside his toque. He died of apoplexy in the following year.

※　※　※

SOURCES: "Anezin & Horan," *Boston Traveler* (June 11, 1862): 4; "Dissolution of Co-partnership," *Boston Daily Advertiser* 102, no. 15258 (July 11, 1863): 3; "The President in Philadelphia," *Philadelphia Inquirer* (June 17, 1864): 1; "Banquet to the Brave," *Philadelphia Inquirer* (June 12, 1865): 3; "A Glance at the Parker House," *Boston Traveler* (January 11, 1871): 1; [Obituary notice,] *Salem Register* (June 13, 1881): 2.

George M. Ardoene 1824–1886
Providence, RI

Italian confectioner and caterer George Ardoene (born Giovanni) came to Providence, Rhode Island, in 1847. Shortly after the cessation of the Civil War, he emerged as the finest caterer in the city and the confectioner against whose creations all others were measured. Ardoene's confectionery at 221 Westminster Street supplied fancy cakes, jellies, preserves, and pastries throughout the 1860s. The building also served as a catering office where he prepared the usual cold dishes found on reception tables—boned turkeys, chicken salad, and lobster salad. In the winter of 1865, he enlarged his store, building a dining parlor and rebuilding the bakery. He rebranded the store the Ardoene Cake Confectionery and Ice Cream Saloon.

In the 1860s, most of Providence's eating houses followed the increasingly antiquated practice of having the dining room below street level. The Metropolitan Oyster Rooms, the Merchant's Saloon (under the Merchants Bank), and Hopkins Eat House fed diners in dim cellars. Ardoene's brightly lit dining room at the back of 221 Westminster seemed in contrast a place both cheerful and modern. Women felt comfortable lunching there. Their patronage may have been responsible for the expansion of his catering business during 1866. By autumn, he no longer listed the confections he vended in his advertisements, but announced that he could furnish the necessaries and ornamentals for "Parties, Weddings, Balls, Dinners, Suppers, Fairs, Festivals, and all Social Gatherings." Ardoene amplified his catering business by actively participating in social organizations, including Providence's St. John's Lodge No. 1 of Freemasons.

By 1867 Ardoene had become the sine qua non of civic celebration in the city. Whether it was the Good Will Fire Company's reception for regional firefighters, or the forty-ninth anniversary of Odd Fellowship in America, or the dedication of John Kendrick's new harness factory, Ardoene spread the tables with a splendid array of cold dishes, from prepared meats to ice creams. Business was so great that he purchased the other old wooden buildings on Westminster, many of them eighteenth-century structures, and razed them. In partnership with B. F. Gilmore, Ardoene built four contiguous brick buildings spanning the block. By Christmastime, the new building was ready for the candy and confection trade. On January 18, 1869, the new, luxurious dining room opened. If the old hall had made rivals appear dowdy, the new salon made them appear perversely antiquarian. A reporter visited on December 19, shortly after the confectionery shop portion of the business had opened. This is what he saw: "His windows show some splendid specimens of ornamental work, and round on his counters and shelves, are the specimens of his handiwork, which, in quality is unexceptionable, comparing favorably with the noted establishments elsewhere in the country." In an age paranoid about adulterations, the reporter assured the readers of Providence that "using pure materials, he is enabled to present the public with articles not deleterious, but free from all unwholesome substances." On January 18, Ardoene announced, "The saloon is arranged in the best style, where will be served cooked to order all dishes usually called for at a first-class establishment. The bill of fare will be complete in its variety of Cold Meats, Oysters, Pastry, Confections, Cakes, Creams, Ices, &c, &c."

For five years the papers rang with accolades about Ardoene's banquets, then in 1874 a notice appeared indicating that Ardoene had retired from the confectionery business, turning his store over to L. A. Tillinghast. Ardoene wished to devote his efforts to event catering. Finding that he needed a restaurant kitchen and bakery to support his efforts, he affiliated in November 1876 with the Café St. George at 157 Westminster Street run by Charles Cole and Ardoene's son, John. By 1880 Ardoene's fame as a caterer had become so great that he catered events in Boston. A menu taken from an event he catered toward the end of his active career conveys the character of his large-scale banquets.

BILL OF FARE

Salmon, with Mayonnaise   Boned Turkey, jellied
Pickled Oysters
Chicken Patties   Oyster Patties
Champagne Ham
Leg of Mutton, Caper Sauce
Chicken Salad   Lobster Salad
French Rolls
English Pickles   Olives
Plain and Fancy Cake
Charlotte Russe
Vanilla   Coffee   Lemon   Chocolate
Strawberry Ice Cream
Biscuit Glace   Roman Punch
Orange, Lemon Ice
Coffee   Tea   Lemonade
Bouillon

The meal contained both hot dishes and cold. There was nothing unexpected or innovative about the menu, but the invariable commendation of Ardoene's work over his life was the quality of his preparations. He was Providence's most reliable practitioner of first-class event food. It was not unusual for caterers who emerged out of the confectionery field to stress execution over creativity.

Sometime in 1885, Ardoene had an intimation that his life was growing short. He booked passage to Italy and spent months touring the countryside around Genoa, revisiting the scenes of his boyhood. He returned to Providence and died content. His passing was reported in newspapers as far away as Worcester, Massachusetts.

☀   ☀   ☀

SOURCES: "Cakes and Confectionary," *Providence Evening Press* 12, no. 80 (December 16, 1864): 3; "Cake Confectionery and Ice Cream Saloon," *Providence*

Evening Press 13, no. 38 (April 27, 1865): 2; [Advertisement,] *Providence Evening Press* 17, no. 48 (November 9, 1866): 2; "Reception of the Good Will in Patiences," *Trenton State Gazette* 85, no. 138 (September 14, 1867): 3; "Handsomely Dedicated," *Providence Evening Press* 18, no. 109 (January 21, 1868): 2; "New Confectionery Store and Saloon," *Providence Evening Press* 20, no. 83 (December 19, 1868): 2; "George M. Ardoene," *Providence Evening Press* 20, no. 106 (January 18, 1869): 2; "L. A. Tillinghast," *Providence Evening Press* 32, no. 81 (December 18, 1874): 1; "Café St. George," *Providence Evening Press* 36, no. 66 (November 29, 1876): 2; Oliver Ayer Roberts, *The California Pilgrimage of the Boston Commandery Knights Templars* (Boston: Alfred Mudge & Son, 1884), 30; "Gelb & Norton," *The Industrial Advantages of Providence, R.I.* (Providence: James P. McKinney, 1889), 113.

Emanuel Pierre Bret 1825–1892
New Orleans; Galveston, TX

For a generation, the Girardin House at 77 Avenue L in Galveston was Texas's temple of fine dining. Emanuel Pierre Bret created its cuisine during its heyday in the 1870s. Hired by steward L. Romanet in late 1873, Bret adapted French technique to the seafood of the Gulf of Mexico, making the dining room of Girardin House the mecca of southwestern bon vivants.

Opened in 1873, the Girardin House accommodated 100 guests, operated on the European plan, and boasted a level of artistic décor unmatched between New Orleans and San Francisco. A novelty in the city was its restaurant designed to accommodate "ladies and families, thus supply a want long needed, and which cannot fail to be appreciated." À la carte service "in the best style" was available from 6:00 a.m. to 12:00 midnight. The Girardin grew famous, too, for banquets vying with the Tremont Hotel for the event business, and often prevailing because of "the abundance of the finest vintages of the world" maintained in the cellars.

Bret emigrated from France to New Orleans in 1858 and was chef-hotelier of the Merchant's Hotel in that city at the outbreak of the Civil War, taking over its management from James DeBaun in 1859. His property assessment in the 1860 census was $10,000. Located on the corner of Canal and St. Charles Streets, the Merchant's Hotel had a restaurant added to the premises in summer of 1861 befitting Bret's ambitions. The federal occupation of New Orleans during the Civil War ruined Bret. He and his wife, Bridgit, moved to Galveston, Texas, to remake their lives. He was forty years old.

Bret opened a restaurant on Galveston's Market Street in a row of frame buildings and set himself up as a public caterer. His dinner for the French Society Ball in winter 1869 won plaudits in the press. This prospered until a substantial part of his neighborhood was destroyed in an arson fire in early December 1869. The French restaurant was completely consumed. He quickly sought out another location, opening a restaurant near Marchand's Grocery on the corner of H and Twenty-Fourth Streets.

In 1872 Louis Romanet, restaurateur of the Commercial Restaurant on Market Street before the Galveston fire, assembled the capital needed to fund his vision of a moderate-size luxury hotel. To head the cuisine department, he recruited the finest French chef working in the city, Emanuel Pierre Bret. Bret, having just suffered the loss of his seven-year-old son, Alexandre, surrendered his eating house and joined the Girardin House staff. There he would reign the undisputed archon of fine dining in Galveston until his death in 1892.

※ ※ ※

SOURCES: "The Merchant's Hotel," *New Orleans Times-Picayune* (September 17, 1859): 2; *United States Federal Census, New Orleans, 1860, Ward 3*, 238; "The Merchant's Hotel," *New Orleans Times-Picayune* (September 11, 1861): 2; *United States Federal Census, Galveston, Texas, 1880, District 5*, 10; "Ball of the French Society," *Flake's Bulletin Galveston* 6, no. 102 (February 6, 1869): 5; "The Late Fire," *Flake's Bulletin Galveston* (December 8, 1869): 2; "Girardin House," *Galveston Tri-Weekly*, 32, no. 156 (October 3, 1873): 3; "The Deep Water Problem," *Galveston Weekly News* (December 9, 1880): 5; "The Girardin House," *Houston Daily Post* 8, no. 116 (May 15, 1888): 18; "County Court," *Galveston Daily News* (September 22, 1892): 8.

Fritz Huppenbauer 1825–1902
Württemberg, Germany; New Orleans

Fritz Huppenbauer was a native of Württemberg, Germany, where he received his culinary training. He emigrated in the wake of the political repression following the revolts of 1848, made his way to Ireland, then departed for New Orleans in March 1849. He found ready employment as a steward.

"Fritz" (he would become a one-name celebrity in the city) combined considerable charm and great business acumen. He earned the support of the Camors brothers—among the smartest restaurateurs in the city. Andre Camors backed

Fritz's takeover of the Commercial Restaurant at 52 Customhouse Street in 1852. The eating house's name announced its intended clientele—businessmen. For seven years, Fritz pushed the palates of cotton brokers, tradesmen, and merchants beyond the oyster, the steak, and the fried potato. In November 1859, he assumed control of a grander establishment, the United States Restaurant. This restaurant, founded by partners Eugene Berger and Charles Lebel in 1850, enjoyed a prime site for street trade on Bienville, previously occupied by Estingov's.

A New Orleans writer in 1875 observed:

> It is a universally conceded fact that nowhere outside of Paris is there to be found such restaurants as in New Orleans; and even in that great city there are few which can presume to rival our best in elegance, comfort, or in the excellence of the cuisine. United to the natural fondness of display which is a characteristic of the American, their establishments have the taste and style of the French. And taking advantage of the plentiful supply of delicious fish, flesh and fowl to be found in this country, they have imported the most noted cooks to be found in the old world to prepare them of their tables.... Among those which have done more than others in thus elevating the business to the proud pinnacle which it occupies, is the United States, kept by Mr. Fritz Huppenbauer ... a cook who would rank with the most celebrated artists of France.

However, excellence could not insulate Fritz from the effects of the national financial depression that bottomed out in 1876. He was forced to give up the United States Restaurant.

In spring 1877, Huppenbauer became proprietor of the Commercial Restaurant and Hotel on 107 Customhouse Street. A year and a half later, in October 1878, he filed for bankruptcy. By spring 1879, he managed the Spanish Fort Hotel on Bayou St. John until M. Micholet hired Huppenbauer away for his more fashionable West End Hotel at New Lake from 1880 to 1883. When E. F. Denechaud took over management of the resort, importing French chef François Cabruges, Fritz retired, living off the ample income of his real estate investments. He died peacefully revered by an ample family in 1902.

※   ※   ※

SOURCES: "Commercial Restaurant," *New Orleans Times-Picayune* (October 17, 1852): 3; "United States Restaurant," *New Orleans Daily Advertiser* (November 7, 1859): 2; "Dinner of the Pelican Cricket Club," *Daily Delta* (May 30, 1860): 2; "The United States Restaurant," *New Orleans Times* 12, no. 6660 (September 1, 1875): 9; "Commercial Restaurant," *New Orleans Times-Picayune* (March 13,

1877): 1; "Bankruptcy," *New Orleans Times-Picayune* (October 8, 1878): 5; "Spanish Fort Hotel," *New Orleans Times-Picayune* (April 27, 1879): 4; "West End Hotel," *New Orleans Item* (July 21, 1880): 1; "Deaths," *New Orleans Item* (May 7, 1902): 8.

John Burroughs Drake 1826–1895
Cincinnati, OH; Chicago

Hotelier John B. Drake became a name in the culinary world of the United States when he instituted an annual game dinner in Chicago, first in the Tremont House, then in the Grand Pacific Hotel. The thirty-three annual dinners became the most famous culinary events in the United States from the 1860s to the 1890s. Supplied by market gunners from Canada, the Rockies, and hunters from the Midwest, the dinners attracted luminaries from the worlds of politics, the arts, and industry. The demand for invitations grew so intense that it was said that thousands of petitions for a place at the table sat in the file cabinets of Drake's secretary.

Drake's love of game derived from his life as a sportsman. Professionally, he had experience working the front of house in hotels as a teenager in Cincinnati, when he was a clerk at the Pearl Street House in 1845. The letter of recommendation that secured him this first job was the most precious relic Drake retained throughout his life, something he showed to presidents, railroad titans, and matinee idols. When the Burnet House opened in Cincinnati, Drake served as chief clerk, learning the hospitality business in all of its dimensions. He found that he loved the public and cherished the effort to provide them the most sumptuous experience at the least expense with the most accommodating staff.

In 1855 he bought a quarter share in the Tremont House, the finest hotel in Chicago. He presided over it until the Great Chicago Fire consumed the building in October 1871. While the fire was burning, he purchased the Old Michigan Avenue Hotel on the corner of Michigan and Congress, betting that the flames would be halted before they reached that juncture. When the smoke cleared, he owned the only hotel on the South Side spared by the flames. He made a fortune in the months after the fire, enough to lease the newly erected Grand Pacific Hotel in 1874. The large, impressive structure became the favorite haunt of railroad executives and politicians in Chicago. He managed the hotel until 1895.

The first game dinner was held at Tremont House during Drake's first year as partner in 1855. The early feasts benefited from the plentitude of wild animals in the West. Only after the Civil War, eleven years into the ritual gathering,

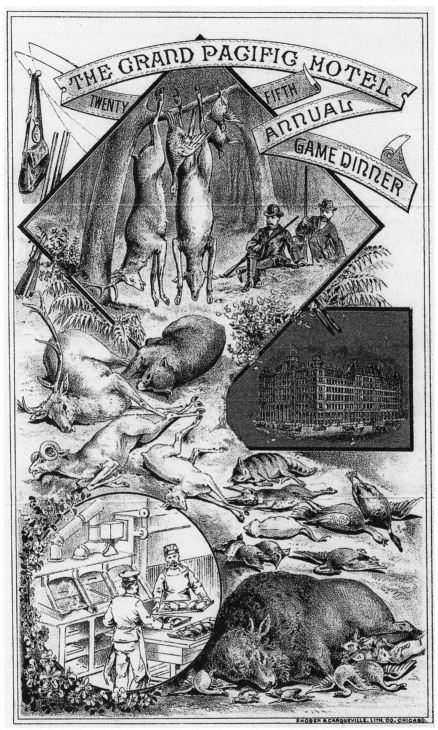

"The Grand Pacific Hotel, Twenty-Fifth Annual Game Dinner" (1884). Menu. Shober and Carqueville Lithography Company, Chicago. From the Henry J. Bohn Collection, Menus: The Art of Dining. Photograph: University of Nevada, Las Vegas University (http://digital.library.unlv.edu/objects/menus/3774).

did the newsworthiness of the feast become apparent to newspapermen. The early bills of fare were simple lists of animals consumed—no mention of pastries, vegetables, fruits, or beverages. The feasts took place on the second weekend in November until the Great Fire. For three years afterward, the feast was suspended, but in 1875 Drake revived the rite at the Grand Pacific: on the twentieth-anniversary weekend, 500 guests assembled. "The menu comprised over 50 varieties of game, including several kinds of duck, three kinds of squirrel, stuffed coon and possum, and the lesser varieties of the feathered tribe, from a meadow lark to a prairie chicken, and all kinds of wild game from the far west." Because the revived feast became an emblem of the will to prevail of Chicago, it became a civic ritual of immense consequence from 1875 onward. A mark of its public character may be seen in the admission of women at the table from 1875 onward, the serving of desserts, and the termination of the feast with a dance.

In the centennial year, the first comprehensive menu of the feast appeared:

SOUP

Game   Chicken Broth

FISH

Baked Red Snapper, Port Wine Sauce

BOILED

Leg of Mountain Sheep   Black Bear Ham

Wild Turkey   Buffalo Tongue   Beef Tongue

ROAST

Rib of Buffalo   Saddle of Bear

Saddle of Antelope   Saddle of Black-tail Deer

Prairie Chicken   Canvas-back Duck

Wild Goose   Black Duck   Wild Turkey

Spotted Grouse   Mallard Duck   Red-head Duck

Butter-ball Duck   Blue-bill Wigeon

Ruffled Grouse   Blue-winged Teal

Green-winged Teal   Pin-tail Duck

Broad-bill Duck

BROILED

Jack Snipe   Fox Squirrel   Gray Squirrel

Quail   Partridge

VEGETABLES
Boiled Potatoes   French Fried Potatoes
Mashed Potatoes   Baked Sweet Potatoes
Turnips   Spinach   Celery   Succotash
Stewed Tomatoes   Green Peas

ENTREES
Ragout of Squirrel, a la Rancoise
Black-bird Pie, American Style
Venison Steak, with Mushrooms
Oysters, Escalloped in Shell

ORNAMENTAL DISHES
Boned Wild Turkey, in Plumage
Black Birds on a Tree
Gelatine of Partridges in Nest
Prairie Chicken on Soele
Boned Quail in Feathers
Les Pigeon Domestique, sur la Grange
Black Squirrel, en Larbre
Canard Truffs, au Naturelle

PASTRY
Charlotte Russe   Plum Pudding, Wine Sauce
Cream Cakes   Meringues, a la Crème
Cocoanut Cakes   Macaroons

DESSERT
Apples   Oranges   Figs   Nuts   Malaga Grapes
Roman Punch   Vanilla Ice Cream   Pears

COFFEE
Fountain, with Game and Fish
Bon Bons, Flowers, and Ornaments

The menu falls precisely into two parts—the first courses are Anglo-American game dishes. From the entrées onward, French banquet cuisine dominates. Indeed, a course of ornamental dishes—the *pièces montées*—indicates that Drake had a classically trained French chef working the kitchens of the Grand Pacific— Pierre Caluori. He was assisted by Tyler Gaskell. Antelope, elk, and mountain sheep joined the roll of consumed creatures in 1877. Loin of buffalo, jack rabbit, and sand hill crane supplemented the list in 1878. Moose and woodchuck appeared in 1880.

In 1893 Drake gave the Thirty-Eighth and final game dinner, a feast that also marked his fiftieth anniversary in the hotel business. The later feasts were prepared by chef C. Wolf. The Buffalo, elk, and antelope had disappeared from the bill of fare. Cinnamon bear was the most exotic of the dishes served. Drake retired shortly thereafter, closed the Grand Pacific, and died in 1895. His son, John Drake Jr., rehabilitated the hotel. John Jr. did not renew the famous game feasts.

✳   ✳   ✳

SOURCES: "An Elaborate Game Dinner," *New York Evening Post* 65 (November 27, 1866): 2; "A Day's Happenings," *Chicago Sunday Times* (November 14, 1875): 5; "Drake's Game," *Daily Inter Ocean* 4, no. 201 (November 15, 1875): 2; "Drake's Delight," *Daily Inter Ocean* 5, no. 200 (November 13, 1876): 8; "A Gastronomic Triumph," *Daily Inter Ocean* 6, no. 198 (November 12, 1877): 8; "Fit for the Gods," *Daily Inter Ocean* 7, no. 202 (November 18, 1879): 8; "An Epicurean Feast," *Daily Inter Ocean* 22, no. 238 (November 19, 1893): 10–11; "John B. Drake Dead," *Daily Inter Ocean* 24, no. 234 (November 13, 1895): 1.

Jean-Georges Torrilhon 1826–1881
Paris; New York

Jean-Georges Torrilhon came to Manhattan in 1856 from the Haute-Loire in France and established himself as a charcutier, grocer, and restaurateur of the first rank. He would make a fortune in gastronomy, lose some of it in real estate, give much of it away to the victims of the Franco-Prussian War, and after turning fifty suffer increasingly from asthma. He died beloved but pitied by New York's French community at the age of fifty-five. During his heyday in the early 1870s, before the economic depression, his restaurant, J. G. Torrilhon & Cie, at 344 Sixth Avenue was a carnivore's dreamland. Torrilhon claimed in 1872 that he could provide anything that one might imagine in the way of "charcuterie fin, jambons, jamboneaux, daubes, galantines, saucissons, viands, volailles et gibiers." Pâtés of various sorts—foie gras, veal, ham—were unsurpassed in the city, some of them being made by Lesage of Paris.

Torrilhon had perfected his skills as a chef at the Maison Chevet in Paris. He came to New York on the invitation of Antoine Bailly, successor to Paul Jauvin, whose Ancienne Maison Jauvin on 188 William Street was a Manhattan landmark. They went into partnership in 1856, and it was there that the "Charcuterie et Comestibles" approach was perfected. The partnership thrived until November 1861, when Bailly decided to return to France. Torrilhon retained the William Street restaurant and opened up stalls at 43 and 45 Tomkins Market. During this period, he chose to identify himself as a charcutier. In October 1865, Torrilhon consolidated all of his business at 378 Sixth Avenue, a twenty-four-room hotel with French dining room. He happily pursued the life of a hotelier-restaurateur until 1869.

In April 1869, Torrilhon lost his wife, Sophie-Eugenie, who died at age twenty-nine. His grief at this loss can be ascertained by the extraordinary monument he erected to her memory in Greenwood cemetery—"a handsome temple supported by four columns, stands on a square block of Italian marble, and inside the temple is the figure of an angel about to drop a festoon of flowers upon the tomb." A widower, he expended his profits on raising his daughter and a younger brother in France who became a priest. He determined to leave the house of his grief and erected a new building at 344 Sixth Avenue. A year after Sophie-Eugenie's death, he announced his change of location and an association with chef Paul Dietrich.

From the time of establishing Maison Torrilhon, Jean-Georges threw himself into the associational world of Franco-Americans, belonging to several societies, including the Société Culinaire Philanthropique. Indeed, his temple made of sugar, salmon, and jam at the 1872 Société Ball was generally considered the greatest *pièce montée* exhibited that year. Yet the public action that most endeared him to the Franco-American communities was posting news and casualty lists from the Franco-Prussian War of 1870–71 at his restaurant. It provided the most current and thorough account of the conflict for over a year. He was later the moving force of the Société Française de Bienfaisance collecting relief for the victims of the war and the later Civil War with the Commune.

Torrilhon's great moment of national notice took place in March 1873 when he catered Ulysses S. Grant's inaugural ball in Washington, DC. At the supper, reporters noted how the president destroyed half a truffled capon and made a "practicable breach in a huge pate de foie gras." Members of the press were given an elevated table at the event, capable of viewing the 350-foot banquet table. Torrilhon received a special letter of commendation from the president's chief of staff that was published widely in the French-language press.

Torrilhon loved the feasting associated with holidays, and his advertisements for July Fourth and New Year's Day promised epicurean carnivals. He first undertook the special holiday production of pâtés and cold cuts for the Fourth of July holiday in 1866, when running the Torrilhon House Hotel. While the patriotic summer festival appeared as an all-meat affair, vegetables in winter had enough mystique for the chef to announce fine artichokes. He also touted cheeses—Neufchâtel, Pont l'Évêque, and Camembert.

In 1876 Torrilhon moved his restaurant operations to 110 Sixth Avenue, instituting a sixty-cent table d'hôte, including wine. The 344 West Sixth Avenue premises were wholly devoted to the production and sale of charcuterie. Torrilhon's problems with asthma became increasingly pronounced in 1878. He turned over the restaurant to his assistant Georges Roth. The restaurant's steward, François Martin, became so proficient in judging pâtés and charcuterie that he went into business for himself in 1879, setting up a delicatessen at 176 Seventh Avenue. When Torrilhon's debility finally precluded work in 1879, he turned over 344 West Sixth to B. Bergmann, who would move the business immediately to Third Avenue.

Torrilhon's final two years were difficult, his suffering alleviated only by the attentive care of his daughter and the concern of a multitude of friends in the city. He died in midwinter of 1881.

❋　❋　❋

SOURCES: "Au Gastronome," *Courrier des Etats-Unis* 38, no. 36 (February 12, 1856): 3; "Dissolution de Société," *Courrier des Etats-Unis* 32 (February 7, 1862): 3; "Avis Important," *Courrier des Etats-Unis* 15 (July 3, 1866): 3; "Sophie-Eugenie Torrilhon" [obituary], *Courrier des Etats-Unis* (April 14, 1869): 3; "Cities of the Dead," *New York Herald* 34, no. 193 (July 12, 1869): 8; "Changement de Domicile," *Courrier des Etats-Unis* 114 (May 13, 1870): 3; "Faits Divers," *Courrier des Etats-Unis* 311 (December 30, 1870): 2; "Le Bal des Cuisiniers," *Courrier des Etats-Unis* 33 (February 8, 1872): 2; [Advertisement,] *Courrier des Etats-Unis* 158 (July 4, 1872): 3; "La Soiree d'Inauguration," *Courrier des Etats-Unis* 55 (March 6, 1873): 1; "Faits Divers," *Courrier des Etats-Unis* 61 (March 13, 1873): 1; "Charcuterie," *Courrier des Etats-Unis* 292 (October 19, 1879): 3; "M. Georges Roth," *Courrier des Etats-Unis* 307 (November 7, 1878): 3; "Jean-George Torrilhon" [obituary], *Courrier des Etats-Unis* 58 (February 24, 1881): 2.

John A. Gray Sr. 1827–1911
New York; Washington, DC

At the close of his presidency in 1837, President Martin Van Buren hired ten-year-old John Gray as a waiting boy. His mother was Jane Gray, the African American house servant of Attorney General Henry D. Gilpin. Gray's first professional memories were accompanying the ex-president northward out of the nation's capital to visit New York. Serving Van Buren for eighteen months out in the country at Lindenwald Farm, Gray returned to the District of Columbia in 1842 and attached himself to Captain Steadman of the United States Navy, serving as his ward-room boy on the *North Carolina*, the *Hudson*, and the *Washington*. During this period, Gray learned the essentials of food preparation and presentation, superintending the captain's (later the commodore's) mess.

From 1850 through 1857, Gray was caterer and steward for Secretary of War C. M. Conrad, running the entertainments at the old Hunt mansion in Washington, DC. Gray's skill managing receptions and entertainments caused him to be hired out to cater ceremonies hosted by Jefferson Davis, Postmaster Hall, and the secretary of the navy.

Gray commented on the extravagance of public entertainments held by Southern statesmen during the period. He commended Jefferson Davis for his free and easy manner, quickness at repartee, and his fondness for jokes. He recalled that Daniel Webster had his snuff box put on a plate and passed around the table after dinner so everyone might have a snort and a sneeze.

His success managing public receptions enabled Gray to become a restaurateur and public caterer in 1857. He functioned both as headwaiter and caterer at most of his events. He staged events for many of the important government figures of the age. "I served at the inauguration ball supper of General Taylor, under Mr. Gautier at Mr. Pierce's and at Mr. Lincoln's reception, to Mr. Chase. . . . I served the supper at Grant's inaugural ball."

In spring of 1869, Gray erected a three-story hotel and restaurant on Vermont Avenue near the intersection with K Street. This stylish Italianate town house designed by Adolph Cluss had lunette windows, porticoes, a bay window, and balustrades. It was the finest small hostelry in the city and proved popular among white patrons until Gray determined in 1871 to open its party rooms and accommodations to African Americans. This initial experiment failed after six months, breaking up the business. It was at this juncture that Gray turned to politics. In 1871 Grant appointed Gray, along with Frederick Douglass, to serve as a member of territorial Washington DC's Council of Legislative Assembly. This meant his involvement in a host of public activities. In 1872, for instance, Gray became a member of the Board of Trustees of DC's "colored schools."

Gray's political career ended in 1874, and he returned to the life of a caterer and hotelier. In 1875, he improved a three-story brick town house on the north side of I Street between Fourteenth and Fifteenth. Gray knew that culture mattered as much as schooling in the formation of civil society, and so reopened the doors of this restaurant-hotel to African Americans. As the *Washington Bee* recalled a quarter of a century afterward, Gray's "house was the finest in the city, notwithstanding the fact that his hotel was the recipient of the leading white people in this country, Mr. Gray recognized the merits of educated and refined negroes." This time there was no falloff in custom. And Gray sought financial security by developing a second stream of revenue.

From the 1850s through the '70s, the Gentlemen's Club became an increasingly central institution of sociability and cuisine. After the Civil War, Gray became steward of the Metropolitan Club, then traveled to New York to direct entertainment and sustenance at the Washington Club. From 1880 to 1883, he served as steward at the Army-Navy Club. Certain of these appointments he served concurrently while managing his hotel.

In 1883 Gray became a restaurateur and hotelier again, outfitting a town house on Seventeenth Street between O and P that he named the Gray Mansion. After a decade of operation, Gray expanded his hospitality business, partnering in a restaurant, Gray & Costley, that catered to the African American elite at 1313 E Street NW. A liquor store and cigar stand occupied the ground floor; and the public dining rooms, the second.

In 1900 Gary took a central part in the formation of the Union League, an association of all the African American businessmen in Washington; he accepted the post of founding vice president.

※　※　※

SOURCES: "Improvements," *Evening Star* (April 26, 1869): 4; "John A. Gray," *Critic-Record* (June 29, 1872): 2; "The Gray Mansion," *People's Advocate* (December 15, 1883): 3; "He Has Served Great Men," *Evening Star* (October 26, 1899): 14; "Afro-Americans for Business," *Evening Star* (1900): 12; "Washington in 1867," *Washington Bee* 19, no. 40 (February 23, 1901): 1; Wilhelmus Bogart Bryan, *A History of the National Capital*, 3 vols. (New York: Macmillan & Co., 1916), 2:592–93; John De Ferrari, *Capital Eats* (Charleston: History Press, 2013), 102.

John Ludin 1827–189?
New York

Born in Colmar, Alsace, France, on September 24, 1827, John Ludin (born Jean) emigrated with his wife, Agnes, to New York in 1852 at age twenty-five. Steven Van Rensselaer hired him to be the inaugural chef de cuisine at his Metropolitan Hotel, a 600-room steam-heated urban palace occupying an entire city block at the juncture of Broadway and Prince Street. Because the hotel was run on the American plan, with the price of occupancy including the provision of three daily

Augustus Fay, "Metropolitan Hotel, New York" (ca. 1855). Lithograph. Miriam and Ira D. Wallach Division of Art, Prints and Photographs, Print Collection, Eno 261 (1659134). Photograph: From the New York Public Library.

meals, Ludin's workday extended from breakfast to supper. His competence at this task is attested by an over two-decade administration of the kitchens, including the rough transition in 1871 from the original management to that of Richard Tweed, the son of the notorious "Boss Tweed" of New York's Tammany Hall.

New York's French newspaper, the *Courrier des Etats-Unis*, sent a reporter to critique the inaugural banquet on September 1, 1852. He declared that if Ludin maintained the excellence of food displayed in the first service, the gourmets of New York would bless the Metropolitan Hotel. He did, and they did. Nearly two decades later, his eminence had won him the honorific title of "Professor," and reverent visitors to his culinary domain in the Metropolitan described him thusly:

> The Professor was a gentleman of about two hundred pounds' weight of ruddy countenance, which ruddy countenance was no doubt caused by the constant re-
> flection of large fires in kitchens all over the world. . . . A strong, hearty Gaul this,
> with fixed principles, I could see for myself, and a hot temper withal, it was palpa-
> ble, as he rattled the saucepans on the long table in the kitchen, of which he was
> lord and master.

The kitchen of the hotel was vast for that age, eighty feet by thirty-five, with fifteen-foot ceilings. Portraits of Ludin at work in this kitchen make evident that his cooking depended greatly on temperature control. He made his chowders over moderate heat using thermometers to monitor the process. The refrigerator, a walnut and oak chamber, was "as large as a moderate tenement house" and could accommodate 200 tons of ice beside the fresh meat and vegetables.

Ludin's cooking served three salons that faced upon Broadway and Prince Street. The windows of these dining rooms contained some of the earliest plate glass in the city, single panes that cost $900 apiece to manufacture.

During the final months of the proprietorship of the Leland brothers, when custom diminished and cost ballooned, they encouraged Ludin to project himself publically—to become a cultural oracle of cuisine. He took up the pen and published a series of weekly reflections on "The Dinner Table . . . what to place on the table, and how to prepare it." Featured in the *New World*, one of Frank Leslie's subsidiary publications, these plainspoken discussions of preparations and dinner service were pitched to the housekeeper, not the professional chef or gourmet. They do, however, evince an earnestness in acquainting the public with the fundamentals of solid cookery, and the series—from January through March—was the first by a professional chef not touting a nutritional philosophy or sumptuary creed published in a mass-market periodical.

When Richard Tweed assumed control of the Metropolitan, he was more concerned that Ludin express himself filling the table than writing about it. For the banquet inaugurating his proprietorship of the hotel, Tweed gave Ludin carte blanche for the feast. The chef worked for a week to fashion the following statement in the style of a cold collation:

SUPPER
Saumon Froid a la Ravigote
Buisson de Crevettes
Bastion d'Anguilles a la Moderne
Galantine de Dinde en Globe sur Soele
Filet de Boeuf a la Garfield
Pain de Foie Gras Historie
Chaux Froix Metamorphose
Pate Froid de Gibier aux Truffes
Langue de Boeuf a la Jelle
Chaux Froix de Becasse aux Olives
Salades de Volaille et de Homard Decorees
Petits Poulets Rotis
Jambon de Virginie

CONFECTIONERY
Jelle au Marashin
Charlotte Russe a la Parisiene

ICE CREAMS
Napolitaine
Chocolate

ORNAMENTAL PIECES
General Washington Mounted (design of the firm)
Franklin representing the Press
Liberty
Representation of President Lincoln
Irish Harp
Kiss Group
Lyre of Caramels mounted with Nougat
Representation of a Jockey Race
Transparent Pyramid
Fruit Meringue Basket
Variety
COFFEE A LA FRANCAISE

One notes the prominence of *pièces montées*—exhibition food—in the presentation. The great French chef and gastronomic theoretician M. A. Carême had made such works an important demonstration of the chef's mastery of the same mimetic processes that undergird the representational work of painting, sculpture, and literature. Ludin had been educated in this most playful form of culinary creativity and brought it with him to New York. When Ludin became president of the Société Culinaire Philanthropique in 1868, he made the display of such works a central feature of the annual balls and exhibitions of this most important institution of culinary sociability.

By 1872 Ludin tired of Tweed's view of hospitality and switched allegiance to the Windsor Hotel. Edward Schelcher took over administration of the Metropolitan. At the Windsor, Ludin operated as the operative chef de cuisine, while Eugene Mehl, chef de cuisine at the Brevoort House, was nominal chef. In his fifties, Ludin grew increasingly set in his ways and difficult to work with, particularly after the death of his wife, Agnes, in 1877. The problems finally climaxed in summer of 1881, during his season spent at Cranston's West Point Resort Hotel on the Hudson. Waiters at the hotel revolted at the quality of food that Ludin served them, calling it putrid. The accusation masked a series of contentions that had grown between the wait staff and the temperamental chef.

Shortly thereafter, Ludin realized that the conditions of the profession had changed in a way that made him anachronistic. He left cooking and became a merchant importer of foodstuffs. He pursued this business until about 1890, when he retired. He returned to France in 1894.

✳ ✳ ✳

SOURCES: "Courrier de la Ville," *Courrier des Etats-Unis* 29, no. 255 (September 3, 1852): 2; *United States Federal Census, New York, 1860, 1870, 1880*; John Ludin, "The Dinner Table," *New World* (February 19, 1869): 19; "The Metropolitan, the Great Broadway Caravansarie," *New York Herald* (August 20, 1871): 8; "Le 'Metropolitan' Hotel," *Courrier des Etats-Unis* 203 (August 21, 1871): 2; "The Metropolitan Hotel Grand Reopening," *New York Herald* (August 29, 1871): 2; "The German Cook's Festival," *New York Herald* (December 11, 1873): 3; "Hotel Waiters Revolt," *New York Times* (September 12, 1881): 3; Passport Application #6704, January 17, 1894, New York, NY.

George Speck Crum 1828–1914
Saratoga, NY

George Crum ran a restaurant, Crum House, at Saratoga Lake from 1860 to 1890, that expressed memorably the vernacular camp cookery of New York. Half Huron and half African American (his father was a black jockey at the Saratoga racetracks), Crum spent his youth and young manhood as an Adirondacks guide, hunting, trapping, and cooking for visitors to the northern New York wilderness areas. Born in Saratoga, his culinary education began while doing scullery work at the Sans Souci Inn at Ballston Spa. A party of hunters staying at the spa contracted Crum to accompany them to the Adirondacks as a cook. He stayed in the region for a dozen years before returning to Saratoga.

Early in the twentieth century, after Crum's death, stories began to emerge that he created the Saratoga chip (the potato chip), when working at the Lake House for Cary B. Moon. No testimony from the early days of the Saratoga fried potato (i.e., the 1850s and '60s) attributed its origin to anyone other than Moon. Crum's creation of the chip is one of the great oral folktales of American culinary history. It runs as follows. In 1858, while working at the Blue Moon Lodge, Crum had an encounter with a dissatisfied customer. The customer returned a plate of thick-spliced fried potatoes, demanding they be cut thinner and fried crisper. The second version had a similar demand. To spite the customer (Crum was a notoriously temperamental fellow), he shaved them paper thin, salted them, and threw them back in the boiling fat till they were crisp enough to shatter. The customer was ecstatic, and the Saratoga chip was loosed upon the diet of hungry Americans. One hungry American who savored the chip was William Vanderbilt, who bankrolled Crum's venture as a restaurateur.

"George Speck Crum." Woodcut engraving from "A Summer Dinner at Crumm's," *Springfield Republican* (September 14, 1894): 9.

The irony of the story is that none of the several extensive descriptions of Crum and his ménage written during his lifetime mentions him preparing Saratoga chips. The Crum House thrived for thirty years on parties of well-heeled spa-goers trekking from the spa hotels to the modestly dressed eatery. "The dining room is a plain room, with clean, bare, pine floor, cane-bottomed chairs, and an unadorned, scrupulously clean table." A contemporary commented on the menu: "The variety of dishes is small, but each one is cooked to perfection. Bass caught in the lake an hour before they are eaten, chickens raised on the place freshly killed, potatoes grown on the side-hills, making them dry and mealy, and corn grown just outside the kitchen door and plucked after you have given your order for your dinner." Other visitors expanded on the menu somewhat, noting that trout, partridge, woodcock, and wood duck were available in season. Also available in the harvest months were "potatoes hashed with cream, green corn, and a plain salad of tomatoes, cucumbers, or lettuce." An honest cookery, highlighting the quality of the local ingredients, Crum's offerings contrasted with the cosmopolitan cuisine of the spa dining rooms. Indeed, the most elaborate preparation of any dish served was that of the hashed potatoes, "which are cooked by his squaw wife," Nancy. Nancy also baked delicious homemade bread.

Crum used no recipes. When asked by diners to supply a description of his preparations, he indicated he could not do so. But in 1894, he invited a guest to witness him at work in the kitchen and transcribe what he saw:

The range is built of brick, and has three arch-shaped flues running up from the ground. These are covered at the top with iron gratings, on which charcoal fires are built, the smoke being carried up through holes in the sheet-iron hood over the fire. As soon as he had built three bright, crackling fires of charcoal, Crumm [*sic*] set about preparing the food for dinner. He took from the ice-chest three fine lake bass, which he had already skinned, and laying them on the meat-board, sprinkled them plentifully with pepper and salt; then he rolled them in cracker crumbs. Leaving them in the crumbs for a moment, he took three young chickens from the ice-chest, all split for broiling, and laying them on another board, seasoned them well with salt. The fires were now ready, and placing the chickens on an iron broiler standing over the center fire, he turned attention to the fish.

"Do you fry your fish in lard?" I ventured to ask.

"No," was the reply; "butter is good enough for me."

Taking out a large agate frying-pan with a handle four feet in length, he put five heaping tablespoonfuls of butter in it; then, without melting the butter, as it was rather soft, he put the fish in, and rolled it over and over in the butter. Then he thrust the pan directly over the burning coals under the broiler where the chickens were.

He shook the fish pan almost continuously, and the butter boiled and bubbled up about the fish and cooked them a delicious brown.

A man then came in with the corn, which he had just plucked from the fields. . . .

It was now 10 minutes since the fish were put in the pan, and, taking a long-handled griddle knife, Crumm deftly turned them over to brown on the other side. In five minutes more they were done and laid on a hot platter. The fish were the very perfection of the culinary art, and no fish ever tasted like them.

When I returned to the kitchen the corn had been taken from the kettle, having boiled just 12 minutes. It was served on a platter folded in a napkin.

Crumm took the chickens from the boiler and laid them on a hot platter and poured over them a gravy of melted butter, which had just a little water in it; then, sprinkling with pepper and salt, he sent them to the table with the potatoes, which were in an uncovered vegetable dish. "Never cover potatoes," said Crumm: "it spoils them."

While the eyewitness in 1894 identified Nancy Crum as the spouse in charge of potatoes and baking, earlier commentators noted that Crum had two wives. "Crum married an Indian squaw, Hester, with a marvelous sunning for cooking vegetables. When his gastronomy became famous he calmly married a bright mulatto, Nancy. The bigamous combination works to perfection."

Sharp-eyed witnesses also determined what appeared to be butter was in actuality a basting concoction that Crum called "Nonsuch Sauce."

Take a cup of water, a cup of butter, a cup of olive oil, a lot of pepper. Mix steadily on the fire, but never to the boiling point, and when the mixture becomes soft and smooth like mayonnaise baste the fish and bird with it, constantly turning them over every few seconds. As it streams over in the fire it raises a blue, devilish flame, which forms a slight crust on the skin of the game and imprisons all the juice. A steak or chops can be done the same way, but with the more delicate texture of fish and birds the effect is overpowering.

George Crum left off serving dinners in the 1890s. His 1914 obituary credited him with the invention of the Saratoga chip. At least five other persons claimed it as well. His fame in the eyes of visitors to the Crum House during his lifetime lay in his skill as a cook of game and fresh vegetables.

✻   ✻   ✻

SOURCES: "A Summer Dinner at Crumm's," *Springfield Republican* (September 14, 1894): 9; "One Day Worth Living," *New York Herald*, no. 216 (August 4, 1889): 6; Elizabeth L. Tompkins, "Wields a Gridiron," *Daily Inter Ocean* 22, no. 142 (August 13, 1893): 2–9.

Louisa Drouilhat 1828–1895
San Francisco; Portland, OR

From the Civil War to 1881, Louisa Drouilhat presided over one of San Francisco's most characteristic French restaurants. She came to San Francisco when husband, Jean Drouilhat—a billiard table maker who won the gold medal at the World's Fair and Castle Garden Exhibition in London in 1851—came from New York to serve as foreman of San Francisco's Excelsior Billiard Manufactory Company in 1856. As Jean Drouilhat bought out his partners and became a sole proprietor, Louisa sought a property that she could convert to a boardinghouse. According to municipal tax assessment lists, Louisa Drouilhat began running an eating house in 1864 at her husband's retail space at 817 Montgomery Street.

During the early 1870s, the Drouilhats undertook several hotel and restaurant ventures. By 1870 Louisa was maintaining a restaurant (at 507 Pine Street) affiliated with the Gailhard Hotel (711 Commercial Street). In 1873 the Drouilhats were co-proprietors of the Stanford Hotel on Townsend Street. In 1874 Louisa resumed proprietorship of 711 Commercial Street and there experienced some of the travails of intimate contact with the public. A local waitress was murdered, slashed across her throat, and the young male murderer committed suicide in the hallway of an upper story of her hotel. It was believed the waitress had abandoned her husband and he then tracked her down to exact revenge.

Throughout the 1870s, the Pine Street/Commercial Street House was known interchangeably as the Gailhard Hotel and Drouilhat's Hotel. There Louisa served two meals—a brunch from 10:00 until 2:00, and a dinner from 4:30 to 7:30. She was known for her egg dishes: omelette à la Lyonnaise, farcied eggs, and poached à la crème. An attraction of her dinners was a half-bottle of California claret for fifty cents. Louisa Drouilhat, "celebrated French dinners—the finest in the city," may not have rivaled Jules Arthur Harder's banquets at the Palace Hotel in the 1870s, yet the meals served at her restaurant at 711 Commercial employed the best ingredients in the market and were prepared by a schooled cook. Her poached salmon and fricasseed haddock became signatures. Throughout the 1870s, Louisa Drouilhat and Ysabel DeVilladon were the sole female restaurateurs listed in the San Francisco directory of commercial eating establishments (160 restaurants listed on average per year).

In the 1880s, Louisa Drouilhat felt commercial competition pinching their profits, so she moved her restaurant to 308 Sutter. But private rooms and a private entrance were not enough to attract new diners to an old name. She did not hesitate when she concluded that the market had passed her by. So Jean and Louisa moved to Portland, Oregon, where Madam Drouilhat opened a restaurant named after herself at 65 Morrison Street. She later determined that 81 Washington would be a better location for business and moved there in 1885, renaming her eating house the Star of Portland Restaurant. Jean continued to make billiard tables in the basement until his illness and retirement in 1893. Louisa Drouilhat died on November 22, 1895.

❊ ❊ ❊

SOURCES: "Restaurant de Gailhard Hotel," *California Journal und Sonntags-gast* 362 (May 6, 1877): 7; "Terrible Tragedy," *San Francisco Bulletin* 37, no. 87 (January 19, 1874): 3; *United States Federal Census, 1870, San Francisco*, 2nd Precinct, 47; "Excelsior Billiard Table Manufactory," *San Francisco Bulletin* 2, no. 57 (June 13, 1856): 1; United States IRS Tax Assessment List, 1864, District 1, San Francisco, San Mateo Special Lists, M756, 2; "Stanford Hotel," *California Journal und Sonntags-gast* 165 (July 27, 1873): 2.

John Gaston 1828–1912

New York; Washington, DC; Macon, GA; Newport Springs, FL; Memphis, TN; Little Rock, AR

When restaurateur Balthazar Roth built Cincinnati's St. Nicholas restaurant into a bastion of haute cuisine after the Civil War, he regarded only one restaurant in the interior of the country as a rival for the title "the Delmonico's of the West"— Gaston's in Memphis, Tennessee. By happenstance, Memphis became home to John Gaston, one of the finest French chefs in nineteenth-century America, immediately after the Civil War. Gaston would maintain an exalted standard of cuisine in the region for half a century.

Born in Bordeaux and raised in his grandfather's Parisian boardinghouse and café, John Gaston (born Jean) contracted to be a galley cook/steward on one of the Le Havre to New York steam vessels during the political troubles of 1848. He worked in ship galleys for two years before settling in New York. He worked briefly as a waiter at Delmonico's, refining his knowledge of cuisine by monitoring the restaurant's kitchens. After a brief season as cook for Secretary of State Lewis Cass in Washington, DC, Gaston headed south to become chef at Brown's Hotel in Macon, Georgia, and then at the Newport Springs Hotel in Florida, before arriving in Memphis on the eve of the Civil War. Gaston affiliated with the Confederate forces during the war, but the precise nature of his service cannot be determined. He may have been a provisioner. The Confederate defeat left him penniless and sick, succored by his fellow countryman and Memphis grocer John Pelegrin.

Gaston recovered late in 1865 and began rebuilding his culinary career. He hired himself out as a grill man at the Gold Eagle Restaurant at 20 Madison Street. With money saved from work and the loans from the Société de secours mutuels of Memphis, he opened a restaurant in 1866 at 44 Adams Street. The *Memphis Daily Avalanche* in June 1866 printed the first advertisement for what would become the great landmark of Memphis cuisine: "To have a clear head a man must have his meals regularly, and they should be of the best materials, sound food and well cooked. Gaston has a happy faculty of filling up without surfeit; he has everything that is wanted, and it is cooked right." The ad copy seems haunted by the dearth and illness that prevailed during the recent war. It should be noted that from the first the restaurant was called "Gaston's"—"the Commercial" was the designation of one of the two dining rooms in the building when, in 1867, Gaston pursued a female clientele. He advertised himself as "John Gaston's Ladies' Restaurant" to indicate that his was not a purely masculine space, that it also served luncheons and ice cream to refresh shoppers, and that it had an elegant décor. The ladies had their own saloon, separate from the

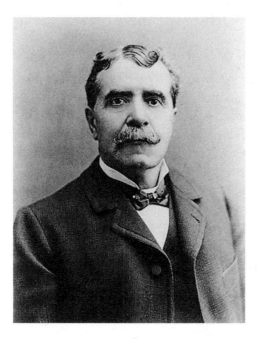

"John Gaston" (ca. 1890).

commercial room. While Gaston's succeeded in winning a daytime women's custom, the evenings retained a masculine aura; indeed, odd eruptions of male misbehavior would trouble the restaurant until it moved in 1870 to Court Street. The strangest of these would be a derringer duel in the dining room between a deputy sheriff and a man about town on September 12, 1870, over whether porterhouse steak typically has a bone in it or not.

Securing capital through a partnership with U. Ozanne, Gaston moved his restaurant to a larger space on Court Street in spring of 1870. It would be "the only establishment in the city where a gentleman can go a get dinner, supper or breakfast a la carte, and served in style." He determined to bank upon the renown of its name in the region, opening a branch at Little Rock, Arkansas, 135 miles away from Memphis, under the direction of his associate chef, Louis Chretien. (Chretien would buy out the partnership and take full control of the restaurant in 1873.) Next, Gaston opened a mobile branch on the *Belle of St. Louis*, a steamer plying the Cairo to St. Louis run in 1872. But the bulk of his effort went to improving and expanding his Memphis headquarters. In 1872 Gaston installed naptha gaslight fixtures in the dining room, enabling late-evening suppers during the winter months.

Gaston's old friend John Pelegrin formed the Société de secours mutuels of Memphis in 1859 to consolidate a Gallic community in the region. Its anniversary banquets, held at Gaston's restaurants after 1866, were occasions of speechifying (putting aside the rancor of the Civil War and embracing the Union was a yearly refrain, the nobility of French culture, another) and revelry. Because the restaurant faced the offices of the *Public Ledger*, the kitchen's offerings appeared frequently in the papers. The appearance of barrels of fresh oysters was hailed in print. Near the first of May, notice appeared of the first strawberries of the spring season. When Gaston secured the exclusive agency of three of the finest brands of champagne (Heidsieck, Grand Vin Médaille, and Sillery Mosseux) for the region in December 1877, readers were alerted. The early arrival of barrels of shad from Savannah came to the knowledge of lovers of roe and planked shad in late December 1878. While news of delectables predominated, the occasional public interest story appeared—like the distraught reaction of a table of gentlemen to a plate of escargots (labeled as periwinkles on the menu)—that suggested the extent to which fine dining remained an adventure to Americans in the 1870s and '80s. Furthermore, one must conclude that the sort of cuisine Gaston prepared depended on a great deal of ingredients brought from elsewhere to supplement the locally sourced meat, game, and poultry. Gaston's cuisine was more cosmopolitan than local.

The installation of Billy Bingham as manager of the restaurant and hotel in October 1877 marked an important juncture in the life of the restaurant, with Gaston concerning himself more with cuisine than hospitality. Bingham's hiring had been necessitated by Gaston's expansion of his enterprise. After his restaurant had "been made famous throughout the United States for its celebrity in the gastronomic world," Gaston decided to expand his premises on Main and Court Streets to include sixty guest rooms on three floors. Furnished in the latest mode and equipped with heaters in every room, the hotel offered elevator access to the upper floors, public spaces, a library, and convenient water closets. In 1877 it was the one deluxe hotel in the city. Its success was pronounced and necessitated an expansion to a hundred rooms and the addition of a billiard parlor and bar. Gaston's Hotel would house a parade of celebrities from presidents to poets from the 1870s through the '90s. Oscar Wilde would sleep and sup there while in Memphis. Sportsman Meriwether Lewis Clark Jr. would end his life by suicide there in 1899.

The popularity and expansion of Gaston's Hotel suffered an interruption in 1878 when yellow fever devastated the city, leading to the closure of many businesses. While the hotel was shuttered, Gaston kept the restaurant open to nourish the population of single persons in the city who regularly boarded. The devastations of "Yellow Jack" were so great that many believed the city was doomed as an "unhealthy locale." The price of real estate in Memphis fell, and when the market bottomed, Gaston went in buying. The wealth of his holdings would sustain his family into the twentieth century and provide a foundation for the benefaction of the John Gaston Lying-in Hospital. The hotel reopened in October 1879 and remained open for the remainder of Gaston's life.

SOURCES: "Gaston's Restaurant," *Memphis Daily Avalanche* 8, no. 141 (June 10, 1866): 3; "John Gaston's Ladies' Restaurant," *Memphis Daily Avalanche* 9, no. 134 (June 8, 1867): 3; [Move notice,] *Memphis Appeal* (April 20, 1870): 4; "Serious Affray," *Memphis Public Ledger* (September 13, 1870): 3; [Notice of Gaston's visit to France,] *Memphis Public Ledger* (September 3, 1871): 3; "The Belle of St. Louis," *Memphis Public Ledger* (February 24, 1872): 3; "More Light," *Memphis Public Ledger* (June 17, 1872): 2; "Special Notice Gaston's Restaurant," *Little Rock Morning Republican* (November 12, 1873): 2; "The First Run of Shad," *Memphis Public Ledger* (December 28, 1874): 3; "French Society Banquet," *Memphis Public Ledger* (May 19, 1875): 3; "Mr. Billy Bingham," *Memphis Public Ledger* (October 22, 1877): 3; "The French Restaurant and European Hotel of Memphis," *Memphis Public Ledger* (November 12, 1877): 3; Louis Gimbell, *John Gaston, Citizen* (Memphis: privately printed, 1930); John Gaston, *Memphis Commercial Appeal* (May 25, 1969): 258.

Joseph Baptiste Peyroux 1828–1887
New York

In the 1870s, Joseph Baptiste Peyroux simultaneously supervised the cuisine of two hotels, the Clarendon and the Everett House. Only Eugene Mehl in New York risked the same degree of multitasking. An active member of the Société Culinaire Philanthropique, Peyroux participated in every campaign to succor orphans, assist cholera relief, and rebuild fire-ravaged cities that the Société launched. He could afford these benefactions, for astute investments in Manhattan real estate had increased his wealth to $200,000 by the time of his death on June 15, 1887.

A native of Bordeaux, Peyroux underwent classical training as a cook and pastry chef before coming to the United States in 1852 at age twenty-four. He rose to the rank of chef de cuisine at the Clarendon Hotel in 1860 and held that post until his death twenty-seven years later; it was one of the longest tenures of a hotel position in nineteenth-century New York. He was admired by his fellow professionals for one sweet dish particularly, pains à la duchesse:

PAINS À LA DUCHESSE
Ingredients: One pound of sifted flour, one pound of butter, two glasses of water, twelve eggs, ¼ pound of sugar, a grain of salt, the juice of half a lemon.

Thomas Sully, *Eliza Leslie* (1844). Oil on canvas, 36 × 26 in. (Acc. No. 1861.1). Photograph: Courtesy of The Pennsylvania Academy of the Fine Arts, Philadelphia. Pennsylvania Academy purchase.

James Akin, "Philadelphia Taste Displayed, or, Bon-Ton Below Stairs" (1828). Colorized lithograph, Kennedy and Lucas. James Prosser's Oyster House. Photograph: HSP Medium Graphics Collection, Historical Society of Pennsylvania.

Antoine Alciatore (ca. 1860). Oil. Photograph: Courtesy of Antoine's Restaurant, New Orleans, Louisiana.

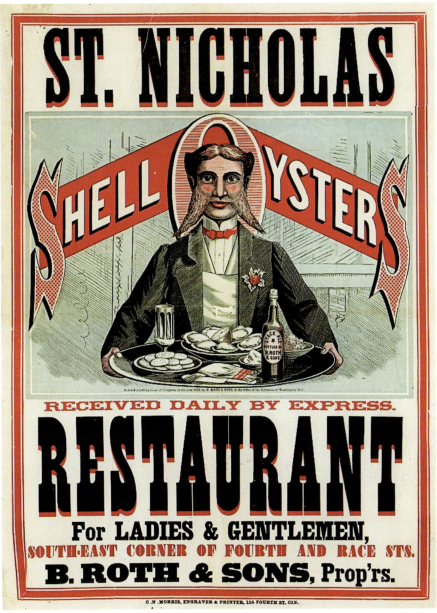

"St. Nicholas Restaurant. Shell Oysters, Received Daily by Express" (ca. 1878). Poster. C. S. Morris, Cincinnati, printer. Photograph: Library of Congress, Prints and Photographs Division (LC-DIG-pga-02243).

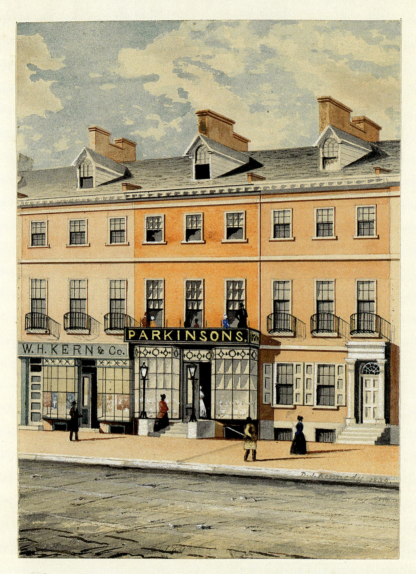

Parkinsons Ice Cream Saloon and Con-
fectionary Store, South side of Chestnut, below 8th
in 1839.
                                         D. J. Kennedy.

"Parkinson's Ice Cream Saloon and Confectionary Store, south side of Chestnut below 8th in 1839." David Johnson Kennedy Watercolors. Photograph: Historical Society of Pennsylvania.

MENU

Oysters on Half Shell. — *3 00*

SOUP.

Bisque aux Ecrevisse.   A la Cresy. *10*

FISH.

Boiled Salmon. *6 60*   Fried Smelts Tartar sauce. *3 00*

RELEVEE.

Sweetbreads larded aux Petit Pois.   *18 00*

COLD AND ORNAMENTAL DISHES.

Boned Turkey aux Truffles.   *30*   Patèe de fois Gras, —
Horn of Plenty,   Bass, sur Mer, —
        Ham, en Bellevue.

ENTREES.

Filet of Beef aux Champignons.   *25 00*
     Capons à la Godard aux Truffles,   *15*
            Lamb Chops à la Jardiniere,   *5 00*

Punch Napolitaine.   *5*

ENTREMETS.

Asparagus,   String Beans,   Stewed Tomatoes,   Green Corn, *10*
            Baked Mashed Potatoes,

ROAST.

Saddle of Mutton,   *5*   Turkey. *10*

RELISHES.

Anchovies,   Olives,   Pickles,   Spring Radishes. *3*

GAME.

Canvas Back Duck.   *16*

SALADE.

Mayonaise of Chicken.   *5*   Mayonaise of Lobster. *5*

ORNAMENTAL PASTRY.

Harp of Ireland,   Temple of Liberty,   Pillar of Flora.
Column of Fame,   Sultanes of Fruit,   Washington.

ENTREMETS SUCRES.

Meringues Imperiales,   Charlottes Modernes,
Champagne Jelly,   Blanc Mange.
Assorted Cakes.   Tutti Frutti Ice Cream.

Fruits and Dessert.

COFFEE.

ST. JAMES HOTEL,   NEW YORK.

Antonio Sivori, "Menu, St. James Hotel, New York" (St. Patrick's Day, 1870). Henry Voigt Collection, "The Life and Times of Antonio Sivori, Part 1, New York, 1869–1881," *The American Menu*, http://www.theamericanmenu .com/2014/02/the-life-and-times-of-antonio-sivori.html (accessed February 14, 2014).

John Rubens Smith, *Southwest View of Sanderson's Franklin House, Chestnut Street, Philadelphia* (ca. 1844). Watercolor. John Rubens Smith Collection. Photograph: Library of Congress, Prints and Photographs Division (LC-USZC4-3672).

Tabor Studio, "Grand Dining Room, Chinese Restaurant, Dupont Street, San Francisco" (1882). Hang Fer Low Restaurant. Photograph: Courtesy of the Bancroft Library, University of California, Berkeley (BANC PIC 1905.06485:046—PIC).

"Palmer House Dining Room" (1875). Ryerson and Burnham Archives. Photograph: Art Institute of Chicago.

"West Entrance to Tampa Bay Hotel, Tampa, Fla." (ca. 1910). Florida News Company postcard.

Lüchow's Dining Room (1905). Schultz Art Company, Hamburg, postcard.

MR. PROSPER GREVILLOT,
Delmonico's Famous Chef.

"Mr. Prosper Grevillot, Delmonico's Famous Chef." From *The Chef Magazine* 1, no. 3 (April 1910): cover.

"Betty Wilson Cooking Schools, Nashville (Season 1915–1916)." Handbill.

Hotel Alcazar, St. Augustine, Florida (1902). Photograph: Library of Congress, Prints and Photographs Division (LC-DIG-ppmsca-18186).

"Palatial Restaurant, 8th Floor. Simpson Crawford Company Store" (ca. 1904).
Postcard of dining room. Souvenir Post Card Co., New York.

Olympic Hotel, Seattle, Washington (ca. 1915). United Hotels postcard.

"Clarendon Hotel, Fourth Avenue and Eighteenth Street, New York" (1870). Clipped Stereograph. Photograph: Library of Congress, Prints and Photographs Division (LC-USZ62-80752).

How to use them: Put the water in a sauce-pan with the sugar, salt and half the butter. Place the pan on the fire and let it boil once, then take it off and work the flour into the consistency. Stir it on the fire until it becomes a light paste, at least until the butter floats on the top, then immediately take off, stirring it constantly; add in one egg, as soon as well mixed, add another, so on until all the eggs are used, the rest of the butter, and finally the lemon. When finished it should be a light paste, and be able to drop from the spoon with a slight resistance, so that it will not spread in the pan. Must be cooked immediately in loaves, in a slow oven. When done open each one and fill the insides with jam or any kind of jelly. They can be made very small.

He won another sort of renown for his witty food sculptures at the annual exhibitions of the Société. His masterpiece in this line, shown at the Metropolitan Opera House, was the huge and hilarious "Anarchist Salmon Chasing Frogs." He was among the most widely known and liked cuisiniers in the profession and was considered the life of the party at the Société's annual gatherings. The office of steward of the balls devolved to him early in the 1880s, and some felt that the exertions of running these events contributed to his death by typhoid pneumonia.

When one wields the knives for a long time, one begins to search for amusement and relief from routine. For a man of active imagination such as Peyroux, this sometimes entailed ventures into areas of cookery beyond haute cuisine.

One of his more amusing ventures was designing at the Clarendon Hotel an echt English menu to celebrate the sixtieth birthday of Queen Victoria in May 1879. The dishes—classics (clichés?) of the English table—appear in a French order of dishes in the menu.

MENU

SOUPS
Green Turtle   Beef Broth

FISH
Boiled Salmon, Egg Sauce

BOILED
Tongue, Caper Sauce   Ham

ENTREES
Veal Cutlets, with Mushrooms   Beef a la mode   Baked Lamb Pie

ROAST
Ribs of Beef   Saddle of Mutton   Turkey, with Currant Jelly

RELISHES
Radishes   Green Onions   Horseradish   Lettuce, Salad Mayonnaise

VEGETABLES
Asparagus   Green Pease   Cauliflower   Tomatoes   Mashed Potatoes

DESSERT
Blackberry and Cherry Pie   Jelly and assorted Cakes
English Plum Pudding, Brandy Sauce
Apples and Oranges   Nuts and Raisins
COFFEE AND COGNAC

Peyroux's health began to decline in 1885. The proprietors of the Clarendon realized that they needed to secure a successor to the chef and contracted with Valere Braquehais in France to come to New York and take over the Clarendon's kitchen. Peyroux's one stipulation in the search was that they find someone expert in food sculpture, since the Clarendon had become distinguished for the exhibition of these pieces. He died two years later

✳ ✳ ✳

SOURCES: "The Refinements of Dining," *New York Daily Graphic* (April 15, 1876): 9; "Britannia's Queen," *Portland Oregonian* (May 26, 1879): 3; "Pour les Naufragés," *Courrier des Etats-Unis* 1 (January 6, 1884): 1; "Les funérailles de M. Peyroux," *Courrier des Etats-Unis* 145 (June 18, 1887): 1; "Personal and Political," *Springfield Republican* (June 26, 1887): 4; "A Chef's Triumphs Ends," *New York Times* (June 17, 1887): 8. "The Famous Chef of the Clarendon Hotel," *The Critic* 7, no. 10 (July 1887): 321; "Pains a la Duchesse," *Société Culinaire Philanthropique, To Their Friends and Patrons* (New York: Société Culinaire Philanthropique, 1888), 17.

Thomas R. Tully 1828–1883
Charleston, SC

The protégé and culinary heir of Nat Fuller, the greatest caterer of nineteenth-century Charleston, Tom Tully won renown under his own name in the era after the Civil War. Stationed in King Street, he furnished "Mince Meat, Turkeys, Game, Jellies, etc., to all his friends, and in fact, to all and every one who know what is good, and are willing to pay for it." Tully knew that custom depended upon publicity, so made certain that regular donations of "good things" appeared regularly in the offices of the *Charleston Courier* in the 1860s. He treated the compositors as well as the editors, winning special favor throughout the print community. Publicity and skill enabled him to become the chief caterer in the Lowcountry after the death of Nat Fuller. Fuller additionally bequeathed to him his place in the Charleston Game Market (stalls Nos. 15 and 16). Every morning from dawn to 10:00 a.m., Tully offered birds, venison, fowls, chickens, geese, ducks, eggs, and "New York Celery." He trained Alfred J. Castion in game butchery and cooking, and in 1881 Castion went into business for himself in stall No. 17, next to Tully. Castion would become a major Charleston caterer and restaurateur.

Tully had the good fortune to be born into a free black family settled on Edisto Island, South Carolina. This enabled him to leave the provinces for Charleston seeking training as a baker. Around 1853 he attached himself to Nat Fuller, sixteen years his senior, when Fuller began his takeover of the city game market. Fuller instructed Tully in meat cooking, pastry work, baking, and confection. He remained associated with Fuller for six years, during the period when

Fuller became the major caterer in the city and had established an office at 68 King Street. In 1859 Tully left, seeking a position of more autonomy. He partnered with the free black pastry chef Martha Vanderhorst in a pastry shop and lunchroom at 117 King Street. In 1859 business had proved sufficiently profitable to enable a move across the street to 124 King Street, a building that contained rooms large enough to accommodate club meetings. Vanderhorst and Tully announced that they could serve "gentlemen's Suppers, Dinners, Meetings." Tully's signature dishes—"Black Cakes, Fruit Cakes, and Cakes of Every Kind"— received conspicuous mention in the notice. From September 1859 to summer 1863, their business stood on the east side of King Street just below Queen (a site now occupied by a parking garage), at the edge of the area destroyed by the great fire. This site became the clubhouse of a number of associations, including the Charleston Ancient Artillery Society. In late 1863, Vanderhorst and Tully moved their dining room to the southwest corner of Rutledge Avenue and Mill Street (a section of streetscape obliterated by the erection of St. Francis Hospital). This became the resort of the Fellowship Society. On April 18, 1866, their partnership dissolved, and Tully returned to his old stand at 124 King Street. By April 25, 1867, less than six months after Fuller's death, the *Charleston Courier* declared Tully "the rightful reigning prince of caterers."

From 1867 to his death in October 1883, Tully was the most imaginative public banquet cook in the city. Whether operating the saloon on a steamer excursion for a fraternal association or supplying the anniversary dinner for one of Charleston's many societies, Tully brought the finest appointments, prepared the most suitable suppers, and employed the smartest and most efficient staff of any public chef in the Lowcountry. He also charged top dollar, a practice that inspired no little grumbling and eventually led to an erosion of custom when members of his staff went into business for themselves, becoming his rivals and using his own recipes. Among traditionalists, however, only Tully would serve— whether to secure a Christmas turkey and mince pie or to cater a daughter's wedding banquet. His typical society dinner can be adduced by the following bill of fare, noteworthy for its incorporation of haute cuisine classics with Lowcounty vernacular cookery. This was served for the St. Andrew's Society in December 1866:

BILL OF FARE

FISH
Rock Fish, lemon sauce; Fried Whiting; Scalloped Oysters; Fried Oysters

ROAST
Turkeys, gravy sauce; Geese, apple sauce; A la mode Beef; Mutton, mint sauce

SALT
Ham, Tongue, Round of Beef

SIDE DISHES
Fricasseed Chickens, with mushrooms; Pigs' Feet, tomato sauce; Stuffed Peppers, Haggis

GAME
Wild Turkey; Venison, currant jelly; Ducks; Grouse; Pheasants; Partridges; Chicken Salad; Lobster Salad

VEGETABLES
Rice, Potatoes, Green Peas, Asparagus

DESSERT
Fruit Cakes, Jelly Cakes, Apple Pies, Cranberry Pies, Peach Pies, Prune Pies, Small Tarts, Calve's Feet Jelly, Ice Cream, Charlotte Russe
FRUIT—Coffee

If adults thought of sumptuous fare spread on a banquet table when Tully's name was spoken, children associated him with the seasonal treats of Christmastide. His King Street eating house became a wonderland of turkeys, iced cakes, candies, jellies, and pies. For a generation after the Civil War, Charlestonians thought the holiday hollow without a Christmas pie from Tully. "Mince pie and the fame of Tully are inseparably connected. In richness of mince meat and delicacy of pastry, his is an unapproachable pie." He was assisted in his preparation of these treats by his employee, cook Frank Rouse.

Tully's status as a cultural treasure was attested by his published obituary, the only one published for any chef, cook, or caterer from Charleston in the nineteenth century.

DEATH OF A CULINARY ARTIST
Thomas R. Tully, the well-known coloured caterer, died at his residence in King street yesterday morning. Tully was essentially and peculiarly one of the landmarks of Charleston. He was born on Edisto Island in November, 1828, and he came to the city while a boy. Here he picked up such an education as could be obtained by free persons of color, and at an early age developed the instincts and genius of a culinary artist. His early education was acquired under the tuition of Nat Fuller, who will be remembered by old Charlestonians as the leading caterer of Charleston. Tully, however, soon outstripped his teacher, and went to the front of the profession in a city where the work of gastronomic artists was always prop-

erly appreciated and handsomely rewarded. For nearly half a century the name of "Tully" has been associated in this city with every occasion worth remembering in the way of good living. For nearly half a century Tully had served the suppers of the Hibernian and Fellowship Societies, of "The Cincinnati," the German Friendly Society and all other associations that delighted to meet around the festive board and discuss the good things of life. Tully had no peer in the preparation of oysters and shell fish. His "stews" were unapproachable, no one could touch him in "fries," no one to this day has ever attained the art of frying an oyster fully and his deviled crabs and deviled terrapin were unequalled. In the matter of preparing "daubes" Tully had no peer. After the war he had a large business, but he seemed unable to realize the results of the war and his prices were found to be too high. He had besides turned out several apprentices, and the bulk of the catering business was transferred to other caterers. Still it was acknowledged that no one could equal Tully in preparing a feast, and those who desired epicurean repasts, independent of expense, always went to Tully. His latest and brightest achievement was a dinner given here in compliment to Gen. Fitz Lee last year—a repast which it is said has never been equaled anywhere in the South. The gourmands who had transferred the preparation of their monthly dinners elsewhere were seriously discussing the propriety of resuming their relations with Tully when his death was announced. Tully had always lived in King street. He was a staunch Democrat in politics, but always conservative in views. His wife died last year, and his only son about five years ago.

His closest relation, John Tully, consigned the caterer's goods to the public auctioneer. On November 20, 1883, the "Administrator's Sale" was held at 124 King Street. The list of goods for auction remains the most thorough inventory of what a successful caterer required to service the public banquet trade in the last half of the nineteenth century in a southern city:

Wagons, Carts, Harness, Ice Cream Churns and Tubs, Ice Boxes, Kitchen Utensils, Stoves, Bake Pans, Dog Irons, Fairbanks' Scales, Molds, Tables, Marble-Top Dress, Stone Mortars large and small, Wash Tubs, Bedsteads, Wooden and Iron Mattresses, Chairs, Stools, Washstands, Poultry Coops, Step-Ladders, Safes, Chests, Copper Bottles, large and small Iron Cauldrons, Waiters, Fancy Cake Molds, Cupboards, Cruet Stands, Coffee Urns, Mahogany Tables, Extension Tables, Wire Safes, Ice Coolers, Knives, Spoons and Forks, Chafing Dishes, Lounge Mirrors, Book Cases, Show Cases, Fenders, Shop Counters. A large amount of Crockery, Glassware, such as Cut Glass Decanters, Cake Dishes, Wine Glasses, Colored Sauterne and Claret Glasses, old-fashioned Decorated Punch Bowls, Dishes, Covered and Uncovered Soup Tureens, Plates, Cups and Saucers, Sugar Dishes, Milk Pots, Glass Water Jugs (cut glass,) Jelly Molds, Fruit Dishes very old, large Glass Cake

Dishes, Ice Cream Dishes, Champagne Glasses, Show Glasses. . . . Table Cloths, Doylies, Aprons, Towels. Plated Candlesticks, Carpets, China Ornaments, Shades, Glass Candle Chandelier, Umbrella Stand and Hat Rack, Stuffed Birds, Mahogany Sideboards, Mahogany Card and Centre Tables, Bohemian Glassware, Spittoons. And generally all the Crockeryware, Utensils, &c. used in carrying on the business of caterer by the late T. R. Tully.

Perhaps numbers of his many pupils purchased these items. Most of Charleston's African American hotel cooks had trained under him—Henry Carroll, Jeremiah Seabrook, and Walter Dennison of the Charleston Hotel; Porter Brown of the Waverly House; and Thomas McNeill of the Pavilion Hotel. Tully's protégé William G. Barron became the next banquet caterer in the lineage of black event chefs in Charleston. Alfred J. Castion was also a major restaurateur and pastry chef.

✳   ✳   ✳

SOURCES: *United States Federal Census for 1850*, Parishes of St. Michaels and St. Philips [Charleston, SC], 128; "Vanderhorst & Tully," *Charleston Courier* (September 16, 1859); "Charleston Ancient Artillery Society," *Charleston Courier* (December 11, 1861): 2; "Green Turtle Soup, Fins and Steaks," *Charleston Courier* (August 13, 1863): 1; "Fellowship Society," *Charleston Mercury* (March 5, 1864): 2; "Notice," *Charleston Daily News* (April 20, 1866): 1; "One Hundred and Thirty-Seventh Anniversary of St. Andrew's Society," *Charleston Daily News* (December 1, 1866); "Tully," *Charleston Courier* 68, no. 21500 (December 24, 1869): 1; "Acknowledgment," *Charleston Courier* 67, no. 21493 (December 16, 1869): 1; "For Sale, Rice Birds!" *Charleston News and Courier* (October 16, 1877): 2; "A Christmas Skyrocket," *Charleston News and Courier* (December 21, 1878): 2; "Notice—A. J. Castion," *Charleston News and Courier* (October 5, 1881): 2; "Administrator's Sale," *Charleston News and Courier* (November 18, 1883): 4.

Anthony Astredo 1829–1896
New Orleans; San Francisco

If John Galpin was the one butcher who became an adept at cookery in New Orleans, Anthony Astredo was the sole fruiterer who did so. He devised an ingenious business model for Astredo's Oyster Saloon, 16 Royal Street. At the beginning of June each year, he would send notice to his clientele that he had "closed his restaurant for the summer season, and is now prepared to furnish the Choicest Fruit the market affords." When Gulf oysters came into season—in early September—he would reopen his restaurant. His favorite variety of Gulf oyster was Cook's Bay, and his favorite preparation, fried. By 1855 business had proved so brisk that he opened a second oyster bar at the corner of Circus and Gravier, and a fruit outlet on Canal.

Unlike the bulk of the city's fruit sellers, who were natives of Malta, Astredo was a native of Palermo, Italy. The scale of his operation dwarfed that of his competitors, being assessed at $10,000 on the eve of the Civil War. Better capitalized than his competitors, he entered into a partnership with Colonel John Hebron of Vicksburg, the foremost orchard man of the southern Mississippi Valley, to be the sole retailer of his peaches, pears, and apples. Astredo announced that he would supply produce "by the million, thousand, box, barrel or dozen." He promoted exotica, selling pomological experiments, such as the Japanese plums grown by G. F. Sturm in Algiers. Astredo is probably responsible for introducing the loquat to New Orleans.

During the Civil War, Astredo served as a sergeant in the first company of the Cazadores Españoles Regiment of the Louisiana Militia. During the war, a trip northward to Richmond in 1862 provoked questions about his loyalty to the Confederacy. Younger brother John (1839–1901) attempted to dispel the rumors, but the experience soured Anthony upon his fellow citizens. After the armistice, he moved westward, opening a saloon on the corner of Montgomery and Green Streets in San Francisco. He was the first transmitter of New Orleans–style cookery to what would become the culinary capital of western American. His legacy in New Orleans was continued by his brother John, whom he trained as a boy and teenager at the Royal Street restaurant.

John Astredo, in partnership with Manuel Delerino, opened the Excelsior Oyster Saloon and Restaurant at 595 Magazine Street in October 1872. John recalled to the public his familial connection with Anthony, the "Oyster King" of the city. The Excelsior achieved a measure of fame for its signature dish—an oyster roll called "the peacemaker"—"Old man of bad habits, if you want peace at home go to Astredo's restaurant, 595 Magazine Street, and get a well fried oyster loaf for your lady." This was an ancestor of the present po'boy. John's fame would fully flower with the opening of Astredo House at New Lake End in 1879. Here John would focus upon the quartet of resort dishes—pompano, blue fish, Spanish mackerel, and soft-shell crabs—earning a repute that had newspaper blurbers recalling the heyday of Miguel and Boudro at Milneburg before the Civil War. John's success was such that he turned the Excelsior over to Terry Tranchina. Indeed, Astredo House proved so profitable that after fifteen years of operation, John had amassed enough wealth upon which to retire. In 1894 he sold out to Tranchina and Joe Oliveri of Leon's Restaurant. In 1901 John was killed by a lightning bolt while sitting on an iron bedstead in a guest house in Mississippi. Anthony Astredo operated a saloon in San Francisco, married Abigail Waite of Vermont, and fathered seven children. He died in 1896 and was buried in Woodlawn Memorial Park in Colma, California.

✷ ✷ ✷

SOURCES: "Anthony Astredo's Oyster Saloon," *New Orleans Times-Picayune* (October 19, 1853): 2; "Astredo Branching Off," *New Orleans Times-Picayune* (September 13, 1855): 2; "Crescent Restaurant and Oyster Saloon," *New Orleans Times-Picayune* (September 22, 1855): 3; [Notice of closing,] *Daily True Delta* (June 11, 1859): 5; "Fruit! Fruit! Fruit!," *Daily Creole* (July 23, 1856): 3; "Astredo," *New Orleans Times-Picayune* (January 21, 1862): 2; "Anthony Astredo," *Daily True Delta* 25, no. 77 (February 19, 1862): 1; "The Peacemaker," *New Orleans Times-Picayune* (October 20, 1880): 4.

George T. Downing 1829–1903
New York; Boston; Newport, RI; Albany, NY; Washington, DC

The supremely ambitious and talented son of Thomas Downing, antebellum Manhattan's famous purveyor of oysters and game, George T. Downing became the foremost caterer in Newport, Rhode Island, and then Washington, DC. An astute African American politician as well as chef, his Republican Party connections secured him in 1868 the position of keeper of the House of Representatives restaurant for the United States Congress. When Democrats found themselves in control of the House, he was voted out of his position in 1876. He was the most talented caterer to have held the post during the nineteenth century.

Taught by his father, Thomas, to present himself in public with maximum dignity, George was a leonine man—majestic, still, and capable of gravity or grace. In a sketch from 1885, an admirer wrote, "The commanding figure and kingly bearing of Downing are too well and generally known to require description." He was reared in a tradition of militant Christianity that combined benevolence and righteousness. When a schoolboy in New York, "single-handed and alone he often fought his way through gangs of insulting white children, and, leading other colored boys, he sometimes drove the white fellows from the streets." He was first educated at Charles Smith's school on Orange Street in Manhattan, then at the Mulberry Street School, a hotbed of African American

Vogt Bros., "George T. Downing" (1882). Wood engraving. Schomburg Center for Research in Black Culture. Photograph: From the New York Public Library (1804236).

communal formation in New York. He attended and graduated from Hamilton College.

George followed his father in organizing his friends and allies into formal associations. At age fourteen, he formed his classmates into a reading and conversation club. Later in life, he assisted in organizing the Grand United Order of Odd Fellows and would serve as its grand master. He became an important Royal Arch Mason as well. As a young man, George became one of the Committee of Thirteen that resisted the enactment of the Fugitive Slave Law in New York. He knew exquisitely well the benefits and disadvantages of political parties. His political engagements were famous to the point of notoriousness.

He repeatedly addressed the public via letters to newspapers indicating his adherence to the "High Tariff" and the Republican nominees in elections. His contemporaries said his "skill in combining the stew political with the stew bivalvular has never been excelled in any age or clime." President Andrew Johnson's attempt to cast himself Abraham-like in the role of savior of the black man was a fanciful bubble "pricked with the point of his oyster knife." Commercial Republicans loved Downing's strict advocacy of pro-business policies. Downing had less love for others of his party and had a sharp eye for the racial contempt within the ranks of the Republicans: "There is a lack of due respect for colored men on the part of the republican party." For this reason, he advocated radical reform within the party, becoming the moving force in the formation of the Sumner Club. His invariable goal in political advocacy was to actualize freedom for newly liberated African Americans after the Civil War by vesting them with the rights enjoyed by white enfranchised citizens. Upon his death in 1903, his elegists remarked that his passing "removes perhaps the last link of the chain of strong characters of the race, who were active in the anti-slavery cause and the agitation for complete citizenship succeeding emancipation."

In the postwar period, as the Republican Party became increasingly estab-lishmentarian and racist, Downing threw his support to Democratic candidates in Rhode Island, provided they voted for civil rights. In 1884 Downing wrote, "As long as the republican party regarded them as bagged black ducks they would not be treated with much respect. They should show that they were live birds, with the power of using their wings and seeking another home." He be-gan to advise generally this switch in affiliation. He later became increasingly independent in his political convictions, suffering expulsion from the Colored Political Club in Newport. Yet his authority and authenticity were so great that those who expelled him were marginalized by the move. Downing's role in moving the African American vote toward the Democratic Party became more dramatic every year in the 1880s and '90s. He even addressed southern demo-crats about the utility of black supporters.

Downing's life as a caterer initially consisted of extending his father's oys-ter provision enterprise to Boston (a catering office at 176 Tremont that offered "French and other Dishes"), Newport, and Albany. In 1846 he moved his res-idence from New York to Newport, where he catered to the summer colony. In 1854 he built the Sea Girt Hotel, which was destroyed by arson in 1860. Un-daunted, he constructed the famous Downing retail block on Bellevue Avenue in Newport, a supremely successful business venture. When Judah Touro's benefaction of $10,000 proved insufficient to purchase the undeveloped land that would eventually become Touro Park in Newport, Downing supplied the shortfall. He loved Newport and regarded it throughout much of his adult life as his home. He was offered the post of Collector of the Port but refused it because of his commitments in Washington and his activities on behalf of black liberty and suffrage generally.

As keeper of the restaurant of the House of Representatives in Washington, he used catering as a means of accessing political power. The conduct of the cuisine and appointments were frequently delegated to his trained assistants. He knew how the rich and powerful loved to dine, and his comfort in the prox-imity of the powerful made him the ideal provider of pleasure and also the ideal conduit of African American appeals for patronage. It was generally known in Washington that no black could secure a diplomatic post without Downing's ac-tive support. His up-to-date engagement in political affairs made him the ideal conversationalist at a Washington political dinner. As a matter of course, he was asked to "join the table" at many serious discussions undertaken by groups he hosted. When expelled as keeper of the House of Representatives restaurant in 1876, President pro tempore of the Senate Thomas W. Ferry gave George Down-ing the position of keeper of the Senate restaurant.

In 1878, as an homage to his father, Thomas, George T. Downing opened a branch of his culinary empire at a site three doors down from his father's first oyster house on Broad Street in Manhattan. In 1880 he opened a restaurant in Albany, New York. Several of Downing's friends, wealthy patrons who had known his work in Newport, convinced him that the capital of New York State stood in need of high-class caterers and restaurateurs. Since Albany was a nexus of political power, Downing agreed to open a branch of his empire there. At the first of the year, Downing moved into No. 7 High Street, a town mansion formerly occupied by Hon. Henry Smith. It was outfitted as a deluxe restaurant. The menu featured "oysters in every form, game, terrapin, salads, Pate Truffe." Downing's decade owning fashionable clothing stores in Newport gave him the eye to create the décor of the house. It became the loveliest dining place in the city during the 1880s.

Downing never lacked money and regularly purchased tracts of urban land. He had also been gifted a large tract of the Adirondack wilderness by a Quaker woodsman that became the subject of protracted litigation after his death between his heirs and several New York millionaires. Downing's financial independence gave him a liberty that few African Americans enjoyed in the nineteenth century. He was untrammeled in thought and speech, and he was a political pragmatist who aggravated doctrinaire members of both Republican and Democratic Parties. The collection of his public writings remains one of the outstanding projects to be undertaken by African American scholarship.

❋   ❋   ❋

SOURCES: "George T. Downing on the Radical Republicans: A Bivalvular Boomerang," *New York Herald* (April 29, 1871): 6; "George T. Downing," *S. F. Elevator* 8, no. 23 (September 14, 1872): 3; "Minor Offices," *Evening Star* (November 29, 1875): 2; "Downing F. R. S.," *Newport Mercury* (February 12, 1876): 2; [Notice on appointment as keeper of the Senate restaurant,] *Alexandria Gazette* (July 27, 1876): 2; "Home News," *New York Tribune* (October 9, 1878): 8; "Colored Men at Dinner," *New York Tribune* (January 11, 1884): 4; "George T. Downing, Esq.," *People's Advocate* (January 12, 1884): 2; T. McCants Stewart, "George T. Downing, A Sketch of His Eventful Life," *Cleveland Gazette* (May 2, 1885): 1; "George T. Downing a Colored Mugwump," *New York Tribune* (August 29, 1885): 8; "George T. Downing" [obituary notice], *Cleveland Gazette* (August 1, 1903): 1; "Senators and Other Public Men Often Consulted Negro Restaurateur," *Boston Herald* (December 28, 1919): 47. Two caches of George Downing manuscripts survive—in Howard University's special collections department, and in the DeGrasse-Howard collection at the Massachusetts Historical Society.

Emile Gerot 1829–1889

Newark, NJ; Richmond, VA; Healing Springs, VA; Buffalo, NY

In the decade following the Civil War, French chef, restaurateur, hotelier, and wine merchant Emile Gerot gave the ex-capital of the Confederacy—Richmond, Virginia—a vision of gustatory splendor that defined worldliness and cosmopolitanism in terms alien to traditional tidewater planter visions of paradise. Gerot tempted and troubled, becoming a kind of test case of the southern imagination. Would Gallic pleasures supplant the comfortable old mainstays of Virginia food and drink? Would the trauma of defeat be drowned in a glass of claret and forgotten in a fricassee? A testament to Gerot's art was that, for a time, the answer was yes. From 1865 to 1874, Gerot's restaurant, wine store, and European hotel made Richmond a pilgrimage spot for devotees of haute cuisine. Perhaps ambition thwarted him. Gerot's attempt to ramp an excellent restaurant into a European-style hotel enacted a program inbred in French cuisiniers rather than responding to the needs of the Virginia public. What is certain is that during the two years that Gerot's European Hotel was open, it supplied luxuries in which few Reconstruction-era Southerners could afford to indulge. In the end, he auctioned the premises, sailed to France to shore up relationships with wine brokers, and moved to Buffalo, New York—then in the midst of a post–Civil War boom—to introduce that city to vintage and French cuisine.

Emile Gerot came to the United States in 1861, establishing a wine import company and saloon in Newark, New Jersey. His initial establishment was located on Market Street. It became the favorite resort of Newark's political parties and periodically suffered from melees when debates over policy escalated into brawls with chair smashing and tumbler tossing. In September 1862, Gerot moved to 155 Market Street, opening the Restaurant Francais, a venue more refined and ambitious than the beer and wine parlor on Market. It became a local center of sociability, the haunt of the Union Party, and the home of the Irving Reunion, a club of literary bachelors. In 1865 Gerot allied with several French expatriates in Newark to stage performances of the Theatre Française at the Green Street Hall. In early 1866, he realized that the defeat of the Confederacy presented an opportunity for entrepreneurs to rebuild the institutions of civilization in the South. He determined to move to the old capital of the Confederacy, Richmond, Virginia, selling his Newark restaurant to Jacob Wambold and Richard W. Post. Yet before establishing a house in Richmond, Gerot returned to France to establish alliances with suppliers of fine French ingredients.

Gerot's French Restaurant at 911–913 Bank Street, between Ninth and Tenth Streets in Richmond, immediately established itself as the superlative eating house in the city. "One need not blush to take a prince there accustomed to Parisian luxuries and cooking, to get a sumptuous dinner or any other meal. His wines, in quality, accord with his cooking." There were fascinations at Gerot's besides cuisine. He owned a cat "said to be nearly four feet long from tip to tip." As in Newark, Gerot imported and sold Bordeaux and Burgundy wines retail at his restaurant. He also attempted to monopolize the quality cigar trade in the city.

In 1870 the popularity of his restaurant enabled him to establish a more luxurious branch at 912 Main Street. (He retained the Bank Street building as a retail wine store.) When members of the press were treated to an introductory dinner on October 31, the more traveled members of the assembly declared that "there is no French restaurant south of New York more complete than that of Mons. Gerot." During the summer seasons, Gerot migrated to Healing Springs, in Bath County, Virginia. In late September, he would reopen his Richmond establishments. While serving his regular meals, Gerot also catered suppers and banquets off premises. In April 1873, he catered the Knights of Pythias banquet at Virginia Hall, filling "three long tables with everything in season suitable to the demands of the occasion, and all was most handsomely arranged with great skill and taste."

In summer 1873, Gerot rebuilt his two offices connecting the Main Street restaurant with the Bank Street store by building an edifice in the center of the block with rooms for boarding. In August, he announced the opening of Gerot's European Hotel, supplying meals on the European plan. Its basement was used as a bar. The first floor boasted a handsome dining room. The third floor had several private dining chambers. The handsome four-story stucco façade with iron veranda was one of the finest fronts on Bank Street. The hotel had fourteen airy rooms and did "a large and thriving business." But it entailed entirely more work than Gerot could manage easily. By November 1874, he was ready to give in, having worked as a hotelier a little over a year. The property was put up for auction in mid-November 1874—at the sale, bidding stopped a thousand dollars below the $36,000 reserve price.

During its brief year of existence, Gerot's hotel burnt itself into the consciousness of Virginia's literati and social elite. In a humorous sketch printed in the January 6, 1874, *Richmond Whig* entitled "What I Did with My Fifty Millions," Moses Adams fantasizes the sorts of luxuries he would indulge when he came into a bonanza. When the first box of gold pieces came in, "I went straight to Gerot's, ordered a nice little supper to be sent to a room up-stairs which I engaged for the night, and with the supper a bottle of his best champagne, a bundle of the finest cigars." When the supper arrived it was "as nice a one as heart could wish," yet while regarding the French fare, Adams found himself longing for "ashcake and buttermilk." Gerot had neither. After puffing through some cigars, Adams found himself longing for his old pipe or a chaw of tobacco. Gerot's challenge: enticing a population habituated to old pleasures to culinary novelties and European luxury. Yet during its brief period of existence, Gerot's hosted several memorable banquets, perhaps none more festive than that held in September 1873 when Richmond's French citizenry gathered to celebrate the evacuation of German troops from France—the effectual end of the Franco-Prussian War.

Sometime in 1874, with France at peace and Gerot's growing discontent at being a hotelier, including harassment by various bands of temperance women, Gerot determined to return to France and set up in the import wine trade again. He put the European Hotel up for sale, left for Europe, and when he returned in December 1875, on the *Labrador*, he set out for Buffalo, New York. There he purchased a property at 18 and 20 West Eagle, quickly found that it was unsuitable, and relocated to 325 Main Street, establishing the French Restaurant and wine retail store. He trained his son Alfred in the dual business of being a wine merchant and restaurateur, and during the 1880s the marquee of the French Restaurant read "E. Gerot & Son." It became Grover Cleveland's favorite haunt in the city. The establishment defined high-end restaurant dining in Buffalo until December 27, 1883, when a gas explosion occurred in the rear of the building, destroying the kitchen and blowing out all of the building's glass windows. Chef Billy Purcell and assistant Charles Rehard suffered extensive injuries. When the establishment reopened in 1884, Gerot had invented an ingenious ladder scaffold fire escape for the building, a design that he patented. In 1885 Madeline Gerot, Emile's wife, died. Emile began turning over the business to his son Alfred. Emile died in 1889, and Alfred appeared as sole proprietor of the French Restaurant in 1890. Alfred would eventually sell out to his brothers in 1900, move to the West, and itinerate as a chef, serving in Kansas City as the private chef of Charles W. Bishop; in Austin, Texas, as chef of the Driskoll Hotel; and in Houston, as steward of the St. Anthony's Home.

❊   ❊   ❊

SOURCES: [Fight at Gerot's saloon,] *Newark Daily Advertiser* (November 29, 1861): 2; "Board of Excise," *Newark Daily Advertiser* (September 3, 1862): 2; "E. Gerot," *Newark Daily Advertiser* (October 15, 1863): 3; "The Irving Reunion," *Newark Daily Advertiser* (April 5, 1864): 2; "Theatre Francaise," *Newark Daily Advertiser* (March 21, 1865): 3; "First Class Restaurant," *Newark Daily Advertiser* (April 2, 1866): 3; "A French Restaurant," *Richmond Whig* 46, no. 94 (November 26, 1867): 1; [Gerot's cat,] *Alexandria Gazette* (February 1, 1868): 2; "Dinner to the Press," *Richmond Whig* 49, no. 87 (November 1, 1870): 3; "The Pythian Banquet," *Richmond Whig* (April 18, 1873): 3; "Gerot's European Hotel," *Rich-*

mond Whig (August 12, 1873): 3; "That Valuable Property Known as Gerot's European Hotel," Richmond Whig (November 13, 1874): 2; [Sale failure,] Alexandria Gazette (November 18, 1874): 2; Moses Adams, "What I Did with My Fifty Millions," Richmond Whig 2 (January 6, 1874): 4; [Notice of the Richmond Banquet,] Courrier des Etats-Unis, no. 214 (September 9, 1873): 1; "Temperance Bands in Richmond," Daily State Journal (March 3, 1874): 1; "Involuntary Ascension," Boston Herald (December 28, 1883): 1.

Mohican Hill 1829–1906

Denver, CO; Salt Lake City, UT; Western Railroads

The free African American chef who brought fine dining to Denver on the eve of the Civil War, and who spent the final decades of the nineteenth century as a private chef cooking on the kitchen car of railroad moguls during their transits of the Southwest, Mohican Hill headed west across the Santa Fe Trail in 1859 when the politics of his native South became so militant that war seemed the only conceivable future. Hill's initial destination was Cañon City, Colorado, but he moved to Denver in 1860 to become chef at the St. James Hotel. The discovery of gold in Colorado and the seating of a branch of the United States Mint there in 1860 made the city a boomtown, with multitudes appearing daily seeking food and accommodation. In autumn 1862, Hill opened the Star Restaurant in Denver. A description of a banquet at the restaurant for Ford & Brother for seventy-five persons on New Year's Day of 1864 suggests the scope of Hill's abilities: "Soup—oyster and mock turtle; roast—no less than eight dishes, comprising among others, turkey, rabbit, antelope and the more common meats; boiled—five additional meats. There were several side dishes, ten relishes and five varieties of vegetables, with sauces and condiments in endless profusion."

Hill's greatest fame as a cook derived from his work at two restaurants of the postwar period: from 1863 to 1873, the Stone Restaurant (which he owned); and from 1874 to 1882, the Bon Ton Restaurant on 243 Fifteenth Street (where owner Martin Welsh employed him as chef). During their periods of operation, both restaurants were regarded as the finest dining spots in Denver. The Bon Ton had the best wine list of any establishment between St. Louis and San Francisco. The Bon Ton failed sometime in 1883, at which juncture Hill became chef at the Hotel Brunswick. In 1885 the master of Salt Lake City's Fulton Market, "Coffee John," hired Hill to be "the presiding genius in the culinary department of the

Fulton market." Yet Hill did not find the Mormon metropolis as congenial as Denver and returned within a year.

Hill and his brother C. B. Hill presided over the most spectacular culinary event of nineteenth-century Denver when they staged a barbecue for 4,000 citizens and visiting Texans at the Denver Stockyard in spring of 1888. The menu was rustic: "barbecued beef, 'possum, bread, cheese, pickles, and beer." A partaker observed, "The dinner was the most superb, from a hungry man's standpoint, ever given in Denver, because there was plenty to eat, and of the best."

In the later 1880s, Mohican Hill left off serving the public to become the private chef of D. H. Moffat, president of the Denver and Rio Grande Railroads. When that railroad was consolidated into the larger Rio Grande and Western Railroads, Hill became chef on the dining car of Col. D. C. Dodge, president. Though maintaining a residence in Denver with his wife and nephew, Hill spent most of the year from April through October on the rails. He died of pleurisy in 1906. A native of Nashville, Tennessee, he arranged the transportation of most of his family to Colorado.

✳ ✳ ✳

SOURCES: [Mayor Cook Regimental Dinner at Star Restaurant,] *Rocky Mountain News* (January 29, 1863): 3; "Ford & Brother," *Rocky Mountain News* (January 6, 1864): 3; [About wine at the Bon Ton,] *Denver Rocky Mountain News* (February 20, 1882): 8; [Fulton Market hires Mohican Hill,] *Salt Lake Evening Democrat* (March 14, 1885): 1; "Banquet and Barbecue," *Denver Rocky Mountain News* (April 1, 1888): 3; "Pioneer Colored Chef Passes Away," *Denver Post* (April 20, 1906); "Mohican Hill, an Old Time Chef, Is Dead," *Denver Republican* 28, no. 110 (April 20, 1906): 11; "Came to Denver in Slavery Days," *Rocky Mountain News* (April 21, 1906): 11.

𝔏ew 𝔅oman 1830–1882
Cincinnati, OH

Cincinnati's "jolly Baron" of *gemütlichkeit* after the Civil War, restaurateur Lew Boman (born Ludwig Baumann) gained fame for offering good value for fine fare in his establishments. His famous Boman's Restaurant amalgamated an American institution—the oyster saloon—with a German *Gasthaus*. The oysters were sourced from the Chesapeake Bay, and his oysterman, Billy Stopl, became

THE BRIGHTON HOUSE AS IT APPEARED IN 1850.

"The Brighton House as It Appeared in 1850." Pen-and-ink illustration from *Historic Brighton: Its Origin, Growth and Development* (Cincinnati, 1902), frontispiece.

so famous a figure among the city's gastronomes that he set up in business for himself in 1874. Bowman's love of seafood and energy in sourcing it made his restaurants the sole Cincinnati venue for celebrated dishes such a Caribbean green turtle soup and skate wings.

Boman was born in Unter-Schoenthal, Württemberg. His parents emigrated to Ohio in 1832 when he was two years old. His culinary training took place on an antebellum riverboat, the *Lexington*, a floating palace of cuisine. At age sixteen, he was hired as a steward and served until the steamship exploded on the lower Ohio in 1855. He was one of the lucky few to survive the blast, which convinced him to seek employment on terra firma. His first establishment, the Globe Coffee House (1856), was on Broadway near the Cincinnati riverfront, but when businesses migrated farther east in the city, he relocated and renovated the old Woodruff House on Sycamore into a billiard parlor and luncheon saloon in partnership with Phil Tieman. There his reputation first burgeoned as his lunches became the talk of the business set. The partnership dissolved shortly after the commencement of the Civil War.

Boman took over management of the Brighton House, then somewhat outside the city precincts. It "became the great 'road house' of the surrounding territory. It was the headquarters for stock men and owners of fast teams." During the war, the favorite Sunday excursion of genteel citizens was to ride out to Brighton House and enjoy a repast. The specialty of the house was roast beef.

When the war ended and the army support contracts evaporated, the stockmen scattered. Boman moved back to the city center, opening the St. Charles at 99 West Third Street. His sumptuous suppers earned him the designation "the Great" Lew Boman. This famous temple of Cincinnati gastronomy flourished, despite a gas explosion in 1869, until 1872, when Boman concluded that he had "made enough money out of the craving stomachs of his fellow townsmen." In reality, asthma and kidney stones prompted him in the mid-1870s to move to suburban Avondale, where he set up an upscale roadhouse in the General Melancthon Wade mansion. It operated as a summer resort. Its clientele could not support the expense of its pretension. Meals were conducted à la carte, and the wine list was the best in the city. Boman was forced to reestablish an eatery, the Merchants' Lunch Room, in the basement of the Burnet House hotel, downtown at 21 West Fourth Street. It proved as successful as every other restaurant he had created. He ran both Avondale and his downtown restaurant concurrently until his death in 1882 from asthmatic complications. The fame of the restaurant was such that it remained viable for years after the master's death, run by his widow, Almina Boman.

SOURCES: "Gas Explosion in a Restaurant," *Cincinnati Daily Inquirer* 33, no. 363 (December 29, 1869): 1; [Sells St. Charles restaurant,] *Cincinnati Commercial Tribune* 32, no. 124 (January 4, 1872): 8; *Cincinnati Commercial Tribune* 37, no. 9 (September 21, 1876): 8; "Billy Stopl," *Cincinnati Daily Enquirer* 32, no. 135 (May 16, 1874): 8; "A Famous Caterer Gone; Death of Lew Boman at His Residence in Avondale," *Cincinnati Daily Gazette* (June 17, 1882): 5; [Obituary notice,] *Cincinnati Commercial Tribune* 42, no. 263 (June 17, 1882): 4.

The

THIRD ERA
1865 to 1885

THE FRENCH HEGEMONY AND THE
NATIONALIST REACTION

Jules Arthur Harder 1830–1915

New York; Saratoga, NY; Savannah, GA; Long Branch, NJ; San Francisco; Los Angeles; Monterey, CA; Honolulu

Author of the great lost culinary masterwork of nineteenth-century American cookery, the man largely responsible for bringing haute cuisine to California, and one of the most brilliant practitioners of culinary exhibition pieces, Jules Arthur Harder was born in Alsace in 1830. His initial training occurred in Paris under Jean-Louis-François Collinet, the brilliant chef who created sauce Béarnaise and les pommes soufflés. Harder underwent seven years of training in the various branches of cuisines.

A job offer from Lorenzo Delmonico to work as an associate chef at Delmonico's drew Harder to New York in 1852. During his ten years in the kitchen, his name did not appear in print once. Yet within the professional community of chefs, his reputation had grown. When Delmonico's chief rival in New York, the Maison Dorée, approached Harder in 1862 to become chef de cuisine, the Alsatian accepted. He replaced Charles Ranhofer, hired by Lorenzo Delmonico to be chef de cuisine at Delmonico's. During Harder's few years at the Maison Dorée, some city gastronomes thought the restaurant superior to Delmonico's. Money lured Harder to the kitchen of New York's Union Club. From thence, he was hired to be the French chef at the Union Hall hotel in Saratoga and headed the culinary department in 1869 when the hotel was rebuilt as the Grand Union, the largest resort in the United States.

Lorenzo Delmonico had watched his former employee rise to higher eminence. He was expanding the Delmonico's empire in New York to three branches. Chef Charles Ranhofer had urged Delmonico to hire Harder to be chef de cuisine at the Fifth Avenue branch in 1871. But this seemed to Harder simply a recapitulation of his labors. From 1872 to 1873, Harder cooked a season in Savannah, Georgia, but the death of his three-year-old son, Theodore, from disease drove him north again in May 1873 to head the kitchen of the Long

Branch Hotel in New Jersey. The owners of the Long Branch, the Lelands, had plans for Harder and for expansion on the West Coast.

When Warren Leland came west in 1875 to build a world-class hotel in San Francisco, Jules Harder accompanied him to mold the kitchen of the Palace Hotel, the landmark of California cuisine. Harder would preside over every great occasion in the city for a dozen years, feeding presidents, royals, opera divas, sportsmen, and plutocrats. During his time at the Palace, Harder offered some candid observations on presidential eating habits.

> I consider President Arthur the best liver of any president we have had. He eats well and eats with judgment. He was not considered such a good liver when I remember him at the Union Club and Delmonico's but that he did know to live is evident from the way he lives now. Gen. Grant dines well now, but I remember him at the Grand Union when he was first made President, and he did not know much about dining then. After his trip around the world he showed great improvement. President Hayes never drank any wine at his dinners, and therefore did not know how to dine. I was ten years with Delmonico. I was with the Union club. I was at the Grand Union in Saratoga; in fact, for twenty-six years I have prepared dishes for all classes of noted people, and President Hayes was the only one I met who did not drink wine with his dinner.

Harder was largely responsible for the design of the Palace Hotel kitchens and the outfitting of the banquet halls. Perhaps of greater long-term consequence, Harder secured the finest seed from French and eastern American sources for garden produce and put it in the hands of California farmers, so that vegetables would have a quality commensurate with that available in the markets of New York. In 1879 he organized the various culinary professionals in the city into the "Culinary, Confectioners' and Bakers' Association," over which he presided.

That same year he superintended the greatest banquet staged in California in the century, a feast for 1,400 in honor of Ulysses Grant at Belmont estate, home of Senator Sharon. It cost $28,000 and was legendary in its lavishness. He was assisted in his endeavors by the Milanese confectioner Horatio Raffa and four French under-cooks, including Henry LeCante, his assistant. Another cook he brought was the ex-slave Muffin Tom, whose egg muffins with cane syrup—a recipe Tom learned during his boyhood in South Carolina—became a famous New York street food and later the exclusive delectation of the Grand Union Hotel in Saratoga.

While many of Harder's dishes became part of the repertoire of American cooks, his greatest contribution to popular taste may have been to widely familiarize the taste of tarragon through his "green goddess" salad dressing.

Harder was among the most literate of the nineteenth-century chefs. His reference library was legendary and his bound portfolios of menus from great European and New York banquets contained thousands of volumes. While in San Francisco, he determined to write a general treatment of cookery treating ingredients available in North America. A Los Angeles reporter in 1886 described the project: "Harder has written a work entitled the 'Physiology of Taste,' which comprises six large volumes of four hundred pages each. Dissertations on the instructions how to cook every known article of food are given." Harder's own mission statement read as follows:

> To embrace the whole list of food articles, their selection, treatment, and best method of preparing them for the table, showing how the utmost value can be obtained from every edible designed by the Almighty for the comfort and nourishment of mankind.

In 1885 Harder self-published volume 1 of this magnum opus, treating vegetables. It is the only cookbook of the century that reveals how chefs made use of the rich variety of vegetables generated by American horticulture during the 1800s. The *California Daily Alta* of July 12, 1886, reported that volume 2 was nearing completion. "It will treat solely of fish, and will embrace a full description of each species native to the salt and fresh water of the North and South American coast." It and subsequent volumes never went to press. Given the unprecedented richness of the first volume, the non-publication of the other five volumes constitutes the greatest loss to American culinary literature from the formative era of the country's cookery. Do we have any idea what might be found in volumes 2 through 5? A scant few recipes survive: "Chicken with Cream Sauce, Vermont Style," "Croquettes of Sweetbreads," among others.

A decade later, in December 1886, Harder was hired to be the chef de cuisine at the first great luxury hotel in Los Angeles: Nadeau House. But the death of Remi Nadeau and an inheritance struggle prompted Harder to move to the Hotel Del Monte in Monterey in 1888. After a decade in the kitchen at the Del Monte, the Macfarlane family lured him to Honolulu to become head chef at the Royal Hawaiian Hotel in November 1898. He found that his teenage children did not thrive in Hawaii, so they moved back to San Francisco in 1900. There he and his wife, Mary engaged in real estate development, building a structure at 628 Shotwell Street, and selling numbers of lots he had accumulated in the 1870s. His son Antoine went into hotel management at the Oakland Hotel. Jules Harder died in San Francisco in 1915.

※　※　※

SOURCES: [Palace Hotel hiring notice,] *San Francisco Evening Post* (July 12, 1875): 4; "A Saratoga Cuisine," *Oneida Circular* 12 (September 6, 1875): 36; "Faits Divers," *Courrier des Etats-Unis* 70 (March 11, 1879): 2; "The Art of Dining," *Evening Star* (June 26, 1883): 3; "Three Famous Banquets," *Los Angeles Herald* (February 26, 1902): 3; "The Palace Hotel," *Newport Daily News* (August 5, 1875): 1; [Obituary notice, J. J. Theodore Harder,] *Courrier des Etats-Unis* 22 (January 27, 1873): 3; "The Nadeau's New Cook," *Los Angeles Daily Herald* (December 2, 1886): 5; "Hawaiian Hotel Changes," *Hawaiian Star* (November 22, 1898): 1; Jules A. Harder, *The Physiology of Taste; Harder's Book of Practical American Cookery, Volume 1: Treating of American Vegetables, and All Alimentary Plants, Roots and Seeds* (San Francisco, 1884).

Elizabeth Kettenring Bégué 1831–1906
New Orleans

In the pantheon of great chefs, more than a few owe their glory to a single dish; some to their handling of great banquets and public events; others to their invention with a region's ingredients in restaurant dinners; and still others to their confectionery skill. Only one won fame for breakfast, the inaugural meal of the day: Madam Bégué. Her eating house in New Orleans began humbly to supply late breakfasts (déjeuner à la fourchette—we would call them brunches today) to butchers getting off work from the morning selling; she finished her life a national celebrity, one of the landmarks of the Vieux Carré. Bégué's Exchange at the corner of Madison and Decatur Streets was an odd landmark, an austere room at the top of a flight of "narrow and old sanded stairs." Two long tables, end to end, dominated the narrow room around which thirty visitors sat to enjoy the one meal that Bégué prepared, a hearty breakfast that lasted from 11:00 a.m. until roughly 2:00 p.m. One witnessed the meal being made in the sunken kitchen opposite. The meal began with bread and wine and ended ritually with a small cup of coffee "over which cognac poured over two lumps of sugar, is burned." Eight to ten courses were served per sitting. The dishes were substantial, examples of a Creolized cuisine bourgeoisie. Menus survive from various years and seasons. This came from April 1904:

River Shrimp on Ice

Celery   Radishes

Omelet a la Espagnole

Chicken a la Jardiniere

Liver a la Begue

Spring Lamb, Salad a la Romaine

Roquefort and Gruyere Cheese

Apples

Café Noir   Pousse Café

Elizabeth Kettenring Bégué was German by birth, a native of Bavaria. She came to New Orleans in 1853, the same year that New Orleans's other great professional woman chef, Sophie Dorn Flêche (Madame Eugène), emigrated from Alsace to Louisiana. Elizabeth's brother Phillip Kettenring was a butcher in the New Orleans market. She secured a job as cook in the kitchen of Dutreil's Café, at the site of the old Spanish Arsenal opposite the market. Louis Dutreil, the proprietor, courted and married his cook, Elizabeth Kettenring, and the house became famous among the butchers for the breakfast served at 11:00 a.m., the hour when the meat market closed. Dutreil died in 1875. Widow Dutreil ran the café for two years. In 1877 she convinced Hypolite Bégué, one of the butchers, to tend bar for her in the first-floor saloon beneath the breakfast room. They proved congenial coworkers, married in 1880, and renamed Dutreil's "Bégué's Exchange."

For four years, Bégué's was known primarily to market to men for its déjeuner. In autumn 1884, New York writers visiting New Orleans to report on the World Cotton Exposition happened upon it and began spreading the word among a network of theatrical people, authors, and epicures. The locale was quaint, the breakfast as splendid as dinner. In 1889 Creole novelist T. C. De Leon in a chapter of his nationally serialized novel, *Creole and Puritan*, entitled "Dejeuner a la Fourchette" portrayed Bégué in the character of Madame Pietro Bartol, and her breakfast (although the dishes were drawn from the repertoire of Madame Eugène). By 1890 the butchers were gone, tourists having supplanted them. By the mid-1890s, reservations were required a week in advance. A spate of newspaper articles in 1897 institutionalized Bégué's breakfast as an iconic experience for visitors to New Orleans.

Documenting Bégué's lavish spreads became a literary subgenre in turn-of-the-century travel writing.

1901: Pineapple, with port wine; coffee, chicken a la Creole, spaghetti, with shrimps, liver a la Begue; anchovy salad, mutton heal with Creole sauce; stuffed tomatoes, potato omelet, French rolls, New Orleans loaf, nuts, coffee.

1905: Promptly at 11 the first course is served which on the day of our visit was shrimp salad, with pepper sauce, then boiled fish with potatoes closely followed by oysters a la Newberg or a la Begue for such a dish was never tasted before or since. By this time our stock of adjectives was so diminished that we said little, but wondered what next. At this stage of the meal Monsieur Begue (he was formerly a butcher in the French market) enters with an immense omelette which he carried around the table and exhibited to the guests. Upon cutting it was found to be filled with sweetbreads. Such a delectable dish but it was really becoming a question where we could stow away the cauliflower with egg dressing which came next. The delicious broiled mutton chops and peas were merely tasted much to our regret. Madame ended this feast with fruit, coffee, and cheese. And the way those who knew how drank their coffee at Madam Begue's! In the first place the coffee is strong, the blackest of black. Into a spoon very old brandy is poured, then lighted and allowed to pour into the coffee.

Several rituals attended the breakfast—Hypolite Bégué's whistle announcing to the waiters the time to produce the first course. His sitting at the head of the table, with a guest of honor at the far opposite of the long table. At the end of the meal, the guest books with their inscriptions were produced for inspection. Celebrities from Walt Whitman's to Julia Marlowe's names appeared. The bill was produced: $1.25 per person including wine.

In the 1890s, Madam Bégué consented to teach classes to young wives of the city. These took place in the later afternoon. A highlight of this instruction was her dictation of numbers of her recipes, intoned slowly and precisely for the women to copy. She told her students, "I am willing you should know all I know, but as long as I live and we make our living out of this restaurant, don't tell anyone any of the secrets I have told you." By the turn of the century, however, the fame of her breakfast had grown so great, it was inconceivable that her custom would diminish if the recipes were published. So she undertook the task of preparing a cookbook of her works—including directions on her famous liver, as well as "Kidney with Tomato Sauce," "Eggs a la Eugene Field," "Stuffed Eggs," "Oyster Soup," "Jambalaya of Chicken," "Stuffed Sweet Peppers," and

"Spaghetti with Shrimp." The Southern Pacific Railroad funded the printing and distribution of the book, *Mme. Begue and Her Recipes*, as a tourist promotion to visit New Orleans. It was the first cookbook published by a professional chef in New Orleans. It was sold at the restaurant at the end of the meal.

Madam Bégué died after half a year's illness in 1906. Hypolite Bégué shortly thereafter married Françoise Laporte, Elizabeth's assistant. Marie Augustine Françoise Laporte was the daughter of Jean Laporte and was trained in the culinary arts by his second wife, Sophie Dorn Flêche (Madame Eugène). Under her regime, a dinner was added to breakfast. The restaurant continued in this fashion until the death of Hypolite Bégué in 1917.

In summer of 1918, Madam Françoise Bégué moved the restaurant from its famous location next to the market to the Old Absinthe House, then filed for bankruptcy in October 1918. The location reopened a month later with new proprietors and it, too, in time died a slow, sad death.

SOURCES: T. C. De Leon, "In the South, Part II, of Creole and Puritan," *Lippincott's Magazine* (October 1889): 472; "A Good Little Breakfast," *Washington Evening Star* (June 30, 1897): 12; "Famous Creole Cooks," *Denver Post* (April 7, 1898): 4; "Breakfast at Begue's," *Kansas City Star* 21, no. 362 (September 14, 1901): 12; "Sunshiners Greet National Leader," *New Orleans Times-Picayune* (April 8, 1904): 8; "Mecca of the Epicure," *Omaha World Herald* 40, no. 225 (May 13, 1905): 16; "At the Famous Begue Exchange," *Baltimore American* (October 31, 1905): 6; "Mme. Begue Now Memory," *New Orleans Times-Picayune* (October 20, 1906): 10; "Famed Cook Dead," *Macon Telegraph* (November 19, 1906): 4; "A Famous Cook," *Charleston News and Courier* (December 21, 1906): 8; "Hypolite Begue," *New Orleans Times-Picayune* (April 5, 1917): 21; "Madame Begue, Famous for Cuisine, Now Is Bankrupt," *New Orleans Item* (October 4, 1918): 11.

Francesco Martinelli 1831–1899
New York

An inspirational chef whose restaurant on Fifth Avenue and Sixteenth Street in New York became the favorite haunt of American painters and illustrators, Francesco Martinelli was born in Lucca, Italy, and came to America as a sailor on the *Constellation*. Shortly after arriving in the United States, he opened a small restaurant on Third Avenue that adapted Luccan approaches and dishes—frying, mixing grains and beans into his soups, roasting and stewing rabbit, crafting pasta made with many eggs, and fashioning salt cod dishes—to American ingredients and tastes. This restaurant on Third Avenue quickly attracted a following, causing him to move to larger quarters on Fourth Avenue. By this time, his cooking had become sufficiently famous to tempt the managers of the Everett House to experiment in hiring an Italian rather than a French chef. The experiment lasted a season before the Everett House called upon Joseph Baptiste Peyroux to restore Parisian cuisine to the dining room.

Martinelli, undaunted, opened a restaurant at 136 Fifth Avenue and Sixteenth Street, the stand that would make him beloved among the fine artists in the city. Martinelli had installed a long table in the cellar reserved for the artists, many of whom were associated with the National Academy of Design. Recalling the table at Charles Pfaff's famous cellar of the 1850s, it had a Bohemian aura, and Martinelli's cuisine had more exotic appeal than Pfaff's pancakes. The restaurant also became a favorite New York venue for class and regimental reunions. For $1.25, one received a five-course table d'hôte dinner. In 1884 Italian visitor Dario Papa pronounced the room and table setups beautiful, and the fringed, bound, and printed menu imposing.

Martinelli made a fortune and, flush with cash, returned to his homeland in 1884. He left his restaurant in the hands of Paul Brignoli, who within months was under arrest for selling liquor without a license; Brignoli quickly learned the ways of a New York restaurateur, paid his fines, and went back into business as Francesco Martinelli's successor. Brignoli kept Martinelli's name and banked on his reputation into the 1890s, when 136 Fifth was purchased by the publishers of *Judge* comic magazine, who tore down the building to erect an eight-story editorial office.

Francesco Martinelli's Italian sojourn lasted three years before boredom prompted his return to Manhattan. He wished to open a restaurant, but his name was taken. Martinelli bet that New York's citizens would migrate to the area around Barclay Street and make it fashionable. His prophecy proved groundless, and the Italian restaurant he settled there bled money. Finally, he pulled out and relocated at Cortlandt Street and enjoyed steady trade until his death on the eve of the twentieth century.

※   ※   ※

SOURCES: "Where the World Dines," *Washington Capital* (December 12, 1875): 6; Dario Papa, *New York* (Milano: Giuseppe Galli, 1884), 328; "Martinelli's Manager Under Arrest," *New York Tribune* (July 3, 1885): 5; Ernest Ingersoll, *A Week in New York* (New York: Rand McNally, 1891), 49; [Obituary notice,] *New York*

Tribune (December 25, 1899): 5; Albert Parry, *Garrets and Pretenders: Bohemian Life in America from Poe to Kerouac* (New York: Dover, 1960), 89.

John Michels 1831?–1874

New York; New Orleans; Boston; Niagara Falls, NY; Columbus, OH; Springfield, OH

A danger of the culinary profession has always been the easy proximity of alcohol and food. For those endowed with huge appetites, indulgence could grow dangerous. A toxic mix of stress, power, and temptation could coalesce into madness in persons lacking great strength of judgment and will. The tragic fate of John Michels, the Flemish-born Parisian-trained chef whom Lorenzo Delmonico imported to New York in 1858, was a signal history of the dangers of certain kinds of genius in the kitchen. A brilliant culinary technician, a master of six languages, a musician, a lover of literature, and a man of volatile passions, Michels could ignite into a knife-waving, screaming monster when his brain was inflamed by liquor.

His talent as a chef won him extraordinary indulgence from his employers. Delmonico paid him a $3,000 annual salary for four years before he was discharged. (Though it should be said that newspapers habitually inflated the dollar amounts of chefs' salaries during the nineteenth century to make them more provocative.) Though the Civil War was raging, Michels chose to accept E. O. Hall's invitation in late 1862 to become chef at the newly reopened St. Charles Hotel in federally occupied New Orleans. Michels demanded $300 a month. His appearance prompted an unexpected wartime revival of the culinary greatness of the hotel. An 1863 dinner hosted by Dr. Zacherie captured Michels at his most masterful:

> Nothing was lacking that might be desired by the epicure or bon vivant, no thing to indicate our restricted supplies of the luxuries of the table. The dishes were as many, as varied, as *recherches* as in the St. Charles's palmiest days; as were also the wines, which surely came from cellars stocked for years ere the terms "blockade" and "contraband" became familiar to our ears. . . . It was remarked by some of the guests—traveled gentlemen—that not even in the most celebrated of the Paris restaurants or hotels, had they ever sat down to a more elegant Dinner.

The financial depression in New Orleans after the end of the Civil War made life there too difficult. Michels went to Boston to serve as successor to chef

James H. W. Huckins at the Parker House after he departed in June 1865. The even-tempered Harvey D. Parker found Michels too difficult, and his stay in the kitchen lasted scarcely a year. Michels then went to the International Hotel at Niagara Falls for a season. Word of his instability began spreading throughout the East.

In 1868 Michels became chef of the Neil House in Columbus, Ohio, located opposite the state house. "Michels signalized his appearance in Columbus by an interruption at the Opera House. A member of the Company, fulfilling an engagement there, was singing a difficult piece rather indifferently, when Michels jumped upon the stage and pushing the singer aside began to render the music himself, creating a sensation in the audience which at once brought the new comer into notoriety." The incident was a portent of craziness to come. He threatened dishwashers with a cleaver and assaulted an under-chef. He was discharged for drunkenness. To make ends meet, he worked for a short period in a Columbus Restaurant, and finally the Lagonda House in Springfield, Ohio.

His wife separated from him in the wake of his discharge from the Neil House and restricted his access to his three children. His inability to control his drinking, his poverty, and his melancholy from restricted access to his children led to his suicide by ingesting arsenic in January 1874.

✳ ✳ ✳

SOURCES: "The St. Charles Hotel," *New Orleans Times-Picayune* (December 5, 1862): 2; "Dr. Zacherie," *New Orleans Times-Picayune* (March 7, 1863): 2; "Suicide of a Celebrated Cook," *Atlanta Constitution* (January 8, 1874): 2.

Lexius Henson 1832–1892
Augusta, GA

Georgia's most accomplished African American restaurateur, Lexius Henson ran Augusta's sole house of fine dining during the last half of the nineteenth century. He was born in Columbia, Georgia, the son of William James Henson and Pinckney Henson. The construction of the canal enabled the family to relocate to Augusta. It that city, Henson learned the art of catering, probably working in the kitchen of the Globe Hotel. What is evident is that when he emerged as a proprietor immediately after the Civil War, he knew both the front- and back-of-house dimensions of running a commercial bar and dining room.

Henson's Exchange Saloon and Restaurant, located on Ellis Street, combined a masculine oyster raw bar and cigar stand with a ladies' restaurant on the second story of the building. Henson served breakfast, a ladies' luncheon, dinner, and supper. "Oysters, fish and game of all kinds are served up in elegant style." A novelty of the ladies' restaurant was that service was conducted by an all-female staff. The clientele of Henson's restaurant were exclusively white. Attempts by African Americans to be served beer in the saloon were rebuffed on several occasions. In an episode on March 1875, "Lexius . . . told them that that was a white man's bar, and that they ought not to try to injure his business in that way." The date of the episode suggests this was an experiment to see whether Georgia would enforce the newly passed Civil Rights Act. Barrooms, however, were one public place not covered by its equal access mandates.

The irony of the episode lies in Henson's own Republican radicalism in the wake of the war. Immediately after the Civil War, he was one of the twenty-six members of Augusta's Sumner Convivial Association. He founded his Exchange Saloon shortly thereafter, and among its first employees (1868) was the young John Hope, who would become one of the major black intellectuals of the late nineteenth century.

The 1874 illustrated *Handbook of Augusta* lauded Henson's restaurant:

Augusta has long needed a first-class restaurant, and Lexius has fully supplied the Avant. His establishment is now equal to any in the South, and up to the standard of excellence maintained by the best restaurants in New York and other large cities. The ladies' restaurant, which is entirely separate from the rest of the establishment, is very handsomely fitted up. A fine Brussels carpet is on the floor, lace curtains adorn the windows, and the tables are dazzling with snowy linen and bright silver. Everything that the New York, Savannah, Charleston and Augusta markets afford may be called for by the patrons of the restaurant. The articles are cooked in excellent style and the prices charged are reasonable. The visitor to Augusta will find as good a breakfast, dinner, supper or lunch at Lexius' as anywhere in the South.

In autumn 1875, Henson began preparing meals on notice. He could do this because his lines of supply for oysters and game had solidified. His bar boasted the "choicest whiskies, brandies, wines, etc." To insure the favor of Augusta's newspapermen, Henson dispatched periodic free feasts to the editorial offices. In September 1877, Henson dispatched a liveried waiter with a platter of "oysters on the half shelf flanked by a bottle of Heidsieck."

From 1875 to 1886, the Exchange Saloon and Restaurant hosted most of the major public banquets staged in the city, including anniversary fetes for the Freemasons. Henson supplied the classic dishes in season—green turtle soup, terrapin stew, oysters. But he had a particular love of vegetables, which he grew on his farm near Augusta. "Some fine specimens of large, clear early rose potatoes have been raised upon the place of Lexius Henson, near the city." He had a horticulturalist's love of superb produce.

In August 1883, the expansion of his business caused Henson to move his restaurant and saloon to 627 Broad Street into what had been a stylish iron-front store. The "bar, cigar stand and oyster counters" occupied the ground floor; the private parlors and dining room occupied the second. The habit of women dining in a restaurant had by then become sufficiently normalized that he did not have to advertise a separate room accommodating ladies. Unfortunately, the financial dimensions of this move proved contentious. He immediately began looking for another locale and in 1885 purchased the old newspaper office, the Chronicle Building.

Throughout the later 1880s, a political war on alcohol was being waged on hotel and restaurant owners by elected city officials. The use of undercover agents to plead for Sunday drinks provoked ire in the city's hospitality trade. When hosts complied with the pleas, information was passed to the police and a fine demanded. Repeatedly, the city extracted $50 fines from Henson, the proprietors of the Planters Hotel, the Windsor, and Moss & Johnson.

During the glory years of Henson's reign over Augusta's haute cuisine, his brother Charles, a self-effacing, proficient, and economical man, served as his junior partner. In 1891, however, Charles's prudence could not rescue his brother from the ill effects of lawsuits and a business downturn. Creditors seized the saloon but quickly realized its value lay largely in the skill of its proprietor. Furthermore, Henson owned substantial Broad Street property. After newspaper announcements of the failure, hard negotiations began between Henson and the Georgia Railroad Bank. The saloon was reconstituted with the Henson brothers in charge, though Charles from this era on predominated. It may have been because Lexius's health was failing. In October 1892 Lexius died. Charles kept the saloon operating until shortly before his death in 1908.

※　※　※

SOURCES: John L. Maxell and Pleasant A. Stovall, *Handbook of Augusta* (Augusta: Chronicle & Constitutionalist Book and Job Printing, 1874), 75; "A Ladies' Restaurant," *Augusta Chronicle* 313 (November 13, 1874): 4. "Civil Rights," *Augusta Chronicle* (March 9, 1875): 4. "Notice," *Loyal Georgian* (March 3, 1866): 2; "Exchange Saloon and Restaurant," *Augusta Chronicle* (November 28, 1875): 3; "The First of the Season," *Augusta Chronicle* (September 22, 1877): 8; "Brevities," *Augusta Chronicle* (June 28, 1883): 6; "Lexius Henson," *Augusta Chronicle* (August 29, 1883): 6; "Old Chronicle Building Sold," *Augusta Chronicle* (June 4, 1885): 8; "The City's Haul," *Augusta Chronicle* (May 25, 1887): 8; "Failure of Rich Colored Barkeeper," *Charleston Post and Courier* (January 21, 1892): 2; "Lexius

Henson Fails," *Columbia State* 1, no. 334 (January 21, 1892): 1; "Hyams vs. Miller, Trustee, et al.," *Reports of Cases of Law and Equity Argued and Determined in the Supreme Court of Georgia, September Term, 1883*, vol. 71 (Atlanta: Harrison & Co. 1885), 608–19.

George E. Johnston 1832–1888
Charleston, SC

African American chef George E. Johnston enjoyed his greatest fame as a cook while in the employ of hotelier Colonel Thomas S. Nickerson, first at the Charleston Hotel, then briefly at the Moultrie House, before overseeing the kitchen at the newly opened Mills House in 1853. Colonel Nickerson's father, J. H. Nickerson, had moved to Charleston in 1843 after mastering the management of hotels in Baltimore while proprietor of Barnum's Hotel. The Barnum Hotel had won national fame for its cuisine, exploiting the rich ingredients of the Chesapeake Bay prepared in a cosmopolitan Anglo-French style. The Nickersons adapted this approach to the bounty of South Carolina. George E. Johnston was trained by the Nickersons, eventually taking charge of the kitchen in the mid-1850s. The position that Johnston held did not accord to our twenty-first-century notions of a chef. He was in charge of buying wines, training and superintending wait staff, as well as preparing menus. The quintessence of the Nickerson-Johnston approach to cuisine may be found in several menus from the mid-1850s for association banquets at the Mills House. The order of the meal was French, as were many of the entrées. Roasts and game, however, tended to be prepared in the English style. The bill of fare for the Anniversary Dinner of the Chamber of Commerce February 1, 1856, is one example:

SOUP
Turtle, a la Francaise, a la Reine, Colbert

FISH
Boiled Fresh English Salmon, from the River Severn, au beurre d'anchois
Bake Shad, Madeira sauce
Boiled Salmon Trout, a la Maitre d'Hotel

RELEVES
Fillet de Boeuf, pique aux Champignons
Capon Braisee, a la Regenee

"The Mills House, Charleston, South Carolina." Wood engraving from *Gleason's Pictorial Drawing Room Companion* (December 10, 1853).

Boiled Leg of Mutton, Caper sauce
New York Turkey, with oysters

ORNAMENTAL COLD DISHES
Galantine de Dinde, aux Truffes, garni d'atelets
Pattie de foie en Bel-Vue, garni d'atelets
Marcassain, a la jelle, a la Joinville, garni d'atelets
Jambon de Westphalia, garni d'atelets
Galantine de Capon, garni d'atelets
Dine Farcie, a la algeriene
Aspic d'huitres, en Bel-Vue
Pattie de Gibier, a la Francaise
Mayonnaise d'homard decoree
Langue de Buffalo decoree, a la moderne

ENTREES
Filet de dindonneau, Bigari aux Truffes
Noix de Veau pique, a la Monglasse
Caille touffe, a la Perrigeux
Vol-au-vent d'huitres, a la Bengeomel

Chartreusse de Pegions, a la Francaise

Filets de Pheasants, a la merechal

Turhaat de Fillet de sole, a la conti

Slami de Becasse, a la Mazarin

Fillet de Poulle prairein, a la Royale

Fillet de Canetonus, a la Bourgignomie

Petits Poullets, a la Rienne, a la simian

Riz de veau pique, aux pitites poie

Filet mignion d'agneau, a la Biron

Vilet de volaille, a la Corbette

PLAT VOLANS

Terine de foie gras Strasbourg

Croquette de volaille, a la Reinne

Ponquitte au Kirsch

Petits Bouchits garni d'un Salpicon

Fried Oysters

RELISHES

Sardines   Anchovies

Olives   Pickles

Currant Jelly   Quince Jelly

Lettuce   Celery   Etc.

VEGETABLES

Green Peas

Stewed Tomatoes

Celery, au jus

Asparagus

New Potatoes

Irish Potatoes

Spinach, au beurre

Turnips, a la Cream

ROAST

Loin of Beef

Turkey, stuffed with Oysters

Saddle of Mutton

New-York Capon, Truffle sauce

Baked Ham, Champagne sauce

GAME

Canvas back Ducks

Grouse   Wild Turkey   Pheasants

Saddle of Venison, Cranberry sauce

Broiled Quail, on Toast

PIECES MONTEES

Mercury on a triumphal Arch

Fountains of Neptune

Naval Trophy

PYRAMIDS

Candied Fruits, etc.

PASTRY

Lafayette Pudding, Madeira Sauce

Plum Pudding, Brandy Sauce

Meringue, Champagne Jelly

Almond Souffles   Mince Pie

Peach Tart   Chocolate Cake

Ratafia Baskets   Cream Pie

Tartlets   Grape Jelly Tart

Apple Meringue

Bouches de Dames

DESSERT

Vanilla Ice Cream

Oranges   Apples   Bananas   Dried Fruits

Coffee and Liqueurs

WINES ORDERED

Pale Sherry   Madeira   Hocks   Champagnes   Clarets

With Colonel Nickerson's ample funding, Johnston could stage dinners on a scale that only Nat Fuller and Eliza Seymour Lee could rival in the city during the antebellum heyday of fine dining in the decade before the Civil War.

George E. Johnston was born in Georgia in 1832. Shortly after the Civil War, he married pastry cook Rosa Cross (1842–1877), ten years his junior, with whom he had two children, Florence and George G. Johnston In the spring following the Union occupation of Charleston in February 1865, Johnston announced his intention of opening a restaurant "second to none in the country." The city, however, lacked the economic resources to support a restaurant with fare of the sort that Johnston had regularly served in the 1850s. Nor were the ingredients readily available to prepare many of the dishes that had graced his former bills of fare. The building at 61 Hassel Street was modest in size, suited for the retail sale of foods and wines, as well as the service of lunches and dinners. The disparity between aspiration and what could be managed in 1865 is revealed in two advertisements that appeared in the *Charleston Courier*. The first, announcing the plan, appeared on April 19. The last, describing "George's Restaurant," describes the rather standard items Johnston offered to diners and boarders.

FIRST CLASS RESTAURANT.—Mr. George E. Johnston, well known to the old habitués of the Charleston Hotel and Mills House, has opened a first class restaurant at No. 61 Hazel street, South side, between Meeting and Kings streets, where the Proprietor will be happy to again meet all his old friends. He intends to keep a restaurant second to none in the country. His bar will be supplied with the very best of wines and liquors, both imported and domestic, and his table furnished with the best of everything to be found in the market. The old friends of the Charleston Hotel and Mills House will be glad to hear of this announcement.

In the years after the Civil War, Johnston discovered a truth that culinarians in many American cities had figured out: more money was to be made vending wine and liquor retail than from serving fine food to the public. Gradually, George's Restaurant morphed into a mixed retail space: part grocery, part cook shop, part tavern, and mainly a wine and liquor store. Those who made money in the food service business had to have a mobile service (such as caterer Tom Tully) or be housed in a hotel.

Much of Johnston's energy in the postwar years was channeled into African American associations, particularly the Freemasons. He was, in 1865, one of the movers in the organization of the Union Lodge of the Ancient York Masons. In 1874 he presided as king of a newly organized lodge of the colored Royal Arch Masons. Eventually the associational world lured him back into the kitchen. In 1876 he supplemented his retail work by becoming steward of the Carolina Club, a role that he undertook for six years. The steward handled the cuisine, oversaw the maintenance of the property, directed the wait staff, and ordered the wine. This revival of service was relatively short-lived. In 1883 he returned to his grocery-liquor store full-time. He died on August 25, 1888, and his passing merited no notice in the public papers. Johnston's central role in Charleston cuisine had been forgotten. Tom Tully, who had died five years previously, had an obituary that extolled him as a genius.

SOURCES: "Chamber of Commerce Annual Festival," *Charleston Courier* (February 12, 1856): 1; "First Class Restaurant," *Charleston Courier* (April 19, 1865): 3; "George's Restaurant," *Charleston Courier* (October 23, 1865): 3; [Union Lodge 1 of the Freemasons meets,] *Charleston Courier* (September 19, 1864): 2; "Master's Office," *Charleston News and Courier* (October 31, 1893): 5.

Dominico Paretti 1832?–189?
New York

Italian-born and French-trained, Dominico Paretti came to New York in 1858. In 1861 he was hired by F. Martinez, who had come from San Francisco's Barnum House Hotel to open the deluxe French restaurant Maison Dorée, a New York clone of the famous Parisian restaurant run by M. Verdier. The New York Maison Dorée was located on Union Square at 42 East Fourteenth Street. Paretti tended the kitchen during the extraordinary burgeoning of luxury in New York during the Civil War, when the restaurant secured the most magnificent service of plate in North America for the benefit of the restaurant's diners. As a reporter noted in 1864, Delmonico's and Maison Dorée were the places of resort for the "jeunesse dorée cros, on Opera nights more especially; and a gay and goodly show do they make in the resplendent salons, with their lady companions all so exquisitely and richly dressed." Another group made the Maison Dorée their particular resort in New York—Manhattan's Jews—so much so that the *Jewish Messenger* suggested that the restaurant's baker learn to prepare unleavened bread so as not to lose clients during Passover. Paretti was obliged to service three meals: dinners and late breakfasts in the main dining room, and luncheons in the ladies' salon, an "installation magnifique" operating midday exclusively for the use of women shoppers and their occasional male escorts. It cannot be determined whether Paretti or Fernandez initiated the historic comparative tasting of Château Margaux with the red wines of Hungary that took place in September 1865.

In November 1865, a cultural critic bemoaning the "present low tide of our domestic cooking" proposed that society arrange for a waiter from one's local restaurant to take an order in the morning and later deliver dinner at the appropriate house. He noted that only Delmonico's and Maison Dorée did this at present for New York society, and that one was obliged to pay "fancy prices." Sentiments similar to these may have prompted banker Wooster Sherman to

"Maison Dorée" (ca. 1866). Stereoscopic photograph, American Views, New York. Robert Dennis Collection of Stereoscopic Views (Coll 91-F209). Photograph: From the New York Public Library (G91F209_019F).

hire Paretti from the restaurant to be his household chef. Paretti was shortly thereafter hired away by newspaper mogul James Gordon Bennett Jr. Educated in France, Gordon Bennett took over management of the *New York Herald* in 1866. An unconventional man with strong appetites, an athletic bent, and a sociable inclination, his dinner parties were legendary in the late 1860s. Paretti well served Bennett's love of Parisian-style cuisine and fine wine until 1871.

Paretti returned to public cuisine when Peter Gilsey launched his luxury hotel, Gilsey House, on the corner of Twenty-Ninth and Broadway. Once it had been well established, Paretti worked stints at the Union Club and the Buckingham Hotel before settling into the kitchen of the Park Avenue Hotel in 1883. At the Park Avenue, he instituted a brigade organization in the kitchen and made a particular effort to secure the best fish in market. He took the restaurant away from the traditional game and red meats emphasis that dominated hotel restaurants in the 1870s.

⁕ ⁕ ⁕

Sources: "The Proprietor of the Maison Dorée," *New York Herald*, no. 9080 (July 21, 1861): 6; "The Gilsey House," *New York Commercial Advertiser* (April 17, 1871): 3; "The Vast Prosperity of New York," *New York Herald* (January 19, 1864): 4; "Maison Dorée," *Courrier des Etats-Unis*, no. 30 (February 5, 1862): 4;

"Les Vins de Hongrie," *Courrier des Etats-Unis*, no. 214 (September 13, 1865): 2; "Town Gossip," *Frank Leslie's Illustrated Newspaper* (November 11, 1865): 3; "Local Items," *Jewish Messenger* 17, no. 13 (March 31, 1865): 108.

Felix J. Déliée 1833–190?
New York

Certain chefs ascended the heights of popularity in nineteenth-century America without opening public restaurants. In the middle of the century, the European penchant for taking certain meals within the safe harbor of one's private club infected America's major cities. Manhattan boasted several such sociable refuges. These elevated Felix J. Déliée to the heights gastronomic esteem. Déliée, a native of France, came with his younger brother Charles to the United States in 1855. Felix was engaged to preside over the kitchen of the Union Club in Manhattan. The stir he created with his classic French fare prompted the rival Manhattan Club to hire him away early in the 1870s. It was during this period that he assumed the presidency of the Société Culinaire Philanthropique, presiding over its affairs in 1878. His greatest fame, however, came when he served as caterer to the New York Club.

Club dining operated in a different financial stream than the restaurant or hotel dining room. Breakage of plates and glassware was charged to the offending club member's account. Restaurants passed through to the customer the extortionate prices that provisioners charged for early season delicacies; the club dining rooms did not. "Turtle soups, terrapin stew, and game purees are not doctored in the clubs as served in the run of public restaurants, consequently there is little profit resulting therefrom to the club." Conversely, the club menus featured very few plain dishes, so the price of a meal was commensurately exalted. Alcohol was consumed steadily at the club, while at restaurants there tended to be a mix of bingers and abstemious diners. Déliée did not have to bother with preparing plain dishes for the feeders who inevitably came into public restaurants in any of his club positions. He cooked for only the most prestigious of New York's sociable companies.

Unusual among the French-trained culinary professionals of his time, Déliée harbored no proprietary grip over his dishes. He had little inclination to secrecy and believed that expertise at the range elevated the chef de cuisine over the cook. Consequently, he took up the pen and began publishing menus and recipes in the pages of the *New York World*. This was such an innovation that rival newspapers burlesqued it as a Democratic Party plot to debilitate the populace. "When the *World* began to give its bills of fare I at once began to eat through them, believing that M. Déliée was a good chef and the *World* men well-known and recognized gourmets. I am not as well now as I was before I began the process. I have lost thirty pounds of good muscle, my stomach is a source of discomfort, my teeth are out of order, and I am becoming slightly bald at the top of my head." While menus had been an adjunct of public dining since the mid-eighteenth century in the French- and English-speaking spheres, menu theory—the sequential ordering of dishes in seasons—became a Parisian fascination in the mid-nineteenth century. It made perfect sense when one considered the practical considerations of provisioning a large-scale dining institution, such as a hotel, to have generalized seasonal meal templates and more specific weekly projections. Marie-Antoine Carême had supplied the theory of menu formation in his 1822 volumes *Le Maître d'hôtel français*, but Déliée was the first in American print (mid-1870s) to make it the frame for conceiving the preparation of food, rather than the kinds of dishes—soups, meats, vegetables, and baked goods.

In 1884 Déliée published one of the landmark culinary manuals of the nineteenth century: *The Franco-American Cookery Book*, which presented 365 daily menus with the recipes for each dish following. The dishes had a New York market seasonality—that is, fish and game were precisely in season, as they were in the market—but vegetables mirrored the hothouse growth cycles that permitted celery in January. Southern truck produce—strawberries, new potatoes, and English peas—were featured in March. Déliée pointedly stressed soups, entrées, and fish dishes as a correction to the emphasis on baked goods and desserts found in many women-authored cookbooks. Yet Déliée was not blind to certain changes of taste occurring in Manhattan. Fifty salads appear in the book. Fundamental cookery—the preparation of sauces and the clarification of stocks—were treated incidentally in discussions of particular dishes. While the title page trumpeted the presence of "over 2,000 recipes" in the volume, numbers of recipes were complexes incorporating previous preparations. The ingredients drew from both foreign and domestic sources, and the canonical American dishes—terrapin stew, canvasback ducks, gumbo, baked cod, clam fritters, Saratoga chips, shad, Carolina sheepshead (the fish), soft-shelled crabs, sweet potatoes, green turtle, fried chicken, fruit pies—appear in multiple forms. Fritters abound. Twenty-five flavors of ice cream and two dozen additional compound desserts incorporating ice creams appear. As early as the mid-1860s, Déliée had confided to his friend Charles Ranhofer that he believed green turtle soup and terrapin would please the taste of any French gastronome. He did not ignore the contemporary fascination with jellies, both savory and sweet. He provided forty-three recipes. Until the appearance of Charles Ranhofer's *The Epicurean* a decade later, no American-published cookbook supplied so comprehensive a view of European gastronomy engaged with American ingredients and tastes.

The volume immediately ran through seven editions. Déliée parlayed his literary fame into a new position, taking over in quick succession the kitchens of the Manhattan Beach Hotel at Coney Island in 1884 and the Langham Hotel in New York in 1885. Toward the end of the century, he became the caterer to the Manhattan Club.

※　※　※

SOURCES: "Gastronomie Internationale," *Courrier des Etats-Unis*, no. 304 (December 24, 1866): 2; "Dreadful Effect of the World's Menus," *New York Daily Graphic* (September 16, 1876): 2; "Le Fleau," *Courrier de Etats-Unis* (September 29, 1878): 2; Felix J. Déliée, *The Franco-American Cookery Book* (New York: G. P. Putnam, 1884); "Business of the Clubs," *New York Times* (January 2, 1887): 5.

Edward Schelcher 1833–1911
Cincinnati, OH; New York; Saratoga, NY

A titan in height and girth, chef Edward Schelcher loomed over the culinary scene at Saratoga from the 1870s through the '90s as master of the Grand Union Hotel's kitchens. During the three months of the resort season, he presided over four chef specialists in national styles—French, German, English, and Italian—and twenty-eight additional undercooks and operatives. With a daily seating of approximately 1,100 guests, the Grand Union's daily consumption of stock averaged 1,800 pounds of beef, 1,500 whole chickens, 25 whole hams, 4,000 ears of corn, and 40 bushels of tomatoes. After summer's end, Schelcher returned to New York, where he superintended the kitchens of the Metropolitan Hotel.

Born in Alsace and trained in German cuisine, Schelcher came to the United States in 1857, settling in the midwestern seat of German culture, Cincinnati. He presided over the Burnet House kitchen for a decade, from 1859 to 1869. During this period, the Burnet was the hotel cherished by political luminaries in the city, hosting many campaign banquets and rallies.

Schelcher came to New York in 1869, accepting dual employment at the Metropolitan Hotel in Manhattan (from September to June) and the newly rebuilt Grand Union Hotel in Saratoga (from June through August). He immediately installed himself into the Society of German Cooks, counterpart to the French Société Culinaire Philanthropique active in the city. In the 1876 meeting, Schelcher's food sculpture of a Saratoga horse race (twenty horses and riders, including one spilled next to the lobster salad) became the talk of the exhibition table. As an Alsatian, Schelcher could claim French affiliation. Consequently, he exhibited with the Société. He also promoted purely professional sodalities, such as the Cooks and Pastry Cooks Association, and assumed that group's presidency in 1883. In each of these groups, Schelcher made a name as a superlative creator of exhibition food. The craft and complexity of these creations is suggested by a description from the year of his presidency: "There was a superb centerpiece of white sugar, representing three different kitchen scenes, and on the top was a lifelike hunting group. . . . His skill was also exemplified in a structure of boned turkey embellished with white boars' heads and two swans swimming in a lake of jelly." Perhaps his greatest exhibition piece appeared in the 1887 ball of the Société, an artistic salmon Statue of Liberty with "a suckling pig, in a revolutionary bonnet roupe" that fished in the waters at the foot of the pedestal.

While descriptions of his display food abound, Schelcher devoted equal attention to his meals. He excelled at roasting but refused to employ ovens in the tasks of roasting and broiling. At the Grand Union, he had an immense hearth equipped with jacks and spits. "This roasting before the fire . . . is the secret of the fine flavor of all roasts. No meat cooked in an oven ever tastes the same." Perpetual basting in the meat's juices and butter was the second requisite of good roasts.

Schelcher grew wealthy over the course of his career. A careful, even-tempered man with a firm will and a logical outlet on matters, he occupied his posts at the Metropolitan and the Grand Union longer than any other chef in New York in any similar institution—almost forty years. He built a three-story brownstone town house on East Eighty-Seventh Street and supported a large extended family. His matched white carriage horses were the talk of that sector of Manhattan at the turn of the twentieth century.

✳   ✳   ✳

SOURCES: "Fashion at Saratoga: The Grand Union Garden Party," *New York Daily Graphic* (August 24, 1875): 2; "The Happy Cooks," *New York Herald* (December 12, 1876): 7; "Cooks Away from the Kitchen," *New York Herald* (January 30, 1883): 5; "The French Cook's Ball," *New York Herald* 33 (February 2, 1887): 9; "Good Cooks at Saratoga," *New York Herald*, no. 21181 (August 19, 1894): 8.

Nunzio Finelli 1834–1886
Philadelphia

One of the greatest of Philadelphia's chefs during the mid-nineteenth century, caterer Nunzio Finelli maintained a Chestnut Street restaurant famous for its "fancy dishes." During his final years of operation, his staff included Philadelphia's great mixologist Charles B. Chandler, who made Philadelphians lovers of the cocktail.

In the mid-1880s novel *The Man from the West: A Novel Descriptive of Adventures from the Chaparral to Wall Street*, a witty bon vivant condemned Philadelphia's restaurant scene, yet he clarified, "I must except Finelli's. It is an oasis in the desert of Philadelphia's barrenness. Finelli's fried oysters are justly famous and his spaghetti is nearly equal to that of our own Mosetti's." The bon vivant was referring to New York's great Italian chef, Louis F. Mazzetti. Fortunately, the recipe for Finelli's distinctive version of fried oysters survives:

OYSTERS FINELLI

Parboil a dozen oysters in their own juice. Let them cool off. Take ham bones and veal bones, sprinkle with flour. Put them in a saucepan with butter and nicely brown; wet them with a pint of beef broth. Boil this for an hour. Then strain. Take the juice or liquid and add to it on half pint cream, mixed with a tablespoon of flour. Cook this for fifteen minutes until it thickens. Spread it out on flat pan until it is almost cool. Take each oyster and roll it carefully in the paste until it is almost round. Then let them get gold. After this take white of eggs and make a batter, thoroughly beaten. Dip the oysters in it and roll them in white bread crumbs. Then fry them in pure white lard for five minutes and serve.

Nunzio's father Antonio was a Neapolitan hotelier. In all probability, the young Finelli learned to cook in the hotel's kitchens. He emigrated to Philadelphia in 1858, having served as galley chief on the USS *Constitution*, and was immediately employed as a cook by the Girard Hotel. With the outbreak of the Civil War, he joined Colonel Collis's Zouaves and fought in campaigns in Virginia, and served as cook for General Banks and the Union officers until he was wounded in the Battle of Cedar Mountain, Virginia, in 1862. He was discharged in autumn of 1862 after returning to Philadelphia to recuperate.

When Philadelphia's Union League Club organized in 1863, Finelli served as its caterer, holding that office until 1869; subsequently, he served the club in the capacity of steward for many years. His duties at the clubhouse left him enough time to organize his own restaurant in 1867, the first being Finelli's at 10 South Chestnut. A loyal son of Naples, when the American centennial approached, Fi-

William J. Kuebler, "Nunzio Finelli" (ca. 1885). Albumen photograph cabinet card. Photograph: Courtesy of Norman Goos.

nelli organized a memorial association to erect a statue to Christopher Columbus in Philadelphia. The ten-foot-high likeness cost $18,000, most of which Finelli cajoled out of the city's Italian citizenry or the high rollers who frequented his establishment. The monument was unveiled on October 12, 1876.

In the year of the centennial, Finelli spent $30,000 to open a temple of fine dining at the juncture of Broad and Chestnut. Café Finelli at 1345 Chestnut Street was a trim four-story building, with a wooden arcade protecting the front entrance and the proprietor's name blazoned on the façade between the second and third floors. Café Finelli's mixture of French haute cuisine, roasted meats, seafood, Italian pastries, wines, liquors, and cigars kept it in the forefront of the city's restaurants until 1884, when the national depression forced its temporary closure. Finelli's son William revived it later in the year.

Nunzio Finelli died of kidney failure on March 18, 1886. William Finelli sold an interest in the restaurant to H. D. Watts in December 1886. The restaurant was known as Finelli and Watts until William's death in 1888. Nunzio's second son, Elijah, also entered the restaurant business, keeping a saloon in another portion of town. Because of Nunzio's deep involvement in Masonic life in Philadelphia, his funeral became a major memorial occasion. His body was interred in Mount Moriah Cemetery.

* * *

SOURCES: "Announcement from 'The Office,' " *Trenton Evening Times* (November 25, 1887): 2; "Chapter XXIII, From the Chaparral to Wall Street," *Austin Texas Siftings* 5, no. 50 (April 17, 1886): 7; [Obituary notice,] *New York Tribune* (March 20, 1886): 8; "The Columbus Monument Unveiled," *Daily Albany Argus* (October 13, 1876): 1; Norman Goos, [Nunzio Finelli biographical outline and genealogy,] Ancestry.com: http://trees.ancestry.ca/tree/1398971/person /-1946621959; Norman Goos, "Nunzio Finelli Biography," *Pennsylvania Historical Society Newsletter* (2015).

Jessup Whitehead 1834–1889
Kansas City, MO; Central City and Leadville, CO; Chicago; Jacksonville, FL; Atlanta and Salt Springs, GA; Huntsville, AL

A steward, chef, confectioner, food technologist, rancher, and cookbook author, Jessup Whitehead built a publishing empire in Chicago in the 1880s directed for the most part at culinary professionals rather than housekeepers. His oeuvre includes *The Hotel Book of Breads and Cakes* (1881), *The American Pastry Cook* (1882), *The Hotel Fish and Oyster Cook* (1882), *The Chicago Herald Cooking School* (1883), *The Hotel Book of Soups and Entrees* (1883), *Hotel Meat Cooking* (1883), *Cooking for Profit* (1886), *Whitehead's Family Cook Book* (1887), and *The Steward's Handbook and Guide to Party Catering* (1889). The contents of these volumes were compiled from columns that Whitehead generated for various periodicals and newspapers, particularly for the *Hotel World* in Chicago, the *Chicago Herald*, the *Jacksonville Florida Illustrated Hotel News*, and the *San Francisco Daily Hotel Gazette*. The compilations were for the most part published by his own Jessup Whitehead and Company publishing business located in Chicago. Each of the volumes appeared multiple times, including numbers of posthumous editions issued well into the twentieth century.

A Londoner by birth, Whitehead came to the United States in 1860, becoming a rancher and farmer in Miami County, Kansas. From autobiographical details contained in the later editions of *Hotel Meat Cooking*, it would seem that sometime in the 1870s he became a trained cook working under a Creole confectioner in Kansas City. His initial work took place in the bakery or confectionery departments of western hotels, particularly the Teller House in Central City,

"Hotel Monte Sano, outside Huntsville, Alabama" (ca. 1890). Photograph: Courtesy of Auburn University Archive (IV B 0620).

Colorado, and the Windsor Hotel in Leadville, Colorado. During his Colorado period, Whitehead began inventing kitchen devices. While in Central City in 1877, he registered Patent 200,957, a pastry table, and 200,958, a French-roll molder. In 1879, while Whitehead was at the Windsor Hotel, he registered a patent for a potato slicer. These evidences of Whitehead's concern for the practical problems encountered in the kitchen foreshadowed his work as a culinary journalist in the 1880s. He remained in Leadville until 1883, when he moved to Chicago.

Whitehead went to Chicago probably intending to set up a kitchen devices manufactory. He wound up getting into the business of publishing hotel cookbooks. Jessup Whitehead Publishing Company was domiciled at 183 North Peoria. Whitehead's Oven and Range series of cookbooks enjoyed singular success because he understood, from his experience in western hotels, that the mystification of haute cuisine in New York and the secrecy of the French chef community ill served the explosively expanding hospitality industry. Small cities sprang into existence across the continent, all requiring hotels. In big cities, constellations of minor boardinghouses ringed the cluster of major hotels at city's center. All wished instructions in plain English of the repertoire of popular dishes, seasonal menus, the best practices concerning the storage and stocking of produce, methods for cost containment, and amusing stories about challenges met and overcome. This Whitehead provided in his books. He used English names for dishes, interspersed stories with recipes, and projected a "we are in this together" sensibility that readers found attractive. Whitehead's great insight was that the growth of the culinary business demanded workers on a scale that the old apprentice system could not supply. Schools did not fill the gap. A burgeoning population of kitchen workers stood in need of some sort of instruction. He supplied it. The enormous success of his books (over twenty editions of certain of the titles) attested to the astuteness of his insight, an apprehension gained no doubt from his work in 1883 as a journalist for the *Hotel World* newspaper in Chicago.

Once his editors were in place, Whitehead left Chicago for warmer climes, periodically shipping off manuscripts to be cobbled into volumes. A decade of Colorado and Chicago winters turned Whitehead's imagination southward to the Everett Hotel in Jacksonville, Florida. The Florida fish dishes he learned in this winter resort make up an excellent selection of Lowcountry entrées found in *Hotel Meat Cooking*.

Whitehead served as the inaugural chef for two important southern resorts. In 1887 Whitehead moved to Georgia to head the kitchen at the newly constructed Sweetwater Park Hotel in Salt Springs, twenty miles from Atlanta. Fronting this mammoth wooden resort, there was a 700-foot-long portico that was 30 feet deep. "The dining hall is a model of beauty and excellence, finished throughout with hard woods, the walls decorated with handsome side boards; furnished with extra large, heavy French plate glass." Shortly before the opening on June 20, 1887, manager J. D. Billings declared: "The table will be furnished with every delicacy that the market will afford. The culinary department will be under the supervision of Messrs. Jessup Whitehead and Harry Hill. Mr. Whitehead having a national reputation as author and publisher of hotel cook books, which are used by all the principal hotels in this country." Surely this was the first time a hotel cook was recommended as a master on the basis of writing books about hotel cooking.

A season of spa-style country living drove Whitehead to the city. He spent 1888 as chef for W. F. Stokes's Restaurant in Atlanta. On January 1, 1889, he severed ties with Stokes to head the kitchen at the newly completed Hotel Monte Sano, a health resort constructed in the hills outside of Huntsville, Alabama. Fully opened in 1888, the Monte Sano catered to persons interested in the new exercise as recreation aesthetic promoted by the physical culture movement. Horseback riding, tennis, bowling, croquet, and hiking were the advertised amusements. The building itself, built of north Alabama stone, was meant to serve as the hub of a real estate colony settling in the healthful mountains north of Alabama's malaria line. These healthful settings did not, however, work their benefits on Whitehead, who, in early spring, sickened. He died on May 12, 1889, while at Monte Sano. He was buried in Huntsville.

SOURCES: J. Whitehead, U.S. Patent 200,958, March 5, 1878; "The Famous Spring," *Augusta Chronicle* (May 15, 1887): 2; "The Sweetwater Park Hotel," *Macon Telegraph*, no. 11762 (July 1, 1887): 5; "Jessup Whitehead," *London American Register* (June 1, 1889); "Huntsville and Its Hotels," *New Orleans Times-Picayune* (May 31, 1888): 4; *Atlanta Directory* (1888), 135.

Fred Harvey 1835–1901

New York; St. Louis; Leavenworth, KS; eighty-four restaurants and hotels in AR, AZ, CA, CO, KS, IL, LA, MO, NM, NV, OH, OK, TX

Stringing his restaurants like jewels along railroad lines, Fred Harvey adorned the West with fine dining, enticing eastern tourists with savory plates to accompany the sublime views. He was the pioneer restaurateur of the American West.

His was a classic "American Dream" story. A Liverpudlian of seventeen, he emigrated to the United States and hired out as kitchen help in a New York eatery. A year later, he ventured southward to New Orleans and nearly died there in the yellow fever epidemic of 1853. After his recuperation, he moved to St. Louis and spent two years selling jewelry before entering into the restaurant business in 1856. This thrived until the Civil War led to a split with his partner. Harvey spent the Civil War working as a railway agent. In 1865 he settled in Leavenworth, Kansas, working as a ticket agent. He would rise through the ranks quickly.

While working as a Chicago, Burlington, and Quincy western freight agent, Harvey learned the austerities and discommodities of American rail travel. Only the most frequented routes in the North had dining cars. In the West, eating houses at depot towns served tinned meats on tables lacking napkins and sanitary flatware. Lame and elderly servitors carried food to the tables. Partnering with Jep Rice, Harvey opened an eating house at Wallace, Kansas, on the Kansas Pacific Line in 1873, and another at Hugo, Kansas (later Colorado). In 1874 he then opened a restaurant at Florence, Kansas, a stop on the Atchison, Topeka and Santa Fe Railway. At this juncture, the Hannibal and St. Joseph Railroad employed him. With three eateries up and running, Harvey approached the manager of the Santa Fe Railroad in February 1875, proposing to create at-

"Fred Harvey," St. Louis (ca. 1857). Tinted photograph. Daggett Harvey Jr. Collection (HP.2011.01). Photograph: Courtesy Palace of the Governors Photo Archives, New Mexico History Museum, Santa Fe.

tractive restaurants along the line as a way of advertising the railroad. Legend has it that the manager wept and embraced Harvey.

Harvey tackled the problems of provision and accommodation sequentially. First he set up restaurants at stops along the line, then hotels at the major stopping-off points. Finally, in 1893 he ran the dining car service on the Atchison, Topeka and Santa Fe. He began in Topeka in 1876, opening a restaurant that created an immediate sensation. He sunk his profits into expansion. Concentrating on areas from the Midwest to the Pacific, Harvey opened during his lifetime fifteen hotels, forty-eight railroad restaurants, and thirty dining cars in the subsequent twenty-five years. Provisioning proved an issue, particularly since he insisted that no canned foods be served at any of the places bearing his name. He made Hermosillo, Mexico, a center of vegetable and fruit production. He contracted with Yaqui Indians to secure green turtles, since turtle soup and turtle steaks were staples of his menus. He co-partnered with several cattlemen to secure beef for his tables. The XY brand of cattle on the 600,000-acre ranch outside Hallock Station, Nevada, was his. He also subsidized the creation of dairy farms in Prescott, New Mexico; Las Vegas, Nevada; and other southwestern locales. Over the last decades of the nineteenth century, he made Kansas City a major provisioning depot for the western railroads.

Recruiting staff became as important as provisioning for Harvey over the years. Securing young talented cooks, he always paired an old cook with a younger and constantly circulated his talent through his empire until the supremely proficient chefs were installed at his hotels. His waitresses were trained to adhere to a strict routine. He hired for intelligence and attractiveness among the lower classes of the East (his sister in Michigan vetted the candidates), and the Harvey Girl became a signature of the restaurants. Harvey's efforts to secure talented waitresses became easier when legends of the ability of girls to woo and wed wealthy ranchers wended their way eastward.

Harvey was the first individual to have constructed a food system serving a chain of restaurants dispersed geographically over hundreds of miles. While restaurants with multiple branches existed prior to Harvey's railroad restaurants of the late 1870s (think of Delmonico's multiple branches in New York, with a short-lived outpost in San Francisco), none tackled the logistic complexities posed by creating institutions of hospitality in the southwestern desert. Harvey's was a heroic effort, and his contemporaries recognized it. "Keeping a hotel on the frontier in the early days was no amusement. Supplies were hard to get: shipments were irregular and competent cooks and waiters were as scarce as saints." Perhaps the greatest challenge in the first decade of his work was securing potable water. The Santa Fe Railway manufactured steel tanks to haul spring water and aided in the construction of storage towers in places where rainfall was sparse or seasonal. During the thirty years Harvey actively engaged in the hospitality business, he introduced refrigerators, cold storage warehouses, and hotel steam heat.

Certain of his businesses were co-partnered with the railroad, others were contracted, and the hotels were run independently. Yet his close affiliation with such a highly capitalized and rationally managed business afforded him advantages when establishing restaurants in towns run by local monopolies that wished to charge exorbitant amounts for supplies. He could source elsewhere; he could wait out any organized boycott, and the quality of his food invariably determined the tastes of the populations in his favor.

Of Harvey's long list of hotels and restaurants, several stand out for their historical importance. The Montezuma Hotel opened in Las Vegas in 1882 and was the first great temple of hospitality in a city that would explore the hotel as an art form. He chose the city for its hot springs, reckoning that it would become an invalid destination. It was to supply this hotel that Harvey established lines with Guaymas and Hermosillo, Mexico in Mexico. And it was here that he faced down a barroom full of rowdy cowboys shooting the bottles off the back bar, grabbing the leader by the collar and flooring him. When the butchers of Las Vegas attempted to organize a cartel and force the price of meat up 20 percent, Harvey's lawyers and out-of-state supplies disrupted the market rigging.

When the Atchison, Topeka and Santa Fe Railway announced the intention of inaugurating a dining car service in summer of 1891, Harvey worried that his restaurant and hotel empire would be rendered redundant, and that the railroad might actively discourage passengers from patronizing his eating houses.

He filed a restraining order in the state circuit court of Chicago to prevent the railroad from instituting the service. The action occasioned the renewal of his monopoly on depot restaurants along the Santa Fe line for two years and opened negotiations for Harvey's undertaking the dining car service.

While Harvey established the parameters and the dining experience in the West, and arbitrated the rise and fall of cooks through his system, he did not ever perform in a kitchen of a Harvey House during his twenty-five-year reign as boss. Still, his provisioning system, refrigeration system, and centralized management directives shaped the contents of menus from Chicago to San Francisco, from Denver to El Paso. All menus were predominately English, with French "light" entrées—"Roast Sirloin of Beef Au Jus," "Lobster Salad au Mayonnaise"—and vegetables appeared conspicuously (perhaps because fresh vegetables inspired greater reverence in the desert regions of the West), and hot dishes balanced cold preparations evenly. No Texican or Native American items appeared on the menu, despite Harvey's commercial sponsorship of Southwest tribal material culture for the tourist souvenir trade. Oysters, lobsters, and fish appeared regularly on Harvey House menus after the spread of refrigeration technology. Rapid transportation by railroad enabled the widespread uniform offering of a generic cosmopolitan cuisine at every point in the Harvey empire. The hallmark of restaurant chains—the standardization of menu—was achieved in the early 1880s by Harvey, largely provisioned west of the Mississippi but also reflecting no Native American or local foodways. Harvey knew his clientele—eastern tourists with a set experience of what constituted first-class cuisine. In 1992 George H. Foster and Peter C. Weiglin published their excellent culinary archive, *The Harvey House Cookbook: Memories of Dining Along the Santa Fe Railroad*, supplying both menus and recipes from the 1880s onward.

After 1885 Harvey's health declined. He suffered from neuralgic disorders and, finally, cancer. In 1899 his health worsened to the point that he gave up direct oversight of his company. He had trained his sons in the business, and they continued it after his death from cancer in 1901. At the time of his death, Harvey's company serviced 12,000 miles of railway with dining cars, restaurants, and hotels. These included the Frisco lines as well as the Santa Fe. The quality of service offered in his restaurants and hotels forced any competitors in the depot towns to upgrade service and food or unprofitably serve the lowest class of patron in a region. Hence Harvey and his successors are credited with forcing improvement of cooking generally in the region.

※　※　※

SOURCES: "Some Facts about Fred Harvey, Caterer," *Cleburn Morning Review* (May 20, 1813): 8; "Fred Harvey to Have Dairy in Las Vegas," *Albuquerque Journal*

(February 6, 1907): 7; William E. Curtis, "Curtis Tells How Fred Harvey Stated Gigantic Hotel System," *Daily Oklahoman* 22, no. 333 (Mary 14, 1911): 7; "Meat Inspection," *Santa Fe New Mexican* 26, no. 29 (March 25, 1889): 4; [Dining car injunction,] *Prescott Weekly Journal Miner* (August 12, 1891): 1; [Obituary notice,] *Kansas Semi-Weekly Capital* 23, no. 13 (February 12, 1901): 3; "The New Siloam: Opening of the Magnificent Hotel at the Hot Springs of Las Vegas New Mexico," *Daily Inter Ocean* 11, no. 26 (April 26, 1882): 9; "Ranches of 'Cattle Kings,'" *Kalamazoo Gazette* (August 29, 1882): 3; Stephen Friend, *An Appetite for America: How Visionary Businessman Fred Harvey Built a Railroad Hospitality Empire That Civilized the Wild West* (New York: Bantam, 2010).

Eugene Laperruque 1835–191?
Paris; Le Havre, France; New York; Lakewood, NJ

Next to Charles Ranhofer, Eugene Laperruque stood foremost in the ranks of the French masters of haute cuisine in the Gilded Age. He presided over four temples of fine dining in New York: Delmonico's, Hoffman House, Café Savarin, and the Plaza Hotel. In his forty years in the industry, his greatest fame lay in the execution of public banquets. While numbers of his contemporaries were more creative in the formulation of dishes (Ranhofer, Jean Roth), or more knowledgeable about the range of ingredients and culinary traditions (Jules Arthur Harder), no one equaled Laperruque in the management of deluxe, public dining.

Lorenzo Delmonico recruited Eugene Laperruque in 1875, installing him as chef de cuisine at the branch of Delmonico's at Twenty-Sixth Street. A master of banquet logistics, Laperruque had presided over several famous public feasts in Europe—for instance, the seating for 1,400 at the reception for the Republican politician Léon Gambetta, home secretary of the Third Republic. He served several households throughout the 1860s—the prince of Montmorency, the marquis of Lorne, and Princess Louise. In the early 1870s, his center of operations became the Elysée Hall at Le Havre, where he staged his own banquets.

Lorenzo Delmonico secured Laperruque when the chef traveled to Canada serving the marquis of Lorne, governor general there. Laperruque worked for Delmonico until an offer in 1884 to become the head of the Hoffman House restaurant tempted him away. During this period, Laperruque trained his nephew Charles in the culinary arts. During Laperruque's benign reign at Hoffman House, the restaurant gained a reputation as a first-rank establishment. Yet management feared Laperruque's power. In 1890 the owners attempted to exert control, extending the authority of the hotel manager over the kitchens. The

Joseph Byron, "Eugene Laperruque in the Office of the Café Savarin, New York" (1902). Photograph: Museum of the City of New York, Joseph Byron Collection (2F3XCSTW40L).

chef and the entire staff went on strike, declaring the manager's assertion of rule "a usurpation of [Laperruque's] authority and tantamount to a statement he was not performing the duties of his office properly." The management attempted to buy the loyalty of the chef's assistants by an across-the-board hike in pay of $25 a month; but all to a man paraded from kitchen in rank order. A crowd of 200 witnessed the exodus. Laperruque would be replaced by chef Gustav Nouvel.

From late 1890 to early 1894, Laperruque served habitués of the winter resort the Lakewood in Lakewood, New Jersey. Reputedly "the most elegantly appointed winter resort in the United States," the Lakewood accommodated 600 guests and boasted a half-mile of enclosed glass piazzas filled with tropical plants. Located sixty miles south of New York in the coastal pine forest inland from Manasquan, it was a favorite getaway of Manhattanites and particularly loved by President Grover Cleveland and his wife.

Finally, in 1894 Laperruque took over the Café Savarin, replacing chef Adrien

Tenu. One of Manhattan's shrines of French cuisine, Café Savarin had been created in 1889 on the ground floor of the Old Equitable Building in Manhattan. Laperruque ran the establishment with his usual imperial presumption, and within a year had inspired in manager George W. Rand an exasperation resembling that of the manager of the Hoffman House. When Rand attempted to assert his prerogatives, Laperruque performed a second walk-out with his entire staff. This time, however, the banks and brokers who patronized the restaurant demanded of Rand that the chef be reinstated. This happened quickly. Laperruque remained in this position until retiring in 1905. In 1907, when the newly opened Plaza Hotel dangled a salary of $8,000 a year for his skills, Laperruque returned to the kitchen. This was the highest wage paid in the city at that juncture. In the early 1880s, when he worked as caterer at the Hoffman House, Laperruque had been paid $5,600, making him second in the scale of compensation only to Charles Ranhofer of Delmonico's, who earned $6,000 per annum. At the Hoffman House, Laperruque commanded twenty-one cooks, pastry cooks, and ice-cream makers. He spent as much as $55,000 for one banquet. In a 100-by-50-foot kitchen, Laperruque prepared "ten kinds of soups, innumerable hors d'oeuvres, releves, entrees, roasts, sorbets, ices, and des[s]erts."

Laperruque had mastered several of the arcane arts of the kitchen. He was an excellent sugar sculptor, could carve masses of suet into the shape of lions and dogs, and fashion scenes of carved vegetables suspended in translucent blocks of gelée. He regularly won medals at the annual exhibitions of the Société Culinaire Philanthropique, including the great gold medal of 1908.

When asked in 1909 about the transformations in cookery over his thirty-plus years in America, Laperruque without hesitation replied that the most salutary development was the turn away from frozen poultry—commonly kept in cold storage for months during the 1880s before preparation—to entirely fresh, directly sourced, chickens and capons.

When asked at the end of his career about the greatest banquet he ever supervised, he named the Washington Centennial Ball at the Metropolitan Opera House in April 1889. This entertainment included a reception for 6,000 guests and a sit-down banquet for 800 persons including the president of the United States. The menus for each portion of this event reveal the highest aspirations of haute cuisine in America at the end of the nineteenth century. Laperruque was assisted by chef Busse. The buffet table for the reception featured:

CHAUD

Consomme clarifie en tasses for 6,000 people

Cape

Huitres poulettes

Bouchees a la Reine

Terrapin Maryland
Croquettes de Volaille
Thimbales Venitiennes
Filet de boeuf pique, sauce poivrade
Chapon au just

FROIDS
Saumon au Beurre de Montpellier
Basse rayee a la Borgia
Truite saumonee a la Bayardere
Filet de boeuf a la Russe
Aspics de foies-gras en belle vue
Jambon historie
Buissons de truffes du Perigord
Pate des canards
Aspics de langues a l'Imperiale
Noix de veau a la Ravigotte
Galatine trufee a la gelee
Chaufroid d'ortolans
Agneau de printemps roti
Becassines et pluviers a la gelee
Sanwiches de foies gras
Salade de Volaille
Salade de Homard

SUCRERIES
Gelee aux fruits
Gelee Rubanna
Charlotte Russe
Charlotte douce
Meringues a la crème
Gaufres Chantilly
Biscuites des Princes
Brioches
Savarins
Gateaux
Petits-fours

GLACES
Vanille

Pistache

Framboise

Café

Ananas

PIECES MONTEES

The banquet—staged on April 30, 1889, at 8:00 p.m.—included thirty-six cooks and assistants manning the carving tables. The menu ran as follows:

HORS-D'OEUVRE VARIES.

POTAGE

Tortue verte

Hors-d'oeuvre chauds

Petites timbales a la ministerielle

POISSON

8 Saumons du Kanebec, sauce Hollandaise

(each being presented on an oval socie four feet long and admirably decorated)

Salade de concombres a lay Mayonnaise

Omees a l'Anglaise

RELEVES

Filet de boeuf pique, sauce Madere

Champignons sautés

Haricots verts

ENTREES

Ris de veau, a la Toulouse

Petits pois, a la Francaise

Caisses de Becassines, a l'Americaine

Flageolets au Veloute

Aspecs de foies gras

Parcelles

Sorbets a la Presidence

ROTIS

Poulet de printemps au cresson

Salade Russe

Glace fantasie

DESSERTS

Petits fours

Mottoes

Gateaux

Fruits

Pieces montees

CAFÉ

Petits pains Viennois

Certain of Laperruque's classic preparations have been preserved and published in *The Plaza Hotel Cookbook*.

❋   ❋   ❋

SOURCES: "A Great Banquet Hall," *Repository* 3 (April 22, 1889): 7; "Hoffman House Cooks Striking," *New York Herald* 245 (September 2, 1890): 4; "A Celebrated Chef," *Worcester Daily Spy* (May 21, 1894): 6; "A Quick Change in the Café Savarin," *New York Tribune* (September 28, 1897): 5; "Société Culinaire Philanthropique Holds Its Forty-Second Annual Ball and Contest," *New York Tribune* (February 7, 1908): 14; "Chef Says Kitchens Improve," *Rockford Republic* (August 20, 1909): 9; "High Salaried Cooks," *Augusta Chronicle* (August 21, 1910): 22; "The Café Savarin," *The Alarm Clock* 6 (May 1, 1926): 1.

Nellie Murray 1835–1918
New Orleans; Chicago; Paris

In the 1890s, Nellie Murray catered every significant ball and society party in New Orleans. She seemed to the city's elite tastemakers the culmination of "a line of the famous Creole cuisinieres of Louisiana that made our dining-rooms and cuisines the rivals of Paris in the old days." An African American savant of Creole household cookery (as opposed to the explicitly French cuisine of the city's fine restaurants), Murray had been born into slavery on the plantation of Governor Paul O. Hebert at Bayou Goula. A house servant, Murray had been trained as a hairdresser, but her interest lay in the kitchens, where her mother served as Hebert's cook. She haunted the cook fires and learned by imitation.

After the Civil War, Murray gravitated to New Orleans, still attached to the Hebert family as a salaried servant. Because Adolph Hebert had married Eliza

"Nellie Murray." Wood engraving from "Woman's World and Work," *New Orleans Times-Picayune* (March 18, 1894): 28.

Miller, a connection was made to that genteel New Orleans family. Nellie became the cook of Eliza's sister-in-law, Mrs. Thomas Miller, and she worked for Mrs. Miller through the 1870s.

Murray said of her training:

> I really don't know. I had always a taste for and fondness for cooking. It just grew in me, and while chef de cuisine at Mrs. Thomas Miller's I learned from that elegant lady, who entertained a great deal, exactly how things should be done, and all about arranging menus, decorating tables and serving nicely. I made it a point to get all the recipes I could. Many ladies, seeing my interest, were very kind to me, and gave me recipes for dishes in which they excelled or were especially interested. So I have just gone on gathering knowledge and skill till I became sought after for my good dishes and pretty way of decorating tables.

Murray left Mrs. Miller's employ sometime in the mid-1880s, purchased a house on Delachaise Street, and contracted to be cook for Mrs. Frank T. Howard and her daughter Annie. One stipulation of her employment was that she could undertake events for other persons. Word of mouth spread of Murray's skill through the network of society women. By 1888 the demand for her was so great that she didn't need a household position. Instead, Murray became the first-call caterer of every society woman. Her scrupulous appointment books had a primary and a backup engagement for every day of the year.

In 1893 she was invited to supervise the cuisine at the Louisiana Mansion House at the World's Columbian Exposition in Chicago. Those who sampled her Creole dinners raved, and the popularity of the dining room gave rise to a crush of customers and a workload that became unbearable. She resigned before the end of the fair and returned to New Orleans and employment with the Howard family. In 1894 Mrs. Howard proposed that Murray accompany the family on a voyage to Europe to serve as chef and personal assistant. Murray agreed and experienced the cooking of Paris (where she resided with Annie Howard for six months), Berlin (where she lived for a year), Vienna, Bucharest, Bern, and London. In Paris, Murray recognized the profound affinity of the food of New Orleans with that of the French capital. "I could see New Orleans and her people in everything that was said and done and cooked. Especially cooked." When Miss Annie Howard married in England, Murray returned to Louisiana in 1896 to resume life as a freelance caterer.

With a practical and synthetic culinary imagination, Nellie Murray adapted the lessons of her European experience to the demands of Louisiana.

> Last winter a lady came to me and asked me to prepare "Fillets de Sole." Now, we have no such fish as sole in New Orleans. When I was in England I ate sole for the first time. I examined the fish. It looked very much like our flounder. Few people eat flounders here in New Orleans. The people over the lake sometimes eat them. The sole is of a darker meat than the flounder caught in our lakes. Well, I have often prepared "sole a la cardinal" from flounders here, but never ventured on the real sole. I think that we may do it now with perfect safety. Just take the fillets tenderloins of the flounder and prepare them as the English do the sole and your finest Englishman cannot tell the difference.

Murray's active life as a caterer lasted until approximately 1906, and then she took positions in various old New Orleans families of her acquaintance—with the Stauffers and the Whitneys. From 1896 to 1906, when newspapers mentioned Murray's work at an event, she was invariably designated as "New Orleans' foremost caterer." Of the many events she catered, perhaps the most interesting was the March 1903 National American Woman Suffrage Convention. The convention directors made a point of securing the service of a woman professional to supply them. "An elegant luncheon was served yesterday, the caterer being the famous Nellie Murray."

In 1916, at age seventy-four, she retired to live with her nephew, at which point she quarreled with his mother—her sister, Marce Andrews—who brought suit, trying to seize Murray's ample bank account. Andrews did not succeed. Nellie Murray died peacefully and well cared for at her nephew's home in early spring of 1918. In 2016 a group of culinary professionals in New Orleans under the direction of Dr. Zella Palmer staged a feast to honor Nellie Murray's accomplishments; the proceeds of the feast went to underwrite costs of for a film biography of another female chef of New Orleans, Leah "Dooky" Chase.

SOURCES: "Nellie Murray," *New Orleans Times-Picayune* (March 18, 1894): 28; "Nellie Murray on European Cooking," *New Orleans Times-Picayune* 60, no. 315 (December 4, 1896): 3; "Women Who Stand for Equality," *New Orleans Times-Picayune* (March 21, 1903): 3; "Legal Clash over Richs of Dusky Maid of Society," *New Orleans States* (January 21, 1917): 4; [Obituary notice,] *New Orleans States* (March 25, 1918): 11.

Wong Ah Cheok 1836–1897?
San Francisco

Wong Ah Cheok took over the landmark Hang Fer Low Chinese Restaurant (later, Hang Far Low) at 713 Dupont Street, San Francisco, in the late 1860s and made its cuisine the standard for Chinese cooking in the city for the next fifty years. Reputed to be the leader of the Hop Sing Long group, a political gang, Cheok tried to keep himself beneath public notice. There were, alas, occasions during which Cheok came to public attention, such as during a gun battle with the rival Suey Sing secret society in August 1881, after the Suey Sing tong raided the Hop Sing Long temple. Though three of Cheok's group were wounded by gunfire, the predominance of Hop Sing Long tong in the Sixth Ward was reasserted.

More consequential in the long term than the turf battles over political dominion in Chinatown was Cheok's enterprise in building Hang Far Low (Apricot Flower House) into the "Chinese Delmonico's," as it was called, the foremost banquet house of Chinese cuisine in the city, an institution so famous and long-lived in public memory that it would survive the earthquake of 1906, being relocated to 725 Grant Avenue, continue as a landmark into the 1960s, then undergo a transmutation into Four Seasons, becoming the favorite hang-out of the beat poets.

When Cheok gained ownership of the restaurant, it had already operated for some time. Two cooks—Lee Yup and Quoi Bok—had cooked in the restaurant since its founding in the early 1850s. Cheok added baker Ah Hung and an additional cook, Sun Suey, to the staff. At a three-story building at 713 Dupont, Cheok presented a three-tier layer cake of dining options. On the ground floor was a store for Chinese ingredients and a meal counter for quick dishes. On the second floor was an eating house for regular boarders. And on the third floor

Tabor Studio, "Grand Dining Room, Chinese Restaurant, Dupont Street, San Francisco" (1882). Hang Fer Low Restaurant. Photograph: Courtesy of the Bancroft Library, University of California, Berkeley (BANC PIC 1905.06485:046—PIC).

was a luxuriously decorated banquet hall for events. Here the greatest moments in nineteenth-century Chinese cuisine on the West Coast were enacted.

The first glimpse of the cuisine from Hang Far Low dates from 1853, when adventurous reporters from the *San Francisco Whig* dined at a banquet hosted by merchant Key Chong, eating sea cucumbers, stewed acorns, dried oysters, periwinkles, lobster, birds' nest, and several dishes completely unintelligible to the diners. During its initial decades, the cuisine was orthodox Cantonese. "No Americans ever eat there." Only after Cheok added the splendid third story in 1872 did the space acquire the cultural mystique that made adventurous Euro-Californians curious to experience the culinary mysteries. Part of the attraction was the extraordinary décor of the building façade. The third-floor balustrade was painted in bright "alternate stripes of red, yellow, blue and green." To accommodate Californians, European wines were served at banquets.

In the 1870s and '80s, Hang Far Low became the first-choice venue for public banquets in the Chinese community. Whether bidding farewell to the Chinese consul or welcoming a new male child to the families that led the Chinese Six Companies, the community assembled on the third floor with an eight- to twelve-course meal. An 1881 banquet with the General Consul and King "Kalakance" (King Kalākaua) of Hawaii was reputed to have been the most elaborate staged in San Francisco to that time. The menu: "Birds-nest, white snow fungus, imperial fish brains, preserved birds' eggs, sharks' fins, fish maw, mushrooms and bamboo shoots, young and tender; stewed duck with Sentsen sauce, chicken with satow dressing, turtle stew, melon seeds, pear wine, Chinese oranges, and preserved nuts." While other restaurants emerged in the 1890s that emulated Hang Far Low's style—notably Hoey Sen Low, Yoot Cheong Low, and Yuen Fong—none could supplant it as the center of civic life.

The earthquake of 1906 destroyed the restaurant completely. It was rebuilt a short way up the street, which was renamed Grant Avenue in the resuscitated city. Cheok had passed over control in the 1890s to his relations in the Wong family. Bo Wong realized that the revived restaurant had to suit tourists' tastes, so he devoted one floor of the restaurant to chop suey and the top floor to classic Cantonese cuisine. It had the most resonant brand name of any Chinese restaurant in the city in the early twentieth century, receiving prominent notice in all the tourist guides to city life and dining.

✳   ✳   ✳

SOURCES: *United States Federal Census for 1870*, San Francisco, 6th Ward, Sheet 14; "Chinese Restaurant," *San Francisco Bulletin* 35, no. 37 (November 19, 1872): 3; "A Chinese Feast," *San Francisco Bulletin* 43, no. 125 (March 5, 1877): 2; "H.I.C.M.S.C.," *Cleveland Leader* (February 21, 1881): 3; "The Chinese Must Go," *San Diego Sun* (August 3, 1881): 1; "A La Chinois," *San Francisco Bulletin* 68, no. 144 (September 21, 1889): supplement 4; "Eyes Opened in Wonderment," *Cleveland Plain Dealer* (April 18, 1897): 3; "Judge Campbell on Chopsticks," *San Francisco Call* (February 21, 1897): 8; Judy Yung and the Chinese Historical Society of America, *San Francisco's Chinatown* (San Francisco: Arcadia, 2006), 17; Andrew Coe, *Chop Suey: A Cultural History of Chinese Food in the United States* (New York: Oxford University Press, 2009), 123-24.

Anthony Edward Faust 1836–1906
St. Louis

Anthony "Tony" Faust, St. Louis's celebrity restaurateur during the Gilded Age, was one of the great personalities in American cuisine. Obsessed with cheese, he summered every year in Europe, searching out obscure local varieties and bringing them to his namesake restaurant. Born in Germany, Faust emigrated to the Midwest and found the German-American world of Missouri to his liking.

"Tony Faust's Restaurant and Fulton Market, St. Louis" (1888).

He grew up bilingual and wandered between the German and English languages when excited or playing cards with his friend August "Augie" Busch, the brewer. (Tony's son Edward would marry Augie's daughter Anna). Faust's English was flavored with a light lisp. His wholehearted barking laugh erupted after the punch lines of jokes with such violence that it would inspire laughter in turn. He presided over a splendid restaurant on the corner of Broadway and Elm Street.

Faust came to St. Louis in 1853, worked briefly as an ornamental plasterer, settling in French Town, on South Broadway. His career as a plasterer ended in 1861 when a soldier accidently discharged a rifle while on parade, wounding Faust in the side. He opened a saloon and restaurant in 1862 at Broadway and Chouteau at a time when Auguste Furcy's French restaurant at 48–50 Olive Street provided an international standard of fine dining for the city. Furcy's supremacy partly depended upon the importation of the finest wines, foie gras, charcuterie, and confections. Faust embraced the insight, albeit looking to Germany rather than France. In 1871 he moved to the corner of Fifth (Broadway) and Elm, occupying a prewar building there. He called his place Tony Faust's Oyster House and Restaurant. The restaurant combined cosmopolitan hotel fare with a strong admixture of German favorites. In the 1870s, his specialties included brook trout, oyster stew, and sauerbraten. The men's dining room served Anheuser beer on draft. He would later have Anheuser brew a Faust label beer for use in the restaurant.

A fire in 1877 forced a rebuild of the restaurant, including an early rooftop garden. In 1878 Faust secured the adjacent building and started the Fulton Market, a produce and import emporium whose collection of sausages, cheeses, fruits, and vegetables became legendary. The late 1870s saw a concerted effort to upgrade the quality of food served at the restaurant. Important in this endeavor was Faust's securing the services of Edouard Birmel (1834–1894). Born in Kehl, Germany, and apprenticed in the famous Spa at Baden-Baden, Birmel mastered both the German cookery of his homeland and the French style of resort cooking. In St. Louis, Birmel was hired in 1866 by Isaac Gildersleeve to be chef of the Everett House. Faust poached him from Gildersleeve and reveled in supplying Birmel the finest ingredients from both sides of the Atlantic. Faust realized the ingredients themselves could generate a second revenue stream, and so stocked the Fulton Market with Indian spices, coffee, and pomological exotica.

From 1888 to 1889, upon securing an additional ten-year lease to the lot, Faust tore down the old restaurant and rebuilt it as a two-story fireproof building. The basement operated as a canning operation for "Faust's Own" brand oysters and a sausage factory. The output stocked the Fulton Market next door. The gentlemen's dining room occupied the first floor; the ladies' dining room, the second floor. In this space, Birmel built a cosmopolitan list of American classic dishes. Consider his list of fish, meat, and game on September 6, 1889:

FISH. Ready to Serve.

Boiled Codfish, Beurre noire 40   Broiled Spanish Mackerel 60

FISH. To Order.

Lobster (whole) 60   Lobster broiled (whole) 75

Lobster (half) 30   Lobster broiled (half) 40

Pompano 60   Blue Fish 50

Red Snapper 50   Soft Shell Crabs 75

Fresh Mackerel 40   Haddock 75

Frog legs 75   Striped Bass 50

Spanish Mackerel 60   Flounder 40

Codfish 40   Halibut 40

BOILED.

Beef Tongue Polonaise 30   Spare Ribs and Sour Kraut 30

ENTREES.

Sirloin of Beef, Baden Baden 50   Chicken Pot Pie, a l'Anglaise 50

Frog Legs Fried, sauce Remoulade 60   Macaroni au Gratin 20

Oyster Pattie 25

ROAST.

Ribs of Beef 40   Loin of Beef 40

Leg of Veal 40   Spring Lamb, Mint Sauce or Peas 50

Leg of Mutton 40

GAME, ETC.

Squab on Toast 40   Young Chicken, whole 75

Venison Steak 60   Young Chicken, half 40

Wood Duck 50   Teal Duck 50

Wood Cock 75

Contemporary descriptions indicate that Faust's sense of décor combined excess with exoticism. The ladies' saloon was "provided with expensive and artistic furniture, the flooring being of polished mosaic pavement and as smooth as glass; the walls richly painted in oil pictures and portraits." From 1888 the entire restaurant boasted electric lighting, employing arc lamps. It was the first public building in the city with electric light. When he opened Faust's New Cabin in 1898, he made a German baronial resort—"The walls are decorated with carved mahogany, while the ceiling is finished in tapestry."

Game was always a significant element on the autumn and winter menus of Tony Faust's, and the restaurateur, having come into the business well before the populations of wild animals began to decline in the American interior, never countenanced the conservation laws put into place in the last decades of the nineteenth century. Prairie chickens served out of season at Faust's appeared on the menu as "Virginia Owls." When arrested in 1889 for violations, he "declared his willingness to plead guilty to the charge and to pay his fine or to break rock as the honorable court might elect."

Tony Faust retired from active management of the restaurant in 1902, handing the business over to his son. His retirement was devoted to special projects, such as collaborating with August Lüchow of New York on a Bavarian-style beer house at the St. Louis World's Fair and setting up a branch of Faust's in New York. He died in Wiesbaden in 1906 during one of his annual summer jaunts. The restaurant did not survive the migration of the theater district out of its neighborhood and closed in 1916.

※ ※ ※

SOURCES: "French Restaurant," *Daily Missouri Republican* 30, no. 200 (August 27, 1851): 3; J. A. Dacus and James W. Buel, *A Tour of St. Louis* (St. Louis: Western Publishing Co., 1878), 297–98; "'Virginia Owls' Restaurant," *St. Louis Republic* 82, no. 21636 (September 6, 1889): 2; "Our Electric Lighting," *St. Louis Republic* 85, no. 22884 (February 5, 1890): 3–25; "A. E. Faust," *St. Louis Republic*

82, no. 21919 (June 16, 1890): 3–24; "Snap Shots of Well-Known St. Louisans," *St. Louis Republic* 89, no. 209 (January 24, 1897): 6; "Owed Success to Bullet Wound," *New York Times* (September 29, 1906); James Faust-Busch Family Papers, A2309, Missouri History Museum Archives.

Sophie Dorn Flêche
(Madame Eugène) 1836–1906
Baton Rouge, LA; New Orleans

Madame Eugène, the empress of nineteenth-century New Orleans restaurant cookery, presided over three important Louisiana kitchens: the Gem Saloon in Baton Rouge during the later 1850s, Le Pellerin (the Pilgrim) in New Orleans from 1860 to 1879, and Moreau's from 1880 to 1887. A native of Reichshoffen, Alsace, in France, she emigrated with her husband, Eugène Flêche, to Louisiana in 1853. At age seventeen, she was a fully trained pastry chef when she began her career as a confectioner in a New Orleans kitchen. She became a name in 1858 when she took over the Gem Saloon in Baton Rouge and made it the best restaurant in Louisiana outside of New Orleans.

In 1860 restaurateur Auguste Broué, after presiding over Le Pellerin for nineteen years and introducing curry to Louisiana's pantry, had grown weary of business and wished to retire to France. He had trained no successor, so he invited Madame Eugène to take over his legacy. She accepted. Under her management, the restaurant on 15 Madison Street (known alternately as Flêche's, the Pilgrim, or Le Pellerin) became the particular resort of the theatrical set. When Giulio Adamoli visited New Orleans two years after the end of the Civil War, he listed four restaurants as the pinnacle of New Orleans dining: the dining room of the St. Charles Hotel, Moreau's, the Cosmopolitan, and Flêche's. He did not list Victor's, the famous restaurant maintained by the Martin family.

Because women played such a significant role in the world of the traveling theatrical companies, and because catering to women had become in the 1850s one of the national preoccupations of high-end restaurateurs, Madame Eugène's success as caterer to actresses and actors in part depended upon her embracing luncheon as a meal at Le Pellerin. She abandoned the traditional late breakfast, the déjeuner—a meal that became the special preserve of Flêche's contemporary Madame Bégué. Madame Eugène instituted the lunch in its place. In response, the ladies of New Orleans flocked to her midday meal, detouring from shopping expeditions on Canal Street into the Quarter to lunch at Le Pellerin.

Women's preference for Madame Eugène's cuisine in New Orleans had several consequences. When Charles Rhodes, proprietor of Moreau's Restaurant—one of the city's great institutions—retired in 1880, instead of turning it over to his son, he entertained Flêche's offer to assume control of the restaurant. Installed on Canal Street, Madame Eugène made Moreau's the finest French restaurant in the city. Rival establishments were abandoned by the city's bon vivants—Victor's suffered its great decline after the death of Georges Martin in 1873, and Antoine's after the death of Antoine Alciatore in 1874 and before the ascension of his son Jules in 1891. A second consequence was the sisterly embrace of the city's women, who adopted Madame Eugène as an honorary Creole home cook, including her recipes in the landmark 1885 collection *The Creole Cookery Book*. She was the only professional chef in the city to be accorded such an honor. She was neither Creole nor a home cook.

Her crawfish bisque recipe was nationally famous and appeared repeatedly in print during the 1880s. But a more precise sense of her art can be obtained by the recipes included in Mrs. Washington's *The Unrivalled Cook-Book*:

PUREE OF SNIPE À LA CRÉOLE (MADAME EUGÈNE)

Snipe should always be kept *four days* at least, before cooking. Never pluck them until you are ready to cook them. Hang them in a cool, dry place. Take a dozen snipe, pluck them and draw them; cut off all the meat, and put it aside, with the entrails, in a mortar; put the remains of the birds in a saucepan with bouillon, parsley, laurel leaf, a clove, and two glassfuls of white wine; boil this till it is reduced to half, and strain it; pound your birds and entrails in a mortar with three ounces of fat pork, moisten with the above sauce, and pass this puree through a colander; put it in a saucepan, let it heat through without boiling, and serve on a dish surrounded by fried croutons.

SWEETBREAD CROQUETTES À LA CRÉOLE (MADAME EUGÈNE)

Soak the sweetbreads an hour in warm water, and blanch them in boiling water until the larding needle can pass through them without tearing them; cut them in dice; cut the same quantity of mushrooms, also, in dice; stew them together in a little white sauce; make them into shapes like a pear, sticking a clove in the end; powder them with bread crumbs and fry; serve with a tomato sauce.

SALPICON (MADAME EUGÈNE'S ENTRÉE)

Make a white roux; moisten it with bouillon and a glassful of white wine; add a soup bunch, salt, and pepper; let it boil and thicken; take for your ragout equal portions of whatever cold meats, fowl, game, livers, ham and tongue, mushrooms, bottoms of artichokes, you may have, and cut them in little dice; let them simmer and color; take out the soup bunch; thicken the sauce with a little flour if necessary; fill little pâtés and vol au vents, and serve.

The only menu of a meal from Madame Eugène's heyday dates from 1877, when she prepared a version of the Maryland feast (terrapin stew, oysters, canvasback duck) for a dinner in honor of Sheriff T. H. Handy.

She was a widow when she ruled over Moreau's. In 1887 she married the retired merchant Jean B. Laporte, returning Moreau's to Charles Rhodes. The delights of domesticity would be brief. In 1890 her married daughter Sophie Flêche Ecuyer died, leaving four young children. In 1892 Jean B. Laporte died. Madame Eugène moved into the Ecuyer household to raise her grandchildren. Absorbed in these domestic duties, she lost touch with the culinary world she once dominated. In 1908, when Walter Hale published an elegy on old New Orleans and its delights in *Uncle Remus Magazine*, he thought that Madame Eugène had returned to France to live out her life in Provence. He did not know she had died peacefully, a beloved Alsatian grandmother in the Ecuyer household, in 1906.

SOURCES: "Madame Eugene's Restaurant over the Gem Saloon," *Baton Rouge Daily Advocate* (October 23, 1858): 1; "A Prophet Is Not without Honor Except in His Own Land," *New Orleans Crescent* (March 14, 1866): 2; [Madame Eugène as "worthy successor of Victor"], *New Orleans Times Picayune* (January 27, 1874); "Victor's Restaurant Burned," *New Orleans Times Picayune* (January 11, 1877); "A Pleasant Occasion," *New Orleans Times-Picayune* (December 21, 1877): 2; Christian Women's Exchange, *The Creole Cookery Book* (New Orleans: T. H. Thomason, 1885), title page. "Jean B. Laporte" [obituary notice], *New Orleans Times-Picayune* (September 2, 1906): 8; Giulio Adamoli, "Letters from America: 1867, III," *The Living Age*, no. 313 (1922): 37; George Augustus Sala, *America Revisited* (1882; reprint, New York: Arno Press, 1974), 3; Rien Fertel, "Creole Cookbooks and the Formation of Creole Identity in New Orleans, 1885–1900" (MA thesis, New School for Social Research, New York, May 2008).

Henri Mouquin 1836–1933
New York

Swiss restaurateur Henri Mouquin became in the 1870s and '80s one of the champions of French cuisine in New York City. He also became the most enterprising wine merchant in Manhattan. His restaurant at 149 Fulton Street had a retail wine store on its back end, fronting Ann Street, that offered the most

William Glackens, *At Mouquin's* (1905). Oil on canvas, 122.4 × 92.1 cm. Jeanne-Louise Mouquin and restaurateur James Moore. Friends of American Art Collection. Photograph: Art Institute of Chicago.

spectacular stock of fine vintages available in nineteenth-century America. A satellite store operated at 33 Park Place, and a branch of Mouquin's restaurant opened on Sixth Avenue below Twenty-Eighth Street in the early 1890s.

Mouquin nearly single-handedly popularized escargots on the menus of American French restaurants from 1888 to 1890. Because the snails thrive in the alkaline vineyards of Burgundy and were a natural adjunct to those vintages, Mouquin began importing cases in the late 1880s. When customs agents opened the first case to come into the Port of New York, the snails escaped the crate and crawled all over the office, much to the consternation of the agents. They were doubly distressed when they learned that the snails did not appear on the lists of dutiable importations. By 1894 Mouquin imported 20,000 to 30,000 snails a week from November through March, trans-shipping crates to San Francisco and Los Angeles, as well as provisioning the hotels of New York and Philadelphia. In 1894 Mouquin's chef provided the first published instructions on the preparation of escargots to the American public in the pages of the *New York Tribune*:

ESCARGOTS À LA BOURGUIGNONNE

First of all, put the snails in cold water, shell and all, for twenty-four hours. This dissolves the chalky matter in the shell more or less. Then place them in warm water for half an hour. They should then be drawn from the shell and placed in a deep pan and boiled for three hours with carrots, thyme and laurel leaves for flavor. Then put them back in the shell, close the openings with a past of crack dust, butter, garlic, chervil, eschallotes, chives and tarragon. Then bake them for two minutes over a very hot fire.

ESCARGOTS À LA BORDELAISE

Immerse it as before in cold and hot water; draw it from the shell and boil it, as in the other style, slowly. Then pour over it a wine sauce, flavored with eschallotes and garlic. Then hold it for a few minutes in a sauce-pan over a very hot fire. Italians often add mushrooms. These are the best ways to cook snails.

Born in Switzerland, Mouquin emigrated to the United States in 1854. Welcomed by his uncle Morel Mouquin, the young Henri was immediately taken to Delmonico's to work as a waiter. According to Mouquin family tradition, he headed west to St. Louis after working a season at Delmonico's. In 1857 Henri returned to New York, petitioned his uncle for financial backing, and opened a modest eatery at 95 Fulton. This early bistro, like his subsequent restaurants, doubled as a store for import foods. Henri's earliest specialty was Swiss cheese. In May 1862, he moved his business to 81 Nassau Street and opened a lunch salon as an adjunct to his cheese store. Once established, he sent to Switzerland for his sweetheart, Marie Julie Grandjean. They married and she took control of the kitchen. The early reputation of the restaurant depended upon her onion soup and her bouillabaisse. Madame Mouquin retired from the management of the kitchens in 1866 to raise children, and various chefs, the most famous of whom was François Sarniguet (1829–1884), superintended the cuisine. Despite Mouquin's service in eastern Virginia during the Civil War, the business prospered under the watchful eyes of his uncle and wife. During the Civil War, he expanded onto 83 Nassau Street, a building with a capacious cellar, and began the importation and storage of wines. By 1869 the business had become so large that he moved to the building at 141 Fulton that extended through the entire block and had a second entrance on 20 Ann Street. He divided the premises into his restaurant (Fulton side) and wine store (Ann side). The size and locale caused him to expand from his usual lunch business to dinner service.

By 1871 his reach as an importer enabled him to supply the best materials in

Europe, consequently elevating his restaurant into the first sphere of continental gastronomy in the city. While fake foie gras was served all over Manhattan, Mouquin served up Strasbourg's finest. A French commentator observed that if it was truffled turkey, green turtles, fresh peas, mushrooms, past, game or fish, Westphalian hams or Wilshire bacon, fresh or dried fruit, or cheese one wished, Mouquin's was the place to visit in Manhattan.

By 1882 Mouquin claimed that his cellars housed the strongest collection of vintages of the "Médoc, Fronsac, St.-Emillion, Barsac, Bourgogne (Côtes d'Or), Beaujolais, Maconnais, Chablis, Rhin, Hongrie, Suisse, Espagne, Portugal, Madere, Muscat de Frontignan, Malvoisie et Tokay" in the United States. Indeed, he became the principal agent for the producers of Bordeaux in the country. In 1886 Henri secured a similar position with the producers of Cognac. Mouquin's dominion over the American market for fine wine was not without its travails. In midwinter of 1888, an electric fire broke out in his wine cellar at Fulton, causing a $1,000 worth of damage. Mouquin's ability as a broker and his faithfulness as a partner made the fire but a momentary distraction in his expanding network of agencies and affiliations. His ads from the 1890s list the names of those whom he represented, whether the celebrated exporter of Tokay, Palugyay & Sons in Hungary, or the Madeira House of Rutherford and Browne. Also in 1890 he made his initial foray into the fine olive oil market, importing the pressings of Feyret & Pinson of Bordeaux.

In the early 1890s, Mouquin opened an upscale French restaurant on Sixth Avenue with an orchestra to accompany dinners. It was stylistically more Parisian than Sherry's and atmospherically more carefree than Delmonico's, and so won the hearts of New Yorkers who revered the most modern sort of French cuisine. The Sixth Avenue restaurant even featured prominently in the romance novels of the 1900s. The wine store continued to thrive on Fulton, with Henri devolving increasing amounts of responsibility on his son, Louis Mouquin. After fifty years in business in New York, Henri retired and settled in the bucolic warmth of York, Virginia. He died at age ninety-six in 1933, deploring in his last breaths the damage done to fine dining by Prohibition.

※　※　※

SOURCES: "Changement de Domicile," *Courrier des Etats-Unis* (May 5, 1862): 4; "Faits Divers," *Courrier des Etats-Unis* 118 (May 22, 1865): 2; [Advertisement,] *Courrier des Etats Unis* 104 (May 3, 1869): 3; "Le Réveillon," *Courrier de Etats-Unis* (December 23, 1871): 4; "Le Bazar Suisse," *Courrier des Etats-Unis* 89 (March 30, 1879): 2; "Mulled Claret, Fire Breaks Out in Mouquin's Wine Cellar," *New York Herald* 19 (January 19, 1888): 9; "The Way to Cook Snails," *New York Tribune* (March 11, 1894): 15; "Henri Mouquin Tells of His 60 Years as a

Restaurant Keeper," *New York Sun* (April 20, 1919): 6; "Henri Mouquin Dead," *Lawrence Journal-World* (December 25, 1933): 2; Mouquin family history: http://history.mouquin.com.

Charles Ranhofer 1836–1899
Paris; New York; New Orleans; Washington, DC

Charles Ranhofer died in 1899 the arch wizard of haute cuisine in America. His cookbook, *The Epicurean*, published in 1894, was indifferent to translating its dishes to the skills of the home cook and revealed unambiguously the chasm between professional creativity and common cookery. A grimoire of French and American cooking, *The Epicurean* revealed the guild secrets—the finesse of saucing, the gnosis of flavor pairings—and gave final permission to chefs to publish their findings without fear of another stealing one's creations and reputation. Publication became publicity rather than bald exposure of one's proprietary knowledge.

Ranhofer had been the chef de cuisine at Delmonico's for over three decades. He had been installed as honorary president for life of the Société Culinaire Philanthropique, the society of Franco-American chefs in New York that nurtured the community's welfare. His career and life story has calcified into a chain of legends. Here are the tales in rough chronological order.

Chef at Sixteen

Born in St. Denis, son of the chef of the Restaurant du Commerce there, Charles Ranhofer departed the family at age twelve to apprentice in the kitchen of the patisserie Fleuret, Boulevard de Madeleine, Paris. He mastered the art, secured his certificate, and immediately secured a position as head baker at Mercier. Ranhofer was quick to act upon opportunity, and he shifted positions to be head baker at Malpiece. Bakers' hours did not much agree with him it would appear, and he left to work as assistant to the brilliant pastry chef Mollard, steward of Prince Henin of Alsace. A year into his tutelage, while working at the chateau at Mongratan, Prince Henin and Mollard fell to fighting over the temperature of an ortolan pâté. Mollard exited and Ranhofer, but sixteen at the time, experienced a field promotion to chef de cuisine. He learned large-scale provisioning, banquet planning, and the timing of courses on the fly. Eventually, the routine of a provincial palace wore on Ranhofer. He resigned, returned to Paris, and began working with the well-connected caterer Benois, then with restaurateur

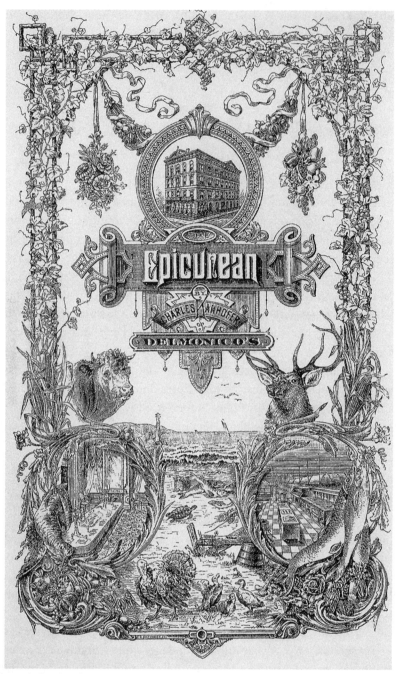

Charles Ranhofer, *The Epicurean: A Complete Treatise of Analytical and Practical Studies on the Culinary Art* (New York: Charles Ranhofer, 1894), title page.

Leserteur. Ranhofer's time with Prince Henin enabled him to reenter aristo-cratic service. He managed the kitchens of both the Duc de Noailles and Baron Rothschild for a season, before consenting to accompany a Russian diplomat dispatched for service to the United States.

Ranhofer in New Orleans

The Russian consul in 1855 was billeted for service in New York. Ranhofer did not much like Waverly Place, home base for the consul in New York, or Wash-ington, DC, with its French restaurant scene dominated by Charles Gautier the confectioner, for whom he also worked briefly. Wanderlust brought him to New Orleans, a spot so congenial that he worked there for four years, from 1856 to 1860, with François Lefevre, heading the second of Lefevre's two sweet shops and luncheon saloons located on the corner of Royal and St. Peter Streets. This place catered primarily to women lunching during midday shopping expedi-tions. Ranhofer became entirely acquainted with the pantry of American ingre-dients during his time in New Orleans and the repertoire of New Orleans chefs. This 1856 lunch menu may be the first American bill of fare surviving from Ranhofer:

Galatine Truffée   Mayonnaise de Volallte

Turkey, trufee   Westphalian Ham

Beef Filet   Stuffed Tongue

Vol au venia, with Mushrooms

Suprème de Volaille   Salmon filet à la Tartare

Culasse-de-poulard, à la maréchale

Charlotte Russe   Rum Jelly   Maraschino

Rice and Milk   Café au lait   Black Mocha, &c.

Beaujolais Wine   Bordeaux Wine

Grave sec   Chablis

Lucel Muscat   Fontignan

Tokay   Champagne

As the political climate grew increasingly rancorous in 1860, Ranhofer re-turned to Paris. His sojourn there would be brief.

Lorenzo Delmonico Secures Ranhofer

Hotelier F. Martinez of San Francisco's Barnum House Hotel in late 1860 moved east intent on creating a restaurant in Manhattan that eclipsed every other in the United States, including Delmonico's. The Maison Dorée (borrowing the name of the famous Parisian restaurant) on Union Square brought the San Francisco meal format—déjeuners, lunches, dinners—dispensing with supper. To lead this ambitious house, Martinez brought Ranhofer from Paris in early 1861 and hired Domenico Paretti as his assistant. Immediately the epicures of New York took notice. Indeed, the response was so enthusiastically favorable that Ranhofer decided not to work in someone else's kitchen and set up his own restaurant instead. Partnering with Eugène Charve, an established figure in New York, Ranhofer opened the Café-Restaurant du Commerce at 426 Broadway in late August 1862. Meanwhile, Martinez replaced Ranhofer by hiring chef Jules Arthur Harder from Delmonico's Chambers Street branch. Lorenzo Delmonico needed a replacement for Harder, and someone to lead the new branch on Fourteenth and Broadway. By February 1863, Delmonico determined he had to break the Charve-Ranhofer partnership and hire Ranhofer to be his chef de cuisine. Delmonico offered two potent inducements: money and power. Early in March 1863, these inducements worked.

Ranhofer at Delmonico's

Though he was not yet thirty when he assumed control of the kitchen at Delmonico's, Ranhofer asserted a level of control over the restaurant's operation unprecedented in the three decades of the institution's existence. He not only prepared the daily bills of fare and banquet menus, he also asserted control over the purchase of provisions, a matter that had been previously conducted by members of the Delmonico family. In the 1870s, Siro Delmonico would work in tandem with Ranhofer in the purchase of supplies for the restaurant, handling the money transfers to vendors. Ensconced in an upscale mansion (the Moses H. Grinnell House) on Fourteenth Street and Broadway, Ranhofer fed a generation of socialites, financiers, statesmen, and bon vivants. His influence upon the restaurant's cuisine was immediate, with a new attention to the appearance of food (the color of sauces could not repeat, nor could the color of roasted meats; banquets had to have at least one spectacle piece in the hall as a focus for attention). In order to bring a standard of technique in the kitchen, he instituted in the 1870s a school in his kitchens, a more formal scheme than apprenticeship. There he trained numbers of the important chefs of New York: Charles Lalonette of the Hotel Buckingham, Emil Herderer who catered President Grover Cleveland's inaugural dinner, chef John Wendling of the Lotus Club, and his various assistants at Delmonico's.

Despite the French orthodoxy of the kitchen technique that Ranhofer championed, he in no sense believed that an immutable canon of dishes—a standard repertoire—must be performed at Delmonico's. (His Delmonico's colleague Louis Ragot did believe this.) Ranhofer thought that the chef de cuisine should have a culinary imagination and create new pleasures for diners. Throughout his career, Ranhofer invented or reinvented dishes, and the most famous of these became standard presentations around the globe: baked Alaska in 1867, eggs Benedict in 1868, lobster Newburg in 1876, and avocado salad in 1893.

Departure from New York

The financial depression of the early 1870s disrupted lives at every level of society. While Delmonico's experienced a drop in trade, of substantially greater consequence was the massive unemployment in Manhattan and the potential for social unrest. To fend off wide-scale starvation, the city of New York and various private institutions set up a network of precinct soup kitchens. Lorenzo Delmonico and Ranhofer set up their own network of soup kitchens at 2 South William Street, Chambers Street, East Fourteenth Street, and 22 Broad Street. These served as many as 12,000 persons a day, mostly laborers and their wives, on fish chowder and beef soup. Ranhofer personally oversaw the composition of the soups. Besides the proteins, observers noted that "there are plenty of potatoes and onions in the chowder, as well as some other vegetables." Consumers judged it "excellent."

The financial downturn caused Lorenzo Delmonico to reconsider the future of his business. He concluded he must relocate his main branch from the Grinnell House, which was too small, to a venue located in a more fashionable district. He settled upon Fifth Avenue and Twenty-Sixth Street. When he informed Ranhofer in January 1876, Ranhofer indicated his intention to retire. This he did, turning over the kitchen to his assistant M. Sallouette. He departed to France with the intention of establishing a business for himself. He ran the Hotel American at Enghien-les-Bains, the lakeside resort on the northern fringe of Paris, for three years before acceding to the repeated appeals of Lorenzo Delmonico to return and preside over the kitchen at Twenty-Sixth Street.

Ranhofer in the Underworld

When Ranhofer returned to New York in early May 1879, his eminence inspired general awe and fear. "Chef" was the title he chose. He descended into the below-grade kitchen complex at Fifth Avenue and Twenty-Sixth to find a roomful of cooks he had personally trained. He never raised his voice. The tilt of an eyebrow or a sideway turn of his wrist were enough to convey his displeasure. Persons would be discharged on the authority of a frown. He preferred efficiency in communication, which meant minimal conversation. Once the provision lists had been dispatched, the menu set, the dishes allocated, his forces would be set into motion. He could lay a banquet for 300 on two hours' notice. From working with him, his forty-two underlings knew the sequence of the preparations, the pace, and the finishing of the dishes. He regularly worked fourteen- to sixteen-hour days. His uncomplaining industry, his unflappability, and his omni-competence won him reverence among the crew and in the profession at large. He brooked no questions and sought only the approbation of Lorenzo Delmonico, whose self-possession and reserve Ranhofer admired. When Charles Crist Delmonico assumed control of the empire, Ranhofer assumed an avuncular concern for the young proprietor and walked him through the kitchen world, expounding the method of its operation in detail.

Ranhofer's office, a minuscule space, stood at the heart of several rooms. To one flank, four roasting ovens were manned by four chefs of his own training and eight assistants who did the butchering and prepping of roasts and grilled items. Three persons operated the ice-cream section, and two men handled cakes and confections. Three bread bakers operated around the clock preparing loaves. A floating staff of eight young assistants served to assist where needed. Two men were employed to scour pots, roasting pans, and kettles, and ten women (Ranhofer found their attention to detail in cleaning superior to men) labored as dish scrubbers. Eugène Garnier, Delmonico's maître d'hôtel, shared Ranhofer's love of precision, expertise, and serenity of service, and held the wait staff to strict promptitude of delivery when dishes emerged from the kitchens. A speaking tube connected Ranhofer with Garnier. Communications among the staff tended to be functional—and the quiet both of the kitchen and the dining room was always a matter of comment for witnesses of Delmonico's operations. All the wines, coffee, and cheese in an evening's repast, whether for a banquet or a solitary patron, came under the aegis of the maître d'hôtel.

Ranhofer the Reformer

Within the rather hidebound precincts of the Société Culinaire Philanthropique, the most consequential association of French chefs in New York, certain inflexible preferences concerning banqueting prevailed. They were visible in the annual dinners and exhibitions. Foremost among these was the preference for the old French style of service in which all the dishes in a course (there were generally three courses per banquet) were laid out simultaneously on the table; this required extraordinary coordination in cooking and had quite an effect as visual spectacle. The usual recourse to chafing dishes and bains-marie to keep dishes warm until service led to some unfortunate results. "The entrees are apt to lose many of their finer qualities by the very act of being cooked and dressed beforehand." In contrast, the Russian system of service suits those who prefer to eat food very hot and do so very quickly. No hot dish is placed on the table. All meats are cut up as needed, in the kitchen or pantry, placed on a platter and brought to groups of ten diners, passed about, with each taking what one wished. Dishes are brought in serial sequence from the kitchen. Ranhofer's innovation, which he called the American service, is detailed in *The Epicurean.* The menu, created by the chef, stands as a guide, specifying the order of dishes; each guest has one for reference. The appearance of food is entirely scripted by the menu. The amount of protein on the menu is a function of diner gender—all-male gatherings featured more roast meats—women in the company dictated light and fancy dishes. If there is a guest of honor from a foreign place, the chef must feature some of the characteristic dishes of the guest's homeland. "Offer on the menus all foods in their respective seasons and let the early products be of the finest quality and only use preserved articles when no others can be obtained." Ranhofer's menus permitted services that presented multiple dishes at one time—in the French style—or single dishes in sequence. The use of the menu as organizer of service was the hallmark of his innovation.

The Epicurean

The scale of Delmonico's enterprises and the size of its staff caused Ranhofer to make use of writings, for record keeping as well as formulation and menu planning. Since the early 1870s, his kitchen school had caused him to record dishes as formulae for study and revision. A hallmark of a Delmonico's chef from the 1850s onward was the recourse to writing. Jules Arthur Harder and Alessandro Filippini both employed their records to generate landmark cookbooks. Of contemporaries in New York unconnected with Delmonico's, only Felix J. Déliée had as much recourse to writing. After Harder, Filippini, and Déliée had all published cookbooks supplying views of professional kitchen craft, Ranhofer, as he contemplated retirement, determined to publish a monument to his creations. *The Epicurean*, after two years of composition, appeared in spring of 1894. It contained over four thousand recipes that claimed to be simplified for general consumption. But a careful reading indicates that the simplification consisted only in a more ample exposition of preparation than a trained professional would need. The processes depicted in the majority of the preparations were in no way simple. Interwoven with the cooking formulae were observations on nutrition, economy, sanitation, order, the aesthetics of appearance, waste, and punctuality. The presentation in terms of style was efficient, intent on instruction rather than amusement. Ranhofer appeared authoritative rather than congenial, direct rather than witty. Yet the treasury of information he presented supplied the most thorough exposition of high-end Franco-American cuisine available from the first age of American fine dining. Its instructions are substantially more useful than Auguste Escoffier's, if one's intent is to prepare dishes, and consequently its influence has been felt more keenly in the professional world of cooking than in public adoption of its insights. Contemporary reviewers called it encyclopedic, but it does not have the organization of such works. They were paying lip service to the scope and thoroughness of Ranhofer's treatment of the preparation of meals. Since its publication, *The Epicurean* has remained a canonical text of American cuisine, a linchpin of an important cookbook collection, and a resource for chefs practicing transatlantic haute cuisine.

When Ranhofer died in 1899, the obituaries highlighted his long service at Delmonico's and this culinary masterwork as the significant matters of his life.

✳   ✳   ✳

SOURCES: "J. [*sic*] Lefevre," *Daily Picayune* (March 14, 1856): 2; "Maison Dorée," *Courrier des Etats-Unis* 37, no. 308 (December 31, 1860): 10; "Ouverture," *Courrier des Etats-Unis* (August 25, 1862): 4; "Café-Restaurant du Commerce," *Courrier des Etats-Unis* 39 (February 16, 1863): 3; "The Delmonico Soup Kitchens," *New York Herald* 39, no. 80 (March 21, 1874): 5; Charles Ranhofer, *The Epicurean* (New York: C. Ranhofer, 1894); "Serving a Public Dinner," *New York Sun* (October 28, 1894): 8; "Culinary King Ranhofer," *Washington Evening Times* (October 12, 1899): 6; "Charles Ranhofer," *New Orleans Times-Picayune* (October 20, 1899): 4; "The King of Cooks," *The Red Cloud Chief* (November 2, 1900): 2; "A Culinary Encyclopedia," *Boston Sunday Herald* (June 3, 1894): 28; William Grimes, *Appetite City* (New York: North Point Press, 2009), 58.

Francis J. Kinzler 1837–1897
New York

Chef Francis Kinzler suffered one of the great indignities of any culinary professional in nineteenth-century Manhattan—he ran a great New York hostelry, the Hotel Brunswick, into bankruptcy in 1885. While it was not an unusual course from the European perspective to transmute from chef to hotelier, Kinzler's superb judgment with the saucepan and stockpot did not translate to a mastery of cash flows when financing the hotel's rehabilitation. It wound up in the hands of an assignee.

Kinzler came to the United States from France and opened a small eating house on the corner of Eleventh Street and University Place, a space that would be later become Solari's, famed for its "absolutely private" second-floor dining rooms favored by New York's underworld bosses. In the 1860s, Lorenzo Delmonico hired Kinzler to be a sous-chef at Delmonico's. When James L. Mitchell

"Hotel Brunswick, New York" (ca. 1885). Stereoscopic photograph. Robert N. Dennis Collection of Stereoscopic Views. Photograph: From the New York Public Library (MFY Dennis Coll 91-F209).

and Charles H. Reed secured the lease of the Hoffman House in 1869, intending to make it a temple of cuisine, they secured Kinzler's services. A partnership rift between Reed and Mitchell in late 1872 led Mitchell to undertake the erection of a rival hotel on the corner of Fifth Avenue and Twenty-Sixth Street with a parallel ambition for fine fare. Mitchell hired Kinzler away from the Hoffman House with a promise of partnership. Mitchell ran the front end, Kinzler the kitchen, and the Brunswick prospered; indeed, it became the resort of the smart set in New York in the late 1870s.

A prose portrait of the Brunswick during the centennial year vividly conveys the qualities of the culinary department:

It possesses a large kitchen. Every inch of cellar space extending from Twenty-sixth to Twenty-seventh street along Fifth avenue is devoted to cooking and other preparation of tables for dining. Every fish, every kind of game, every article of table goods has been carefully assorted and laid away in a place assigned to it. Without a spark of light the chef could descend into the kitchen and lay his hand at the first trial upon any cut of meat that may be ordered, and it would be found in absolute readiness for the fire. There is as much discipline among the assistants and scullions as on board a man-of-war. So thoroughly is the work systematized that it is as easy to fix the responsibility for a bad roast as it is to fix the responsibility of a theft of a mint. The dinners prepared are marvels of culinary excellence and artistic displays. They cost from $5 to $50 per plate according to the completeness of the menu, the number of musicians, the display of flowers, the cost of getting up the menu, and the amount and value of the wines and liquors ordered.

One famous Brunswick dinner prepared by Francis Kinzler with the aid of Sebastian Nouvelle on February 10, 1876, had the following menu:

HUITRES EN COQUILLE
Cotes de Rion

POTAGES
Printanier a la Royale   Tortue Verte   Vinto de Pasto

HORS D'OEUVRES
Varies   Pates chauds a la Russe

RELEVES
Coquilles Saint Jacques   Saumon a la Hollandaise

ENTREES
Filet de Boeuf pique a la jardinière   Caisses de Ris de Veau, Pompadour
Cauteau Lacaussade   Brunswick Private Stock

LEGUMES
Haricots verts sautés au beurre   Petits Pois a la Francaise

PIECES FROIDES
Galantine de Volaille, Historiee   Aspic de Homard, Bagration
Sorbet au Kirsh

ROTIS
Selle de Mouton, Anglaise   Canvas-back Duck (Salade laitue et celery)
Chateau Lachaise

ENTREMETS SUCRES
Charlotte Parisienne aux pistaches   Corbeille Meringuee
Sultane d'Oranges a la Reine   Nougat Modern

PIECES EN GLACE
Le Lion   Locomotive
Compotes   Corbeilles de Fruits   Assiettes Montees

The success of the Hotel Brunswick's cuisine depended on Kinzler's eye for talent. He rivaled Lorenzo Delmonico in his ability to detect disciplined, imaginative employees. Besides Nouvelle, Kinzler had Sebastian Michel and Eugene Chaude as assistants. Both were talented practitioners of exhibition food.

Mitchell's death in 1883 forced Kinzler into the role of a front-of-house manager. The 1885 crisis led to eleven years of financial and legal maneuvering before Kinzler and Rebeca B. Mitchell put the hotel in receivership with liabilities of $524,447 and assets of $379,154. The closure of the Brunswick so disheartened Kinzler that he retired to live with his son in Newport, Rhode Island. He died in 1897.

※ ※ ※

SOURCES: "Le Réveillon," *Courrier de Etats-Unis* (December 23, 1871): 4; "The Refinements of Dining," *New York Daily Graphic* (April 15, 1876): 9; "Chef Kinzler's Failure," *New York Times* (February 6, 1885): 5; "A Receiver for the Brunswick," *New York Tribune* (January 28, 1896): 12; "Francis J. Kinzler," *New York Tribune* (February 18, 1897): 7.

Gustave "Gus" Jaubert 1838–1920
Lexington, KY

In any population of saloon keepers, café owners, eating house proprietors, and oyster cellar men in the cities of nineteenth-century America, there was invariably one or two persons who intuited a higher calling than providing food, drink, and temporary shelter. Some came to love the community in which they served, understood the need of people for a space for festivity, a sense of occasion, and splendid fare. In the case of saloon keeper Gus Jaubert of Lexington, Kentucky, this sense of calling emerged over the course of a thirty-year career that began just after the Civil War and lasted to the end of the century.

A native of New York, he came to Louisville, Kentucky, with his French parents in 1842. His younger sister, Virginia, who worked as a greeter in the saloon, was born in Lexington in 1853, where the family had moved shortly before. During the Civil War, young Jaubert enlisted and eventually became cook with

Mullen Studio, "Gustave Jaubert" (ca. 1890). Lexington, Kentucky. Albumin photograph. Photograph: Courtesy of Barbara Koch-McGhee, Atherton House, Louisville.

General John Morgan's cavalry. During the weeks of deprivation endured by the unit, Jaubert improvised a stew of leftovers, using blackbirds as the chief protein. He called it burgoo. This stew—with chicken substituted for blackbird—became Kentucky's signature dish during Reconstruction.

In 1867 Jaubert opened the Magnolia Saloon, "where everything suitable for the palate can be supplied," on the corner of Short and Mulberry Streets. It enjoyed success, encouraging Jaubert to seek a larger building. He found one at 18 North Mill and moved in during the summer of 1870. For much of the 1870s, he had from twenty to twenty-two rivals in the business, but only the saloon at the St. Nicholas Hotel challenged him when it came to the quality of food and drink. It was the only establishment in the city that regularly served green turtle soup,—that favored dish of American fine dining.

In the 1880s, having established his restaurant as a fixture in Lexington's gastronomic firmament, Jaubert began the career for which he became nationally famous—as caterer for political barbecues and public events. It was Jaubert who developed the distinctive preference of Kentucky for barbecued lamb that persists to the twenty-first century, and then there were the cauldrons of burgoo. The first occasion he served burgoo in quantity took place in Ashland in 1882, when he cooked 1,750 gallons of the savory stew. Later in life, he claimed his first barbecue took place in Sayres Woods in 1886 in connection with the congressional campaign of James B. Beck. By 1888 the scale of the events that he catered became enormous. He employed as his assistant in these outdoor feasts Samuel Oldham Jr., an African American barbecue specialist, who became famous from 1890 until his death in 1896.

Jaubert's barbecue and burgoo became so celebrated that every element on Kentucky's political spectrum called upon his services, despite his own affiliation with the Democratic Party. Confederate veterans or an encampment of the Grand Army of the Republic (GAR), Democratic stump meetings or Republican conventions, commercial conclaves or religious revivals—if the hosting bodies aspired to public significance, they erected the big tent, trenched the eighty-foot pit, and called in Jaubert. By the 1890s, the burgoo had transmuted into "Gus Jaubert's famous burgoo." As many as 150,000 people attended the 1895 GAR encampment at which he barbecued "forty-five beeves, 384 sheep and 241 shoats. Following were the ingredients of fifteen thousand gallons of burgoo: 300 bushels of tomatoes, 300 bushels of potatoes, 900 dozen ears of green corns, eight barrels of onions, sixty dozen fat hens and other ingredients in proportion." If the hosts wished variety, Jaubert offered to fry catfish as well.

Jaubert remained tight-lipped about the recipe of burgoo until old age and infirmity caused him to leave off catering. He offered the following to reporter Edwin Carty Ranck on November 29, 1914:

> Nobody but a crazy man ever puts whisky in burgoo. The kind of burgoo I make—the kind that has been drunk all over Kentucky, Indiana, and Ohio—is made of vegetables and meat alone. If you want to make, say, a gallon of burgoo, take a gallon of water and put in a whole chicken and a beef shank, cut up into small pieces. Keep this cooking until the meat is well done. Then put in four ears of green corn, cut off the cob; half a dozen tomatoes, a dozen potatoes, and three onions, all cut up very fine. This mixture must be stirred continuously to prevent scorching, and water must be added from time to time, as is necessary. It takes from two to three hours to cook burgoo properly, and when you take it off the stove it should be light brown in color and very thick.

One notes that the recipe says nothing about the seasoning, which was known to contain a good deal of pepper.

Jaubert sold his saloon in 1901 to Melven Sheerer after thirty-four years of operation. Almost immediately, the Normandy hired Jaubert to make his signature dish, which it made available every day it was open. Jaubert continued catering several barbecues each year into his mid-seventies.

When he died at age eighty-two in the winter of 1920, M. Kaufman, an old friend, addressed his spirit in a newspaper meditation. Kaufman did not recall the great festivals that had made Jaubert's name famous; rather, he wrote of incidents in the first months of his career as a restaurateur: "When you came back from the Civil War, where you had contended for the right, as you saw it—as you did in all things—you opened a coffee house and do you remember how you were wont to send buckets full of soup to the needy and suffering and how the poor newsboys came to your place and none ever left hungry? No one knows how many poor stranded souls lived on your bounty; for you never let your left hand know what the right one did."

The needs and the pleasures of the community were always Jaubert's primary concern.

✳ ✳ ✳

SOURCES: *Lexington Directory* (1867), 90; *United States Federal Census, 1870,* Lexington Ward 2, 33; "Shelbyville's Louisville Southern Barbecue," *The Climax* (May 30, 1888): 1; "Deaths and Funerals," *Lexington Morning Herald* 26, no. 366 (December 1, 1896): 5; "Jaubert," *Lexington Herald* 34, no. 248 (September 4, 1904): 4; "Cooking Is Unique as Crowd Is Great," *Lexington Herald* 37, no. 115 (April 25, 1907): 8; Edwin Carty Ranck, "A Kentucky Burgoo-Master," *Lexington Herald* (November 29, 1914): 3; "Noted Burgoo Maker and Wife Wedded 50 Years Ago Today," *Lexington Herald* 286 (October 13, 1918): 13; "In Memory of Gus Jaubert," *Lexington Herald* 90 (March 3, 1920): 2; Federal Writers Project, *Kentucky: A Guide to the Bluegrass State* (New York: Harcourt, Brace and Company, 1939), 354.

Eugene Mehl 1838–1910
New York; Long Beach, NY; St. Paul and Lake Minnetonka, MN; San Diego, CA; Brigantine Beach, NJ

In France the ambition of every good cook is to become chef, and of every capable chef to become the proprietor of a substantial hotel. Alsatian Eugene Mehl fulfilled that ideal life plot with panache. He had finished his kitchen apprenticeship at age sixteen, when he came to the United States in 1854 and immediately found employment in the kitchen of the Brevoort Hotel. He rose through the ranks, serving in the various kitchen offices before elevation to chef de cuisine. Mehl's management of that office commanded the respect of his professional colleagues in Manhattan. They elected him to the presidency of the Société Culinaire Philanthropique in 1871.

Mehl oversaw the cuisine of the Brevoort House in the era when it became favored by New York's Bohemian arts community. From 1859 to 1882, he led the kitchen of this small aristocratic hostelry distinguished for its lack of a bar-room; for its ability to cater to the refined tastes of European royals, such as Prince Albert (who resided there during his 1870 sojourn in America) and the Grand Duke Alexis of Russia; and for its herb gardens fronting Fifth Avenue. The service was decidedly old-fashioned: the 6:00 p.m. late dinner was presented on silver and porcelain. "The waiters were all marshaled by a steward, and at the tap of a bell they came into the dining room in procession, put their dishes down on the tables with a flourish, and lifted the silver covers as one man, with the precision of a military drill. The guests of the hotel usually wore evening dress." During the summers after 1880, Mehl worked at Long Beach, a new resort erected on Long Beach Barrier Island in Nassau County.

He was lured away from the Brevoort only when offered a partnership in the running of the Windsor Hotel. Mehl managed the back of house, his partner the front, and they shared the profits. When the owner of the Windsor died and his son ran the business into the ground, Mehl took his $100,000 savings and entered into the career of a hotelier, managing in 1889 the Hotel Ryan in St. Paul concurrently with the Lafayette Resort Hotel in Lake Minnetonka, Minnesota, in the summer. Jessup Whitehead preserved a menu from Mehl that shows the classicism of his French cuisine in the early 1890s:

BLUE POINTS SUR COQUILLE

POTAGES
Bisque de crevelles   Consomme d'Orsay

HORS D'OEUVRES
Varies
Petites bouchees au salpicon

POISSONS
Bass rayee a la Hollandaise   Filet de sole a la Joinville
Concombres   Pommes croquettes

RELEVES
Selle de chevreuil a la Cumberland
Jambon d'ourson au chasseur
Tomates farcies

ENTREES
Cotelettes de pigeonneaux chevaliere
Petits pois Francais

Poltrine de cailles a l'Andalouse
Quenelles de perdreaux a la St. Hubert
Flabeolets a l'Anglaise
Ballettines d'ortolans a la Periguex
Fonds d'artichauts, Lyonnaise

SORBET
Lucullus

ROTI
Poule de prairie   Sarcelles
Salade escarole

PIECES MONTEES
Paniers garnie aux fruits   Pyramide en nougat
Chalet Suisse   Chapelle Turque
Vues du Lac Minnetonka
Corne d'abundance
Chemin de fer du Northern Pacific entrent dans le tunnel Mullen

SUCRES
Pudding a la Tyrolienne, sauce sabayon
Glace Napolitaine   Bavarois au chocolat
Petits fours assortis
Fruits   Fromage   Café

VINS
Chateau Yquem   Amontillado
Johannisberger Cabinet
Chateau Cos d'Estournel, '74
Roederer   Pommery   Chateau Lafite, '65
C'os de Vougeot
Liqueurs

This idyllic arrangement collapsed when Mehl's beautiful daughter ran away with a black bellboy, then after a fortnight of adventure, tired of romance and returned home. The resulting scandal forced Mehl to look for a place to escape the whispers.

He took over the Hotel del Coronado in San Diego in 1895, partnering with U. F. Newlin in its management. Sharing power did not sit well with Mehl, so he departed after only a season, taking over the Holland House, an ocean-side resort hotel at Brigantine Beach, New Jersey, which he managed for six years. He retired a millionaire in 1901.

✳ ✳ ✳

SOURCES: "An Englishman's Tribute to the Brevoort House, New York," *Christian Union* 8 (October 15, 1873): 309; "New Resort," *New York Times* (July 18, 1880): 5; "Hotel Notes," *Amusement Bulletin* 1, no. 2 (December 1889): 14; Albro Martin, *James J. Hill and the Opening of the Northwest* (St. Paul: Minnesota Historical Society, 1891), 257–64; [Daughter's elopement,] *Hickory Press* (September 28, 1893): 1; Jessup Whitehead, *Hotel Meat Cooking*, 7th ed. (Chicago: Jessup Whitehead Publishing, 1901), 364.

John W. Conway 1839–1899
Santa Fe, NM

Santa Fe's absorption of cosmopolitan style into its Spanish colonial culture took place gradually. John Conway's renovation of the Bon Ton restaurant in 1887 marked an important juncture, for its excellent fare, roasts, and East Coast oysters appealed to the Hispanic elite as well as to the Anglo contingent seeking refinement. Every substantial town in the New Mexico territory had a version of the Bon Ton—McKnight's Bon Ton Saloon in Las Vegas (when the town was still part of New Mexico) was the prototype. The Miles Brothers' Bon Ton restaurant in Las Cruces had "a good feed corral connected" with it, and after April 1891, "a French cook and new waiters." Santa Fe opened its version of the "splendid saloon" in 1883, when C. Chambers opened the Bon Ton restaurant on San Francisco Street. Dishes were served up à la carte by short-order cooks. But Chambers lost money on the business and sold it to Harry S. Welsh in December 1885. Welsh thought that securing oysters would improve the business. But vending meals at 25 cents a person was no way to stockpile money. John W. Conway decided he knew what needed to be done to make the Bon Ton splendid and profitable and took over in 1887.

Born in Ontario, Canada, and raised in St. Louis, John Conway joined the Union army at the outbreak of the Civil War, serving first as a drummer, then a teamster. He remained in service after the war, stationed in the western districts, coming to Santa Fe in 1879 after leaving the army. For a year he worked as an employee of the Fischer Brewery. His interaction with the brewery's customers interested him in saloons. In 1880 he opened the City Beer Hall. His experience running the hall convinced him he knew the public taste and could make a success of the Bon Ton where others had failed. In 1887 he took over the restaurant, remade its menu, and commenced advertising its attractions, repeatedly asserting the first-class character of his establishment, contracting with the finest cooking talent he could secure (often from Denver or San Francisco), and promising "fish, oysters and sweetmeats can be had here at a moment's notice and done to the queen's taste in any desired style." Conway ran both hall and restaurant from 1887 until his death.

Nothing forces one to improve like having a rival, and in caterer Will C. Burton, Conway had a redoubtable competitor. Proprietor of Billy's Plaza Restaurant in the late 1880s and '90s, Billy Burton took to publishing his menus in the papers. "Maccaroni la Italiene, Croquettes de Homard, Bouchees aux huitres" were the featured entrées on Sunday, December 15, 1888. It was the oyster that enabled Conway to prevail in the contest on the gustatory level. But as fundamental to his success was his conviction that in Santa Fe, good eats must be paired with amusement. At the Bon Ton, he constructed a billiard room and a ten-pin bowling alley contiguous to the beer saloon. At the short-order counter or the café dining room, one could have Kansas City beef steaks, fish, game, Baltimore oysters, "spring chickens, game in season, frogs legs, the finest fruits and vegetables." If one was a stranger to the city, one could secure lodging in one of the upstairs rooms.

Early in the 1890s, Conway took his son, John V. Conway, into the business. His wife, Maria, managed the front of house. Expanding the number of rooms for transient guests to eighteen, he took to calling his place "the Bon Ton Hotel." In 1897 he took over the old Fischer Brewery site, converting it into an outdoor beer garden, a sandwich shop, and an indoor recreation area in the old malting house. He led an active civic life, serving as officer in local associations and city councilman. Having married into the local Martinez family, Conway made certain that Hispanic interests were served. His son John V. managed the local baseball team and was viewed as belonging equally to both the Anglo and Spanish communities in the city. When he married Delfinn Gonzales in 1893, John V.'s status as a youthful leader of Santa Fe's Hispanic community was cemented.

When John W. Conway died in early 1899, his wife and son took over the restaurant, saloon, and beer garden and kept them operating into the twentieth century. John V. would rename the hotel the Normandie and retain Bon Ton as the name of the restaurant within the establishment in 1905.

※ ※ ※

SOURCES: "Special Notices," *Newmans' Semi-Weekly of Las Cruces* (April 2, 1881): 3; "Special Notices," *Newmans' Semi-Weekly of Las Cruces* (April 20, 1881): 3; "Chambers & Co.," *Santa Fe New Mexican* (December 30, 1885): 1; "For the

Holidays," *Santa Fe New Mexican* (December 15, 1888): 4; "Menu Billy's Plaza Restaurant," *Santa Fe New Mexican* (December 15, 1888): 4; "J. W. Conway's Bon-Ton Restaurant," *Santa Fe New Mexican* 26, no. 233 (November 22, 1889): 1; "The Bon Ton Hotel," *Santa Fe New Mexican* 34, no. 117 (July 9, 1897): 4; "Death of John W. Conway," *Santa Fe New Mexican* 36, no. 24 (March 18, 1899): 4; "Round about Town," *Santa Fe New Mexican* (December 31, 1899): 4; "Minor City Topics," *Santa Fe New Mexican* 36, no. 25 (March 20, 1899): 4; "Bon-Ton Café," *Santa Fe New Mexican* 37, no. 81 (June 5, 1900): 5; Christmas Menu, 1891, Restaurant-ing through History: http://restaurant-ingthroughhistory.com/tag/santa-fe-restaurants/.

Victor Dol 1840–1911

New Orleans; Havana; Montréal; San Francisco; Los Angeles

When Los Angeles transitioned from being an outpost of civilization to the bustling hub of Southern California in the last quarter of the nineteenth century, Victor Dol supplied the high-style cuisine that attested to the city's cultural adequacy. A radical leftist who became a real estate millionaire, a chef in New Orleans, Cuba, Canada, and San Francisco before coming to Los Angeles, Dol was a quasi-mythical figure. His place in Los Angeles was secured by another legendary figure, Benjamin "French Louis" Flotte (1814–1888).

The quasi-mythological father of haute cuisine in Los Angeles, Flotte excited the epicures of early 1870s California at the Oriental Restaurant, a one-story structure opposite the Pico House on Main Street. The restaurant, despite its name, was not Asian, but French (from the perspective of California, Paris was in the "East," too). Flotte was an anarchist who had repeatedly been imprisoned in France for incendiary writings, visionary plots for governmental restructuring, and active participation in the agitations of 1848 and 1871. He had settled in San Francisco in the mid-1850s (he would keep a house there until 1874) and opened a successful restaurant, but returned to Paris during the outbreak of the Franco-Prussian war. He was present during the short-lived Commune, but returned to California after its failure, coming to Los Angeles and setting up the Oriental Restaurant.

In Flotte's kitchen, Charles Casson—an ex-member of the culinary staff under chef Giuseppe Ranieri of Emperor Maximilian I of Mexico—presided, a fortunate survivor of the crack-up of the empire. In 1873 Flotte moved his enterprise up to the Downey block at Main and Temple Streets, leaving Casson in charge of the Oriental. At Main and Temple, Flotte operated in the brick-

"Victor Dol" (ca. 1908).
Photograph: Neighbor-
hood News Online, Los
Angeles, http://the
neighborhoodnewsonline
.net/history/our-history
/585-popular-living-history
-tour-is-back.

paved, fountained courtyard of that elegant structure. Renamed the Commercial Restaurant, Flotte's place became the foremost scene of fine dining and celebration in the burgeoning city. The press of business was so great that the aging restaurateur began to seek a partner. He learned that his niece Felicie's husband, Victor Dol, was operating a restaurant in San Francisco (Dol & Bigne). In late 1876, Flotte invited Dol to become a full partner in the most successful dining business in Southern California. It promised substantially greater financial security than competing in the cutthroat world of San Francisco dining. So, early in 1877, Victor came to Los Angeles, taking over the kitchen of the Commercial. For the last two decades of the nineteenth century, he managed the finest restaurants in the city: first the Commercial and then the Maison Dorée. The latter constituted the standard against which any other was judged in the city.

Born in Cuers, France, Victor Dol left his native village and parents at age thirteen to apprentice as a cook in Paris. There he absorbed the doctrines of socialism along with the techniques of French cooking and baking. He would retain throughout his life a strong concern for the welfare of workers and suspicions concerning the concentration of power in the hands of oligarchs. Dol donated substantial amounts of money to socialist parties and causes throughout his life. At the age of seventeen, he emigrated to New York and was briefly employed there before arriving in New Orleans in 1858. In 1862 he met Felicie Marvardy, a young woman who also hailed from Cuers, and married her.

During the Civil War, Dol made his way to Cuba and in the 1860s worked in Havana. In the mid-1870s, he worked in Montréal. Thence he traveled to San Francisco in 1873, went into partnership with Vincent Bigne setting up the Nevada restaurant at 412 Pine. (It would later be renamed the Maison Dorée.) Dol became a naturalized citizen of the United States in San Francisco on October 23, 1876, shortly before receiving his invitation to come to Los Angeles. He arrived in Los Angeles circa 1877 to take over the Commercial Restaurant. "Dol kept up the traditions of the place and even increased them. His customers comprised the elite of Los Angeles and of Southern California." He served dinners in the French style, accompanied by "an excellent French vin ordinaire" without extra charge. For 75 cents, "a Bordeaux wine of capital grade" would be brought to the table. In 1889 his success became so great he had to move, taking over a house at 229 West First Street next to the Times building, and naming the new restaurant, again, the Maison Dorée. It offered a businessman's lunch for 25 cents from noon until 2:30 p.m. Its culinary artistry flourished in the dinner evening hours.

Dol was a versatile and expert artist. Some indication of his range can be had from a menu of dishes he prepared for lunch in 1895 to honor the visit of Chevalier Bertolini and the officers of the Italian warship *Cristoforo Colombo*:

RELISHES
Anchovies, Mortadella di Bologna

SOUP
Consomme a la Royale, Sauterne Wine

FISH
A la Cristoforo Colombo, Tartar Sauce

ENTREES
Chicken liver and Risotto, a la Milanese
Lamb Chops, a la Toscana, with Petit Pois
Chicken, American style, with Asparagus a la Parmigiana
Turkey, with Salad, a la Romana
Omelette a la Marguerita

WINE
Chianti

DESSERT
Fruit, Cakes, Italian Champagne

Because the restaurant was a large-scale consumer of fish and vegetables, Dol determined in the early 1890s to get commercially involved in the harvest of seafood. In June 1891, he partnered with J. L. DeJarnatt in the creation of the American Fishing Company operating out of Los Angeles.

In the 1880s, Dol began directing the profits from the restaurant into purchasing Los Angeles real estate. His wife, when not raising the family's two daughters, superintended the development of these properties. From 1888 until the death of his wife, Felicie, in 1898, Dol grew enormously wealthy from land holdings. Whenever he and Felicie sold a lot, they would immediately invest in another and became significant landlords by the end of the century. He retired from his restaurant when she died, selling it to Emil Camus. In 1904 he married Tatiana Sicilinski, moved to Santa Monica, and lived in peaceful retirement there until his death in 1911.

✳   ✳   ✳

SOURCES: [Notice: Opening of the Maison Dorée,] *Los Angeles Herald* (January 4, 1889): 6; "Certificate of Partnership," *Los Angeles Herald* (June 10, 1891): 7; "Distinguished Visitors," *Los Angeles Herald* (March 6, 1896): 3; "Deaths," *Los Angeles Herald* (March 19, 1898): 12; "Famous Old Time Restaurants Here," *Los Angeles Herald* (July 2, 1905): 3, 30; "Post Office Site Almost Cleared—Downey Block Demolition Little Slow," *Los Angeles Herald* (May 15, 1905): 3; "In Memory of Brother Pioneer Victor Dol," *The Annual Report of the Los Angeles County Pioneers of Southern California for the Years 1913-14* (Los Angeles, 1914), 15-16; "Victor Dol," *A History of California and an Extended History of Los Angeles and Environs*, 3 vols. (Los Angeles: Historical Record Company, 1915), 2:189; Michel Cordillot, "Benjamin Flotte," *La Sociale en America: Dictionnaire biographique du movement sociale, 1848-1922* (Paris: Les Editions de l'Atelier, 2002), 187-90.

Magdalena "Lena" Frey Fabacher 1840–1914
New Orleans

When German-born grocer and tavern keeper Franz Joseph Fabacher (1829–1897) left off retailing in 1879 in New Orleans, he became a keeper of an eating house and saloon. His Alsatian wife Lena enabled him to become something more—the most popular restaurateur in 1880s Louisiana. The Fabachers opened a modest saloon on Gravier Street. The location did not encourage traffic, so within a year they removed to Royal Street. The new location would become in one decade the most profitable and popular restaurant in the French Quarter on the strength of its Creole-style cooking and modest pricing. When the restaurant finally closed in 1915, a memorialist observed that its success depended greatly on the talent of Lena Fabacher, the original chef de cuisine. "Mrs. Fabacher was a famous chef, one of the first of the women who made a restaurant in New Orleans famous by her cooking ability. She ran that business with an iron hand."

Lena's discipline was noteworthy, for she ran the kitchen of Fabacher's despite raising twelve children, the last of whom, Jacob, was born after the move to Royal Street. The oldest boy—Joseph Henry—had left home by the time the restaurant opened. Eighteen-year-old Lawrence would be Lena's chief aide in the kitchen and eventual successor as manager after Lena retired in 1894. Lena was Joseph Fabacher's third wife, the first having been Mary Anna Frey, Lena's older sister, whom Joseph divorced. Lena gave birth to the first seven children in Louisiana without being formally married to Joseph (the ceremony finally took place on July 27, 1874). Lena was eighteen and living in New Orleans when she gave birth to John Henry Fabacher, the man who would bring modern rice planting to Acadia Parish.

The Frey family hailed from Rosenwiller, Bas-Rhin, in Alsace. They had moved to Louisiana sometime prior to 1852, when Lena was still a young girl. Her training in Creole cuisine, therefore, took place in New Orleans in the 1850s, during the period when the first great woman caterer of New Orleans, the Alsatian Sophie Dorn Flêche (Madame Eugène), was establishing her career in the city.

Lena Fabacher began work at Fabacher Hall on Gravier in 1879. Its reputation for quality burgeoned shortly after opening. An 1880 newspaper reporter observed the customers could enjoy "as fine a repast as possibly can be spread in the city." The clientele consisted of neighborhood people, and the profit made from the markup on the sale of Lemp's St. Louis lager beer. In late 1880, the Fabachers moved to the corner of Customhouse and Royal Streets. The next years would see the business's expansion into the adjacent buildings, beginning with 1882's rental of Shepard Mansion on the Customhouse Street side of the restaurant. After this addition, the business was advertised as "Fabacher's Royal Restaurant, Oyster Saloon and Hotel." The lodging component of the business would diminish in importance as the food exploded in popularity. In 1887 a celebrant observed that Fabacher's "feeds more people than any similar place in many states, and gives employment to a large number of persons, and is in every way a prominent concern. Its aim has been to furnish the best food and the most reasonable rates and its prosperity is the best sign of its popularity and success."

Cost was kept low by arranging exclusive provisioning arrangements with certain farmers and oystermen. The latter were important, for a distinguishing mark of the offerings was that "during the summer fine oysters in every style were to be had." The menu for the most part was in English—the exception being a quartet of fishes served *au gratin*—pompano, sheepshead, red snapper, and trout. Sheepshead was also Lena's featured fish in bouillabaisse. While she did offer a red fish court-bouillon, better versions were served in the city. Her frog legs and shrimp creole, however, had no rivals. Lena's lunch offerings included creole beefsteak and tripe à la creole. "Fabacher's Restaurant has a reputation for good cooking, polite attention and moderate charges. Upon this principle it has grown to be the largest, handsomest and most popular restaurant in town." Part of its immense popularity derived from its effective display of food in picturesque tableaux in the front window on Royal Street, particularly in holidays. The arrangements were the work of the young Lawrence Fabacher.

Joseph periodically went to Europe to import wine and beer. Son Lawrence ran the front of house and was the driving force behind the electrification of the dining rooms in the mid-1880s. Fabacher's was the first electrically illuminated restaurant in New Orleans.

Lena presided over the kitchens for the dinner service. Because the restaurant remained open all day and all night, she hired a staff of cooks to perform her wishes, among them Max Richter and W. Brechtel. Lena's vision of cuisine deviated from the French haute-cuisine standard embodied by Moreau's, Victor's, John's, Antoine's, and the hotels. She incorporated dishes from the Creole home-cooking repertoire and, in certain respects, predicted the rise of the Creole eateries in the 1890s and 1900s. One noteworthy dimension of the restaurant was its avoidance of the priciest vintages and its care securing vin ordinaire of the best quality to pair with its dishes.

A fire on June 11, 1894, did minor damage to the restaurant, but prompt action by the firefighters saved the building. The next day, Lawrence Fabacher assured the public that the dining room would be open as usual. It was about this time that Lena retired from the kitchen, permitting her lieutenants to take charge of the cook stoves. Fabacher's remained an important restaurant until 1915, when the new "quick service" restaurants ate away at its customer base. Lawrence had become absorbed in the manufacture of Jax Beer.

※　※　※

SOURCES: "Our Firefighters," *New Orleans Item* (March 4, 1880): 4; "Lemp's St. Louis Lager Beer," *New Orleans Item* (March 20, 1880): 4; "Fabacher's Royal Restaurant, Oyster Saloon and Hotel," *St. Landry Democrat* (October 21, 1882): 8; "Fabacher's Restaurant," *New Orleans Times-Picayune* (December 21, 1884):

2; "Christmas at Fabacher's," *New Orleans Times-Picayune* (December 25, 1887): 7; "A Card," *New Orleans Item* (June 12, 1894): 5; Genealogy: http://www .birkenhoerdt.net/getperson.php?personID=I54534&tree=Suedpfalz.

George W. Harvey 1840–1909
Washington, DC

Founder of the most famous oyster house in Washington, DC, and a master of tidewater cuisine, George W. Harvey possessed both skill and wit. Opening his namesake restaurant on the eve of the American Civil War, his initial clientele drew largely from the ranks of the Union army. Partnering with his brother Thomas in 1856 in a produce business, George had the inspiration of opening an oyster restaurant on the Philadelphia model in 1858 in an old brick blacksmith shop at Eleventh and C Streets northwest, across from the Carust Theater. The brothers' original business plan was to cater the theater balls and service the theatrical community. They would also supply oysters wholesale to institutions in Washington. The coming of the war and the discovery of Harvey's oyster saloon by the soldiery altered that plan. For many, the feast at Harvey's on the eve of deployment became the image of plentitude that haunted men's imaginations during the periods of camp privation.

The great labor in an oyster house is shucking the bivalves. Whether fried, stewed, or eaten on the half shell, oysters had to be opened, work that required manpower and time. In 1862, it was reported, "Men stood around in hundreds clamoring for cooked oysters of all sorts. No force of waiters and cooks that Harvey commanded could supply the demand fast enough." Harvey hit upon the expedient of steaming the oysters, creating an effective new way of serving quantities piping hot and quick from the steam pot. The steamed oyster was such an innovation that President Lincoln became a consumer. The Harvey brothers secured their supply of oysters from the entire Chesapeake Bay region and "were the first to introduce many well-known brands of oysters such as Lynn Havens, Winter Harbors, Horn Harbors, York Rivers and many others." Lynn Havens had been an established brand for a generation before Harvey embraced them.

In 1867 the restaurant moved to Pennsylvania Avenue and Eleventh Street, and pointedly presented itself as a venue in which men *and* women could dine: Harvey's Old Established Ladies' and Gentlemen's Oyster Saloon and Restaurant. It was the second restaurant in the city (Gautier's was the first) to make exclusive accommodations for women. Gentlemen dined on the first floor; ladies dined on the second. In 1869 George bought out his brother Thomas's interest

"Harvey's Old Established Ladies' and Gentlemen's Oyster Saloon and Restaurant" (1877), advertisement.

in the establishment and in the oyster supply business as well, including the leases on oyster beds throughout Maryland and Virginia.

The menu at Harvey's drew heavily from the bounty of the Chesapeake Bay, adjusting offerings to the season: in September and October, "Crab Flake à la Harvey"; in November and December, "Broiled Canvasback Duck"; in January and February, "Stewed Terrapin"; in March, "Planked Shad"; and from September through April, "A Peck of Steams" and "Pigs in Blankets"—the restaurant's famous oyster offerings. Harvey himself won international renown for preparing the three central dishes of Chef François Lagroue's famous Maryland Feast for Baltimore's Maryland Club: rare breast of canvasback duck, terrapin à la Maryland, and Lynn Haven oysters. When Sir Thomas Lawrence wished to re-create the Maryland Feast in London, he transported Harvey across the Atlantic to oversee its creation.

Harvey's personality contributed to the cachet of his restaurant. "He was a man of quiet dignity, good judgment, and native ability. Men of mark who went to his place found in him a pleasant companion, one who could discuss with [them] the questions of the day and whose unfailing courtesy added to the charm of a meal at his restaurant." Many of the clubs in the nation's capital met in the room at the rear of the restaurant's second floor and extended to Harvey an honorary membership. Whether the Canvasback Club or the Dining Club of the New York Delegation in Congress, Harvey was granted a seat at the table. These all-male sodalities bestowed upon Harvey the honorific "Colonel."

Harvey's hospitality did not necessarily extend to certain African American gentlemen. In 1888 he was brought before the court in the District of Columbia for refusing to serve E. M. Hewlett, in violation of the Civil Rights Law. While the restaurant had served other African Americans in the 1880s, Harvey personally refused Hewlett's request to supply some fried oysters, citing Hewlitt's reputation as an activist who regularly appeared in restaurants, provoking scenes, and leaving without paying the bill. Hewlitt dropped the charges before the jury made a finding. The restaurant employed several African American cooks and waiters, the most famous being "Old Randolph," who had worked with the Harvey brothers as a freeman before the Civil War and remained as a fixture in the dining room for forty-eight years. Sam Brown manned the raw bar for forty years. Both retired with pensions.

Harvey himself retired from business in 1906, selling the restaurant. He died of heart disease three years later.

⁂ ⁂ ⁂

SOURCES: "A Bivalvular Feast," *Washington Evening Star* (November 4, 1865): 2; "Civil Rights in Restaurants," *Washington Evening Star* (May 29, 1888): 5; "Harvey's," *Washington Evening Star* (December 16, 1902): 55; "The First Steamed Oysters," *Charleston News and Courier* (June 3, 1906): 23; "Steamed Oyster Inventor Is Dead," *Cleveland Plain Dealer* (May 6, 1909): 1; "George W. Harvey Dead," *Washington Evening Star* (May 5, 1909): 2; "Long Trip of a Famous Cook," *Grand Rapids Press* (May 21, 1909): 16.

Emeline Jones 1840?–1912
Baltimore; New York; Long Branch, NJ; Washington, DC; Point Comfort, MD

Gentlemen's clubs after the 1850s became places where fine dining flourished in America's major cities. Club cooking became greatly influential in haute cuisine generally when the signature feast of Baltimore's Maryland Club—Lynn Haven oysters, canvasback duck, terrapin à la Maryland, crab salad, hominy cakes, celery salad—convinced French-trained chefs that American local ingredients and preparations possessed sufficient distinctiveness and quality to be incorporated into the repertoire of haute cuisine. The dishes for the Maryland Feast had been adapted by François Lagroue in the 1850s from preparations by African American caterers in the Chesapeake region. Clubs throughout the Northeast in the latter decades of the nineteenth century featured the Chesapeake dishes on their menus. Some reasoned that securing an experienced African American cook from Maryland or Virginia would be more authentic and economical than hiring a French- or Swiss-trained chef. Emeline Jones was the most famous of these club cooks, preparing the banquets of the Carlton Club of New York in the 1870s.

Born into slavery on the estate of Colonel Benedict William Hall of Eutaw, Maryland, near Baltimore, Emeline Jones had been trained as a house servant as a girl. Hall's daughter Elizabeth married Horatio Whitridge and took Jones with her to his house in the Little Gunpowder District of Baltimore. Here Jones grew into womanhood and perfected her cooking skills, preparing meals for the merchant Whitridge. Prior to the Civil War, Whitridge freed Jones, who made her way to New York in 1864, working as private cook to insurance executive Daniel Fearing at his mansion on the corner of Fifth Avenue and Fifteenth Street. One of the guests at the Fearing mansion was "the prince of good fellows" John Chamberlain, a sportsman, hotelier, and entrepreneur. In 1868 Chamberlain began developing Long Branch, New Jersey, into a gambling mecca. The erection of Monmouth Raceway and its Club House in the late 1860s accomplished this. He secured Jones to cook for the Club House.

Because he invested in a stable of racehorses as well as the track and the Club House, Chamberlain failed to profit from the Long Branch venture. He departed, next determining to give the nation's capital a world-class gambling club. Smitten with Jones's dishes, Chamberlain brought her with him from Long Branch to be chef for his Washington Club House. Located in the former enclave of the British legation, this gentleman's retreat when opened in 1874 was hailed as "the most elaborate and spacious gaming house and restaurant in the United States and cost $90,000." A reporter commenting on the cuisine of the club remarked, "The cook, Emeline Jones, is the well-known colossal quadroon woman who has roasted and stewed so daintily at Long Branch."

Chamberlain undertook the management of the Carlton Club in New York and brought Jones with him to supply the cuisines. The Carlton Club became during the later 1870s the nexus of the sporting and political worlds. "No dinner of congressman or senator was considered complete without Emeline's Southern specialties." Presidents Garfield, Arthur, and Cleveland devoured her dishes and attempted to secure her services in the White House—to no avail. Chamberlain paid her well and treated her with a deference and affection that earned her loyalty. Chamberlain permitted her to hire out her services to other entities. During the holiday season in New York, Wall Bakery on Sixth Avenue engaged Jones to make mincemeat pies and rolls. These became famous citywide. Chamberlain also gave her carte blanche to hire assistants in the kitchen for banquet work. Jones considered it her responsibility to train and give practical experience to African American bakers and cooks, particularly those coming from Baltimore and Philadelphia. She was responsible for launching the careers of John Lucas, Hiram Thomas, Horatio Butler, James W. Mars, Vernon C.

Murray, and William Heydiger. She trained Mrs. Fanning C. Jarvis to be her successor.

When Chamberlain opened his resort hotel, Chamberlain's, at Point Comfort, Maryland, he brought Jones southward from New York whenever a major banquet required extraordinary treatment. After the closure of the Carlton Club in 1886, he offered her a permanent position there.

Emeline Jones's repertoire of recipes has survived in surprising detail. Her expertise in the Chesapeake style of southern cooking was so preeminent among practitioners in the North that newspaper reporters repeatedly interviewed her during the 1890s and 1900s. The oral transcripts they printed provide the most revealing window on the accomplishments of African American caterers in the Gilded Age. First, a general characterization of her club fare at the Carlton: "Canvasbacks made the fame of the establishment. Woodcock 'on toast' (served with the head on) was a special dish at the late suppers, and fried sweetbreads with mushroom sauce another. Farcis crabs in Emeline's hands were a far cry from the dried-out meat mixed with bread crumbs usually found masquerading under that title. She mixed the meat with a rich cream sauce, put it back in the shell and placed it in the oven until slightly browned." Her recipes come down in both paraphrased and near-verbatim form.

APPETIZER

An "appetizer" which regards as one of her best productions is intended to take the place of the oyster course at dinner. It is composed of the breast of chicken chopped fine, with capers, celery, parsley and one truffle, also chopped fine, and salt anchovies cut into small pieces. The whole is squeezed through a napkin, salt and pepper and mayonnaise dressing added and one spoonful on a single lettuce leaf is served.

She favored five soups for banquets, the classic consommé royal, purée of chicken, green turtle, crab gumbo, and chicken and okra soup.

CRAB GUMBO SERVED WITH RICE

Everything has to be fried in the pot first for the gumbo, the ham and chicken, some of the crabs raw, some of the okras, a little onion, and it is all cooked brown, and I throw in a can of tomatoes, that takes up all the brown. Then I pour in enough water to make soup for twelve or fourteen people, according to the size of the dinner, perhaps three or four quarts, and cook for several hours. I crack all the little fins and claws, and put those in to boil to give the full flavor of the crabs. I scald the other crabs so that I can handle them and clean them, and there will be about half a dozen to put on to boil until they are done, and I pick out all the meat and have it clean and ready for use. When the soup is cooked it must be strained through a French colander, and then you have a rich stock. That must be put back in the pot and thickened with a little cornstarch or flour, and the remainder of the okras are sliced in, and the last thing the meat of the crabs is thrown in. Before the soup is served it must be skimmed to get off the fat: then you have a nice creamy soup just thick enough, and not pasty: thin-sliced okras and the meat of the crabs, and the soup is thoroughly flavored.

Oysters were the sine qua non of Chesapeake fine dining. Emeline Jones had several preparations.

GRILLED OYSTERS

Have the griddle ready as for hot cakes. When the oysters are drained perfectly dry touch the griddle over with butter. Lay the oysters carefully on the host surface with a spoon. The oysters must be so dry that they will begin to brown immediately, and to get them in this condition they should be strained through a colander and then spread on a coarse towel.

SPICED OYSTERS

To one gallon of selected oysters add three tablespoonfuls of salt; let them come to a boil; take the oysters out and put them in cold water and strain the liquor. Take enough of the liquor to cover the oysters; add one pod of red pepper, half ounce of pepper-corns and a few blades of mace. To each quart of liquor add 30 cloves and one gill of vinegar. Boil the liquor with the spices and vinegar for two or three minutes, drain the oysters and pour the boiling liquor over them.

Her entrées ran from standard banquet fare, such as fillet of sole with shrimp sauce, roast beef, a saddle of mutton, and boned capon. To these she added her southern specialties, the canvasback and broiled red duck. She served the breasts somewhat rare and sliced with side dishes of celery salad and fried hominy cake. Another southern standard was baked country ham.

OLD VIRGINIA HAM

There are a good many people in New York who keep those old Virginia hams, the Todd hams, hanging in their cellars, and they like those for dinner. They are served with a salad, or with broiled larded breasts of chicken. The ham has to be soaked two days and two nights, then it is pashed, and put in a deep boiler with part water and part cider, plenty of cider and a cup of sugar. If you can't get cider I use a cup of vinegar with the sugar. Then it has to simmer for four hours, or, if it is small, not so long, and never stays until it is thoroughly done. The cider has softened it, and when it is ready, I put it in a pan and remove the skin, put on a little sugar and cayenne pepper, and brown it in the oven, basting it with champagne. That is the way to cook those Todd hams—bake until they are just nice to slice. Serve it hot, with champagne sauce, with just a little over it to make it moist.

Many persons attempted to secure from Jones her famous recipe for stewed terrapin. Count Canino published a version obtained from the lips of John Chamberlain, one that lacked fundamental details about length of cooking.

STEWED TERRAPIN

Boil the terrapin until tender, pick out the meat carefully, save all the natural juices, make a sauce of fine cream and the best butter, put the terrapin meat and juice into a stewpan with the sauce, bring to a boil, pour in a wineglassful of madeira and serve very hot.

In 1898 a reporter inferred other aspects of her preparation and published the following elaboration in the *Trenton Evening Times*:

Take four terrapin (red legs), put them into boiling water in which a tablespoon of salt has been added. Boil two or three hours, or until the red skin on the feet and toe nails and shell can be easily removed. Use everything but the entrails, being careful not to break the gall bag in the liver: but if by accident you should do so, then wash in cold water. Make a dressing of half a pint of thick, rich cream, one tablespoon of flour rubbed into nearly half a pound of butter, boil half a dozen eggs hard and mash the yolks with a little cream, season by adding salt, red and black pepper and one-quarter of a teaspoon of ground mace, add sherry and serve.

Of vegetables, she regularly prepared potato croquettes, puffed sweet potatoes, green peppers stuffed with creamed rice, and green beans. One of the more interesting of her preparations was stuffed tomatoes, which she recommended as an accompaniment for boned broiled shad or for women's luncheons.

STUFFED TOMATOES

I always tell people to get the hot-house tomatoes, and not the Southern ones. They are smaller and very tender, and any one who likes tomatoes and most people do, can eat a whole one. Then they do not have to be cut, and they look much nicer. I remove the skin first by pouring a little boiling water over them. I always see that done myself, and they are not left standing in tomatoes. Then I scoop out the top and fill them with French dressing and put them away for two or three hours while it soaks into them, and they become thoroughly flavored. Then I chop the cucumbers, add a little whipped cream, horse radish, grated fresh from the root—that which comes from bottles is not good for anything—and mix with a little vinegar and salt—it does not require pepper with the radish—and fill the tomatoes. . . . The tomatoes are thoroughly chilled by being put into a dish of salt and ice.

When grapefruits started appearing in New York markets in some numbers in the 1880s, she experimented to devise a chilled grapefruit refresher.

CHILLED GRAPEFRUIT

The pulp [of the grapefruit] was removed and well mixed with white grapes and maraschino. It was then sweetened and a little Santa Cruz rum added, after which it was put in a freezer. For serving it was returned to the skin, which was cut in the shape of a basket.

Chamberlain's death in 1896 prompted a transformation of her career. One of his sporting circle, John Daly, hired her to run once again the kitchen in the Club House at Long Branch during the three summer months of racing. During the remaining nine months of the year, Jones worked out of her home, catering banquets and parties for the men's clubs and for society women. There she worked until her retirement. During her final protracted illness, the Société Culinaire Philanthropique, New York's famous French chefs' society, paid for her care and support, and also for her funeral. She died midsummer of 1912, remembered and celebrated by a culinary community that she had nurtured. Obituaries inaccurately attributed the creation of the Saratoga chip (potato chip) to her.

※　※　※

SOURCES: "A Gorgeous Gaming Place," *New York Daily Graphic* (December 20, 1874): 3; "Personal Points," *Kansas City Times* (October 20, 1886): 4; "Long Branch Memories," *Kansas City Times* (August 26, 1888): 4; "Terrapin, Salt and Fresh," *Trenton Evening Times* (April 18, 1898): 5; "An Old-Fashioned Cook," *New York Times* (December 31, 1899); "Some Points on Cooking," *Fort Worth Morning Register* 5, no. 130 (March 15, 1901): 4; "Keeps It a Secret," *Grand Rapids Press* (January 12, 1903): 8; "Noted Cook Dead, Emeline Jones," *Cleveland Gazette* (July 20, 1912): 1.

Frederic Mergenthaler 1840–1902
Paris; St. Petersburg, Russia; New York; San Francisco

The talented successor to Jules Arthur Harder as chef of San Francisco's Palace Hotel, Fred Mergenthaler was a native of Strasbourg. He had been trained in Paris and almost immediately went into royal service, working for the queen of Holland, the Grand Duke Alexis of Russia in St. Petersburg, and finally the king of Prussia. He arrived in the United States in 1872 and worked in New York kitchens as a staff chef at Delmonico's, the Hotel Brunswick, the Hoffman House, and Café Savarin. In 1887 he was appointed with much fanfare chef de cuisine of the Palace Hotel but was deposed when E. L. Thorne became hotel manager in 1890. Mergenthaler ran a very successful French restaurant on Bush Street, San Francisco, for two years. Kitchen unrest at the Palace characterized the period following Thorne's appointment. Finally, in January 1892, after burning through three chefs de cuisine, the Palace Hotel was compelled to restore Mergenthaler to command of the kitchen. Thereafter he enjoyed a ten-year dominion over the cuisine of the hotel, until his death in 1902.

On January 8, 1892, Mergenthaler took over the kitchen of the Palace Hotel after a two-year debacle initiated by its hiring of M. Dubois, the Vanderbilt family chef in New York. Promised a salary of $300 a month after a trial month's payment of $250, Dubois walked out when his second month's paycheck was for $250. Apparently the first month's work had convinced the hotel's steward that Dubois would not work out, so he had contracted with another Parisian chef, Andreas, to come and assume control of the kitchens. Andreas lasted a brief term, succeeded by chef Duprue. Duprue eventually found himself at odds with management and walked out in early January 1892, accompanied by twenty other kitchen employees—all French. Four would return the next day when they learned that Mergenthaler had been reemployed. Observers noted that the ethnic composition of the kitchen was made cosmopolitan by Mergenthaler's rule, with French, German, Swiss, and Scandinavian staff members.

Mergenthaler's cuisine was equally cosmopolitan, combining American game, French entremets, and a liberal supply of vegetables cooked plainly. A Thanksgiving menu from his initial stint at the Palace Hotel conveys his hyphenated approach to cuisine.

OYSTERS
Blue Points
Oysters on the Shell

SOUP
Consomme des Sportsman
Cream of New Peas
St. Germain

HORS D'OEVRUES
Cucumbers   Olives   Caviar Russe   Salted Almonds
Celery   Radish

FISH
Escalops of Salmon Venitienne

Broiled Shad a la Polonaise

Pommes Raphael

RELEVES
Saddle of Bear a la Stanly   Capons, Oyster Sauce

Ham, Glace au Champagne

Boiled Grouse, with Brussels Sprouts

ENTREES
Borchette of Lamb

Sweetbreads, Puree of Chestnuts

Papilettes of Tenderloin of Beef a la Clarmont

Mouse of York

Ham a la Chantilly

Aspice of Fat Goose Liver, Strabourgeise

Courstades of Cherries

Portugaise, Punch a la Cardinal

ROASTS
Prime Roast Beef

Lamb, Mint Sauce

Mallard Duck, Currant Jelly

Young Turkey, Cranberry Sauce

SALADS
Celery, Heart of Lettuce and Eggs

VEGETABLES
Sweet Potatoes   Cauliflower   String Beans

Fried Salsify   Peas   Tomatoes   Rice

Mashed Potatoes   Hominy, cold

GAME
Pate   Bone Capon, a la Jelly

PASTRY
English Plum Pudding   Mince Pie   Peach Tartlette

Croquette de Messina   Assorted Fancy Cakes

Meringue, a la Crème   Bonbons

Biscuit Glace a l'Italienne
Vanilla Ice Cream
Fruits   Dessert   Coffee

Mergenthaler believed that "Californians are more French in their culinary tastes than any other people in the United States." He had obviously not visited New Orleans. Among his distinctive culinary convictions, he believed that eating radishes for dinner ruined one's stomach; they were exclusively a breakfast vegetable. "A glass of Vermouth Torreno before a meal makes a wonderful difference in the enjoyment of the feast." Salted almonds were an invariable adjunct to any meal with which wine was served, since they had a magical effect in bringing out the virtue of a vintage. Appetizers—such as caviar, anchovies, and stuffed olives—were excellent aids to digestion. Plum puddings and mince pies were barbarities.

From 1892 until his death in 1902, Mergenthaler maintained the exalted standard of the Palace Hotel's cuisine. Ernest Arbogast then took control of the Palace Hotel's kitchen.

❋   ❋   ❋

SOURCES: "'Frisco's Thanksgiving Menu," *New York Evening World* (November 27, 1888): 2; "A Pot Boiler," *New York Herald* 112 (April 22, 1890): 9; "Kitchen Rulers," *San Francisco Call* (January 8, 1892): 7; "Chef Mergenthaler Airs His Culinary Philosophy," *San Francisco Morning Call* (December 21, 1892): 8; "Well Known Chef Dead," *Denver Post* (January 6, 1902): 1.

Agnes Moody 1840–1903
Chicago; Paris

Born a slave on a plantation in Hagerstown, Maryland, Agnes Moody fled north at the age of twelve to Canada in the company of nine other fugitives in 1852. The Underground Railroad secreted her on the passage to Canada. As a teenager, she availed herself of the liberties of that northern country, learning to read and write and cook. The rigors of the Fugitive Slave Law kept her north of the border until the defeat of the Confederacy. In 1866 she moved to Chicago. There she became a famous clubwoman and caterer. She achieved international renown in 1900 when the US Commissioner General Ferdinand Peck appointed her to present traditional American corn dishes—corn soup, flapjacks,

"Agnes Moody" (1900).
Photograph: Chicago
Public Media.

corn dodgers, corn bread, hoecakes, corn pone, and corn muffins—at the World Exposition in Paris.

Agnes was a specialist in corn cuisine. She "knew how to prepare more delicious corn concoctions than any other living person." At the corn kitchen in the American Building, she personated "Aunt Jemima," the famous Louisiana household cook of legend and advertising fame. Moody became a celebrity. Indeed, cornmeal cookery became a fad in Paris. "Groceries where the wealthy were wont to purchase their staples found it necessary to add the maize meal to their stock and chefs by the hundred who were engaged at the great houses were sent to the corn kitchen where Aunt Jemima was chief potentate to learn the ways of making different kinds of corn bread." The Countess de Castellane brought her as a guest to her chateau for a week. The US Commissioner of Agriculture in Paris held a reception in her honor and awarded her a Tiffany Gold Medal adorned with a shock of corn and an inscribed notice of merit. Because corn was viewed in France as a fodder crop, Moody's dishes performed a transformation of public opinion about its palatability for human consumers. Moody observed, "I am generally diffident concerning statistics, but in the beginning I baked an average of 1,000 corn cakes each day, and soon the average rose to 2,500. During the exposition I baked in round numbers 135,000 corn cakes, pones and loaves."

Moody supplied an ethnographic history of cornmeal to American reporters:

The Indians were first to use maize for food and in slavery, of which I am a product, the colored people were given ground corn as the principal article of food. They were allowed white flour only seldom: indeed, these occasions were so rare that the slaves in my section of Maryland called it "heaven dust." Our people are natural cooks, and in their efforts to make the corn meal palatable they improved upon each improvement until corn bread was generally more acceptable than wheat. Finally the fame of corn bread reached the "big house," and now the dinner is not complete in many Southern homes unless corn bread in some form is a part of it.

Married to Benjamin Moody, also an ex-fugitive slave from Maryland, Agnes operated as a caterer from her home on Dearborn Avenue in Chicago. She probably secured her custom from the extraordinary web of organizations in which she participated. In every one of these associations—the Daughters of Tabor, the Wayman Circle, Colored Eastern Star, Grand Household of Ruth–Odd Fellows, Woman's Christian Temperance Union—she served as an officer and orator. Moody was a founder of the National Association of Colored Women and served as vice president at the time of her Paris sojourn. Her skills as an orator brought her before the public on many occasions from the mid-1870s to 1901. Some performances were memorable. In December 1893, at the great reception of Frederick Douglass held in Chicago at the time of the World's Columbian Exposition, Moody, who "spoke for the 'Mothers of the Race,' talked so facetiously and pertinently as not only to bring forth loud applause, but also to deeply move 'the Old Man Eloquent' himself."

There can be little doubt that Agnes Moody's skill at expression mattered as much as her skill with Indian meal to Commissioner Peck when he selected her to be the corn advocate in Paris. However much newspapers wished to visualize her in light of a mammy stereotype, this eloquent activist for civil rights and women's public presence understood that she was an ambassador for African American foodways and the corn farmers of the American Midwest.

After Moody's return to Chicago in 1900, she began experiencing symptoms of heart disease. She remained active as a speaker and clubwoman well into 1901 before her condition declined to a point that forced her inactivity. She died in 1903 and her memory was celebrated with an extraordinary outpouring of affection by the African American community of the Midwest.

※　※　※

SOURCES: "The Southern Negro," *Kalamazoo Gazette* (June 1, 1892): 2; "In Honor of J. H. Hopson," *Daily Inter Ocean* 12, no. 17 (April 10, 1893): 3; "The Douglass Reception," *Cleveland Gazette* (December 9, 1893): 1; "Colored Eastern Star," *Daily Illinois State Register* (August 10, 1898): 4; "A Local Awakening," *Indianapolis Freeman* (July 29, 1899): 1; "A Colored Chef in Paris," *New Orleans Times-Picayune* (May 20, 1900): 24; "Mrs. Agnes Moody," *San Antonio Express* 34, no. 434 (April 2, 1900): 4; "In Paris," *Wisconsin Weekly Advocate* (May 24, 1900): 1; "The Windy City," *The Colored American* (June 23, 1900): 9; "Aunt Jemima Makes Corn Pone," *San Jose Mercury News* (December 30, 1900): 18; "Race Echoes," *Iowa State Bystander* (December 14, 1900): 8; "Letter of Thanks," *St. Paul Appeal* (April 25, 1903): 4; "Mrs. Agnes Moody Won Fame with Corn Cakes," *Cleveland Gazette* (May 9, 1903): 2.

Joseph Seyl 1841–1921
Chicago

Joseph Seyl guided the kitchens of Chicago's Palmer House for almost half a century, when it ranked among the first-tier hostelries in the United States. Born in Prussia on July 6, 1841, he came to the United States when he was eighteen, settling in Chicago in 1859. He worked as second cook in several restaurants during the 1860s, finally rising to head cook.

Potter Palmer hired Seyl to be chef de cuisine at the first Palmer House in 1871. Seyl's loyalty during the hiatus in business caused by the Great Chicago Fire won Palmer's respect and abiding friendship. When the rebuilt Palmer House opened on State Street in 1873 after heroic rebuilding efforts, Seyl was installed as steward, an office that encompassed the duties of both chef and chief provisioner for the Palmer House. He would superintend the food over forty-five years, remaining a fixture in the face of a host of crises, including the installation of a rival food vendor, Anderson & Anderson's Oyster House, under the hotel in 1875, the great tenant walkout of 1884, and the discharge of the wait staff in May 1890 when the waiters unionized and struck. When Potter Palmer sold out to the Chicago Hotel Company in 1904, Seyl had become so much a Chicago institution that no thought was given by the new management to his replacement.

For many years, the Palmer House promoted its banquet facilities. One inducement to non-Chicago guests was Seyl's inclusion of a signature "home dish" in the visiting group's menu. For instance, when the Maryland Society feasted at the Palmer House in 1898, they delighted in seeing "Oysters and Biscuits from Home on the Menu." Another of Seyl's touches was to festoon the dining halls with vines, flowers, and ferns secured from Chicago's greenhouses. While dinner menus for hotels abound, few survive from this era for luncheons. Seyl's menu for President Grover Cleveland's Palmer House lunch of October 5,

"Palmer House Dining Room" (1875). Ryerson and Burnham Archives. Photograph: Art Institute of Chicago.

1887, proves an exception. Cleveland's well-known taste for meat and homey fare was aptly served:

COLD MEATS
Roast Beef   Spring Lamb   Turkey
Smoked Beef

HOT MEATS
Tenderloin Beef Steak   Lamb Chops
Poached Eggs on Toast
French Fried Potatoes   Hot Corn Cakes
Tea and Coffee

Seyl behaved in the rather self-effacing manner of culinary professionals of an earlier generation. He never sought to place his name in the papers, or desired to be called out for a toast at a banquet or to name recipes after himself. Instead, he let his employer Potter Palmer bask in the spotlight. When his younger contemporaries organized the Chicago Epicures Club, a sociable assembly of chefs who prepared their finest dishes for one another, Seyl chose not to join.

His life was his work, and his work was in the "back of the house," despite being denominated a steward.

A cadre of German chefs controlled the city's major kitchens. They competed for business with great seriousness and made banqueting a spectacular matter. The ten-course dinner became their métier. Chef C. Wolf, a brilliant inventor of kitchen appliances as well as chef de cuisine, reigned over the Grand Pacific Hotel. Chef George F. Segar ruled the kitchen of the Auditorium Hotel. Joseph Seyl controlled the Palmer House, and his assistant, Adolph Hieronymous, took over the Albion Restaurant in the Pullman Building in 1894. August Ratz held a variety of hotel posts. Edward Pfeiffer operated as steward of the Iroquois Club. Le Ciarcoschi, a Swiss chef, presided over the Leland Hotel. French chefs—Frederick Compagnon, Charles Laperruque, Thomas Pierrot, Louis du Verdier—held relatively minor posts in the city.

Seyl's long residency as chef de cuisine enabled him to view some of the great alterations in cooking and dining of the late nineteenth and early twentieth centuries. He witnessed the eclipse of the coal range by gas, the electrification of the kitchen, and the entire delocalization of city food by Chicago's many transportation lines. What he found most shocking was the rise in food prices. Charging a nickel for a roll and butter at the Palmer House restaurant, an item long given gratis in 1915, provoked a public meditation of the days when a dozen eggs cost five cents in Chicago. With some regret, he realized the golden age of modest prices would never been seen again in America's big cities.

Retiring at age seventy-six in 1917, Seyl was the dean of hotel chefs in America. He lasted so long because he ignored the culinary fashions that roiled Paris and New York. "He ran his kitchen along original lines, specializing in foods prepared in family style, and of the savory, hearty, appetizing kind that have made the Palmer House dining rooms popular places of resort for more than forty years."

❋   ❋   ❋

SOURCES: "New Oyster House Under Palmer House," *Chicago Sunday Times* (November 14, 1875): 6; Menu, January 9, 1884, *Palmer House Chicago American & European Plans* (Chicago: S. D. Childs, 1884); "Hotel Guests Enraged," *Cleveland Plain Dealer* 40, no. 92 (April 17, 1884): 4; "A Story of Success," *Trenton Evening Times* (April 1, 1886): 5; "A Distinguished Guest," *Daily Inter Ocean* 16, no. 195 (October 6, 1887): 2; "Cold Dinners," *Cleveland Plain Dealer* (May 19, 1890): 1; "True to the Old State," *Baltimore Sun* 122, no. 75 (February 11, 1898): 2; "Joseph Seyl, Dean of American Chefs, Retires," *Hotel Monthly* 22 (1917): 54; "What They Say," *Hotel Monthly* 30, no. 346 (1922): 61.

Auguste Valadon 1841–1890
New York

In the city of New York, the restaurant and the club dining room were most often the preferred places of consumption for gastronomes, until the burgeoning of the hotels in the 1870s. Auguste Valadon at the St. James, Antonio Sivori of Delmonico's, and Sebastian Nouvelle of the Hotel Brunswick led the brotherhood of chefs in improving banquet menus in the city hotels to rival the best in the world. Valadon stood distinct from his brethren for his literacy. He owned the great culinary library in the city, and perhaps because of his bookishness gained a reputation for being a classicist—one who cherished the dishes found in canonical works such as Marie-Antoine Carême's *L'Art de la cuisine française au dix-neuvième siècle* or those of the conservative school of Third Empire chefs such as Urbain Du Bois. While Valadon believed that creativity could exist in the kitchen, he also believed that circumstances in America—that lack of culinary patrons to call out the genius of talented chefs—precluded American hotels from being the vanguard of innovation in the culinary world.

A menu for a party of fifteen at the St. James early in the Centennial Year of the United States conveys Valadon's firm adherence to classic Parisian-style French food.

POTAGES
Consomme a la Nelse   Puree a la Reine

FLANES
Casserole de riz a la financiere   Galatine a la gelee

RELEVES
Turbot sauce homard   Rosbif a l'Anglaise

ENTREES
Fellets de canetons, a la Macedoine   Cotelettes d'Agneau,
aus petits-pois   Poulards a la fermiere
Salade de homard a la gelee

BOUTS
Croquembouche de choux   Biscuit a la vanilla

ROTIS
Poulets nouveaux   Becasses et mauviettes

LEGUMES

Haricots-verts a la Grancaise   Seakae au veloute

ENTREMETS

Savarin au rhum   Gelee de fruits, garnie   Biscuit a la crème

Pouding a la Chateaubriand

The service was à la Russe, that is, dishes served in sequence by course. The number of dishes employing gelatin was prophetic of culinary fashion for the period from 1876 to 1890.

A collection of Valadon's recipes was published in Edwin Troxell Freedley's 1879 compendium, *Home Comforts; or, Things Worth Knowing in Every Household*. Yet true to his classicist instincts, his renderings of cream sauce, curry sauce, sauce maître d'hôtel, bread sauce, and piquante sauce provide little not found in dozens of presentations in other cookbooks. For novelty, the recipe for "Cream Fried" deserves recollection:

> Take a quarter of milk and boil it. Then put in another pan half a pint of cream, two ounces of corn starch, half a pound of sugar, flavor to taste, and six yolks of eggs; mix well and pour this into the boiling milk; stir all well together, and quickly pour into a flat pan to cool; cut it up into round or square pieces; bread as rice croquettes; fry and serve hot, well-powdered with sugar.

Valadon was a member in good standing of New York's Société Culinaire Philanthropique and won commendation for his "Hercule portant la terre" sculpted of sugar in the 1878 Bal Des Cuisiniers.

In 1881 Valadon left the St. James for the Victoria Hotel on the corner of Broadway and Twenty-Sixth Street. He remained active in the annual culinary exhibitions and contributed a sculpted sugar Neptune and a pyramid of lobsters to the 1890 fete weeks before his death in March.

※   ※   ※

SOURCES: "The Refinement of Dining," *New York Daily Graphic* (April 15, 1876): 9; "Le Bal Des Cuisiniers," *Courrier des Etats-Unis* 38 (February 7, 1878): 2; Edwin Troxell Freedley, *Home Comforts; or, Things Worth Knowing in Every Household* (New York, 1879); "Le Bal Des Cuisiniers," *Courrier des Etats-Unis* (February 7, 1890): 1.

Fernand Fere 1843–19??
New York

Revered chef of the Astor House in New York during the 1870s, Fernand Fere was a pillar of the French expatriate community in Manhattan. No one worked more effectively on committees than Fere, a sociable, efficient man with a ready smile, a tiny pocketbook full of observations, and abounding energy. When France dispatched a delegation of officials in 1881 to honor the centenary of the Battle of Yorktown, Fere and Gustave Nouvel of the Hoffman House served as the culinary representatives of the reception committee. In 1882 Fere ascended to the presidency of the Société Culinaire Philanthropique, the principal association of culinary professionals in the city. During his presidency, the Société absorbed the smaller Société Fraternelle des Cuisiniers in New York. In April 1882, Fere accomplished the single greatest work ever undertaken by the French expatriate community: convening an assembly of all the various French associations in New York, the Union des Sociétés Françaises, under his directorship. Not a Bastille Day, Mardi Gras, or Franco-American anniversary of the 1880s and '90s took place without Fere's active participation.

Born in Morley and educated in Havre, Fernand Fere had emigrated to New York in 1870, part of the wave of chefs seeking their fortune in the years after the American Civil War. He presided over the Astor House for much of the latter 1870s and early '80s. He became an American citizen in 1887, but on every public occasion he made clear that he was Franco-American.

Fere's devotion to France in politics, art, and gastronomy would periodically inspire satire. In May 1882, for instance, he attempted to assay an American menu at the Astor House, producing the following:

SOUP

Cream of Lobster   Beef broth with new vegetables

RELISHES

Olives   Anchovies   Sardines   Chow Chow Pickles

FISH

Kennebec boiled salmon with Victoria sauce and new potatoes

RELEVES

Sugar cured hams glaces, champagne sauce   Pork & Beans, Boston Style
Boston Brown Bread

```
                    ROCKAWAYS, HALF-SHELL

        GREEN TURTLE            COLBERT            CHICKEN CONSOMME

    BOUCHEES, LUCULLUS                           BOUDINS OF CHICKEN
        CAVIARE               ANCHOVIES               OLIVES

    BOILED SALMON, COULIS D'ECREVISSES          BROILED DELAWARE SHAD
        CUCUMBER SALAD                           POTATO, DUCHESSE

            ROASTED FILET OF BEEF, HUSSARDE

    SWEETBREAD LARDED, MONTPENSIER
        SPRING CHICKEN FRIED, STANLEY
            BREAST OF MALLARD DUCK, CHASSEUR
                GRILLED SQUAB ON TOAST, CRESSES
                    RICE CROQUETTES, MAISON D'OR

            PATE DE FOIE-GRAS

            SORBET EN SURPRISE

    SPRING LAMB, MINT SAUCE    TURKEY, GIBLET SAUCE    RIBS OF PRIME BEEF
                PHILADELPHIA CAPON, TRUFFE

        SLICED TOMATOES         CELERY          LETTUCE SALAD

            BAKED STUFFED TOMATO, CREOLE
    NEW ASPARAGUS   CREAMED SPINACH   GREEN PEAS   SWEET POTATO CROQUETTE
        EGG-PLANT FRITTER   OYSTER-PLANT, POULETTE   NEW BEETS, BUTTER SAUCE
            STEWED TOMATO   BOILED ONIONS   BOILED POTATO   MASHED POTATO

                SOUFFLE PUDDING, MADEIRA
    RHUBARB PIE    FRANGIPANE TART    STRAWBERRY SHORT CAKE    ECLAIRS AU PUNCH
        GATEAU, ST. HONORE        SAUTERNE JELLY        CHARLOTTE RUSSE
            ASSORTED FANCY CAKES        NESSELRODE PUDDING GLACE
                WALNUT CARAMELS    STUFFED POTATOES, FROZEN

        PINEAPPLE CHEESE                      ROQUEFORT CHEESE
            FRUIT                 COFFEE              NUTS

    SUNDAY, MARCH 29, 1891
```

Fernand Fere's menu for Easter Sunday, March 29, 1891, at the Plaza Hotel, New York. From the Henri Bettoni Collection. *Menus: The Art of Dining.* Photograph: courtesy of the University of Nevada, Las Vegas University, http://digital.library.unlv.edu/u?/menus,2336.

ENTREES

Tenderloin of beef, Bearnaise style   Green peas   Sweetbread, larded, tomato sauce

VEGETABLES

Baked macaroni with cheese, home style   Spinach   Summer Squash

ROAST

Lamb, mint sauce

DESSERT

Plum Pudding, Rum Sauce   Ice Cream   Coffee   Chocolate   Fruit   Cheese

A commentator observed, "It will be seen at once that the styling of this dinner as America was, to use the gentlest word, a fiction. The solitary representative of American culinary fame was a small, greasy slice of pork, secreted in the centre of some dozen ancient beans."

As a French chef, however, Fere had few equals, and was just as adept at fermenting Alsatian sauerkraut as he was making a classic such as Quenelles de lapin—a dish enshrined in Viard's *Le Cuisinier Royal*. Here is Fere's 1882 updating of that canonical rabbit forcemeat:

> Bone some rabbits and extract all the nerves. Pound well in a mortar, and strain through a hair sieve. Soak some bread crumbs in milk, bouillon or hot water. When well soaked put them in a new, white cloth and squeeze as tight as possible, so no liquid remains, pound well, and strain the same as the meat. Have some butter, free it of all its lumps, equal quantities of meat, bread and butter. Mix well together, adding salt, pepper, a little grated nutmeg, and a little ground allspice. Beat up well and throw in one egg at a time, until you have consumed five. Two entire and the yolks of three, if your meat is still too thick add another. When sufficient, put a little in a saucepan to taste if seasoned properly. Whip the three remaining whites to a froth and add them to the forcemeat, stirring all the time, with a wooden spoon. Take from the mortar and reserve for culinary purposes.

In 1883 Fere turned the kitchens of the Astor House over to Charles Babin and moved to the Broadway Hotel at No. 1 Broadway. His replacement would be shot and killed by waiter Joseph Ott on November 8, 1886. It was from the kitchens of the Broadway Hotel that Fere dispatched most of the food for the Société banquet of 1885, over which he had charge.

Fere had a fascination with the chemistry of food preparation. When David Wesson hydrogenated cottonseed oil to produce what we now call Crisco, Fere convened the culinary community in New York to explore the possibility of the substance as a replacement for butter (concerns about whether it communicated tuberculosis were then prevalent). He invited the press and the cooking community to his restaurant in the Washington Building at No. 1 Broadway in May 1884 to experience a feast created employing cottonseed margarine.

Fere's love of innovation extended to kitchen technology. When industrial-size natural gas ranges began to be manufactured in the mid-1880s, Fere organized a demonstration at Tammany Hall in February 1887. "A large range with three or four double compartments, heated by gas, had been placed in the north-west corner of Tammany Hall, and it was about this that the company gathered." A table extended in front of the range, and it was loaded with sirloin and porterhouse steaks, mutton chops, chicken and lobster croquettes, joints, rolls, biscuits and other substantials and delicacies ready to be cooked. The assembly was satisfied and "Resolved, That we here now encourage the indorsement of said range and recommend it, and believe it to be the most economical in the market." For a period from 1888 through 1890, Fere operated as an agent for the gas range manufacturers as well as laboring as a chef.

When the luxurious Plaza Hotel opened overlooking Central Park in the winter of 1891, Fere was hired to preside over its cuisine. Among his challenges at the Plaza was Walz Vetta's widely publicized Bohemian dinner of early November 1892. Vetta, a wealthy Texan, invited his guests to imagine whatever dishes and entertainments they wished upon arriving, and they would be satisfied. This dinner without a menu became newspaper fodder across the United States, and Fere apparently complied with every wish impromptu.

Throughout the early 1890s, Fere suffered from gout. It became so debilitating that he was forced to step down as chef of the Plaza in early 1894. His place was taken by a traditionalist who had this to say about the gas ranges that Fere had installed in the kitchens of the Plaza: "We have them, but I won't use one of them. Give me charcoal first, then hard coal—but no gas or electricity. For toast or waffles I use the gas, for there is no delicate flavor to be emphasized. We also boil large quantities of vegetables by gas—when we do not steam them—but for broiling nothing is so perfect as charcoal. We use three bags a day here in our range."

In 1897, at age fifty-four, he returned to his native county to consolidate inheritances there. He never returned to the United States.

✳ ✳ ✳

SOURCES: "La Reception des Delegues Francais," *Courrier des Etats-Unis*, no. 301 (October 27, 1881): 1; "Faits Divers," *Courrier des Etats-Unis* (January 29, 1882): 4; "Union Des Societes Francaises," *Courrier des Etats-Unis*, no. 132 (May 14, 1882): 4; "Scarcely American Fare," *The Sun* (May 28, 1882): 1; "Pour remplacer le beurre," *Courrier des Etats-Unis*, no. 122 (May 21, 1884): 2; "The French Cook's Ball," *New York Herald* 34 (February 3, 1885): 9; "A Gas Cooking Séance," *New York Herald* 43 (February 12, 1887): 3; "Quenelles de Lapin," *Société culinaire philanthropique de New York: To Their patrons and Friends* (New York: Société Culinaire Philanthropique, 1888), 70; "Dinner without Menu," *New York Herald*, no. 316 (November 11, 1892): 5; "Big Chefs Express Views," *Philadelphia Inquirer* 131, no. 15 (July 15, 1894): 19; United States Passport Application of August 9, 1897.

Maria Parloa 1843-1909
Portsmouth, NH; Wolfeboro, NH; Isle of Shoals, ME; Boston; New York

In the nineteenth century, the cooking school supplied to American women an introduction to standard kitchen practices in settings alternative to the practice-based apprenticeship system of culinary training found in Europe and hotel restaurants in the United States. Located in the major American cities, the cooking schools operated under the direction of a single matron, who lectured an audience of women while working at dishes in a demonstration kitchen. The lecture demonstrations touched upon best practices for cooking and baking, a repertoire for household or boardinghouse fare, economy in the purchase of food, and nutrition. Maria Parloa, who opened Miss Parloa's School of Cooking in Boston in 1877 and who lectured on advanced cooking techniques at the Boston Cooking School during its founding seasons of 1879-82, was among the greatest of these public instructors. In 1882 she founded the New York Cooking School. After 1887 she became the most famous itinerating lecturer on cooking techniques in the United States until the turn of the twentieth century.

Born in Massachusetts in 1843, she absorbed the seriousness of the New England physical culturists concerning hygiene, diet, and exercise. She was apparently orphaned at an early age and, in the New England tradition, educated in cookery with the thought of making her a hired household cook. Her skills, however, were such that she found ready employment in New England small hotels. During her late teens and early twenties, she worked seasons in New Hampshire at the Rockingham House in Portsmouth (the most historic hostelry in that city, first constructed in 1785 and still in operation as a hotel and restaurant), the Pavilion Hotel in Wolfeboro (open only during June through early October in the 1860s), and the McMillan House in North Conway (a summer wilderness resort opposite Peaked Mountain). Most famously, she worked the Appledore Hotel, a resort venue on Maine's Isles of Shoals. The modest pay and seasonal remuneration of these jobs took their toll on Parloa, and in 1871 she enrolled in classes to become a schoolteacher. She found winter employment in a school in Mandarin, Florida, where Calvin Stowe, Harriet Beecher Stowe's husband, ran a mission chapel and school.

Her career as a culinary lecturer began in New London, Connecticut, in 1876. She had come north to address a meeting in that city being held to raise funds to buy an organ for Calvin Stowe's Florida church and spoke about the art of cookery. Her performance stirred such interest that she instantly found herself in demand. A group of women organized the funding for the opening of Miss

"Maria Parloa" (ca. 1890).
Maria Parloa Collection.
Photograph: Courtesy
of Bethel Public Library,
Bethel, Connecticut.

Parloa's School of Cooking in 1877 at 174 Tremont in Boston. Installed in the upper floor of a Colonnade Row house, her demonstration kitchen was outfitted with "low tiles and Morris draperies." During the refitting of the space, she enrolled with Boston's best elocution teacher to improve her oral delivery to a professional standard. She maintained her school until 1882. Concurrently, she lectured at the Boston Cooking School established by the Women's Education Association of Boston down the street at 158½ Tremont, speaking on alternating Sundays about fancy dishes.

She self-financed the opening of the New York School in October 1882. Headquartered in a building at 222 East Seventeenth Street, she held daytime classes there throughout the week, alternating lectures with practice classes in a large kitchen. In her advertisements, she made clear the seriousness of the endeavor. "It is not intended merely to provide an afternoon's diversion for occasional auditors at the public lectures or demonstration lessons, nor simply furnish a round of merry times for pupils in practice classes." The first New York class dealt with cream of celery soup, chicken à la tartare, pigs in blankets, charlotte russe, and royal diplomatic pudding. She would also contract out with churches, hospitals, and local associations to conduct special neighborhood classes in the evenings, so that working women did not have to travel across Manhattan for instruction, but could hear and see her demonstrations at places within walking distance of their homes. The New York School operated for five years, closing in June 1887 when the demand for Parloa's services had become so general that touring made more sense than convening school at a central location. From

1887 onward, she crisscrossed the eastern United States, with an occasional foray southward, holding lectures in nearly every place aspiring to be a city. In New York after 1887, she took to holding classes in Madison Square Garden, when her audiences by then numbered in the thousands. The mass classes could be irksome, for many came wanting recipes for fancy dishes, rather than instruction in more needful matters, such as baking bread.

Parloa possessed several virtues necessary for her calling. She had a systematic turn of mind, capable of analyzing and laying out cooking and baking processes with a clarity that the uninstructed could grasp; she possessed great sororal affection for women and respected their efforts at self-improvement, a care manifested in the patience in her interactions with students and a complete lack of condescension dealing with them; and, finally, she possessed a journalist's skill in writing factual information. She became a magazine columnist on the topic of home economics, and then one of the most important cookbook authors of the last quarter of the nineteenth century. She, Mary Virginia Terhune (known by her pen name, Marion Harland), and Sarah Tyson Rorer were the triumvirate of kitchen oracles that American women heeded when setting up house. At the time of her death in 1909, Parloa's cookbook titles had sold a half-million copies. The sequence of important titles is as follows: *The Appledore Cook Book: Containing Practical Receipts for Plan and Rich Cooking* (1872), *Camp Cookery: How to Live in Camp* (1878), *First Principles of Household Management and Cookery: A Text-Book for Schools and Families* (1879), *Miss Parloa's New Cook Book: A Guide to Marketing and Cooking* (1881), *Miss Parloa's Kitchen Companion: A Guide for All Who Would Be Good Housekeepers* (1887), *Choice Recipes* (1893), *Miss Parloa's Young Housekeeper: Designed Especially to Aid Beginners* (1893), *Home Economics: A Guide to Household Management* (1898), *Canned Fruit, Preserves, and Jellies: Household Methods of Preparation* (1905), *Preparation of Vegetables for the Table* (1906), *The Government Cook Book: Economical Use of Meat in the Home* (1910), and *Chocolate and Cocoa Recipes and Home Made Candy Recipes* (posthumous 1911).

Of these many volumes, *Miss Parloa's Young Housekeeper* became particularly important, often given as a bridal gift to a newlywed woman, much as *The Joy of Cooking* or the *Betty Crocker Cookbook* were for later generations. In the foreword of that landmark work, Parloa wrote:

> Wherever I have gone in the last 15 years in following my calling as a teacher of cooking, earnest appeals have been made to me to plan my next book for the especial benefit of those who have just begun, or who are about to begin, to keep house for two or three. The young wives want to know how to buy supplies for a small family; how to cook economically and well; what to do with food that is left over from any meal, and numerous other things pertaining to their daily work. At

last I have set about telling them. They will find that it is not necessary to have an immense income in order to live well.

Parloa made wholesomeness the culinary ideal of the home. Yet her instructions treated other matters as well, including a particularly valuable section on cooking for invalids and children suffering from illness.

Culinary topics dominated Parloa's lecturing and writing during the 1880s. General household management—furnishing, cleaning, and keeping records for a house became central in her instructions of the 1890s. She provoked controversy with her advocacy of hardwood floors over carpets. After the turn of the twentieth century, and at the behest of the US government, Parloa turned attention to food preservation—making preserves and jellies, canning, drying, and pickling. Her one major contribution to the alteration of prevailing American tastes was her insistence on making breakfasts simpler, smaller, and more digestible. She worked in concert with the cereal advocates of the physical culture movement in this campaign.

While Parloa belonged to a group of women hailed as scientific instructors on cookery and household management, she did not stress nutritional chemistry in her cookbooks or infection theories in her household management manuals. She realized expositions of Liebigian chemistry had less potency as an attractor of public attention as the ideal of food purity. Teaching the practice of sanitation, in the end, probably enacted more good than any exposition of hygienic theory. Her astute sense of public interest was honed while working on the editorial staff of the *Ladies' Home Journal* during the late 1890s and early 1900s. During the final decade of her life, when the US government engaged Parloa to write on food preservation and economical cookery, it also encouraged her to treat medicine and food chemistry more explicitly. Her lectures post-1901 are thus decidedly more academic in their treatment of nutrition, the chemistry of cooking, and the danger of pathogens in the kitchen.

Miss Parloa interrupted her work as a culinary instructor periodically to undergo tutelage herself. In the summer of 1878, she traveled to London and Paris to study food processing and preparation. In France she witnessed the techniques of French butchers—their quick drainage of fluids and inflation of cavities and arteries with a bellows—a process she advocated repeatedly in magazines and lectures. When her interests turned to household management in the 1890s, she toured England, France, and Germany from 1894 through 1896 absorbing the latest thought on domestic economy and hygiene. Parloa's single condition, and her ample income from book sales and lecturing fees, enabled her to live wherever she pleased and travel wherever she wished. In the final years of her life, she settled on Bethel, Connecticut, as a congenial and healthy place of residence. She died during gallstone surgery in 1909 and bequeathed her fortune to the town, a portion of it to be reserved for the construction of athletic fields for the town's youths. The Boston Public Library received her collection of cookbooks and housekeeping guides.

✳   ✳   ✳

SOURCES: "Pure Food and Music," *New York Herald* 278 (October 4, 1872): 7; "Miss Parloa's Cookery School," *New York Tribune* (October 30, 1882): 5; "Cooking as an Art," *Evening Star* (November 18, 1882): 2; "Lectures in Cookery," *New York Tribune* (October 30, 1883): 2; "Miss Maria Parloa," *Trenton Times* (June 17, 1887): 2; "Maria Parloa Was Bride's Best Friend," *Boston Herald* (September 5, 1909): 23; "Maria Parloa and Her Cook Books," *Trenton Evening Times* (August 31, 1909): 6; Kiyoshi Shintani, "Cooking up Modernity: Culinary Reformers and the Making of Consumer Culture, 1876–1916" (PhD diss., University of Oregon, 2008).

The
GILDED AGE
1885 to 1919

FAME AND THE MASTER CHEF

Charles E. Rector 1844–1914
New York; Chicago; Washington, DC

In 1884 Charles E. Rector opened the doors of his game and seafood restaurant, Rector's, on 187–192 Clark Street in Chicago. Few restaurants in the nineteenth century won so instantaneous and universal favor and fame. It became the favorite resort of traveling men, nouveau riche couples, turfmen, and bachelors about town. Getting a "bird and a cold bottle" became the slogan of the kind of informal glitz that Rector popularized in Chicago. Rector's also enjoyed an immense midday business lunch trade.

Born in New York, Rector was raised in the Frontier House Hotel in Lewistown, New York, of which his father was proprietor. He absorbed public hospitality as a boy, and at the outbreak of the Civil War he enlisted. At war's end, found himself in Washington, DC, where he took a job as a government clerk but was fired when budget austerity caused his office to be disbanded. A friend secured him a job as conductor on a New York streetcar. Rector's career as a restaurateur began in the 1872 as steward of a dining car on the Pennsylvania Railroad, working the Chicago–New York route. "Breakfast, dinner, and supper were from the same card, with bacon and eggs, ham and eggs, or steak as the chief feature."

Rector eventually disembarked the train for a life in Chicago. He kept bar at Charlie Kern's saloon, but the decisive experience in his early career took place when he was barkeep in the saloon of the Brown Hotel. There Rector witnessed a hotelier of genius, M. Kinsley, improve his house into the first rank of American hostelries. He witnessed how style, publicity, amenities, and staff contributed to public favor.

With money earned from his barkeep's salary, Rector secured the lease of a cellar saloon on the corner of Monroe and Clark. He served oysters and obtained backing for his enterprise when he hit upon the idea of serving oysters off-season, secured from northern waters where there was no interdiction of tonging or dredging in "non-r" months. The saloon had as its emblem a brass griffon, which Rector would use ever after as his icon. Rector made his reputation with oysters, but in the 1880s he expanded the oyster saloon's offerings to include a whole range of seafood. In 1891 he doubled the space and number of rooms, cleared out the harsh arc lights for incandescent fixtures, and expanded the area of the house devoted to women. One lesson Rector learned from his days as a barkeep stayed with him during his years as a restaurateur: keep connected with the city's political power structure. He served as alderman of the Twenty-Eighth Ward in the city.

The success of his Chicago restaurant and his conviction that Rector's manifested a more unbuttoned, less ostentatious version of the high life than that offered by Delmonico's or Sherry's impelled him to open Rector's in New York in 1899. Leasing a new building constructed by Charles T. Barney, next to the Hotel Cadillac on Broadway at Forty-Fourth Street in Times Square, it had the audacity to be across from the new and final main branch of Delmonico's. The two restaurants opened almost simultaneously, and they offered a stark contrast. Delmonico's was classical, elegantly austere, quiet, and tranquil; Rector's was loud, late, ornate, and it did not stint on champagne or the signature lobsters.

Rector's New York was the first of the "lobster palaces." It won favor with the theatrical set particularly and, indeed, was celebrated in song and in the farce *The Girl from Rector's*. Rector realized that fashionability was a fragile thing, and that he could not compete with established temples of haute cuisine in the long run if he did not pay attention to the culinary end of matters. Rector's own sense of culinary excellence was French. He once told a reporter that American food had no distinctive character or individuality, except "in the far south, perhaps, but nowhere else." He took as a professional model the Parisian restaurateur Mourier, who ran the Café de Paris, Foyot's, d'Armenonville, and Pre Catain. He admired Mourier's creativity as a chef and decisiveness as a proprietor. Rector dispatched his son George, then a law student at Cornell University, to Paris to learn French cuisine. Apprenticing at the Café de Marguery, George returned after substantial instruction and practiced his art in the kitchens of Rector's. He remained with his father until 1909, when his father organized the company that would transform his restaurant into a luxury hotel. Chef George Rector set up an independent restaurant on Long Acre Square and would enjoy a long public career as a culinary personality.

The menu at Rector's began with eleven different oyster preparations and clams casino. The soup offerings were perfunctory. Then came the signature lobsters—in croquettes with sauce à l'anchois, split and broiled with chili sauce, split and deviled, cold with tartar sauce, stuffed with crab and bread crumbs, and cold deviled. Almost as many crab recipes were available, including a Newburg. There were surprisingly few hot entrées—sweetbread, lamb, chicken, and filet mignon. Game featured red head duck (the canvasback had become scarce in the eastern flyway by 1899), venison, grouse, snipe plover, and partridge. There was a surprising abundance of cold dishes—the traditional banquet dishes of caterers and sandwiches. Salads also abounded. Desserts were canted toward ice creams rather than cakes and jellies.

After establishing his successful New York restaurant, Rector determined to expand on the East Coast and overseas. He sold the Chicago restaurant, which was renamed the Café Royale by its new proprietors (the space would finally shut its doors in 1919). In 1901 Rector went to London to obtain an option on the Hotel Walsingham site, intent on razing it and building a new American hotel in its place. Rival Louis Sherry apparently made an offer on the same property. In the end, neither project was built. But Rector, after the success of the New York operation, realized that expansion was the chief way to raise revenue exponentially. He opened a third branch of his restaurant empire in Washington, DC, a move that strengthened his brand but did not, in the end, fatten his wallet.

In 1910 Rector, having witnessed the decline of the Delmonico's empire with the death of Charles C. Delmonico, determined to build his own restaurant-hotel complex on the site of his restaurant. The $3 million Rector's hotel was elegant, classy, and, well, rather Delmonico-esque and stodgy. All of the raffish character of his New York restaurant had been expunged. So the Broadway Johnnies of New York passed it by. Mayor Gaynor's 1:00 a.m. closing order for Manhattan entertainment venues cramped the style of New York nightlife. In the provinces, another difficulty arose. A poster advertising the Broadway musical farce *The Girl from Rector's*, with a leggy showgirl seated on a lobster being borne aloft by a well-fed waiter, had spread across the continent in advance of the touring musical. It "gave residents of Kansas City and Pittsburgh very salacious ideas of the New York hotel." By 1912 Rector knew his great creation to be a failure. His heart disease—something which had periodically incapacitated him since 1907—began to persist. In 1914 he died in the old gambling resort of Long Branch, New Jersey, after a protracted illness.

✳   ✳   ✳

SOURCES: "Extensive Improvements," *Daily Inter Ocean* 20, no. 173 (September 13, 1891): 17; [Alderman Rector,] *Chicago Eagle* (January 1, 1898): 1; [New York real estate notice,] *New-York Tribune* (January 24, 1899): 12; "American Hotel in London," *New York Tribune* (August 22, 1901): 8; "George Rector," *New York Sun* (June 22, 1909): 12; "Kingpin of Chefs," *Salt Lake Tribune* (February 13, 1910): 20; "Christmas Gift for 'Great White Way,'" *Elkhart Truth* (December 13, 1910): 2; "Thanks U.S. for Firing Him," *Kansas City Star* 31, no. 287 (July 1, 1911): 10; "The Poster That Put the Ban on Rector's," *San Francisco Call* (July 6, 1913): 19; Menu, New York Public Library Collection; "Charles E. Rector Dies," *New*

York Times (September 23, 1914): 7; "Charles E. Rector Dead, Famous for Cafes in Two Cities," *Duluth News Tribune* 46, no. 157 (October 4, 1914): 1; "Too Many Irons in the Fire," *Seattle Daily Times* (February 9, 1919): 10; "Rector's, New York City, 1899–1919," the *American Menu*: http://www.theamericanmenu .com/2015/08/rectors.html.

Edward Charbulak 1845–1929

Saratoga, NY; New York; St. Louis

A native of Moravia and trained in the Austrian apprenticeship system, Edward Charbulak came to the United States in the wake of the Civil War to become a sous-chef under chef Ludin at the Metropolitan Hotel in Manhattan. Yet he won fame in the 1870s in the United States while cooking at the Grand Union Hotel in Saratoga, New York, during the summer seasons. Terse, commanding, and left-leaning in politics, he cut a distinctive figure in the society of the New York spas. His Austrian-honed skills at fish and pastry cookery won him respect among his professional colleagues. At the Metropolitan, he endured the financial and managerial uncertainties of the house—its seizure for bankruptcy in March 1871, its festive reopening in August of that year, and a destructive fire in 1872. These travails bothered the orderly Moravian, so after his Saratoga summer in 1872, he removed to St. Louis. There he found an Americanized version of German culture that suited him greatly. He became the chef at Barnum's Hotel in St. Louis in autumn of 1872.

When Barnum's began declining in the early 1880s, Charbulak transferred to the Southern Hotel, a historic hostelry rebuilt after a fire in 1877, equipped with a state-of-the-art kitchen. Because Charbulak had experienced the challenge of serving the miscellaneous tastes of the public at the Grand Union Hotel in Saratoga, he quickly adapted from the Austrian cuisine of his training to the provisions found in the American market. He characteristically moderated the French menu during his hotel career in St. Louis. His Americanization is particularly visible in his holiday menus of the 1880s and '90s. This Christmas menu from the Southern Hotel from 1888, the last year of the old hotel, well conveys the extent of his Americanization:

Blue Points

Terrapin, Aux Quenelles Radishes

Consomme, Dauphine, Salt Almonds

Celery

Benjamin West Kilburn, "We wait your pleasure, Southern Hotel, St. Louis, Mo., U.S.A." (ca. 1885). Stereograph of E. Charbulak's staff and restaurant interior by James M. Davis, New York. Photograph: From the New York Public Library (MFY Dennis Coll 90-F436).

Small Patties of Oysters, Supreme

Broiled Charleston Shad, a la Maitre d'Hotel

Julienne Potatoes

Roast Sirloin of Beef

Browned Mashed Potatoes   Asparagus

Turkey, Chestnut Dressing

Sweet Corn   Baked Sweet Potatoes

Young Pig, Apple Sauce

French Peas   Haricots Verts

Sweetbreads Pique, Aux Truffles

Cutlets of Pheasant, Puree of Artichokes

Orange Fritters Glace au Kirsch

Champagne Punch

Roast Larded Quail, Bread Sauce, Mallard Duck, Grape Jelly

Galantine of Prairie Hen

Fresh Lobster, Mayonnaise

Boned Turkey, en Gelee

Russian Caviar on Toast

Chicken and Lettuce Salad

English Plum Pudding, Brandy and Hard Sauce

Assorted Cake   Apple Pie

Charlotte Russe   Mince Pie

Confectionery   Pumpkin Pie
Ice Cream in Form
Roquefort, Edam, Sage Cheese
Bent's Crackers, Cider
Fruit, Coffee

One presumes that this feast was served in banks of chafing dishes on a buffet table. Spanish mackerel and leg of boar appeared on the Christmas 1890 bill of fare.

During Charbulak's tenure, the Southern was one of the foci of social life in St. Louis, with a heavy banquet trade, club sittings, and receptions. Charbulak's organizational skills made him invaluable to the management, and he remained actively employed at the Southern well into his sixties.

※   ※   ※

SOURCES: "Marshal Sharpe Seizes the Metropolitan Hotel," *New York Tribune* 30, no. 9354 (March 30, 1871): 5; *St. Louis, Missouri, City Directory, 1873*, 171; [Menu,] *St. Louis Republic* 81, no. 21381 (December 25, 1888): 8; "A Happy Holiday," *St. Louis Republic* 83, no. 22112 (December 26, 1890): 5; "Palate Ticklers," *St. Louis Republic* (September 16, 1894): 27; "To-Day at the Hotels," *St. Louis Republic* (December 25, 1888): 8.

Louis Charles Fleury Lallouette 1845–1915
Paris; New York

Trained as a pastry cook in Paris, Charles Lallouette in the later 1860s worked as head pastry chef in several Parisian hotels and noble households before ascending to the post of chef de cuisine at the Grand Hotel in Paris. While he served in the household of the Empress Eugenie in Paris, he worked alongside Charles Ranhofer. When Ranhofer became chef de cuisine at the main branch of Delmonico's, Ranhofer's cousin established the connection and proffered the invitation to come to New York. Lallouette worked for a period in the 1870s as chef at the Fourteenth Street branch of Delmonico's and later at the Fifth Avenue house. Ranhofer includes one of Lallouette's menus as an exemplary meal in *The Epicurean* (1894). The Hotel New York offered him a position in late 1875 as chef de cuisine, replacing E. Mercier. Lallouette accepted and inaugurated that hotel's heyday as a culinary destination in New York.

"Charles Lallouette."
Duotone from "The Science of Cookery," *Leslie's Weekly* 81 (October 24, 1895): 270.

In 1877 the Hotel Buckingham lured him away with a part partnership in the business. He remained in that position for twenty years. While at the Buckingham, Lallouette faced a number of challenges, perhaps none so steep as satisfying the desires of the Ichthyophagous Club, the devourers of sea creatures, which met regularly in the 1880s. They demanded seasonal fare and novelty. One of Lallouette's menus from this group dates from 1885 and violates the club brief only in insinuating a vegetable or two in the mix and a filet of beef.

Blue Points

Extract of Razor Clams

Bisque of Starfish   Vin de Graves

Radishes   Celery   Olives   Royal Sherry

Squid fried (Chondopterygien)

Winkles, Burgundy Fashion

Sea Spider Crab a l'Infernal

Cray Fish du Potomac

Liebfraumilch

Cucumbers   Hollandaise Potatoes

Skate, Cream Sauce (Acandopterygien)

Crevaile a la Marseillaise

Sea Robins baked a l'Amphitrite

Salmon (Royal Fish), Parisian style

Baisson of Lobster, Tartare Sauce

Pontet Canet

Filet of Beef

Mushrooms and Tomatoes Farcies   French Peas

Stewed Terrapin, Buckingham style

Ichthyophagous Punch

Broiled Teal Duck   G. H. Mumm's Cordon Rouge

Lobster Salad   Crab Salad   Lettuce Salad

Neapolitan Ice Cream   Fruit Jelly   Assorted Cakes
Fancy Pyramids   Fruit   Cheese
Café   Liqueurs

Here is the recipe for a more conventional fish dish from his repertoire, fillet of sole magny, which appeared on the menus of the Hotel Buckingham repeatedly during the 1880s.

Separate the fillet of one or more soles, place in a vessel with butter, shallots, chopped onions. Add white wine and mushroom juice, raw oysters and mussels, salt and pepper, cover with bits of butter, and place on the fire to boil, then cover and bake for five or six minutes to finish the poaching. Then place the fillets on a serving dish, array the oysters and mussels around them. Make a Normandy sauce and nap the fillets with it, adorn it with three or four large mushrooms, and crown with spiced red shrimp.

After his retirement, Lallouette visited his native land on a regularly basis. During a visit in summer of 1915 to Nice, he died of esophageal cachexia.

❋   ❋   ❋

SOURCES: "How Art Caters to Appetite," *New York Herald* (March 17, 1895): 4–8; Recipe translation by David S. Shields; "The Science of Cookery," *Leslie's Weekly* 81 (October 24, 1895): 270; American Consular Service Death of a Citizen Abroad Notice, July 22, 1915.

Louise Volkmann 1845–1922?
New York

Vegetarianism enjoyed a powerful transformation from philosophy to public practice in the 1890s, when the Pure Food Movement gained adherents in the wake of the tubercular milk scare and growing concern about the unsanitary conditions and animal cruelty of the meatpacking industry. After a banquet in 1892 hosted by Mrs. Le Favre in New York for the Vegetarian Society, there was a conviction that the movement had grown to an extent that warranted the creation of a restaurant. The Vegetarian Café opened on 240 West Twenty-Third Street on February 5, 1895, announcing:

With right good will to all mankind
And animal creation,
We mean to show the world at large
A vegetarian Celebration.

The mistress of ceremonies at this celebration was Mrs. L. Volkmann. The bill of fare reflected the movement's embrace of "temperance, thrift, and purity" by making a virtue of simplicity:

SOUP
Entire Wheat Bread   Gluten
Potato Cakes   Lima Beans
Baked Macaroni with Cheese
Holland Vegetable Cutlet, Tomato Sauce
Potato Salad
Rice Pudding   Pie
Oranges   Apples
Tea   Coffee   Chocolate

Volkmann, realizing that her enterprise required mystique, would not reveal the constitution of the Holland cutlet, nor the other tofu-like bean preparations that rotated with it on the menu—the Swedish, Danish, and Norwegian cutlets, all sauced à la Provençal. Volkmann's own Scandinavian heritage was referenced in the names of these dishes.

Reporters noted that three sorts of persons appeared in the restaurant: regular boarders who were adherents to the vegetarian cause, novelty seekers, and the economists who sought nourishment at a fraction of the cost of a steak dinner. The forty members of the Vegetarian Society made a point of boarding regularly at the café. But some of the neighborhood drop-in trade were mystified by the absence of meat, as reported in a humorous sketch entitled "No Fish, Flesh, or Fowl" in the *Watertown Daily Times* on May 13, 1895.

Volkmann insured that the bill of fare at the Vegetarian Café mirrored seasonal availability and manifested variety. Fruit soups alternated with lentil and tomato; "spaghetti with tomato sauce, baked cauliflower, and flageolette beans" were menu regulars. The American penchant for fruit pies was ingeniously served and diners assured that crusts were made from butter not lard (Cottonlene, or Crisco, had not yet been rehabilitated from its bad reputation as a lard adulterant). Volkmann built public interest by periodically staging "feasts"— for instance, a June strawberry feast featuring strawberry lemonade, strawberry fritters, shortcake, and ice cream.

Realizing that her core clientele consisted of diners with various strong sumptuary convictions about animal cruelty, nutrition, or the effects of diet on psychology, Volkmann also issued occasional public sermonettes and dicta. She claimed she could "work twice as hard as she could when living upon meat."

Volkmann's cuisine, like much vegetarian cuisine in the twentieth century, wrestled with the yearning for the taste of meat that haunted converts to the vegetable. One of Volkmann's great concerns was to create meat substitutes that approximated the taste of cutlets and steaks. She also realized that women were often the most determined adherents to the cause, and that these women might be married to men who savored meat. To these spiritual sisters she assured them that "a skillful cook can make dishes into the preparation of which no animal substance enters so like meat foods in taste that the difference can hardly be noticed."

A native of Kiel, Germany, Louise Carstensen graduated with honors from that city's conservatory of music. In 1864 she married Carl A. Marckenthuen of the English merchant marine but was widowed in 1871. She then emigrated to the United States with her second husband, Reverend Amandus Volquarts. After his death in 1882, Louise set up a private music school in New York. Her marriage to wealthy landscape gardener Max C. A. Volkmann in 1888 prompted her to leave off teaching and devote her energies to causes that moved her passions. She was a missioner in the prisons, a supporter of various New York hospitals, president of the Independent Women's Suffrage League of New York, organizer of the National Provident Union, and the creator of the Vegetarian Café.

The Vegetarian Café lasted two seasons before Volkmann's interests moved elsewhere. She became an astute broker of Manhattan real estate and after the turn of the twentieth century split her residence between Newport, Rhode Island, and New York. The example of her restaurant, however, inspired similar establishments in other cities, in Boston in 1897, and later in San Francisco and San Jose, California. Yet commercial success for vegetarian dining did not come about until Bernarr Macfadden opened his chain of Physical Culture restaurants in American cities in 1904. Connecting the diet to the body beautiful instead of the avoidance of carnage dissipated the sanctimoniousness that troubled vegetarianism in the perceptions of the masses.

※　　※　　※

SOURCES: "Here's a Plot to Ruin Butchers," *New York Herald* (March 13, 1892): 4; "First Vegetarian Café in New York," *New York Herald* (March 17, 1895): 4–5; "A Strawberry Feast," *Denver Post* (June 24, 1895): 5; "It's Good for Vegetarianism," *Kansas City Times* (May 19, 1895): 21; John Leonard, *Women's Who's Who of America* (New York: American Commonwealth Co., 1915), 840.

Frank Xavier Mivelaz 1846–1928 and Louis L. Mivelaz 1854–1901

Louisville, KY; Memphis, TN; Little Rock, AR; Fort Smith, AR; Vicksburg, MS

Swiss-born chef Frank Mivelaz brought fine dining to Little Rock, Arkansas, in partnership with his younger brother Louis L. Mivelaz (born in Kentucky in 1854), the ambitious restaurateur and hotelier. In 1881 both brothers left significant positions—Frank as chef de cuisine at the Louisville Hotel in Kentucky, Louis as chef and steward of the Peabody and Gaston Hotel in Memphis—to open the Capital Hotel Restaurant in Little Rock. The outgoing Louis operated as proprietor, Frank as chef. The earliest information about offerings dates from 1882, when Louis announced that the kitchen was serving up the first oysters, frog legs, and prairie grouse on August 8—early indeed for the first named of the items. As with all hotel restaurants of any pretension, wines, liquors, and cigars featured prominently in the saloon; a local innovation was its emphasis on mixed drinks.

For the first two years of the enterprise, Frank cooked on a brick range. In September 1883, the restaurant purchased a $500 state-of-the-art steel range. A tour of the premises after the range's installation noted an enormous icebox "packed with prairie chicken, quail, venison, white fish, trout." The restaurant seated seventy-five for breakfast, dinner, and supper. For banquets and special occasions, Louis would construct a grand exhibition piece, such as the wax castle with knights he erected in 1886 for a Knights of Pythias celebration.

In 1884 Louis and Frank's brother Lawrence opened a restaurant under the McKibben Hotel in Fort Smith, Arkansas, an establishment boasting the same high-end $500 range as that at the Capital Hotel Restaurant.

In April 1881, a fire ignited in the Capital Hotel, destroying the wooden portions of the kitchen and melting the silver. Uninsured, the Mivelaz brothers suffered $1,500 in damages, yet opened the hotel and secured breakfast for guests as though nothing happened. When the damage was repaired, Frank sought to demonstrate unequivocally that his cuisine was the best offered in any restaurant in the state. The regular bill of fare in December 1888 announced the following:

BREAKFAST

Fruits

Tenderloin Steak   Fish   Turkey-hash on toast

Eggs (any style)   Potatoes   Buckwheat cakes   Sausage or Spare-ribs

Coffee   Tea   Milk

"Capital Hotel, Little Rock, Arkansas" (1892). Photograph: Courtesy of the Butler Center for Arkansas Studies, Central Arkansas Library System.

DINNER

Soup L'Italian pasta, Aux Fine Herbs

Tenderloin of Trout, Tartare Sauce

Turkey with dressing   Roast Ribs of Beef, drip Gravy

Roast of Veal with French Peas

Acutee of young Squirrel (Hunter's style)

Apple Fritters, Cream Sauce

Vegetables—Green Peas   Baked Mashed Potatoes

Egg-plant, drawn butter   Roast Sweet Potatoes

Celery   Chicken Salad   Radishes

Pastry—Mince Pie   Cabinet pudding

Rhine Wine   Punche Frappe   Black Coffee

SUPPER

Steaks of Chops   Assorted Cold Meats

Salads   Eggs to Order   Corn-Beef Hash

Mush and Milk   Cakes with Maple Syrup

Fruit Sauce   Hot Rolls   Biscuits   Toasts

Cold Turkey

Coffee   Tea   Milk

The improvements were not restricted to the menu. In 1889 an expanded dining hall was outfitted on the second floor and a billiard parlor installed. In

1893 the hotel recapitalized. Frank was not listed among the partners. Then, in summer of 1893, Louis took control of the Carroll Hotel on Clay Street in Vicksburg. This luxury accommodation aspired to be the finest hotel in Mississippi, yet it did not have the customer base to thrive. After two years of trying to wrestle the hotel to profitability, Louis abandoned the project, moving to Memphis to run the Waldorf Café and Hotel. For the final six years of his life, Louis's corpulent smiling presence was a familiar sight in the city. He died suddenly by apoplexy ascending the stairs in his hotel after dinner in October 1901.

In 1894 Lawrence moved from Fort Smith to Little Rock to open the Merchant's Cafe, but a shake-up in the management of the Richelieu Hotel in the city afforded him an opportunity to become a hotelier as well.

⁂   ⁂   ⁂

SOURCES: "Capital Hotel Restaurant," *Arkansas Gazette* (June 4, 1881): 4; "Capital Hotel Saloon," *Arkansas Gazette* (April 22, 1883): 5; "Local Paragraphs," *Arkansas Gazette* (September 7, 1883): 8; "Clean as a Parlor," *Arkansas Gazette* (September 13, 1883): 5; "Good News for the Boys," *Arkansas Gazette* (January 18, 1884): 8; "The Castle at the Banquet," *Arkansas Gazette* (May 23, 1886): 5; "Local Items," *Arkansas Gazette* 126 (April 10, 1887): 4; [Advertisement,] *Arkansas Gazette* (December 11, 1888): 4; "Louis Mivalez's Future Scheme," *Arkansas Gazette* (January 19, 1890): 4; "Preparations for the Opening of a New Hotel," *New Orleans Times-Picayune* (July 3, 1893): 6; "A Change," *Arkansas Gazette* (July 4, 1896): 5; "Hotel Man Dropped Dead," *Columbus Daily Enquirer* 42, no. 235 (October 15, 1901): 2; [Louis Mivelaz, Mortuary notice,] *New Orleans Times-Picayune* (October 15, 1901): 4.

Gustav Nouvel 1846–1906
Nantes, France; Halifax, Nova Scotia; New York; Chicago

Chef Gustav Nouvel made the Hoffman House in New York a major outpost of haute cuisine in the United States during the 1870s. Born into a family of hoteliers in Bretagne, France (his parents operated the Hotel de France and the Hotel du Cheval Blanc), he learned cuisine in the kitchens of his family's establishments. He finished his training as a pastry cook in Nantes and had a varied career in a variety of European hotels, before coming to America as steward of an English regiment stationed in Halifax, Nova Scotia. He fell in love with

"Gustav Nouvel" (ca. 1885). Wood engraving from newspaper clipping. Photograph: From the New York Public Library, Print Collection (1804943).

America, determined to remain, and ventured southward to New York in 1870 with his wife, Amelia.

Nouvel entered New York's culinary scene as a club cook, catering first for the Merchants Club from 1870 to 1871, then the Union Club in 1872. He also catered for the Dakota for a brief period before replacing Francis Kinzler as chef of Hoffman House in 1873. Kinzler had made Hoffman House a byword of gastronomy. Nouvel maintained its exalted reputation.

A thoroughly professionalized cook, Nouvel presided over the Union Culinaire Cosmopolite in the United States as president. In 1881 he met with Fernand Fere, the head of the Union Universelle de l'Art Culinaire (United States branch), in order to negotiate the amalgamation of both organizations. This resulting association would assist the placing of trained European chefs and confectioners in appropriate positions in American institutions. The Union vetted immigrants to determine whether they were artists or pupils and placed persons accordingly. For a period in the 1880s, the Union also operated as a guild employment bureau for culinary professionals of French and Belgian nativity. One aspect of Nouvel's professionalism was his conviction that print culture must be used to discipline and educate cooks. He was one of the proprietors of the journals *L'Art Culinaire Americain* and *La Cuisine*, the organs of French cuisine in the United States.

Nouvel was trained in the spectacular style of Parisian public event dining and was a master of fanciful displays incorporating sculptures of lard, sugar architecture, and translucent blocks of gelatin containing miniature villages made of carved vegetables. One such—"Neptune et Venus dans le Bosphore"— became the talk of the chef's masquerade ball in winter 1878.

Like most French-trained chefs, Nouvel had learned his craft on a coal cook-stove. While numbers of hotel kitchens used gas stoves, Nouvel continued to employ coal until 1895, when the cheapness of natural gas made the economies of coal untenable. After switching, he wondered at his resistance: "The experiment has thoroughly convinced me that gas has great advantages over coal, and that it is certain to come into universal use for fine cooking." Convenience—the lack of a necessity to reduce coals to embers versus the instant-firing gas—proved decisive. The temperature control of gas proved particularly important in controlled-fire preparations, such as crepes and egg dishes, for example, as in his signature dish:

EGGS À LA CASTELIANE
Prepare six soft poached eggs and wrap them in six French pancakes already stuffed with durcels of fresh mushrooms. Bread them à l'Anglaise and fry. Serve on bread crusts and garnish them in the middle with demi-glace or Madeira sauce, with truffles rognons and crete de gos. Serve cold.

On October 22, 1875, Nouvel became a United States citizen. He presided over the Hoffman House kitchen until 1884, when he was supplanted by Eugene Laperruque. Nouvel returned to the Union Club to serve that famous club dining room. Laperruque's autocratic tendencies finally prompted management of Hoffman House to restore Nouvel to his old position in 1890. Nouvel presided over Hoffman House through the 1890s, including the six-month renovation at the end of 1894. When the hotel reopened on New Year's Day 1895, Nouvel unleashed his imagination, creating a display in the center table of the barroom that had newspaper reporters rhapsodizing: "The center piece was a marvelous production representing a mammoth salmon riding in state in a boat propelled in part by sail and in part by a swarm of nymphs and mermaids, who pushed it through a turbulent sea full of accompanying dolphins, mermen, sea horses and other mythological things in sugar."

In 1898 the Grand Pacific Hotel succeeded in luring Nouvel to Chicago; the overture succeeded because the hotel also agreed to hire Rudolph Busse, the steward at Hoffman House and Nouvel's trusted colleague. Nouvel remained in Chicago for a brief two years, returning to New York and resuming his culinary career there on Lexington Avenue. He turned sixty in 1906 and died shortly thereafter.

※   ※   ※

SOURCES: "The Cook's Masquerade," *New York Herald* (March 22, 1878): 4; "New Cooking Schools," *New York Herald* (November 19, 1881): 4; "What We

Owe to the Hens," *Boston Herald* (April 7, 1895): 31; "Hurrah for 1895!" *New York Herald* (January 2, 1895): 4; "The Science of Cookery," *Leslie's Weekly* 81 (October 24, 1895): 270; "A Leading Chef's Testimony," *New York Tribune* (October 30, 1897): 11; "Notes and Personals," *Hotel Monthly* 6, no. 59 (February 1898): 16; New York Death Notices, 1906.

Benjamin Franklin Simms 1846–1897
Baltimore

One hallmark of success as a caterer was to expand one's business beyond one's home city and become the supplier ("provisioner") of desirable ingredients to a region or the nation. African American caterers in the post–Civil War South had an advantage in setting up such wholesale custom in that most of the fishermen and turtle hunters in coastal regions were black. Benjamin Franklin Simms of Maryland exploited his African American network of suppliers in the Chesapeake to set up a national reputation as a provider of terrapin, oysters, and ducks.

Born in Annapolis, Simms grew to manhood at a time when terrapin à la Maryland had been elevated to the signature dish of Chesapeake fine dining and a fixture on club menus in the big cities of the North. Born a freeman, Simms spent his teen years after the armistice working as a servant to merchant Lennox Birkhead, who brought him from Annapolis to Baltimore. Once in Baltimore, Simms attached himself as assistant to Henry Jakes, the foremost African American banquet cook in Maryland during the middle decades of the nineteenth century. He learned every aspect of the caterer's craft: securing ingredients, cooking the dishes, staging the banquet, hiring the wait staff, and providing the entertainment. One of Simm's tasks for Jakes was to deal with the fishermen and terrapin hunters who supplied the region's favorite ingredients. When Simms went into business for himself, however, he did not enter direct competition with his mentor, instead opening a sweet shop at 1045 Cathedral Street.

Simms used his connections among confectioners in other eastern cities as a base for inquiring about the demand for other sorts of products—particularly Chesapeake game. Because confectioners had close connections with grocers and market sellers, Simms's overtures produced hard information about where demand for game was most intense. He began supplying Chesapeake products to grocers and market men across the continent in the early 1880s. He made terrapins, canvasback ducks, and hams his stock in trade. "To clubs and hotels in New York, Chicago, Philadelphia and San Francisco Simms ships the good things, and his name was well known to connoisseurs."

Simms stockpiled his profits as a game broker until he had enough cash and credit to equip himself with a caterer's rig of serving dishes, flatware, and stemware. He then set himself up as a banquet cook in Baltimore. Some idea of his art may be gleaned by a menu he prepared in 1892:

Oysters Half Shell

Consomme

Terrapin

Roast Turkey, Currant Jelly

Potato Croquettes   String Beans   Asparagus

Canvas-back Duck

Hominy   Currant Jelly   Plain Celery

Smithfield Ham   Lettuce

Leibfraumilch

Ices   Cakes   Wafers

Coffee

Liquors   Cigars

He specialized in cooking regional fare in his banquets and became Jakes's successor as foremost caterer in Maryland. Yet it was the resonance of his name as a national supplier that accounted for his success when assigned the task of supplying food at the Maryland Building at the 1893 World's Columbian Exhibition in Chicago. The public knew that Simms meant quality, and so flocked to the Maryland eating hall on the Midway.

The feasts on the Midway were one of the last moments when the general public could partake of canvasback duck and terrapin with some assurance they were consuming what was advertised, as wild populations of both creatures were plummeting at the end of the nineteenth century. The misrepresentation on menus of yellow-bellied sliding turtles as terrapin and red-head duck as canvasback duck became ubiquitous. One of Simms's enduring merits was his supply of the authentic ingredients to hotels at a time when there was little surety of obtaining them elsewhere.

❋   ❋   ❋

SOURCES: "Thanksgiving Dinners," *Baltimore Sun* 112, no. 6 (November 23, 1892): 6; "Saddlery Association," *Baltimore Sun* 11, no. 158 (November 16, 1892): 8; "Caterer Simms Is Dead," *Baltimore Sun* 122, no. 26 (December 16, 1897): 10.

William G. Barron 1847–1900
Charleston, SC

Born into slavery in Charleston, South Carolina, William G. Barron was liberated at age eighteen and attached himself to caterer Thomas R. Tully to learn the art of cookery. Tutored at Tully's restaurant at 128 King Street, Barron was trained in every aspect of the business—preparing cuisine, managing on location cooking, directing service, securing entertainment, and doing cleanup. From approximately 1867 to 1872, he worked as Tully's assistant. Alfred Castion, Barron's principal commercial rival in the 1880s and '90s, took over as Tully's assistant in 1873. In the 1870s municipal records, Barron is listed as a private servant; since he catered events for the South Carolina Jockey Club, his employer may have been the club's treasurer, John C. Cochran. In 1882, Barron determined to conduct business on his own, he decided to challenge his teacher directly by running a restaurant and event catering business simultaneously. He found a building at 1 State Street, near Broad Street, a heavily trafficked location. Barron's success was so great that in 1884 he had Henry Oliver erect a new building at the site. Opening on October 15, 1884, with a celebratory lunch, attendees declared that Barron's Hall "is as neat in outward appearance as it is comfortable within." The second floor had a spacious hall measuring twenty-five by forty-three feet. It had a seating capacity of two hundred. The first floor was devoted to his store and catering office. From 1884 to 1892, Barron's restaurant was one of the four most successful in the city not housed in a hotel; Patjen's on East Bay, the Grand at 278 King Street, and C. W. Meyer's at 108 Meeting Street were the others.

Within a year of going independent, Barron's popularity as a caterer began to eclipse that of Tully. After the great caterer's death in 1883, Tully's eulogist recalled that "after the war he had a large business, but he seemed unable to realize the results of the war and his prices were found to be too high. He had besides turned out several apprentices, and the bulk of the catering business was transferred to other caterers. Still it was acknowledged that no one could equal Tully in preparing a feast, and those who desired epicurean repasts, independent of expense, always went to Tully." The eulogist no doubt referred to Barron, the most conspicuous of Tully's former apprentices. In 1880, for instance, Barron secured the contract to cater the annual meeting of the Agricultural Society of South Carolina, a job long serviced by Tully. Barron also catered the Ladies Memorial Association in April 1880. He undercut Tully on price and by simplifying the bill of fare for banquets. One finds the same classic catering dishes featured since the 1830s in Charleston—oysters, crabs, turkey, ham, capon, and various salads—but with less variety and no French affectation.

Inventory of Personal property of Estate of William G. Barron deceased

50	punch glasses (large)	3		1 50
18	" " (small)	2		36
131	tumblers	1½		1 95
97	wine glasses	1	¢ a piece	97
1	Coffee pot (large)	10		10
7	" pots (small)	25		25
1	tea kettle	10		10
1	kerosene oil stove	35		35
7	Tables	25		1 75
4	meat boxes	15		60
1	tub	10		10
1	heater	50		50
8	benches	5		35
3	slabs	10	¢ a piece	30
100	forks (old)	05	¢ " "	1 00
83	" (new)	10	¢ " "	8 30
114	knives	01	¢	1 14
20	" old	01		20
8	salad dishes	25		25
166	Teaspoons	1		1 66
3	Butter knives	5		15
2	punch bowls	150	the 2	1 50
31	saucers	1		31
48	cups	1		48
5	cake plates	25		25
6	fruit dishes	20		20
1	Coffee Urn	25		25
3	Silver trays	25	¢ a piece	75
107	Dinner plates	3	¢ " "	3 21
88	Breakfast "	3	¢	2 64
96	soup plates	3	¢ " "	2 88
20	Large flat dishes	15		3 00
				37 35

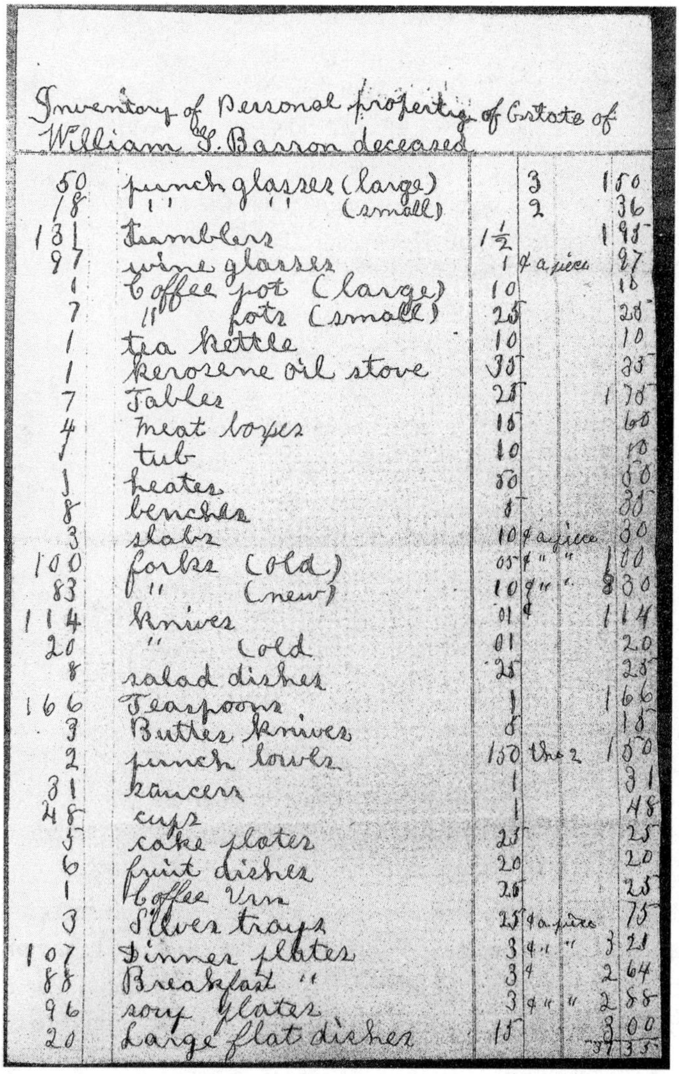

"Inventory of the Personal property of Estate of William G. Barron deceased" (1900). College of Charleston. Photograph: South Carolina Historical Society Manuscripts.

Here are two bills of fare—one from an 1885 ball held by the Porters Central Benevolent Association, a highlight of African American sociability on the yearly calendar, the other an 1899 banquet from the Fellowship Society.

BILL OF FARE 1885

Davis's Diamond Ham
Smoked Tongue
Beef a la Mode

Roast New York Turkey

Stewed Oysters

Petit Pois

Mixed Pickles

Dessert

Vanilla Ice Cream   Plum Cake

Lemon Ice Cream   Large Cake

Small Cake   Vanilla Ice Cake

BILL OF FARE 1899

Stewed oysters

Devilled crabs   Oysters patties

Roasted turkey

Ferris's ham   Smoked tongue

Stuffed shad

Olives   Pickles

Philadelphia Capon   Brown gravy

Crab salad   Potato salad

Boiled Irish potatoes   Green Peas

Rice   Asparagus

Vanilla ice cream   Lemon ice cream

Assorted cakes   Fruits

This is Tully's repertoire without the flourishes—roasted turkey instead of boned and galantined; capon and gravy instead of capon and champignons.

The cycle of business that Barron followed was seasonal. His restaurant shuttered in June, and he traveled into the Carolina mountains to cater at the summer resorts (primarily Flat Rock). In September, he returned and reopened both the catering business and the restaurant. His saloon room remained active through the summer.

In the 1890s, when Barron reigned as the unchallenged eminence among city caterers, he became an honorific colonel. Notices of his work in the newspapers began to assume a formula: "The supper was served in the height of style. Col. Barron was the caterer and he ministered to the cravings of the inner-man as few are able to do." His designation as "Colonel" may have resulted from his repeated employment by various South Carolina military companies, such as Colonel John C. Minott's Berkeley Cavalry, on their bivouacs and anniversary celebrations. In the later 1880s, these encampments came to resemble festivals, and the victualing was an elaborate process. For the 1888 Bivouac of the Charleston Battalion at Greenville, Barron reported that he would obtain "his meats from the Greenville and New York markets. He will also arrange to have daily shipments from Charleston of fresh fish, shrimps and vegetables." One of the purposes of the encampment was to acquaint men from other regions of the splendor of Charleston cuisine; "the mountaineers will have an opportunity of feasting on fricasseed shrimps a la maître d'hotel, clam chowder, broiled whiting, fried porgie, soft-shell crabs and other seaside delicacies served in the most appetizing style."

In 1892 Barron moved from No. 1 State Street to No. 12, opposite Chalmers. His old space was leased by his chief rival, A. William Ristig, who made it the site of his restaurant until Barron resumed control of the hall in 1897. He prospered there until contracting typhus in late August 1900. His obituary notice in the *Charleston News and Courier* observed, "Barron had considerable reputation in Charleston for his cooking and he was best known as Barron the caterer. For a good many years he had been serving families in this city, and many banquets and fine suppers were gotten up under his direction. Barron had a big reputation for the fine qualities of many of his dishes, and by his death one of the most conspicuous figures in the catering line is removed from Charleston." He was survived by his wife, Rebecca, who kept the business going for several years with the aid of her son, William Jr. An inventory of his catering equipment resides in the collections of the South Carolina Historical Society.

✵ ✵ ✵

SOURCES: "The Agricultural Society," *Charleston News and Courier* (January 10, 1880): 1; "Ladies Memorial Association," *Charleston News and Courier* (April 17, 1880): 1; "Minott's Mounted Men," *Charleston News and Courier* (February 24, 1883): 1; "Matters in the State," *Charleston News and Courier* (April 30, 1883): 1; "The Agricultural Society, 'Barron's,' " *Charleston News and Courier* (October 15, 1884): 8; "The Mutual Aid Picnic," *Charleston News and Courier* (May 14, 1885): 1; "Feeding the Soldiers," *Charleston News and Courier* (July 7, 1888): 8; "The Ambassadors of Trade," *Charleston News and Courier* (May 4, 1889): 2; "Good Fellows All," *Charleston Evening Post* (March 9, 1899): 5; "Cotton Kings in Council," *Charleston News and Courier* (December 12, 1890): 8; "Removals," *Charleston News and Courier* (October 10, 1892): 3; "All Around Town," *Charleston News and Courier* (September 16, 1892): 8; William G. Barron, Estate Papers, South Carolina Historical Society, Charleston, SC.

Joseph Pio Campazzi 1848–1922

*Rio de Janeiro; New York; Saratoga Springs, NY;
Albany, NY; Quebec; Tampa Bay, FL; Augusta, GA*

While certain dishes and vegetables from Italy had become installed in the foodways of the United States during the nineteenth century, the regional cuisines of Italy came to America conveyed by immigrant families in cities, and not, for the most part, by trained culinary professionals. A scant handful of chefs—led by Luigi Mazzetti in New York and including John Baggi of the Bristol Hotel, Joseph Paltenghi of the St. Cloud Hotel, D. Peretti of the Union Club, and Domingo Gianini of Delmonico's—presented refined versions of Italy's many culinary scenes. Joseph P. Campazzi belonged to that rare company.

Campazzi began his career at age nineteen as cook on Prince Amedeo of Savoy's frigate the *Maria Adelaide*, and he worked two years before the enticements of Rio de Janeiro lured him onto land. Having successfully concluded its war with Paraguay, the empire of Brazil was commencing its golden age under emperor Dom Pedro II. Campazzi used his connections with Italian royalty to secure a position as a chef in the imperial household. During Dom Pedro II's tour of Europe from 1871 to 1872, Campazzi accompanied the royal party as chef. When the imperial family returned to Brazil, Campazzi chose to cross the Atlantic with another destination in mind—New York.

On September 8, 1872, the following advertisement appeared in the classified section of the *New York Herald*: "A First Class Man Cook, Late in the Service of the Emperor of Brazil, speaking French, Spanish, Portuguese, Italian and a little English, wishes a situation in a private family or a first class hotel; best references. Apply to J. Campazzi, 36 East Houston St." He worked three years as chef for a private family before being hired in 1875 as chef of New York governor Samuel J. Tilden. After Tilden's failed candidacy for the presidency, Campazzi decided he would change his métier from private chef to the powerful to a public caterer at major hotels.

During the summer months, Campazzi installed himself as chef of the United States Hotel in Saratoga Springs, New York, serving the spa set. It remained the constant in his life for the subsequent decades as he occupied a variety of hotel kitchens for a season or two on an almost experimental basis. At various times, Campazzi presided over the kitchens of the Manhattan Beach Hotel, the Tampa Bay Hotel, the New Frontenac in Quebec, the Lakewood Hotel, the Kenmore Hotel in Albany, and the Plaza Hotel in Manhattan. His greatest moment as a chef occurred while he reigned over the kitchens of the Murray Hill Hotel in New York in the mid-1880s. The hotel's staff was contracted in 1885 to cater President Grover Cleveland's Inaugural Ball. The menu, which catered to

"West Entrance to Tampa Bay Hotel, Tampa, Fla." (ca. 1910). Florida News Company postcard.

Cleveland's taste for French fare, demonstrated Campazzi's thoroughly cosmopolitan talents:

HOT DISHES
Clam broth   Consomme

COLD DISHES
Turkey, ham, beef, boned turkey, tongue, pickled oysters, pate de foie gras

SALADS
Chicken   Lobster

ORNAMENTAL DISHES
Salmon, a la Neptune
Striped bass, au Bearre de Montpelier
Boned capon, a la Murray Hill
Bastion, a la Democrat
Pate of game, a la Rossini
Pain de foie-gras, a la Regence
Beef tenderloin en Bellevue
Boned pheasant with truffles
Russian salad (four seasons)
Fountain de Liberte

ICES AND CREAMS
Orange, lemon, pineapple, vanilla, chocolate, Neapolitan

CAKES, FRUITS, ETC.
Assorted cakes, fruit, cheese, nuts, rains, coffee

WINE LIST
Cordon Rouge, G. H. Mumm & Co.
Grand Seo, Jules Mumm & Co.
Extra Dry, G. H. Mumm & Co.
Veuve Clicquot, yellow label, Schmidt & Peters

While the Gallic resonance of this menu might suggest an abandonment of Campazzi's Italian heritage, in the following year he made a point to New York reporters that "he was an Italian cook and did not belong to the French Société" in Manhattan. Nor did he exhibit in the annual exhibitions of the Société Culinaire Philanthropique because "he [didn't] think that Italian pieces look well to French judges."

The most lucrative of his hotel residencies proved to be at the Manhattan Beach Hotel where he managed to save $30,000 in the early 1890s. This he applied to partnership with George McKane, brother of the imprisoned scam artist John Y. McKane, in establishing a restaurant. The business proved a disaster. "Campazzi engaged then in real estate speculation and then ran a fruit stand. Finally he lost all his money and his mind." He was committed to the Amityville asylum. A year in the sanitarium restored his senses, and he was released in 1895.

Campazzi rehabilitated his career by attaching his fortunes to the developers who sought to make Florida a winter paradise for chilled northerners. H. B. Plant's Moorish revival Tampa Bay Hotel, one of the great resorts of the 1890s, brought Campazzi to preside over the fourteen-member staff. Once installed in the Florida resort scene, Campazzi reverted to his usual peregrinations. He presided for three years at the Hotel Ponce de Leon in St. Augustine and two seasons at the Breakers in Palm Beach. He then went to Augusta, Georgia, in 1908, becoming chef of the Hampton Terrace Hotel. He staged a memorable banquet for William Howard Taft there late in 1908. After a year as chef of the US receiving ship *Colorado*, he returned to Palm Beach to be chef at the Royal Poinciana Hotel. An indication of his distinctive style as a chef can be adduced by the recipe of this resort entrée:

SUPREME OF CHICKEN SAN JUAN HILL
Draw and singe two good-sized milk-fed, tender chickens. With a small sharp knife separate the breasts and the fillet mignons. Take the breasts, flatten lightly and give them an oval shape, point at one end. Place in a sautoir which has been

lightly buttered. Make four crosswise incisions in each fillet mignon and insert quite deep a small round of truffles the size and thickness of a penny. Lay the fillets lengthwise over the supreme, having first given the supreme a very light coat of white of egg just where the fillets are to be placed. Cover with a round piece of buttered paper and place on one side. With the remainder of the chicken make two quarts of broth well flavored with celery, onions, a little thyme and a couple of bay leaves. Use one pint to make a supreme sauce and use the rest as follows: Take a small saucepan, put in it four ounces of butter, one small onion chopped fine, two ounces lean raw ham cut in small square pieces. Cook a few minutes until it assumes a golden color. Add the rest of the broth and one and a half cups of rice. Stir well and let boil for twenty-five minutes. When nearly cooked add the following articles, all cut in very small squares: half a green pepper, half a red pepper, twelve canned French mushrooms, one truffle, and one tomato. Dip the tomato in boiling water to remove skin and also remove the seeds. Lightly mix the whole. Place the sautoir containing the supreme on the range for one minute; then place in a hot oven for fifteen minutes. Watch carefully so the supreme will not become brown. Place an inch thick layer of rice on a round platter. In the center make a cone of the rice five inches high. Place the supreme around the cone, leaning each of the four pieces against the cone in an upright position. Have four croutons the same shape and size as the supreme, dipped in supreme sauce. Sprinkle them with very finely chopped parsley and place in an upright position between the supreme. Have the supreme sauce very hot. Pour some around the platter and serve the remainder separately.

Campazzi retired in 1917, lived with his three grown children in New York for three years, then moved with his daughter to Newton, Massachusetts, where he died in 1922.

✳ ✳ ✳

SOURCES: [Advertisement,] *New York Herald* (September 8, 1872): 9; "The Supper," *Boston Herald* (March 5, 1885): 1; "Poems in Pastry," *New York Herald* (December 17, 1886): 3; "M'Kane's Friend Again Sane," *New York Tribune* (August 14, 1895): 12; G. Hutchinson Smyth, *The Life of Henry Bradley Plant* (New York: G. P. Putnam's Sons, 1898), 189; "Jos. P. Campazzi," *Augusta Chronicle* (February 8, 1909): 8;. Archie Croyden Hoff, "Supreme of Chicken San Juan Hill," in *Roasts and Entrees of the World Famous Chefs* (Los Angeles: International Publishing Co., 1914), 29–30.

"Harry" Lee King 1848–1900

New York

In the final decades of the nineteenth century, eight Chinese restaurants lined Mott Street and Park in Manhattan. The greatest of these restaurants, Chung Fah Low (rendered as "The Live and Let Live"), occupied number 11 Mott Street and operated under the aegis of Tom Lee, whose import company was one of the thriving enterprises in New York's Chinese community, and who headed the Loon Ye Tong, a quasi-criminal organization at war with the Tong of Wo Kee over control of illicit enterprise in New York.

Lee King presided over an establishment more functional than decorous on the second floor of the building. The dining room accommodated "half a dozen small wooden tables ranged around the sides, and one larger table in the center." The walls bore luridly colored American lithographs and placards bearing adages in calligraphy. The kitchens were crowded with ingredients. In 1884 Edwin H. Trafton, a reporter, toured the cooking spaces of the restaurants and spoke with Lee King, identifying him by the generic name for a Chinaman used in American papers, "Ah Sin." Trafton's report is the richest back-of-house portrait of an early East Coast Chinese restaurant that survives from the nineteenth century.

> Carefully plucked ducks, from which the blood had been skillfully drained and carefully preserved to be subsequently utilized by the cook, lay in ghastly piles, while various other kinds of unidentified meats and some vegetables were in different stages of preparation to tempt the palates of fastidious patrons. In vessels of peculiar workmanship fashioned like witches' caldrons in miniature, were mysterious broths containing masses of unknown things of pungent odors, which were, in fact, various sorts of food dried in China, now being soaked into a consistency that would render them grateful and more or less easily to be masticated additions to the forthcoming dinners of New York gourmets. Along with packages of rice, I noticed a box of American-made starch.

King had come to New York in 1876, leaving his family behind in China. Very few Chinese women (from two to six) resided in Manhattan in 1880. King's spouse and child remained in China for the first years he presided over Chung Fah Low.

King catered principally to the Chinese community in the city, so his cuisine hewed to the classic banquet style, supplying a *Gzuh* (a spread of dishes). Several classes of *Gzuh* might be had—a first-class spread entailed about forty dishes; a second-class, twenty-eight courses; a third-class, eighteen; and a

C. Bunwell, "Harry Lee King." Wood engraving from Edwin H. Trafton's "A Chinese Dinner in New York," *Frank Leslie's Popular Monthly* 17, no. 2 (February 1884): 184.

fourth-class, only eight dishes. These were made for any number of people up to twelve. When Trafton dined there in 1884, the bill of fare included birds' nest soup, bull-fish, dried oysters, Chinese codfish, duck, pork, rice, tea, and wine. But descriptions of substantially more elaborate dinners have survived. One of these dinners celebrated the christening of Tom Lee Jr. on April 1, 1882.

Sometime during the 1890s, the restaurant's ownership came into the hands of Horn, Hung, Low and Company. By this time, a farm in Long Island growing Chinese vegetables had expanded the availability of non-imported items on the menu.

The building in which Chung Fah Low operated had some notoriety in the records of New York's police department. The top floor of the rickety antique structure was given over to prostitution. The eighteen-year-old Suen Yee, a Chinese sex slave, was rescued by police from Lee Khi's vice den in May 1890. When Lee first arrived in New York in the late 1870s, opium was consumed in bunks in the backyard of 11 Mott. The cellar of the building was given over to *fantan*, the gambling game to which some Chinese were addicted. In 1894 a riot ensued in the restaurant when headwaiter Lee Gong confronted a group of *fantan* players who attempted to stiff on their bill. Cutlery flew and shots were fired.

In 1894 Lee King spoke with reporters about the disinclination of the Chinese, even evangelized immigrants, to celebrate Christmas and instead focused all celebration on the New Year. He had appended the Anglo name Harry to his usual appellation at this juncture. In the interview, he averred, the Chinese cherished New Year's because they "stop work, eat much fruit, have big dinner—$16 for eight people—drink rice wine, pear wine; eat birds' nest."

At some juncture in the late 1880s, King brought his spouse and child from China. The experience apparently got him involved in the smuggling of other Chinese into New York, an action for which he was arrested but not tried on two occasions. Lee King died on February 26, 1900, having worked in New York nearly a quarter of a century.

✳ ✳ ✳

SOURCES: "A Chinaman's Heir," *Truth* (April 2, 1882): 1; "Reforming Chinatown," *New York Herald* (June 19, 1883): 8; Edwin H. Trafton, "A Chinese Dinner in New York," *Frank Leslie's Popular Monthly* 17, no. 2 (February 1884): 183–87; Woo Chin Foo, "Chinese Restaurants," *Current Literature* 1, no. 4 (October 1888): 318 (reprint from the *Cosmopolitan*); "Enslaved in Free America," *New York Herald*, no. 148 (May 28, 1890): 3; "John Chinaman Sticks to His Own Day," *New York Herald*, no. 354 (December 20, 1891): 8. "Chinese in Wild Panic," *New York Herald*, no. 308 (November 4, 1894): 4; "They Went A-Slumming," *New York Tribune* (January 17, 1899): 7; *United States Federal Census, 1890*, New York, Manhattan, District 1-34, sheet 25; "Two More Chinamen Arrested," *New York Tribune* (July 10, 1904): 9.

Jeanne Marie Bouisson Esparbe 1849–1923
New Orleans

Presiding over the kitchen of Maylie's, the much-beloved New Orleans restaurant-saloon, from its opening in 1878 until 1923, Jeanne Marie Bouisson Esparbe (who went by Marie) prepared a French table d'hôte cherished by the all-male clientele for four decades. She was one of three women who dined at Maylie's prior to Prohibition in 1919.

Married to Hypolite Esparbe, a French-born butcher at the Poydras Market, Marie began preparing a brunch—*déjeuner à la fourchette*—for the market men that was served a little after the market's closing bell at 11:00 a.m. (The mealtime would be shifted to 10:30 a.m. after the turn of the century.) From this hungry brotherhood evolved an all-male sodality of diners who made the eating house—the Maylie and Esparbe restaurant—their favored resort for almost two generations. At first, the establishment consisted of two neighboring

From "Madame Esparbe, famed by feasts in Maylie's Gives Tourist Recipes," *New Orleans States* (January 12, 1916): 1.

houses, Nos. 1001 and 1007 Poydras Street—occupied by Bernard and Hanna Maylie and by Hypolite and Marie Esparbe, respectively. Marie was Hanna's sister, and during a visit from Lacave, France, in 1870, had fallen in love with Hypolite, married, and moved in. Her cooking ability put both families in mind of the opportunity to refresh the butchers of the market. From the beginning, a partnership was envisioned in which Hypolite ran the bar and Bernard managed the front-of-house and the business finances. Marie plied the stoves and ovens.

"The morning breakfast soon drew so many patrons that it became an institution and thrifty French people were growing rich. Later the dinner was added and today [1916] many of the most celebrated men in the country remember with pleasure meals they have eaten at Maylie's." Diners congregated at the bar and partook of beverages until the meal was announced. Then the customers would file into the dining room and take a place at one of two long tables. Every seat was invariable occupied. The offerings were bistro fare:

Boiled crabs with cream gravy and mountains of snowy rice if it was a Friday; spaghetti with rich tomato sauce and highly seasoned daube, if it was Monday; sweet breads, veal pie, with a crust that Dickens would have immortalized; crisp salads, two of them, one at the early stage of the meal, the other later, with the roast preceding the dessert of ginger snaps and cheese and fruit. Always there was chicken or turkey and roast beef, mutton, veal or pork falling in smoking tempting slices from the carving knife.

One dinner bill of fare suggests the heroic amount of food offered at a sitting:

Beef Soup

Salaam Sausage

Bouillie

Boiled Sweetbreads with Boiled Potatoes

Chicken Saute with Onions

Scrambled Eggs

Rib Roast with Lettuce Salad

Roquefort Cheese

Fruit and Cake

The sausage was Marie's version of the Lyons sausage—the Bouillie was her signature dish—a brisket of beef boiled to exquisite tenderness and served with mustard.

Some of the recipes that Marie released in 1916 indicate ancient and classic modes of preparation:

CRAB STEW

Slice an onion into small pieces and place in boiling grease; then add one spoonful of flour to a dozen hard-shell crabs, thoroughly cleaned, and place in pot together with one-half a can of tomato paste, add a little water in order to make a short gravy. Boil for about one hour. Just before serving add one raw egg, mixed with a large piece of butter. Serve.

SWEETBREADS, FRICASSEED

After sweetbreads have been thoroughly cleaned place in strainer and scald: then take a sliced onion and place it in boiling grease and add a spoonful of flour and put in the sweetbreads, and white wine with a little parsley. Allow it to cook for about forty-five minutes.

In these recipes, Marie left out the most important dimension of her cooking—the seasoning. New Orleans gastronomes recognized "Mme. Esparbe's marvelous sleight of hand in flavoring her sauces and compounding her Creole delicacies." None of this is captured in these laconic transcripts. While white wine might be incorporated in individual dishes, the finished plates were invariable served with a bottle of red vin ordinaire, until the Volstead Act drove bottles from the table.

Maylie's closed in August 1920 because of "Prohibition and the high cost of food." The closure was short-lived, lasting from the end of spring until September 15. Indeed, the hiatus turned out little different than the suspension of the restaurant's business during summer, which had been usual in the 1900s when the Bouisson sisters vacationed in Mandeville. From autumn 1920 until her death three years later, Marie Esparbe plied the large brick range in the courtyard, near the ancient wisteria vine that emerged from the floor and through an aperture in the roof. When she died in early May 1923, the city's gastronomes recognized that an era had ended. Madame Bégué, the other great exponent of the *déjeuner à la fourchette*, had died in 1906. Devotees feared that a French brunch in the old style would no longer be available in the city. Certain of these fears were justified. Marie's nephew John Maylie overthrew the old policy of stag dining. The tables no longer sported claret. Another chef stood at the old brick range. Only Madame Esparbe's recipes remained.

Maylie's continued long after Marie's death, suffering the loss of the main building through road expansion in the 1950s, and shuttering in 1986 and again in the wake of Katrina. The memory of Madame Esparbe's cuisine, however, has been kept alive through the publication of *Maylie's Table d'Hote Recipes*, edited by Eugenie Lavedan Maylie in 1950.

✳   ✳   ✳

SOURCES: "Madame Esparbe, Famed by Feasts in Maylie's Gives Tourist Recipes," *New Orleans States* (January 12, 1916): 5; "New Orleans Weeps as Maylie's Closes Doors," *Duluth News-Tribune* (August 22, 1920): 7; "Famous Restaurant will Reopen Doors," *New Orleans Times-Picayune* (September 5, 1920): 12; "Madame Esparbe, Famous as Cook, Will Delight No More Epicures," *New Orleans Times-Picayune* (May 10, 1923): 2; "Mme. Esparbe," *New Orleans Times-Picayune* (May 14, 1923): 8; "Old Café Stove Glows 61 Years," *Trenton Evening Times* (September 27, 1937): 9.

Alessandro Filippini 1849–1919
New York; Bernardsville, NJ; global port cities

Lorenzo Delmonico hired Alessandro Filippini—fresh off the boat in 1866—to work at Delmonico's on Fourteenth Street. Hailing from the same Swiss canton as the Delmonico family and having newly finished his culinary apprenticeship in Lyons, Filippini proved a congenial spirit to Lorenzo, Siro, and Charles—orderly, tireless, and a master of detail. Filippini became one of the pillars of that dining empire in New York for a quarter century. After proving himself at the mansion as an assistant to Charles Ranhofer, he was elevated to chef man-

"Alessandro Filippini."
From *The Table* (New
York, 1889), frontispiece.

ager at the Broad Street branch of the restaurant, where he ran the kitchen for
seventeen years. He then took charge of the five-year experiment at the Equitable Building (a branch intended to service the dry goods district). When
Charles C. Delmonico decided to close down 341 Broadway in 1891, Filippini
was determined to go into business for himself, leasing two floors of a building
at 337 Broadway. He had by this time published *The Table* (1889), a cookbook
supplying a year of menus and associated recipes that won substantial praise—
"undoubtedly the best cook book that has been written for years"—for its exposition of Franco-American cuisine.

His decision to go independent inspired intense regret in Charles Delmonico, since Filippini had, after the death of Siro Delmonico in 1881, assumed
the role of chief provisioning officer for the Delmonico's empire, scouring the
markets every morning before sunrise for the best meat, fish, and produce and
buying for the four branches of the restaurant. Each morning, Filippini would
visit every Delmonico's branch to examine the larder and the daily levels of
consumption to guide the next day's purchase. It was said in 1890 that no one
in New York better knew the value of food, the quality of ingredients, or the
best sources. His white-streaked coal-dark hair was immediately recognizable
to every important grocer and vendor in Manhattan. He had also won a strong
following among the dry goods merchants who did not wish to see him removed
uptown.

When opening his namesake restaurant at 337 Broadway, Filippini hoped that
offering his food at more modest prices than those that prevailed at Delmonico's would attract more custom than had graced his old venue. On the ground
floor were a bar, café, and luncheon counter. The principal dining room radiated

from the head of a handsome stairwell rising to the second floor. Three private dining rooms for meetings lined the back of the dining gallery. He also arranged that the cooking take place in an adjunct building, so odors would not invade the dining room. But the inability of the neighborhood population to support a commercial-scale eatery, the failure that had prompted Charles Delmonico to close 341 Broadway, afflicted Filippini's enterprise as well. It remained open scarcely for two years, going into receivership in June 1893 with liabilities of $95,713 and actual assets of only $8,623. A cholera scare in summer of 1893 exacerbated Filippini's slide into debt.

To repair his fortunes, Filippini immediately became involved in the management of the Hotel Somerset in Bernardsville, New Jersey. Yet overseeing the Somerset kitchen hardly availed him of his foremost skill set—his knowledge of New York's provision markets. Filippini's skills as a master of provisions and expert food planner were coveted by a number of institutions. In 1897 he became the chief food officer for the International Navigation Company, inspecting the mess operations of a fleet of transatlantic and transpacific vessels of the Merchant Marine. His struggle to impose a standard of performance in a large number of galleys while suiting the taste of a mix of ethnicities traveling on the oceanic liners proved successful, winning the praise of the governors of the company. His experience of markets, ingredients, and cooking methods around the globe, particularly his engagement with Japanese treatments of seafood and Chinese handling of ingredients, led to a cosmopolitanizing of Filippini's conception of food in the first decade of the twentieth century. Contracting with Doubleday, Page and Co., Filippini published in 1906 *The International Cookbook*, again organized as a year of menus with associated recipes. With the aid of Doubleday, Filippini commenced a syndicated series of columns about food in 1909, reporting the results of his experiments. Carried in major metropolitan papers (the *Boston Herald*, *Denver Post*, *Philadelphia Inquirer*, etc.), his internationalized recipes bore names such as "Eggs Calcutta" and "Salad Interlaken."

No major chef of the nineteenth century exploited print more extensively than Filippini. Pierre Blot, the culinary lecturer, never established a successful restaurant or hotel career before establishing his cooking school in New York and publishing *What I Eat and How I Make It* in 1863. With the publication in 1890 of *The Table: How to Buy Food, How to Cook It, and How to Serve It* in New York (released concurrently in London as *The Delmonico Cook Book*), Filippini offered a version of haute cuisine adjusted to the larders and labor scale of the private family. Few professional chefs fretted that the secrets of professional cookery were being revealed in all their arcane precision. Indeed, Filippini's colleagues marveled at an imagination that could generate a year's worth of menus for breakfast, luncheon, and dinner that was attentive to the seasonal offerings of the market. Filippini, following Lorenzo Delmonico, was a meal modernist. He did not recognize the old breakfast-dinner-supper cycle of meals. By dinner, Filippini meant a meal served at 6:00 p.m. and later. Only the New York Hotel (resort of the old Knickerbockers) retained the old 3:00 p.m. sitting for early dinner in the era after the Civil War. The other admirable dimension of the book in the eyes of his colleagues was the convenient calendar of market items—fish and produce—by month of availability. While Thomas F. DeVoe's famous *The Market Assistant* of 1867 was more exhaustive and descriptive, Filippini's calendar was far easier to consult quickly.

When Delmonico's ex-chef Charles Ranhofer, noting the success of Filippini's book, published his landmark *The Epicurean* in 1894, he made no adjustments to the larders and abilities of home cooks. Ranhofer published the guild knowledge of the highest level of culinary professionals in the United States, and in an instant the secret doctrines of the kitchen were laid bare for the inspection of the public. As happens whenever an adept reveals the most powerful mysteries, members of the brotherhood took offense. After 1894 the question whether to profit from airing the proprietary knowledge of a kitchen was a perpetual temptation of the professional chef.

Filippini, once committed to the path of publication, kept to it. He revised and expanded *The Table*. In 1892 he published *100 Ways of Cooking Fish* and *100 Ways of Cooking Eggs*. These were followed by 1893's *One Hundred Desserts*. All three volumes of the Charles L. Webster Publishing's Handy Volume Culinary series were amalgamated into a single volume entitled *300 Culinary Receipts*. All of these early works were composed intermittently during free moments amidst work. While the volume on eggs enjoyed particularly popularity, posterity has found the brief book on fish and seafood preparation the most useful of the trio.

Long ocean voyages supplied the leisure hours that enabled Filippini to render *The International Cookbook* of 1906 entirely more polished. Doubleday, too, put far more money into editorial refinement of the text and promotion of the work in newspapers. Indeed, their success enabled Filippini to cease his endless crossings of the oceans and enjoy a life of leisure with his family in Manhattan in the 1910s.

※　※　※

SOURCES: "A Famed Old Hostelry," *New York Herald* (March 29, 1886): 21; "A Change by Delmonico," *New York Tribune* (December 9, 1890): 2; "A New Down Town Restaurant," *New York Tribune* (February 3, 1891): 3; "To Open a New Downtown Restaurant," *New York Tribune* (March 14, 1891): 4; "Snails on the Table," *Cleveland Leader* (April 10, 1892): 17; [Advertisement, Hotel Somerset,] *New York Tribune* (May 15, 1893): 8; "Filippini Couldn't Make It Pay," *New York Tribune* (May 16, 1893): 1; "Business Troubles," *New York Herald* (June 1, 1893): 15; "A Vocation Followed by but One Man," *Philadelphia Inquirer* 141, no. 30 (July 30, 1899): 5; Mr. Filippini's Sea Duty," *Shenandoah Herald* (August 25, 1899): 4; "Delmonico Recipes from Famous Chef," *Boston Herald* (October 31, 1909): 41.

Louis F. Mazzetti 1849–192?

New York; Washington, DC

Louis F. (born Luigi) Mazzetti left a significant mark on New York dining in the nineteenth century. A native of Milan, Mazzetti was the first Italian-trained chef to be employed by Delmonico's Restaurant, and he introduced the kitchen staff there to the characteristic dishes of cuisine Milanese—risotto, osso buco, and brasato. Mazzetti came to New York in 1867 after finishing his apprenticeship and was hired immediately into Delmonico's kitchen.

In 1873 Ulysses S. Grant, expanding the scope and splendor of state dinners, hired Mazzetti as White House chef, charged with public dinners, while Lucy Fowler, the cook of Grant's first term, stayed on to prepare breakfasts, baked goods, and family meals.

Upon Mazzetti's return to New York in 1877, he opened a restaurant at 867 Sixth Avenue that he named after himself. During the summer, he gardened at a farm in Stroudsburg, Pennsylvania, growing produce for his restaurant. An inquisitive and inventive man, Mazzetti patented an ice cream mold in 1883 and made the confectionery counter of his restaurant one of the glories of Manhattan. He became an American citizen on July 19, 1880, and returned briefly to Milan in the summer of 1886.

In the mid-1880s, Mazzetti began to suffer from severe respiratory problems. These coalesced into a full-blown case of tuberculosis. He retired to his farm, cared for by his wife and in the company of his young son. In September 1887, reports came from Pennsylvania that he died at age thirty-eight of tuberculosis. His worldly goods were distributed to his wife, Sophy, with the exception of a good ring bestowed upon his brother Antonio.

❋   ❋   ❋

SOURCES: "Funeral of Well-Known Caterer," *New York Tribune* (September 27, 1887): 7; United States Passport application, June 7, 1886, #6590, State of New

York; *Report of the New York Produce Exchange* (New York: De Leeuw, Oppenheimer & Myers, 1887), xi; *New York Wills and Probate Records*, Wills, Vol. 0387–0389, 1887–1888, 461–43.

Sarah Tyson Rorer 1849–1937
Philadelphia; New York; Washington, DC

America's "Queen of Domestic Science" became the oracle of hygiene in home cookery in the period from 1878 to the First World War. Sarah Tyson Rorer's initial base of power was a cooking school organized by the New Century Club of Philadelphia. Realizing she could dictate the curriculum without interference if she exercised complete control, Rorer resigned the club's institution and formed her own Philadelphia Cooking School in 1882.

From this central school, Rorer taught two generations of young women to be teachers of cooking, each generating an ancillary cooking school somewhere else in the country. A writer in 1913 observed, "Her graduates now preside over cooking schools scattered all the way from the Atlantic to the Pacific coast, and even into Canada." Rorer realized that her graduates would not be hired as hotel or restaurant chefs because of the exclusivity and organization of the Eurocentric brotherhoods that ran the profession. So she developed connections that enabled women to dominate the cooking staffs in hospitals and schools, as well as the traditional domination of the boardinghouse trade.

Born Sarah Tyson Heston in Bucks County, Pennsylvania, she was the favorite child of Dr. Charles Heston, a manufacturing chemist. Educated in private schools in Buffalo and Aurora, New York, Sarah Heston cultivated chemical science. While always drawn to cookery, she did not become a close student of nutrition until having to care for her physician father when he returned from service in the Union army as an invalid. The family moved to Philadelphia in 1860. She married W. A. Rorer, a man too traditional in his sense of marital roles adequately to accommodate his wife's sense of vocation and her need to express her talents. The marriage would dissolve in 1896.

Rorer's talents were amplified by several qualities of character. She was singularly quick of perception, decisive in her judgments, and direct in her interactions with other persons. Her aura of earnestness, her clarity of expression, and her self-possession vested her with authority. She valued facts over opinions, findings over feelings, and experimental knowledge over intuition. She was tireless in her exertions, systematic in her initiatives, and self-critical in

"Sarah Tyson Rorer."
From *Mrs. Rorer's
Philadelphia Cookbook*
(Philadelphia: Arnold,
1886), frontispiece.

her assessments of her works. Though not greatly religious, she observed that
the effectiveness of organized religion depended upon its media—its writings,
its preaching, and its Sunday school catechisms. She determined to master the
arts of writing and oratory to convey her message to a wide-ranging public.
Her monthly newsletter, *Household News*, eventually became absorbed in the
national monthly, the *Ladies' Home Journal*. Her lectures, first delivered within
the confines of her school, were polished and elaborated into public vehicles
delivered on lecture tours to local athenaeums, women's clubs, and civic associations. She learned, for instance, to employ wit in her public lectures to combine
amusement with edification.

Her labors to improve her communicative skills resulted in a self-confident
mastery of pen and podium, yet these successes could scarcely have prepared
her for the unprecedented popularity of her 1884 *Cook Book*, or the even more
successful *Philadelphia Cook Book* in 1886.

In 1903 Rorer closed the Philadelphia Cooking School. She would subsequently take contracts to teach nutrition at Harvard University for its extension
program and for the University of Pennsylvania in Philadelphia.

In 1905 Rorer, with business partners, set up two restaurants in New York
bearing her name that would embody her principles. Serving moderately priced
food, prepared simply and attractively for middle-class people, the restaurants
incarnated her criticism of the extremity of haute cuisine. Located at 42 Broadway and 55 New Street in Manhattan, they were managed by former pupils.
Since Rorer resided in Washington, DC, she did not participate directly in their

operations. When both enterprises failed in the summer of 1907, creditors attempted to secure payment from Rorer and the papers declared, incorrectly, that she was insolvent when they had gone bankrupt in September.

Rorer took an intense interest in the social condition of women. A feminist, she repeatedly advocated the vote for women, the establishment of vocational training for women, and the creation of social services that could prevent poor women from falling into lives of prostitution and crime. Her views provoked sharp criticism in the South when she lectured there. Yet she did more than simply talk about aiding poor women, volunteering with the Bedford Street Mission in Philadelphia, and teaching a class in the slums on how to perform domestic work. She had erected at her own expense a model working-man's home designed for optimal economy and efficiency.

During the Columbian Exposition of 1893, the Board of Lady Managers, recognizing Rorer's efforts to improve the condition of women, bestowed upon her the superintendence of the model kitchen in the famous Woman's Building. There, for two hours every morning, Rorer lectured on dietetics. While many of her insights into the chemistry of nutrition and best daily diet proved sound (she disparaged margarine and championed olive oil), she retained some of the century's trepidations about dyspepsia and the bad effects of eating raw foods. She advised Americans, for instance, to eat bananas cooked, not raw.

※　※　※

SOURCES: Mrs. Talcott Williams, "The Most Famous Cook in America," *Ladies' Home Journal* 14 (February 1897): 7; "Mrs. Rorer on Restaurant Extremes," *Idaho Statesman* (October 8, 1905): 2–10; "Famous Cook Is Alleged Bankrupt," *Aberdeen American* (September 28, 1907): 3; "Woman's Progress," *National Labor Tribune* (October 28, 1909): 6; "Woman Who Has Brought Fine Art into Cooking," *Trenton Evening Times* (November 30, 1913): 16.

Jules Chatain 1850–1918?
Shreveport, LA; Fort Worth, TX

French cooking came to Texas by way of Louisiana, both in its Creole and classic forms. The hotels and restaurants of Galveston, Houston, Fort Worth, Dallas, and San Antonio at various points at the beginning of the twentieth century proudly advertised their embrace of the Gallic style in cookery. For a period during the first decades of the twentieth century, it prevailed over the Mexican-Texican cuisine that eventually became the regional signature. The pioneer chefs who established high-level French cooking and expert Creole cooking in the state tended to be men in their thirties. An exception was French-born Jules Chatain, who in June 1907 opened a landmark French restaurant in the Melba Hotel Building at 1105–07 Houston Street in Fort Worth. Having kept a fine restaurant in Shreveport from 1900 to 1907, the fifty-seven-year-old Chatain came to Fort Worth and opened the French Restaurant. It quickly won many devotees to his culinary vision. By 1910 the expansion of his clientele prompted Chatain to build an annex to his dining place, then a second dining room in 1912.

A leonine man with heroic mutton-chop sideburns that flared out from his cheeks and beneath his chin, Chatain fit the public perception of chef as a kind of divine monster. His visage stared out at readers of the *Fort Worth Star-Telegram* in the daily ads that he placed in the classified section. Chatain began his career at age twenty in his native France but did not come to America until he was fifty. The circumstances are unclear why he would choose to uproot himself from Europe at so advanced an age. His first establishment, the New York Restaurant at 522 McNeill Street in Shreveport, offered that booming oil town solid French fare using local ingredients. He conducted his Shreveport and his Fort Worth places in tandem with his wife, Mary (Madame Chatain), who supervised the service. A menu of a banquet held by newspapermen in November 1909 indicates the character of his art. It benefited from the bounty of the harvest.

RELISH

Celery Tomatoes Manzanilla Olives

Oyster Cocktail a la Rochambeau

Riesling wine

SOUP

Mock Turtle with sherry wine

FISH

Tenderloin of trout with Tartare sauce

Parisienne potatoes White wine

ENTREES

Tenderloin of beef French green peas

Zinfandel wine

Bouche a la Reine

ROAST

Squabs on toast   Lettuce salade

Rum omelette

Cheese Camembert, crackers

Blue ribbon beer

DESSERT

Cakes and fruit

Café noir a la Chatain

Cigars—Jose Vila

The stranglehold of continental beverages on French menus has been over-thrown in Chatain's bill of fare. California zinfandel and Pabst Blue Ribbon have insinuated places toward the end of the repast. While the classic French order of dishes has been maintained, menu French has been minimized, and the multiplication of dishes per course has been reined in.

Chatain's French Restaurant in Fort Worth opened at 7 a.m. daily to serve breakfast; the midday meal was its principal seating. Evening feasts were re-served for banquets, such as that described above. On most days, it did not serve dinner. This approach made it singularly successful during the decade of its operation before the chef's ill health prompted its closure in 1918.

❋   ❋   ❋

SOURCES: "French Restaurant," *Fort Worth Star-Telegram* 25, no. 131 (May 19, 1907): 10–11; [Advertisement,] "French Restaurant," *Fort Worth Star-Telegram* 25, no. 147 (June 4, 1907), first cover; "J. Chatain, Announcement!" *Fort Worth Star-Telegram* 27, no. 288 (October 31, 1909): 12; [Advertisement,] "J. Chatain Host to Newspaper Men," *Fort Worth Star-Telegram* 27, no. 299 (November 11, 1909): 12.

Emil Hederer 1850–1907
New York; Philadelphia

Running a major hotel kitchen requires great personal resources. Some manage to imbue command with grace, and hard work with a spirit of collaboration. Others glory in power and revel in coercion. Emil Hederer—chef of the Waldorf, Rector's, and the Bourse in Philadelphia—chose the dictatorial path, often to great personal cost.

"Emil Hederer." Wood engraving from "Chef's Banquet," *Philadelphia Inquirer* (March 15, 1898): 3.

An Alsatian, Hederer came to New York in 1876, hired by John Jacob Astor to be his household chef. Hederer's early career in the city was spent satisfying the palates of billionaires—the Astors, the Lorillards, and the Belmonts. Like many of his countrymen, Hederer discovered the city's markets abounding in fine vegetables, seafood, and meat. There was but one deficiency: mushrooms. Hederer determined to arrange for the supply of culinary-grade fungi. Unfortunately, when he sought a cultivator, he encountered a flimflam artist, Anthony Muzzarelli, who owned a patch of land on Hudson City Heights known as "Old Brewery Frosen." Hederer sunk $5,000 into the scheme, crediting Muzzarelli with having "a mysterious secret process for the production of fresh mushrooms." It did not take long to become disabused of this fantasy.

Chefs made their reputation among the profession in New York by their performance in exhibitions by the various culinary associations. In 1882 the Union Universelle pour le Progrès de l'Art Culinaire staged a grant Alimentary Exposition in the city. Hederer was appointed treasurer of the event (an office he may have secured by aggressively seeking recovery of his lost investment in the mushroom debacle). His success in financing the Exposition cemented his reputation as a reliable fellow.

The exposition work brought him to the attention of hotelier George Boldt, who hired him away from the plutocrats to run the Bellevue Hotel in Philadelphia. This situation was a trial run for Boldt's grand ambition—to make the Waldorf Hotel in New York the byword of haute cuisine. Being satisfied that Hederer could handle the job, Boldt then installed him in the state-of-the-art kitchen of the Waldorf in Manhattan. Some people respond to power well; Hederer did not. Egotism bloomed, and a volcanic temper blossomed. Cooking is a collaborative art, particularly in a hotel. At the Waldorf under Hederer, it became a matter of performing what the autocrat wished. He found at least one loyal lieutenant, Victor Hirtzler, who accomplished whatever the chef wished. Others found the circumstances less sufferable and a kitchen revolt ensued. Boldt replaced Hederer with Xenophon Kuzmier in May 1893. Hederer migrated to Rector's. Unfortunately, once installed at the head of a kitchen again, Hederer's megalomania was reactivated. Charles Rector had less patience than Boldt, firing Hederer almost immediately, but not before assistants had harvested a dozen of the chef's signature dishes.

One interesting dimension of Hederer's repertoire was his interest in and mastery of English comfort food. This culinary cosmopolitanism proved congenial to moneyed Americans. One wonders whether it was in the service of John Jacob Astor, who was notoriously immune to the charms of refined Parisian cookery, that the chef perfected the following:

BEEFSTEAK PIE

Take a nice piece of beef, rump or sirloin, cut it in small slices, slice also a little raw ham, put both in a frying pan with some butter and a small quantity of chopped onions, let them simmer together a short time on the fire, or in the oven, add a little flour and enough stock to make sauce, salt, pepper, chopped parsley and a little Worcestershire sauce as seasoning, add also a few sliced potatoes and cook together for about twenty minutes; put this into a pie-dish with a few slices of hard boiled eggs on the top, and cover with a layer of common paste. Bake from 15 to 20 minutes in a well heated oven. All dark meat pies can be treated precisely the same way, if poultry, leave the potatoes out.

In the wake of the ouster from Rector's, Hederer removed to Philadelphia and the kitchen of the Hotel Stenton, where he would labor from 1894 to 1897. Then Carl G. Essner, an old colleague from the chef's time at Philadelphia's Bellevue Hotel, came seeking his services. Essner has seen that Hederer could manage a kitchen without verbal abuse. Essner had served as a steward at the Waldorf as well and witnessed the things that triggered the chef's temper. A group of Philadelphia businessmen had hired Essner to run a deluxe dining facility named the Bourse. Located on the eighth floor of the Bourse Building (at the corner of Merchant and Ranstead Streets), the restaurant became the preferred scene of dinner negotiations in the city. Numbers of his diners were his backers, and they encouraged Essner's effort to create a splendid scene for dining.

Stepping from the rapid running elevators one is ushered into a Turkish room, from which all the glare of light is excluded, and the impression is one of oriental splendor. Soft rugs, cushions, divans and hanging curtains in a kaleidoscope of colors are everywhere. Opposite is the ladies' waiting room, which is in white and gold, and a step to the left is the ladies' dining room. This will accommodate 200 guests. The walls of light blue are met with a heavy wainscoting of mahogany and from the ceiling hang heavy chandeliers of gold.

There were four private dining rooms, and a gentleman's dining room seating 250. Essner knew he had to secure a chef as splendid as the décor. He obtained Hederer. Visitors declared it the "finest public dining hall in the city."

Hederer found a circumstance congenial to his temper and made the Bourse a temple of fine dining from 1897 until his death in 1907. Hederer's friend Essner, however, fell into financial distress, first in staging the inordinately expensive inaugural ball for President William McKinley, then entering into a costly partnership deal with Charles Rector. In 1899 Essner began directing money from the Bourse into a personal account; he was detected and disappeared before being called to account. Fortunately, the Bourse had ample financial resources and Hederer could continue plying his art.

Hederer's move to Philadelphia may have been helped by a second possibility that piqued the chef's sense of ambition. A National Epicurean College had been organized in the city under the direction of Richard Cronecker. Hederer was approached to be on the governing board. As visionary and useful as this institution appeared, it expired before Hederer himself did in 1907.

SOURCES: "Law aux champignons," *New York Herald* (June 10, 1880): 11; "L'Exposition Alimentaire," *Courrier des Etats-Unis* (March 26, 1882): 4; "Cooks Go Out in Two Hotels," *New York Herald* (May 19, 1893): 7; "The Bourse Restaurant," *Philadelphia Inquirer* 133, no. 125 (November 2, 1895): 4; "Bourse Restaurant, Its Doors Thrown Open for Inspection by the Public," *Philadelphia Inquirer* 133, no. 126 (November 3, 1895): 7; "Inauguration Plans," *Philadelphia Inquirer* 136, no. 12 (January 12, 1897): 2; "The Terrapin at the Supper," *Washington Evening Star* (February 20, 1897): 2; "The Inaugural Ball Supper," *Washington Evening Star* (March 2, 1897): 9; "Closing Accounts," *Washington Evening Star* (March 6, 1897): 11; "Hotels Change Hands," *Philadelphia Inquirer* 136, no. 99 (April 9, 1897): 11; "Caught on the Fly," *Philadelphia Inquirer* (October 8, 1897): 4; "Chefs Banquet," *Philadelphia Inquirer* (March 15, 1898): 3; "In McKinley's Honor," *Philadelphia Inquirer* 139, no. 120 (October 28, 1898): 5; "Wants Bourse License," *Philadelphia Inquirer* 142, no. 154 (June 3, 1900): 2; [Mortuary notice,] *Philadelphia Inquirer* (August 2, 1907): 7; William Grimes, *Appetite City: A Culinary History of New York* (New York: Macmillan, 2009), 140.

Urban Sobra 1850–1896
Chicago

For a period in the 1880s and early '90s, the young Urban Sobra was the most accomplished French chef in Chicago. He presided over the kitchens of two of the city's great institutions, the Hotel Richelieu (from 1887 to 1894) and the Auditorium Hotel (from 1895 to 1896). There were some who considered him the greatest culinary technician in the United States. Jovial, well-informed, fluent in English and Spanish as well as his native French, he stood at the heart of Chicago's world of culinary professionals until illness began to afflict him in 1894. It is difficult to determine from the surviving testimonies whether the illness was psychological or physiological. Sobra resigned as chef of the Auditorium in May 1896. Four months later, he died from asphyxiation caused by an unlit gas jet. His wife, Leona, believed the death accidental, indicating that the couple had planned a trip to France.

Sobra underwent the traditional training by apprenticeship in France and served for a period in the French army during the Franco-Prussian War. He became steward of several ships of the French fleet in the latter 1870s and early '80s, including the vessel that transported the French delegation to New York to celebrate the centenary of the Battle of Yorktown, perhaps the greatest festival of Franco-American feeling of the last half of the nineteenth century. During the transit, Sobra served as chef to General Georges Ernest Boulanger. When he arrived in New York, he stayed in the city working as a hotel cook and living on Christopher Street in Greenwich Village. Shortly after the Hotel Richelieu opened in Chicago in autumn 1885, H. V. Bemis engaged Sobra to serve as chef. He did so because he was determined to supply in Chicago "a cuisine second to none," a gustatory experience superior to any available in the city. When Bemis's contemporaries said he made a mistake erecting so luxurious a hotel in Chicago—"he should have built the Richelieu in New York"—Bemis retorted that he wanted to prove that Chicagoans could "dine as well here as they can at the Hoffman or Delmonico's." Sobra warranted the truth of that claim.

Bemis had made his fortune in the brewing industry before becoming a hotelier, and he knew the power of alcohol in hospitality. Few could have predicted the extremes to which his cellar building would extend in assembling "the largest and finest assortment of choice wines to be found in America." This provided Sobra an extraordinary complement to his creations, a cuisine "not surpassed by any on this continent." He was creating that cuisine when the Crystal Banquet Room on the top floor ignited from a faulty flue in 1891, nearly destroying the hotel. He stayed through the reconstruction in 1892, serving as chef de cuisine until Bemis put the hotel in receivership in early 1895.

During his tenure at the Richelieu, Sobra's banquet cooking became nationally famous. In 1889 a rumor circulated that President Harrison had tapped him as White House cook (Hugo Zieman, the Richelieu's headwaiter, had signed on as White House steward). Sobra resented the idea that he would surrender the office of hotel chef to become the cook for "a private family." Within the community of French chefs, there were those who ranked him above Charles Ranhofer in his management of dishes. In 1893 Leon Mathieu, the chef of Milliard's, an extraordinary French restaurant in Omaha, observed, "Sobra, the chef of the Hotel Richelieu, Chicago, is the greatest cook in the United States. He receives a salary that a congressman would jump at." When the World's Columbian Exhibition was staged in Chicago in 1893, many visitors trekked north to Michigan Avenue to the Loop to experience the legendary fare. Of the banquets for visitors staged during the exhibition year, the September 1893 celebration of Russian culture hosted by Commissioner General Gloukhovsky gained particular fame. W. B. Bender suggested the menu that Sobra prepared. It began with a tide of caviar.

Canape a la Russe

Hors d'oeuvres varies

Consomme Printaniere Royal

Filet de Turbot farcie   Au Vin Blanc

Pommes Persillades   Concombre

Aloyan de Boeuf a la Chiron

Petites Bouchies a la Motglas

Asperges de Bordeaux   Hollandaise

Sorbet de Curacoa

Faisan Roto au Cresson

Salade de saison

Glace de Fantasie

Petits

Fromage

Café

In the year after the exhibition ended, particularly during the last half of 1894, the Hotel Richelieu suffered a downturn in business. It was at this juncture that Sobra responded favorably to an overture by the Auditorium Hotel to take over its kitchens. H. V. Bemis put the Richelieu into financial receivership in summer 1895.

During his years at the Auditorium, Sobra suffered increasingly from his debility. He abandoned his position shortly before the invasion of the Republican Party convention in summer of 1896. He died before summer's end.

There were odd features to Urban Sobra's life that diverge from that of the usual cuisine artist. One was his enduring friendship with General Boulanger, war minister of France. They corresponded regularly. The general, who greatly admired Chicago, came to visit Sobra shortly after he became installed as the chef of the Richelieu. In turn, Boulanger extended to Sobra an invitation to come to France. When Sobra visited France in 1889, he found the country disturbed by Boulanger's agitations for another war with Germany. A political movement had formed around the general that would come close to installing him as dictator in a coup d'état.

Another strange dimension had to do with his wife, a large, voluptuous, and passionate woman with a love of court proceedings. In 1891 Mrs. Sobra wrongly accused J. B. Newman, a tourist from Springfield, of stealing her diamonds. Her canvassing of the city's pawnbrokers, however, finally revealed the real culprit, a man named Manning who greatly resembled Newman. Her published apology did not forestall Newman's suit seeking $10,000 recompense for the damage to his reputation. While his lawsuit did not succeed, the adventure would prove consequential for Mrs. Sobra. During her search for her diamonds, she met Jacob Franks, wealthy president of the Rockford Watch Company. "From this chance meeting . . . a strong attachment sprang up between them." After Urban Sobra's death, Marguerite Leona claimed that during the two years of mourning, Franks approached her, declared love, won her affection, proposed, but postponed the date of marriage, and was ultimately guilty of breach of promise. In 1903 Mrs. Sobra sued for $75,000. The case fell apart when it was revealed in court that during the time she was supposedly engaged to Franks, she went on an unchaperoned night trip to Milwaukee with a Mr. Ferguson, who, it turned out, was a detective hired by Franks. On the stand, Mrs. Sobra claimed she was drugged when that trip was taken. The jury judged the claim hardly credible and found for Mr. Franks.

※   ※   ※

SOURCES: "Le general Boulanger a Chicago," *Courrier des Etats-Unis* 96 (April 21, 1888): 1; "War's Stern Alarm," *Daily Inter Ocean* 18, no. 170 (September 10, 1889): 1–7; "He Feels Hurt," *Daily Inter Ocean* 17, no. 334 (February 21, 1889): 1–6; "Mr. Newman at Home," *Daily Illinois State Register* (October 13, 1891): 6; "Completely Vindicated," *Daily Illinois State Register* (November 24, 1891): 6; "About Cooking and Cooks," *Omaha World Herald* (January 22, 1893): 14; "Cheers for the Czar," *Daily Inter Ocean* 22, no. 185 (September 27, 1893): 1–10; "The Hotel Richelieu," *Cincinnati Post* (November 13, 1894): 2; "Richelieu a Success," *Daily Inter Ocean* 24, no. 134 (August 5, 1895): 7; "Death of Noted Chef Urban Sobra," *Daily Inter Ocean* 25, no. 155 (August 26, 1896): 8; "Franks

Case on Trial," *Rockford Republic* (May 2, 1903): 8; "Franks Said He Did Not Promise," *Rockford Republic* (May 1, 1903): 5; "Franks Side of Sobra Case," *Rockford Republic* (May 7, 1903): 7.

Adrien Tenu 1850–1901
Paris; Monaco; Vienna; Stockholm; New York

When the Société Culinaire Philanthropique began staging annual public exhibitions in the 1880s, several chefs became stars for *pièces montées*, sculptural exhibition pieces made of food. Among the greatest artists of spectacle food was Adrian Tenu of the Café Savarin in Manhattan and later the Fifth Avenue Hotel. Tenu alternated between striving for unlikely verisimilitude or shock value in his creations. Summer—a scantily clad nymph made of mutton tallow clutching a bouquet of wax flowers—or a salmon outfitted as Neptune.

Apprenticed in the patisserie of Julien Freres in Paris, Tenu learned pastry cooking by its greatest French practitioners. Three years training earned him a cherished spot in the Grand Hotel, where he worked for four years. This résumé gave him entrée into any kitchen in Europe, and he availed himself of the opportunity, crossing the Continent as inclination drove him: two years at the Hôtel de Paris in Monaco, a year at the Grand Hotel in Vienna, and three years at the Grand Hotel in Stockholm. Lorenzo Delmonico heard about the wandering genius and secured his services for the Twenty-Sixth Street branch of Delmonico's, the last cook that Lorenzo would hire before his death. Tenu had not worked there half a year when robber baron Jay Gould hired him to be his private chef at what was then considered a scandalously high salary. It did not take long for Tenu to discover that Gould's favorite dish was tripe and onions.

Adrien Tenu was thought to be "the handsomest chef in town," particularly after he left the millionaire's employ in 1882 and became a public caterer at the Hotel Brunswick, a position he held through 1888. "He wears a black mustache, a becoming cap, and is just heavy enough to be imposing." Among the culinary community in New York, his work at the Brunswick brought him admiration, particularly for his impeccable taste and for his quiet authority presiding over a corps of cooks. When the developers who erected the Equitable went looking for someone to man the deluxe Café Savarin in their building, Tenu was their primary target. It proved a spectacular space, with a capacity for 3,000 diners during the lunch hours from 11 a.m. to 3 p.m. The Café Savarin ranked third or fourth behind Delmonico's and Sherry's in terms of fashionability among Manhattan restaurants. One dimension of Tenu's work at the Café Savarin was

"Adrien Tenu." Duotone from
"The Science of Cookery," *Leslie's
Weekly* 81 (October 24, 1895): 270.

serving as caterer for the well-heeled Lawyers' Club that also occupied the Equitable Building. In 1894 he left for the Hotel Fifth Avenue with Eugene Laperruque, coming to it as successor. One of his recipes dates from his three-year
stint at the Hotel Fifth Avenue:

EGGS OUDINOT

Take three hard boiled eggs, split lengthwise and remove the yolks. Chop the yolks
and add half the amount in bulk of cooked and chopped fresh mushrooms. Mix
gently with a tablespoonful of Bechamel sauce, season with salt, pepper and nutmeg, and garnish the empty white pieces of the eggs with this stuffing. Dilute a
little Bechamel sauce with a tablespoonful of cream and a small piece of butter.
Put a part of the sauce on the bottom of a baking pan, enough to cover it, and lay
the eggs on it and cover with the rest of the sauce. Put a pinch of Parmesan cheese
on each egg and bake for 10 minutes.

The culmination of Tenu's career as a culinary artist came in 1896, when he
was recruited to be the chef at the Waldorf Astoria. His reign over the kitchens
was relatively short, for Tenu expired during the great Fourth of July heatwave
of 1901. He numbered among two hundred citizens whom the 98-degree heat
felled. He would be followed in the Waldorf kitchen by Rene Anjard.

Tenu published two recipes during his tenure as chef of the Waldorf, both
treating reed birds, including a version of the classic reed birds on toast.

REED BIRDS

After the birds are singed and split and the intestines have been removed, put a
skewer through them; broil over a brisk fire about three minutes: serve on toast
with maître d'hôtel butter.

ROASTED IN SKEWERS

Remove the gizzards and pouches from the birds, cut the legs half way up and cover with bards of fat pork cut very thin: thrust small skewers through them and roast from six to seven minutes in a very warm oven; unwrap, salt and dress on buttered toast, garnished with watercress and lemons; serve with gravy in a bowl.

During Tenu's quietly efficient dominion over the Waldorf Astoria kitchen, hotel steward Oscar Tschirky, "Oscar of the Waldorf," saturated the magazines and newspapers with his recipes, aesthetic dicta, and food criticisms. Included in his publications were items that Tenu had created in the Waldorf Astoria kitchen. Oscar's self-aggrandizement ran to appropriating for himself the honor of creating the most famous dish ever to emanate from the kitchens, the famous salad bearing the hotel's name. Though Oscar suggested in his cookbook that he was the originator, Tenu created it—with equal portions of sweet apples, celery, both chilled and diced, seasoned and served in a mayonnaise dressing on a lettuce leaf. Others took up the Waldorf salad, adding walnuts, watercress, orange sections, and even red peppers. But Tenu offered it in stunning simplicity—apples, celery, mayonnaise dressing—and it has lived for well over a century. Many food writers have permitted themselves to be the instruments of Oscar's vainglory; it is time to put a halt to the misattribution. The steward only assembled the salad; he did not create the formula.

※　※　※

SOURCES: "Poems in Pastry," *New York Herald* 351 (December 17, 1881): 3; "L'ouverture du café Savarin," *Courrier des Etats-Unis* 7 (January 9, 1888): 1; "Les Bal de Cuisiniers," *Courrier des Etats-Unis* 31 (February 5, 1890): 1; "Artists in Gum Paste, Mutton Tallow and Wax," *New York Herald* 31 (January 31, 1892): 9; "What We Owe to the Hens," *Boston Herald* (April 7, 1895): 31; "The Science of Cookery," *Leslie's Weekly* 81 (October 24, 1895): 270; "French Cooks and Their Art," *New York Herald-Tribune* (January 29, 1896): 4; "Best Way of Preparing Reed Birds," *Boston Herald* (October 16, 1898): 32; "Death of a Chef," *Dallas Morning News* (July 7, 1901): 3; "Fruit Salads," *New Orleans Times-Picayune* (February 16, 1902): 24.

Valere Braquehais 1851–1920?

New York; Saratoga Springs, NY; St. Augustine, FL; Fort Lee, NJ

An artistic and visionary French chef, Valere Braquehais gained fame in New York as the master of the kitchens at the Clarendon Hotel, one of Manhattan's boutique "family hotels" of the Gilded Age. It was located on the corner of Fourth Avenue and Eighteenth Street.

Braquehais famously presided over the Chef's Ball of 1894, when drunk prostitutes got out of hand and caused a ruckus. In the subsequent legal hearing, Braquehais provided the Société Culinaire Philanthropique's financial records, indicating that members of the New York police force in attendance had been paid off to prevent the fete's shutdown as an immoral exhibition. The luster of his reputation somewhat diminished, Braquehais sought a situation at the head of another institution, the equivalent of Clarendon, outside of New York. Finally, in 1898 he found what he sought, far to the south, and became chef at the Hotel Ponce de Leon in St. Augustine, Florida, one of the greatest southern resort hotels. There, assisted by Andrew Dellera, Braquehais assayed resort banquets and tourist dinners during the winter months until 1902.

In 1902 he returned to the New York metropolitan area, settling near the Palisades on the New Jersey side of the Hudson River. His insertions into public notice were few and strategic. In 1907 he sent a letter to the *New York Herald Tribune* advocating consuming the spleen of ruminant animals. From 1902 to 1908, he became one of the movers in an association erecting a monument on the site of the Revolutionary Battle of Fort Lee in New Jersey. The final portion of his culinary career was spent as chef of the Terminus Restaurant in Fort Lee, New Jersey, a post he held until 1917.

Classically trained in France, Braquehais came to New York in 1885 during the culinary boom of the 1880s to work at the Clarendon Hotel. He also contracted during the summers to head the kitchens of the United States Hotel in Saratoga Springs, New York. He maintained close relations with the Parisian scene, and when the Eiffel Tower was erected in 1888 for the Exhibition Universelle of 1889, Braquehais secured plans and constructed a sugar replica for the Société Culinaire Philanthropique Ball of 1888. New Yorkers had a view of the completed structure in glassy miniature before Parisians saw the iron original. For his enterprise, Braquehais was appointed banquet director of the 1889 Ball. During the 1889 Ball, he was voted into the presidency of the Société.

During the year of Braquehais's presidency, France and the United States celebrated the 100th anniversary of the Fall of the Bastille. Chef Braquehais's fourteen-year-old daughter Fernande supplied the climax of the New York fes-

"Valere Braquehais."
Wood engraving from
"Frank W. Sanger's
Story," *New York Tribune*
(December 6, 1894): 13.

tivities; after the parade of Franco-American associations, she presented Mayor
Grant with a huge red, white, and blue floral bouquet from the Société. The
handsome mayor's embarrassed thank-you kiss in the French style provoked a
delighted uproar in the crowd, "the climactic incident" of the celebration. Braquehais presided over the Société from 1889 to 1894.

Besides being a masterful chef, Braquehais was regarded as a first-rank
sculptor, capable of molding improbable media, such as mutton tallow, into tor-
sos and busts that appeared to be "an excellent imitation of Italian marble." He
maintained a separate studio in the basement of the Clarendon for the preparation of his display *pièces montées*, the exhibition of which was a highlight of the
annual French Chef's Ball in New York. His 1892 bust of Vice Admiral Gervais,
the recently appointed commander of the French fleet, was so visually arrest-
ing that a drawing of it appeared in the January 31, 1892, issue of the *New York
Herald*.

In 1898 Braquehais moved his family southward, becoming chef of the Hotel Ponce de Leon resort in St. Augustine, Florida. This deluxe accommodation
boasted interior decoration by Louis Comfort Tiffany and kitchen ranges by
Francis Morandi and Son. Entirely electrified, the hotel technology equaled the
most advanced in New York, London, and Paris. Braquehais greatly enjoyed
having his family stationed in St. Augustine and remained in the position longer than any other of the resort's early chefs. A menu from February 22, 1899,
documents the sort of fare that he offered visitors to the resort during its midwinter season:

MENU

Blue Point Oysters   Little Neck Clams
Green Turtle   Clear Cream of Asparagus

Canapes of Caviar a la Russe

Celery   Olives   Salted Almonds   Brandy   Peaches

Boiled Red Snapper, Sauce Cardinal Broiled Pompano, Maitre d'Hotel

Slice Cucumbers   Potatoes, Martha

Filet of Beef Pique, Montrogue

Terrapin, Baltimore Style

Fried Chicken, Maryland

Tomatoes Farcies, Parisienne

Pineapple Fritters au Kirsch

Lalla Rookh Punch

Ribs of Prime Beef   Ducking   Apple Sauce

Saddle of Mutton, Currant Jelly

Cauliflower   Hollandaise Minced Spinach with Egg

Boiled Rice   String Beans   Stewed Tomatoes

Boiled New Potatoes   Mashed Potatoes

Baked Sweet Potatoes

Quail on Toast au Cresson

Tomatoes, Mayonnaise

English Plum Pudding, Hard and Brandy Sauce

Lemon Cream   Meringue Pie   Cherry Pie   Charlotte   Chantilly

Washington Cake   Glace Petits Fours   Ponce de Leon

Assorted Cake Jelly   Menthe Confectionery

Tutti Frutti Ice Cream   Strawberries with Cream

Fruit   Nuts   Raisins   Figs

Foreign and Domestic Cheese, Crackers

Coffee

After his return to New York circa 1903, Braquehais became involved in the effort to make Fort Lee, New Jersey, a Revolutionary Historic Site.

⁜   ⁜   ⁜

SOURCES: "La tour Eiffel en sucre," *Courrier des Etats-Unis* 313 (December 31, 1887): 1; "Artistic Wonders in Sugar," *New York Tribune* (February 3, 1888): 5; "High Art in Cookery," *New York Tribune* (February 6, 1889): 7; "La Société culinaire philanthropique," *Courrier des Etats-Unis* 82 (April 5, 1889): 1; "Artists in Gum Paste, Mutton Tallow and Wax," *New York Herald* 31 (January 31, 1892): 9; *Saratoga Springs, New York, City Directory 1892*, 111; "At the Family Hotels," *New York Tribune* (December 8, 1893): 3; "Frank W. Sanger's Story," *New York Tribune* (December 6, 1894): 12–13; "The Spleen as Food," *Elkhart Daily Review* (October 24, 1907): 2 (syndicated story); Menu, Hotel Ponce de Leon, St. Augustine,

February 22, 1899, New York Public Library Menu Collection, 1899–207; *United States Federal Census, 1900*, Borough of Manhattan, 1, 107, sheet 6.

Jean Roth 1851–1909
New York

French-trained Jean Roth came to New York at the invitation of Lorenzo Delmonico to serve as chef de cuisine at the branch of Delmonico's at 112 Broadway. Through much of the 1880s, Roth worked with Domingo Gianini and Charles Ranhofer, presiding over the Delmonico's culinary empire in Manhattan. He was paid $4,800 annually; Alessandro Filippini worked as his assistant.

In 1892 Roth presided over the restaurant at the St. James Hotel. During his tenure there, he contributed to a project among New York's chefs to imagine the ideal Christmas feast with this recipe:

CREAM OF ARTICHOKES, MORLAISSIENNE

Take half a dozen fresh artichokes, trim off all the great parts of the leaves; mince, blanch and drain them. Put in a saucepan two ounces of good butter; when very hot set in the artichokes and fry them colorless; moisten with two quarts of broth; let boil until the artichokes are done. Drain and mash them in a mortar; pass through a fine sieve.

Put the puree back in a saucepan; dilute with its own broth, adding a pint of cream sauce. Stir it on the fire to a boiling point; take off the fire; remove all fat; thicken the soup with six raw egg yolks, one quart of cream and four ounces of fine butter.

Cut some stale bread in small squares, dried in the oven. Season the soup with salt, pepper and nutmeg to taste. Serve the bread separately on a napkin.

Throughout the 1890s, Roth served as a minor officer of the Société Culinaire Philanthropique and regularly showed sugar sculptures in the annual exhibitions. In 1895 Roth changed venues, taking over the kitchens of the Hotel Netherland on New York Avenue. During this phase of his career, he began experimenting with American and West Indian dishes. His "Pepper Pot" became a signature preparation at the turn of the twentieth century:

Make a good, strong chicken broth. Thoroughly clean and parboil some raw honeycomb tripe, and cut in small squares; also the same amount and shape of potatoes, a little ham cut in smaller squares and fresh green peppers to taste. Boil the whole in chicken broth with a raw ham bone until the tripe is cooked, stir in flour thickening with a little curry powder to taste. Add a few fresh tomatoes, peeled and seedless, cut in small pieces and so come to a last boil.

Roth ascended to the presidency of the Société Culinaire Philanthropique in 1904. While he was in the presidential chair, he was forcibly retired from his position at Hotel Netherland. His manager observed, "Roth got into his head that he owned the kitchen—in fact, the hotel—a mental aberration common to cooks." Roth's departure marked the eclipse of the hotel as a New York culinary destination.

※　※　※

SOURCES: [New York chef salaries,] *Daily Illinois State Journal* (May 13, 1884): 4; "An Ideal Dinner," *New York Herald* (December 23, 1894): 3–7; "French Cook's Ball Tonight," *New York Daily Tribune* (February 2, 1904): 6; "A Shake-Up at the Netherland," *Broadway Weekly* 3, no. 69 (June 9, 1904): 18.

Charles Henry Smiley 1851–1911
Chicago

Chicago's foremost caterer at the beginning of the twentieth century combined extraordinary congeniality and a Chesterfieldian dignity. Son of an African American slave who had escaped to St. Catharines, Canada, Charles Henry Smiley was born on October 5, 1851. In 1866, after threat of recapture had vanished with the armistice, his parents moved back to the United States, in Philadelphia. Smiley was fifteen and he worked as a laborer.

Smiley came to Chicago in 1881 and hired himself out as a janitor and waiter. Serving society parties acquainted him with the requisites of setting up a successful business as an event caterer. He opened an office on Twenty-Second Street and enjoyed ready success. His attention to detail, his taste in appointments and decorations, his ingenuity in conceiving presentations and entertainments—all vaulted him to the top of his profession. When hotelier and grocer Louis D. Beman built the 1,000-seat shingle-style Rosalie Music Hall at South Park Station, he hired Smiley in July 1886 to run the Red Roses Café. Smiley used the luxurious kitchen of the café as a catering office.

Smiley stockpiled money from jobs throughout the later 1880s. Finally, in 1894 he designed and built his headquarters at 76 Twenty-Second Street, developing it into "the largest and most complete of its kind in the country." It was estimated to be worth $100,000. He staffed it entirely with African Americans, becoming one of the significant employers of blacks in the Midwest. He knew talent when he encountered it and gathered around him a staff of experienced and ingenious people. His party manager, the man responsible for décor and settings, was Major John C. Buckner, an astute politician as well as caterer. In 1901 he threw a party to honor his employees at his home. Mr. Libonati's mandolin orchestra played, Mr. Samelson's floral bouquets perfumed the room, and confectioner Robert Reichert's ice-cream sculptures melted while the kitchen produced the following for Smiley's associates:

BLUE POINTS
Boiled Salmon, a la Mayonnaise
Baked Ham
Scalloped Oysters   Cold Roast Turkey
Pickles   Celery
Potato Salad   Chicken Salad
Fancy Molds of Ice Cream
Assorted Cakes   Black Coffee
Cheese   Crackers
Cigars

A civic-minded man, Smiley campaigned actively for civil rights and education, practiced extensive charity, and spoke at many public meetings, including Booker T. Washington's Colored Business Men's Convention in summer of 1900. Besides the welfare of his race, Smiley had one other passion—fine horses. He owned a stable of fourteen, some thoroughbred, others workhorses, including his favorite, a jet black workhorse named Prince.

In late 1901, Smiley began to suffer from health issues. He persevered through the summer of 1902, then sold his business "at a handsome figure," intent on a life of recreation and travel. Upon his death in 1911, he left $3,000 to the University of Chicago to endow a scholarship for worthy African American students.

※　※　※

SOURCES: Julius N. Avendorph, "Charles M. Smiley, One of Chicago's Leading Citizens and Foremost Caterers, Dies," *Broad Ax* (April 1, 1911): 2; "Charles Henry Smiley," *Indianapolis Freeman* 13, no. 52 (December 19, 1900): 5; "Charles H. Smiley, the Chicago Caterer Entertains in Honor of His Assistants," *Indianapolis Freeman* 14, no. 4 (January 26, 1901): 3; "Caterer Smiley Retires,"

Colored American 9, no. 18 (August 16, 1902): 11; "Chicago Women Want Souvenirs," Fort Worth Morning Register (January 17, 1901): 7; "Hon. John C. Bruckner, Soldier, Statesman and Hero Passed Away," Broad Ax (December 20, 1913): 1; "The Café of Red Roses," Hyde Park Herald 5, no. 22 (July 24, 1886): 6; [Smiley's horses,] Wisconsin Weekly Advocate (April 4, 1901): 1; [Erection of Smiley's building,] "Doings of the Race," Cleveland Gazette (August 11, 1894): 2.

Frederick Compagnon 1852–1926
Chicago; San Diego; Los Angeles

Chef of Chicago's Grand Palace Hotel when that hostelry opened at the corner of Clark and Indiana Streets in 1890, Frederick Compagnon had established his reputation as a caterer in the world of gentlemen's clubs. He had served as chef at both the Chicago Club (from 1879 to 1884) and the Union League Club (from 1885 to 1887) in the city. Yet his enduring fame resides in being the chef who opened San Diego's iconic Hotel del Coronado.

Born in Switzerland as Pierre Frederic Compagnon, he was trained in Paris. The twenty-seven-year-old cook and his wife, Mary, emigrated to the United States in the winter of 1879, settling in Chicago. He changed his name to Frederick P. Compagnon. Almost immediately, Mary gave birth to a daughter, Louise Jacqueline Compagnon. Frederick became a naturalized citizen on October 28, 1884.

In 1887 John B. Seghers, the manager of the Union Club in Chicago, enticed Compagnon to join him in his new management venture, the resplendent Hotel del Coronado being built in San Diego. (In the twenty-first century, the "Del" remains the most emblematic of Southern California hotels.) Compagnon arrived early, recruited a splendid team of associates, and began the politicking needed to get sufficient attention and money from the owners. In February 1888, he warned of disaster if a sufficient number of cold storage lockers were not supplied. (Among other details in his plaint was the revelation that all the meat to be used in the hotel was to be shipped from San Francisco.) Paid $200 a month, given accommodation in a private house, he supplied Parisian fare with a Pacific twist. Since the hotel supplied guests with three meals a day on the American plan, Compagnon and his staff worked virtually around the clock. Yet Compagnon was a man always in search of amusement, ready to join manager Seghers and champion Frank Owens in the billiard parlor. To astonish bathers, he bounded into the waves wearing a silk top hat as well as his swimsuit. In June 1889, he secured two sea lion pups to liven up the hotel aquariums and ponds. In March 1890, Compagnon resigned, and his sous-chef, Antoni Gorra,

East view of the Hotel del Coronado, San Diego, California (1888). Photograph: Hotel Del Coronado History Collection.

was elevated in his place. He left in April, sojourned briefly in San Francisco, and returned to Chicago, intent on setting up as a hotelier-chef. As a stopgap, he resumed his stewardship of the Chicago Club until his hotel was ready. (This Club was also under the management of the Seghers family.)

He took no chances, since his own money was at risk. The Grand Palace Hotel did not aspire to be the house of epicures; too many fine Chicago chefs catered to wealthy gastronomes. Instead, it catered to midwestern businessmen on trips to Chicago; its cuisine did not aspire to cosmopolitan brilliance, but aimed for wholesomeness and good taste. The solid values and dependability of his cooking was advertised in a host of newspapers published in small midwestern towns. It took four years of supplying the unimaginative tastes of this clientele before the boredom drove him to terminate his experiment in being a proprietor and caterer. He felt happier employed in another man's kitchens. So he secured the position of chef in Chicago's Victoria Hotel in 1895. There he trained his son Frederick P. Compagnon Jr. in the kitchen arts, making him a French-trained, though American-born, pastry chef. Junior would make a culinary career in San Francisco in the early twentieth century.

During the 1890s, Compagnon was a fixture of Chicago's culinary scene, an officer in the Gastronomic Club, the city's famous company of culinary professionals located at 55 Dearborn, and host of several of their dinners. In 1895 his "Striped Bass en belle veue," garnished with meat jelly and tartar sauce, was the centerpiece of the club's banquet table. In 1896 he brought a game pâté. Because Compagnon boasted skill as an instrumentalist as well as a cook, he frequently was tasked with assembling and leading the "orchestra" that provided musical accompaniment to the club's nights of frivolity.

Upon the death of his wife in 1903, Compagnon determined to leave Chicago. His son suggested removing to the West Coast, and Compagnon migrated to Los Angeles, where he operated a restaurant until his death in 1926.

※ ※ ※

SOURCES: "Brevities," *San Diego Daily Bee* (May 30, 1887): 1; "The Grand Opening," *San Diego Union* (February 21, 1888): 5; "Billiards," *San Diego Union* (July 1, 1888): 1; "Coronado Beach," *San Diego Union* (June 7, 1889): 6; "Across the Bay," *San Diego Union* (June 30, 1888): 8; "Coronado," *San Diego Union* (March 27, 1890): 8; "Personal," *San Diego Union* (April 9, 1890): 8; [Antoni Gora,] *San Diego Union* (May 2, 1890): 5; "Chefs at a Feast," *Daily Inter Ocean* 24, no. 21 (April 14, 1895): 6; "Eat of Their Own Baked Meats," *Daily Inter Ocean* 24, no. 362 (March 21, 1896): 6; "Chefs to Entertain Consomme Manufacturers," *Daily Inter Ocean* 25, no. 242 (November 21, 1896): 9.

Jose Gestal 1853–1916
Boise, ID

In the latter half of the nineteenth century, Hispanic restaurants began appearing in some numbers in Florida, California, and the southwest territory. Only in Texas, New Mexico, and Arizona were they categorized as Mexican restaurants. Elsewhere, they were termed Spanish. Those that catered to a local Hispanic population made no claims about the refinement or novelty of their food. Some that sought crossover trade from local Anglo communities attempted fusion cuisines. In the 1870s, Chono Nebades of San Luis Obispo, California, in his Spanish La Vos de Mejico restaurant, offered Hispanic-, French-, and American-style food. Francisco "Frank" Costa in Fresno did much the same in the 1880s. There were, however, a handful of restaurants in the West, authentically Hispanic in style, that were embraced by the entire community—Native, Anglo, and Chicano. The Basque-Spanish restaurant of Jose and Narcisa Gestal in Boise, Idaho, became one such institution in the 1880s and '90s. This Basque couple took the salt cod, peppery lamb stew, and omelet laced with chili that became standard western Basque fare and offered it to the public for a decade beginning in 1884, before becoming one of Idaho's pioneering horticulturists and larger sheepherders.

Boise had few places of public dining in the last decades of the nineteenth century—the Pacific Chop House on Main Street, Mrs. Morden's Palace Restau-

Gestal Building, Boise, Idaho (ca. 1890). Idaho State Historical Society. Photograph: Idaho State Archives (2040-A).

rant, and the restaurant at the Natatorium Rest. When it opened on Idaho Street between Seventh and Eighth, Gestal's second Spanish Restaurant was a revelation—a jaunty brick building seventy-five by twenty-five feet, with sixty feet of the depth devoted to the dining room. A second floor contained private dining rooms, and every space was decorated by Narcisa's paintings and flowers from her garden, including the "bleeding heart." A second building was erected on the adjacent lot that became a boardinghouse noteworthy for its electric lights, hot and cold running water, and bathrooms.

Born in Santa Inés de Moark, Coruna, Spain on June 5, 1853, Jose Gestal signed on as a cook on the Spanish steamship lines at age eighteen and had circumnavigated the globe by the time he was twenty. In 1885 he came to Boise as a member of the Basque settlement in Idaho, entering the restaurant business, operating at a site now occupied by the state capitol building. There he developed a following among the miners and cowboys who peopled Boise.

> The delicate and tempting plats which garnished his bountifully supplied table— all for the moderate sum of two "bits"—tempted many a hardy miner and many a daring cowboy to invest his last quarter in a square meal, instead of rashly endeavoring to double it by "bucking the tiger" at the fascinating game of faro or the deep and mysterious game of "craps." Passers-by, who were not patrons of the senor's sale a manger, had their souls stirred, aye, even their very stomachs by the delicate aroma of garlic which was wafted upon the evening breeze as they wended their weary way homeward after a hard day's work.

After five years at the one-story brick building on the corner of Idaho and Eighth Streets, Gestal erected his new brick Spanish Restaurant farther down Idaho

Street. From 1890 until summer of 1894, the Gestals offered the citizens of Boise splendid breakfasts, including lamb chops and eggs. Breakfast morphed into a noontide meal, the restaurant would close at 2:00 p.m. and then reopen for dinner at 5:00 pm. Though a barroom operated in conjunction with the dining room, the Gestals grew increasingly discontented with the customer difficulties arising from overconsumption. In the 1890s, Idaho remained an unbuttoned territory not much given to the temperance cause.

On July 1, 1894, the Gestals notified the public that they were retiring from the restaurant business to devote themselves to hothouse plants. Narcisa Gestal had opened a greenhouse in 1893, and the profits realized by her plants eclipsed those of the restaurant. In the following year, the restaurant building was leased to Will H. Davison. He styled it the Restaurant and Short Order House. In 1900 Davison sold the building to I. W. Pfost and used the proceeds to become a sheep farmer.

✳   ✳   ✳

SOURCES: "La Vos de Mejico," *San Luis Obispo Tribune* (August 7, 1875): 7; "J. Gestal's New Spanish Restaurant on Idaho Street," *Idaho Statesman* (October 16, 1891): 5; "The New Restaurant," *Idaho Statesman* (November 17, 1891): 5; "Spanish Restaurant," *Idaho Statesman* (January 26, 1894): 3; "Has Bought Sheep," *Idaho Statesman* (November 23, 1900): 8; "Death Comes to Jose Gestal," *Idaho Statesman* (May 11, 1916): 5.

Jules Weber 1853–1940
New York

The genius of some resides in their tongue, of others, in the mind. Alsatian Jules Weber's great gift was for social organization. Indeed, from 1884 onward, he was the essential man in the institutional world of French cuisine in the United States, chairing the employment agency that settled the majority of Francophone culinarians in their jobs, and presiding over New York's most important societies of French expatriate life and culinary professionalism.

Weber's training was typical of a professional chef, serving his apprenticeship at the highly regarded Maison Rousseau in Alsace. He emigrated to New York in 1873 and was soon hired as a pastry cook at M. Purcell's Metropolitan restaurant. His skill led to a rapid promotion to the position of chef. Yet he quickly grew impatient at the scope of enterprise, left, and took a position at the

Astor House working under the revered Fernand Fere. Fere urged that Weber join the Société Culinaire Philanthropique, a recommendation that had importantly consequential results. Fere also suggested that Weber seek employment in places where his organizational skill and culinary imagination might shine untrammeled by kitchen bureaucracy. So Weber left the Astor House to preside over the dining room of the Merchants Club. The restrictions of clientele at the club began to irk Weber, so he quickly left to be chef at Maresi's restaurants. Sportsman Pierre Lorillard, dining at Maresi's, was so impressed with a dish prepared by Weber that he offered to increase Weber's salary if he would become his chef at Newport and his New York town house. This Weber did, stockpiling his salary. He had grown tired of the vagaries of cooking to satisfy other people's whims. He was determined to serve the culinary profession in other ways—as employment broker and importer.

In mid-1884, Weber opened a placement bureau for "cuisiniers, patissiers, confiseurs, boulangers, glaciers, sommeliers et garcons et filles de cuisine" at an office at 100 West Forty-First Street. The incorporation of kitchen-prep women in this list suggests the thoroughness with which Weber conceived the professional world of his colleagues. He would oversee its operation until 1905, when he turned the agency over to his brother George. One reason he could undertake the role of job broker was his deep involvement in the associational world of French expatriates, particularly French chefs. In 1880 Weber became secretary of the Société Culinaire Philanthropique, and in 1885 he would be elevated to the presidency, where he served until 1889. Weber was concurrently a commissar of the Société Française de Bienfaisance in New York. He would become president of that organization in the 1890s.

Having noted the enormous wealth generated by the import business conducted by Henri Mouquin, Weber commenced his own business in 1887, specializing in importing foie gras from his native Strasbourg. (He claimed in later life to have force-fed geese as a boy.) The late 1880s saw the United States awash in fake foie gras—liver pâtés concocted of lard and chicken livers flavored with Madeira. Having established a sterling reputation in his work placing chefs, his former clients looked favorably on his sourcing of French delicacies. Almost immediately Jules Weber, Inc., proved solidly profitable. He expanded the business's offerings carefully, adding sevruga caviar and Crouzat wine sauces. After noting the perpetual shortage of green turtle in northern restaurants, in 1905 he outfitted a factory ship for cruising the Caribbean to capture turtles and process and can the meat for use by chefs.

In 1927 Weber endowed the Jules Weber Foundation intended to provide financial support to culinary professionals who suffered bad fortune. The Société Culinaire Philanthropique was named as trustees, and the foundation survives as an enduring legacy of Weber's regard for his colleagues.

SOURCES: *New York Passenger Lists, 1820–1857*, ship name: Milton, arrival date: June 19, 1854; "Société Culinaire Philanthropique," *Courrier des Etats-Unis*, no. 298 (October 23, 1881): 7; "Monsieur Jules Weber," *Courrier des Etats-Unis*, no. 25 (January 29, 1885): 3; "La Fête de la Société Française de Bienfaisance," *Courrier des Etats-Unis*, no. 137 (June 10, 1886): 1; "Canning Turtle Aboard Ship," *National Provisioner* 32 (January 7, 1905): 44; [Crouzat wine sauces,] *New York Hotel Review* 16 (October 7, 1922): 66; "An Interview with Jules Weber," *Hutchinson News*, May 20, 1937, 7; Otto Gentsch, "Portrait D'Alsacien," *Alsace New York* 7 (Spring–Summer 2009): 3.

Paul Gilardoni 1854–1905
Mobile, AL; Birmingham, AL

Birmingham, Alabama, became a culinary destination when Paul Gilardoni made the New Metropolitan Hotel restaurant a temple of the cuisine of Lombardy, Italy, at the outset of the twentieth century. Gilardoni had moved to Mobile, Alabama, after a career in the Italian military in the late 1870s, opening a confectionery store on Dauphin Street. The business failed, forcing him to hire out as a cook at the Independence Saloon. He aspired to be a proprietor, but the business climate of Mobile did not permit this. In 1887 he transplanted to Birmingham and opened a café at 209 Twentieth Street. Gilardoni's pastries made the café's reputation, enabling him to move to a more spacious venue and expand his menu at 109 Nineteenth Street. Something of a wit, and wishing to deflate the hyperbole of newspaper advertising, Gilardoni hailed Paul's Café as "the Only Second-Class Eatery in the South." In truth, it was the most stylish and cosmopolitan public dining room in Birmingham. Wishing to diversify his business, he devised a scheme to plant vineyards on 170 acres of land he purchased in North Lake. Gilardoni then brought his brother Louis and his family over from Italy to oversee his pomological enterprise.

In August 1900, Gilardoni partnered with hotelier Emil Lesser to open the Metropolitan Hotel. When the partnership was announced in the Birmingham papers, the reporter opined, "Paul is one of the few really great chefs and restaurateurs in the South—an educated, experienced caterer, who combines art and science in the preparation of epicurean dishes." The restaurant served a merchant's lunch for 30 cents and dinner, and would cater events in the private dining rooms on the second floor. The Lombardy emphasis on polenta, lard, pork,

Metropolitan Hotel, Twentieth Street, Birmingham, Alabama (1902). Photograph: Courtesy of Birmingham Public Library.

and rice mapped rather smoothly upon southern taste for grits, lard, pork, and rice—so the Italian-southern fusion cuisine that Gilardoni offered on his menus was a far cry from the pasta and tomato sauce offerings of contemporary Italian restaurants in America. His background in confectionery, too, suited a regional food culture in which cheap sugar had occasioned a turn toward desserts.

The Gilardoni brothers belonged to that class of immigrant entrepreneurs never satisfied with a single enterprise. Besides orchards, farms, hotels, and cafés, they became involved in graphite mining in the hills near Birmingham during the 1890s.

Gilardoni's cuisine thrived until his death in 1905. All told, Birmingham enjoyed the creations of this culinary artist for a decade, the most memorable period in the city's food history until the end of the twentieth century, when it became once again a destination for food lovers.

✳ ✳ ✳

SOURCES: [Advertisement,] "Paul's Café," *Birmingham Age-Herald* 21, no. 139 (April 14, 1895): 17. "To Become Americans," *Birmingham Age-Herald* 23, no. 31 (February 23, 1897): 1; "Charge of It," *Birmingham Age-Herald* (August 8, 1900): 1; "Birmingham's New Hotel Is a Beauty," *Birmingham Age-Herald* 27, no. 135 (November 1, 1900): 6.

Augustino G. Ferera 1855?–1900?
Fresno, CA; Seattle, WA

Sometimes modest-sized cities had the good fortune to host cooks with superlative talent. If the small city harbored ambitions, a hotel or restaurant that expressed taste and style might become a source of civic pride. Fresno, California, in 1890, had Ferera's. Its period of operation was short and spectacular, sufficiently memorable to become fixed in the city's culinary memory.

Located at 1827 Mariposa Street, this outpost of haute cuisine evolved out of an earlier venture, A. Mitrovich's Restaurant and Oyster House in the Fresno Opera House. A. Mitrovich and A. G. Ferera, "the best cook in the state," served "Regular French Dinners" from noon to 7:00 p.m. In October 1887, the partnership dissolved, with Mitrovich returning to his middle European home. Ferera ran the business under the old name until the formal final dissolution of the business in December 1888. In February 1889, a commodious and well-situated restaurant on South J Street run by Henry Ratto failed because of the proprietor's lack of enterprise. Ferera and partner W. L. Doty secured the property, proposing to "conduct the restaurant on a first-class basis." Ferera indicated that the bill of fare would resemble that of Edward Marchand's at the Poodle Dog, in San Francisco. "Gus" Ferera supervised the cuisine, while Doty dealt with the wine and cigars. Ferera indicated that the preeminence of his fare would arise from an aggressive campaign "to secure everything in the market" in Fresno and to source from San Francisco when Fresno was lacking.

Ferera and Doty's restaurant quickly became the center of civic revelry in

Fresno. The associations held their banquets there, and the kitchen catered the meetings of the city's municipal government.

Ferera operated as steward in the restaurant, hired Ratto to be the head cook (Ratto's liability was improvidence, not lack of talent at the stove), and Ah Sing to serve as assistant cook. The pairing proved volatile, with kitchen spats sometimes leading to assaults and fines. Over the course of 1889, Ferera grew increasingly uncomfortable with the restaurant's location. Though it was near Fresno's principal bank, houses of prostitution were springing up along J Street. In October, he removed to the Denicke Building on Mariposa Street.

When Ferera's reopened in November, it rebranded itself as a French and Italian restaurant. Ratto severed his relationship with the restaurant. Ferera jettisoned Doty and sold half interest in the venture to his brother Antonio Ferera.

During the winter of 1890, Gus Ferera catered a series of banquets that impressed diners as being the finest ever eaten in Fresno. The Press Club banquet of March 4, 1890, generated a menu in its well-considered plates and classicism matched any offered at a restaurant on the West Coast during the late nineteenth century:

HUITRES SUR COQUILLE
Hors d'Oeuvres, Pate de Foie Gras
Olives d'Espagne avec Anchois
VIN, Chablis

POTAGE
Poulet a la Reine
VIN, Sherry

POISSON
Mountain Trout a la Maitre d'Hotel
VIN, Haut Sauterne

ENTREES
Poulet Saute a la Marengo
Filet de Boeuf Pique a la Richelieu
VIN, Burgundy

LEGUMES
Petits Pois Francais   Chouxfleurs au Gratin

ROTIS
Dinde Farci aux Truffes

Salade de Laitue
VIN, Pommery Greno Sec Frappe

ENTREMETS
Omelette Souffle

DESSERT
Gateaus   Fruits   Fromage
Café Noir au Kirsch a la Ferera
Havana Cigars

The menus of three of these winter feasts made the pages of the *Fresno Morning Republican*. But the expense registered here was great. In April, the building suffered substantial damage from a defective roof. The expenses proved too great for Ferera to cover. He went into arrears and abandoned the business. His old cook, Henry Ratto, swooped in to occupy the premises. On May 28, 1890, the paper announced the existence of "Ratto Restaurant. Formerly Ferera's."

Ferera moved to Seattle, Washington, and became steward of the Maison Tortoni.

※　※　※

SOURCES: "Mitrovich's Restaurant," *Fresno Republican Weekly* (March 20, 1887): 5; [Partnership dissolution notice,] *Fresno Morning Republican* (October 2, 1887): 3; "Ratto's Restaurant," *Fresno Morning Republican* (February 12, 1889): 3; "A Chinaman Fined," *Fresno Morning Republican* (October 13, 1889): 3; "Closed for Removal," *Fresno Morning Republican* (October 15, 1889): 3; [Notice of partnership with brother,] *Fresno Morning Republican* (December 11, 1889): 4; "Fresno Press Club," *Fresno Morning Republican* (March 5, 1890): 3.

Louis Sherry 1855–1926
New York; Long Branch, NJ; Narragansett, RI

No event more clearly marked the disaster for fine dining that Prohibition wrought than the closing of Louis Sherry's namesake restaurant in Manhattan in 1919. Realizing that the financial footing upon which haute cuisine rested had been undermined—the revenue of the sale of wines and liquors—this greatest of early twentieth-century restaurateurs abandoned the hospitality sector and

"Louis Sherry." Duotone
from Moses King's *King's
Notable New Yorkers* (New
York, 1889), 389.

became a commercial confectioner. He turned to sugar as his mainstay, manufacturing and distributing for retail sale chocolates and high-end ice creams.

Sherry's exit from the restaurant world resembled in certain particulars his entrance into it. After serving as busboy at Wendell House, waiter and head-waiter at the Hotel Brunswick, and steward of the Hotel Elberon (a resort at the summer gambling mecca of Long Branch, New Jersey), Sherry became in 1883 a purveyor, offering "fancy cakes of every name and nature, of ice cream of every imaginable flavor, and ices of every possible kind" at a shop at 662 Sixth Avenue. These confections were the sine qua non of society parties and receptions. Yet other things were also needful for catering, particularly banquet staples such as "sweetbread, lobster, salmon, dried oysters, deviled crab, chicken salad," and terrapin. From the first, Sherry's ambition was to be a caterer. He had identified a weakness in Delmonico's domination of the high-end banquet trade in New York: the restaurant empire wished all of the revelry to take place in one of the branches of their chain only. Yet many wealthy clients wished to stage events at their own town mansions and estates. Charley Delmonico was reluctant to send staff out to do private catering—only chef Antonio Sivori did this service. Sherry put himself forward to serve the desires of those who fancied home-based parties and receptions. Sherry's success in the home hospitality business forced Delmonico's to develop a party chef division, under the command of chef Prosper Grevillot.

From an early age, Sherry possessed three qualities that made him a preeminent caterer and, later, restaurateur: ambition, a love of the ritual dimensions of dining and celebrating, and an exquisite aesthetic sensibility. During the 1880s, when Sherry first established himself as a rival to Charley and Charles C. Delmonico, most of his clients thought him French. While his father was a French-Canadian who emigrated to Vermont and set up as a carpenter in St. Albans, his mother was a daughter of an old Vermont family; Louis Sherry was a native-born American. He formed his ambition to become a caterer at the age of fourteen. Sometime in the 1890s, he floated a story that his initial experiences in the hotel business were as a busboy in a Montreal Hotel—the story appears to have been a fabrication to explain his fluency of his French. The truth of the matter appears in another interview he gave in 1902 concerning his early days on the wait staff of the Hotel Brunswick in New York. In order to become a successful waiter, he realized, he must learn French. "I made the French waiters give me practice. I got it down pretty well and almost everybody believes that I am a born Frenchman. If I say I am a Vermont Yankee, they are sure that it is a joke." Sherry should have added that his father spoke Canadian French around the house when he was a boy.

Securing employment at the Hotel Brunswick was a stroke of good fortune—or perhaps a surprisingly astute youthful calculation. It was, in the later 1870s, one of the temples of French cuisine in North America, under the command of chef Francis Kinzler. Sherry "went into the kitchen whenever he could get away from his duties" and learned to cook. He helped the cooks free of charge and, he says, "took my pay out by asking questions. I kept that up for the seven years while I was at the Brunswick." While securing an on-the-job culinary education, he was also schooled in taste by listening to the conversation of the epicures and bon vivants who flocked to Kinzler's dining room to experience the cuisine.

Sherry's stint as steward at the Long Branch resort supplied him with a $1,300 nest egg and the backers to enable him to open his shop and catering office in 1883. In 1884 he hired A. Armand, a talented assistant chef from Delmonico's convinced that the new proprietor Charles C. Delmonico was casting a cold eye at him. To ensure that he had income during the summer, when Manhattan's social scene shut down, Sherry contracted to run the casino and restaurant at Narragansett Pier in Rhode Island. He would spend every summer developing the scene at Narragansett until the great fire of 1900 destroyed the resort. (Sherry's chef J. Keller would invent the dish "Clams Casino" at his resort in the 1890s.) The question remains—how did an ambitious, largely self-educated young man from Vermont in a sweet shop on Sixth Street and his culinary sidekick, a disgruntled castoff of Delmonico's, successfully challenge the most established, celebrated house of haute cuisine in America? Ambition only counts for so much.

Sherry levered himself into importance with fashionability—modishness at a time when Delmonico's became hide-bound by traditionalism. The death of both Lorenzo and Siro Delmonico in 1881, the financial debacles of Charley Delmonico in 1883 and his death in 1884, forced their heir, Lorenzo's grandnephew Charles Crist, to adopt the Delmonico name and protect the legacy by embracing Delmonico's traditionalism. Every ball and reception occurred in one of the Delmonico's venues, causing a growing crush in the company. In September 1883, Sherry went to Paris to learn the state of cuisine and service there firsthand. What struck him was the ancillary decoration at banquets—the flowers, hand-painted menus, sculptures, exhibition dishes, and linens. He determined that he would only provide the best—and would charge top dollar—and that he would personally attend to every job. At first he did not get major commissions. "Delmonico and Pinard were old and proved, while I was an experiment. I must establish a reputation with the small orders. They were slow in coming but they came. A small breakfast here, a lunch there, and so on. Nothing could be better than what I sent out, nor served better, nor on daintier table service, and, I may add, no bills could be stiffer."

Sherry's uncompromising pursuit of tastefulness, beauty, and bonhomie in his catered events earned him word of mouth. His willingness to work in the client's home proved one of the determinative dimensions of his success. If one wished superb cuisine, Sherry would provide it. If one desired an extravagant gesture, he would provide that as well. A description of the Rhinelander/Kipp engagement dinner of spring 1888 suggests how much he learned about festive décor from his Parisian sojourn:

> In the center of the polished table a miniature lake was arranged, above which ferns and lilies nodded and swayed and in which fishes of varied colors darted, the whole surrounded by tropical plants and glowing parterres of flowers. Small electric lights were arranged about the lake and in the center a fountain tossed its spray, while a colored glass ball lighted by electricity rose and fell in the crystal jet. A wealth of tropical foliage and bloom transformed the banqueting hall into a bower of beauty in which tiny colored electric lights flashed and flowed, and each of the twenty courses Manhattan enabled the lighting effects. Sherry's showed characteristic foresight in making the acquaintance of a pioneer New York electrician.

By summer 1889, Sherry's client book had grown to such an extent that he ventured an expansion that, according to a contemporary observer, "astonishes every hotel man and café manager in the city. He has rented one of the largest houses on Fifth avenue, standing on the corner of Thirty-seventh street, and is now having it completely rebuilt inside so as to provide it with a large public dining room, a ball room and several private dining rooms." Sherry could not have undertaken such a costly enterprise if he did not have some substantial champions in the world of New York society, old-line tastemakers who had grown tired of the scene at Delmonico's. After opening Sherry's Restaurant in late 1889, the champions made themselves visible. Mrs. William Astor gave a New Year's Eve ball and supper at Sherry's, and her daughters staged two further events. By the second week in February, Sherry's had been installed as the new thing in the bon ton. Mrs. Astor's "endorsement is of more actual value to Sherry than would be the name of an Astor at the bottom of a note for a quarter of a million."

Sherry's restaurant gained the favor of the younger set of the moneyed class. The décor—pastels, mirrors, tropical plants—stood distinct from any place in the city. Sherry's greatest anxiety was the cuisine. Delmonico's had the most talented chef in the western hemisphere, Charles Ranhofer. Sherry hired a sequence of talented collaborators: chef Xavier Wertz, at the first Sherry's at Thirty-Sixth Street and Fifth Avenue; the youthful prodigy chef Pasquale Grand, at the second Sherry's, the distinguished 1898 Sanford White–designed building on Fifth Avenue at Forty-Fourth facing the last Delmonico's building; and, finally, the ex-Delmonico's chef Jean Boileau.

Sherry's greatest contribution to the history of American restaurant cuisine was his revolution in marketing the image of the good life. He projected an exuberant yet elegant youthfulness in his restaurants, repeatedly suggesting that the best qualities of Continental cooking and style were found at Sherry's, combined with the technological innovation, showmanship, and love of the new typical of America. His rivalry with Charles C. Delmonico gave high society a cultural drama that drew national interest. He made himself a brand—an arbiter of taste—and an advocate of new modes of eating and socializing. Though trained in cuisine, the only widely published recipe linked to his name is a treatment of strawberries.

STRAWBERRIES À LA LOUIS SHERRY

Louis Sherry, the caterer, believes that sugar and cream destroy the natural flavor of the strawberry. Instead of cream Mr. Sherry use lemon juice. For each quart of strawberries he used the juice of one lemon and five or six tablespoons of powdered sugar. The strawberries, the sugar and the lemon juice are stirred up together a few minutes before being served. "It is much better to serve the berries at as near as possible the temperature at which they are packed."

One of Sherry's ambitions was to assimilate to his dining rooms and ballrooms the theatrical permissions of Broadway. Music was an accompaniment of dining at various times. Sometimes this stirred up controversy, as in the infamous *Little Egypt* performance at a bachelors' dinner held by H. B. Seeley on December 19, 1896, that led to a police raid. Sherry turned this rather infamous episode into a grand occasion for publicity, suggesting the edginess of entertainment at Sherry's. The key to success for Sherry was that he managed to escape censure, to burnish his reputation for cultural innovation, and to avoid the impression that he was engaged in the sort of nouveau riche lobster-palace sensationalism that attached to new rivals like Rector's.

After Sherry left off his summertime involvement at the Narragansett Pier at the beginning of the twentieth century, he was periodically rumored to be involved in any number of major hospitality projects—hotels in London and San Francisco, a restaurant in Paris. An ugly divorce proceeding in 1908 heated these rumors. Sherry's great reward in his work lay in his personal engagement in the event. Having nominal control of simultaneous events (the Lorenzo Delmonico model) had little to no attraction for Sherry. When Prohibition came in 1919 and the merriness and revelry of the social world evaporated overnight, Sherry shuttered his Broadway palace. It became a bank. He secured backing from the owners of the Waldorf Astoria to develop a line of confections for retail. Louis Sherry Ice Creams and Louis Sherry Chocolates with its distinctive lavender box became the Häagen-Dazs of the 1920s through the '50s.

National advertising commenced in November 1919. For someone who delighted so wholeheartedly in the caterer's craft, retirement for Sherry was difficult. Periodically in the early 1920s, he continued to cater events in New York. He died in his apartment in the New Amsterdam Hotel, leaving his fortune as an endowment for the Presbyterian Hospital.

SOURCES: "A Dinner at the Gramercy," *New York Tribune* (October 24, 1883): 5; "Island Resort," *New York Herald* 195 (July 13, 1884): 17; Richard Edwards, "Louis Sherry," in *New York's Great Industries* (Chicago: Historical Publishing Company, 1884), 171; "Lucullan Feasts," *Denver Rocky Mountain News* (July 6, 1888): 2; "Midsummer in New York," *Boston Herald* (July 21, 1889): 24; "Astor Ladies Countenance Sherry Against Delmonico," *Boston Herald* (February 9, 1890): 24; "Your Winter Breakfast," *Boston Herald* (October 30, 1892): 31; "Sherry's Spring Delicacies," *Kansas City Star* 17, no. 237 (May 13, 1897): 4; "New York Daily Letter—the Rise of Louis Sherry," *Cleveland Plain Dealer* (August 11, 1902): 4; Associated Press, "Sherry's, Epicure's Mecca, Will Close," *Daily Illinois State Register* (May 6, 1919): 1; "Louis Sherry, Noted Café Man, Born Here 71 Years Ago," *St. Albans Daily Messenger* (June 11, 1926): 2.

Jean Galatoire 1856–1919

New Orleans; Birmingham, AL

Equally famed as a restaurateur and a sportsman, Frenchman Jean Galatoire founded one of the longest-lived of New Orleans restaurants, one that in the twenty-first century has come to represent Creole tradition. The founder of Galatoire's came to New Orleans via Mexico, where he had been a successful steward in Vera Cruz. (The July 26, 1876, passenger list of the SS *City of Mexico*, Vera Cruz to New Orleans, lists him as "George Galatoire" and his occupation as "student.") A native of Pardies, Base Pyrenees, France, he arrived in the city in 1876 and hired on as a waiter at Germain Espy and J. A. Lahargu's Commercial Restaurant at 107 Customhouse. Two years later, at age twenty-two, he was managing the famous Boudro's Restaurant at Milneburg for Philip Billman.

Serving as steward for one of the great resort restaurants of Louisiana prepared Galatoire for the responsibilities of being a restaurateur. He could not raise the capital, however, so he spent a season as steward at Marchal's Restaurant before convincing Louis A. Trapet, who managed the Spanish Fort Hotel during the summer seasons, to enter a partnership. They opened the Pelican Exchange on the corner of Canal and Basin Streets. The Pelican Exchange advertised "the choicest of salt water oysters and the finest wines and liquors that can be had at reasonable prices." During this period of his life, he used "John Galatoir" as his public name. While managing the front of house at the Exchange, Galatoire kept up a feud with his former employer Jules Marchal. This erupted into violence in late spring of 1883 when Marchal was arrested for assault and battery on Galatoire. He did not contest the charge, though he himself bore wounds from a blunt instrument. At about the same time, Galatoire's partnership with Trapet dissolved, the latter hiring on with Tresconi to run the Washington Hotel saloon during the summers. Galatoire sought a new partner and found one in Jean Rannou. On September 22, 1884, Galatoire opened John's Restaurant at 19 Union Street, the site of Marchal's until Jules's divorce from Marie J. Rannou, when she took possession of restaurant. In July 1886, Galatoire married Gabrielle Marchal, closed his restaurant, and left immediately for Birmingham, Alabama.

From 1887 through 1896, Galatoire was the most accomplished caterer in Birmingham. Running the Old Alabama Club at 210 Twenty-First Street, Galatoire oversaw the festivity of the city's social season from 1887 to 1889. The unwillingness of the club to increase his emolument led to a break. He established John's Saloon and Restaurant, serving French fare and seafood, at 106–108 Twenty-First Street. The Old Alabama Club meanwhile languished after the crisis. By 1894 the club was forced to vacate its premises. Galatoire returned to New Orleans in 1896.

"Jean Galatoire" (late nineteenth century). Photograph: Courtesy of Galatoire's Restaurant, New Orleans, Louisiana.

Galatoire's march into culinary celebrity began in October 1903, when he opened a restaurant at 121 Dauphine Street in New Orleans. Almost immediately it became a favorite venue for club banquets. Its initial motto was conventional—"Everything the market affords, a la carte and table d'hote"—but the food well exceeded the standard offered in New Orleans. When the space at 209 Bourbon once occupied by Victor Bero became open in 1905, Galatoire moved his establishment there. During this period, he joined the French Society, participating in the anniversary Bastille festivals at the fairgrounds, and became a champion of the French opera, probably at the insistence of his friend Victor Bero. Sometime between 1905 and 1908, he reverted to his birth name, Jean Galatoire.

One impetus to his return to a Gallic identity was the arrival of his nephews, Justin (in 1902), Leon, and Gabriel (in 1905), from France to assist in his enterprise. Jean Galatoire trained them in all aspects of the business—cuisine, provisioning, banquet catering, event planning, and dining room management. While Justin served some time in the kitchen, the food at Galatoire's was performed to Jean's specifications by a series of cooks. The wait staff was under the expert direction of Rene Cazaubon.

The year 1909 marked the ascension of Galatoire's to the first rank of New Orleans cuisine, a restaurant that could be spoken of in the same sentence with Antoine's. The menu was French, and in contrast to the cuisine of Jules Alciatore at Antoine's, not given to improvisational flights of fancy; rather, classicism was the order of the day. Fish were prepared meunière amandine. Shrimp marguery, chicken financière, and Brabant potatoes rarely left the menu.

An avid horse lover, Jean Galatoire proved instrumental in the revival of horseracing in New Orleans in 1914. During the last five years of his life, he came to be regarded as a sportsman of the first importance.

Kidney disease began to incapacitate Galatoire in 1917. He turned over the management of Galatoire's to his trio of nephews. He died with an estate valued over a half-million dollars, and a restaurant whose name was a byword for New Orleans French tradition.

❋   ❋   ❋

SOURCES: *Soard's New Orleans Directory, 1875*, 305; *Soard's New Orleans Directory, 1877*, 290; "Louis Trapet," *New Orleans Item* (September 30, 1880): 4; "The Murder of John Walker," *New Orleans Times-Picayune* (August 22, 1882): 3; "First Recorder's Court," *New Orleans Times-Picayune* (June 5, 1883): 3; "Marchal's," *New Orleans Times-Picayune* (June 30, 1883): 2; "Opening," *New Orleans Times-Picayune* (October 5, 1884): 7; *Polk's Birmingham, AL, City Directory, 1890*; "Ordinances on First Reading," *New Orleans Item* (October 30, 1903): 7; "Galatoire's Restaurant," *New Orleans Item* (January 9, 1905): 3; "Fourteenth of July," *New Orleans Times-Picayune* (June 21, 1908): 16; National Archives and Records Administration, Washington, DC, *Passenger Lists of Vessels Arriving at New Orleans, Louisiana, 1820-1902*, National Archives Microfilm Publication, M259, Roll #59.

August Lüchow 1856–1923
New York; St. Louis

Proprietor of New York's iconic German restaurant at the turn of the twentieth century, August Guido Lüchow emigrated from Germany in 1879, and in the next year secured a position as barkeep at Baron Otto von Mühlbach's beer hall on 110–112 East Fourteenth Street in Manhattan. Legend holds that when von Mühlbach made noises about retiring, Lüchow approached a regular customer,

Lüchow's Dining Room (1905). Schultz Art Company, Hamburg, postcard.

piano manufacturer William Steinway, whose showrooms stood on the street opposite. He supplied the loan in 1882, enabling Lüchow to purchase the establishment, thereby keeping Steinway's favorite luncheon spot open. Renamed Lüchow's, the restaurant and beer garden became the haunt of musicians and composers, a performance venue of two generations of instrumentalists, and the site of the formation in 1909 of ASCAP, the historic institution protecting creators' copyrights.

By the mid-1880s, Lüchow secured exclusive American rights to import two German beers that would make his restaurant nationally famous—Würzburger Hofbräu and Pilsner. When H. Von Tilzer wrote the Tin Pan Alley drinking song "Down Where the Wurzburger Flows," Lüchow's restaurant became a mythic locus of gemütlichkeit. August discovered he didn't need to invest in advertisement to distribute his beer brands to saloons across the continent. Because musicians lived an itinerant life, word of mouth spread through the German communities and amateur music networks across the country.

The restaurant was known for several of its creations. In Lüchow's estimation, the bockwurst was definitive. Once, as a joke, a Hot Springs, Arkansas, hotelier secured some from the chef of Lüchow's restaurant and served them to August Lüchow, inviting comment. But Lüchow's prejudices were so great he refused to eat the item placed before him, once he noted that his host's chef was Italian.

Taking a cue from European practice, Lüchow's instituted a calendar of festivals in the 1890s, each celebration having distinctive beverages and dishes: the March Bock Beer Fest, the May Wine Fest, the Octoberfest, and Christmas (oxtail soup, poached carp, goose stuffed with chestnuts, cream-braised onions, and plum pudding). In connection with these fests, a German accordion band serenaded diners. In the years following Lüchow's death in 1923, this dimension of the restaurant's character became more pronounced, eclipsing the orchestral serenades (sometimes with Victor Herbert conducting) that characterized Lüchow's golden age. Consequently, the later Lüchow's was a decidedly more touristic and middle-brow restaurant than when August presided.

Yet August Lüchow himself experimented with the vulgar, kitschy version of German festivity in 1904, when he and Tony Faust of St. Louis collaborated in creating a mini-Tyrolean village and ski chalet at the St. Louis World's Fair. The largest eating space at the fair, it had a capacity of serving 8,000 persons. "Flower girls, brought over from Europe, moving about among the tables in their peasant dress, and two mixed choruses of Tyrolean singers in native costume, one band containing fourteen persons, and the other twelve, give a true Tyrolean flavor to the whole picture. The yodelers were especially selected from the finest singers in all Tyrol." With such cultural window dressing conspicuously featured, the food became decidedly secondary.

During the first decade of the twentieth century, Lüchow's immersion in the society of musical personalities ignited a desire to become an impresario. For several years he stalked the manager of the Irving Place Theatre, attempting to take the house over and install Gustav von Seyffertitz as director. He lobbied for the importation of German operettas. He was rebuffed in 1905. But Lüchow's instincts were sound. *The Merry Widow* would premiere in 1907, leading to an operetta boom on Broadway that would not recede until the mid-1920s. Lüchow finally secured management of the Irving Place Theatre in 1909.

One of the consternations of Lüchow's career was provoked by the outbreak of the First World War. As the most conspicuous German venue of hospitality in the city, it became in 1914 a gathering place of Austro-German patriots. Indeed, a group of 800 marched from the German consulate in New York and invaded the restaurant in early August 1914 for an impromptu venting session. As British propaganda turned public opinion against Germany, the restaurant's Germanness became a problem. Lüchow removed the umlaut over the *u* in his last name on the restaurant's exterior signs. A lurid American flag was printed on the cover of its menus—a flag with sixty-five stars!

The chefs employed at Lüchow's were anonymous creatures. Publicity centered on the famous consumers or on the host. Even George Luks famous modernist painting *The Chef at Luchow's* did not supply a name for the subject. When Jan Mitchell compiled his *Lüchow's German Cookbook* in 1952, he did not have a trove of traditional recipes from the restaurant's kitchen to serve as the basis of his text; rather, he attempted to construct the most evocative collection of German recipes traditionally prepared in the United States.

⁕   ⁕   ⁕

SOURCES: "Tyrolean Alps on the Pike a Great Meeting Place," *New Orleans Item* (August 29, 1904): 3; "Notes of Folks and Doings in Stageland," *Charleston Evening Post* (March 22, 1905): 3; "Lends Theatre for German Plays," *New York Tribune* (May 27, 1909): 7; "Announcement," *San Diego Union* (April 12, 1913): 5; "Guests at Hot Springs Feel Real Joy in Living," *Richmond Times Dispatch* (December 6, 1914): 46; "German War Fever at White Heat Here," *New York Sun* (August 4, 1914): 3; "Luchow's Puts 65 Stars in Flag," *New York Sun* (June 24, 1917): 2; "August Lüchow gestorben," *New Yorker Volkszeitung* 46, no. 201 (August 22, 1923): 2; Jan Mitchell, *Lüchow's German Cookbook* (Garden City, NY: Doubleday and Co., 1952).

Rufus Estes 1857–1939
Nashville; Chicago; American Railways

Employment as a steward on a Pullman service train stood foremost among salaried positions for talented African American cooks at the turn of the twentieth century. But to be considered for a position, one had already to have mastered kitchen skills. Rufus Estes, one of the greatest Pullman stewards, began his career as a culinary professional as a cook's assistant at the Hemphill Restaurant on Church Street in Nashville, Tennessee, in 1873. Founded after the Civil War, the restaurant moved to a spacious building across from Nashville's Masonic Hall in 1870. Originally boasting a saloon done up in "magnificent style" and two kitchens (the second dependency would burn up in 1873), the establishment had expanded and morphed into Hemphill's European Hotel and Restaurant by the time Estes was hired. Hemphill's ambitions in the culinary field can be seen in banquets such as the fish feast of February 1872, when they served "halibut, salmon, smelt, lobster, et id omne genus"—items sourced far from central Tennessee. From the first, Estes learned his art in the most cosmopolitan kitchen his native region possessed.

Rufus Estes was born into slavery in Murray County, Tennessee, in 1857, his mother the property of D. J. Estes. He told of the travails of his early life in the introduction to his 1911 cookbook, *Good Things to Eat*. Estes spoke of child labor during the Civil War, his brothers' flight to join the Union army and their eventual sacrifice of their lives, and his mother's travails and loss of health. The remnants of his family moved to be with his grandmother in Nashville in 1867. Estes worked at odd jobs to supplement the family's income until he was hired at age sixteen by Hemphill's chef.

Estes experienced a five-year kitchen apprenticeship in Nashville. He also worked front of house as a waiter. When he turned twenty-one, he left to seek his fortune in Chicago. Estes was hired as chief line cook at $10 a week by Charles Martell, whose French Restaurant stood at 77 North Clark Street. It was during the brief two-year sojourn with Martell that Estes refined his skill at saucing, one of the things that made him something more than a line cook in the eyes of the Pullman Company when they hired him in 1883.

Pullman hired Estes for the elite service corps that manned the private cars used by traveling dignitaries. During the duration of travel on the rails, a VIP would be assigned a steward to prepare meals, perform personal services, and serve as butler, if needed. Interactions could be close during the week it took to travel from coast to coast, so congeniality mattered as much as culinary talent in a private car steward. Estes served many of the famous of the 1880s and '90s—opera singers such as Adelina Patti and Emma Calvé, US presidents Grover Cleveland and Benjamin Harrison, as well as evangelists, royals, explorers, scientists, and actors. Estes's skills could suit all tastes from the down-home cooking loved by Maurice Barrymore to the French finesse desired by Ignacy Jan Paderewski.

State laws frequently required the president of a passenger rail company to ride and inspect every mile of track under his control. Hence each railroad had a specially outfitted presidential car, designed to serve any need the CEO had during his protracted peregrinations. In 1897 Arthur Stilwell—president of the Kansas City, Pittsburg and Gulf Railroad network—hired Estes to be his steward. The chef presided over a state-of-the-art galley at the rear of the $20,000 touring car. When Stilwell's syndicate failed and the rail lines and touring car fell into the hands of John "Bet a Million" Gates, Estes stayed on for an additional eight years. Estes attributed to Gates the idea of publishing a treasury of his dishes for general use.

Upon turning fifty, Estes determined to leave off traveling. He had always kept a house at 3209 Dearborn in Chicago, where he decamped between tours. In 1907 he left the railways for good to become a corporate cook in Chicago, serving the midday meal to executives of the Illinois Steel Company at 3408 Church Street. In the evenings, he socialized with members of the Appomattox Club, a civic association that combined mutual entertainment and the betterment of the race. Estes periodically catered the club's elaborate events and won the name "Captain Rufus." He had a theme song composed for him by J. Edward Green, fellow member and leader of the Eighth Regiment Orchestra.

1911

"Rufus Estes." Duotone from *Good Things to Eat, as Suggested by Rufus* (Chicago: Published by the author, 1911), frontispiece.

During his affiliation with the Appomattox Club, Estes was invariably the chairman of the House Committee.

In his sixties, Estes became less tolerant of Great Lakes winters. He reflected on the salubriousness of Southern California, a region he had repeatedly visited on the rails. Late in the 1910s, he moved to Ceres Street in Los Angeles (not too far from the current fashion district) and worked in a café. He is listed as a restaurant cook in both the 1920 and 1930 Los Angeles census. He died, after a brief illness, in 1939.

No other Pullman chef left so thorough a documentation of his repertoire of dishes as Rufus Estes in *Good Things to Eat*. The format of the volume hearkened back to the narrative (sans measurement formulae) recipes of the era when he learned cookery in the 1870s. Certain recipes contain commentary (for instance, how to cook a well-done steak without reducing the exterior to carbon) and tips based on broad experience. The contents were shaped to a large extent to the larder available on the railroads (more root vegetables than leafy greens, more stockyard beef than saltwater fish). The dessert section was canted to pies rather than confections and cakes; the breakfasts featured eggs and griddle cakes. Dinners included French fare, along with American meats and potatoes. Estes's own tastes insinuate themselves throughout the collection—he loved chestnuts, and they crop up in every section of the book. He favored stuffings and forcemeats. Intermingled among the cosmopolitan fare expected on continental trains were a select few dishes from his Tennessee home: peanut soup, a selection of fritters, and that classic creation of the mountain South, green tomato pie:

GREEN TOMATO PIE
Take green tomatoes not yet turned and peel and slice wafer thin. Fill a plate nearly full, add a tablespoonful vinegar and plenty of sugar, dot with bits of butter and flavor with nutmeg or lemon. Bake in one or two crusts as preferred.

Estes's formality about the craft of cooking—his presumption that any reader would know how long to bake the pie and at what temperature—suggested he had no intention of instructing a tyro. Still, there were moments when he assumed the pose of an instructor bestowing a sacred formula to a class of initiates—for instance, here is a maxim that could not have been spoken before the lettuce craze of the 1890s: "Fish should never be served without a salad of some kind."

※ ※ ※

SOURCES: "Restaurant Removed," *Nashville Union and American* (January 25, 1870): 4; *Chicago Business Directory, 1882,* 818; "A Brilliant Function," *The Broad Ax* (January 10, 1903): 1; "Grand Ball and Reception," *The Broad Ax* (October 12, 1907): 2; "Appomattox Club Notes," *The Broad Ax* (February 5, 1910): 1; "Mr. Rufus Estes as an Author," *The Broad Ax* (May 6, 1911): 2; Rufus Estes, *Good Things to Eat, as Suggested by Rufus: A Collection of Practical Recipes for Preparing Meats, Game, Fowl, Fish, Puddings, Pastries, Etc.* (Chicago: Published by the Author, 1911), 8.

Prosper Grevillot 1857–1923
New York

The last in the line of classically trained French chefs who supervised the cuisine at Delmonico's in New York, Prosper Grevillot was the favorite cook of Charles Crist Delmonico, whose death in 1901 ended the ascendency of that famous restaurant empire. Grevillot cooked at the Twenty-Sixth Street branch, then later at the Forty-Fourth Street one.

Born in France, Grevillot was brought to America at age seventeen to cook

"Mr. Prosper Grevillot, Delmonico's Famous Chef." From *The Chef Magazine* 1, no. 3 (April 1910): cover.

for a private family in New York. In 1875 Lorenzo Delmonico hired him as a cook's assistant. His ability and attention to detail attracted the attention of chef Eugene Laperruque, who upon the opening of the Twenty-Sixth Street restaurant brought Grevillot with him as larder cook. Laperruque guided the advanced training of Grevillot.

Because advancement could be slow in the Delmonico's world, Grevillot decided in 1880 to accept the job of chef entremetier at the Hotel Brunswick, then trying to maintain a hard-earned reputation for excellent cuisine. He worked at the Brunswick until 1883, when Charles Delmonico rehired him to be the outside parties chef for the Delmonico chain. His resourcefulness and his social tact kept him in this position until 1891, until he was appointed chef of the Broad Street branch during its final years of existence (from 1891 to 1893). When the Broad Street building was torn down in 1893, there was no head chef position open, so Grevillot accepted the post of assistant chef to the legendary Charles Ranhofer at the Forty-Fourth Street house. Ranhofer's death in 1899 elevated Grevillot to the highest position in the Delmonico's empire. He remained chef of the flagship branch at Forty-Fourth Street from 1899 until 1912.

As the last of the Delmonico master chefs, he rose to public prominence after both Alessandro Filippini and Charles Ranhofer had published books about the dishes that had made the restaurant famous in the nineteenth century. Hence, Grevillot's treatments of the Delmonico's canon of dishes never took book form. Yet early twentieth-century magazines do manage to preserve close to a dozen of Grevillot's favorite dishes. Here are two of the most noteworthy of that body of recipes:

TO TRUFFLE POULTRY

This operation consists of brushing and peeling the truffles, cutting the wrinkled surface off as thinly as possible. The size of those chosen must be in proportion to the bird that is to be truffled, for instance, take larger ones for a pullet, a partridge and so on. Pound the truffle peelings adding about the same quantity of fat pork as there are peelings, and continue to pound till it forms into a paste, then add the same quantity of very white raw chicken livers. Pound again altogether and put in half the weight of fresh butter, salt and pepper; mix all thoroughly. Take the forcemeat from the mortar and mix into it the peeled truffles in the following proportions: A twelve-pound turkey will take two pounds of truffles, a six-pound capon one pound of truffles, a three-pound chicken half a pound of truffles, and so on according to the size of the bird. Line the inside of the neck with a slice of fat pork, cover this with broad slices of truffles, and insert the above prepared truffles half into the neck part, and the other half into the rump part, truss for roasting. The neck part must be well stuffed so that the breast has a plump appearance, and sew up the apertures so that none of the dressing can escape.

MARROW PUDDING À LA BARTHOLDI

Unnerve, chop, pound and pass through a sieve six ounces of marrow or beef kidney suet or else half of each; work it with eight ounces of powdered sugar, the yolks of ten eggs and add twelve ounces of breadcrumbs soaked in a gill of rum and half a gill of cream; salt six ounces of candied apricots, cut into eight inch squares, six ounces of cherries cut in four, and two ounces of angelica. Mix well and stir in ten very stiffly beaten egg-whites. Butter and flour a cone-shaped mold, pour in the preparation and cook in a baine-marie for one hour. Unmold and pour a Bichoff sauce over the pudding prepared as follows: Two gills of white wine, two gills of syrup, lemon and orange peel, cut into Juliennes, shredded pistachios, nine ounces of Malaga raisins, currants and Smyrnas softened in water. Heat without boiling.

Like many of the chefs at Delmonico's, Grevillot used the French language in his kitchen directions. Half of his surviving recipes are written in his native language, including noteworthy versions of "Pigeonneau à la Mora," "Filet de Bass à la Parisienne," "Mignons d'Agneau aus Épinards," and "Potage de Poulet au Riz à la Moderne."

Grevillot appears to have retired in 1912. He lived an additional eleven years before dying peacefully in Nassau, Long Island.

⁂ ⁂ ⁂

SOURCES: "High Cooks to the Rich," *Kansas City Star* 27, no. 141 (February 5, 1906): 7; "Prosper Grevillot," *The Chef* 1, no. 3 (April 1910): 7; "Société Culinaire Philanthropique," *New York Hotel Record* 14 (January 1915): 31.

Pierre Borel 1858–191?
New York

Named after an ancestor who was a famous French alchemist, Pierre Borel came to the United States in 1873 to perform culinary chemistry as assistant to Eugene Mehl at the Windsor Hotel at 575 Fifth Avenue. He would eventually succeed Mehl as chef de cuisine and presided over the Windsor's kitchens until the great fire on St. Patrick's Day 1899 that destroyed the seven-story edifice and killed over eighty occupants. The fire did not begin in the kitchen.

For all his talent as a chef, Borel possessed many of the worst attributes found in those whose power gave them near-absolute rule over a domain. He was a martinet, dismissive of points of view that did not mesh with his own, and given to verbal if not physical abuse. When the *New York Herald* reporters decided to write about breakfasts as an aid to home cooks, for instance, and inquired whether a traditional "English" breakfast was ever served at the Windsor, they wrote: "He would have nothing to say about the English meal; it evidently wasn't worth consideration from his point of view." The French fare that he proposed as the start to the day included a cut of beef so rare and so expensive, "Chateaubriand trianon," a double tenderloin, that no home cook would use it. He suggested white wine and coffee with brandy as appropriate accompanying beverages.

If the English breakfast inspired contempt in Borel, the English Christmas dinner, a fixture in American hotels, inspired a passive-aggressive response. Borel advertised its availability yet treated it in an offhand manner. A news report concerning the Windsor's feast deserves extended quotation, for its account of Borel's manner:

> After all the circumlocution befitting the dignity of so great a personage, I was ushered into the presence of that monarch in his Tartarean realms. He graciously handed me the bill of fare in rough draft, dated December 25, 1889. From it, at my request, he made such a selection of dishes as would, in his opinion, constitute a fit Christmas dinner for a good representative of the Anglo-Saxon race. He did this with the remark that his dinner on Christmas was not very much better than that on all other days. M. Pierre Borel, when I asked him to designate whatever dishes were especially his own, replied with great dignity that he often invented dishes for his guests, but on principle never gave to them his name or that of the hotel.

The menu Borel chose was as follows:

Clear green turtle soup
Timbale Talleyrand
Broiled shad, maitre d'hotel sauce
Spring lamb   Asparagus
Chicken fricassee, Lucine
Redhead ducks   Green peas
Plum pudding
Fruit
Coffee

Having both asparagus and green peas at Christmas suggests that Borel was on good relations with greenhouse gardeners in the metropolitan area with extraordinary talents at forcing vegetables.

Borel was paid $200 weekly as chef de cuisine at the Windsor, the bulk of which he applied to various real estate speculations in the city and the upkeep of an estate in the South of France. He refused to join the Société Culinaire Philanthropique, the principal social club of French chefs in New York, and did not send exhibit pieces to the annual balls, indicating that the hotel's proprietor thought it an unnecessary expense; but there is reason to believe that this was a concocted excuse. A reluctance to spend money that did not suit his own purposes was Borel's ownmost pathology. This did not become apparent until his divorce proceedings from his wife, who ironically was named Genereuse. In 1894 she asserted that

> after being treated shamefully for years her husband finally turned her out of the house he owns in Williamsbridge. While they lived together she says he did not al-

low her enough money to keep the [four] children properly clothed or to supply the table with the necessaries of life. He allowed twenty-five cents a day for support of each member of the family. She asserts that he kept her in constant fear. He had a loaded revolver in the house, and he occasionally fired bullets through her hair to subdue her. He also owned a poisoned dagger, which he threatened to use on her. She says he has saved $28,000 in money.

Borel countersued his wife for abandonment. The court sided with Mrs. Borel, granted a divorce, and ordered that he pay $25 a week in alimony.

After the destruction of the Windsor, Borel returned to France, where he retired to his estate in Provence.

A chef must demonstrate extraordinary talent in order to compensate for the wretchedness of such behavior in both professional and personal life. Does the following justify it?

SALMIS OF WOODCOCK À L'AVIGNONNAISE

Select six plump woodcock, clean well, withdrawing the intestines and discarding the gizzard. Chop the intestines with three chicken livers and three smooth shallots, season well with pepper, salt and chopped parsley and cook in a stewpan. Cover six small slices of toast with the mixture. Remove the breasts of the woodcock and cook in the oven. Chop the remaining portions of the bird and moisten with catsup sauce, white wine demi-glace sauce the essence of truffles, and cook together. Dress the breasts on the stuffed toast, draining half the sauce over the same, and serving the remainder separately.

※　※　※

SOURCES: "Hommes qui Préparent les Festins," *L'édition du Dimanche du News* (January 1885): 6; "Christmas Feasts from Many Sources," *New York Herald* 356 (December 22, 1889): 21; "Winter Breakfasts," *New York Herald* 304 (October 20, 1892): 31; "Borel's Poisoned Dagger," *New York Herald* 305 (November 2, 1894): 4; [Notice of alimony,] *New York Tribune* (March 31, 1896): 12.

Xenophon Kuzmier 1858–1932
Philadelphia; New York

One of the most irrepressible of New York's great chefs, Xenophon Kuzmier was hired by Philadelphia's Stratford Hotel in 1884 to preside over its kitchens. A

Hotel Savoy, New York (ca. 1895). Duotone. Blanchard Press, New York, postcard.

native of Austria, he learned to cook in the kitchen of Princess Demidoff, sister of Napoleon II.

Kuzmier became a force in the national culinary community when his exhibition piece "Le Grandeur des États-Unis" tied for first honors at Philadelphia's chefs ball and exhibition in winter of 1892. In an entirely edible sculpture, Uncle Sam welcomed representatives from nations around the globe to the country.

The Hotel Savoy in New York made a talent raid in 1893 on the Stratford's kitchen, securing Kuzmier with a salary reportedly in the $8,000 range. From early in Kuzmier's residency at the Savoy comes a recipe for a north European specialty:

CARP, SCANDINAVIAN STYLE
Take a good sized carp weighing about six pounds, clean and wash it and place in cold water until you are ready to cook it. Turn a bottle of Bordeaux claret into a saucepan, with four tablespoonfuls of honey, half pound of currant jelly, one-quarter pound of Sultana raisins and one-quarter pound of almonds which have been scalded, one-quarter of the skin of an orange, one-half pound of butter, two bay leaves, four cloves, salt and pepper. Boil until the currant jelly is dissolved. Then place the carp in the pan and cook until done. Serve hot or cold. This dish is cooked especially for Christmas Eve.

A ladies' man with a wicked sense of humor, one of Kuzmier's chief amusements was baiting credulous newspaper writers. Whenever asked an asinine question, he concocted outlandish answers. In 1901, when asked what chefs eat, Kuzmier replied, "We absorb food fumes. . . . When one takes and retains in his system through the pores roast beef, mutton and all other health and strength giving foods he does not require them in his stomach." Inevitably, a contingent of fringe thinkers who believed that human beings were evolving away from the ingestion of food took up Kuzmier's remarks and sought him out as a prophet of the stomach-less future. In a second article, Kuzmier made the further tongue-in-cheek observation: "All chefs drink—that is, a great majority, claret being the principal beverage. The heat of the kitchen is so great that liquids are necessary to keep the pores open."

For that portion of humanity who had not yet evolved beyond ingestion, Kuzmier generously supplied a menu for a Thanksgiving dinner later that year:

Celery   Radishes

Canapes of Anchovy

Ox joint, English style

Boiled Sheep's Head, with Horseradish Butter

Boiled Potatoes, with parsley

Roast Turkey, stuffed with Oysters

Cranberries

Stewed Celery in Gravy

Sweet Potatoes, Georgia Style

Winter Squash Cakes Fried in Butter

Green Salad and Cheese

Home Made Plum Pudding

Vanilla Ice Cream

Cakes   Fruits

Demitasse Coffee   Cognac

The "Sheep's Head" referenced above is the fish, not the mammal. Kuzmier favored parsnip or chestnut stuffing if oysters were not available.

In 1908, when the newly constructed Gotham Hotel on Fifty-Fifth Street transformed from a residential house to a tourist hostelry, hotelier Benjamin Cheney hired Kuzmier to head the kitchen, upping his salary. Money greatly interested the chef because he had become smitten with owning real estate. During the latter half of the 1910s, Kuzmier's real estate investments began to reap huge benefits. He owned a 150-acre farm in Long Island and developed 227 lots on the island and another 114 in Hartsdale, New York.

Eight years into Kuzmier's time at the Gotham, he made national news when he "stole a kiss" from newlywed Julia Nish. The twenty-four-year-old bride didn't want to be kissed, but Kuzmier thought that custom entitled him to one. He kissed; she sued. The court decided $1,000 damages were in order. Mrs. Ellen Kuzmier was not amused.

Kuzmier's curious mind turned toward the drying of food. World War I had made the question of how to provide instant rations at the front a matter of concern in the culinary community. It caused Kuzmier to seek out chef Auguste Gay. Together both devised ovens that dried the vegetables and stock for soup into a powder that could be reconstituted with water. He patented the process in 1918. Their discoveries were taken up by Keystone Foods, which began the processing of instant foods in the 1920s.

✳︎ ✳︎ ✳︎

SOURCES: "Annual Ball of Chefs," *Philadelphia Inquirer* 126, no. 19 (January 19, 1892): 6; "The Ideal Christmas Dinner," *New York Herald* 3 (December 23, 1894): 7; "What New York Chefs Eat," *Washington Bee* 20, no. 15 (September 7, 1901): 1; "The Abolition of the Stomach," *New Orleans Times-Picayune* (September 29, 1901): 25; "Thanksgiving Dinners," *Dallas Morning News* (November 24, 1901): 14; "High-Salaried Cooks," *Trenton Evening Times* (August 7, 1910): 23; "Landlord Steals Kiss," *Idaho Statesman* 120 (December 12, 1916): 6; "Food Products Made by New Process," *American Food Journal* 16 (March 1921): 12–15.

François Sartre 1858–1921
Biloxi, MS; Gulfport, MS; New Orleans

A successful restaurateur in New Orleans, Biloxi, and Gulfport, François Sartre brought fine French cuisine to Mississippi and, over the course of his career, incorporated a variety of local Creole dishes into his menus. A native of Bordeaux and apprenticed as a chef there, he came to New Orleans in 1888, contracted as a private cook for the Godchaux family of Reserve, Louisiana. The Alciatore family heard of his work and in 1890 hired him to work in the kitchen of Antoine's Restaurant. He worked there eight years, until taking over the restaurant at the French Opera House on Bourbon Street and making it a destination for the city's gastronomes. In 1895 he hired out to run the Willow Cottage on the Biloxi beach during the summer months. In 1899 he purchased the premises and named it François's Restaurant; it would be the finest on the Gulf Coast from 1899 until 1909.

Sartre became a resident of Biloxi at the turn of the century and an American citizen in 1903. After the death of his wife from yellow fever, he brought his sister and brother-in-law from Argentina to manage the property. In 1903 he opened a second venue, the François Hotel in Gulfport, Mississippi. He gradually turned over the restaurant to his sister and, in 1909, after Mississippi prohibited the sale of alcohol in places of public entertainment, turned the restaurant into a grocery and ship chandlery.

In 1909 Sartre moved to New Orleans to run the Hotel Denechaud. Yet he preferred the life of a restaurateur, so he left in 1910 to open the François Restaurant on "Old 27" Carondelet. Here he became known to every banker, financier, and broker in the city, and the phrase "Fill 'em up, François" became one of the resonant phrases of the French Quarter. In 1919 he bought the 917 Gravier Street building that had housed Henry C. Ramos's Imperial Cabinet Saloon (home of the famous Ramos gin fizz) and with $35,000 outfitted it as the François Restaurant during the First World War. Among the other culinary professionals in New Orleans, he had especially close relationships with the Alciatore family and with Madame Bégué, having hosted her in Biloxi in the summer of 1903.

When the Volstead Act went into effect in 1919, Sartre had stockpiled a substantial amount of liquor and wine. It was an open secret that a drink could be had at François's, and a raid in 1919 found several gallons of whiskey stashed beneath the cashier's table.

After Sartre's death in New Orleans in October 1921, his remains were preserved, then conveyed to Biloxi for interment in June 1922. His estate was valued at $24,174 and went to his three daughters. Sartre's friend A. O. Bourdon became his successor as the reigning savant of Mississippi Creole cuisine. Bourdon partnered with J. M. Barbazan and Rene Cazaubon to keep his New Orleans restaurant operating.

✳   ✳   ✳

SOURCES: "Francois Sartre," *Biloxi Daily Herald* 1, no. 187 (March 18, 1899): 8; "A Social Reunion," *Biloxi Daily Herald* 2, no. 212 (April 24, 1900): 8; [Citizenship notice,] *Biloxi Daily Herald* (February 24, 1903): 2; "Francois Sartre," *Biloxi Daily Herald* 12, no. 107 (December 10, 1909): 8; "Soft Drinks Succeed Liquors," *Biloxi Daily Herald* 11, no. 117 (January 2, 1909): 9; "Biloxi News Paragraphs," *Gulfport Daily Herald* 1, no. 95 (January 22, 1910): 8; "Francois Sartre Prominent Caterer Opens Excellent French Restaurant," *Gulfport Daily Herald* 12, no. 79 (November 15, 1919): 4; [Mortuary notice,] *Gulfport Daily Herald* 24, no. 63

(October 27, 1921): 3; "Francois, Noted French Chef, Dies," *New Orleans Times-Picayune* (October 27, 1921): 6; "Francois Restaurant Owner Left $24,174," *New Orleans Times-Picayune* (December 1, 1921): 5; "Bonds Set in Liquor Cast Against Restaurant Man," *New Orleans States* (October 21, 1921): 5; "Bring Sartre Remains Here," *Gulfport Daily Herald* 24, no. 272 (June 29, 1922): 2.

Betty Lyles Wilson 1859–1924
Nashville

In the early nineteenth century, a woman typically championed a state's cookery—whether Mary Randolph, the "Housewife" of Virginia; Sarah Rutledge, South Carolina's "Housewife"; or Lettice Bryan, the "Housewife" of Kentucky. In the final part of the century, women advocated for the entire southern region. Mrs. Betty Wilson became one of the more celebrated of the avowed "southern cooks." She transported that northern institution, the cooking school, below the Mason-Dixon Line and used newspaper publicity campaigns to acquaint home cooks from Kentucky to Florida with the regional repertoire of dishes.

When Betty Wilson emerged as a conspicuous voice in the culinary print world in the 1890s, she differed from previous oracles to housewives by jettisoning any appeal to a sense of family duty, didacticism about nutrition, or economy. Her keywords were *change*, *newness*, and *pleasure*. Among the questions Wilson addressed to would-be attendees of her school: "Do you like new housekeeping ideas?" "Won't you be happy to have interest, more pleasure, and an added zest in housekeeping during the coming season?" Wilson was all about the aesthetics of liberation from routine. Paradoxically, the newness that she promised came about from introducing young women to the best parts of an old tradition.

Part of Wilson's traditionalism was her conscious identification with that central authoritative figure through which the female oracles of state cuisine spoke: the housewife. I am a "house-keeper and homemaker," she declared before every lecture. Yet she simultaneously embraced a second less domestic identity as "Uncle Sam's Cake-maker." Cakes, of course, had been that category of preparation for which many a domestic cook won local renown—the most ornamental of kitchen productions displayed at a church bake sale or civic receptions could make one's name and create a demand for one's wares. Mastery of cake making stood at the heart of Wilson's appeal: "And then her cakes—cakes that are marvels of beauty—cakes that melt in the mouth—little cakes—

Betty Wilson
Cooking Schools

NASHVILLE

SEASON
1915-1916

Yours for service

Betty Lyle Wilson

"Betty Wilson Cooking
Schools, Nashville
(Season 1915–1916)."
Handbill.

big cakes—the President's own cake—cakes for your own family use—cakes for special occasions—all are yours for the asking."

From 1897 to the First World War, "one of Mrs. Wilson's unequalled fruited cakes, decorated in her own matchless way, finds place of honor on the table of the President of the United States." Dispatched from Wilson's bake shop in Nashville, Tennessee, these holiday cakes made her public reputation. Yet it was not fruitcake that captured the imaginations of the women who flocked to her public demonstrations. Midway through the 1890s, Wilson began working up elaborate icings on her cakes—rococo butter cream flourishes, subtly color harmonized architectures of fondant and sculpted sugar. These homemade eye dazzlers suggested to household cooks—in a way that hotel chef exhibition pieces did not—that a do-it-yourself baker might create spectacular cakes.

Wilson's personal journey as a baker began in an invalid's bed as a young wife and mother in Nashville. Weak and stir-crazy, she roamed her house in a wheelchair until venturing into the kitchen one day. "A book lying on the table in the kitchen caught her eye, and on picking it up it fell open, and on the page the first words were 'Recipes for Easy Cake.'" She gathered the materials and set to work. Her first rough product gave her so much concrete satisfaction that she set on teaching herself the art. Entirely instructed in the techniques of baking by cookbooks, she built on her competencies by experiment, particularly in the decoration of baked goods. In her classes she always supplied one cake recipe that was both simple yet distinctive. She presented her recipes as sparse formulae.

NEIL ROSE CAKE

Whites of 6 eggs.

3 cups of flour.

1¾ cups of granulated sugar.

1 cup milk or water.

1 light cup butter.

3 level teaspoonfuls of baking power.

Flavor to taste.

Color 1–2 batter a delicate pink and put layers together with desired filling.

When the success of her presidential cakes made her reputation, she realized that if she were to make cooking and baking a profession, she must expand the scope of her preparations. The last decades of the nineteenth century made the sandwich (both as appetizer and as luncheon staple) an increasingly important category of production. Wilson suggested that mastery of the sandwich was a hallmark of women's kitchen craft. She was the first to elevate sandwich making to a first-tier kitchen mystery among the professional cooks who appeared regularly in print.

Instructed by print herself, Wilson realized her professional path lay in print as well. She began writing pieces for magazines. In 1914 she published *Mrs. Wilson's Cook Book* with the Foster and Parkes Company of Nashville. It combined basic recipes for standard dishes with fancy cakes, salads, and sandwiches. Throughout each section, a selection of classic southern dishes appeared. The cookbook proved a launching pad for her most brilliant career initiative. In 1915 she convinced a number of southern newspapers (the *Lexington Herald*, *Macon Ledger*, *Montgomery Advertiser*, Baton Rogue's *State Times Advocate*) to sponsor a cooking school in the newspaper's city. The papers would build a female readership. They would sponsor her appearance and pay her a fee. Admission to the week-long cooking school would be free. The contents of the course would be epitomized in the daily issues. Wilson, a majestic-looking middle-aged woman with an aphoristic brevity in her speech, magnetized her auditors. Invitations to lecture began pouring in from colleges, hospitals, and women's clubs. But the newspaper-sponsored cooking schools made her the "famous southern cook" of the World War One era. After the war, a second instructional book, *Mrs. Wilson's New Cook Book*—a renovation of the first—appeared, published again by Foster and Parkes. Its most distinctive innovation was the use of brand-name products in the recipes, consolidating a tendency that would dominate printed recipes in women's magazines for much of the twentieth century.

She trained her daughter Mary Lyles Wilson to be her successor as instructor and newspaper cooking expert. Mary would serve as the Piggly Wiggly grocery chain's cooking instructor in the 1920s.

❋   ❋   ❋

SOURCES: "Betty Lyles Wilson Here for First of Talks on Practical Cooking," *Montgomery Advertiser* 86, no. 39 (February 8, 1915): 6; "Questions Put and Answered by Mrs. Wilson," *Lexington Herald* 130 (May 10, 1917): 12; "Betty Lyles Wilson, Uncle Sam's Cakemaker and South's Famous Cook," *Columbus Ledger* (February 19, 1917): 6–7; "Betty Lyles Wilson, South's Great Cook, Tells of Her First Cake," *Columbus Ledger* 31, no. 60 (February 16, 1917): 5; "Who Is Mrs. Betty Wilson?" *Evansville Courier and Press* (April 26, 1917): 10.

Charles Crist Delmonico 1860–1901
New York

When Charles Delmonico, last of the third generation of the proprietors of the famous Manhattan restaurant, died—having frozen to death after suffering a stroke and wandering into the snow in the Orange Mountains in 1884—dominion over America's most famous culinary institution fell to Charles Crist, son of Rosa Delmonico Crist, Charles's sister. To maintain the name, Rosa had her son legally change his name to Charles Crist Delmonico in 1884.

While a teenager, Charles Crist had been taken into the business by his uncles and shown the methods that enabled the supply, staffing, and renovation of the several branches of the restaurant. Lorenzo drilled in him particularly the importance of pursuing the classical rather than the modish in cuisine and décor. When Charles Crist assumed control, every aspect of the running of the empire was already familiar to him, and he embraced his role with aplomb. Under

Byron P. Stephenson,
"Charles Crist Delmon-
ico" (1891). Pen illustra-
tion from "Delmonico's,"
The Illustrated American
(May 16, 1891): 630.

his administration, the branches were reduced to three: the Citadel (the William Street branch opened in 1837), the uptown (between Broadway and Fifth
Avenue), and the downtown (at Fourteenth Avenue and Twenty-Sixth Street).
The uptown branch was the banquet house of high society, the evening resort of
the glamorous, wealthy, and talented. The downtown branch was the luncheon
spot of the financial world and an evening resort of those who favored fine dining over sociability.

He shut the branch at 112 Broadway in 1888, and the 22 Broad Street branch in
1893. He rebuilt the Citadel in 1891. In 1897 he opened the final Delmonico's at
Fifth Avenue and Forty-Fourth Street, a space sufficiently lucrative and efficient
to enable him to close the branch at Broadway and Twenty-Sixth in 1899.

Until the last year of his life a bachelor, he always appeared in tailored suits,
stylish but never conspicuous, sporting a scrupulously trimmed mustache or
beard. A clubman and bon vivant himself, Charles Crist habitually dined at his
uptown restaurant early in the evening and then took supper at the downtown
branch. He was known for the regularity of his habits and the discipline of his
ingestion.

Every afternoon at about 5:30 a tall, well made and handsome man of about 33
years of age walks briskly up Broadway from Twenty-third street and enters the
café at the corner of Twenty-sixth street. His face has none of the flush that suggests high living; on the contrary his eye is clear and alert, while his rather spare
figure indicates a frugal diet, and might well belong to a man engaged in a lively

hustle for an existence. Nor do these signs belie him, for Charles Delmonico is of extremely frugal tastes as to eating and drinking.

Chain-smoking assisted in maintaining this discipline, repressing his appetite. He had two indulgences: fine clothing and the theater.

Charles Crist was generally admired by the arbiters of high society for maintaining the immemorial rules of the house: no unescorted women admitted; no refreshment will be serve to a man and woman in a private room, no matter who they are; any guest who makes himself obnoxious is blacklisted, and the waiters instructed to permit the guest on subsequent visits to sit, but not to be served. Charles Crist impressed long-standing clients by the severity of his tastes. He thought paintings and sconces detracted from the simple nobility of the marble-top tables in the café of the downtown branch, so dictated that the space always have bare walls.

Several challenges faced Charles Crist during his stewardship—in 1893 the International Hotel Waiters' Association attempted to organize Manhattan's restaurants and hotels, including Delmonico's. A May Day 1893 demonstration had a parade of waiters playing the "Dead March from Saul" in front of Delmonico's. "The windows on the Broadway Delmonico's were crowded with guests. Charles Delmonico himself stood in the doorway." Assistant chef Columbin deserted the restaurant and joined the strikers. Delmonico paid his 900 waiters 66 or 83 cents a day. Unlike other restaurateurs, however, he pensioned staff members who had more than a decade's service. He was indignant when reports circulated that he had raised wages capitulating to the labor action: "I have not raised wages here a single dollar, and I don't intend to. I have not taken a single striker back, and never will. I told them to strike if they wanted to and fifty of them went out. Not one of those fifty will ever be employed by me again."

During the first decade of Charles Crist's administration, the yearly profit of the empire hovered around $2 million. Delmonico's kept the prices for items high and a rich mythology of stories developed about provincials indulging themselves in the menu and discovering they lacked the funds to pay the bill (a famous tale dealt with Governor Bill Bradley of Kentucky and politician John T. Yerkes). Another mythology concerned Delmonico waiters who overheard stockbrokers' conversations, played the market accordingly, and amassed great fortunes.

A nagging concern for Charles Crist was the migration of the fashionable world uptown. This prompted him in 1896 to begin negotiations with Theodore A. Havemeyer for the lease of Sherwood House on the corner of Fifth Avenue and Forty-Fourth Street. In 1899 Charles Crist shuttered the building on Twenty-Sixth.

An astute judge of culinary talent, Charles Crist employed several chefs of world renown during his tenure. Foremost among them were Charles Ranhofer and Prosper Grevillot.

Beginning in 1897, rumors began circulating about the state of Charles Crist's health. Chain-smoking took its toll, and he began haunting sanatoriums and spas. His marriage to Jeanne Edwards—a woman whom he met in 1900 in Hot Springs, Virginia—surprised everyone. His death from heart disease in 1901 in Denver surprised relatively few. He sired a son, Charles Crist Delmonico II, during his brief marriage. Charles Crist Delmonico IV is now living.

> He knew everybody worth knowing of all classes—matrons and maids of Murray Hill, actors and actresses of Broadway, bankers and brokers of Wall street, lawyers, publicists, turfmen, editors, educators—he knew them all. Dignified as he was, the leading lady called him Charley; the chief justice and the great financier called him Charley. He was Charley to nearly every one, although occasionally someone called him Del or Delmonico. Address to him, Charley did not smack of familiarity, but rang with affectionate esteem.

During his life, Charles Crist Delmonico shared the proceeds from Delmonico's with his mother, Rosa, his sister and brother, and three other family members. After his death, there was disagreement how the empire should be managed. Delmonico's restaurant did not long survive Prohibition, closing in 1923. Versions were revived periodically during the twentieth century, banking on the magical name.

※   ※   ※

SOURCES: "To Preserve the Delmonico Name," *New York Herald*, no. 17344 (February 14, 1884): 6; Stephen Morley, "Delmonico's Café," *Chicago Daily Inter Ocean* (April 30, 1893): 4–33; "Waiters Parade for Higher Pay," *New York Herald* 122 (May 2, 1893): 9; "Cooks Go Out in Two Hotels," *New York Herald* 130 (May 10, 1893): 7; "To Tip or Not to Tip," *Charleston News and Courier* (June 20, 1893): 5; "Delmonico's—How the Famous Establishment Is Conducted," *Cincinnati Post* (October 18, 1893): 2; "New Home for Delmonico's," *New York Tribune* (March 4, 1896): 12; "Famous Restaurant Closed," *Illinois State Journal* (May 14, 1899):11; "Delmonico Is Soon to Marry," *Philadelphia Inquirer* 142, no. 132 (May 12, 1900): 3; "One of the Famous Delmonicos," *Denver Post* (September 29, 1901): 4; "Stories of Delmonico," *Morning Olympian* (October 13, 1901): 4; "Death of C. C. Delmonico," *New York Times* (September 21, 1901): 7.

J. Valentine Seitz 1861–1916
Boston

A pillar of the Boston culinary scene from the 1880s until his death on the eve of the First World War, J. Valentine Seitz was trained in Germany and came to the United States in 1881 to head the kitchen at the Hotel Vendome on Commonwealth Avenue. At the time, it was in the vanguard of hospitable amenities and gastronomy among Boston's hotels. The Parker House, in order to secure some of Vendome's luster, hired Seitz away, and he operated as chef there through the latter 1880s. In 1891 a disagreement with management sent Seitz to the Hotel Brunswick, where he became a fixture.

The Brunswick, because of its large, well-appointed meeting rooms, was a favorite meeting place for Boston's many clubs and associations. Seitz became a specialist in large-scale evening dining. He won the profound respect of the brotherhood of chefs for his expert management of the 1,200 seating of the convention banquet of the Association of Manufacturers shortly after the turn of the twentieth century. A token of this respect was his election to the presidency of Boston's Epicurean Club, the society of chefs and stewards devoted to the exploration of good food. Like New York's Société Culinaire Philanthropique, Boston's Epicurean Club held annual exhibitions showing off the chefs' mastery of food sculpture, sugar architecture, and baking. In 1907 the witty Seitz portrayed himself in tallow and vegetables "seated in an auto, complete with steering wheel, brakes, controlling levers and lights, while in the tonneau reposed a game pate surrounded by hand-made wax roses."

During Seitz's tenure at the Hotel Brunswick, he created a signature dish that became a necessary offering at Boston's club dinners:

BREAST OF CHICKEN BRUNSWICK

Cut the breast off a chicken; take off the skin and wing bone, split it lengthwise nearly in two; chop two cooked fresh mushrooms and a small truffle very fine; mix it with a little chicken force meat and stuff the split breast with it. Cover the breast with a thin layer of force meat and sprinkle some chopped ham and pistachio nuts over it. Cook the breast slowly for about 15 minutes in a flat saucepan in the oven with butter and a little sherry. Cover the breast with buttered paper. When cooked dish it up on a crouton and surround it with fresh mushroom sauce.

Seitz himself partook of the sociable spirit of Boston's clubmen. In 1890 he became a member in good standing of Boston's Germania Lodge of Freemasons and remained active in its affairs for the remainder of his life.

Hardworking, competent, and professional, he remained energetically in

Hotel Brunswick, Boston (ca. 1906). Detroit Publishing Company (019617). Photograph: Library of Congress, Prints and Photographs Division (LC-DIG-det-4a13540).

charge of the culinary department of the Hotel Brunswick until his death on May 27, 1916.

❋   ❋   ❋

SOURCES: "Favorite Dishes of the Chefs of Boston's Clubs and Hotels," *Boston Herald* (January 1, 1905): 34; "Exhibition in Talbot and Paul Revere Halls Weds Art and Humor," *Boston Herald* (February 26, 1907): 14; [Obituary notice,] *Boston, Massachusetts, City Directory, 1916*, 1768.

Leon Surdez 1861–1947?
New York; Philadelphia; Springfield, MA

Leon Surdez came from Switzerland to New York at age nineteen in 1880. He attracted the attention of Charles Delmonico, who hired him as cook at one of the downtown branches of Delmonico's. Quickly rising through the ranks, Surdez became chef de cuisine in 1888. He worked thirteen years all told at Delmonico's, eight as head of one of the branches. After that, he spent three years as chef de cuisine at the Waldorf Astoria. In 1896 he was enticed to Philadelphia to manage the kitchens of the Hotel Walton at a salary that "would make the eyes of many a professional man open wide." The Manhattan Hotel, desirous of making a name for cuisine, hired Surdez in 1898, bringing him back to New York.

While lionized by epicures and newspaper writers, Surdez suffered from the abuse of a wife, Honorine, whose volcanic temper horrified neighbors and made home life intolerable. Tumults from Surdez's domestic life appeared periodically in New York's papers. He separated sometime in the early 1890s and divorced her after eight years of marriage in 1896. Relationships, however, can be complicated, and Leon remarried Honorine, living with her in Manhattan in the first decade of the twentieth century.

A half dozen of Surdez's recipes saw their way into print during his career—renditions of classics, such as broiled marrow on toast and beef tenderloin with béarnaise sauce, as well as novelties, such as chicken à la Cleopatra. Of particular interest were Surdez's egg recipes from 1893 to 1896, when he was chef at the Waldorf.

EGGS CANADA

Take two fresh tomatoes, dip them in hot water, in order to remove the skins. Cut a slice in the top large enough to retire the seed or interior, break one raw egg in each tomato; mask with cream sauce, cover your tomato with the removed slice, place the tomato in a buttered saucepan, and let cook slowly for eight or ten minutes. Dress them on a very hot plate, surrounded with Madeira Sauce.

RUM OMELET

Put six eggs, a third as much milk, and a teaspoonful powdered sugar in a bowl together, and beat enough to mix, but not to make too light. Set a half cup of rum where it will get warm. Put a tablespoonful olive oil or butter in a frying pan and pour in the omelet before the butter gets hot enough to make the omelet stick on the bottom. This omelet should not be cooked through, and the brown outside rolled in, but should be shaken and shaped in the further side of the pan, as soon as the edge is cooked enough to fall over into the middle, so that the omelet is not a cake, but a soft, cooked mass with pointed ends and thick center. A broad bladed knife is useful to help shape it. Have an iron wire red hot in the fire, and when the omelet is done slip on to a hot dish, dredge the top with powdered sugar, mark with bars across the sugared top, pour the rum around, set it on fire and serve.

In 1895, when the *New York Herald* requested a Thanksgiving menu that reflected American ingredients and dishes, Surdez supplied an elaboration of chef François Lagroue's famous Maryland Feast of the 1850s, adding turkey and substituting Shinnecock oysters for Lynn Havens.

Shinnecock Oysters

Cream of Fresh Mushrooms

Amontillado Pasado

Mouse of Smelts, with Oyster Crab Sauce

Salad of Cucumbers

Cream Sauce

Barsac

Coquille de Ris de St. Jacque

Roast Vermont Turkey, Chestnut Stuffing

Timbale of Spinach

Potato Cornucopia

Champagne

Punch Eyvette

Terrapin, Chesapeake

Old Madeira

Canvasback Ducks

Celery Salad   Fried Hominy

Chambertin

Old Fashioned Pumpkin Pie

Ice Creams

Fruit   Fancy Cakes

Coffee

He preferred to cook on a seven-foot range with a firebox in the center and ovens on both sides. The range sported a bain-marie filled with boiling water to one side and a detachable grid iron on the surface.

After working at the Walton, Surdez returned to New York to work as a chef at the Manhattan Hotel for a decade. In 1911 Surdez removed to Springfield, Massachusetts, serving as the chef at the newly opened Kimball Hotel, and then in 1913, to the Hotel Worthy. In 1915 he returned to New York. In the 1920s, he retired to Bergen, New Jersey. He then moved to Dade County, Florida, during World War II.

※   ※   ※

SOURCES: "A Cook in Hot Water," *New York Herald*, no. 271 (November 28, 1888): 4; "What We Owe to Hens," *Boston Herald* (April 7, 1895): 31; "The Waldorf's Chef Sued for Divorce," *New York Tribune* (May 23, 1894): 3; "Thanksgiving Dinner Menus," *New York Herald*, no. 328 (November 24, 1895): 5-4; "Model Kitchen as It Should Be," *New York Herald*, no. 21356 (February 10, 1895): 3-4; "Caught on the Fly," *Philadelphia Inquirer* 134, no. 177 (June 25, 1896): 7; Max

Kuhn, *All Happy* (New York, 1905), 120; Emma Paddock Telford, "Rum Omelet," *San Diego Evening Tribune* (August 1, 1906): 7; "New Kimball Hotel Opens for Guests," *Springfield Republican* (March 20, 1911): 12; "Kimball Gets the Worthy," *Springfield Republican* (January 2, 1913): 10.

Fernand Alciatore Sr. 1862–1928
Paris; Marseilles; New Orleans

Proprietor of the restaurant La Louisiane, Fernand Alciatore was the eldest son of Antoine Alciatore, creator of Antoine's. Fernand's initial culinary education took place in his father's kitchen in New Orleans. In 1878, the year of the Paris World's Fair, he went to France as a fifteen-year-old to finish his training. Legend holds that he accomplished this at Au Petit Marguery under the famous Nicolas Marguery. At age seventeen, he became a chef at Le Grand Hôtel de Marseilles. He returned to New Orleans in 1882 to establish himself in business and to marry. His uncle Louis and aunt Ann Bezaudun in 1900 invited him to help run the restaurant and hotel they founded in 1881, La Louisiane.

Louis Bezaudun (1854–1911), born into a culinary family in Marseilles, was working as chef at Le Grande Hôtel de Noailles, when he was summoned to New Orleans to serve as chef at Antoine's upon the death of Antoine Alciatore in 1874. He married Antoine's sister Ann. From 1874 to 1881, Louis directed the kitchens of Antoine's before determining that he would like to found his own restaurant featuring some of the dishes of his home—bouillabaisse, tripe à la mode de Caën, sauces laced with Pernod. Bezaudun, in typical French fashion, wished to run a hotel as adjunct to the restaurant; it would be under the management of Madame Bezaudun. They located it at the Zacharie House, an elegant brick town house of the 1830s, at Nos. 717–19 Customhouse Street, near Royal in the Vieux Carré.

Fernand Alciatore, among other culinary arts, mastered butchery when in France. He returned to New Orleans, married Louisa Marchand in 1882, and entered the retail meat trade, offering the choicest cuts offered in the city. Located first on Conti, his store was at 54 Bourbon Street until 1893, when he opened a restaurant with the poetic name A La Renaissance des Chenes Verts at 902 Metairie Road—out at City Park adjacent to the historic dueling grounds. This rural resort became economically feasible by the paving of Alexander Street out to the location. His success in this enterprise attracted the attention of Bezaudun. In 1901 Bezaudun invited Fernand to become co-proprietor of La Louisiane. Alciatore took control of the kitchen, and in 1904 he brought in his son "Ferd.

"Fernand Alciatore and His Children" (ca. 1910?). Photograph: Courtesy of Cynthia Bozzone.

Jr." to operate as steward in the front of house. Bezaudun gradually retired from the business, and by the time of the general renovation of the building during summer of 1909, Alciatore was listed at sole proprietor. Customhouse Street was renamed Iberville.

One sign of Fernand Alciatore's influence on the restaurant's cuisine was the elimination of table d'hôte service; everything was offered à la carte, except on Christmas and New Year's. Only then did Alciatore prepare a set menu. In 1912 he contributed the following New Year's menu to the public to suggest how the feast might be done in traditional New Orleans French style:

Aspic Surpris
Bisques Crabes

Pompanos—Lion D'Or

Pommes Duchesse

Supreme Becassines en Caisse

Chous Fleurs—Gratin

Poulet Grain—Truffe

Salade Panache

Omelette Souffle

Café   Moka

Orange Brulot

Alciatore made it known he did not much favor turkey as a holiday dish because of its tendency to dry out. Another thing that Alciatore did not favor was sweet tea. When questioned about the import ban on absinthe imposed in 1911, Alciatore opined, "That tea you Americans drink is worse than absinthe—yes—you drink it all day long—especially that colored tea—that does more harm than absinthe—that's why you Americans are all so nervous: you drink tea the whole time—that colored stuff." One notes that Alciatore in no way considered himself an American, despite his Louisiana nativity.

In 1912 Alciatore made his son Ferd Jr. a full partner in the business. Ferd Jr. was the moving force behind a second renovation of the building in late summer and early autumn of 1914, constructing a new ballroom to exploit the social dancing craze sweeping the nation and expanding the dining area extensively. The Saturday-night dances became one of the most popular diversions of the city in the later 1910s.

The Bezauduns and Fernand Alciatore had operated and improved a property they leased from others. In 1920 Alciatore purchased the building fee simple. While Prohibition troubled the business of many restaurants, the 1914 move toward dancing and social occasions kept business thriving at La Louisiane through the 1920s. During this decade, Fernand stepped back from the operation of the business, content to have his son maintain control. When Fernand died in 1928, there was no crisis in succession or vision. The unexpected death of Ferd Jr. in January 1931, however, provoked the first of a series of transfigurations that would make La Louisiane one of the most long-lived and changeable of the classic New Orleans restaurants.

※   ※   ※

SOURCES: "Restaurant de la Louisiane," *New Orleans Times-Picayune* (April 20, 1900): 15; "Chat," *The Harlequin* 1, no. 44 (May 12, 1900): 2; "Restaurant and Hotel de La Louisiane," *New Orleans Item* (December 28, 1901): 7; "News and Notables at the New Orleans Hotels," *New Orleans Times-Picayune* (December 26, 1903): 4; "Restaurant de la Louisiane," *New Orleans Item* (September 9, 1909): 5; "Louis Bezaudun, Famous Chef, Dies of Gout," *New Orleans Item* (November 5, 1911): 1; "Ban on Absinthe Hits Antique Saloons," *New Orleans Item* (December 14, 1911): 1; "A 'Fine' New Year's Dinner," *New Orleans Times-Picayune* (December 29, 1912): 46; Frank Schneider, " 'Louisiane' Surrenders to Giddy Age," *New Orleans Item* (November 20, 1914): 21; "Restaurant de la Louisiane Renovated," *New Orleans Times-Picayune* (November 15, 1914): 24; "Cynthia St. Charles Letter," *New Orleans Item* (November 22, 1914): 12; La Louisiane restaurant history booklet "L'Histoire de la Louisiane"; "Orleans Cuisine Draws Visitors to La Louisiane," *New Orleans Times-Picayune* (February 21, 1927): 19; "Elder Alciatore, Artist in Cuisine, Claimed by Death," *New Orleans Times-Picayune* (April 3, 1928): 4; "Local Landmark Offers Visitors a Feast," *New Orleans Times-Picayune* (June 18, 1986): 58.

Gustave F. M. Beraud 1862–1932

New York; Denver; Seattle; Kansas City, MO; Chicago; San Antonio; Houston

Gustave Beraud was a genius, a scoundrel, and the chef who brought world-class dining to Kansas City, San Antonio, and Houston in the first decades of the twentieth century,

Beraud was born in Les Fains, France, on January 20, 1862. He rose through the stations in various hotel kitchens around France. Beraud reflected on the usual course of culinary training for French chefs in 1901—two years of apprenticeship under a master in a hotel, lodging on premises and eating in the kitchen, learning first to scour pots, then scale fish and clean vegetables. The apprentice scrutinizes the cooking going on around him, is finally permitted to cook simple dishes, assist in events, and, if judged competent, sent out to serve special dinners for private families. "He learns to make game pies, patties of different kinds, fillet of sole and things of that sort. And while he learns cooking he learns, also, how the dishes are to be served." To become a finished chef, the aspirant, after completing his apprenticeship, goes to a pastry shop and learns baking, preserves, and confections for an additional two years. His masters, the local mayor and sometimes the chief of police, sign a certificate attesting to the cook's successful completion of his course of study and readiness for professional employment.

This had been Beraud's experience. In 1886, while working in a Parisian hotel, he attracted the attention of Cornelius Vanderbilt's chief of staff, who hired

Newspaper advertise-
ment for Beraud Cafe,
Kansas City. From
Kansas City Star (June 16,
1903): 5.

him as chef in 1884. After serving Vanderbilt, Mrs. William Waldorf Astor hired Beraud to be the chef of the Astor household in New York.

Beraud first came into public notice in the United States as a swindler. In October 1887, a young Frenchman named Henri Dumay came to New York, boarding with Beraud. During his stay, Dumay became smitten with Beraud's wife and disappeared with her. Beraud wrote Dumay's father informing him that his son had been arrested for theft and that 6,000 francs had to be telegraphed immediately to Beraud to forestall Henri's incarceration. The older Dumay sold his assets to provide the sum. Beraud sent the following telegram in return: "Lawyer sends formal withdrawal. Money received. My life is ruined, for your son has abducted the wife of his benefactor, me. Obliged to sell everything. Crazy with grief. Money received does not pay half for us. I forgot momentarily to say I will make your unfortunate son take first steamer. Hope he will have remorse some day." The elder Dumay immediately grew suspicious, dispatched the French consul in New York to the Astor residence, and found that Mrs. Beraud had returned to Gustave the day after payment was received. As reporters observed, "It looks very much as though Mrs. Beraud was in the conspiracy, too." Beraud was arrested. He was released only after the return of the money; he immediately departed New York.

Beraud calculated he would have to get beyond the range of New York gossip columns to secure a position. He spent 1889 and 1890 as chef of the Denver Club, and 1891 and 1892 helming a restaurant in Seattle. In 1893 he thought the talk had subsided sufficiently to venture a return to New York. For six years, he worked at various hotels, choosing to work at second-rank establishments to keep from stimulating much public recall.

In 1899 Kansas City opened the world-class Baltimore Hotel, a marble temple with a state-of-the-art kitchen. Beraud accepted the position of chef de cuisine and recruited a staff of six French and German cooks from eastern hotels to serve him. Beraud wished to generate public interest in good cooking that would make the Baltimore Hotel's dining room the focus of a perceived new era in Kansas City cuisine. He created elaborate food sculptures in the hotel's grill room that became the talk of the city and the subject of newspaper stories. In winter of 1901, Beraud began a column in the *Kansas City Star* instructing home cooks in haute cuisine classics and renovating home-cooking standards, while also making them more appealing. The key articles in the 1901 series were as follows:

"How to Roast a Chicken"
"Leg of Mutton with Beans"
"Fried Chicken"
"Frying a Quail"
"Oyster Cocktails & Omelet Soufflé"
"Broiled Turkey & Turkey Soup"
"Lobster a la Newberg"
"How to Bake a Red Snapper"
"Egg Toast with Turkey"
"Fried Fish with Sauce"
"To Make a Queen Pudding"
"Stewed Beef a la German"
"Sweetbreads"
"Baked Indian Pudding"
"Shortcake"
"Omelet & Lamb Kidneys"

Because "Baked Indian Pudding" shows a French chef coming to grips with American ingredients and culinary tradition, it serves as a graphic picture of Beraud's culinary practice.

Indian corn and a few other good things may be united in a way that will result in the product called "baked Indian pudding." It will be found that the pudding is a product in which are combined in equal measure economy, taste, and health. It is economical because none of the raw materials of which it is composed are costly, and it is healthful because its ingredients are plain and wholesome. Also it tastes good when served with "hard sauce."

To begin the mixing of the baked Indian pudding . . . "you see that I have before me only a large pan, rather shallow. Into this as you see, I pour a quart of water."

Having done this he set the pan on the stove and watched it meditatively. Soon the water began boiling and the chef took a quart of yellow Indian meal in his left hand, and with a spoon in his right he poured the meal slowly into the water stirring it all the while with the spoon. He poured the meal slowly, so that the water would penetrate and scald each particle of it.

"Now," he remarked, "I set the pan on the side of the stove, where there is no heat, and stir into it one tablespoonful of butter, one half cup of molasses, one half teaspoon of cinnamon, the same quantity of mace and four eggs." Beraud did this very rapidly. His movements are so rapid and his hands as skillful that it is interesting to watch him at his work.

Continued the chef: "After you have mixed in your spices and eggs, butter and molasses, add a pint of milk. Stir it all up very thoroughly. Don't let there be any lumps in it. Then shove the pan filled with the raw pudding into the oven. And have your oven medium hot." . . .

When the [pudding] had been absorbing heat in the oven from three-quarters of an hour the chef took the cover from it and again shut it up in the oven.

"The top will grow brown in color," he said, "and that's the way we want it to look." It was only a few minutes afterward that Beraud again looked into the oven. The surface of the pudding was golden. He took it out of the oven. And then he turned it into a pan.

"Slice it off with a knife like cake," he said, "and it is good either hot or cold. If you don't eat it all the day that it is made save it until the day following. It will be good then."

The healthfulness of food—a matter only touched upon at the outset of this piece—was an enduring concern for Beraud. He paid particular attention to nutritional claims made by the vegetarian wing of the American physical culture movement. Given Kansas City's involvement in the meat trade, Beraud's boldness in advocating a vegetable diet had a heroic quality. "Meat is not a necessary article of diet and in a short time I think the American people will outgrow the habit. Very little meat is eaten in France, which is a nation of epicures. . . . The Beef Trust should not alarm us. . . . We ought to be glad the Beef Trust has increased the prices of meat, because we eat too much meat anyhow." Beraud published menus with no red meat as a guide to home cooks and indicated that those who thought they needed such protein should look to fish and chicken if they couldn't swear off flesh entirely. Beraud paid particular attention to the qualities of the vegetables he served and developed a partnership with the Brus Brothers outside of Shawnee Mission, Kansas, to supply him the highest-quality produce.

Beraud's ambitions conformed to the model career envisioned by many French chefs: apprenticeship, service as an assistant chef in an institution, appointment as chef de cuisine at a reputable institution (club, aristocratic household, or hotel), and finally the proprietorship of a hotel. On July 3, 1902, Beraud resigned as chef of the Baltimore to partner with King and Ketner in the management of the Midland Hotel. James Ketner covered the front of the hotel and Beraud the cuisine, signing a three-year contract with owners Hale and Ream in Chicago. The owners of the Baltimore Hotel did not savor the prospect of having Ketner and Beraud renovate the Midland into a rival. They went to Chicago and bought the Midland in September. They delivered in September an ultimatum to Beraud: either return to the Baltimore or set up as an independent restaurateur. The owners of the Baltimore would not abide him as a competitor in a hotel. This became clear when George Chamber started negotiations for the purchase of the Century Hotel and floated the possibility of Beraud's operating the kitchen.

While mulling his options, Beraud took a temporary position as chef of the University Club of Kansas City. Finally, in December 1902, Beraud's Café opened at 123 West Eighth Street, a high-end restaurant with banquet facilities and an on-site catering capacity. Unfortunately, the banquet trade could not support a restaurant with such a high price point for its dishes. In early April 1903, financial difficulties caused Beraud to transfer ownership to trustee Michael H. Aaron. By extraordinary exertions, Beraud secured the $7,500 demanded by creditors and the café remained open. Never a flourishing institution, it would expire, and in 1907 Beraud took over as chef of the Grill Room of the newly built Sexton Hotel. Beraud recommended that the hotel build a fish pool in which patrons could net the creatures to be prepared for supper. A year in charge of the Sexton convinced Beraud that he had accomplished everything that could be accomplished as a culinary professional in Kansas City. He accepted an invitation to become steward and chef of the Welling Hotel in Chicago. Chicago, however, supplied no solace. Used to being the biggest culinary star in a city, he found little to satiate his vanity in a culinary scene boasting several star chefs. The growing oil prosperity of Texas began causing him to look for situations in one of the established Lone Star cities.

In 1910 Beraud became steward of the St. Anthony Hotel in San Antonio. For the next dozen years, bidding wars would take place between establishments in Houston and San Antonio for his services. He would serve at various times in the Bender Hotel in Houston, the Gunter in San Antonio, the Rice Hotel in Houston, and the Hot Wells Hotel (a summer tourist destination) in San Antonio. In every venue, he raised the level of culinary artistry, championed local ingredients, and projected an ideal of refined service.

Beraud became fascinated with fruit cultivation during his Texas sojourn and planted a fig orchard in Colorado County. He became a major force in the Texas Fig Growers Association and supplied Houston with fruit and vegetables throughout the 1910s. His concern with pomology prompted him to explore new introductions, and in 1918 he was among the first to serve the honeydew melon as the maître d'hôtel of the Bender Hotel in Houston.

❋   ❋   ❋

SOURCES: "Gotham Gossip," *New Orleans Times-Picayune* (May 11, 1888): 2; "Will Open Today," *Kansas City Journal* (June 10, 1899): 5; "France's Trained Cooks," *Kansas City Star* 21, no. 209 (April 14, 1901): 5; "A Corn Delicacy, by Beraud," *Kansas City Star* 21, no. 223 (April 28, 1901): 10; "Menus without Any Meat," *Kansas City Star* 22, no. 218 (April 23, 1902): 5; "Vegetables and Our Ills," *Kansas City Star* 22, no. 278 (June 22, 1902): 5; "Beraud with the Midland," *Kansas City Star* 22, no. 290 (July 4, 1902): 1; "Comfort in the New Section," *Kansas City Star* (June 9, 1907): 7; "A Chicago Hotel for Beraud," *Kansas City Star* 71, no. 287 (November 30, 1908): 1; "Former Astor Chef to Be Head Steward at New Rice Hotel," *Houston Chronicle* (May 18, 1913): 49; "Honeydew Melon Will Be a Bender Delicacy," *Houston Chronicle* (September 21, 1918): 10.

Joseph Coppa 1862–1949
Paris; Guatemala City; San Francisco

A native of Turin who received his training in Italian kitchens, refined his pastry-making skills in Paris, and launched his professional career in Guatemala, Joseph Coppa (born Giuseppe) trekked northward to San Francisco in 1899 and found culinary fame there in late 1903 as proprietor of Coppa's Restaurant, 628 Montgomery Street, the headquarters of Bohemian San Francisco. In the remains of restaurant after the earthquake and fire of 1906, Coppa prepared the first restaurant meal for survivors of the disaster served in the city. The building was one of the few reasonably intact after the disasters, though its décor had been singed.

Coppa brought his wife, Elizabeth, and brother, Victor Louis Coppa, to San Francisco in 1899 after having presided over a restaurant in Guatemala City. A skilled chef, he immediately found work in Martinelli's Restaurant in the Commercial Hotel. Adolfo Martinelli would have found Joseph's Piedmontese style of cooking congenial. (The Martinelli brothers, San Francisco's foremost pasta makers, produced Piedmontese agnolotti and tagliatelli). The promise of higher

"Joseph and Victor Louis Coppa" (1940). Ex-photo morgue, *San Francisco News*. Photograph: Courtesy of San Francisco History Center, San Francisco Public Library.

pay lured him into Calixte Lalanne's kitchen at the Poodle Dog Restaurant, then the finest French restaurant on the West Coast. A small group of devotees, "the fuzzy bunch," tracked him from Martinelli's to the Poodle Dog. This group of painters and writers, objecting to the exalted prices and precious décor of the city's palace of haute cuisine, urged Coppa to establish his own café. They assured him that they would be faithful patrons and also supply publicity.

Coppa's Restaurant opened in autumn of 1903 on the ground floor of a commercial building. Immediately the Bohemian Club installed itself at the central table and commandeered the walls as an art gallery. The painters Xavier Martínez, Perry Newberry, Portner Garnett, and sculptor Robert Aitken appointed themselves the committee of décor in 1905, after a photographic exhibition in the spring. When the images came down, the committee broke out their crayons and chalk and adorned the gray backing paper with caricatures of club members. But the artistic transformation of the restaurant began when Coppa applied his lurid Italian color sensibility (garish gold and regal red) to a re-papering of the interior. The artists thought it awful but proposed a remedy. On a Sunday when the restaurant was closed, the artists broke out their brushes and chalks and began drawing allegories: the poet and the lobster finding common cause in Bohemia; Beauty holding aloft baked fish and fowl; Father Time languishing on his back under the clock. After an initial burst of energy, the decoration of the restaurant languished until the arrival of Xavier Martínez from Mexico. He contributed a fanciful image entitled "Before the Gringo Came," an illustration of Coppa's Restaurant in early 1904 before the public arrived to gawk at the Bohemians. He also supplied the famous frieze of black cats skirting the ceiling. While the Bohemians were largely a male sodality, there were two regular women attendees to the table and two women who dined occasionally.

Numbers of menus survive from Coppa's pre-earthquake heyday. His cuisine combined local dishes—abalone soup, Dungeness crab soup, sand dabs—with northern Italian dishes: tagliatelli with mushrooms and truffles, ravioli, tortellini, risotto. Yet Coppa's stint in Guatemala inflected his cuisine as well. One recipe preserved in Clarence E. Edwords's 1914 guide, *Bohemian San Francisco*, reveals a singularly creative take on ingredients:

CHICKEN PORTOLA À LA COPPA

Take a fresh cocoanut and cut off the top, removing nearly all of the meat. Put together three tablespoonfuls of chopped cocoanut meat and two ears of fresh, green corn, taken from the cob. Slice two onions into four tablespoonfuls of olive oil, together with a tablespoonful of diced bacon fried in olive oil, add one chopped green pepper, half a dozen tomatoes stewed with salt and pepper, one clove of garlic, and cook all together until it thickens. Strain this into the corn and cocoanut and add one spring chicken cut in four pieces. Put the mixture into the shell of the cocoanut, using the cut off top as a cover, and close tightly with a covering of paste around the jointure to keep in the flavors. Put the cocoanut into a pan with water in it and set in the oven, well heated, for one hour, basting frequently to prevent the cocoanut's burning.

Because the writers in the Bohemian circle loved to fictionalize their world, numbers of literary portraits exist of Coppa's, its decorations, and the company. Perhaps the most transparent representation occurred in Gelett Burgess's novel, *The Heart Line* (1907), under the cognomen "Fulda's."

In April 1906, Coppa's survived the San Francisco Earthquake. It became the instant target of looters, who stole food, smashed china, and ruined the murals. Its habitués collected in the street at nightfall, then located Coppa at the Presidio.

It took little persuasion to induce him to go back to his ruined restaurant and prepare a dinner, such as had made his place famous among artists, writers, and other

Bohemians, in the days when San Francisco was care-free and held her arms wide open in welcome to all the world. It was such a dinner as has been accorded to few. Few there are who have the heart to make merry amid crumbling ruins of [what] they held dear in the material world. . . . [I]t marked the passing of the old San Francisco and the inauguration of the new.

Coppa had found a case of claret in the cellar that the National Guard soldiers had not pillaged.

Coppa built his restaurant anew at 423 Pine Street near Montgomery. As an act of solidarity, many of the old clientele returned. But there were no surreal murals—the gatherings of the painters and poets seemed more and more a re-enactment of an unselfconscious camaraderie no longer possible. Coppa did, however, offer his walls as exhibition space. The publication of Burgess's novel in 1907 had attracted the gawkers and tourists. In June 1908, the *San Francisco Call* observed that "the local artists no longer feast at Coppa's." They took up residence in a "quaint hostelry" on Telegraph Hill, posted a sign over the door that read "No Philistines need apply here," and barred the door when other than artists sought entrance. They had migrated to Carmel-by-the-Sea.

The new location faltered, and Coppa sold out to M. L. Chelli in 1910. He kept the name alive and ran the restaurant through 1914. Meanwhile in 1910 Coppa established his Pompeian Gardens—or Coppa's Villa, San Rafael, as it came to be known. There he tried to maintain the cuisine that made his name before the earthquake. He returned to the city on the eve of World War I, open-ing an Italian eatery at 540 Washington Street (known locally as the red paint restaurant). In the early 1920s, he migrated to 120 Spring Street. He would re-main there until his relocating to 239 Pine Street in the 1930s. His son Victor was involved in a business on Jackson Street. In the early 1920s, he supplied recipes of his classic dishes on the back of San Francisco's Fairy Macaroni packages.

He died in San Rafael on January 13, 1949, at age eighty-eight.

✳   ✳   ✳

SOURCES: "Guatemala from South America," *San Francisco Call* (August 30, 1901): 7; Laura Bride Powers, "Bohemian Club Is the Foster-Parent of Art," *San Francisco Call* (December 11, 1904): 19; Mabel Croft Deering, "San Fran-cisco's Famous Bohemian Restaurant," *The Critic* 48, no. 6 (June 1906): 523-26; "Freak of Frisco Fire," *Mills County Tribune* (May 15, 1906): 4; "Books Review," *San Francisco Call* (November 3, 1907): 13; "Artists Find New Haunt on the Hill-side," *San Francisco Call* (June 14, 1908): 36; [Coppa's Villa,], *San Francisco Call* (April 6, 1910): 7; Clarence E. Edwords, *Bohemian San Francisco* (San Francisco: Paul Elder & Company, 1914), 36-39; "Café Owner Succumbs," *San Diego Union*

(January 14, 1949): 11; Warren Una and Joseph Henry Jackson, *The Coppa Murals: A Pageant of Bohemian Life in San Francisco* (San Francisco: Book Club of California, 1952).

Jules Louis Alciatore 1863–1934
New Orleans; Marseilles; Paris; New York

On October 1, 1891, Madam Julie Alciatore, widow of Antoine Alciatore, surrendered control of Antoine's restaurant, leasing it to her sons Alexandre and Jules Alciatore. Alexandre had handled the front-of-house duties at Antoine's during the 1880s. Jules was chef de cuisine of the Pickwick Club in New Orleans, the foremost epicurean brotherhood in the city. Immediately they hosted a feast for the press announcing a new era in the landmark French Quarter restaurant. Soon after Jules Alciatore took to the gazettes announcing dishes being featured on the new menu: "Tripes a la Mode de Caen," "Crevettes Marinerre," "Poulet en Cocottes." The innovations eventually provoked a contention between Julie, Alexandre, and Jules, leading to Jules's departure. Alexandre elevated François Sartre from sous-chef to chef de cuisine at Antoine's while Jules Alciatore opened Jules' Restaurant ("the Delmonico of the South") in the Pickwick Club building on the corner of Canal and Carondelet Streets. The Alciatore family quickly realized the error of its ways and begged Jules to return. After an electrical fire broke out in the Pickwick Club on March 15, 1894, Jules relented, returning to 65 St. Louis Street in late March 1894.

Conceived during one of his father's rare military leaves during the Civil War and born in 1863, Jules Alciatore combined a public school education with a rigorous kitchen apprenticeship from 1869 to 1874 under his father. At age sixteen he shipped to Paris and finished his education, staging at the Maison d'Or, Boissier's, and the Grand Hotel at Marseilles. He worked as an assistant to chef Brabant of the Rue Montmartre in Paris and apparently spent a summer in Strasbourg learned to make foie gras under Louis Henri and learning the secrets of sugar sculpture with Aron Feitel. In May 1884, Alciatore returned to the United States from Bordeaux, a fully finished cook, disembarking in New York. Family legend tells that during the transit the ship's cook fell ill and Jules Alciatore cooked in his stead without pay. So grateful were the passengers that they contributed a purse to his welfare.

In New York, Jules Alciatore presented himself to Jean-Baptiste Martin, whose Restaurant Martin on Ninth Street at University Place ranked among the finest in the city. Martin served a daily à la carte brunch and dinner priced at $1

"Jules Alciatore" (ca. 1900). Tinted photograph. Photograph: Courtesy of Roy Guste, Roy Guste Photography, New Orleans.

from 5:00 to 8:00 p.m. During the period when Alciatore worked in Martin's kitchen (1884–86), the restaurant featured the following daily specials:

Monday: Tête de veau à la vinaigrette
Tuesday: Bouillabaisse
Wednesday: Ragoût de mouton
Thursday: Fricandeau piqué à Poseille
Friday: Rale au beurre noir
Saturday: Pieds de mouton à la poulette
Sunday: Boeuf braisé froid à la gelée

In 1883 the Pickwick Club, a sociable association founded in 1856, erected a building at 140 Canal Street designed by Isaac J. Knapp of New York. The picturesque building housed one of the finest dining rooms in the city and a professional-grade kitchen. For years it lacked a culinary artist worth the space. In 1886 Jules's mother convinced him to return to New Orleans and serve in a dual capacity as special events caterer for the Pickwick Club and chef at Antoine's. Jules reestablished himself in the city of his birth, living at the restaurant at 65 St. Louis, while handling the Pickwick Club banquets.

Like his father, Jules Alciatore was a creative chef. In 1899 he devised his most famous dish—oysters Rockefeller—an oceanic substitute for escargots bordelaise. It was a baked/broiled concoction of oysters, greens (most now use spinach), butter, herbs, absinthe, and breadcrumbs. This in itself would ensure Alciatore's immortality in the pantheon of American chefs, but his importance was substantially greater. By 1900 he was transforming New Orleans restaurant fare, moving it away from classic French hotel cuisine to something more Mediterranean in its European dishes and Creole in its Louisiana dishes. In 1901 Alciatore advertised risotto, ravioli, and shrimps à la Moriniere. The restaurant had moved to 713 St. Louis Street near the Hotel Royal.

In 1903 Jules, a lover of "the only real French Opera House in the United States," created a tradition of extending the operating hours of the restaurant to accommodate the late-night opera crowd. After the turn of the century, the opera became one focus of identity for that portion of the population that the English-language newspapers were calling increasingly "the French colony" in Louisiana. Alciatore conspicuously participated in every institution of the French colony—the opera, the Société Française, and the St. Louis Cathedral. In 1909, for instance, he collaborated with his older brother Fernand and the two other great French restaurateurs of the city, Jean Galatoire and Frank Lamothe for a Bastille Day picnic with the following menu:

Soupe a la Tortue

Vol-au-Vent a la Toulouse

Roti de Veau

Poulets de Grain

Jambon de York

Salade Bourgeoisie

Crème a la Clace   Gateau

Café—Demi-Tasse

Supplying the sorts of ingredients that drew high-end custom—game, fresh oceanic fish, turtles—at times proved difficult. Alciatore had a network of market hunters in New Iberia and parts inland who supplied him. When conservation laws began to be enacted and enforced with some rigor after the first decade of the twentieth century, Alciatore found himself being cited by game wardens and inspectors regularly. Unmarked boxes of quail, snipe, and rabbits addressed to Alciatore were seized in January 1911.

In 1912 oysters Rockefeller had gained such widespread favor in the United States that Alciatore began advertising that he was the inventor. The dishes that enjoyed particular favor in the 1910s included oysters à la Ellis, soufflé of pompano, and poulet à la Pupiniscoscoff. At this juncture, the reputation of Antoine's eclipsed that of the great hotel dining rooms. Yet Jules Alciatore and his colleagues in the New Orleans restaurant world made common cause in 1918 against the rising tide of Prohibitionist sentiment in the United States. New Orleans had never been a dry city, and the prospect of a ban on alcohol made most restaurateurs realize that they would be forced to conduct illegal liquor sales if the Volstead Act passed. Nineteen eighteen proved to be a year of bad portents with World War I in Europe and the suicide on July 4 of the restaurant's oldest employee, manager Julius Touya, who shot himself in a city park when he learned he possessed an incurable medical condition. Jules Alciatore had to identify the body of the man he had known since he was a boy learning to cook at the restaurant.

When Prohibition arrived, Antoine's compensated for the lack of alcohol by a frenzy of created dishes. Each year four or five new items were announced, but several enduring themes of the decade were (1) the prominence of escargot dishes—escargots à la Sloilamelopinto, escargots à la Pupiniscoscoff, (2) ingenious chicken dishes, and (3) well-publicized specialty dishes made for visiting dignitaries—such as an oysters and foie gras dish for Ferdinand Foch in 1922. By 1923 Alciatore decided he would evade the law. The authorities cited Antoine's for illegal liquor sales in October of that year and convicted Alciatore in 1924. At the trial, Alciatore defended himself by indicating that he was out of the country when the illegal sales occurred. More important than his contretemps with the Prohibition officers was his hiring of Camille Averna in 1922. This chef from Palermo cooked beside Alciatore for a decade, imbibing the entire repertoire of the restaurant—the classics dating from Antoine Alciatore's day such as pompano en papillote, the French classics such as l'écrevisse à la cardinal, and his various inventions. When illness prompted Jules to turn management of the restaurant over to his son Roy in 1930, Averna was there to insure the whole legacy of dishes, including the signature café brulo diabolique—brandy, citrus, cinnamon, lump sugar, black coffee, and coffee liquor ignited in a silver bowl.

When Jules Alciatore died of protracted illness in September 1934, his passing was mourned by epicures and culinary professionals on both sides of the Atlantic. He left behind him a repertoire of New Orleans dishes, an example of creativity within a distinct tradition of food, and a body of wise sayings that deserve the attention of any lover of cuisine:

If you smoke between courses, don't come here; eat off the arm of your chair in a lunchroom. The food will taste the same, both places.

A restaurant is a place where dollars are exchanged for food. Neither should be counterfeit.

If you come to a first-class restaurant for first-class food and service, bring a first-class pocketbook. If you have to figure the cost, you can't afford it.

The best food in the world grows right here around New Orleans. If all New Orleans cooking was equal to New Orleans food, New Orleans would have to be bigger than New York to accommodate the rush.

SOURCES: [Alexandre and Jules Alciatore assume management of Antoine's], *New Orleans Item* (October 2, 1891): 4; "Jules Restaurant," *New Orleans Times-Picayune* (February 11, 1894): 9; "Jules Restaurant," *New Orleans Times-Picayune* (February 23, 1894): 5; [Advertisement of return to Antoine's,] *New Orleans Times-Picayune* (March 23, 1894): 5; "Hotel Louis Martin," *Courrier des Etats Unis* 93 (April 18, 1889): 4; "Antoine's" *New Orleans Times-Picayune* (September 1, 1901): 16; "Fourteenth of July Fittingly Celebrated," *New Orleans Times-Picayune* (July 15, 1909): 12; "Quail, Snipe and Rabbits Seized," *New Orleans Item* (January 3, 1911): 3; "Famous for Its Cooking," *New Orleans States* (January 22, 1916): 8; "Antoine Manager Commits Suicide as Women Pass," *New Orleans Times-Picayune* (July 4, 1918): 3; "Plans Supreme Dish for Palate of Foch," *New Orleans Item* (December 4, 1921): 18; "Jules Alciatore Found Guilty of Liquor Sale," *New Orleans Times-Picayune* (March 28, 1924): 16.

Mary Anastasia Wilson 1863–1926?

New Orleans; Heidelberg; London; Lake Como; Italy; Philadelphia

Queen Victoria's personal chef Mary Wilson was born and christened Marcelle Anastasia Hinkks in New Orleans. Her mother ran a small pastry shop in that city and her family was steeped in the Creole tradition. At age seventeen she was hired as a kitchen girl in the St. Charles Hotel in New Orleans and there learned the rudiments of hotel cookery. When she turned twenty-one, she sailed to Paris to complete her education. She worked five years with M. Soirée and an additional five years under E. Simone, the renowned pastry chef. She then hired on as a sous-chef at the Café Royale in Paris at the time when it was the Prince of Wales's favorite table. During a conversation over her meat pasties, the prince prophesied that she would one day become chef at Buckingham Palace.

Marcelle Anastasia, however, wished to learn more of the science of food—the chemistry of nutrition and the processes of fermentation and cooking. So she went to Germany. At Heidelberg University, she absorbed Justus von Liebig's nutritional science. Much of the practical dimensions of the German food science courses were intended for the victualing and nutrition of the German armed forces. She spent a year applying what she knew to the logistics of food preparation for the army. She left Germany a thorough dietitian and returned to Paris to instruct dietetics at the Paris Academy.

At this juncture, Buckingham Palace was looking for a chef who could manage the newly installed gas kitchen in a scientific and economical manner. The Prince of Wales inquired at the Paris Academy, recalled Marcelle, and upon learning that she now taught method in nutrition and kitchen management, he hired her to be Queen Victoria's chef. Marcelle became Mary and began speaking English. During her five years as chef to Queen Victoria, Mary Wilson became obsessed with the principles of economy as they applied to food. She abhorred waste and began calculating the value of every ingredient and every act of kitchen labor. Later in life, when she toured the United States lecturing housewives on home economics, her grasp of economies of scale was unequaled among any food professional at the beginning of the twentieth century.

When Victoria could only ingest liquids at the end of her life, Wilson reckoned her usefulness over. Physicians ruled the royal diet. She left the palace for the Continent, contracting as stewardess to the American House at Lake Como. Her two years' tenure there enabled her to make a thorough acquaintance with northern Italian cuisine. By age thirty-five, she had mastered Creole cookery, Parisian pastry cooking, and Italian cuisine. After brief service as the personal chef of Count Leo Monnosky of Russia, she returned to the United States in 1900.

Wilson established a cooking school in Philadelphia at the Children's Homeopathic Hospital, instructing women in household management and nutrition. When the United States entered into World War I, Wilson's unique experience in military food logistics and her expertise in nutrition prompted authorities to request that she set up a school to instruct US Navy cooks. She did this in 1917 at the Philadelphia Naval Yard and taught the rudiments of cooking to hundreds of enlisted men during the duration of the war. She performed the work pro bono, for which she was appointed a lieutenant commander of the US Navy.

After the war, her deep concern about urban poverty and the poor food habits it engendered prompted her to conduct free classes to poor mothers on economy and nutrition. Her fame enabled her to support herself by writing for the *Ladies' Home Journal*, serving as the food editor for the *Philadelphia Public Ledger*, and undertaking lecture tours, particularly in the South. Each summer she conducted a summer school at the University of Virginia in domestic science. In 1920 the Lippincott Company published *Mrs. Wilson's Cook Book: Numerous Recipes Based on Present Economic Conditions*. Targeted at women with modest household budgets, Wilson's compendium stressed baked goods, basic meat dishes, and puddings. Within a year it had gone through three printings.

※　※　※

SOURCES: "Queen's Chef Now Teaching Sailors," *Philadelphia Inquirer* (June 15, 1918); "Victoria's Chef Coming to Richmond," *Richmond Times Dispatch*

(March 30, 1919): 45; "A Queen's Cook Now Teaches the Poor," *Kansas City Star* 30, no. 48 (January 7, 1920): 8; *Mrs. Wilson's Cook Book: Numerous Recipes Based on Present Economic Conditions* (Philadelphia: J. B. Lippincott & Co., 1920).

Herman J. Berghaus 1864–1944
Boston

Chef of Boston's Young's Hotel from the 1880s to the 1920s, Herman J. Berghaus was a native of Berlin and took his kitchen apprenticeship there. He emigrated at age sixteen in 1881, settling in Boston and finding immediate employment in hotel kitchens. He was appointed the chef of Young's Hotel when he was twenty-two and there led a staff that included 10 cooks, 6 bakers, a butcher, 24 kitchen girls, 3 confectioners/ice cream makers, and a steward. He would enjoy extraordinary longevity as a professional cook, becoming in the late 1930s the grand old man of Boston dining. Part of his eminence derived from his central role in founding Boston's Epicurean Club in 1894. This society of culinary professionals convened "for the purpose of the maintenance of a reading room, where members may meet for literary and social entertainment, and for educating members to a higher degree of proficiency in the Art of Cooking, and for extending aid and relief to unfortunate and needy members." A friendly, creative fellow, Berghaus remained beloved of his brethren.

An article about a tour of Boston's major hotel kitchens in the September 16, 1894, *Boston Daily Globe* depicted the stocky young chef manning the broilers in the subterranean kitchens of the hotel. It described an immaculately clean, complicated, energetic, and well-organized realm crowded with provisions: "100 pounds of cod, 75 pounds of haddock, 25 pounds of halibut, 25 pounds of salmon, 6 pounds of turbot. 10 pounds of Spanish mackerel, 1¾ dozen fresh mackerel, 4 dozen frog legs, 1½ dozen flounders, 2 quarts of clams, 3 dozen perch, 4 pounds of butterfish, 5 pounds of striped bass, 2 pounds of cod's tongues, 45 pounds of salt cod, 6 pounds of smoked salmon, 3 gallons of oysters to fry and broil."

His famous dishes included a potato salad that many New England household cooks imitated and his recipes for broiled game birds:

ROAST REEDBIRDS A LA FORD
Remove the gizzards and clean a dozen birds. Stuff with sweet potatoes, roll each bird in a slice of bacon, put on a skewer and roast the birds in a hot oven for seven or eight minutes, and serve on slice of fried hominy with some nice white chicory.

SALMI OF REEDBIRDS EN BLAIZER

Take one dozen very rare roasted reedbirds, put in a chafing dish with a pinch of salt and one of pepper, add a little chopped shallot, the juice of a lemon, one ounce of butter and a glass of good old Madeira or Burgundy wine; let simmer for a second or so, then add some grated bread crumbs, cook a minute longer and serve. This is fit for the gods.

Berghaus belonged to that school of culinary professionals that believed an American cuisine would apply the best Old World technique to the best American ingredients. Hence his reed birds make use of fried hominy wafers and sweet potatoes rather than crackers and forcemeats as accompaniments and stuffings. This would be the path that in the twentieth century led to a refined American style of cooking.

✳   ✳   ✳

SOURCES: "Founder of Epicurean Club of Boston Dead," *Boston Herald* (May 23, 1944): 13; *Epicurean Club of Boston and Vicinity Constitution*, Massachusetts Archive; "Epicurean Club Formed," *Boston Daily Globe* (October 2, 1894): 2; "Hotel Kitchens," *Boston Daily Globe* (September 16, 1894); "Best Way of Preparing Reed Birds," *Boston Herald* (October 16, 1898): 32.

Louis C. Billotte 1865–1924
New York; Boston; Charleston, SC

Boston's most reputable French restaurant at the beginning of the twentieth century was Ernest Mieusset's, the favored destination of the city's epicures and the meeting place of persons who loved to talk about cuisine as well as eat it. "Chef Louis" (as he was called) presided over the kitchen of Mieusset's during its days of glory from 1896 to 1906.

Trained in France, Billotte emigrated to New York in 1882, where he worked as "second cook" in the Hotel Martin, then in the Hotel Brunswick under Sebastian Nouvelle. He was elevated to the status of chef when he contracted to prepare the cuisine at New York's Knickerbocker Club. At this juncture, in July 1889, Billotte became a citizen of the United States. Club cookery failed to provide the challenge Billotte craved, so after three years he moved to Boston, heading the kitchen in the Berwick and Madison Hotel for a season before settling at the old Hotel Reynolds on Washington Street. His time there coincided with that hotel's brief preeminence in the city. In 1895 he was enticed to go southward to Charleston to preside over the New Charleston Hotel kitchen. He did not, however, find the kitchen culture there to his liking and immediately returned to Boston to conduct cuisine at Mieusset's.

While at Mieussett's, "Chef Louis's" devotees bombarded him with requests for recipes. Consequently, a rich manuscript literature of his preparation survives in personal recipe collections. Certain of the dishes found their way into print occasionally.

FROG LEGS MADELEINE

For one dozen frogs' legs: Three chopped shallots, one quarter-pound of fresh mushrooms cut in slices; put in a sauté pan two ounces of butter, the mushrooms and frogs' legs, fry for five minutes; moisten with half a glass of white wine. When the frogs' legs are done remove on a dish, add a tablespoonful of veloute sauce, two yolks of eggs, one ounce of butter, season to taste with salt, red pepper, the juice of a lemon. Pour this over the frogs' legs and mushrooms, with four pieces of heart-shaped toasted bread and shopped parsley.

The death of Ernest Mieussett in late 1906 marked the end of that restaurant's status as the temple of Boston cuisine. Afterward, Billotte partnered in the restaurant Blaha & Billotte at 5½ Broad Street, working there until World War 1.

※　※　※

SOURCES: *Charleston, South Carolina City Directory*, 1895, 228; 1900 United States Federal Census, Massachusetts, Plymouth City, Brockton City, 1093, sheet 5; "Favorite Dishes of the Chefs of Boston's Clubs and Hotels," *Boston Herald* (January 1, 1905): 34; "Mieusset's All to Wife," *Boston Herald* (July 9, 1907): 5.

Adrian Delvaux 1866–1954
Reims, France; Paris; Chicago; Kansas City, MO; Columbus, OH

"The Great Adrian" was chef of the Baltimore Hotel when it epitomized stylish life in Kansas City, Missouri, after the turn of the twentieth century. Belgian by birth, French by training, Delvaux began his professional life in the kitchens of Le Grand Hôtel, Reims, and then worked as sous-chef at the Bristol Hotel in Paris. In 1890 he was hired to be chef of the Chicago Club in Chicago. His tenure would be short, finding better remuneration in the Congress Hotel and then the Auditorium Hotel. In 1903 he moved to Kansas City, Missouri, to become chef de cuisine at the most luxurious hotel in the city, the Hotel Baltimore, replacing Gustav Beraud.

When Delvaux walked into the kitchen, the Baltimore had only two rivals west of New York for size and amenities: the Palmer House in Chicago and Brown's Hotel in Denver. Adrian Delvaux knew precisely the opportunity standing before him—an exquisite venue in a city ambitious for commercial and cultural distinction. Delvaux wholeheartedly embraced his role as oracle of the good living.

Delvaux knew how to engage the public interest. When the Baltimore hosted a show of the Boston Terrier Association and the hotel hosted sixty canine guests, he made sure that a reporter from the *Kansas City Star* witnessed his consultation with the meet organizer determining what would be most healthful and savory for the show dogs to eat. At Christmastime, he erected a joke Christmas tree in the hotel kitchen festooned with odd culinary adornments.

One of the culinary fashions at the turn of the century was cooking dishes *en papillote*, enclosed in a paper bag to concentrate flavors and juices. In 1911 Delvaux assured the readers of Kansas City that the method could be used for vegetables as well as the chops and fish that were its usual applications. He periodically fulfilled his civic responsibility to inform household cooks of tweaks that made home preparations more savory or suitable. In 1907 he demonstrated a means of making a southern staple—fried chicken—more interesting as a smothered chicken:

> Mr. Delvaux seasoned the pieces of chicken with salt and pepper and rolled them in flour. Then he washed a dozen pods of okra and cut them into thin slices, throwing away the stems. He peeled and sliced a medium sized onion, cut one-quarter pound of ham in half-inch dice and chopped fine one small green pepper. Then he fried the chicken and ham until they were brown and put them into enough smoking hot lard to half cover them. To this he added the okra, onion, pepper and enough broth to cover all. It was then seasoned with salt and stewed gently until both chicken and vegetables were tender. When the broth became thicker than ordinary gravy while cooking he added a little boiling water. "It is usual to serve a dish of plain boiled rice with the chicken."

The technical range of Delvaux's cooking is best conveyed by his contributions to Archie Hoff's 1913 International Cooking Library series of cookbooks. Delvaux's recipes appear in the volumes on roasts and entrees, on desserts, on chafing dish specialties, and on dainties. Among the most interesting of his contributions was his "Roast Saddle of Venison, Sweet Sour Sauce." While the name of the sauce might conjure the pineapple and vinegar abominations of the mid-twentieth century, Delvaux's sweet sour came from the play of port wine, lemon, and currant jelly.

ROAST SADDLE OF VENISON, SWEET SOUR SAUCE

Take a saddle of venison weigh[ing] seven or eight pounds, remove outer skin, lard the saddle and place in a braising pan to which has been added chopped onions, carrots and a mixture of spices. Place about six ounces of soft butter on saddle and set in hot oven for fifty minutes, or longer if necessary. Remove saddle from pan. Place in pan one-half cup of flour; let same get nice and brown; add juice of three pounds of tomatoes and about one pint stock. Cook together for fifteen or twenty minutes; then strain this juice through a fine sieve into another sauce pan. Add to this one-half cup currant jelly and the peeling of one lemon. Set back on fire and boil for five minutes. Skim off top and strain, after which add the juice of one lemon, one glass Port wine and season to taste with salt and paprika. Serve this gravy with your saddle of venison.

Being located in one of the great centers of meatpacking in the United States made Delvaux attend to the fine points of roasting and grilling. He became a devotee of the highest grades of meats—what the packing trade called holiday beef—growing increasingly interested in the world of butchery and the market for shorthorn cattle. As his judgment of meat grew expert in the 1910s, he became convinced that his knowledge might occasion the improvement of the quality of meat available from Kansas City. In 1917 he cast off his toque. He bought out A. Weber's meat and grocery market and became a provisioner of beef. In two years he built the business into "the largest meat market and grocery in Kansas City." His eye for quality became legendary, and he was loved by cattlemen because he spent aggressively to get supreme-quality beef; he invariably formed the top of the market. A farm—like the Warren Mitchell farm in Platte County, Missouri—that brought Delvaux's top price reckoned his purchase a "real triumph."

In 1920 Delvaux's success prompted H. D. Newhart to leave off managing the Baltimore Hotel to join him as partner in the meat market. Delvaux's movement into the wholesale and retail meat trade did not mean an entire abandonment of his culinary enterprises. His skills as a charcutier enabled him to create Delvaux Sausage, the best product of its sort vended between Chicago and New Orleans.

He continued managing his meat-processing company until the mid-1920s when heavily capitalized meat packers began buying up quality local meat outlets. Bought out in 1925, he donned his whites and returned to the kitchen as chef of the Hotel President. When the Depression roiled the hospitality business in Kansas City, Delvaux moved to Columbus, Ohio, to run the Neil House for several years. When he retired in 1939, he returned to Kansas City, the scene of his greatest triumphs and home of his daughter and son-in-law. When he died in 1954, papers across the nation noted the passing of "The Great Adrian," the man most closely associated with the golden age of Kansas City dining and the greatest moment of its prominence as a source of quality beef.

❋   ❋   ❋

SOURCES: "How to Tempt a Hot Weather Appetite," *Kansas City Star* 27, no. 317 (August 4, 1907); "Paper Roasts at a Hotel," *Kansas City Star* 32, no. 50 (November 6, 1911): 1; "A Joke Tree at the Baltimore," *Kansas City Star* 32, no. 99 (December 25, 1911): 2; Archie Croydon Hoff, *Roasts and Entrees of World Famous Chefs* (Los Angeles: Universal Publishing, 1914), 20; "Dogs Are Hotel Guests," *Kansas City Star* 37, no. 89 (December 16, 1916): 1; "Local and Personal," *National Provisioner* 57 (September 22, 1917): 40; "Some Meat Prices Fall," *Kansas City Star* 38, no. 166 (March 2, 1918): 2; "A Weber Meat & Provision Co.," *Kansas City Star* 83, no. 225 (September 18, 1920): 9.

Oscar Tschirky 1866–1950
New York

A waiter whose genius for organization and his talent for command vaulted him into the role of manager of the dining rooms of the Waldorf Astoria Hotel, Oscar Tschirky—"Oscar of the Waldorf"—commands interest in the way he appropriated the role of public arbiter of taste in American print media shortly after the turn of the twentieth century. He was not a chef (Adrien Tenu ruled over the Waldorf Astoria kitchen). He was not a restaurateur whose vision of cuisine at the turn of the twentieth century changed the course of fine dining, such as Louis Sherry or Charles E. Rector. Rather he was a food publicist, a genius at projecting a vision of the high life, and his hotel's importance, into print. As such, he stands as the model of the media culinarians—the public oracles (James Beard, Lucius Beebe et al.) about American cuisine who would proliferate after the Second World War.

Tschirky came to the United States in 1883 from Neuchâtel, Switzerland, and rose through the ranks of a series of important American hostelries and restaurants: busboy at the Hoffman House in the last days of its importance, waiter at a branch of Delmonico's in the early 1890s, maître d'hôtel at the Waldorf Hotel when it opened in 1893. When the Waldorf amalgamated with his neighbor, the

Benjamin J. Falk, "Oscar Tschirky" (ca. 1900), cabinet card.

Astoria Hotel, after 1897, Oscar superintended the combined dining facilities. When Thomas M. Hilliard retired as manager of the Waldorf Astoria in 1906, Tschirky took his place, earning a reported salary of $25,000 per annum. He ran the hotel with two other triumvirs, W. H. Marshall and W. H. Barse.

Oscar's importance to the Waldorf Astoria became apparent as early as 1901 when George C. Boldt, the CEO of the hotel, learning of Tschirky's plan to resign and set up an independent restaurant in New York, invited him into partnership of the hotel. He received an estimated quarter million dollars' worth of stock, a portion of which he immediately cashed out to expand his estate on the shores of Lake Mohonk in rural New York. Oscar's "chicken farm," run by his son, resembled a Swiss chalet and was eventually converted into a resort for culinary professionals.

Certain traits of character enabled Oscar's rise. He had a "sticky" memory, capable of recalling faces and names of customers despite years between visits. He had a genial, suave manner to guests, and an autocratic demeanor to his subordinates. He had an acute sense of order, a tactful way with words, and a perfectionist's eye for detail. But his greatest genius was in branding. He wore formal evening wear in the dining room. He contractually stipulated that his name would be "Oscar of the Waldorf"—no Tschirky. He instructed hotel staff to refer to him as "Mr. Oscar." He perfected a nod—a dignified, familiar bob of the head—that became a badge of social recognition in New York.

After Prohibition killed off Sherry's and Delmonico's restaurants, and after hubris brought Charles Rector's hospitality empire into bankruptcy, Oscar found himself in the 1920s as the face of what survived of fine dining in Manhattan. He banked on that conspicuousness, and honors began to come his way: a citation by the king of Romania, the Belgian government's La Medaille d'Or de l'Ordre de la Couronne, and finally appointment by the French government as Chevalier of the Ordre du Mérite Agricole. The citations were conspicuously displayed in his office.

However personally gratifying the honors may have been, their significance paled in comparison with the name recognition he enjoyed among the American public. Throughout the first decades of the twentieth century, he was constantly appearing in the newspapers: demonstrating how to carve a Thanksgiving turkey (1908), mixing up a Waldorf salad (chef Tenu's creation, but so associated with Oscar that James Beard would later attribute it to him), and speaking in favor of women waiters during the manpower shortage of World War I. Some of these articles suggested that he was a chef and that he prepared private dinners for customers. He did not dispel these rumors. And there is no doubt that he could perform the chafing dish items and assemble and dress salads, work that befell waiters in the 1890s. Yet there was an audacity in publishing a cookbook, *Recipes by Oscar of the Waldorf-Astoria* (J & G. Cox, Ltd., 1920). Certainly most of these dishes derived from the repertoire of chef Tenu.

Oscar presided over the removal of the Waldorf Astoria Hotel to its new premises in 1931 and occupied his office long enough to see a biography written about him in 1943. He retired to New Paltz, New York. When he died in 1950, he knew that he had contributed materially to the survival of fine dining in America during the period between the two world wars when it stood in most peril.

※　※　※

SOURCES: "Oscar of the Waldorf, His Unique Position in New York's Largest Hotel," *Kansas City Star* 19, no. 239 (May 14, 1899): 11; "Partners for the Waldorf," *San Antonio Express* 36, no. 172 (June 21, 1901): 2; "From Waiter to Manager," *Baltimore Sun* 138, no. 12 (March 15, 1906): 12; "Oscar, the Famous Autocrat of the Big New York Hotel's Dining Room, Promoted," *Boston Journal*, no. 23734 (April 6, 1906): 8; "Good-by to Men Waiters," *Kansas City Star* 39, no. 90 (December 16, 1918): 1; Nunnally Johnson, "Oscar: Head Waiter to Chevalier," *Canton Repository* (June 8, 1924): 56; James A. Beard, "Mushy Apples Mar Majesty of Waldorf," *Portland Oregonian* (November 30, 1972): 44.

John Young 1866–1920
Baltimore

Born in the first year of liberty in Rappahannock, Virginia, African American caterer John Young was "a scientist, an artist and an alchemist" to those who tasted his diamondback terrapin and fried chicken. He left Tidewater, Virginia, for Baltimore in 1883, intending to be a Pullman porter on the Chesapeake and Ohio Railway. When he failed to secure a position, he was hired on as a waiter and kitchen aid by Henry James.

In the 1880s, waiters and stewards frequently took over the task of preparing chafing dish preparations in hotel banquets and club dining rooms. Young became the greatest of the figures who transmogrified from waiter to caterer. His initial post was at the famous Maryland Club in Baltimore. There he learned to make a "Terrapin a la Maryland," the signature dish of Chesapeake cuisine and a fixture of fine dining in club dining rooms and restaurants along the eastern seaboard in the 1880s, following this recipe:

> Carefully cut up two terrapins . . . place them in a saucepan with half a wine-glass of good Madeira wine, half a pinch of salt, and a very little cayenne pepper, also an ounce of good butter. Mix well a cupful of good, sweet cream with the yolks of three boiled eggs, and add it to the terrapin, briskly shuffling constantly, while thoroughly heating, but without letting it come to a boil. Pour into a hot tureen, and serve very hot.

Young moved from the dining room of the Maryland Club to the Hotel Rennert, where he became captain of the waiters and master of the chafing dishes. In the 1890s, he served in a similar capacity in the Baltimore Club and the Athenaeum Club, but he became nationally famous as the steward of the Elkridge Hunt Club, one of the great fox-hunting sodalities of the American elite at the turn of the twentieth century. During his seven-year residence as steward, he mastered the entire repertoire of game and seafood cookery. While there he also made two sets of connections that would serve him in good stead in subsequent years—a chain of African American suppliers of terrapin and ducks from the eastern shore, and a list of well-heeled Americans from Europe and North America who had sampled his work and desired more.

In 1905 Young set up business for himself as a caterer, working out of his house at 134 Richmond Street. One component of his business was to serve as provisioner of diamondback terrapin to wealthy clients throughout the United States. Shipping barrels of dormant turtles via rail to Chicago, Boston, and New York, he had a steady income as a wholesaler. In Baltimore he became the first-call caterer for fashionable events—weddings, association banquets, and anniversaries. He was the regular caterer of the Bachelor's Cotillion in the city. He supervised all the events at the Baltimore Yacht Club as well. "To attempt to list all the Baltimoreans who knew John Young by his works would be like reprinting a blue book. " He died of influenza at age fifty-four after an illness of two months.

※ ※ ※

SOURCES: Alexander Filippini, "Terrapin a la Maryland," in *One Hundred Ways of Cooking Fish* (New York: H. M. Caldwell, 1892), 99; "Fox-Hunter Entertained, Luncheon Give at the Elk Ridge Club," *Baltimore Sun* 22, no. 81 (February 18, 1898): 10; "Guests of Miss Jenkins," *Baltimore Sun* 122, no. 85 (February 23, 1898): 10; "Seeing the B. and O.," *Baltimore Sun* 135, no. 12 (May 28, 1904): 6; "John Young Is Dead," *Baltimore Sun* 66, no. 154 (May 13, 1920): 24.

Emile Bailly 1868–1930
Paris; Berlin; Frankfurt; London: Monte Carlo; Paris; New York

When the management of the St. Regis Hotel in Manhattan secured chef Emile Bailly from the Pavilion Royale in Paris in 1903, it charged him with making the high-end hostelry famous with its cuisine. Specifically, they directed him to create a signature dish bearing the hotel's name that would galvanize the culinary world. After weeks of experimenting and failing to fashion a revelatory item, Bailly decided there were other ways to compete with the Waldorf Astoria. He observed that Oscar Tschirky ("Oscar of the Waldorf") had made himself a public oracle about taste while he was a headwaiter by an aggressive projection of his opinions in print. Oscar branded himself. Bailly followed suit. He made the acquaintance of the editors of women's magazines and the New York offices of the various news syndicates. He adjusted his appearance, trimming his beard into a rakish Vandyke and appearing everywhere in his toque and whites to accord with the public image of a French chef. He cultivated a poetic prose style and wrote his own copy. From 1907 to 1915, Bailly's recipes, reflections, and pronouncements appeared everywhere. Local papers from El Paso to Oshkosh printed his "secrets" to superlative cooking. In A. C. Hoff's 1913 International Cooking Library, a book series presenting recipes from "World Famous Chefs," Bailly's contributions were ample and conspicuous.

Stuart Travis, "Dining Room, St. Regis Hotel, New York" (1905). Photograph: From the New York Public Library, Art and Picture Collection (809528).

Born in Paris, Bailly had a classic kitchen apprenticeship of five years, including a year devoted to pastry. He spoke of his education in a syndicated story in 1909. A talented cuisinier, he was hired to be assistant to the chef of the Russian ambassador in Berlin. He first became chef de cuisine in that same city, at the Adlon. He then moved to the more commodious Frankfurter Hoff in Frankfurt, Germany. He served a stint at the Carlton in London. He became known as one of the premier chefs in Europe during his tenure as chef at the Grand Hotel in Monte Carlo. Thence he went to the Pavilion Royale in Paris, perhaps the great restaurant of its age. He was working there in 1903 when lured to New York only by the promise of a salary in excess of $12,000 per annum, the highest offered by any New York hotel. At the Grand Hotel in Monte Carlo, he trained an assistant, Edouard Panchard, whom he brought with him to the St. Regis as sous-chef. Panchard would himself become a major force in New York cuisine in the 1910s as chef of the Hotel McAlpin. Bailly, meanwhile, did not entirely sever his connection with the European scene. At the end of the hotel season in late May, he would surrender the kitchens of the St. Regis to Panchard and return to Paris for the summer.

The kitchens over which Bailly reigned in the St. Regis seemed to visitors a "wonderland": "The floors are of marble, the walls and ceilings are of glistening white tiles, and the tables and counters are of heavy plate glass. Even the air here is better than that of the outside world. It rises through openings so devised that before all the ranges there is always a current of clean, pure air." Bailly had 33 cooks working under him; and an additional 117 waited, cleaned, or performed prep work. Two butchers cut meat on a twenty-four-hour cycle.

Bailly came to the St. Regis at a moment when fine dining in New York had turned away from the excesses of the Gilded Age. The multiplication of dishes at each course had been pared down to one or two items. In 1905 he published a menu reflecting his ideal $15 dinner, a meal sans wine and sans special decorations:

Caviar

Potage Renaissance

Clear Green Turtle

Agneau de Printemps

Haricots Verts   Pommes Nouvelles

Jambon de Virginie aux Epinards

Filet of Capon a la Genin

Poussins Rotie

Mignardise de Foies-Gras

Salade

Glace Mousse aux Fraises

Fromage

Café

This did not mean the St. Regis eschewed decorative food and confection. Its studio rivaled those of Sherry's and Delmonico's. "With creams, sugars and lees serving as their marble a half dozen sculptors are busy, and though their fairy masterpieces are as evanescent as some of the fortunes spent for them, they are in their very mutability all the more desirable to St. Regis patrons."

Bailly understood haute cuisine to be an art that stressed the freshness of ingredients, the immediacy of preparation, and the delicacy of flavor. Though in command of a bank of refrigerators, he minimized the time that food was allowed to sit in the icebox. He critiqued industrial-scale preparation of food and the cult of speed (the fast lunch): "It is the essentially American idea of having everything ready, or done on a big scale so as to economize time and labor, that has done most toward reducing eating to mere feeding in America." He was the prophet of the fast-food nation, yet his words of woe did little to stem the rush toward greater speed, convenience, and anonymity of food preparation.

Bailly, however, did not reject every dimension of mass consumption and marketing. Heeding his employer's demand for a consumable with the St. Regis name blazoned on it, Bailly had his staff blend "St. Regis Special Brand Coffee," a roasted blend marketed by the Mutual Coffee Company.

Since 1890, newspapers had learned the value of publishing recipes to build a readership of women household cooks. Two types of contributors dominated the papers—home cooks and celebrity chefs. The celebrity chefs usually contributed simple dishes from the basic repertoire that could be imitated by the home cook. In March through May 1912, Bailly syndicated a series of articles entitled "Cooking Secrets of Famous Chef: By Emile Bailly, Chef at the St. Regis, N.Y." The dishes were basic: mayonnaise, sauce tartar, cardinal sauce, stuffed squab, lobster salad, chicken croquettes with tomato sauce, strawberries Mannon. In other articles he told how to pick a Thanksgiving turkey or bake a spicy pumpkin pie. Yet the fullness of Bailly's art appears only in those recipes he contributed to Hoff's 1913 cooking guides. He is the principal author of *International Dessert and Pastry Specialties of the World Famous Chefs* (1913) and his prefatory defense of "dainties" as a category of preparation compels close attention because of its appreciation of honey in confectionery work in an age when cane sugar was supplanting its place.

In the mid-1920s, Bailly's health began to decline. He returned to France and attempted to recuperate at his home in the suburbs of Paris but died in 1930.

⁂ ⁂ ⁂

SOURCES: "The Gentle Art of Cooking at Its Highest in America," *Tampa Tribune* (January 29, 1905): 16; Emile Bailly, "What French Cookery Is," *Kansas City Star* 26, no. 146 (February 10, 1905): 13; "A Million a Day for Dinner," *Seattle Daily Times* (May 21, 1905): 43; "Hotel Seeks a Famous Dish," *New York Times* (January 11, 1908): 9; "How to Pick Your Turkey," *Daily Illinois State Journal* (November 22, 1911): 8; A. C. Hoff, *International Dessert and Pastry Specialties of the World Famous Chefs: The Dessert Book* (Los Angeles: International Publishing Co., 1913), 1–36; "Hints for Delicious Dishes Prepared by Emile Bailly," *Fort Worth Star-Telegram* 30, no. 153 (June 18, 1922): 4; [Obituary notice,] *New York Times* (March 29, 1930): 19; "Memoirs of Chef Emile Burgermeister," *Golden Toque Newsletter* (March 2006): 3–4.

Eugene Habisreutinger 1868–192?

Zurich; Geneva; Paris; New York; Saratoga, NY; Asbury Park, NJ; Newport, RI

In Europe once a cook had finished his apprenticeship and secured a place in a major hotel kitchen, his most typical career path had him serving a season in several restaurants and hotels, crossing borders and familiarizing himself with different national cuisines. Cosmopolitanism of culinary outlook insured maximum adaptability when moving to a new position. Eugene Habisreutinger was one such kitchen cosmopolitan. A native of St. Gall, Switzerland, who apprenticed in Zurich as a pastry cook, he began his professional career in Geneva as an assistant hotel cook. Two years of experience equipped him to seek employment in Paris. He stationed at in the kitchens of the Continental Hotel and learned the art of banquet cooking. When his bank account ran dry after months of unremunerated labor, he secured a well-paying position at the Mentone. Hearing of the lofty salaries paid experienced French cooks in the United States, he emigrated in 1886. (He would later tell census workers he came in 1882.)

He used a job offer at the Hotel Brunswick as his warrant for coming to America, yet his stay at that hotel was short. He surveyed the culinary landscape of New York, seeking positions that offered higher salaries and greater scope for creativity. In quick succession he served at the Troy Club and the Tuxedo Club before finally securing in 1900 a position as the sous-chef at Sherry's, then rivaling Delmonico's in reputation as the most fashionable restaurant in New York.

During the summer, when restaurants closed in Manhattan, Habisreutinger worked as one of three associate chefs at the United States Hotel in Saratoga, New York. He realized when he returned to New York in September 1892 that he would remain in a subordinate position at Sherry's if he remained. He migrated from Sherry's to another New York culinary temple, Hoffman House, working under chef Gustav Nouvel in the hope of becoming his successor. Nouvel did not wish to step aside, so, finally, in 1897, he secured the position of chef de cuisine at the Coleman Hotel, Asbury Park, New Jersey, in 1897. During the winter, when the New Jersey resort closed, he oversaw cuisine at the Breakers in Newport, Rhode Island. During the 1890s, he was an active participant in the Société Culinaire Philanthropique.

Fluent in English, French, German, and Italian, he was an ideal resort chef, able to communicate with the international company of visitors. The hotel company that employed him at the Coleman Hotel and the Breakers would ramp up kitchen quality at its other resorts—at the West Superior Hotel in Minnesota, for instance—by having Habisreutinger perform short-term residencies. Two of the chef's spring menus from his residence in Minnesota survive—one is noteworthy for the appearance of "Chop Suey a la Woo Lo," a dish he learned from Admiral Dewey's Chinese chef:

DINNER, SUNDAY, APRIL 26

Forked Rivers on half shell
Chicken Okra a la Creole

Cream of Celery au Croutons Souffle

Radish   Queen Olives

Canape a la West Superior

Boiled Live Salmon, Sauce Hollandaise

Potatoes Ponte Neuf

Chop Suey a la Woo Lo

Petite Pate Toulouse

Lobster a la Newberg

Imperial Punch

Roast Prime Ribs of Beef, dish gravy

Long Island Ducklings, Apple Sauce

New Spinach with Eggs

Asparagus with Melted Butter

Mashed Potatoes   Browned Sweet Potatoes

Salad de Cobilins

Fresh Rhubarb Pie   Fancy Cakes

Neapolitan Ice Cream

Roquefort Cheese   American Cheese

Bintz Crackers   Demi Tasse

Habisreutinger endured the taxing responsibilities of a resort chef for a decade before opting to return to New York to become chef of the Lambs Club, the famous society of theatrical personalities. Certain of his dishes from this last station of his career—Malayan fish cakes and wild goose a la terrapin—showed Habisreutinger's creativity and his global cosmopolitanism. The following item, besides its novelty, had the recommendation of being able to be performed with any fish at hand:

MALAYAN FISH CAKES

Take any kind of fresh fish, skin and bone it and then chop it fine with four medium sized mushrooms. To one pound of the fish add two yolks of eggs, one teaspoonful of Bengal chutney, salt, pepper and nutmeg. Mix all together thoroughly. Mound into small cakes, roll in cracker meal and fry in clear, hot butter. Serve with brown curry sauce.

❋   ❋   ❋

SOURCES: "Art in the Chef's Work," *New York Times* (January 29, 1896): 3; "Superior Hotel Has Paris Chef," *Duluth News-Tribune* (May 3, 1903); "Chop Suey the Way Admiral Dewey Liked It," *Duluth News-Tribune* (April 26, 1903): 3; "New Dishes by a Famous Chef," *Idaho Statesman* (January 19, 1913): 2.

Jose Sanroman 1868–1947

Los Angeles

In Los Angeles, competition among a community of Mexican restaurateurs led to an efflorescence of traditional cookery. The pioneer of these establishments was Jose A. Quiroz y Cia's Rockford Restaurant at 604–606 North Main, a combined confectionery and eating house employing cooks expert in the vernacular style in the 1890s. Tamales, enchiladas, and albondigas were prepared to order, and meals would be sent out to families if need be. His competitor Jose M. Salazar offered menudo, chili con carne, carne seca, and enchiladas at his Cinco de Mayo Restaurant at 535 New High Street. Ismael Durazo's Restaurant Mexicano at 414 North Main offered the best chiles rellenos in turn-of-the-century Los Angeles. The most ambitious restaurateur to emerge in the neighborhood was Jose Sanroman.

Sanroman's El Progreso Restaurant opened up at 228 Aliso Street in 1911. The next year he purchased Ismael Durazo's old place at 414 North Main, installing Pilar Pardo as cook. He manufactured tamales and tortillas in-house, having a corn mill in the food preparation space. In 1916 Sanroman sold the name and mill to Pardo. Her El Progresso continued to offer tamales and tortillas made from scratch through World War I. Sanroman, meanwhile, opened a larger establishment—a restaurant, tortilla factory, and store at 107–109–111 North Spring Street.

He conceived his restaurant and emporium to be a Mexican supper club and tienda. At the Gran Restaurant, Sanroman diners were entertained with singers and strolling musicians. He determined on the eve of the First World War to create the city's, indeed the nation's, greatest Mexican restaurant—"Este Restaurante es el único netamente mexicano en todos los Estados Unidos." It occupied numbers 107 and 109 of the building complex, while 111 Spring housed his Tienda de Abarrotes y Fábrica de Tamales. His chicken and beef tamales were offered at the store freshly made. He also sold the entire range of chili peppers, queso blanco, carne seca, and panocha (the pudding).

Sanroman's cuisine in the restaurant was equally varied: mole de Guajolote, refried beans in the style of Vera Cruz, baked sheep's head, barbeque, pepián de gallina, nopalitos, and rice served in the various regional Mexican styles. Breakfast was served at 6:00 a.m., and service continued until 10 p.m. After the passage of Prohibition in 1919, the restaurant notified the public that it only served beverages condoned by law. Its usual custom in 1919 was over eight hundred diners a day. During the early 1920s, the restaurant remained a vital scene of Mexican cooking, but by mid-decade the grocery had become more profitable.

RESTAURANT DE SANROMAN

JOSE SANROMAN, Propietario

El Mejor Restaurant Hispano-Americano. ♪ Lugar Cosmopolita.

Exquisitos Platillos mexicanos
Departamentos reservados para familias. :
Servicio rápido e inmejorable.
Música y Variedades. : : :

Abierto todo el día y en la noche, hasta la 1 de la mañana.
Ofrece listas de precios al alcance de todas las fortunas. : :

Telefono:
Main 8441

TODOS LOS ALIMENTOS SON FRESCOS. ESPECIALIDAD EN TAMALES

107-109-111 N. SPRING ST.   ♪   LOS ANGELES

SANROMAN TAMALE FACTORY

JOSE SANROMAN, Prop.

Oferta especial a su numerosa clientela: Tamales por mayor a precios sumamente bajos. Carne seca, 50c. libra; Panocha, 2 lbs. por 25c. Pastas, 2 lbs. por 15c. Queso blanco, 25c. lb. Chile piquín, 75c. lb; y otras muchas mercancías. Chile colorado 30c. lb.

TAMALE Y CAFE, 5 centavos   Phone, Main 4571
136 N. SPRING ST.   Los Angeles, Cal.

Restaurant de Sanroman. Advertisement from *Prensa Los Angeles* (December 8, 1917): 3.

Indeed, it was a fixture in the life of Angelenos searching for authentic ingredients and spices well into the Depression.

❋   ❋   ❋

SOURCES: "The Rockford Restaurant," *Los Angeles Union* (November 21, 1896): 3; "Restaurant Cinco De Mayo," *Monitor Mejicano* (July 9, 1898): 3; "El Progreso Restaurant," *Regeneracion Los Angeles* (February 25, 1911): 3; "Vesubio Café," *Prensa Los Angeles* (August 31, 1918): 6; *Los Angeles City Directory, 1912*, 1344; "Restaurant de Sanroman," *Prensa Los Angeles* (December 8, 1917): 3; [Ad for singers,] *Correo Mejicano* (October 18, 1917): 5; "Sanroman," *Prensa Los Angeles* (June 8, 1918): 6; "El Progresso Restaurant," *Prensa Los Angeles* (August 31, 1918): 6; "Gran Restaurant Sanroman," *Heraldo de Mexico* (August 23, 1919): 8.

Henry C. Dousseau 1870–1913
Brussels; Paris; New York; St. Augustine, FL; Boston

The only major culinary artist to hail from Luxembourg in the United States, H. C. Dousseau apprenticed at the world-famous Maison Bourse in Brussels. He rose through the ranks of the kitchen in a trio of Brussels institutions: the Grand Hotel, the Hotel du Grand Miroir, and the Restaurant a l'Eperon d'Or. A skilled pastry chef, he then sought employment in Paris at Flamands. Word of his imaginative handling of classic confections and his skill at banquet cooking wended its way to his native country. The Duke of Luxembourg installed him as the chef of event cooking at the Luxembourg palace.

In spring of 1893, Dousseau came to America to become associate chef of the Savoy Hotel with chef Albert Winsbach after the short and messy reign of Xenophon Kuzmier in the kitchen. Dousseau's intention, however, was to secure absolute sway over a cuisine at maximum pay. Young and temperamental, he shifted employment rapidly to the Netherlands and then the Metropole Hotel in New York. Familiarity with the scene caused him to realize that higher salaries with less onerous event work might be had as chef at one of the major gentlemen's clubs in the city. So he undertook stints heading the kitchens of the Colonial Club, the Democratic Club, and the Wool Club. In the summers he hired on as private chef for millionaire Augustus W. Mott's schooner, *Magic*, and his rival Commodore Caldwell Hart Colt's yacht, *Dauntless*. These cruises acquainted Dousseau with the burgeoning resort scene in Florida.

From 1896 to 1899, he presided over the kitchen of the Alcazar Hotel resort in St. Augustine, Florida, pioneering the employment of the state's citrus in cuisines. He then returned to New York to become chef from 1899 through 1902 at the Oriental Hotel in Manhattan Beach. In 1902 he moved to Boston to preside over the cuisine at the Union Club. The recipe for the signature Union Club dish was printed in the *Boston Herald* in spring of 1905:

PLANKED SADDLE OF MUTTON A LA UNION CLUB
Garnish an oak or maple plank with a fancy border of duchesse potatoes; cook a saddle of mutton to point; put it on the plank and around the saddle dress bouquets of French peas, haricots vert, Brussels sprouts and a nice head of cauliflower. In the interstices of the bouquets put noisette and soufflé potatoes Serve in an ice boat of gravy, another of currant jelly and one with hollandaise ice.

Dousseau enjoyed the culinary sociability of Boston, joining the Epicurean Club, the society of the city's chefs and caterers, and participating in the competitive dinners until his departure from the city in 1907, when he returned to

Hotel Alcazar, St. Augustine, Florida (1902). Photograph: Library of Congress, Prints and Photographs Division (LC-DIG-ppmsca-18186).

Manhattan to become chef of the Metropolitan Club. He reactivated his membership in the Société Culinaire Philanthropique and took second place at the annual food sculpture contest in 1909 for a life-size sugar rendering of an English setter. Sometime in 1911, Dousseau purchased property in Long Island City. He died in his Long Island home in 1913.

※ ※ ※

SOURCES: "Cooks Got Out in Two Hotels," *New York Herald* (May 10, 1893): 7; "Favorite Dishes of the Chefs of Boston's Clubs and Hotels," *Boston Herald* (January 1, 1905): 34; "Chef of Café Martin Wins Prize at Ball," *New York Herald* (February 5, 1909): 6.

Pierre Buisson 1871–1945
New York; Middlesboro, KY

During the end of the nineteenth century, the shopping emporium morphed into the department store. In the major cities of the United States, multi-story towers

"Palatial Restaurant, 8th Floor. Simpson Crawford Company Store" (ca. 1904). Postcard of dining room. Souvenir Post Card Co., New York.

of commerce arose and entered into a fierce competition for the carriage trade. The presumption of the retailers was that during the daylight hours the moneyed daughters and wives of the upper and upper-middle class did the shopping. In order to cater to their wishes, the department store began incorporating within it ladies' restaurants—dining rooms specializing in lunch, confections, tea, and coffee. Pierre Buisson, a hotel and club chef, presided over the greatest of these dining rooms during the first decade of the twentieth century, the eighth-floor roof parlor of the Simpson-Crawford Department Store in Manhattan. Capable of seating 1,200 guests, decorated in turquoise and pale yellow Louis XVI revival wall and ceiling treatments, and vivid with electric lights and crystal, Buisson's dining room became one of the joys of shopping. In the summer the side walls were removed and palm trees installed to make it an open-air roof garden. Nahan Franko's orchestra serenaded guests from 12:15 to 2:15 each afternoon.

Born in Haute-Loire, France, Pierre Buisson came to the United States in 1889 as a teenager and apprenticed in New York in the kitchens of the Hoffman House, a bastion of French gastronomy in the country. He trained under Gustav Nouvel. With such a background, he easily secured employed as a sous-chef at the Waldorf Astoria. In search of emolument, he accepted terms as chef de cuisine of the Marie Antoinette Hotel, which in turn brought him to the attention of the management of the well-endowed Rittenhouse Club in Philadelphia. He cooked there in 1899. How, precisely, a chef for a very old-boy Philadelphia gentleman's club came to be considered ideal for accommodating the tastes of discriminating city women is a mystery.

To demonstrate that accepting a position as chef at a metropolitan department store in no way meant lowering of the exaltation of his cuisine, Buisson in 1904 competed for honors at the annual chefs ball, and his food sculpture, the "towering 'Les Quatre Saisons,' . . . received a place of honor in the middle of the hall. It was built in tiers, composed of good things peculiar to the different seasons and about the base was a small regiment of soldiers drilling."

What is not a mystery is that seven years of such service sated him on department store catering, and he returned to the more encompassing culinary practice associated with hotel dining. On January 1, 1908, he became chef of the Hotel Prince George in Manhattan. From this period comes one of his chief creations:

KERNEL OF LAMB, PRINCE GEORGE

Preparing for four persons have on hand four French artichokes and four kernels of lamb cut from the loin. Boil the artichokes for 20 minutes and then clean them thoroughly, scooping out enough of the insides to make room for the kernels of lamb. Meanwhile fry the kernels until medium done. Place them inside the artichokes and cover with hot Colbert sauce. This sauce is prepared by mixing a cup of strong beef tea with a pound of fresh butter, the juice of two lemons and some fresh chopped parsley. After the sauce has been poured over the artichokes the dish is ready. It should be served on a heated silver platter.

When custom at the Prince George began to falter in summer of 1909, Buisson began looking for another venue. He found it in the newly erected Great Northern Hotel on Fifty-Sixth and Fifty-Seventh Streets in Manhattan. He relocated there with Victor Boisack as pastry chef on September 1, 1909.

With the collapse of dining in New York occasioned by Prohibition, Buisson found himself trekking into the center of the country for employment. It is a period difficult to document, but it can be ascertained he spent time at the Hotel Cumberland in Middlesboro, Kentucky, in the early 1920s. He returned to New York later in the 1920s, retiring to Queens with his wife, Eliza.

✳   ✳   ✳

SOURCES: "Chefs Works on Display," *New York Times* (February 3, 1904); "Mr. Pierre Buisson," *Colorado Spring Gazette*, no. 10233 (April 13, 1909): 5; Simpson-Crawford Department Store, http://daytoninmanhattan.blogspot.com/2011/12 /exclusive-1902-simpson-crawford-dept.html; "Favorite Dishes of New York Chefs," *Colorado Springs Gazette*, no. 10233 (April 13, 1909): 6; "The Great Northern Hotel Staff," *New York Hotel Record* 8 (1909): 3; "Local Briefs," *Middlesboro Daily News* (December 22, 1922).

Henri D. Fouilloux 1871–19??

Paris; Rome; Cleveland; Chattanooga, TN; Dallas; Youngstown, OH; New Orleans

A restless, enterprising chef who shaped fine dining in both Cleveland and New Orleans in the United States early in the twentieth century, Henri Fouilloux received his training in the Maison Arwaud in Paris. His first professional placement was in the kitchens of the Hôtel du Rhin, Paris. He spent his twenties as a private chef working for Baron de Neuflize in Paris, then the American ambassador in Rome Vayne McVeah, Count Moroni Pecci at Rome, Pope Leo XIII at the Vatican, and finally diva Madame Nellie Melba. He was chef at the Grand Hotel in Rome when he was enticed to America by the promise of an exalted salary at one of the country's most luxurious hotels, the Hollenden.

Cleveland's place in the culinary firmament at the beginning of the twentieth century was secured by the luxurious Hollenden Hotel. Fouilloux presided over the kitchens during that hotel's greatest fame, from 1903 to 1906. The Hollenden was the scene of many culinary adventures during Fouilloux's superintendence. In 1906 the kitchen introduced alligator tails to Cleveland with much public fanfare, Fouilloux and steward Frank Holden having been fascinated by reports of their popularity in Florida resort hotels. "It is creamy in color, tasting a little like frogs' legs, but with a more pronounced gamy flavor, juicy-altogether tempting."

In 1907 S. S. Stein convinced Fouilloux to collaborate in the creation of the finest haute cuisine restaurant the city had ever seen. The Savoie Restaurant—located in the Lennox Building on the corner of Euclid Avenue and Ninth Street—became the byword of amusing food. As with most American French restaurants of the era, confections and ice creams comprised an important dimension of the offerings—then regarded essential for the women's lunch trade. The standard service was à la carte, with no alcohol on the menu. A private dining area dominated the second floor for the banquet trade. Of the celebrations held in the restaurant, descriptions of the Bastille Day bash of Cleveland's Société Française la Gauloise (of which Fouilloux was president) were memorable, with a plaster model of the famous prison blown up on premises as the climax of the festivity.

Fouilloux's enterprises expanded when he partnered with Charles Latsch and Gottlieb Mueller in founding the Blitz Filter Company in October 1907. The filter—a ball strainer—was intended for culinary use. Fouilloux changed the name of the business to the Fouilloux Ballon Passoire Company so that culinary professionals knew what the product was. Fouilloux's filter business operated in Cleveland while his career as a chef/caterer took him elsewhere.

Fouilloux became chef of the Hotel Patten in Chattanooga, Tennessee, in 1910; steward of the Hotel Southland in Dallas in 1911; then chef of the Hotel Ohio in Youngstown, Ohio, in 1912. In 1913 he became chef-steward of the St. Charles Hotel in New Orleans. In 1913 certain of his recipes for "Imperial Stew" and "Breast of Mallard Duck Au Porto" were published in A. C. Hoff's anthology, *The Chafing Dish Specialties of the World Famous Chefs* (1913). In 1914 Fouilloux published a classic recipe for the West Indian delicacy long savored in New Orleans:

CLEAR GREEN TURTLE SOUP

Take two pounds of fresh green turtle meat cut in dice with a little chopped onions and a piece of butter. Fry and season with a little paprika, salt, whole pepper and a small handful of odoriferous herbs, such as corienthe, romarin and basilie [coriander, rosemary, and basil]. Put the whole in a two quart stew pan, with a half nice fat hen and little knuckle of veal, two whole tomatoes, half a pint of Samos wine and one gallon of chicken bouillon. Skim the liquid at the first bubbling and move it back to the side of the fire. When the meat is done, drain it, skim off the fat from the soup, pass it through a fine muslin cloth into another stew pan and put in again, one by one, your diced turtle meat with a few dice of black truffles and finish before serving with a glass of Samos wine.

Another of his recipes from the St. Charles Hotel appeared later in the year:

RIS DE VEA (SWEETBREADS) CHANTECLAIR

Take one pound sweetbreads well braised and cut in large dice. Add one dozen coxcombs and kidneys, mix whole with sauce supreme well creamed. Take four nice tomatoes, peel, take off tops like covers, hollow them out and at the last minute put the sweetbreads, etc., into them. Put covers on and let stand in hot oven about one minute. Serve with good veal stock and Madeira.

The outbreak of World War I prompted the patriotic Fouilloux to return to France in 1914. He joined the territorial infantry and won the Croix de Guerre for valor and heroism. When the United States entered the war, Fouilloux was made attaché to the Eighteenth US Field Artillery. When the armistice took place, Fouilloux volunteered his services to the YMCA to assist in the direction of the hotels operated for the accommodation of enlisted men on leave of absence. For his services to the Americans, the Expeditionary Force Headquarters issued a commendation to Fouilloux in "appreciation of the highly meritorious services." Fouilloux conducted the remainder of his career in Europe.

SOURCES: "'Gator Tails Are Newest Delicacy," *Cleveland Leader* (January 14, 1906): 8; "The Savoie Restaurant," *Plain Dealer* (June 3, 1907): 5; A. C. Hoff, "Clear Green Turtle Soup," in *Soups and Consommes of the World Famous Chefs, United States, Canada, Europe* (Los Angeles: International Publishing Company, 1914), 33; A. C. Hoff, *Roasts and Entrees of the World Famous Chefs, United States, Canada, Europe* (Los Angeles: Universal Publishing Company, 1914), 33; "Former Steward in N. O. Hotel Cited for Bravery," *New Orleans Item* (October 26, 1919): 15.

Walter George 1871–1931?

Chicago; Milwaukee

For a period in the late nineteenth century, America's railroads boasted a cadre of expert stewards who cooked for dining cars. Walter George, chief cook of the Pioneer Limited express train in the northern Midwest, was one of the few who transitioned into the restaurant world after the turn of the twentieth century. Restaurateur J. L Slaughter hired him to preside over the kitchens of his New Turf European Hotel and Restaurant in Milwaukee, Wisconsin, during the Christmas season of 1902.

Beginning in 1898, the Pioneer Limited ran between Chicago and Minneapolis via Milwaukee on a nightly basis, the #1 westbound, the #4 eastbound. One of the first named trains, it was famous for its innovations: the first sleeping cars, first electric lighting, and first steam heating of any railroad in the United States. Its dining cars (there were two—one over which Ben Shivers presided, the other by Walter George) had "the reputation of giving the best dining-car service in the states." The staff—cooks, waiters, and conductors—was entirely African American. Prior to contracting with the Pioneer Limited, George had worked for the Illinois Central and lived along the line in Centralia, Illinois. He was a native of Cleveland, Ohio.

George made the best use of his high-tech surroundings, winning accolades for the food served on the rails. Yet for someone ambitious about cuisine, the inevitable restrictions of dishes because of the limitations imposed upon ingredient storage on dining cars set George looking for new opportunities. He would find them in Milwaukee, working for J. L. Slaughter.

Slaughter's New Turf European Hotel and Restaurant opened in April 1902 on Wells Street in Milwaukee, between Second and Third. It was designed as a "first-class colored club and hotel." The European quality of the hotel did not derive from its employment of the European plan of meal service, rather to suggest a non-American, non-racist space in which one could be accommodated. The New Turf suggested that the club dimension of the establishment resembled that of the racing clubhouses at Long Branch, New Jersey, or Saratoga, New York. Its initial cook, Joe Phillips, while competent in the production of ordinary fare, could not handle the event banquets and Sunday meals that would generate the restaurant's gastronomic reputation. Hence Slaughter approached Walter George with the promise of "a more liberal salary than he has yet paid any employee."

A menu from December 14, 1902, suggests the sort of meal that cosmopolitan blacks of the urban Midwest recognized as "high-class gastronomy":

MENU

Blue Points

Celery   Radishes

Consomme, Clear

Tapioca, a la Mont Glas

Baked Whitefish, Tomato Sauce

Potatoes, Julienne

Salmi of Game a la Modern

Cauliflower au Gratin

Banana Fritters, Brandy Sauce

Prime Ribs of Beef

Mashed Potatoes   Buttered Beets

Roast Young Turkey, Cranberry Sauce

Braised Sweet Potatoes   Fried Parsnips

Salad-Lettuce, French Dressing

Cabinet Pudding, Brandy Sauce

Apple Pie

Tea   Coffee   Milk

Price: 50 cents. Service: 5:00 to 8:00 p.m.

The New Turf Café operated on Wells Street until 1906. The editor of Milwaukee's black newspaper in 1905 observed that Slaughter's "café and hotel and his tonsorial department combined in this city is the only one of its kind owned by our people anywhere in this country."

In 1907 John Slaughter relocated to 194 Third Street, jettisoning the rooming house, and concentrating on George's cuisine and an artistic dining atmosphere. The café remained a fixture for some years, but both it and George disappeared from the record on the eve of the First World War. Nevertheless, for a brief period after the turn of the century, Walter George created cuisine at one of the few deluxe centers of black hospitality in the United States prior to the Jazz Age.

⁂ ⁂ ⁂

SOURCES: "Cream City Notes: The Dining Car Boys," *Wisconsin Weekly Advocate* (November 22, 1900): 1; "New Turf Hotel," *Wisconsin Weekly Advocate* (January 4, 1902): 1; "Opening of the New Turf Hotel," *Wisconsin Weekly Advocate* (April 17, 1902): 1; "The Turf Café," *Wisconsin Weekly Advocate* (December 11, 1902): 1; "Walter George," *Wisconsin Weekly Advocate* (December 11, 1902): 1; "Mr. John Slaughter," *Wisconsin Weekly Advocate* (March 6, 1905): 1; "An Announcement," *Wisconsin Weekly Advocate* (August 1, 1907): 1.

Jacques Lescarboura 1871?–1948?

Paris; Madrid; Naples; Munich; New York; Palm Beach, FL

Certain family culinary dynasties crossed the Atlantic in the nineteenth century. As news of the spectacular salaries paid to fully trained French chefs filtered back to France, the sons of established cooking families were determined to gain quick recognition and emolument in New York, Boston, Philadelphia, or San Francisco, rather than endure the slow march up the hierarchy of a first-ranked hotel. Jacques Lescarboura was the middle son of one such professional family. His father had been honored as a Chevalier de Reine in the service of Queen Isabella of Spain. At age thirteen, Lescarboura had learned his craft in the kitchen of the Hotel Bristol in Paris. His first job was as assistant cook for the Rothschild household. Then began the usual seasonal staging at hotels in Madrid, Lake Como, Naples, and Munich. He eventually became chef at the Café Riche in Paris. While working there, he received the summons from Charles C. Delmonico to serve as an associate chef under Charles Ranhofer at Delmonico's. Lescarboura came to the United States with his older brother Desire on June 19, 1888.

Lescarboura had not been long serving at Delmonico's when a temptingly high salary was offered for his services by the newly formed Vaudeville Club, a society of theatrical producers and headlining performers. He accepted and watched as the club succumbed to the overly dramatic sensibilities among the membership. Fortunately, in 1893 the Hotel Marlborough was in need of a chef

Hotel Marlborough, New York (ca. 1910). Rathskeller's separate Ladies' Restaurant to the left. Photograph: Shorpy Historic Picture Archive.

de cuisine, one of sufficient repute to given them some profile in the city dining scene. He was hired and immediately paid dividends in terms of custom and publicity. It was Lescarboura who suggested that a rathskeller might add a distinctive dimension to the hotel's food and drink offerings. It would become a famous New York watering hole.

Lescarboura won renown for his fish preparations, and his boiled "Pompano Moulin Rouge" appeared on the menu of an ideal Christmas dinner compiled by New York's most reputable chefs for the *New York Herald* in December 1894. The recipe is of interest because it representing a decidedly early nineteenth-century approach to saucing that worked well with the distinctively flavored pompano, a Gulf Coast fish popularized in American haute cuisine through New Orleans.

POMPANO MOULIN ROUGE

Split two fish and clean carefully. Season with salt, pepper, nutmeg and the juice of a lemon. Boil them over a moderate fire and when done place in a large dish. For the sauce place a pan on the fire containing one tablespoonful of Worcestershire sauce, two of mushroom catsup and two of melted extract of beef. Cook until it bubbles, then work in slowly one-half pound of good butter, one ounce of anchovy butter, the juice of a lemon, and add a dozen shelled shrimp. Serve the sauce separately. Before sending the fish to the table lay around the edge of the dish slice of lemon cut in fancy styles, and garnish with fresh parsley.

His other stylistic distinction was his predilection for employing fresh flowers in dishes. His "Eggs Flora," for instance, employed two dozen fresh violets, in a mélange of mushrooms and soft eggs.

If Lescarboura embraced American fish and flowers for their flavors, he showed less affection for the national bird. When asked to prepare a Thanksgiving menu in November 1895, he jettisoned turkey and put lamb in its place, though spring chops sit oddly in the midst of an autumn feast.

THANKSGIVING MENU

Blue Point Oysters

RELISHES
Queen Olives   Celery

SOUP
Consomme Stanley

FISH
Long Island Sole, Saute Colbert
Pommes Windsor

ENTRÉE
Spring Lamb Chops, Villeroy
Brussels Sprouts

ROAST
Blackbirds Bardes Sur Rotie
Lettuce and Tomatoes

ENTREMETS
Strawberries   Ice Cream   Sponge Cake
Fruit   Cheese
Coffee

Lescarboura remained chef at the Marlborough until 1914. The outbreak of war in Europe inspired patriotic concern on the part of Lescarboura. He left hotel work to spend five years doing culinary labor for the American Red Cross in hospitals and camps in France and Belgium.

After the armistice, Lescarboura returned to America, becoming chef of the Everglades Club in Palm Beach, Florida. In 1921 or 1922, he returned to France and determined to stay. He left behind his brothers chef Desire Lescarboura in New York and Louis Lescarboura at the Fort Pitt Hotel in Pittsburgh, the latter on the verge of becoming the "Mushroom King of America."

❊ ❊ ❊

SOURCES: "An Ideal Dinner," *New York Herald* (December 23, 1894): 3–7; "How to Cook Your Easter Eggs," *New York Herald*, no. 21412 (April 7, 1895): 2; "Thanksgiving Menus," *New York Herald*, no. 328 (November 24, 1895): 4; "The Science of Cookery," *Leslie's Weekly* 81 (October 24, 1895): 270; A. C. Hoff, *The Chafing Dish Specialties of World Famous Chefs, United States, Canada, Europe* (Los Angeles: International Publishing Company, 1913), 34; Passport Application, March 25, 1921, Florida, Palm Beach; Fred Kelson, *Louis Lescarboura, Mushroom King* (Oxford, PA: Hengwrt Publishing Company, n.d.), 11–13.

𝔏ee 𝔠𝔥it 1872?–1908
Philadelphia

Chinese restaurateur Lee Chit practiced his art at Yen Nom Low at 917 Race Street in Philadelphia for a decade before his assassination in July 1908 on the street in front of his restaurant by hitman George Lee of the On Leong Tong. Chit's cuisine represented the most authentic and refined available in the eastern United States at the turn of the twentieth century.

A reporter from the *Philadelphia Inquirer*, observing through alien eyes the month feast of firstborn male Wong Hun Chung in December 1902, wrote:

> The banquet consisting of sixteen courses, was served in a private dining room on the second floor and was calculated to satisfy the most fastidious Chinese appetite. Such plebian dishes as chop suey, yock a mien and boiled rice were debarred. Only the choicest viands were served. The menu included sharks fins, birds' nests, pigeon wings, rich conserves and candies and the most expensive Oriental delicacies, with rare old wines.

Lee Chit's restaurant opened in 1897 after an 1896 police raid and police scrutiny made the gambling house operating at 917 Race Street shut down. Chit took over the building, probably from his cousin Willie Lee York, active in Chinese gambling circles. Chit's restaurant had a dual identity. To the Chinese cognoscenti, it was Yen Nom Low's; to curious Americans it was a "Chinese Restaurant . . . A Place for the 'Smart Set' and Sight-seers." The latter sort of customer would receive "Chinese-American Food Served in a Genuine Chinese Fashion." Its rivals—the Chinese restaurant at 907 Race Street that offered "Chinese Food—from Soup to Nuts" and the "Select Chinese Restaurant" at 931 Race Street under Hom Kin—could not compete with Chit's talent when it came to Jing cuisine, and so conceded the Chinese banquet business to Chit while competing for the American walk-in trade.

The rivalry between the On Leong Tong and the His Sing Tong served as the context for Chit's assassination. Chit, who conspicuously did not ally with any tong, had thrown considered weight behind the effort of his cousin Reverend Lee Hong to diminish the influence of the Tongs in Philadelphia. Hong's First Chinese Baptist Church Mission had been actively evangelizing and challenging the influence of these criminal associations. In the wake of the killing, much speculation about the motive of George Lee floated in Philadelphia's papers: a romantic rivalry, a tong debt, his being a cousin of Willie Lee York, a local officer of the Hip Sing Tong. For a period of time when York was in prison, Chit had managed York's restaurant on Vine Street as well as his own. Lee used an insanity defense in his trial, claiming that the voice of Confucius instructed him to shoot Chit. The jury did not buy the plea and convicted him.

In the wake of Chit's murder, his restaurant was renamed the Pekin Chinese Restaurant and began advertising in English in the Philadelphia newspapers.

※　　※　　※

SOURCES: "A Chinese Raid," *Philadelphia Inquirer* 135, no. 43 (August 12, 1896): 11; "Chinatown in Holiday Garb," *Philadelphia Inquirer* 147, no. 168 (December 15, 1902): 5; "Native Banquet to Rev. Lee Hong," *Philadelphia Inquirer* 148, no. 106 (April 16, 1903): 2; "Assassin's Shot Kills Lee Chit in Tong War," *Philadelphia Inquirer* 159, no. 15 (July 15, 1908): 1; "One Chink Dead, Two Men Shot," *Wilkes Barre Times-Leader* (July 15, 1908): 3; "Lee Chit's Slayer Heard Confucius," *Philadelphia Inquirer* 159, no. 120 (October 28, 1908): 12; "Verdict Is First Degree," *Philadelphia Inquirer* (October 29, 1908): 8; "Chinatown Keeps Tamest New York," *Philadelphia Inquirer* 160, no. 23 (January 23, 1909): 8.

Emile Burgermeister 1874–1957

London; Monte Carlo; Berlin; Frankfurt; Paris; New York; San Francisco; Seattle

An Alsatian born into a family of cooks, Emile Burgermeister worked single-mindedly in his youth to become a hotel chef. He trained under some of the great talents of late nineteenth-century dining: with Auguste Escoffier at London's Ritz-Carlton and with Emile Bailly at the Grand Hotel in Monte Carlo. He sought to understand the logistics of large-scale service in two Germanic hostelries—the Hotel Adlon in Berlin and the Frankfurter-hof—then refined his understanding of French haute cuisine at the Pavilion Royal in Paris.

When Emile Bailly installed himself as chef at the St. Regis in New York in 1903, he summoned Burgermeister from across the Atlantic to be his assistant. Two seasons of learning American methods and dining-room preferences armed Burgermeister to become chef de cuisine. After a short stint as second in command at the Waldorf Astoria, he traversed the continent, accepting the post of chef at the Fairmont Hotel in San Francisco. In 1909 he additionally became chef of the Thompson-Jaulus Café in that city, a state-of-the-art gas kitchen. He held both positions concurrently.

From his years at the Fairmont come a number of Burgermeister's specialties, including the following:

OYSTER AND FROG LEGS, FAIRMONT

Boil some eastern oysters in their own liquor, skim and drain. Season the frog legs with salt and pepper and prepare the cream of two cups of cream, beaten in with three yolks raw eggs; chopped fine chives and parsley; three ounces of sweet butter and the juice of one lemon. Take sweet butter and let simmer and add a few finely chopped shallots; add the frog legs and fresh mushrooms; steam together for a few minutes. Add one glass white wine, let cool so as to evaporate the acid of the wine, add one cup soup stock, let boil down to half before serving; add oysters and the preparation of cream mentioned above without boiling. Season to taste and serve on dry toast.

LOBSTER GOURMANT

Prepare a mixture of chopped fine whites of celery (tender), fresh raw carrots, two shallots and young onions in proportion; one bouquet of parsley, laurel leaves, thyme. Take the meat of lobster, sauté in butter, add the mixture; pour over a small glass of cognac or white wine. Let simmer, then cool so as to evaporate the acid in the wine, mix two peeled and chopped tomatoes; add the bouquet, let boil; add one cup of cream; reduce to half. Before serving add three ounces

Olympic Hotel, Seattle, Washington (ca. 1915). United Hotels postcard.

sweet butter. Season with salt and cayenne pepper and serve on dry toast. Take out bouquet.

STRIPED BASS GRAND-MERE

Bone a nice, whole striped bass, being careful not to split the back. Season well. Prepare a stuffing of chopped medium onions simmered in butter, one dozen oysters cooked in their own liquor, dried and chopped up, three milk rolls soaked in milk and pressed out, salt, pepper, chopped parsley, nutmeg, and the yolks of three eggs. Stuff the bass and bake on a flat au gratin dish. Pour over some sour cream and sweet butter. Bake in oven forty or fifty minutes without turning the fish, but basting very often with the sauce.

In late 1914, Burgermeister moved from the Fairmont to the Palace Hotel in San Francisco, the original grand hotel of the city, rebuilt after the 1906 earthquake and fire into a spectacular entity. He presided over the kitchens during World War I, negotiating the shortages of salt and other ingredients to the best of his ability.

In 1919 Burgermeister, an amateur photographer, vacationed at the Snoqualmie Falls in Washington State and became enamored of the locale and its ingredients. In 1924 he bade farewell to California, migrated northward, taking over the kitchen of the newly constructed Olympic Hotel in Seattle, and became for the Jazz Age the most conspicuous face of fine dining in the Northwest. He was largely responsible for defining the Northwest as a distinct culinary region in the national culinary imagination. Burgermeister's kitchen at the Olympic was palatial, equipped with 16 gas ranges, 5 soup cauldrons, and 9 charcoal broilers. His automated dishwasher could handle 40,000 dishes an hour. The chef's office had its own shower and sleeping chamber. His staff numbered 75.

In 1935 Burgermeister retired and moved with his wife, Frances, to Santa Clara, California. He would later relocate to Columbia, South Carolina, where he died.

※   ※   ※

SOURCES: "City Can Boast of Magnificent Café," *San Francisco Call* (April 14, 1909): 5; A. C. Hoff, *Fish, Oysters and Sea Foods of the World Famous Chefs, United States, Canada, Europe* (Los Angeles: International Publishing Company, 1913), 28–29; "Olympic Chef Has Cooked for Kings, Queens and Emperors," *Seattle Daily Times* (November 30, 1924): 14; "Behind the Scenes in a Seattle Hotel," *Seattle Daily Times* (March 25, 1928): 73; *Memoirs of Emile Burgermeister* (Columbia, SC: For the Author, 1950); "Olympic Hotel, a History," *Seattle Daily Times* (May 21, 1982): c-31.

Der Doo 1874–1929?
Baltimore; Washington, DC

Baltimore's premier Chinese restaurateur in the decades after the turn of the twentieth century and Washington, DC's most important Asian restaurateur of the 1920s, Der Doo conducted business in the midst of an ongoing war with Chinese secret societies.

After emigrating from China to Baltimore in 1900, Der Doo converted to Christianity, learned English, and dressed in stylish Western garb. He sought political influence in the city's Chinese community. As president of the Chinese Reform Association, an entity that aggressively sought to repress the opium trade, Der Doo inspired the enmity of the "highbinders," Chinese reactionaries who sought control of Chinese commerce in the city through extortion, violence, and trickery. They registered two false mortgages intended to embarrass Der Doo financially; these were proven to be forgeries in court. His enemies then resolved to kill him, but police protection kept him safe. They set Doo's business on fire in 1906, which caused $1,000 in damages to the building. The tong claimed that Der Doo was engaged in an insurance scam, setting his own building on fire, producing two witnesses who testified to that effect. Der Doo was acquitted, countersued the witnesses, and in the course of their trial revealed much about the operation of Baltimore's secret societies. These revelations made the police decide to take aggressive action against the criminal organizations. During a raid by Captain Ward on the 111 Park Avenue stronghold of one tong, an archive of papers documenting the conspiracy against Der Doo was uncovered.

Der Doo began as a restaurateur on Fayette Street in 1900 but immediately found himself in trouble after countering police harassment by dowsing an officer with hot water. He closed the restaurant, opening a grocery and import store at 116 Park Avenue. While managing the grocery, he organized the Baltimore Chinese Empire Reform Association in 1903. Among the goals of the organization was modernization of the form of Chinese government, and particularly to do all in their power "to introduce free schools in China where the females will have the same advantages of education that the girls of this country enjoy." Immediately Baltimore's two tongs (which represented themselves as Freemasonic lodges to the authorities) began to organize against Der Doo. On May 5, 1906, fire broke out at Doo's Wing Ying Ling Company, importers. This was the first act in the attempt to ensnare Doo in an insurance fraud that ultimately failed. In late 1906 Doo marked his legal triumphs by opening the Empire Restaurant at 202 West Fayette Street.

The inaugural feast invited Baltimore civic leaders and members of his association to a banquet with the following courses:

JOW CHE GAI (FRIED SPRING CHICKEN)
Fresh Cann Li Chee
Gai Yong Yen Wor (Minced Chicken with Edible Bird's Nest)
Kwo Che Ap (Duck with Many Kinds of Condiments)
Sam See Chee (Shark's Fins with Sliced Chicken, Ham, Bamboo Shoots)
Si Wo Ap (Boneless Duck with Chinese Parsley)
Bark Neu Kwai Chow (Chicken, Duck, and Squab, with Condiments)
Foony Wong Yin
Far Sang Tong (Chinese Peanut Candy)
Hang Yen Soo (Almond Cakes)
Suey Ching Go (Crystal Cakes)
Sang Sui Li Chee Gon (Chinese Dry Nuts)
Mut Kim Ghet (Golden Lime)
Know Mine Li Chee Gon (Best Chinese Nuts)
Long Sue (Tea)
Snow Pear Wine

Reporters noted that he imported a banquet cook for the restaurant. Within weeks this chef exceeded the variety and excellence of this feast with a New

Year's repast; its bill of fare appeared in Baltimore's papers. Early in the history of the restaurant's operation, Doo decided that he would seek American custom, so he advertised the entire menu of his offerings with English explanations affixed. Among the classic dishes were inserted the Chinese-American clichés devised on the West Coast, chop suey and yak o mein. Interest now affixes to his "Special Dishes":

CHING DONG DONG (ROASTED CHINESE MUSHROOMS)
Sen Lat Cho Gai (Chicken with Chestnuts and Ham)
Gai Lung Sang Chey (Minced Chicken, Ham with Lettuce)
Gai Yong Wong Yo Taw (Brain of Yellow Fish with Minced Chicken)
Gai Yong Yen Wor (Minced Chicken with Edible Bird's Nest)
Kow Chow Ap (Duck with Many Kinds of Fruit)
Kow Cho Gai (Chicken with Many Kinds of Fruit)
Sam See Chee (Sharks' Fins with Sliced Chicken, Bamboo Shoots, etc.)
Si Wo Ap (Boned Duck with Condiments, Chinese Parsley)
Bark Neu Kwai Chow (Chicken, Duck and Squab with Many Condiments)

The menu also explained that meals could be prepared in the Shanghai style, the Peking style, and the Peking Imperial style.

In May 1908 Doo expanded his restaurant empire, establishing a branch at 412 East Baltimore, and a branch on the corner of Ninth and F Streets in Washington, DC. During this time, he was viewed as "the mayor" of Baltimore's Chinatown. It was a shock when federal authorities arrested him and two other conspicuous citizens as conspirators in a scheme to smuggle Chinese persons into the United States via Jamaica. The case amounted to nothing but indicated a revival of the highbinder campaign against Der Doo, which would lead to legal agitations throughout the early 1910s. In 1914 Doo transferred his base of operations to Washington, DC, in part because his education, his mastery of English, and his Reformist agenda attracted the attention of the US State Department, anxious to have a capable interpreter in the heightened international situation of the First World War.

Doo moved into his Far East restaurant at 516 Ninth Street. After acclimatizing himself to Washington, he realized that other locations offered better promise of traffic. He chose a site across from the National Theatre on Thirteenth Street. He characterized his business in 1920 as "an oriental restaurant of the highest character—excellent service—best Chinese cooking—separate rooms for ladies—special attention to after theater parties." He characterized the style of cookery as Mandarin. A second less authentically Chinese branch, the Far East Tea Garden, opened at 1412 New York Avenue under the management of Benjamin D. Fong. The restaurant remained in business through 1928.

❋   ❋   ❋

SOURCES: "Der Doo, the Chinese Reformer," *Baltimore Sun* 138, no. 94 (August 18, 1903): 7; "Chinatown Was Greatly Excited," *Baltimore American* (September 21, 1903): 14; "Trouble in Chinatown," *Baltimore Sun* 137, no. 50 (July 5, 1905): 7; "Der Doo Goes through Fire to Save $1000," *Baltimore American* (May 6, 1906): 9; "Highbinder Mystery Revealed," *Baltimore American* (May 29, 1906): 13; "Society Dines with Der Doo," *Baltimore American* (December 14, 1906): 17; "Chinese to Celebrate Their New Year's Today," *Baltimore American* (February 12, 1907): 13; "Yakomin, An Chair, Shu Ap and Gar Lew Chop Suey," *Baltimore Sun* 140, no. 93 (February 17, 1907): 12; "Der Doo Is a Chinaman with American Notions," *Baltimore Sun* 141, no. 115 (September 8, 1907): 12; "Real Chinese Honeymoon," *Baltimore Sun* 142, no. 12 (February 5, 1908): 12; "Three Chinamen Held," *Baltimore Sun* 147, no. 146 (October 9, 1910): 16.

Victor Hirtzler 1874–1931

St. Petersburg; Lisbon; New York; San Francisco

The chef of the St. Francis Hotel in San Francisco from 1904 to 1926, Victor Hirtzler had been the royal chef to King Don Carlos of Portugal eight years before the monarch's assassination by leftists irate at his indulgence in luxury. A native of Strasbourg, Hirtzler learned cuisine from Emile Faypell, a decidedly more French than German Alsatian restaurateur. His mastery of French cuisine received its most concrete recognition when Hirtzler was hired by chef Eugene Kratz, overseer of French cuisine at the Winter Palace in St. Petersburg. Each dish prepared for the imperial table had to be tested for poison by an officer of the rank of major in the imperial army. In 1905 Hirtzler supplied newspaper reporters with recipes for three of the czar's favorite soups: orockka, pischy, and roussulmeck. He worked at the palace two years before the paranoia there prompted him to leave for Portugal. The pinnacle of his career as a royal chef took place at a banquet for Kaiser Wilhelm in Strasbourg attended by several other monarchs. The menu suggests Hirtzler's accomplishments in the European court style of haute cuisine. The wines are italicized.

LE POTAGE DE GRIVE A LA RUSSE
Lacroute gratinee aux raciness
La julienne au blond de veau

Joseph Byron, "Victor Hirtzler in the Office of the Majestic Hotel" (ca. 1903), seated with the hotel manager. Photograph: Museum of the City of New York, Byron Collection.

La bisque de volaille au beurre d'ecrouvisses Heres

Le saumon du Rhin au vin de champagne

La Turbot Hollandaise

Falkenberger

Le pate chaud de mauviettes

Chateau-Cages

Le sauté de poulet a la d'Artois

Le selle d'agneau aux legumes

JOHANNISBERGER

La Terrine de foie gras aux truffles du Perigord

La poularde du Mans a l'Estragon

Les fonds d'artichauts Mayonnaise

Maces

Na nougat a la Parisienne

Les gateaus d'amandes

Les pains au pistaches

Champagne

Le fromage bavarois aux framboises

Les petits fours friandises

Le cafe Floria

Liqueurs

Hirtzler came to America at the turn of the twentieth century at the invitation of chef Adrien Tenu of the Waldorf Astoria to serve as his second in command. Autocrats, however, do not savor being subordinate to other autocrats, so he quickly decamped to preside over the Hotel Brunswick in New York. Then he served a stint as chef at Sherry's, the quintessential New York haute cuisine venue. His final New York station was the Hotel Majestic on Central Park West and Seventy-Second Street. When the St. Francis opened in 1904 in San Francisco, Hirtzler was engaged as its first chef. He remained with the establishment during its reconstruction after the earthquake and fire that had destroyed the original in 1906. In a short period, chef Victor revised what the West Coast envisioned a French chef to be:

> Little, but with broad shoulders, a Vandyck beard and sparkling eyes, Victor is far from being the sort of person usually pictured by that word—cook. He is an artist. A composer, with a soul for the music of a sputtering roast or the delicious staccato of a broil. A man full of the artistic temperament, alive to the possibilities—the esthetic possibilities—in an entrée or a sauce or the rich blending of harmonies in a masterpiece from the soup pot.

Hirtzler embraced his role as the face of California cooking. When World War I broke out and many of the European-born chefs in the United States returned to victual the troops in France, Germany, Italy, Switzerland, and Belgium, Hirtzler sought to remedy the shortage of chefs by turning the kitchens of the St. Francis into a cooking school, where he would "give lessons free of charge to ambitious young men."

In 1919 Hirtzler published the *St. Francis Hotel Cook Book*, one of the landmark encapsulations of San Francisco's style of cooking. Certain of the dishes have remained fixtures of the establishment, cherished by Hirtzler's successors in the kitchen, such as Paul Debes. One of the highlights of the book was the section on menus. Hirtzler, whose personal collection of menu cards exceeded a thousand items, loved conceiving of novel combinations of dishes.

Hirtzler's search for the best ingredients had him cast a wide net for the specialties of the West Coast. In 1922 he established the mystique of the Olympia oyster by adopting it as the oyster of choice in San Francisco, holding "Olympia Oyster Day" in which dozens of different preparations of the creature were offered.

After a labor action soured the situation at the St. Francis, Hirtzler attached himself to a new project. He did not wish to leave San Francisco, a city that he had grown to love. He engaged to be the inaugural chef of the Mark Hopkins Hotel, under construction at the time he was sacked from the St. Francis.

SOURCES: "In the Czar's Kitchens," *Kansas City Star* 26, no. 29 (October 16, 1905): 11; M. G. Mary, "Victor Hirtzler of the St. Francis Tells Intimate Stories of the Royal Kitchens of Europe," *San Francisco Call* (May 10, 1908): 6; [Hirtzler's menu collection,] *Oregonian* 21, no. 5 (May 26, 1912): 4; "Chef Hirtzler to Train More Cooks," *Salt Lake Telegram* (July 15, 1917): 30; "Great Northern Features Olympia Oyster on Bills," *Olympia Daily Recorder* 20, no. 239 (February 11, 1922): 1; "Earth Feels Good to Chef After Aerial Mishap," *San Diego Union* (July 25, 1926): 20; "San Francisco's Exotic Restaurants," *Oregonian* (May 18, 1958): 81.

Louis Calixte Lalanne 1874–1942
San Francisco

Sometimes the mystique of a restaurant—its connections with the pleasures of a city during boom times, its piquant décor, its raffish company—eclipses the reputations of the chefs who worked its kitchens. Such was the case with the legendary Poodle Dog Restaurant of San Francisco, a French bistro opened on the crest of the gold rush in 1849 and remade repeatedly during the nineteenth and twentieth centuries. Its name and reputation surpassed those of the several chefs who worked its kitchens, even the most accomplished of them, Louis Calixte "Cal" Lalanne, who presided over the cuisine of the third and fourth incarnations of the Poodle Dog.

Born in Bordeaux, Lalanne came to California in 1889, at the age of fifteen, with his entire family. His mother, Mary, was soon widowed, and Ca would remain her support for the remainder of her life. He had been thoroughly trained in France, and the 1889 Oakland Directory indicates that the teenager was employed as a cook. He came to the attention of Pierre Carrere, a veteran restaurateur who was involved in the management of the Poodle Dog Restaurant.

A word about the Poodle Dog Restaurant's history: It moved to 445 Bush Street in 1873 with two longtime employees, Jacob Stork and François Péguilhan, in charge. While there it became with Marchand's Restaurant one of the twin peaks of French cuisine in San Francisco. The Poodle Dog became particularly famous for its wine list. The restaurant's space was relatively modest by Gilded Age standards, so in the 1890s the proprietors looked to larger premises. They could not find what they desired, so they sold the business. In 1895 Antonio Blanco, a restaurateur-developer, bought the rights to the name and cellars and built a temple to high-end consumption six stories tall on the cor-

Ruins of the Poodle Dog Restaurant, San Francisco, after the 1906 earthquake. Photograph: Courtesy of the California Historical Society (FN-32949).

ner of Eddy and Mason Streets. Meanwhile, the old premises were taken over by Pierre Carrere (founder of the Maison Tortoni), Jean Baptiste Pon, and Cal Lalanne, with Pon handling the front of house and Lalanne, the kitchen.

From 1895 to 1906, the year of the earthquake, diners could choose between Blanco's Poodle Dog and Pon and Lalanne's Old Poodle Dog. Blanco's restaurant was a high-priced lobster palace on the model of Charles Rector's Chicago restaurant, charging well-heeled businessmen top dollar for name ingredients—caviar, lobster, venison, champagne. Lalanne was known for making supremely savory dishes from basic ingredients. The dishes were French in execution but named in English on the menu, and were winning to a broad spectrum of tastes. A lunch prepared by Lalanne in November 1906, after the restaurant was reconstituted after the San Francisco Earthquake, reveals his classic approach:

SOUP

Clam Chowder   Sorrel Consommé

FISH

Skate Fish   Brown Butter Salmon
Filet of Sole   Tartar Sand dab
Silver Smelt   English Sole
French Imported Snails   Pompano

ENTREES

Braised Chicken a la Casserole

Veal Tongue Spanish

Shirred Eggs a la Meyerbeer

Kidney Saute Blood Pudding and Sausage Liver Brochetts

Calves' Head   Lamb Chops   Calves' Brains

Boiled Pig's Feet   French Andouillette

Rump Steak

Canvasback   Mallard   Sprig Teal

DESSERT

Assorted.

The variety of ducks, the pompano imported from the Gulf of Mexico, and the classic bistro meats are all noteworthy.

The temporary venue for the post-earthquake Old Poodle Dog was 824 Eddy Street. The community of French restaurateurs had been brought into disarray by the destruction of all of the great houses in the city. Yet enormous solidarity had been nurtured in the community by the extortion controversy in the years before the disaster. When the mayor and his bagmen squeezed protection money from the owners, brandishing the threat of non-renewal of licenses, onetime rivals turned into comrades in their fight against the corrupt government. Cal Lalanne and Jean Pon, having lost their partner Pierre Carrere shortly before the earthquake, thought to strengthen the finances of the Old Poodle Dog by inviting the owners of the destroyed John Bergez Restaurant and Frank's Rotisserie into the partnership. They found renovated space at 415 Bush Street and formed what would be called the Bergez-Frank's Old Poodle Dog. Lalanne remained in control of the kitchen.

For a dozen years the restaurant thrived, a favorite place for club meetings, reunions, and parties. Lalanne's relationship with his partners was congenial until the passage of the Volstead Act initiating Prohibition. Despite the evaporation of profits with the loss of wine revenue, Lalanne wished to persevere. His partner, Camille Mailhebuau, did not. When the restaurant was shuttered, Lalanne opened another restaurant, the Ritz, that would eventually morph into the Ritz Poodle Dog when Cal's son, Louis, inherited it.

A coda: It should be said that there is more groundless mythmaking about the origins of the Poodle Dog than any other restaurant in the United States. Particularly fantastic are a series of stories generated by Blanco in the 1890s that he printed in the publicity for his "New" Poodle Dog. For the history best supported by contemporary documentation from the 1850s and 1860s, see my biography of Edward Marchand.

SOURCES: "Old Pierre Passes Away," *San Francisco Call* (February 14, 1906): 16; Old Poodle Dog Menu, November 30, 1906, New York Public Library, http://menus.nypl.org/menu_pages/38167; "Tell of Money for Ruef Paid for Protection," *San Francisco Chronicle* (December 15, 1906): 2; "Old Poodle Dog, Famed Since '49, Dies of Drought," *New Orleans Times-Picayune* (April 15, 1922): 1; Chris Smith, "Treasures from Famed San Francisco Eatery Find Their Way Home," *Sonoma Press Democrat* (August 1, 2010), http://www.pressdemocrat.com/article/20100801/articles/100809971; Erica J. Peters, "The Poodle Dog," in *San Francisco: A Food Biography* (San Francisco: Rowman & Littlefield, 2013), 114–18.

Jules Dauviller 1877–1918?

Paris; New York; San Francisco

It became a fashion in the 1880s among the wealthiest American plutocrats—the Astors, Vanderbilts, Goulds, Morgans, and Whitneys—to go to Europe and hire a talented young professional to become the family chef. Newspaper reporters became fixated on these private cooks because of the astronomical salaries being paid for their services—$10,000 a year being the break point for newsworthiness, since it eclipsed the salary of most state governors. The favorite places to poach talent in Europe were the kitchens of the royal households or from hotels in Paris, Baden-Baden, or Monte Carlo. Jules Dauviller succumbed to a $10,000 offer from Mr. and Mrs. Harry Payne Whitney and crossed the Atlantic in 1906. They had found him in the kitchen of the Grand Hotel in Paris.

In winter of 1912, arthritis began to afflict Ernest Arbogast, longtime chef de cuisine of the landmark Palace Hotel in San Francisco, to the point that he could not maintain his mobility in the kitchen. He announced his retirement and intention to become a rancher. The management hired Dauviller to become Arbogast's successor. Dauviller understood the responsibilities of taking over an institution. The Palace Hotel chef was supposed to be a local oracle of food. Because Victor Hirtzler at the St. Francis Hotel was so famous, the management of the Palace Hotel urged Dauviller to contribute to the papers. So periodically he offered menus and recipes for home use. Realizing the gap between hotel fare and the home meal, he tended to frame his recommendations as being for Sunday dinner.

Oysters in Half Shell
Consommé Piedmont
Ripe Olives   Salted Peanuts
Boiled Barracuda, Clam Sauce   Potatoes Nelson
Chicken in Casserole, Country Club   String Beans
Fine Herbs   Roast Saddle of Lamb, Mint Sauce, Currant Jelly
Ice Cream   Biscuits   Tortoni   Cake Constantine
Black Coffee

The recipe for "Boiled Barracuda with Clam Sauce" reveals Dauviller's strong faith in the abilities of California's home cooks.

BOILED BARRACUDA

Select a nice piece (about three pounds) of barracuda, trim neatly, place in a saucepan, cover with cold water, add juice of a lemon, salt, pepper, corn and powder, cloves, onions, sliced thin, parsley, bay leaf, thyme, garlic, set on the fire, let boil for 10 minutes slowly and simmer for an equal period. Then remove carefully, dress fish on a hot dish with a napkin, garnish with parsley and boiled potatoes, roll in butter and chopped parsley.

CLAM SAUCE

Select three dozen little neck clams, plunge them in a gill of boiling water with a few leaves of celery; let boil for about 10 minutes. Thoroughly drain them, keeping the liquor. Put in a saucepan one tablespoon butter, heat for a minute, add two tablespoons flour, let cook for five minutes, stirring continuously. Pour in the liquors of the clams, stirring quickly. Let boil for three minutes, season to taste, dilute an egg yolk in a tablespoon of cream and a few drops of lemon juice; pour in the sauce and sharply mix; let cook one minute more. Do not let boil, and add the clams, removed from the shell. Serve in a sauce bowl.

In 1914 when Clarence Edgar Edwords canvassed the city's chefs and restaurateurs for the quintessential regional recipes for his guide *Bohemian San Francisco*, Dauviller opined that the Palace Hotel produced two dishes upon which he would stake his and the hotel's reputation: "Planked Fillet Mignon" and "Cold Fillet of Sand-Dabs, Palace." Because the Pacific sanddab (*Citharichthys sordidus*) was one of the most popular game fishes of the northern California coast, Dauviller's recipe deserves airing as an example of a developing ingredient-driven California haute cuisine.

COLD FILLETS OF SAND-DABS, PALACE

Select six nice fresh sand-dabs. Raise the fillets from the bone, skin and pare nicely and season with salt and paprika. Arrange them in an earthenware dish. Cut in Julienne one stalk of celery, one green pepper, one cucumber, two or three tomatoes, depending on their size. With the bone of the sand-dab, well cleaned, make a stock with one bottle of Riesling, juice of one lemon and seasoning. Add chervil and tarragon. Season to taste and cook the Julienne ingredients with some of the stock. When the rest of the stock is boiling poach it in the fillets of sand-dab, then remove from the fire and let get cold. Put the garnishing around the fillets and put on ice to get in jelly. When ready to serve decorate around the dish with any kind of salad you like, and with beets, capers, olives and marinated mushrooms. This must be served very cold and you may serve mayonnaise sauce on the side.

In 1913 Dauviller contributed substantially to Archie Hoff's International Cooking Library series. His time at the Palace Hotel ended in 1917. Like numbers of other patriotic French chefs in the United States, he responded to World War I by returning to his home country to fight. He then passed from the record of American cooking.

※   ※   ※

SOURCES: "New Chef for Palace Hotel," *Portland Oregonian* 31, no. 10 (March 10, 1912):2; "Sunday Menu," *San Francisco Call* 114, no. 139 (October 24, 1913): 8; Clarence E. Edwords, *Bohemian San Francisco: Its Restaurants and Their Most Famous Recipes* (San Francisco: Paul Elder & Co., 1914), 61.

Emil C. Altorfer 1880–1945
St. Louis; San Francisco; Portland, OR

Hotels drove the development of cuisine in the Northwest. In Portland, Oregon, the Portland, the Imperial, and the New Heathman were central institutions in the exploration of seafood cookery and game of the Northwest. All three institutions at one juncture or another enjoyed the talents of the same chef, E. C. Altorfer.

A native of Switzerland, Emil Altorfer came to the United States as the proprietor of the German House at the St. Louis 1904 world's fair, which was called the Louisiana Purchase Exposition. His authentic German dishes found very potent rivals in the offerings of German-Americans Tony Faust and August Lüchow, served at their kitschy Bavarian mountain house. Yet he made sufficient money to determine that he would remain in the United States. He headed west to California. He was hired as chef at the distinctively three-towered St. Francis Hotel in San Francisco.

Jerome L. Brizzolari was chef of the Portland Hotel, the greatest hotel in Oregon, in the early 1910s. But in 1911 he decided to take over the kitchens of the Willard Hotel in Washington, DC. This set the directors of the hotel scrambling for a replacement. They approached Altorfer with a challenge to his vanity: did he wish to be a second-rank figure in a major city, or the major chef in a city about to become a first-rank metropolis? Altorfer went north in 1912.

Installed in the kitchens of the Portland Hotel, Altorfer explored the world of salmon. Yet more consequential for the twentieth century was his work with potatoes. Oregon had opted for a potato agriculture rather than wheat or corn, and during the First World War grain shortages, Altorfer collaborated with Henry Thiele of the Hotel Benson and several state government officials to promote the adaptability of the potato in baking, cooking, and distilling. Altorfer, despite his German heritage, became a conspicuous American patriot during the war, designing the wartime "substitute diet" in which beef and pork were eliminated in favor of "chicken, fish, rabbit, duck, goose, lobster, clams, sea food, and egg dishes." Another change: "Fried dishes will be avoided whenever possible." The one alteration that endured after the war was the greater prominence of salads on the menu.

Altorfer greatly concerned himself in Oregon's grape and raisin culture. In his explorations, he was aided by his friend and colleague W. Ruffner, whom he hired as pastry cook in 1915. Raisin bread and raisin pastries became staples in northwestern restaurants. Altorfer remained at the Portland Hotel in the 1930s until a desire to change his circumstances prompted him to accept the offer of the Imperial Hotel to be chef, replacing George Arnold before the outbreak of World War II. He remained chef of the Imperial until his death.

✳   ✳   ✳

SOURCES: "Personal Mention," *Portland Oregonian* (April 18, 1911): 4; "Cash Prizes," *Portland Oregonian* (December 19, 1917): 9; "War-Time Menu to Start on Tuesday," *Portland Oregonian* (September 23, 1917): 22; "Spud Show Draws," *Portland Oregonian* (May 15, 1918): 9; "Those Who Come and Go," *Portland Oregonian* (October 12, 1927): 10; "Emil C. Altorfer," *Portland Oregonian* (June 9, 1945): 7.

Edouard Panchard 1881–1956

Vienna; Paris; Baden-Baden; Monte Carlo; New Haven, CT; New York

When appointed head of the kitchens of the Hotel McAlpin in 1913, Edouard Panchard, age thirty-two, became the youngest chef de cuisine in a major Manhattan hotel from the Civil War to the First World War. Young and charismatic, Panchard radiated authority as well as culinary skill.

A Parisian, he apprenticed with his father, chef of the Russian embassy in Vienna, working for Prince Lobanov-Rostocki, a royal with notoriously fastidious tastes. He did stations at several Parisian hotels including a stint as fish cook at the Paris Ritz. After a term in the French army, he worked a season as sous-chef in Baden-Baden. He then went to Monte Carlo. From thence he came in 1904 to America, where he was sous-chef at the St. Regis. He served in similar positions at the Taft Hotel, the New Haven, and the Waldorf Astoria. In late 1913 he became chef de cuisine at the Hotel McAlpin in New York. He had just turned thirty-two.

Panchard leaped to the top of the culinary profession because of his creativity. He had a strong synthetic imagination when it came to combining tastes. It found expression particularly in preparing sauces. His "Exquisite Sauce" became a household sensation when the recipe appeared in syndicated in newspapers in 1915.

EXQUISITE SAUCE

Put two finely minced shallots in a pan with some good vinegar, crushed white pepper, the stems of tarragon and a little chervil. Place on the fire till the vinegar evaporates, then add the catsup, chili sauce and two spoonfuls of puree of red pepper and cook until it is reduced to half of the original volume. Then add some fish broth, bind with the four egg yolks, finish the sauce with ½ pound good butter, strain and serve.

His taste for French traditional fare ran to the unusual, and he introduced Americans to several distinctive dishes, including "Chestnut Croquettes."

CROQUETTES OF CHESTNUTS

Select four pounds of fine, sound chestnuts, slit them on one side and put them to roast in a large perforated pan: cover and toss at times until done. They may also be cooked by placing them on a baking sheet and then in a hot oven to roast without blackening. Skin them, removing both the skins. Pick out twenty of the finest and pound the others to a fine paste. Add, while continuing to pound, two ounces of vanilla sugar and a little raw cream. Pass this preparation through a sieve and put it into a saucepan, beating into it six egg yolks, then dry over the fire while stirring. Pour this on a baking sheet and leave till cold, then divide it into parts, and of each one make a ball an inch and a quarter in diameter. In the center of each ball insert on the roasted chestnuts, split in two. Mold the croquettes to the shape of a chestnut, dip them in beaten eggs, roll in white bread crumbs and fry in very hot, clear frying fat. When done, drain and sponge, sprinkle with vanilla sugar and dress on a napkin.

During this period, Panchard managed the entire Booma chain of restaurants, as well as the Café Savarin, the Claridge, the Trouville at Long Beach, and the Hotel McAlpin. His greatest friend and ally in the city was Louis Diat, chef of the Ritz-Carlton.

During his tenure at the McAlpin from 1913 through 1918, Panchard served his turn as public oracle on culinary matters. During the beef shortages in 1917-18 caused by the First World War, he published a *New York Times* story about using turtle as a beef substitute. To reinforce the equivalency, Panchard took to calling turtle meat "turtle beef" and offered a recipe for "Turtle Beef Creole." When Herbert Hoover, then the US Food Administrator, sought to center American cuisine more directly around corn, Panchard supplied recipes for cornmeal soufflé, chicken hash with polenta, and cornmeal gnocchi. More consequentially, Panchard assumed the office as head of the executive committee of the Chef de Cuisine Association of the United States, the organization that undertook the training of army cooks for the American expeditionary forces. Directing classes on the campus of Columbia University, he exerted great energy in ensuring that rations and cook training far exceeded that which prevailed during the Spanish-American War. At the outset of the war, he wrote General Leonard Wood, saying, "I have fed as many as 25,000 people in one day. If my country needs my services, my resignation will be in the hands of my employers." He was hailed as the patriot chef.

Panchard formulated a set of model menus for the feeding of soldiers. They embodied his vision of mass nutrition and economy:

BREAKFAST
Cereals—oatmeal, hominy, cornmeal mush, force, pancakes, shredded wheat
Meat—sausage, bacon, steaks, salt codfish, liver, hash or eggs
Dry or fresh fruit—prunes, apricots, peaches, apples, fresh apples, pears

DINNER
Soups—vegetable, peas, tomato, onion soup, minestrone, chowder
Meats—pot roast, smoked ham, steak, roast mutton, stew with vegetables, baked beans

Vegetables—spaghetti with tomatoes, sweet potatoes, kidney beans, beans, fish or substitute
Dessert—apple pie, bread pudding, plain cake, stewed fruit, pie, rice pudding with prunes

SUPPER

Meat—macaroni baked with cheese, hamburger steak, mutton stew, cornmeal mush baked with cheese, cold smoked ham, hard-boiled eggs
Vegetables—salad, fried potatoes, sliced tomatoes, potato salad, spaghetti gratin, pickles

DESSERT

Tea buns, stewed peaches, corn bread, rice pudding, pancake with jam, pie, bread and butter pudding
Coffee, tea, bread and butter is served with the meals

Fruits assumed a great deal of weight in Panchard's understanding of nutrition. During the summers of 1915 and 1916, he published newspaper articles replete with berry and fruit recipes. Consequently, there is little surprise in seeing the prominence of fruit on the army menus. During the period of Panchard's service, Louis Paquet assumed control of the McAlpin kitchens.

Panchard's experiments with substituting meats for beef (whale and manatee, which he considered farming with Alexander Graham Bell) caused him to considered writing a book on American national gastronomic likes, dislikes, and eccentricities. This book did not materialize, but in 1919 he produced a much more practical and less philosophical volume, *Meats, Poultry and Game: How to Buy, Cook & Carve, with a Potpourri of Recipes.* His literary ambitions would eventually find expression in his becoming editor of the *Culinary Review* in the period between the wars.

In 1923 Panchard became head of the kitchen of the Majestic Hotel Resort restaurant facing Central Park. He would shortly thereafter become the supervisor for food of the United Hotels Company. In the 1930s he became an editor and official of the national association of hoteliers.

Panchard died of a heart attack in Doctors Hospital, Freeport, New York, on May 28, 1956.

※ ※ ※

SOURCES: "McAlpin Recipes," *Washington Herald* (January 16, 1901): 8; "New Hints on Serving Fish," *Denver Rocky Mountain News* (February 8, 1914): 34; "Secrets of a French Chef," *Macon Telegraph* (February 16, 1915): 6; "King of

Chefs Reveals Deep Secrets," *Boston Herald* (February 21, 1915): 40; "Famous Chef's Method of Using Fresh Fruits," *Kalamazoo Gazette* (July 2, 1916): 6; "Use of Turtle Meat," *New York Times* (September 20, 1917); "Chefs to Train Cooks for Army," *Seattle Daily Times* (May 9, 1917): 9; "To Make Corn King," *Baltimore American* 222 (October 24, 1917): 10; "Panchard—Chef and Patriot," *Lexington Herald* 159 (June 8, 1917): 4; "New Army Men to Be Fed Well at Cantonments," *Wilkes-Barre Times-Leader* (August 15, 1917): 16; "Sea-Cow Now May Become War Food," *San Diego Union* (October 22, 1917): 9; Edouard Panchard, *Meats, Poultry and Game: How to Buy, Cook & Carve, with a Potpourri of Recipes* (New York: Dutton, 1919); "Panchard, Chef, Dies," *Seattle Daily Times* (May 28, 1956): 9.

Louis Paquet 1882–1966
Lyons, France; Paris; London; New York

The creator of spaghetti tetrazzini, the chef de cuisine at the Hotel McAlpin when it generated over 4 million meals annually, and an eloquent public advocate of cuisine in the dark years when Prohibition disrupted the economics of fine dining, Louis Paquet became one of the leaders of the American culinary profession in the second decade of the twentieth century. As president of the Société Culinaire Philanthropique in the era between World Wars I and II, Paquet preserved the culinary profession's sense of purpose through Prohibition, the Great Depression, and World War II.

Son of a chef in the city of Lyons, Paquet learned the rudiments of the art at his father's side. As a teenager he worked as an assistant chef in his father's restaurant, but the provincialism of his home city and tales of the glories of Parisian cuisine prompted him at age twenty-two to depart for the capital. His rise through the kitchen ranks was rapid. He joined the kitchen staff at the Hotel Violet, then worked as sous-chef at the Restaurant Marguery, which was "famous the world over for its delicious fillet of sole," and finally at the fashionable Hotel Meurice. In 1902 he decided to learn what experiences London might afford, becoming second in command at the Café Royal on Regent Street, when it was one of the gastronomic marvels of the city. He labored there until 1907, when his questing spirit determined that he leave for America. Paquet found ready employment in the world of private clubs, serving as chef of the Hardware Club, the Greenwich Country Club, and the Hamilton Club of Brooklyn, when talent scouts from the Knickerbocker Hotel spotted him. He was installed as second in command at the Knickerbocker until a more lucrative offer came from the Savoy.

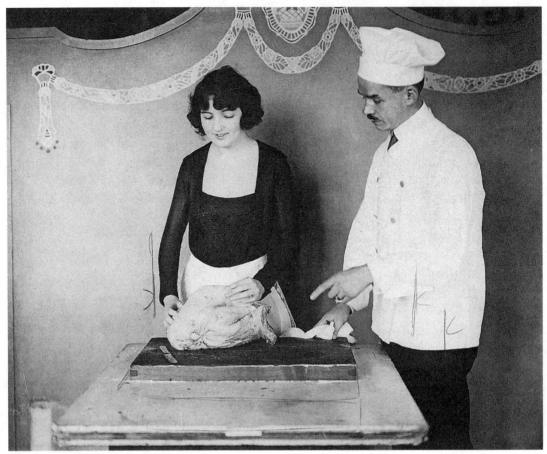

F. M. Kirby, "Louis Paquet instructing" (1919).

Edouard Panchard, who had been retained as chef de cuisine of the Hotel McAlpin when L. M. Boomer opened the immense hostelry in 1912, surveyed the staffs of every important restaurant in the city looking for someone who could serve as his lieutenant. Paquet's skill, efficiency, and pragmatism outweighed his youth in Panchard's eyes. Paquet was thirty when he first cooked in the McAlpin's immense kitchen.

One of Paquet's virtues in Panchard's eyes was his fluency in English, gained during his five years' residence in London. Panchard believed that publicity—particularly chefs' writings printed in newspapers and magazines—were essential in building the brand for a hotel's cuisine. Paquet became a frequent contributor to news syndicates in the 1916–18 period. When Paquet was named chef de cuisine of the Hotel McAlpin in 1919, he immediately began sending stories to periodicals—holiday recipes, recommendations to make home meals memorable, and "tricks of the trade." An example is his suggested menu for a company dinner by simplifying hotel dishes into an impressive but straightforward repast:

CHICKEN BROTH, IN CUPS
Eggs, Columbus Style
Lamb Sweetbreads, Villeroy Sauce
Green Peas Buttered
Broiled Squabs
Lettuce Salad
Parfait, with Chocolate
Macaroons flavored with Lemon
Small Cup of Coffee

Syndicated in early April 1921, this menu reflects the post-Prohibition realities of public dining—no wines accompanying the meal or incorporated into the dishes. With alcohol removed from the rank of ingestibles, an expansion of the sugar dimension of dining took place. He published several articles devoted to cakes, including detailed recipes for lady cake, Savarin cake, English pound cake, honey cake, and chocolate éclairs. Yet his most intriguing recipes are those for confections made from banquet flowers, such as the following:

VIOLET PRALINES

For this, select the violet of Parme, or violet with large flower. Separate leaves from the pistils or green part of the flower: cook them in soufflé sugar (melted sugar); afterwards put them in steamed pot and keep closed airtight, thus holding natural flavor and color of flowers. Quantity of sugar used depends on quantity of violets, as the violet leaves must absorb the syrup made of the heated sugar, and yet will not absorb it all. Next day heat the pot, then spread the leaves on a sieve top to dry. Place the violet leaves in dry powdered sugar, and candy them by placing in a warm place (top of stove) for a few hours to crystalize.

Paquet's interest in the late Victorian fancy for candying flowers may be attributed to his general fascination with the visual dimension of food. He belonged to that generation of French chefs who moved away from the spectacle piece exhibited on the banquet table to the composition of the dinner plate as the focus of visual artistry. In a set of general recommendations to home cooks published in April 1921, Paquet counseled, "Make your meals a picture . . . vegetables should be selected with a thought to variety of color . . . every dish brought to the table should have the appearance of careful arrangement and never must be filled to the brim." Paquet was the first to advocate that the space on the plate contributed just as much to the visual effect as the items to be eaten.

Spaghetti tetrazzini, or chicken tetrazzini, was a dish prepared for opera singer Luisa Tetrazzini when Paquet was chef at the Knickerbocker Hotel in 1908. Served over spaghetti, the dish incorporates diced chicken or turkey, mushrooms, and sliced almonds in a creamy parmesan sauce. Sometimes attributed to Ernest Arbogast of the Palace Hotel in San Francisco, it was a common item of knowledge in the New York professional chef world and in newspaper reportage. Indeed, the opera singer took lessons in its preparation from Paquet.

When the Hotel McAlpin was sold in 1938 to Jamlee Hotels, Paquet assumed an advisory role in the kitchen. His work with national culinary institutions occupied much of his time. He retired to St. Petersburg, Florida, in 1951.

⁂ ⁂ ⁂

SOURCES: "Many Cake Recipes," *Jackson Citizen Patriot* (December 16, 1919): 12; Louis Paquet, "Christmas Dinner in a Great Hotel," *Salt Lake Telegram* (December 18, 1919): 11; "Flowers That Bloom in Spring May Be Turned into Candies and Jam," *San Luis Obispo Daily Telegram* (April 19, 1920): 8; "So This Is the Stuff That Makes Genius," *Charlotte Observer* (November 16, 1920): 2; "You Serve Company? M'Alpine Hotel Chef Tells You Just How to Do It," *Muskegon Chronicle* (April 1, 1921): 20; "How to Make Meals Tasty," *Salt Lake Telegram* (April 14, 1921): 24; Karl K. Kitchen, "Life History of a Chef," *Cleveland Plain Dealer* (May 27, 1921): 18; Mary C. Pickett, "The Men Who Make Hotels Cuisinely Famous," *New York Hotel Review* 16 (October 7, 1922): 61; William S. Burroughs, "The McAlpin's Cuisine," *Esquire* (February 1939): 186; [Obituary notice,] *St. Petersburg Evening Independent*, December 16, 1966, 15-A.

Louis Diat 1885-1957
Paris; London; New York

From opening day in 1910 to closing day in 1951, Louis Diat ruled as the chef de cuisine of the Ritz-Carlton in New York. It was there in 1917 that he popularized vichyssoise, the creamy glacé made of leeks and potatoes that became a twentieth-century menu staple in American restaurants. His contributions to hotel cuisine were collected and published in the best-selling *Cooking a la Ritz* in 1941.

Born in Montmarault in central France, Louis Diat and his younger brother Lucien learned cooking from their mother, Annette. (Lucien would eventually become chef at the Hôtel Plaza Athénée in Paris.) Louis received training as a pastry chef at a Moulins patisserie. His initial positions were at the Hotel Le Bristol and the Hotel Du Rhin. But his professional mastery bloomed under the tutelage of Cesar Ritz while working as chef potager in Paris and at the London Ritz before being tapped to work in New York. A stint as chef of the Carlton House was prep work for launching the kitchen of the new Ritz-Carlton in Manhattan. Auguste Escoffier served as nominal chef de cuisine at its opening, and Jean Millon as chef-steward. Diat served as kitchen manager.

Working in conjunction with Jean Millon, Diat sought to make the Ritz-Carlton a temple of French cuisine. To do this, they defied contract labor laws, recruiting Parisian cooks and importing numbers of them. In 1913 the US government cracked down on this practice, indicting Millon for hiring eight French cooks for the hotel. Millon in defense likened the practice to the producers of opera hiring European divas—when artistry is the salient draw, one goes where artistry abounds. New York had not devised a system for the nurturing of American students into professional-quality cooks. The welter of European talent in the Ritz-Carlton kitchen led to chaos when World War I led to a mass exodus of French and German workers when the countries called up their reserves. Jean Millon joined the transatlantic call in 1914, leaving Diat, who had naturalized shortly after coming to the United States, to assume the duties of provisioner as well as chef. Instead of using the traditional title, chef de cuisine, Diat took to calling himself "Executive Chef."

Diat's friend Edouard Panchard, chef of the Hotel McAlpin and Café Savarin, challenged him to attend more closely to American tastes and serve the new American lifestyle, in particular catering to the distinctive activities of summer. They collaborated in imagining road food for automobile trips, devising in June 1916 menus for a motoring picnic. Here is Diat's:

GRAPEFRUIT COCKTAIL
Cold Eggs with Ham in Tarragon Jelly
Lamb Stew with Spring Vegetables
Cold Roast Chicken with Water Cress
Salad of Asparagus
Strawberry Tart

Diat's lasting contribution to cuisine resulted from his serious engagement with the problem of creating dishes suitable to hot weather. New Yorkers had developed a penchant for jellied soups in the mid-1910s. Indeed, in 1914 Millon had popularized the Russian okroshka, a chilled soup of sorrel, spinach, white wine, and cider. Understanding the popular demand for chilled soups in summer, Diat decided to diverge from the gelatin path, making cold cream the base of potage. He had been working intensively with potatoes through 1916, particularly trying to perfect "Potatoes à la Duchesse," a baked puree of potatoes and eggs. Pureed potatoes and cream would be the building blocks employed in creating crème vichyssoise glacé, Diat's lasting contribution to summer menus. As he recalled at the time of the closing of the Ritz, it was based on a standard home soup of his country, refined by his handling of the pureed potato and cream. A Cleveland woman's reaction to tasting it at the Ritz-Carlton communicates the reasons for its enormous popularity: "The crème Vichyssoise glacee was delicious. It was well chilled. It tasted like a thin, rich cream of potato soup. It was not lumpy or stodgy like cold cooked potato. . . . At an early opportunity I am going to try it at home. On a hot day it proved refreshing."

Prohibition contributed to the crack-up of the restaurant trade in America's big cities in 1919–20. Only the deluxe hotel dining rooms survived, offering a semblance of haute cuisine, stripped of wine. Diat kept the ideal of French fine dining alive in New York, and his work as torchbearer was recognized in the 1940s when *Gourmet Magazine* installed him as its resident arbiter on French cuisine. Under the gourmet auspices, he published cookbooks, *French Cooking for Americans* (1946) and *Sauces: French and Famous* (1951). He died an international culinary celebrity.

※   ※   ※

SOURCES: Louis Diat, *Cooking a la Ritz* (New York: J. B. Lippincott Company, 1941); "Ritz Carlton Chef Is Indicted by U.S. Jury," *Macon Telegraph* (December 4, 1913): 9; "War Touches a New York Hotel," *Boston Herald* (August 4, 1914): 6; "Birth Inspires New Dish," *Rockford Republic* (July 9, 1914): 9; "Picnic Menus Made Up by Two Famous Chefs in New York," *Idaho Statesman* 279 (June 14, 1916): 5; "Potatoes a la Duchesse," *Washington Evening Star* (May 14, 1916): 70; "Picking the First Course for a Dinner at Home," *Cleveland Plain Dealer* (August 25, 1928): 12; Geoffrey T. Hellman, "Diat," in *Secret Ingredients: The New Yorker Book of Food and Drink* (New York: New Yorker, 2009), 421; Louis Diat, *French Cooking for Americans* (New York: J. B. Lippincott Company, 1946); Louis Diat, *Sauces: French and Famous* (New York: J. B. Lippincott Company, 1951); "Louis Diat, of Vichyssoise Fame, Dies," *Dallas Morning News* (August 30, 1957).

Index

Note: *Names in bold indicate biographical entry.*

CULINARIANS

abolition, 15, 70, 145-46, 211

actors, 81-84, 150, 186

advertisement, 5, 21, 30, 37, 44-45, 62, 85, 118, 133, 166, 197, 206, 213, 219, 229, 294, 336, 341, 344, 366, 443, 455, 477, 507; bill of fare, 164, 487, 525; closure, 154, 192; ingredients, 127, 140, 389, 394, 429, 444; mock, 30, 434; naming, 120; no need for, 118; opening, 241, 283

aesthetics, 4, 9-10, 105

African American, 11, 15, 18, 145, 236, 331, 515-17; authors, 448-52; caterers, 15, 28, 39-43, 92, 142, 144, 145-47, 158-59, 177, 188-89, 197-99, 247-51, 260-62, 304-6, 388-89, 426-28, 499-500; cooking, 18, 138, 345-50; exclusion, 277, 344; hoteliers, 197-99, 230-32; politics, 147-48, 197-98, 253-57; restaurateurs, 260-62, 276-78, 279-80, 390-93

agriculture, 3, 5, 535

Alabama, 107-8, 189-90, 293-94, 434-35, 444; Birmingham, 435-36, 444; Mobile, 14, 107-8, 189-90, 434

à la carte, 2, 12, 26, 119, 168, 181, 211, 221, 242, 263, 335, 445, 474, 485, 512

Alciatore, Antoine (chef, restaurateur), 136, 137-38, 314, 473, 485

Alciatore, Fernand (chef, restaurateur), 473-76, 487

Alciatore, Jules (chef, restaurateur), 2, 22, 136-37, 314, 485-89

Alexis, grand duke of Russia, 17, 159, 174

Altorfer, Emil C. (chef), 534-35

Anezin, Augustin François (chef), 97, 216-18

appetite, 4, 71, 91, 275, 285, 467

apprenticeship, 5, 57-58, 76, 87, 137, 176, 250, 311, 319, 338, 386, 403, 416, 419, 432, 450, 460, 480, 485,

486, 491, 501, 503, 510, 536; formalization of, 322; inadequacy of, 294

Archestratus of Gela, 9; "Hedypatheia," 9

Ardoene, George M. (confectioner, caterer), 218-21

aristocracy, 3-4, 10, 18-19, 54, 321, 331, 480; avoidance of, 81

Arkansas, 383, 447; Fort Smith, 383; Little Rock, 383-85, 447

Arnold, George, 184; "Why," 184

asparagus, 55, 125-26, 173, 246, 249, 281, 339, 377, 389, 392, 423, 456, 505, 543

association. *See* club; culinary society

Astor, John Jacob, 104

Astredo, Antonio (restaurateur), 15, 251-53

Astredo, John, 252-53

Augustin, James (caterer, steward), 15, 158-59

Augustin, Peter, 158

Augustin, Peter Jerome, 159

Bailly, Emile (chef, newspaper essayist), 500-503

baker, 10, 14, 35-38, 57, 96, 165, 168, 218-19, 247, 284, 324, 346, 462-64, 491

ball, 13, 47, 56, 79, 90-92, 104, 126, 187, 205, 219, 245, 343, 441; Astor New Year's Eve, 442; Athenaeum Spring, 91-92; Bachelor, 35, 38; catering, 56, 78; Chef's Masquerade, 386-87; Fireman's Ball, 103; Franklin Pierce Inauguration, 133; Free School Association, 168; French Society, 222; Grand State, 147; Grover Cleveland Inaugural, 394-95; Independents Social Club, 166; James Buchanan Inauguration, 133; Jockey Club, 127; Old Guard, 178; Philadelphia Chefs, 458; Porters Central Benevolent Association, 391-92; Purim, 178; room,

ball (*continued*)
63, 79, 475; Société Culinaire Philanthropique, 209, 229, 235, 289, 422–23, 511; St. Cecilia, 127; U. S. Grant Inauguration, 231; Washington Centennial, 301–2; William McKinley Inaugural, 415; Zachary Taylor Inauguration, 92, 231

Baltimore, 13, 16, 38, 163–64, 187–88, 216, 279, 344, 345–46, 388–89, 499–500, 523–25

banquet, 1, 13, 41, 44, 47, 54, 55–56, 76, 86–87, 99, 148, 157, 209, 217, 219, 221, 233, 242, 248–49, 307, 322–24, 347, 356, 439–41, 466, 469; Barnstable Centennial Feast, 91; bill of fare, 220, 234–35, 279–82, 389, 391–92, 411–12, 417, 437–38, 524; Charleston Chamber of Commerce 1856, 279–82; Chinese, 307–9, 398–99, 519–20, 524; cooking, 1, 15, 146–47, 227, 348, 439, 541; Democratic Whig Festival, 99; Denver Stock-yard Barbecue, 261; Empire & Keystone, 174–76; equipment for, 126, 250; Fort Worth Newspaper-men, 411–12; Fourth of July 1850, 147; Fresno Press Club, 437–38; General Benjamin Butler, 211–12; General Gloukhovsky, 417; Grand Canal Dinner, 47; Grand Duke Alexis, Philadelphia, 159; hall, 13, 15, 416, 466; Kaiser Wilhelm at Strasbourg, 526–27; Knights of Pythias, 258; kosher, 166–67; manager, 158; Metropolitan Hotel for Richard Tweed, 234–35; Mount Vernon Fair, 47; Music Fund Society, 41; Philadelphia City Council Feast, 41; Prince de Joinville, 179, 181–83; Richmond Railroad, 206; Schuylkill Fishing Company, 41; specialist, 145, 299, 388, 439, 499, 508; Ulysses Grant S. F., 269; vegetar-ian, 380–81; Washington Centennial, 301–3

Barron, William G. (caterer, chef, restaurateur), 87, 251, 390–93

barroom, 14, 52, 95, 103, 192, 277, 297, 387, 432

beef, 26, 47, 52, 54, 73, 139, 151, 201, 213, 218, 288, 296, 322, 402, 455, 459, 478–80, 495–96, 537–38; à la mode, 25, 69, 99, 127, 130, 246, 248, 391; barbecued, 261; consommé, 26, 200, 246, 362, 402; daube, 33; menu listing, 44–45, 133, 172, 178, 182, 211, 226, 246, 248–49, 281, 311, 321, 352, 357, 362, 363, 377, 379, 384, 391, 396, 412, 425, 505, 515; recipe ingredient, 59, 155, 290, 331, 415, 454, 511, 518; roast, 44–45, 74, 91–92, 127, 130, 137, 147, 164, 201, 262, 281, 298, 311, 348, 352, 357, 363, 377, 384, 396, 401, 412, 505, 515; steak, 33, 61, 64, 81–84, 101, 140, 162, 164, 186, 190, 197, 208, 211, 336, 342, 357; tongue, 172, 211, 226, 311

beer, 18, 51, 66, 91, 257, 261, 277, 312, 335–36, 342; ale, 13, 43, 46, 101, 163; bock, 448; garden, 446–47; lager, 66, 184–86, 195, 311, 341, 412; porter, 13, 65, 85, 163

Bégué, Elizabeth Kettenring (chef, restaurateur, cookbook author), 5, 270–73, 313, 403, 461; *Mme. Begue and Her Recipes*, 273

Benjamin, Ralph, 166

Benoit, George, 54

Beraud, Gustave F. M. (chef, newspaper essayist), 476–81, 494

Berghaus, Herman J. (chef), 491–92

Bero, Victor, 136

Billman, Philip, 111–13

bill of fare. *See Menus index*

Billotte, Louis C. (chef), 492–93

Black Culinary History Group, 11

Blaut, Lazarus, 168–69

Blot, Pierre (amateur cook, lecturer, cookbook au-thor), 7, 201–4, 405; *Handbook of Practical Cookery for Ladies and Professional Cooks*, 202

boardinghouse, 6, 10, 14, 29, 57–58, 86–87, 189, 203, 241, 293, 365, 408, 431

Bogle, Robert, 31, 158

Bohemians, 17, 143, 184–86, 251, 274–75, 332; club, 5, 481–85

Boman, Lew (chef, restaurateur), 19, 261–63

bonbons, 77, 132, 171, 352

bon vivant, 14–17, 26–28, 30, 36–39, 101–2, 221, 275, 290, 314, 322, 440, 466

Borel, Henry, 151–52

Borel, Pierre (chef), 455–57

Boston, 1, 4, 26–32, 49–53, 54, 90–92, 93–98, 145–49, 159–62, 208–9, 211–14, 216–18, 255, 275–76, 382, 469–70, 491–92, 492–93, 508–9; Cooking School, 365–66; cultural politics, 91–92, 148–49, 209

Boudro, Lucien (chef, restaurateur), 109–13, 121, 138, 252, 444

Boulanger, Joseph (steward, chef, restaurateur), 54–56, 66

Bourquin, Lucretia (chef), 98–99

Brady, Diamond Jim, 104

branding, 20–21, 65, 68, 73, 174, 190, 213, 311, 442, 447, 465, 497, 540

brandy, 27, 75, 80, 88, 126, 147, 151, 272, 455, 488; cognac, 34; drops (candy), 173; sauce, 246, 282, 377, 424, 515

Braquehais, Valere (chef), 246, 422–24

breakfast, 13, 45, 51, 74, 94, 95–97, 119, 163, 170, 180, 196, 242, 277, 368, 407, 451, 455–56; late (*déjeuner à la fourchette*), 135, 270–73, 284, 313, 401, 432; menu, 151–52, 210, 271, 383–84, 537; times, 45, 61, 94, 129, 412

Bret, Emanuel Pierre (chef, restaurateur, hotelier), 221–22

Brillat-Savarin, Jean Anthelme, 3, 9–10, 27; *Physiologie du goût* (1825), 3, 9–10

Brisolara, Miguel (chef, restaurateur), 121–22, 139, 252

Brougham, John, 82–83, 150

buckwheat cakes, 42, 101, 215, 383

Buisson, Pierre (chef), 509–11

Burgermeister, Emile (chef), 503, 521–23

butcher, 14, 139–41, 247, 251, 270–71, 297, 324, 368, 400–401, 473, 491, 495, 502

cake. *See* confectionery

California, 3, 20, 150, 188, 268, 353, 382; Fresno, 436–37; gold rush, 119, 195; Los Angeles, 269–70, 337–40, 451; Monterey, 270; San Diego, 328–29; San

Colorado, 260; Central City, 292–93; Denver, 260–61; Leadville, 293

commerce, 10, 12–13

community, 3, 10

Compagnon, Frederick (chef), 358, 428–30

confectioner, 5, 17, 33, 36–39, 50–52, 76–77, 107, 131–32, 169–75, 218–20, 269, 313, 388, 427, 434–35, 439, 491; advertisements, 99; *The Confectioner's Journal* (Parkinson), 20, 174–75; *The Royal Parisian Pastrycook and Confectioner* (Carême), 87; training, 5, 117, 158

confectionery, 13, 20, 31, 36–39, 50, 58, 442–43, 503; cake, 29, 33, 35–37, 39, 77–78, 86–88, 126, 133, 147, 165, 171, 178, 218, 220, 227, 246, 248–49, 282, 339, 352, 377, 380, 389, 392, 396, 402, 412, 424, 427, 439, 451, 459, 462–64, 472, 505, 518, 524, 533, 541; *Hotel Book of Breads and Cakes* (Whitehead), 292; Jewish, 165–68; menu category, 147, 234, 378; recipe, 88; *Seventy-Five Receipts for Pastry, Cakes, and Sweetmeats* (Leslie), 58, 60; shop, 13, 33, 36–39, 50, 76, 87, 102–3, 117, 169–71, 218–20, 407, 434, 506

Connecticut, 366; Bethel, 366–68; New Haven, 536; New London, 366

consumption, 4, 201–2, 368–69, 502; as knowledge, 4; nationalist, 170; supply and, 340, 404

contest, 37, 74, 170–73, 336, 509

Conway, John W. (restaurateur, hotelier), 335–37

cook, 14; American, 54–55; complete, 87; French, 87. *See also* chef; plain cook; private chef

cookbook, 6–9, 16–18, 57–60, 201, 268, 464; *Complete Cookery* (Leslie, 1851), 59; *Cook's Own Book, and Housekeeper's Register* (Leslie, 1833), 60; *The Epicurean* (Ranhofer, 1894), 8, 319, 325–26; *Franco-American Cookery Book* (Déliée, 1884), 7, 287–88; *French Cooking for Americans* (Diat, 1946), 544; gender and authorship, 201, 214, 297; *Harvey House Cookbook* (Goster and Weiglin, 1992), 298; *Home Comforts* (Freedly, 1879), 360; *Hotel Meat Cooking* (Whitehead, 1883), 292–93; *Miss Parloa's Young Housekeeper* (Parloa, 1893), 367–68; *Mme. Begue and Her Recipes* (Bégué, ca. 1900), 272–73; *Philadelphia Cook Book* (Rorer, 1886), 409; *Physiology of Taste; Harder's Book of Practical American Cookery* (Harder, 1885), 7, 260–70; *Recipes by Oscar of the Waldorf-Astoria* (Tschirky, 1920), 498; *Seventy-Five Receipts for Pastry, Cakes, and Sweetmeats* (Leslie, 1828), 58; *The Table: How to Buy Food, How to Cook It, and How to Serve It* (Filippini, 1889), 7–8, 404–6; *United States Cook Book* (Volmer, 1858), 7; *What to Eat and How to Cook It* (Blot, 1863), 7

cooking: Goodfellow's school, 5, 18, 57–58; Parloa's school, 201, 322, 325, 365–66; plain, 6, 156, 203, 214; Rorer's school, 408–9; science, 98, 201–2, 364, 380, 408–10, 489–90; Wilson's school, 462–65

Coppa, Joseph (chef, restaurateur), 5, 17, 481–85

cosmopolitanism, 8, 14, 64, 117, 148, 164, 166, 279, 298, 310–12, 335, 351, 405, 414, 343, 452, 504–5; rejection of, 208, 237

cost, 47, 66, 92, 168, 196, 234, 269, 291, 327, 342, 346, 358, 381, 488

crab, 178, 188–89, 374, 390, 401; deviled, 66, 178, 250, 392, 439; menu listing, 112, 178, 344, 379, 392; recipe, 347, 402, 474; salad, 345, 379, 392; soft-shelled, 42, 89, 111, 121, 252, 287, 311, 393; soup, 347, 474, 483

creole, 135, 293; cookery, 138, 402, 410, 444, 460–61, 487, 489–90; *Creole and Puritan* (DeLeon, 1889), 271; *The Creole Cookery Book* (1885), 314; *de couleur*, 189, 304–7; dishes à la, 162, 272, 342, 504, 537

Crum, George Speck (chef, restaurateur), 236–39

cuisine, 8, 10, 14, 76; nationalism, 10

culinary associations: Boston Epicurean Club, 480; Chicago Epicures Club, 368; Cooks and Pastry Cooks Association, 300; Culinary, Confectioners' and Bakers' Association, 268; French Restaurant Owners, 120; Gastronomic Club, 440; Société Culinaire Philanthropique, 27, 220–21, 240–41, 246, 256, 297, 300, 312, 330, 361, 371, 372, 374, 430, 433–34, 436–37, 444, 515, 520, 550; Society of German Cooks, 300

Dabney, John (caterer, chef, restaurateur), 204–7

Dagnoll, Joseph 10

Daly, Augustin, 186

Dancevich, Lazzaro, 164

D'Arcy, Daniel, 162

Dauviller, Jules (chef), 532–34

debt, 44, 47–48, 53, 196, 405, 520

Deguise, Isaac, 27

Delaware, 89, 159

Déliée, Felix J. (chef, cookbook author), 7, 286–88, 325; *Franco-American Cookery Book* (1884), 287–88

delivered meals, 34, 76, 121, 203, 284–85

Delmonico, Charles, 105–6

Delmonico, Charles Crist (restaurateur), 105–6, 324, 441, 452, 465–68

Delmonico, John, 14, 102–103

Delmonico, Lorenzo (restaurateur), 14, 102–6, 142, 171, 193, 267, 275, 299, 321–22

Delmonico, Peter, 14, 102

Delmonico, Siro, 105–6, 322, 403, 404, 443

Delvaux, Adrian (chef), 493–96

demotic style, 5, 19, 92

De Scheppers, Augustine, 108

dessert, 19–20, 44, 46, 99, 113, 126, 131, 178, 212, 226–27, 246, 249, 282, 287, 304, 339, 353, 362, 375, 392, 412, 435, 438, 451, 503, 538; *International Dessert and Pastry Specialties of the World Famous Chefs* (Bailly, 1913), 503; *One Hundred Desserts* (Filippini, 1893), 406

Diat, Louis (chef), 542–44

Dingeon, Leon, 119

dinner, 33, 45, 61, 128, 168, 333, 406, 451, 540; famous, 171–73, 209, 261, 328, 364; game, 160, 224–28; invitation, 151; music, 106, 318; price, 154, 186, 195, 286, 485–86, 502, 515; private, 83, 133, 180; public, 92, 125,

game (*continued*)

laws, 72; seasonality, 66, 101, 171, 287, 312; venison, 46, 52, 55, 62, 73, 89, 95, 101, 125–26, 130, 133, 151, 164, 190, 211, 227, 247, 249, 282, 375, 383, 494–95; venison recipe, 530

Garrison, William Lloyd, 145

Gaston, John (chef, restaurateur, hotelier), 241–44, 383

gastronome, 4, 16–17, 110–11, 149–51, 201–2, 267, 287–88, 359, 402–3, 429, 460; contest of, 169, 171–74. *See also* bon vivant

"Gastronomic Almanac" (Blot), 202

gastronomy, 3–4, 10, 12, 28, 56, 96, 107, 172, 228, 288, 317–18, 361, 469, 510, 515

Gatewood, William C., 124–27, 129

Gautier, Charles (confectioner, restaurateur), 131–34, 231, 321, 343

gender, 57–58, 278; education, 409–10, 462–63; patronage and, 36, 133, 305, 313, 510; separation, 97, 111, 135, 157, 181, 191, 194, 211, 241, 277, 284, 311, 414, 525

George, Walter (steward, chef), 514–16

Georgia, 130, 171, 382; Atlanta, 294; Augusta, 276–79, 396; Macon, 241; Madison Springs, 86; Salt Springs, 294; Savannah, 11, 267

Germany, 156, 193, 214, 222, 309, 368, 446, 448, 501, 528; Baden, 18–19, 186, 193, 311, 532, 536; Bavaria, 207, 214, 271, 535; Berlin, 167, 306, 491, 501, 521; Frankfurt, 501, 521; Kehl, 311; Kiel, 382; Munich, 516; Prussian, 350–51, 356; training in, 469, 489

Gerot, Emile, 257–60

Gestal, Jose (chef, restaurateur), 25, 430–32

Gilardoni, Paul (confectioner, restaurateur, hotelier), 424–36

Goldsmith, L. E., 192

gourmet. *See* bon vivant; gastronome

Graham, Sylvester, 201–2, 213

Gray, Charley, 95

Gray, John A. (caterer), 230–32

Greeley, Horace, 84

Grevillot, Prosper (chef), 105, 439, 452–55, 468

Habisreutinger, Eugene (chef), 503–6

Halleck, Fitz-Greene, 36–37, 64, 184; "Ode to Fortune," 64; "Ode to Simon," 36

ham, 36, 45–46, 69, 91–92, 99, 133, 140, 188, 218, 228, 288, 377, 390; bear, 226; menu listing, 44, 133, 147, 178, 220, 246, 249, 281, 321, 352, 361, 373, 391–92, 395, 427, 524, 525, 537–38, 543; pie, 33; recipe ingredient, 59, 151, 155, 191, 290, 314, 348, 397, 414, 425–26, 469, 494; Smithfield, 389; Westphalia, 126, 178, 318, 321

Harder, Jules Arthur (chef, cookbook author), 3, 7, 105, 137, 240, 267–70, 299, 322, 325, 350; green goddess dressing, 21; *Physiology of Taste; Harder's Book of Practical American Cookery, Volume 1* (1884), 269

Harvard College, 29–30, 32, 145, 211, 409

Harvey, Fred (restaurateur, hotelier), 295–99

Harvey, George (restaurateur), 343–44

Head, Joseph, 174

health, 4, 12, 34–35, 170, 215, 294, 459, 478–79

Hederer, Emil (chef), 412–15

Helena, MT, 196–97

Henson, Lexius (chef, restaurateur), 276–79

Hercules, 10

Hill, Mohican (chef, restaurateur), 260–61

Hirtzler, Victor (chef), 413, 526–29, 532

Hispanic dining. *See Ethnicities index*

holidays, 45, 56, 70, 81–82; Christmas, 77, 83, 171, 219, 248–49, 376–78, 399, 425, 448; closure on, 56; Easter, 362; New Year's, 45, 70, 82

home cooking, 6–8, 17–18, 41, 85, 175, 189, 314, 319, 342, 406, 408–9, 450, 478, 503; instructions for, 202–3, 366–67, 408–9, 455, 462–64, 479; by servants, 57–58

homosociality, 12, 17, 61, 184–86

hospital, 6, 88, 366, 382, 408, 443, 465, 490, 519

hospitality, 3, 13–14, 58, 61, 78, 91, 94, 149, 157, 199, 224, 448, 455–57, 474, 494, 517–18; administration of, 75; black, 516; industry, 293, 297–98, 495; interracial, 124, 199, 344

host, 3, 77–78, 83, 87, 118, 123–24, 151, 184, 187, 259, 278, 288, 380, 429, 448, 485

hotel. *See Restaurants index for particular hotels*

hotelier, 3, 11–12, 75–76, 95–98, 179–81; French wish to be, 117

housewife. *See* home cooking

Huckins, James H. W. (chef, food processor), 20, 96, 211–14, 217, 276; soups, 213–14

Huppenbauer, Fritz (chef), 222–23

ice cream, 28, 76, 78, 99, 126, 133, 146, 157, 166, 170, 174, 188, 219–20, 287, 375, 381, 512; manufacture, 132, 174, 199, 324, 439–43; menu listing, 147, 174, 178, 227, 235, 282, 353, 362, 378, 380, 392, 396, 424, 427, 459, 472, 505, 518, 533

Indiana, 140; Evansville, 108–9; Indianapolis, 109

Italy, 2, 152, 220, 273–74, 407; cuisine of, 339, 394, 434, 489; nativity in, 2, 121, 122, 176, 218, 252, 273, 284, 290–92, 394, 407; pasta, 138, 272–73, 290, 381, 538, 540–41; regional food, 407, 434, 483, 489; risotto, 138, 339, 407, 483, 487; salad, 33, 36; training in, 151–52, 396, 481

Jakes, Henry, Jr. (caterer), 187–88, 388–89

Jaubert, Gustave "Gus" (caterer, restaurateur), 8, 329–32; burgoo recipe, 331

jelly, 37, 69, 76, 87, 92, 99, 126, 166–67, 171, 190, 215, 218, 247, 287–88, 268, 429; *Canned Fruit, Preserves, and Jellies: Household Methods of Preparation* (Parloa, 1905), 367; hams, 99; menu listing, 133, 147, 178, 211, 212, 220, 234, 246, 249, 280, 281, 282, 321, 352, 377, 380, 389, 424, 533, 543; recipe ingredient, 458, 495, 508, 534

Jennings, Chester, 46

Jewish foodways, 165–69, 284
Johnson, Reverdy, 199
Johnston, George E. (chef, restaurateur), 279–84
Jones, Emeline (chef), 345–50
Julien (Jean Baptiste Gilbert Payplat) (chef, restaurateur), 1–4, 25–29, 32, 34, 49–51

Katzenbach, Peter, 159
Keene, James R., 150
Kentucky, 139, 205, 467; Lexington, 329–32; Louisville, 329, 383, 462; Middlesboro, 511
King, "Harry" Lee, 20, 398–400
Kinzler, Francis J. (chef, hotelier), 326–29, 386, 440
kitchen, 2, 4, 6, 16, 45, 57, 65, 83, 91, 95, 98, 118, 130, 140, 151, 268, 289, 293–94, 322, 358, 376, 433, 449, 478, 528; arrangement, 12, 97, 109, 157, 233, 301, 323–24, 351, 472, 491, 501–2, 522–23; car on train, 260; cookstove, 203, 363, 387, 551; demonstration, 365–66, 410; described, 41, 97, 217–18, 323–24, 327–28, 398, 491, 501–2; duties, 118, 217, 323–24; equipment, 250, 522–34; gender, 57, 60, 121, 327, 464, 489–90; hierarchy, 76, 217–18, 233, 285, 322–24, 327, 346, 412–14; portable, 148; sanitation, 209, 218, 368; slaves, 86; technology, 15, 105, 157, 293, 363, 387, 423, 489–90, 551; training (*see* apprenticeship); walk-out, 300, 351
Korsmeyer, Carolyn, 9; *Making Sense of Taste: Food and Philosophy* (1999), 9
Kuzmier, Xenophon (chef), 414, 457–60, 508

labor, 2, 4, 9, 323, 343, 405, 467, 502, 504, 528, 543
Lakemeyer, Frederick, 118
Lalanne, Louis Calixte (chef, restaurateur), 482, 529–32
Lallouette, Louis Charles Fleury (chef), 105, 378–80
Laperruque, Eugene (chef), 105, 299–304, 387, 453
La Touche, Bertrand, 54
Le Count, Isaiah (caterer, chef, restaurateur), 2, 89–90, 101–2, 158
Le Count, James, 90
LeCounts, Thomas, 39
LeCounts, William, 39
Lee, Eliza Seymour (pastry chef, caterer, restaurateur), 6, 84–88, 127, 282
Lee, John, 86–88
LeFort, Victor (chef, restaurateur), 107–9
Le Rebour, M., 27
Lescarboura, Jacques (chef), 516–19
Leslie, Eliza (boardinghouse cook, cookbook author), 6, 56–60
Leslie, Lydia, 56–57
Letourno, Joseph (caterer, restaurateur), 77–80; U.S. Capitol Refectory, 79–80
literati, 81–82, 185–87, 258, 483
lobster, 65, 74, 139, 308, 360, 363, 439, 449, 530, 535; deviled, 2, 89–90; menu listing, 133, 147, 173, 178,

220, 249, 311, 361, 377, 379, 395, 505; Newburg, 323, 478, 505; palace, 19, 374–75, 443; pudding, 36; recipe, 521; salad, 43, 125–26, 147, 178, 220, 249, 289, 298, 379, 395, 503; sauce, 173; soup, 361
London, 16, 18, 35, 45, 54, 76, 81, 165–67, 239, 292, 344, 368, 375, 490, 501, 521, 539–40, 543
Los Angeles, 20, 269–70, 337–40, 451
Lüchow, August Guido (restaurateur), 312, 446–49, 534
Ludin, John (chef, importer), 232–36
lunch, 14, 36–39, 64, 71–72, 87, 131, 199, 283, 306 342, 419, 447, 464; businessman's, 339, 373, 434, 466; drinking at, 75; introduced, 35, 163–64; menu, 321, 356–57, 530; room, 111, 248, 262–63, 317, 404, 488; women's, 35, 111, 127, 174, 196, 219, 241, 278, 284, 321, 349, 510, 512
luxury, 13, 26, 36, 91, 147, 259, 284, 526; foods, 91, 141; hotel, 269, 285, 374, 385; restaurant, 180

macaroni, 33, 151, 182, 212, 213, 311, 362, 381, 484, 538; pie, 126
Madrid, Frozine (chef, restaurateur), 189–90
Madrid, Manuel, 189
Maine, 94, 135, 171, 218; Liquor Law, 96
maître d', 3, 190, 324, 481, 496–98
Manners, Robert (chef, restaurateur), 89, 100–102
Marchand, Edward (chef, restaurateur), 4, 119–21, 436, 529, 531
market, 7, 10, 45, 47, 51, 73–74, 92, 139, 202, 240, 260, 268, 271, 277, 294, 310–12, 350, 376, 388, 393, 404–6, 413, 436, 445; Faneuil, 52; fish, 100, 105, 285; French, 122, 139, 164, 272; fruit, 252; game, 47, 123, 125, 127, 140–41, 247; gunners, 224–26; mass, 21, 96, 174, 502; meat, 139–41, 495; *Miss Parloa's New Cook Book: A Guide to Marketing and Cooking* (1881), 367; preeminence in, 67–68; rarities, 95; rigging, 297; St. Mary's, 139
Martin, Georges, 136
Martin, Jules, 135–36
Martin, Victor (chef, restaurateur), 134–36, 138, 313
Martinelli, Francesco (chef, restaurateur), 19, 273–75
Martinez, F., 119, 284, 321–22
Maryland, 89, 91, 34, 279, 353–55; Baltimore, 38–39, 187–88, 345–47, 388–89, 499–500
Mazzetti, Louis F. (Luigi) (chef, restaurateur), 19, 105, 290, 394, 408–9
meat, 3, 33, 47, 72; conserved, 33; predilection for, 201. *See also* beef; game; ham; mutton; veal
Mehl, Eugene (chef, hotelier), 235, 244, 332–35, 455
menu, 148, 180. *See also Menus index*
Mergenthaler, Frederic (chef), 350–53
Mexico, 107–8, 135, 296–97, 337, 444, 483, 506
Michels, John (chef), 135, 217, 275–76
Mile, Thomas, 164
Miller, Adrian, 11
Miller, Joseph William, 42; "Prosser's Journey to Heaven," 42–43

Parloa, Maria (chef, lecturer, cookbook author), 6, 18, 365–69; *Miss Parloa's Young Housekeeper*, 367–68

Pasteur, Louis, 201

pastry, 26, 31, 33–34; cook, 32–35, 76–77, 84–88; cooking, 10, 16, 87; shop, 34, 57–59, 87, 117. *See also* confectionery

patriotism, 229, 448, 513, 519, 534–35, 538

Peguillan, Eugene, 120

Pelletier, François-Winceslas (chef), 190–93

Peyroux, Joseph Baptiste (chef), 244–47, 274

Philadelphia, 13, 17, 33–35, 39–43, 56–61, 67, 78, 89–90

pie, 16, 27, 33, 46, 87, 99, 171, 191, 249, 353; beefsteak, 415; black-bird, 227; chicken, 46, 126, 130; cream, 282, 424; fruit, 212, 246, 249, 287, 377, 381, 424, 515, 538; game, 36, 476; green tomato, 452; ham, 33; lamb, 246; macaroni, 126; menu listing, 44–45, 212, 246, 282, 311, 377, 381, 384, 472, 505, 515, 538; meringue, 166; mince, 46, 130, 248, 282, 346, 352, 377, 384; oyster, 34, 44–45, 126, 130, 146–47; pot, 34, 311; pumpkin, 65, 378, 472, 503; quail pie, 45–47; rhubarb, 505; shrimp, 126, 130; veal, 33, 401

pleasure, 2–3, 9–10, 13, 58, 64, 86, 104, 184–85, 255, 257, 259, 323, 333, 463, 529; garden, 61, 78

poetry, 27, 32, 38, 53, 71; "A little learning is a dangerous thing," 32; "Battle of the Bucks," 27; "Communication," 51; "Downing and the Pine Collector," 69–70; "Ode to Fortune," 64; "Ode to Simon," 36–37; "Prosser's Journey to Heaven," 42–43, "The Raven," 71; "Why," 184–85

politeness, 29–31, 101, 158

politics, 73–74, 96, 147–48, 331; Democratic Party, 149–52, 158, 255, 287, 331; Republican Party, 198, 211, 253–56, 277, 417–18; Tammany Hall, 104, 233; Whig, 74

Pollard, Othello (confectioner, chef, caterer, restaurateur), 28–33

Poppleton, Ann (confectioner, restaurateur), 35–39, 58, 64

potato, 192, 223, 238, 272, 331, 349, 389, 451, 535; French fried, 227, 357; mashed, 246, 353, 377, 384, 424, 505, 515; menu listing, 210, 227, 246, 249, 281, 353, 357, 361, 377, 379, 381, 383, 384, 392, 402, 411, 424, 427, 459, 472, 505, 515, 538; recipe ingredient, 192, 414, 509, 533; salad, 381, 392, 427, 491, 538; Saratoga, 141–45, 208, 236–37, 350; soufflés, 151; sweet, 17, 126, 227, 173, 287, 353, 377, 384, 424, 459, 492, 505, 515; vichyssoise, 542–44; white (Irish), 173, 281, 392, 402, 424, 459, 515

Prescott, AZ, 197

president of the United States: Adams, John Quincy, 220; Arthur, Chester A., 219, 279, 357; Buchanan, James, 144; Cleveland, Grover, 219, 311–13, 357, 367–68, 405–6; Fillmore, Millard, 103; Garfield, James, 145, 211, 357; Grant, Ulysses, 240–42, 279–80, 418; Harrison, Benjamin, 201; Harrison, William Henry, 428; Hayes, Rutherford, 279; Jackson, Andrew, 65, 164; Johnson, Andrew, 162, 265; Lincoln, Abraham,

228, 354; McKinley, William, 426; Pierce, Franklin, 144; Polk, James K., 166; Taylor, Zachary, 103, 157, 242; Tyler, John, 201; Van Buren, Martin, 220, 241–42; Washington, George, 21

Prevaux, John, 118

Priet, Pierre, 120

Prior, Adam, 85

profession, 1–5, 87, 108, 245–46, 368, 444, 508; advancement, 187, 255, 278, 491, 515; crisis in, 180; eminence in, 98, 335–38, 387, 427, 437, 499, 547, 550; exhibiting, 136, 185, 424; identity, 5, 78, 211, 260–61, 385; organization, 279, 300, 372, 397, 444, 502 (*see also names of associations*); solidary, 31; training of, 96, 235 443, 501, 553; women, 57–58, 317, 324–26, 368–69, 419, 475, 501; writing for and by, 181, 213–14, 284, 297–98, 303–6, 336–37, 416–17, 475

Prohibition (Volstead Act), 1, 19, 390, 475, 487–88, 506, 511, 531, 539, 541; closures due to, 402, 438, 443, 468, 498, 544

Prosser, James (chef, caterer, restaurateur), 39–43, 89–90

Puritanism, 4, 19, 91, 202

racism, 66, 67–71, 344

railroad, 14, 66, 70–72, 92–93, 122–25, 178, 206–7, 224, 260–61, 273; dining, 373, 450–52, 514–15; restaurants for, 296–99

Ranhofer, Charles (chef, cookbook author), 8, 21, 105, 267, 287–88, 299, 301, 319–26, 403, 406, 425, 442, 454, 468; *The Epicurean* (1894), 325–26

Ranieri, Gustave, 107

recipes, 2, 6–7, 59–60; format, 59; publication, 6–8, 20; unwritten, 7, 87–88. *See also Recipes index*

Rector, Charles E. (restaurateur, hotelier), 1, 4, 19, 373–76, 415, 443, 496, 498, 530

repertoire, 2, 6, 11, 60, 99, 112, 122, 125–26, 146, 154, 168, 269, 271, 293, 321–22, 342, 345, 365, 380, 392, 414, 451, 462, 488, 498–99, 503

restaurant, 1–5, 12, 18, 34, 49–50; branches, 76–77; décor, 3, 62–63, 82–83, 132; design, 132, 199; failure, 195–96; lobster palace, 374–75, 443; motto, 72, 83, 98; national, 65–66; origin, 5, 12, 26–29; restorator, 12, 26–28, 34, 50–51, 94–95; steak house, 83; summer closing, 159. *See also Restaurants index*

restaurateur, 1, 3, 11–14, 19–20, 102–6, 117; successor to, 77, 90, 111–13

Rhode Island, 142; Newport, 52–53, 253–55, 330, 382, 432, 504; Providence, 218–21

Rhodes, Charles, 153–54

Richet, Nicholas, 119

riot, 78, 84, 399

rivalry, 26–28, 44–45, 62, 89–90, 92, 101–2, 118, 153, 166–67, 248, 267, 307, 314, 336, 375–76, 393, 440–42

Rorer, Sarah Tyson (cooking school director, cookbook author), 18, 367, 408–10

Roth, Balthazar (hotelier), 155–58, 194, 241

Roth, Edward N., 157

Roth, Jean (chef), 105, 425–26
rotisserie, 119
Rouillard, Frederick (chef, restaurateur), 28, 49–53, 95, 98
roux, 59, 155, 314
Rubicam, Daniel, 98
Rutjes, Adolph John, 127

Saint-Gaudens, Augustus, 146, 161
saloon, 13, 55
Salt Lake City, UT, 196
San Antonio, TX, 20, 410, 476, 480, 498, 529
San Francisco, 1, 20, 119–21
Sanroman, Jose (restaurateur), 20, 506–7
Saratoga, NY, 141–44, 193–94, 236–39, 267–70, 288–89, 376, 394, 422–24, 503–4; chip, 17, 141–42, 173, 208, 287, 350
Sartre, François (chef, restaurateur), 460–62, 485
sauce, 8, 76, 150–51, 212, 260, 287, 322, 402, 473, 528; anchovy, 126, 374; apple, 248, 377, 424, 505; béarnaise, 267, 471; Bechamel, 420; Bichoff, 454; brandy, 246, 282, 424, 515; bread, 377; caper, 220, 246, 280; cardinal, 424, 503; celery, 211; champagne, 182, 281, 348, 361; chili, 374; clam recipe, 533; Colbert, 511; cranberry, 92, 164, 282, 352, 515; cream, 89, 211, 269, 347, 360, 379, 384, 425, 471, 472; creole, 272; curry, 360, 505; egg, 246; exquisite recipe, 536; fish (Worcestershire), 36, 126, 414, 518; gravy, 211, 248; hard, 377; hollandaise, 303, 505; homard, 359; lemon, 248; lobster, 172; Madeira, 173, 279, 282, 303, 387, 471; maître d'hôtel, 360, 456; mayonnaise, 172, 178, 182, 212, 220, 239, 246, 280, 298, 321, 347, 377, 422, 424, 427, 503, 527, 534; mint, 112, 173, 248, 312, 352, 362, 533; mushroom, 347, 469; Nonsuch, 238; Normandy, 380; oyster, 164, 211, 352; parmesan, 542; pepper, 272; Perigueux, 112, 182; piquante, 360; poivrade, 302; port wine, 226; re-moulade, 311; rum 362; sabayon, 334; *Sauces: French and Famous* (Diat, 1951), 544; shrimp, 348; supreme, 181, 397, 513; sweet and sour, 494–95; tartar, 339, 374, 379, 384, 411, 429; tomato, 172, 249, 272, 314, 362, 381, 401, 435, 503, 515; truffle, 281; veloute, 493; Victoria, 361; Villeroy, 541; wine (claret), 211, 227, 317, 433
Schelcher, Edward (chef, hotelier), 235, 288–89
Schimmelfennig, Alexander (general), 130
Schultz, Louis (chef), 193–95
seasonality, 7–8, 65, 67–68, 73, 111, 117, 125, 130, 135, 160, 168, 186, 189, 202, 237, 277, 336, 344, 379, 511; cookbook reflecting, 287, 325; first appearance, 122, 190, 243, 286
seasoning, 7, 156, 175, 238, 331, 349, 402, 414, 421, 425, 457, 493–94, 513, 517, 534
seating, 12, 111, 151, 299, 469; café style, 12, 180; capacity, 159, 180, 194, 288, 390, 415, 510; refectory style, 12
secret, 6, 18, 143–44, 272, 289, 319, 405–6, 500; "Cook-ing Secrets of Famous Chef: By Emile Bailly, Chef at the St. Regis, N.Y.," 503; society, 30, 523–24
Segar, George F., 358
Seitz, J. Valentine (chef), 469–70
Selves, Georges, 157
Seyl, Joseph (chef), 356–58
Seymour, Sally, 84–86; teacher of pastry cooking, 85
Shadd, Bonaventura, 66
Shaw, Robert Gould, 145–46, 148
Sherman, William T. (general), 130
Sherry, Louis (caterer, confectioner, restaurateur), 19, 20, 375, 438–43, 496
shop, 33–34, 36–38, 50, 65, 77, 99, 139; combined with eating house, 76, 283; confectionery, 13, 50, 84–86, 117, 127, 132, 167, 169–71, 174, 219, 248, 321, 439–40, 463, 476, 489; cook, 119–20, 336
shrimp, 272, 348, 393, 447, 487; creole, 342; menu listing, 271; pie, 126, 130; recipe ingredient, 380, 518; salad, 272
Sieghortner, August Louis (chef, restaurateur), 207–8
signature dish, 6, 8, 21, 89, 99, 111, 144, 151, 154, 175, 248, 252, 330, 356, 374, 377, 388, 425, 469, 499, 500, 508; drink, 488; menu, 345
Simms, Benjamin Franklin (caterer), 187–88, 388–89
Simonet, Stephen (confectioner, chef, restaurateur), 33–35
simplicity, 4, 6, 59
Sivori, Antonio (caterer, chef), 176–79, 359, 439
slavery, 6, 15, 67, 71, 85–88, 122–31, 145, 149, 153, 189, 198, 204–6, 254, 269, 304–5, 346, 353–55, 390, 459; Fugitive Slave Act, 145, 148, 353; *The Miracle of the Slave* (Tintoretto), 148
Smiley, Charles Henry (caterer), 426–28
Smith, Joshua B. (caterer), 15, 93, 145–49
Snider, Jacob, Jr., 174
Sobra, Urban (chef), 416–19
sociability, 14, 103–4, 184, 232, 235, 257, 391, 466, 508
Sommers, Isaac, 167
soup, 12, 21, 26–29, 33, 36, 45; barley, 26; bouillabaisse, 111; celery, 127, 366, 505; chowder, 73, 161, 163, 233–34, 323, 393, 530, 537; court bouillon, 110–11, 122, 189, 342; green turtle, 16, 39, 44–45, 51, 62, 66, 98, 142, 164, 172, 262, 277, 318, 330, 347, 423, 456, 502, 513; gumbo, 59, 155, 164, 208, 287, 347; healthfulness, 25–28, 33; okra, 59; serving time, 94; vichyssoise, 2, 8, 543–44
South Carolina, 59, 171, 248, 269, 462; Charleston, 84–88, 122–31, 247–51, 279–84, 290–93; Columbia, 107
Soyer, Alexis Bénoit, 8, 176
Spain, 89, 121, 431, 516
Sponset, Chris, 157
Steadman, Edmund Clarence, 184
steamboat, 139
Stetson, Charles (colonel), 179
Stetson, James P. M. (hotelier), 179–83

Stevens, Daniel, 124

steward, 3, 10, 14, 91, 103, 107, 138, 142, 145, 156, 157, 160, 176–77, 203, 223, 230, 245, 259, 262, 319, 385, 416, 438, 444, 474, 499; club, 127, 149–50, 158, 199, 214, 232, 283, 290, 499; hotel, 179–80, 351, 356–57, 383, 387, 414, 439, 480; as master of ceremonies, 31, 35, 77–78; presidential, 54; railroad, 373, 449–50; *Steward's Handbook and Guide to Party Catering* (Whitehead, 1889), 292

stylishness, 3–4, 19, 36–39, 105

summer, 50–51, 61–62, 67, 82, 110–11, 140, 255; closure, 252, 402–3; food, 121, 125, 130, 160; garden dining, 174; relocation of chefs, 87, 110, 206, 258, 376, 394, 422, 440, 460, 504; resort, 76, 136, 159, 193, 206, 235, 258, 263, 288, 333, 350, 365, 392, 394, 422, 440, 444, 504; school, 490

Sumner, Charles, 145, 148–49, 199

supper, 13, 33, 45, 83, 90, 94–95, 117, 119–20, 145, 167, 203, 206, 219, 229, 242, 248, 258, 262, 277, 373, 383, 392–93, 442; club, 506; eliminated, 196, 322; "Great Supper," 92; kosher, 166; late, 199, 347; menu, 234, 384, 538; private, 83; room, 132

Surdez, Leon (chef), 470–73

Sykes, William (chef, restaurateur), 44–49, 62, 82

table d'hôte, 2, 13, 52, 180

Taft, George, 161

Taft, Orra A. (chef, restaurateur, hotelier), 159–62

tea, 45, 78, 91, 102, 147, 220, 381, 384, 399, 510, 515, 524; cake, 86, 165; service, 180; sweet, 475

temperance, 19, 74–75, 79–80, 91, 96, 259, 281, 432; Washingtonians Temperance Society, 74; Women's Christian Temperance Union, 355

Tennessee, 242; Chattanooga, 513; Memphis, 242–44, 385; Nashville, 261, 449–50, 452, 462–65

Tennison, Joshua, 65

Tenu, Adrien (chef), 105, 300–301, 419–21, 496, 498, 528

terrapin, 17, 39–43, 46, 55, 61, 66, 74–74, 99, 126, 133, 173, 187, 204, 256, 388–89, 499–500; à la Maryland, 17, 199, 302, 344, 345, 376, 424, 439, 472, 499; deviled, 250; French style, 101; Sandy Welsh's Lunch, 5, 71–74, 94; soup, 111, 213; stew, 40–41, 152, 188, 206, 212, 277, 286–87, 315, 344, 349, 379

Texas, 410, 430; Austin, 259; Fort Worth, 410–12; Galveston, 221–22; Houston, 480–81; San Antonio, 480–81

Thomas, Hiram S., 144

Thomson, James, 76

tomato, 137, 288, 331; green tomato pie, 452; ingredient in recipe, 59, 157, 213, 314, 331, 347, 397, 402, 426, 471, 483, 495, 513, 521; menu item, 173, 227, 246, 249, 272, 281, 352, 380, 381, 411, 424, 515, 518, 538–39; salad, 237; sauce, 249, 272, 314, 362, 381, 401, 435, 503, 515; soup, 213; stuffed, 349; tomatoes frappés à la Julius Caesar, 137

Torrilhon, Jean-Georges, 228–30

Tournoi, L., 154

transportation, 14, 61–62, 78

Trapet, François, 197

Trapet, John P., 197

Trapet, Pierre (chef, restaurateur), 195–97

Tresconi, John, 122

Tschirky, Oscar (steward), 421, 496–98

Tully, Tom R. (caterer, confectioner, restaurateur), 87, 128, 247–51, 283, 390, 392

turkey, 83, 91, 99, 137, 204, 218, 247, 260, 318, 390, 471, 475, 478; boiled, 44, 172, 211; boned, 69, 83, 99, 125–26, 133, 166, 168, 178, 220, 227, 289, 395; galantine, 212; hash, 383; jellied, 125, 220; menu listing, 44–46, 133, 147, 166, 172, 178, 182, 211–12, 220, 226–27, 246, 248–49, 280–82, 321, 339, 352, 357, 377, 383, 385, 389, 392, 395, 427, 459, 472, 515; roast, 46, 92, 126, 133, 182, 206, 246, 392, 427, 459, 472, 515; truffled, 318, 321, 454; wild, 46, 130, 164, 226, 249

turtle, 12, 17, 39–43, 52, 388–89, 433, 537; calipash, 44–47; calipee, 45, 47; clubs, 61–62, 71–75, 194, 211, 246, 286; soup of green, 44, 45, 51, 62, 66, 98, 142, 164, 172, 262, 277, 318, 330, 347, 423, 456, 502, 513; steak, 43, 46, 130, 296. *See also* terrapin

Ude, Louis-Eustache, 18

urban, 15, 125, 196, 232, 515; cityscape, 16; corruption, 19; dining, 13, 18; poverty, 490; real estate, 256

Valadon, Auguste (chef), 359–60

Van Rensselaer, Walter (chef, restaurateur), 14, 162–65

vegetables, 7, 55; absence of, 47; earliest, 95. *See also individual vegetables*

vegetarianism, 18, 380–82, 479; rejection of, 202

Virginia, 67, 124, 132, 171, 290, 317–18, 344, 346, 462, 499; Old Virginia Ham, 348; owls, 312; Richmond, 6, 107, 204–6, 252, 257–58; University of, 490

vocation of cooking, 2, 5–6, 58, 87; women's sense of, 58, 87, 408, 410

Voigt, Henry, 11, 176–77; *The American Menu* blog, 11

Volkmann, Louise (chef, restaurateur), 380–82

Vollmer, William (chef, cookbook author), 7, 213–16; *United States Cook Book*, 215–16

waiter, 3, 10, 14, 55, 89, 94, 119–20, 164, 180, 204, 207, 241, 272, 297, 317, 333, 343, 363, 426, 440, 444, 450; African American, 127, 145, 148, 204, 231, 426, 450, 499, 514; dress, 180, 277, 245; head, 31, 42, 95, 145, 158, 187, 231, 399, 417, 439, 496–97; labor unrest, 235, 356, 467; polite, 168, 180; wage, 95, 145, 199

Walker, William (caterer, chef, restaurateur), 15, 65–66

Ward, Sam (gastronome, amateur chef), 17, 149–52, 208

Washington, DC, 16, 54–56, 65–66, 78–80, 117–18, 131–34, 144, 151–52, 187, 197–200, 213, 230–32, 255–

WOMEN

Holton, Elizabeth, 87
Holton, Mary, 87
Howard, Mrs. Frank T., 305-6
Howe, Julia Ward, 151
Howland, Esther A., 18

Jakes, Mary, 188
Jarvis, Mrs. Fanning C., 347
Johnson, Camilla, 87
Jones, Emeline, 345-50

Kuzmier, Ellen, 460

Lalanne, Mary, 529
Lee, Eliza Seymour, 84-88, 127, 232
Le Fevre, Carrica, 380-81
Leslie, Eliza, 6, 56-61; writings, 58-60
Lincoln, Mary Todd, 18, 133
Lind, Jenny, 209
Louderback, Mary C., 157
Louise (princess of France), 299
Ludin, Agnes, 232

Madrid, Frozine, 189-90
Marchand, Félicité, 119-20
Maylie, Hanna, 100-101
Miller, Mrs. Thomas, 305
Moody, Agnes, 353-56
Mouquin, Marie Julie Grandjean, 317
Murray, Nellie, 304-7

Niblo, Martha King, 61-62
Nish, Julia, 460

Pach, Mrs. J. M., 167-69
Parkinson, Eleanor, 171; *The Complete Confectioner* (1843), 171

Parloa, Maria, 6, 18, 365-69
Payplat, Hannah Horne, 28, 50
Peguillan, Françoise, 120
Pelletier, Jane Lavinia, 192
Pollard, Eupha Brown, 31
Poppleton, Ann, 35-38
Porcher, Mrs. Frances J., 124
Prado, Pilar, 506

Randolph, Mary, 6
Rorer, Sarah Tyson, 18, 367, 408-10
Rubicam, Elizabeth, 98-99
Rutjes, Théonie Mignot, 127

Sobra, Marguerite Leona, 418
Stowe, Harriet Beecher, 153, 365
Surdez, Honorine, 471

Tetrazzini, Luisa, 541
Torrilhon, Sophie-Eugenie, 229
Tresconi, Sarah Brisolara, 122

Vanderhorst, Martha, 248
Van Rensselaer, Emeline Gladding, 164
Victoria (queen of England), 490
Volkmann, Louise Carstensen, 380-82
Vollmer, Anna Barbara Lindenmayer, 214

Washington, Martha, 158
Whitridge, Elizabeth Hall, 346
Wilson, Betty Lyles, 462-65
Wilson, Mary Anastasia, 489-91
Wilson, Mary Lyles, 466
Windust, Sarah E., 80-84

ETHNICITIES

RESTAURANTS

Bank Coffee House (New York City), 61–63
Bank Coffee House (Philadelphia), 101
Barnum House (San Francisco), 119, 284, 321
Barnum's Hotel (Baltimore), 187, 279
Barnum's Hotel (St. Louis), 376
Barron's Hall (Charleston, SC), 390–93
Bégué's Exchange (New Orleans), 270–73
Bellevue Hotel (Newport, RI), 52–53
Bellevue Hotel (Philadelphia), 413
Bender Hotel (Houston), 480–81
Beraud's Café (Kansas City, MO), 480
Billy's Plaza Restaurant (San Francisco), 336
Bishop's Hotel (New Orleans), 162
Blaut and Minsesheimer's kosher restaurant (New York), 168–69
Boman's Restaurant (Cincinnati), 261–62
Bon Ton Restaurant (Denver), 260–61
Bon Ton Restaurant (later Bon Ton Hotel; Santa Fe, NM), 335–37
Boudro's Arcade (West End, New Orleans), 110–11
Boudro's Confectionary and Lunch Saloon (New Orleans), 111
Boulanger's American and French Restaurant (Washington, DC), 54–55
Bourse (Philadelphia), 414–15
Brevoort House (New York City), 235, 332–33
Brighton House (Cincinnati), 262–63
Broadway Hotel (New York City), 363
Brown Hotel (Chicago), 373
Brown's Hotel (Macon, GA), 241
Burnet House (Cincinnati), 193–94, 263, 288

Café Finelli (Philadelphia), 291
Café Royale (Chicago), 1
Café Savarin (New York City), 300–301, 351, 419–20, 537
Canter's Confectionery and Ice Cream Saloon (New York City), 164–68
Capital Hotel (Little Rock, AR), 383–85
Carroll Hotel (Vicksburg, MS), 385
Chamberlain's Resort Hotel (Point Comfort, MD), 347
Chatain's French Restaurant, Melba Hotel (Fort Worth), 411–12
Chung Fah Low (New York City), 398–400
Cinco de Mayo Restaurant (Los Angeles), 506
City Hotel (New York City), 44
City Oyster House (Fish Refectory; Philadelphia), 100–101
Clarendon Hotel (New York City), 244–46, 422–23
Classic Hotel or Attic Bower (Cambridge, MA), 29–30
Clubhouse, The (Washington, DC), 199
Coleman House (Asbury Park, NJ), 504
Commercial Restaurant (New Orleans), 223
Commercial Restaurant (San Francisco), 338–39
Congressional Refectory (Washington, DC), 78–80
Continental Hotel (Philadelphia), 216–17
Coppa's (San Francisco), 5, 482–84

Cornhill Coffee House (Boston), 160
Cornucopia (Philadelphia), 101
Cotton House (Roxbury, MA), 160–61
Crescent Restaurant (New Orleans), 162–64
Crum House (Saratoga, NY), 236–39

Dabney's (Richmond, VA), 206–7
Delmonico's (New York City), 1, 4, 7–8, 17, 102–6, 193, 267, 351, 375, 407, 440–41, 470, 516; Beaver Street, 207; Broadway, 105, 299, 425–26, 466; Chambers Street, 103–4; Fifth Avenue, 105–6, 323–26, 378; Forty-Fourth Street, 454–55; Fourteenth Street, 104–5, 322–23, 378, 403–4, 452–54; Hotel, 104; San Francisco, 196; William Street, 102–3
Dol and Bigne's Nevada restaurant (later Maison Dorée; San Francisco), 338
Downing's Oyster Saloon (New York City), 68
Downing's Refectory (New York City), 68
Downing's Restaurant (Albany, NY), 256
Drouilhat's restaurant (Portland, OR), 240

E. Gerot & Son (Buffalo, NY), 259
Empire Restaurant (Baltimore), 524–25
European House (Washington, DC), 117–18
Everett Hotel (Jacksonville, FL), 294
Everett House (New York City), 244–45

Fabacher's Restaurant (New Orleans), 340–42
Fairmont Hotel (San Francisco), 521–22
Far East Restaurant (Washington, DC), 525
Faust's (St. Louis), 19, 310–13
Ferera and Doty's restaurant (Fresno, CA), 436–37
Fifth Avenue Hotel (New York City), 208–11, 216
Filippini's restaurant (New York City), 404–5
Finelli's (Philadelphia), 19, 290–91
Fountain Inn (Washington, DC), 78
Franco-American restaurant (Washington, DC), 118
Francoise's (Biloxi, MS; New Orleans), 1, 460–62
Franklin House (Philadelphia), 190–92
Franklin Institute Restaurant (Philadelphia), 99
French Opera House Restaurant (New Orleans), 460
French Restaurant (Mobile, AL), 107
French Restaurant (San Francisco), 119–21
Frozine's No. 1 Eating House (Mobile, AL), 189–90

Gadsby's National Hotel (Washington, DC), 54, 65
Gailhard Hotel Restaurant (also Drouilhat's Hotel; San Francisco), 239–40
Galatoire's (New Orleans), 445–46
Galpin's Restaurant (New Orleans), 140
Gaston's French Restaurant and Commercial Hotel (later Hotel; Memphis), 241–44, 383
Gautier's Saloon (Washington, DC), 132–34
Gem Saloon (Baton Rouge, LA), 313
George's Restaurant (Charleston, SC), 282–83
Gerot's European Hotel (Richmond, VA), 257–59
Gestal's Spanish Restaurant (Boise, ID), 430–32

New Metropolitan Hotel (Birmingham, AL), 434–36
New Poodle Dog (San Francisco), 4, 529–31
Newport Springs Hotel (Newport Springs, FL), 241
New Turf European Hotel (Milwaukee), 514–15
New York Coffee House (New York City), 44–46
New York Restaurant (Shreveport, LA), 411
Niblo's Garden (New York City), 61, 63–66, 76

Ogden's Star Hotel (Philadelphia), 99
Old Absinthe House (New Orleans), 1
Old Poodle Dog (San Francisco), 1, 119, 482, 529–31
Olympic Hotel (Seattle), 522–23
Oriental Restaurant (Los Angeles), 337–38

Palace Hotel (San Francisco), 3, 7, 268–69, 350–53, 532–34
Palmer House (Chicago), 356–58
Paretti's (New York City), 19
Paris Restaurant (Evansville, IN), 108–9
Park Avenue Hotel (New York City), 285
Parker's Eating House (Boston), 95
Parker House (Boston), 90, 93, 96–97, 211–12, 217–18, 275–76, 469
Parkinson's (Philadelphia; New York City), 169–77
Paul's Café (Birmingham, AL), 434
Pavilion Hotel (Wolfeboro, NH), 366
Pearl Street House (Cincinnati), 224
Pelican Exchange (New Orleans), 444
Pfaff's Cellar (New York City), 184–87
Pfaff's New Restaurant (New York City), 186–87
Phenix Coffee House (New York City), 80–81
Philadelphia Boarding House (Philadelphia), 57
Philadelphia Eating House (Philadelphia), 99–100
Philadelphia Hotel (New York City), 44
Phoenix House (also Miguel's; Lake End, LA), 121–22
Planter's Hotel (Saratoga, NY), 194
Plaza Hotel (New York City), 301–4, 364, 394
Point Shirley House (Boston), 161–62
Pollard's Refectory (Boston), 29
Pompeian Gardens (San Francisco), 484
Portland Hotel (Portland, OR), 535
Poughkeepsie Hotel (Poughkeepsie, NY), 74
El Progresso (Los Angeles), 506
Prosser's Oyster Cellar (Philadelphia), 39–43

Rector's (Chicago; New York City), 1, 4, 373–75, 414
Rector's Hotel (New York City), 375
Restaurant de Sanroman (Los Angeles), 506–7
Restaurant du Cardinal (New Orleans), 154
Restaurant Martin (New York City), 486–87
Restaurant Mexicano (Los Angeles), 506
Restaurant Victor LeFort (Indianapolis), 109
Revere House (Boston), 209, 216
Rice Hotel (Houston), 480
Richelieu (San Francisco), 196
Ritz-Carlton Hotel (New York City), 541–44
Rockford Restaurant (Los Angeles), 506

Rockingham House (Portsmouth, NH), 366
Royal Hawaiian Hotel (Honolulu), 270
Royal Poinciana Hotel (Palm Beach, FL), 396–97

Sandy Welsh's Terrapin Lunch (New York City), 71–76, 81
Sansome Coffee Saloon and Restaurant (San Francisco), 196
Schultz's restaurant (Cincinnati), 194
Sea Girt Hotel (Newport, RI), 255
Shakespeare House (New York City), 49, 81–84
Shakespear Hotel and Restorator (Boston), 27
Shanly's (New York City), 1
Sherry's (New York City), 1, 4, 441–43, 504
Sieghortner House (New York City), 207–8
Simonet's Restorator (Philadelphia), 34–35
Simpson-Crawford Department Store Restaurant (New York City), 510–11
Southern Hotel (St. Louis), 376–78
Spanish Fort Hotel (Bayou St. John, LA), 223
Stackpole House (Boston), 51–52
Stanford Hotel (San Francisco), 239–40
St. Anthony Hotel (San Antonio, TX), 480
Star Restaurant (Denver), 260
St. Charles Hotel (New Orleans), 162, 275, 513
St. Francis Hotel (San Francisco), 526–29
St. James Hotel (Denver), 260
St. James Hotel (New York City), 176, 359–60
St. Louis Exchange Hotel (New Orleans), 135, 153–55
St. Marks restaurant, Stevens House (New York City), 176–77
St. Nicholas restaurant (Cincinnati), 156–58, 194
Stone Restaurant (Denver), 260–61
Stratford Hotel (Philadelphia), 457–58
St. Regis Hotel (New York City), 500–503, 521, 536
Sweetwater Park Hotel (Salt Springs, GA), 294

Taft Hotel (New Haven, CT), 536
Taft's Hotel (Boston), 161
Taft's Restaurant (Boston), 159–60
Tampa Bay Hotel (Tampa), 394, 396
Tenth Street Hotel (Washington, DC), 78
Tontine Coffee House (New York City), 44
Tontine House (Boston), 90–91
Tremont House (Chicago), 224
Tremont House (Restorator; Boston), 49, 94

Union Club (New York City), 7
Union Hotel (San Francisco), 120
Union Rotisserie (later Louisiana Rotisserie; San Francisco), 119
United States Hotel (Saratoga, NY), 394
United States Refectory (Philadelphia), 89–90

Vanderhorst and Tully's (Charleston, SC), 248
Vauxhall Garden (Camden, NJ), 78
Vegetarian Café (New York City), 380–82

MENUS

RECIPES

APPETIZERS

Appetizer (Emeline Jones), 347

Puree of Snipe a la Creole (Madame Eugène), 314

SOUPS AND STEWS

Beef Tea (James Wormley), 200
Burgoo (Gus Jaubert), 331
Clear Green Turtle Soup (Henri D. Fouilloux), 513
Crab Gumbo Served with Rice (Emeline Jones), 347–48
Crab Stew (Marie Esparbe), 402
Green Turtle Soup (Julien), 26
Ochra Soup (Eliza Leslie), 59

Okra Gumbo Soup (Baptiste Moreau), 155
Pepper Pot (Jean Roth), 425–26
Stewed Terrapin (Emeline Jones), 349
Terrapin à la Maryland (John Young), 499
Terrapin Stew (James Prosser), 40–41
Terrapin Stew (Sam Ward), 152
Tippecanoe Broth (François-Winceslas Pelletier), 191–92

SAUCES

Clam Sauce (Jules Dauviller), 533
Exquisite Sauce (Edouard Panchard), 536
Nonsuch Sauce (George Speck Crum), 238–39

SEAFOOD

ENTRÉES

VEGETABLES

BAKED GOODS

DESSERTS

BEVERAGES